PRECLASSICAL CONFLICT OF LAWS

To better appreciate present-day private international law and its future prospects and challenges, we should consider the history and historiography of the field. This book offers an original approach to the study of conflict of laws and legal history that exposes doctrinal lawyers to historical context, and legal historians to the intricacies of legal doctrine. The analysis is based on an in-depth examination of Medieval and Early Modern conflict of laws, focusing on the classic texts of Bartolus and Huber. Combining theoretical insights, textual analysis, and historical perspectives, the author presents the preclassical conflict of laws as a rich world of doctrines and policies, theory and practice, context and continuity. This book challenges preconceptions and serves as an advanced introduction which illustrates the relevance of history in commanding private international law, while aspiring to make private international law relevant for history.

NIKITAS E. HATZIMIHAIL is Associate Professor of Private Law, Comparative Law, and Legal History at the University of Cyprus. His doctoral dissertation received the Addison-Brown commencement Prize at Harvard Law School.

CAMBRIDGE STUDIES IN INTERNATIONAL AND COMPARATIVE LAW: 153

Established in 1946, this series produces high quality, reflective and innovative scholarship in the field of public international law. It publishes works on international law that are of a theoretical, historical, cross-disciplinary or doctrinal nature. The series also welcomes books providing insights from private international law, comparative law and transnational studies which inform international legal thought and practice more generally.

The series seeks to publish views from diverse legal traditions and perspectives, and of any geographical origin. In this respect it invites studies offering regional perspectives on core *problématiques* of international law, and in the same vein, it appreciates contrasts and debates between diverging approaches. Accordingly, books offering new or less orthodox perspectives are very much welcome. Works of a generalist character are greatly valued and the series is also open to studies on specific areas, institutions or problems. Translations of the most outstanding works published in other languages are also considered.

After seventy years, Cambridge Studies in International and Comparative Law sets the standard for international legal scholarship and will continue to define the discipline as it evolves in the years to come.

A list of books in the series can be found at the end of this volume.

PRECLASSICAL CONFLICT OF LAWS

NIKITAS E. HATZIMIHAIL
University of Cyprus

CAMBRIDGE
UNIVERSITY PRESS

CAMBRIDGE
UNIVERSITY PRESS

University Printing House, Cambridge CB2 8BS, United Kingdom

One Liberty Plaza, 20th Floor, New York, NY 10006, USA

477 Williamstown Road, Port Melbourne, VIC 3207, Australia

314–321, 3rd Floor, Plot 3, Splendor Forum, Jasola District Centre, New Delhi – 110025, India

79 Anson Road, #06-04/06, Singapore 079906

Cambridge University Press is part of the University of Cambridge.

It furthers the University's mission by disseminating knowledge in the pursuit of education, learning, and research at the highest international levels of excellence.

www.cambridge.org
Information on this title: www.cambridge.org/9780521863025
DOI: 10.1017/9781139016674

First published 2021

A catalogue record for this publication is available from the British Library.

Library of Congress Cataloging-in-Publication Data
Names: Hatzimihail, Nikitas, author.
Title: Preclassical conflict of laws / Nikitas E. Hatzimihail, University of Cyprus.
Description: Cambridge, United Kingdom ; New York, NY : Cambridge University Press, 2021. |
Series: Cambridge studies in international and comparative law ; 151 |
Includes bibliographical references and index.
Identifiers: LCCN 2020041335 (print) | LCCN 2020041336 (ebook) |
ISBN 9780521863025 (hardback) | ISBN 9781139016674 (epub)
Subjects: LCSH: Conflict of laws–History.
Classification: LCC K7030 .H38 2021 (print) | LCC K7030 (ebook) | DDC 340.909–dc23
LC record available at https://lccn.loc.gov/2020041335
LC ebook record available at https://lccn.loc.gov/2020041336

ISBN 978-0-521-86302-5 Hardback

Uxori et parentibus carissimis

Historia vero testis temporum, lux veritatis, vita memoriae, magistra vitae, nuntia vetustatis, qua voce alia nisi oratoris immortalitati commendatur?

And as History, which bears witness to the passing of the ages, sheds light upon reality, gives life to recollection and guidance to human existence, and brings tidings of ancient days, whose voice, but the orator's, can entrust her to immortality?

Cicero, *De oratore*, 2.36 (E. W. Sutton trans., Loeb Classical Library)

CONTENTS

FIGURES, TABLES AND MAPS

Figures

Tables

Maps

1 Europe in 1300 from J. Watts, *The Making of Polities: Europe 1300–1500* (Cambridge University Press, 2009)

Finland (Swe.)
Estonia (Den.)
Novgorod
Principality of Novgorod
Livonia
Gotland
Öland
Kurland
Riga
TEUTONIC ORDER
Tver'
Moscow
Vladimir
Königsberg
Danzig
Pomorze
Prussia
Elbing
Marienburg
Lithuania
Gniezno
Greater Poland
Kuiavia
Duchy of Masovia
Sandomierz
Silesia
Lesser Poland
Cracow
Kiev
Margravate of Moravia
Galicia/Ruthenia
Podolia
Visegrád
HUNGARY
Transylvania
Moldavia
Slavonia
Belgrade
Wallachia
Croatia
Bosnia
Bulgaria
SERBIA
Thrace
Albania
ROMAN EMPIRE (BYZANTIUM)
Constantinople
Thessaloniki
Nicaea
Trebizond
Epirus
Osmanli Emirate
Calabria
Athens
Anatolia
Morea
Konya
Cyprus
Crete (Ven.)

1 (*cont.*)

2 Italy from C. Allmand (ed.), *The New Cambridge Medieval History, Volume VII c.1415–c.500* (Cambridge University Press, 1998)

3 The Netherlands from M. Prak, *The Dutch Republic in the Seventeenth Century: The Golden Age* (Cambridge University Press, 2005)

ACKNOWLEDGMENTS

This book is a historical contribution to the study of contemporary private international law. Adopting a historical perspective was a gradual process, as I sought to understand this legal field and its place within the study and practice of law. One way of looking at modern doctrine is as the estuary of past notions, doctrines, and ideas. Such a metaphor highlights the complexity – and unique value – of our own legal environment, but is also an invitation to seek out the very different environments traversed by the main river and its tributaries – shaping them and, in turn, being shaped by them.

This is, accordingly, a story about Medieval, Early Modern, and subsequent jurists and the systems they constructed, as they employed tools both familiar and unfamiliar to us in the present day, dealing with problems we can identify with as well as with now-obsolete aspects of the evolving legal treatment of human existence. These discursive ancestors were children of their time but also strove to bequeath to worlds more different than they could have imagined. We certainly cannot grasp past or present conflicts theories, principles and norms, or potential alternatives, without an appreciation of the world in which they originated and where they are asked to operate. At the same time, so much of conflicts doctrine has shown remarkable resilience across time and space. Context is vital, yet it is clearly not everything.

It is customary to express frustration, or fascination, with the present state of conflict-of-laws doctrine. Indeed, such contrasting feelings have motivated this book. But, at its heart lies an earnest conviction about the value of private international law as a juristic approach to global governance and the management of legal diversity. Private international law is a distinct legal discipline, formed out of the creative tension between the "domestic" institutions and policies of what we conceive as private law, and the "public" or "quasi-public" institutions and aspirations of international governance. Private international law cannot be separated from – but neither should it be subordinated to – either. This socio-epistemological understanding of the legal discipline has informed both my own historical narrative, as well as the book's emphasis on the importance of historical consciousness as well as on the inherent subjectivity of existing historical literature. Cicero's exhortation epitomizes the twin themes of the book: awareness of the oratorical – even instrumentalist – element in the writing of history, as well as hope for its potential to "shed light upon reality" and improve our better selves.

Preclassical Conflict of Laws began its life as a Harvard Law School doctoral dissertation on private international law and comparative legal history. That dissertation – which was awarded the Addison-Brown Prize at the 2003 Harvard commencement and, shortly thereafter, a book contract from Cambridge University Press – possessed many of the qualities and theoretical ambition associated with younger scholars. The overall conception of the dissertation survives in this book, along with many fragments, but that early work has been revised, significantly expanded, and re-revised substantially – albeit intermittently as professional obligations allowed – over a prolonged period, until it was finally completed in the midst of the COVID-19 pandemic. This is, therefore, a different, more mature work: perhaps less theoretically precocious (its author being all too aware of the vastness of existing but unexplored ideas), but more confident in the analysis of Medieval and Early Modern doctrine, the result of hands-on exposure to legal teaching and problem-solving (and more comfortable access to primary sources).

The book owes its existence to a number of people. First among them are my doctoral supervisors, David Kennedy and Charles Donahue Jr.: their approaches were very different from one another but my work clearly carries the influence of both. David introduced me to intellectual legal history, legal theory, critical approaches, and textual analysis. Charlie instilled in me the importance of context and appreciation for the hard toil of legal history. They also gave, by word and example, invaluable advice that I still carry with pride and gratitude. Next comes my third committee member, Duncan Kennedy, our *maître d'armes*, who started my journey in private law theory and the intellectual history of legal doctrine, and another gentle giant, the late Arthur Taylor von Mehren. I am especially grateful to Professor Bernard Audit, my external examiner, for his attention and ideas, as well as to Charalambos Pamboukis, who initiated me to the field of private international law, Joseph Singer, who supervised my master's thesis, and Richard Fentiman, who has influenced the pragmatic turn of my doctrinal outlook as reflected in the completed book. Of the many teachers and mentors

I have been blessed with, I must especially thank, for ideas, encouragement, and leading by example: Anthony Antapasis, Michael Blumm, Thomas Baker, Daniel Coquillette, Anghelos Foustoucos, Constantinos Kerameus, Eben Moglen, Setsuo Miyazawa, Emmanuel Roucounas, Symeon Symeonides, and Spyridon Troianos.

I cannot do justice to all my friends, comrades-in-arms, and colleagues who have contributed to this book. For reading parts of one or more of my drafts, I must particularly single out Ralf Michaels, Mikhail Xifaras, Michael Chatzipanagiotis, Carlos Esplugues Motta, José Augusto Fontoura Costa, Quim Forner Delaygua, Adolfo Giuliani, Emmanuel Guinchard, Saskia Lettmaier, Arnaud Nuyts, Lazaros Panourgias, Ilaria Pretelli, Gian Paolo Romano, Stelios Tofaris, Alexander Trunk, and Spyridon Tzounakas. Petja Toškan, my patient Harvard officemate, has been unfailingly supportive, an intellectual powerhouse, and a friend for life. My work on Latin texts, and growing appreciation for the subtleties of that language, owes a lot to Charles Donahue, my guide to the Medieval mind for over two decades (to whom I owe the translations of Aldricus, Accursius, Carolus, and the anonymous Parisian gloss in Chapter 3), and Spyridon Tzounakas, who introduced me to Stoicism and classical reception in Early Modern texts. My interaction with undergraduate and graduate students was in itself fulfilling but also helped me reflect upon and elaborate more clearly my ideas; I am thankful to all of them, especially to Kyriakos Kyriakides, Rafaella Charalambous, and George Sotiri for rewarding discussions and Christodoulos Christodoulou, who read a complete draft at a critical moment and provided an invaluable reader's perspective. I am also indebted, for their meaningful support, discussions, and friendship to William Alford, Lia Athanassiou, Moritz Bälz, Yas Banifatemi, Bojan Bugarič, Maria Canellopoulou Bottis, Antonis Bredimas, Theodore Christakis, Panagiotis Christias, Aurelia Colombi Ciacchi, Brooks Daly, James Filippatos, Spyridon Flogaitis, Maria Gavouneli, Martin Goyette, Gail Hupper, Michael von Hinden, Dionysia Kallinikou, Haris Konidaris, Katerina Konidaris, Konstantinos Kotoulas, Stacy Koumbis, P.J. Kozyris, Tania Kretsi, Dimitris Liappis, Peter Krug, Carole Moal-Nuyts, Nicholas Mitrokostas, Matjaž Nahtigal, Rossanna d'Onza Garcia, Andreas Papaconstantinou, Nicholas Papaspyrou, Stavros Papastavrou, Sophia Pavlaki, Ioannis Stribis, William Suarez Potts, George Serghides, Costas Synolakis, Jeanne Tai, Andrew Varcoe, Eleftherios Voglis, Nadine Watté, A.N. Yiannopoulos and Dongsheng Zang. Acknowledgments are also due to my fellow SJD travelers and the staff at the Harvard Law School, my colleagues and staff at the University of Oklahoma, the Université Libre de Bruxelles (U.L.B.), and the University of Cyprus.

The work also benefited from the anonymous reviewers of the original manuscript, as well as from presentations made and feedback received in several venues, including the 2007 Annual Meeting of the Law and Society Association in Berlin; the 2013 Comparative Legal History Workshop at the University of Lund; the 2018 Law and Empire in the Longue Durée Workshop at the University of Cambridge; the 2019 International Congress on the Enlightenment in Edinburgh; and a lecture on Medieval Private International Law at the University of São Paulo in 2020 as the manuscript was nearing its final form. An article based on the dissertation's take on Bartolus was published as "Bartolus on the Conflict of Laws" in the *Revue hellénique de droit international*, 60 (2007), 11–69; Chapters 7–10 significantly expand upon and replace that article, but I remain grateful to its readers for feedback. An early version of Chapter 11 was published in the *Dignatio rerum Professor Elias Krispis* (Thessaloniki: Sakkoulas, 2018), 239–264. My essay on "Reflections on the International Dimension of Private International Law" in the *Liber amicorum Nadine Watté* (Brussels: Larcier, 2017), 287–302, includes sections of Chapter 6. Another article, "On the Doctrinal Beginnings of the Conflict of Laws," which has just appeared in the *Yearbook of Private International Law* 21 (2019/2020), 101–133, actually expands upon the argument in Section 3.4.

The initial research for this work was conducted at Harvard and its magnificent libraries, at a time prior to the massive digitization of old books. It was continued at the Université Libre de Bruxelles and the University of Cyprus, my places of employment; Bremen University and the University of Cambridge, where I was generously allowed visiting fellowships; but also over shorter visits at Heidelberg University, the University of Athens, the University of Southern California, Leiden University, the University of Groningen, the British Library, the Bibliothèque Nationale de France, and the Peace Palace Library.

I am also grateful to the Fulbright Program (Greece), the Alexander S. Onassis Foundation (Greece), and the A. G. Leventis Foundation (Greece) for financial support during my graduate studies at Harvard; the Clark Byse Fellowship program and the Reginald Lewis Fund at Harvard; the Crowe & Dunlevy Professorship fund at the University of Oklahoma for funding linked to teaching and professional opportunities; and, of course, the University of Cyprus for funding of my research activities over the past fourteen years.

I owe a great debt to Cambridge University Press. The book would not exist without James Crawford and Finola O'Sullivan. Judge Crawford saw its value at a time when the history of international legal doctrine was much less fashionable, and I was a brash young scholar. I wish I had heeded his warning and published earlier, but I do hope the end result was worth his wait. Finola ensured the completion of the book, with patience, encouragement, and wisdom, and tolerated a significantly larger manuscript than the one in the contract (almost double the size of the original script). I am especially grateful to Marianne Nield, who succeeded in finally getting the elusive and ever-growing script to production, as well as Laura Blake, who skillfully handled production, the production team led by Indra Siddharthan, and Diana Witt, who handled the indexing. I am eternally thankful to my copyeditor, Benjamin Johnson.

No acknowledgement can be enough when it comes to my family. My parents, Emmanuel and Despoina, to whom the dissertation was dedicated, have been patiently awaiting this book, as the conclusion of a long journey for which they set me off, endowed with their values, love, and support. The book itself is the result of my new family. My wife, Tsampika, bore with me all the hardships of this journey, including countless hours of toil and frustration. She was a constant companion, and unbiased arbiter, in my explorations of law and history, providing me with inspiration, courage, personal fulfillment, and the intellectual environment that made this book. To her, I pledge my love and promise new journeys.

1

Introduction

1.1 Prologue

In almost every textbook on private international law, there is a reference to the Medieval and Early Modern jurists who, it is claimed, wrote on the conflict of laws. Such references are often very brief. Some appear to unveil the foundation stone of our whole doctrinal edifice, but many others may look and feel ornamental, of no importance to their author's argument. What matters most is that, when viewed as a whole, these references constitute an integral aspect of our thinking about private international law – an aspect that, it will be argued in this book, is important, if neglected and often misunderstood.

Accordingly, this is a monograph about conflict of laws scholarship in the Middle Ages and the Early Modern period – several centuries that are grouped together in the literature as "theory" or "theories" of statutes. The choice of title, which is explained subsequently in this Introduction, is meant to convey the need to rethink early conflicts doctrine. Medieval and Early Modern scholarship must first be understood in the context of its own time and place. At the same time, these texts have acquired most of their meaning over time: they can thus only be truly appreciated – and, I would argue, truly understood – when viewed from a wide perspective taking us all the way to the present – and to our immediate ("classical") past. Accordingly, we approach the past in the hope of understanding the present, but we must also understand the present (ourselves) in order to gain a meaningful understanding of the people we have come to think of as our discursive ancestors.

This is why, properly speaking, the historical study of Medieval and Early Modern conflicts doctrine in this monograph consists of two detailed examinations of two canonical texts, rather than a comprehensive narrative such as is usually found in conflicts historiography. This is also why the actual historical study effectively constitutes the second half of this work, the first two parts laying the intellectual groundwork.

Conflict of laws today has been described as a tributary stream of past theories and doctines, but it may be more of an estuary: an essential understanding of that fertile and complex area would be important before we start near the river's sources.

This book is an historical contribution to contemporary private international law. At its core, this is a work of doctrinal legal history (with some touches of intellectual history). But its writing necessitated broad reflections about the role of history – and, more broadly, historical consciousness – in private international law. What is "history" for us and how are we reconstructing the past? Does all of this truly matter? If yes, what has been the role(s), in conflicts doctrine, of invocations of the past – and what should we do with that famously "foreign country?" How should the history of private international law be written? From a certain point of view, this book constitutes an introduction to the history of private international law.

From yet another point of view, this book could be seen as an historical introduction to private international law. Exaggerated as such a claim might be, without question this book is motivated by the present-day state of this field. It is inspired by the discussions about the legal treatment – and conceptualization – of transnational activities and about the role of legal scholarship – and practice – in our "globalized" world. To write a history of private international law means also to take account of the foundational concepts and ongoing theoretical debates and concepts of private international law; to trace and seek explanations for, as well as guidance from, the present state of certain conflicts doctrines.

Each of these descriptions has its merits but it only goes far enough in identifying the three themes running through this book: current doctrinal concerns and premises; the role and formation of historical consciousness; and the lessons to be drawn from a historical study and the reasons of the choice of topic. Sections 1.2–1.4 of this chapter are devoted to a preliminary elaboration of these themes. Once the project has been better explained, the next step is to provide the necessary background. The fifth section of this chapter ("1.5: An Historical Outline") provides a brief history of private international law aimed at acquainting the reader with the historical material, perceptions in doctrinal literature and the author's own perspective. The choice of title is explained in that section. The next section ("1.6: Essential Premises") presents the basic concepts and analytical tools underpinning this book: on the one hand, the socio-epistemological perspective of the legal field that leads us to emphasize the notion of private international law as an autonomous discipline (and discursive community) and why this matters; on the other hand, the functional perspective that leads us to an appreciation of the multidimensional governance and other functions that private international law is tasked with performing.[1]

1.2 The End of History for Private International Law?

These are interesting times for private international lawyers across the globe. New national legislation, international instruments, and authoritative academic projects – in matters big or small – proliferate on a global, regional, and national level. The European Union (EU) has already gone further than anyone ever has in achieving the late nineteenth-century dream of international codification. EU instruments are even given uniform interpretation by the European Court of Justice. Regional organizations in other parts of the globe have sought to emulate the EU. The Hague Conference on Private International Law is being made truly global, as its membership expands. The Conference acts sometimes in concert, sometimes in parallel, sometimes in a friendly competition with other international institutions such as the United Nations Commission on International Trade Law (UNCITRAL) and the International Institute for the Unification of Private Law (Unidroit). The role of institutions representing international business – such as the International Chamber of Commerce (ICC) or specialized trade federations – in global rule-making is generally acknowledged. Moreover, under the auspices of these institutions, international commercial arbitration has given rise to a veritable constellation of transnational jursdictional systems. As to national judiciaries, they are achieving a degree of institutionalized communication with each other that gives new meaning to notions of judicial comity.

These are also exciting times for the theoretically minded among us. The upheaval of the "conflicts revolution" has subsided and there is little of the Cold War-era talk of a "crisis" in the conflict of laws. For most scholars today, the key words appear to be consolidation, empiricism, and synthesis.[2] At the same time, the increased complexity of private-law regimes creates new types of problems, which may or may not require new kinds of solutions. The technological revolution challenges our

[1] These ideas are then elaborated in the first two Parts of the book.

[2] See e.g. S. Symeonides, "Private International Law: Idealism, Pragmatism, Eclecticism (general course)," *Recueil des cours*, 384 (2017), 9–385.

fundamental premises about how to draw the best connection between cases and polities. The emergence and proliferation of regulatory law, and especially the increased appetite of regulatory regimes, both national and regional, for reaching beyond their territory, contrary to the traditional notions about public law, pose another set of challenges.[3] These new realities invite the exploration of interdisciplinary insights.[4] Perhaps for the first time, we are also witnessing other legal fields weighing potential lessons from conflicts doctrine.[5]

These are also times of anxiety. Much of the excitement generated in the field over the past generation relates to legislative projects such as the EU Regulations. Yet it is widely – and correctly – felt that "[t]he agenda [these instruments] promote is not the design of optimal rules for choice of law, but rules which serve [the] homogenising project [of European integration]."[6] In general, private international lawmaking has become more controlled by bureaucrats and is sometimes used more to fulfill work quotas and to explain political statements than to effectively resolve real problems. Admittedly, few outsiders would share our lament about the loss of "the brio and intellectual challenge of the subject."[7] But many of the new instruments are not free from retrograde doctrinal positions.[8]

[3] See e.g. the essays in F. Ferrari and D. Fernández Arroyo (eds.), *Private International Law: Contemporary Challenges and Continuing Relevance* (Cheltenham: Edward Elgar, 2019); and M. Lehmann, "Regulation, Global Governance and Private International Law: Squaring the Triangle," *Journal of Private International Law*, 16 (2020), 1–30.

[4] See e.g. M. Whincop and M. Keyes, *Policy and Pragmatism in the Conflict of Laws* (Aldershot: Ashgate/Dartmouth, 2001); H. Muir-Watt, "Aspects économiques du droit international privé," *Recueil des cours*, 307 (2004), 25–383; and F. J. Garcimartín Alvarez, "Regulatory Competition: A Private International Law Approach," *European Journal of Law and Economics*, 8 (1999), 251–270; T. Putnam, *Courts without Borders: Law, Politics and US Extraterritoriality* (Cambridge: Cambridge University Press, 2016).

[5] See e.g. G. Teubner, "Altera Pars Audiatur: Law in the Collision of Discourses" in R. Rawlins (ed.), *Law, Society and Economy* (Oxford: Oxford University Press, 1997), 149–176; the special issue on "Transdisciplinary Conflict of Laws" in *Law and Contemporary Problems*, 71(3) (Summer 2008), 1ff.

[6] R. Fentiman, "Choice of Law in Europe: Uniformity and Integration," *Tulane Law Review*, 82 (2008), 2022–2051, 2049.

[7] C. Forsyth, *Private International Law*, 5th ed (Cape Town: Juta, 2012), 61: "[M]any theoretical questions – classically, how is local sovereignty to be reconciled with the application of foreign law – have been resolved by the wand of European regulation. The brio and intellectual challenge of the subject is much diminished. Legislation is inevitably a political act. So compromise, not principle, shapes the form of the law that emerges."

[8] See e.g. S. Symeonides, "Rome II and Tort Conflicts: A Missed Opportunity," *American Journal of Comparative Law*, 56 (2008), 173–222.

Conflict of laws also appears to face a broader, existential problem. Regardless of which point in time one identifies as the beginnings of conflicts doctrine, or of conflict of laws as a subject, conflict of laws was truly made a distinct, popular subject during the first wave of globalization, between the mid-nineteenth and early twentieth century.[9] This is indeed the period when the very notion – and term –*private international law* comes into being. Private international law, as we know it, was a pillar and a child of this so-called first globalization and it has remained the pillar of global interactions even after its reputed demise – continuing at the same time its doctrinal evolution into a more sophisticated edifice. But, unlike the nineteenth century, our discipline did not seem to attract much enthusiasm from intellectuals and ideologues of the present-day globalization.[10] In fact, contemporary technological and outright developments have coincided with an outright challenge to the necessity and long-term viability of the conflict of laws itself. The EU's Regulations on private international law matters are presented as only the interim stage for large-scale projects for the unification of private law across Europe, with the adoption of a European Civil Code prominent among them. In the legal world of international commerce, the conflicts paradigm is under attack by a coalition of civil and business law professors, lapsed conflicts lawyers, legal theorists, and social scientists. The "terrible and odious practice of the conflict of laws" is deplored, and polemical statements are unearthed to that effect from the past.[11] Others declare the

[9] I do not seek to take part in the debate as to the historical beginnings of globalization, nor indeed attempt a definition. For present purposes it is enough to follow the established view among economists, especially. See e.g. K. O'Rourke and J. Williamson, "When Did Globalization Begin?," *European Review of Economic History*, 6 (2002), 23–50. As the fields of economic history and global history are expanding, it is becoming clear that the Early Modern Era must be seriously considered in order to understand what led to the nineteenth-century developments. See C. A. Bayly, *The Birth of the Modern World, 1780–1914: Global Connections and Comparisons* (Oxford: Blackwell, 2004), 41–42.

[10] There has on the contrary been an increasing effort to address globalisation from a private international law perspective. See e.g. the essays in and the essays in H. Muir Watt and D. Fernandez Arroyo (eds.), *Private International Law and Global Governance* (Oxford: Oxford University Press, 2015).

[11] O. Lando, "Some Features of the Law of Contract in the Third Millenium," *Scandinavian Studies in Law*, 40 (2000), 345–501, 354 quoting Thibaut in translation: "If there is no unity of laws then the terrible and odious practice of the conflict of laws will arise . . . so that in their intercourse the poor subjects will be stuck and suffocated in such a constant maze of uncertainty and shock that their worst enemies could not advise them worse. Unity of law would, however, make smooth and safe the road of the citizen from one state

irrelevance of private international law to international practice.[12] Arbitral proceedings are often presented as operating in a world of their own. Transnational business law, often in the guise of *lex mercatoria*, is presented as a "rival" to private international law; "conflictualists" are contrasted to "internationalists," in a narrative of polar opposition where they are supposed to "represent" two "radically different approaches to the same problem," with an "abyss … separat[ing] their respective schools of thought."[13] Even among those who consider complete uniformity of private law improbable in the foreseeable future, those who regard such complete unity as an aim to strive for outnumber those who regard legal diversity as a value by itself.

The external challenge to the viability of private international law is related to an internal challenge: the doctrinal consciousness of private international lawyers. We have apparently reached an armistice in wars about the method – or methods – used in private international law, due to the exhaustion of everyone involved rather than to a clear victory for any warring faction. In responding to the – theoretical and practical – challenges of the modern world, conflicts doctrine has become more inward-looking, more technical, as well as – perversely – more conceptualist.[14] To paraphrase Gutzwiller, it would appear that in private

to the other, and wicked lawyers would no longer have the opportunity to sell their legal secrets and thereby to extort and maltreat the poor foreigners."

[12] H. P. Glenn, "The Nationalist Heritage" in P. Legrand and R. Munday (eds.), *Comparative Legal Studies: Traditions and Transitions* (Cambridge: Cambridge University Press, 2003), 76–127, 98 ("private international law is now systematically avoided by nearly all those with the knowledge and means of doing so, in favor or international arbitration").

[13] For notable examples of lapsed private international lawyers see e.g. F. Juenger, "The *Lex Mercatoria* and Private International Law," *Louisiana Law Review*, 60 (2000), 1133–1150, notably at 1136–1140 (where Juenger speaks exactly of "the problems of private international law," meaning conflict of laws). See moreover F. Juenger, "Some Random Remarks from Overseas" in K.-P. Berger (ed.), *The Practice of Transnational Law* (The Hague/London/Boston: Kluwer Law International, 2001), 81–89, 81, acknowledging the fear that "[s]uch a new *lex mercatoria* would of course obviate the need for choice-of-law rules," which might cost him and other conflicts lawyers their jobs; this however "never kept [him] from straying beyond the confines of the conflict of laws to ponder the need for a universal commercial law" – and finding his colleagues' "disregard of an emerging reality deplorable."

[14] See e.g. Teubner, "Altera Pars Audiatur," 144–776, who, in advocating "a new law of conflicts" for the collision of discourses, presents – positively – the "traditional international conflict of laws" as possessing "an abundance of circular references, self-references and paradoxes" (159) as well as terms providing "a legal form for oscillating

international law, "method" is everything – but this is often a method isolated from its theoretical foundations and policy implications.

We are thus still arguing as to whether we should remain loyal to the traditional method of "bilateral," "jurisdiction-selecting" rules, which designate as applicable the law of one or another state – *a priori*, in neutral and abstract terms. If not, what is the alternative? Under which criteria can we let the local substantive law determine its own reach? If yes, how do such choice-of-law rules function, and how are they reconciled with devices such as *renvoi* or legal characterization, which – depending on the beholder – manipulate their reach, or facilitate their operation but most certainly complicate things? And what about escape devices, such as the *ordre public* exception or the "unilateral," preemptive application of certain domestic norms to transnational situations? Choice-of-law rules themselves have become more complicated. There are by far more rules, each dealing with very specific, often specialized subject matter. Many of these rules tend to describe in detail the material situation which should trigger the application of "law A" or "law B," and often operate in layers of "exceptions to the exception." All this is accompanied by abstract thinking which often puzzles students and uninitiated lawyers alike.

This industrialization or *grammarization* of legal thinking is not strictly a conflict-of-laws phenomenon, but it certainly characterizes the workings of our field. What is even more remarkable, however, is the intellectual separation of the conflict of laws from substantive law, namely private law. Many private-law concepts and policies have been integrated into the conflicts discourse, new breeds of conflicts rules have an explicit substantive impact and the best doctrinal work includes excellent analyses of the substantive-law stakes. But it still appears as if the conflict-of-laws ideology of substantive-law neutrality has led to a pervasive disregard of policy considerations.

A similar attitude is noticeable with regard to the role of the international aspect of private international law. There are those in the literature who disclaim any "special link" between public and private international law.[15] Others on the contrary stress the importance of the

between inside and outside, for blending the foreign with the familiar, and for the game of confusion of self-reference and hetero-reference" (160).

[15] See e.g. K. Lipstein, "The General Principles of Private International Law," *Recueil des cours*, 135 (1972), 97–230, 168ff; Forsyth, *Private International Law*, 5 ("The word 'international,' thus serves only to mark the existence of those foreign or international

relationship, or the "confluence" of the two fields.[16] What these attitudes have in common is that authors tend to build upon their own view of the international milieu. Private international law certainly impacts international governance; its function and structures may help consolidate or undermine the existence and operation of an international system of sovereign states. Yet that international system appears in conflicts works as immutable, as a given. In fact, a basic reason for the total war declared on private international law by certain "globalists" or "transnationalists" seems to be exactly their aspiration that its demise will help achieve a different global ordering of relations involving individuals, corporate entities, and even political entities.

1.3 An Historicism for the Age of Globalization

"When a scientific province, such as ours, has been cultivated by the unbroken exertion of many centuries, a rich inheritance is offered to us who belong to the present," wrote Friedrich Carl von Savigny in the Preface inaugurating his *System of Contemporary Roman Law*, almost two hundred years ago:[17]

> It is not merely the mass of truth won which falls to our share; every direction essayed by the intellectual powers, all efforts of past time, be they fruitful or abortive, are also good for us as pattern or warning and thus we are in some sense in the position of working with the united powers of centuries passed away. If now we would, through indolence or conceit, neglect this natural advantage of our position and in a superficial treatment leave to chance how much of that rich inheritance is to influence our culture, we should then be dispensing with the priceless benefits inseparable from the nature of real science – the communion of scientific

elements which raise the question of whether the lex fori is the appropriate law to apply, or not"), 70 ("Public international law is no guide for the resolution of conflict problems"); M. Bogdan, "Private International Law as Component of the Law of the Forum (General Course on Private International Law," *Recueil des cours*, 348 (2011), 9–252, 35 ("The word 'international' in 'private international law' has thus a meaning that differs from what the same word means in 'public international law'. It does not have in mind the origin of the rules or the essential qualities of the parties, but refers rather to the cross-border character of the legal relationship involved").

16 A. Mills, *The Confluence of Public and Private International Law* (Cambridge: Cambridge University Press, 2009).

17 F. C. von Savigny, *System des heutigen römisches Rechts*, vol. I (Berlin, 1840), ix ("Vorrede"). Excerpted passages come from F. C. von Savigny, *System of the Modern Roman Law*, vol. I, trans. William Holloway (Madras, 1867), iii. Citations are to the German original.

> convictions and at the same time with the constant, living, progress without which that communion might pass over into a dead letter.[18]

Today, Savigny's words sound so close, and so distant, for those who have chosen as their vocation the legal field of which he has provided the most important paradigm. We must pay heed to his warning of how "superficial treatment," may, "through indolence or conceit ... leave to chance" the role "of that rich inheritance" in our culture.

Savigny's proposed remedy was to synthesize, to restate, "from time to time," the juristic output of the past, and present, "in a unifying legal consciousness."[19] In the past two centuries, our philosophical premises – regarding both history and law – have become more sophisticated, and less assured. Savigny clearly understood how legal discussion is altered by the discovery of new material, and the emergence of new factual problems. With hindsight, we can today claim a superior awareness of the contingency of historical research with its contemporaneous context, and of the inherent contradictions of legal reasoning. But his basic ideas, and ambition, have not lost their value, nor their vitality.

It is the ambition of this book to be part of such "unifying consciousness" of contemporary private international law, to contribute a renewed appreciation of this "rich inheritance" and the "living connection which knits the past to the present."[20] This is a book that tries to adhere to the standards and methodology of legal history, while remaining motivated by presentist concerns – and by the conviction that the study of the history of conflicts doctrine matters in today's world.

History matters, first and foremost, because it can help us better undertand who we are, where we are coming from – and where we are going. What is unique about present-day doctrines, about our problems and aspirations – and what is not. History can help us place things – and

[18] Savigny, *System*, ix–x.

[19] Ibid., x: "In order that this may not happen, it is desirable that from time to time, the researches and gains of individuals should be summarized in a unifying consciousness. The holders of science, living at the same time, are often in sharp opposition to one another; but those contrasts come out still more strongly when we compare all ages. Here our business is not to choose the one and reject the other; the task consists rather in dissolving the perceived oppositions in a higher unity which is the only way to a safe progress in the science."

[20] Ibid., xiv–v: "The essence of [the historical] view rather consists in the uniform recognition of the value and the independence of each age and it merely ascribes the greatest weight to the recognition of the living connexion which knits the past to the present, and without which we recognize merely the external appeareance, but do not grasp the inner nature, of the legal condition of the present."

ourselves – in perspective. It has been suggested that "in private international law, history is everything" – or even that "everything worthy of trying has been tried before." This is certainly not correct. There might be more to the notion of present-day doctrine as an estuary of past ideas and doctrines. There is also educative value to historical narratives.

This brings us to the second reason as to why historical study matters for private international law. Historical imagery, historical narratives abound in present-day discussions of conflicts theory and doctrine. Our modern or "postmodern" discourse is replete with genealogies of favored approaches, with venerated relics, with examples to imitate and/or avoid. "History" is used as an argumentative weapon in the discourse. Like certain kinds of weapons, the impact of historical invocations is not always felt immediately and they may produce effects long after the endeavor in which they were deployed has faltered. An author may offer a historical narrative of dubious accuracy in support of a doctrinal project that is soon dismissed; but his historical imagery might yet live on, often mutating and influencing our perceptions. In that sense, writing a history of private international law has also necessitated the critical examination of the role of existing historical literature in the present-day discourse of private international law.

There is a duality involved in this project. One cannot write history without achieving a certain degree of understanding of the world in which one's subjects lived, and in which they sought to make their own contribution. Such understanding will always remain imperfect: the past shall forever be "a foreign country," and an ever-changing one at that, but we can aspire to a better understanding.[21] It also necessitates a certain degree of detachment from – as well as awareness of – present-day predicaments and sensibilities. But to establish such "living connection," it is not enough to engage in an archaeological exploration of the past. It is important to be explicit and self-aware of the preconceptions with which we, and those before us, approach our material. It is in effect necessary to consider our present condition and aspirations – to place ideas and struggles in perspective, and achieve a certain degree of

[21] D. Lowenthal, *The Past Is a Foreign Country—Revisited* (Cambridge: Cambridge University Press, 2015). The quote ("The past is a foreign country: they do things differently there") is the opening line of the novel by L. P. Hartley, *The Go-Between* (1953). Given that engaging with foreign countries is an important part of the vocation of private international law (and comparative law) scholars, the phrase may aptly describe the challenge involved.

self-awareness. It is also imperative to examine carefully, respectuflly but critically, not only the legacy of those who have already written about the history of private international law but more generally the general position of the past in contemporary private international law – what we could call the *historical consciousness* of private international lawyers.

In a sense, what has already been written – and what is being thought – about conflicts history should serve both as study material and as foil. Study material, in that conflicts historiography developed in a manner parallel to the development of a distinct *discipline* of private international law. And foil, in that conflicts historiography and the overall historical consciousness of conflicts lawyers has constructed an image of the past – and its relationship to the present – which cannot be ignored but leaves much to be desired.

1.4 Revisiting the Early History of Private International Law

In 1913, Joseph Henry Beale, Royall Professor of Law at Harvard Law School and future father of the First Restatement on Conflicts decided to mark the 600th anniversary of the birth of Italian jurist Bartolus da Sassoferrato (1313–1357), by taking a break from his doctrinal pursuits and translating a tract by Bartolus on the conflict of laws.[22] Beale (mis) quoted François Laurent – a nineteenth-century Belgian author who had sponsored a conflicts theory diametrically opposed to Beale's own – as saying that "the substance of truth was found in [Bartolus's] writings and that advocates and judges could do no better than to follow his opinions."[23]

Beale went on to say that:

> In the course of five hundred years, the simple principles which Bartolus laid down became strangely warped and distorted. The various schools of statutists in Italy, France and the Netherlands drew singular conclusions from his expressed opinions and ascribed these conclusions too often to Bartolus himself. Through Dumoulin, Voet, and Huber these new

[22] See *Bartolus on the Conflict of Laws*, trans. Joseph Henry Beale (Cambridge, MA: Harvard University Press, 1914).

[23] Beale, "Introduction" in *Bartolus on the Conflict of Laws*, 10, citing from F. Laurent, *Droit civil international*, t. I (Bruxelles, 1880), 299. This is however a misquotation: Laurent is talking about the authority, unmatched by any other jurisconsult, that Bartolus once enjoyed; he opens the sentence in question with *on disait*. For the phrase attributed to him by Beale, Laurent cites P. Ancharanus, *Iuris quæstionum libri tres*, vol. II, 20 No. 3.

> conclusions became the basis of much modern speculation, through the works of Story, Mancini, and Foelix.[24]

Beale's endeavor was indeed astonishing. One would be challenged to draw many similarities between the conflicts doctrines of Bartolus and Beale (as well as between either of them and Laurent). Beale's skills in Latin, and his knowledge of Continental legal history, left much to be desired.[25] Remarkably, this was not an individual eccentricity: a few years later, Ernest Gustav Lorenzen – the Yale Law professor who would soon thereafter lead the opposition to Bealian doctrine[26] – published a study and a translation of the conflicts tract of Ulricus Huber (1636–1694) – a seventeenth-century Dutch author, widely regarded as the grandfather of Anglo-American conflict of laws.[27]

A century has passed since these two American contributions to the historiography of private international law. References to the Medieval and Early Modern jurists who wrote on conflicts issues and are usually grouped together as "statutists" are very common to this day. A modern casebook, co-authored by one of Beale's successors to the conflict of laws mantle at Harvard Law School, describes Bartolus as the founder of our field, who among other things "re-introduced the 'conflictual method,' . . . introduced the 'unilateral' conflictual method" and provided us with "the first comprehensive, and predictably unsuccessful, attempt to delineate the legislative competence of states."[28]

Admittedly, most such references appear ornamental, or superficial – very few conflicts lawyers can claim to have read Bartolus, Huber, or any other "statutist" text. What is remarkable, however, is the varied imagery of representations of pre-nineteenth century conflict of laws in contemporary private international law. For many, those authors mark the

24 Beale, "Introduction," 10.

25 See Chapter 7 below.

26 Ernest Gustav Lorenzen was one of the advisers employed by the American Law Institute to assist Beale with the Restatement. According to R. Leflar, *American Conflicts Law* (Indianapolis, IN: Bobbs-Merril, 1967), 2: "He ceased to serve after the early sections were written, and he as well as others spoke out frequently from then on against the Restatement approach to the subject." See *American Law Institute Proceedings* 3 (1925), 222ff.

27 E. Lorenzen, "Huber's De Conflictu Legum," *Illinois Law Review*, 13 (1919), 375–418, reprinted in his *Selected Articles on the Conflict of Laws* (1947), 162–165.

28 S. Symeonides, W. Perdue, and A. T. von Mehren, *Conflict of Laws: American, Comparative, International* (St. Paul, MN: West, 1998), 8–9. Three pages are devoted to Bartolus in this short historical treatment, one to Huber and one more to Wächter and Savigny together.

beginning of something, a continuous discourse, which runs to the present. Beale discerned a body of contemporary choice-of-law principles in the fourteenth-century work of Bartolus. Others have discovered, in the High and Late Middle Ages, the origins of contemporary notions or doctrines, such as unilateralism or party autonomy.[29] Some even find resonance with statutist theories and lament their subsequent corruption.[30] There are also those who view pre-nineteenth century conflict of laws as "Paradise Lost" – the time when conflicts issues were dealt with by an international *community* of scholars, unhindered by the legal nationalism and positivism of subsequent times.

However, for all the romance surrounding the distant past of conflicts doctrine, it remains fundamentally an *ancien régime*. Modern literature abounds with examples of authors dismissing opposing theories or doctrines as a mere repetition of statutist theories that have been long forsaken, and probably for a good reason.[31] American conflicts revolutionaries are thus often accused of having simply reprised statutist doctrine.[32] Continental unilateralists are also occasionally dismissed as "neo-statutaires." A learned detractor even characterized the late

[29] See with regard to party autonomy F. K. Juenger, *Choice of Law and Multistate Justice* (The Hague: M. Nijhoff, 1993), 8, 10, 17; and H. Yntema, "The Comity Doctrine," *Michigan Law Review*, 65 (1966), 9–32.

[30] See e.g. J.-L. Elhoueiss, "Personnalité et territorialité en droit international privé," unpublished Doctoral dissertation, Paris II (2000), with regard to the soundness of constructing a system based on territoriality and personality.

[31] See a recent article with a telling title: C. Bisping, "Avoid the Statutist Trap: The International Scope of the Consumer Credit Act 1974," *Journal of Private International Law*, 8 (2012), 35–62, 44: "Statutists were a group of medieval scholars – the founders of private international law – who believed that the application of a statute could be determined by the statute's inherent desire to apply. If there was no such desire, a statute would not apply to an international situation if there were other alternative rules."

[32] See e.g. K. Lipert (ed.), *Historischer Statutismus und Neo-Statutismus der USA* (Zurich: Juris-Verlag, 1979). For more casual references, see e.g. Forsyth, *Private International Law*, 63 ("the great wealth of modern thought in the USA about the conflict of laws is concerned with the revival, in some form or another, of statutism"); Bisping, "Statutist Trap," 44–45 ("A similar approach is taken in modern US conflict of laws under various headings such as 'better law' or 'interest analysis'. Despite many differences in detail, they are basically statutist approaches"); C. Pamboukis, *Idiōtiko Diethnes Dikaio*, (Athens: Nomiki Bibliothiki, 2020), 143 speaking of "functional neo-statutism." See further P. Volken, "How Common Are the General Principles of Private International Law? America and Europe Compared," *Yearbook of Private International Law*, 1 (1999), 85–102, 101 concludes that: "All conflict of laws theories developed on the North American continent during the past 150 years are based on statutists theories. They have all been theories claiming, justifying, or legitimizing the (overtly extended) spacious reach of certain domestic statutes."

nineteenth century school of Pasquale Mancini, which marks the full and conscious break from statutist doctrine, as "sociological neo-statutists."[33] And there are those who appear not to notice the similarities their own theories have to Medieval or Early Modern doctrine.[34] A few others would deny Medieval doctrine to the conflict of laws, by insisting that what Medieval jurists were doing was not really conflict of laws, after all.[35]

Such diversity in perceptions is, to some extent, the result of the diversity of modern doctrinal approaches to private international law. It may also be attributable, in part, to the lack of any recent historical study of statutist doctrine.[36] The historiography of early conflicts law boasts of some great works, which however bear unmistakably the marks of time. Unfortunately, even these works are only infrequently taken into serious consideration in contemporary literature.

This book is an essay on the writing of the history of private international law. In the spirit of the Savignian manifesto adopted to our age, this is a book about antitheses and syntheses: past and present, law and history, history and historiography, theory and practice, the externalities of context, and the internal qualities of the discourse. These complexities

[33] Lipstein, "General Principles," 143ff. See also A. Boggiano, *Derecho Internacional Privado*, 6th ed, vol. I (Buenos Aires: LexisNexis, 2006), 66 uses a similar term (*la escuela neo estatutaria de la Habana*) for Bustamente's doctrine.

[34] For example, L. Barnich, *Les actes juridiques en droit international privé: essai de méthode* (Brussels: Bruylant, 2001) promotes the *locus regit actum* rule as the "paradigm" for conflict of laws. Indeed, the original title of his monograph made express reference to a "lost paradigm." L. Barnich, "Le lieu des actes juridiques: paradigme perdu de droit international privé," unpublished Doctorate thesis, Université Libre de Bruxelles (2000). Barnich traces his rule to the nineteenth century; Medieval and Early Modern conflict of laws is dealt with in less than a page. See Barnich, *Actes juridiques*, 198–199 (aptly titled "Origine de la distinction").

[35] A notable example involves another Harvard law professor, legal historian Sanuel E. Thorne, who claimed, a half-century after Beale's translation and citing Beale's doctrinal work, that what Bartolus was doing was not conflict of laws, but statutory interpretation. See Chapter 2 below.

[36] The tour de force of B. Ancel, *Histoire du Droit international privé* (Paris: Université Panthéon Assas Paris II, 2008) has been the main exception. It has been replaced by B. Ancel, *Elements d'histoire du droit international privé* (Paris: Panthéon Assas Paris II, 2017). The final revision of this manuscript also saw the culmination of very interesting doctoral projects working on the history of private international law for theoretical purposes. See R. Banu, *Nineteenth-Century Perspectives on Private International Law* (Oxford: Oxford University Press, 2018); A. H. Neidhardt, "The Transformation of Private International Law: A Genealogy of the Family Antinomy," Doctoral dissertation, European University Institute (2018).

reflect in the book's structure. As its title indicates, this is a study of conflict of laws in the Middle Ages and the Early Modern Era – a period which we will be calling the *preclassical period*, in contrast to the *classical period* of national legal systems, choice-of-law rules, and general principles that begins in the nineteenth century. A substantial part of the book consists of two detailed case studies, on the conflicts writings of Bartolus of Sassoferato and Ulrik Huber, where we shall attempt to re-create the conflicts doctrine of each, and relate this to their broader aspirations and worldview. Too many studies of preclassical (and subsequent) doctrine have been limited to the presentation of the "general theory" and the foundations proposed by the old writers. On the contrary, the case studies in this book aim at a comprehensive examination of each author's *conflicts treatment*, at considering seriously how its theory and principles are applied to specific doctrinal questions. The doctrinal treatment of specifics is important on its own right, and sometimes more telling than axioms. We shall thus give emphasis on structure, contents and omissions, even *obiter dicta*. This is not simply an exercise in textual analysis: in each case, the author's main conflicts writing will be our starting point, but an attempt will be made to fill in the background, to consider the authors' context as well as to compare them with other figures of preclassical conflict of laws and draw connections.

There are several reasons for the choice of Bartolus and Huber as the subjects of these case studies. They are probably the best-known preclassical jurists, at least in the English-speaking world.[37] Their conflicts tracts constitute extremely sophisticated texts, and their close reading will put to rest many preconceptions about preclassical scholarship – and the tracts themselves. Moreover, Bartolus and Huber represent distinct periods, and styles, in the history of preclassical doctrine and European

[37] Practical considerations also weighted in my choice. These are probably the most easily available preclassical texts to an English-speaker today (each has been translated twice in the twentieth century), and neither is especially lengthy (a reason for their relatively wide circulation in past times). This book should therefore also help the reader to an independent study of these texts. In any case, these have been the most influential texts of their respective periods. Among Medieval jurists, Bartolus has clearly outshone Baldus in this respect. Among the Early Modern Belgian and Dutch jurists, Burgundus and Rodenburgh were influential in their time, and Johannes Voet gave us a lasting monument of the *mos hollandicus*. But Huber's conflicts treatment has had, by far, the more lasting influence, and its study best serves the purposes of this monograph.

legal history.[38] They were legal academics who published on all aspects of legal doctrine, as well as theory. They were important figures in the *ius commune Europaeum*, which has found so much resonance in our time. They both used the Corpus Iuris Civilis as the starting point for their major work (in Latin), and sought to balance the assertive realities of local law against a common – yet evolving – tradition of learned law. They are also very different from each other in style, language, ideas, and subject matter treated.

This book is certainly not, however, a complete history of conflict of laws in the preclassical period. The grand works of classical conflicts historiography, the erudition of Ludwig von Bar, E. L. Catellani, Max Gutzwiller, François Laurent, E. M. Meijers, Karl Neumeyer, and especially the sweeping – and never completed – study of Armand Lainé, will find in this work an admiring interpreter, at best an interlocutor, but certainly not a rival or pretender to succession. On the other hand, these great works are undoubtedly children of their own era – and this firm grounding is part of their greatness. They can find much resonance with modern readers and they have achieved an understanding of the past that is admirable and often unsurpassed. But they use the tools available to them at that time and address the questions relevant to them and their immediate audience. As common as the proverbial expression about standing on the shoulders of giants may be, it is certainly appropriate for our case.

At the same time, the book is about more than preclassical conflict of laws in the strict sense. The study of preclassical conflict of laws properly speaking forms only the second half of the book, with the first half setting the stage, in the manner outlined above, in our quest to establish the "living connection." A critical study of conflicts historiography is needed, if we are to make good use of the available historical literature. In that regard, as in many others, one cannot tell the history of preclassical conflict of laws, without constant references to the classical – and modern – scholarship that has shaped our own views on both conflict of laws and its history. Part I of the book is therefore about the historical

[38] This also explains their choice over either of the two most famous French preclassical jurists, Charles Dumoulin (1500–1566) and Bertrand d'Argentré (1519–1590). Today, they are both presented as the main representatives of the so-called French school of statutes. However, Dumoulin has been characterized, not unfairly, by leading conflicts historians as a continuator of Bartolus and the Italian school. In his turn, d'Argentré certainly found his creative continuation (or culmination?) in Huber and the Dutch school. See Chapter 3 below.

consciousness of private international lawyers; its development, the materials of its formation and the imagery it bequeaths us about preclassical conflict of laws.

This book is also an historical contribution to the study of contemporary private international law. It is undoubtedly influenced by the context in which it is written, by the audience it seeks to address. It is informed by present-day questions and concepts. It is also mindful of the extent to which we tend to view the past in present terms. In an effort to better understand both preclassical doctrine and the path of evolution that has led us to the present moment, it has looked into contemporary ideas and doctrines, reconsidered concepts and was confronted with present-day challenges. Part II draws on modern doctrine, viewed in historical perspective, in establishing the conceptual tools to be used, and questions to be asked, in our historical exploration.

Having explained the perspective and motivations of this book, it is now time to provide readers with the requisite terms of reference. An essential understanding of the field's history is needed first, in order to better explain the fundamental theoretical premises underlying this work in the section that follows.

1.5 An Historical Outline

It is commonly accepted that the defining moment in the history of private international law concerns the full and definitive displacement of pre-nineteenth century doctrine by a new legal paradigm, sometime in the early to mid-nineteenth century. Often described as a "Copernican revolution," this paradigm shift entailed the abandonment of the "statutist" doctrines of ascertaining the spatial reach of statutes in favor of the "Savignian" method of localizing in space the legal relationship.[39]

From the point of view of contemporary doctrinal lawyers, such paradigm shift is indeed Copernican: instead of fitting legal relationships into legal rules, it is now legal rules that are made to fit into legal relationships. But is this truly the whole story? Moreover, how does such a shift in paradigms come about?

[39] The term "Copernican Revolution" was first used by P. Neuhaus, "Savigny und die Rechtsfindung aus der Natur der Sache," *RabelsZ*, 15 (1949), 364–381, 366. See subsequently, O. Kahn-Freund, "General Problems of Private International Law," *Recueil des cours*, 143 (1974), 139–474, 244, 252; J. Kropholler, *Internationales Privatrecht*, 6th ed (Tübingen: Mohr Siebeck, 2006), 13.

1.5.1 *Theories of Statutes, or: Preclassical Conflict of Laws*

The "Copernican" moment is preceded by six to seven centuries of scholarly writings on the conflict of laws, dating to the early stages of the renaissance of legal scholarship in the High Middle Ages. Conflicts doctrine from that period is grouped together as the *theory* – or theories – *of statutes* (*théorie des statuts*; *Statutenlehre*). In fact, what especially Early Modern jurists regarded as "theory of statutes" often resembles what we would today regard as legal theory, statutory interpretation or legal methodogy, and the subjects touched upon would fall under not just private but also criminal or even public law.[40] The theory of statutes did intersect with the conflict of laws, however, given that a major endeavor of these Medieval and Early Modern jurists was to ascertain the reach of individual statutes or customs over people and cases (i.e. what we would today call their personal and territorial scope).

In the beginning, this question was treated on a case-by-case basis, but as scholars moved from analogy to abstraction, the distinction between statutes whose effect extended beyond the lawmaker's territory (*extra territorium*) from those whose effect did not become a principal doctrinal tool. The former statutes were associated to the person and thus came to be called personal statutes (*statuta personalia*). The latter statutes were associated to the territory and came to be called real (*statuta realia*). Over time, an intermediate category was invented, the so-called mixed statutes (*statuta mixta*). As the concept referred to *statuta* with both personal and real elements, it was employed differently by each author, depending on whether his inclination was favorable to *statuta personalia* or *realia*. Rules on legal acts, such as contracts, might have been most commonly classified as mixed statutes.

Throughout this period, legal scholarship vacillated between how to best classify statutes. Should emphasis be given to their actual wording and content? Would classification of cases into more abstract legal categories be more satisfactory – or at least more efficient? Over time, the advent of territorial sovereignty led to stronger identification between rules and territory. As the Medieval fiction of political unity over the entities whose laws conflicted collapsed, but also ideas about the State and law as a tool of statecraft changed, Early Modern authors were also

[40] See M. Sbriccoli, *L'interpretazione dello statuto : contributo allo studio della funzione dei giuristi nell' età comunale* (Milano: A. Giuffrè, 1969); K. Boosfeld, "Die beiden Statutenlehren: Geschichte eines rechthistorischen Missverständnisses," *Zeitschrift der Savigny-Stiftung für Rechtsgeschichte (Germanistische Abteilung)*, 136 (2019), 76–93.

tasked with explaining how the local polity was sovereign yet had to apply another polity's law. The growth of commerce led to a stronger insistence on the need to safeguard the universal effectiveness of legal acts, but also to more diverse rules on ever more problems.

Today, the significance, and context, of the statutists' distinctions are lost. What has registered in our historical consciousness is the notion that the former, binary approach – which we could call the *basic theory of statutes* – corresponds to the primordial tension between personalist and territorialist approaches. The latter, tertiary approach – which we could call the *classic theory of statutes* – represents more mature doctrine thinking, as statutists understood the complexity of factual situations and sought to deal with current problems. At the same time, their doctrine became more convoluted over time, eventually succumbing to a decaying scholasticism.[41] Statutists did nonetheless manage – whether in spite or by means of their baroque conceptualism – to invent, or at least come across, many contemporary doctrines and notions.

The story of statutist doctrine is told in isolation from general legal history and developments in the European legal scholarship of the Middle Ages and the Early Modern Era. In our historical consciousness, statutists and their theories form a unified discourse. The internal dividing lines, as presented in conflicts literature, tend not to challenge this sense of unity; the primary aim of subsequent dividing schemes apparently lies in attributing specific doctrines to a specific writer or school, or grouping certain writers into statutist schools. For the time being, it suffices to note that statutist doctrine is usually divided into three schools – Italian, French, and Dutch – which appear to succeed each other chronologically: the Italian school peaks in the fourteenth century, the French school in the sixteenth century, and the Dutch school in the seventeenth century. On the contrary, not much is usually made of the eighteenth century. A common view – though by no means universally

[41] See e.g. G. Teubner, "De Collisione Discursuum: Communicative Rationalities in Law, Morality and Politics," *Cardozo Law Review*, 17 (1996), 901–916, 901 on Johan Nikolaus Hert: "Invoking systematic construction and elaborate casuistry . . . Hert complexified the so-called statutist method according to which which collision rules determined jurisdiction by analyzing the nature of the statutes involved. Developing a complex rule system for the collision of laws, Hert felt compelled to distinguish the incredible amount of sixty-three different casuistic constellations in order to fight Pascal's Paradox. For this scholarly exercise he became famous, and rightly so. But his immortality in legal circles is based on the desparate sigh which he hove while drawing his tortured distinctions: '*quam sudent doctores*.' How the doctors are sweating!"

held – is that statutist doctrine was in crisis, by the eighteenth century, and that it only survived into the nineteenth century by means of rules in the new national Codes. The standard historical account suggests as principal cause the unraveling of statutist theories and their foundations.[42] Sometimes, extrinsic phenomena have been proposed as additional causes, such as the creation of national legal Codes and legal nationalism, and the rise of international law.

1.5.1.1 History and Prehistory

The last eight or so centuries of doctrinal discussion and writing on conflicts issues are usually distinguished from those preceding eras – notably Antiquity and the Early Middle Ages – where conflicts were dealt with in a different manner, mostly unconsciously. I have chosen to refer to those earlier eras as *prehistorical*, in contrast to the historical era of doctrinal writings on conflicts questions.[43] Prehistory worlds have in fact been featuring in the historical literature, and probably the historical consciousness, of private international law, since the beginnings of conflicts historiography. In another study I have attempted to illustrate how the treatment of Antiquity and the Early Middle Ages in conflicts literature has evolved in reflection to the contemporary preoccupations and method of late nineteenth and twentieth-century private international lawyers.[44] The discussion of prehistory, however, falls largely outside the goals of this book.

[42] See e.g. Juenger, *Choice of Law*, 32, 34, who emphasizes the role of Karl Georg von Wächter in that regard: "Wächter was an iconoclast. He debunked statutists learning, exposed the vested rights theory's circular reasoning and disparaged the comity doctrine. . . . But the influence of Wächter's ideas on European conflict of laws proved to be minimal because his compatriot Savigny soon overshadowed him."

[43] The term prehistory has been used since the mid-nineteenth century to denote "the study of the history of a region prior to the earliest appearance of written records relating to it" (Daniel Wilson, 1851) See also John Lubbock (Lord Avebury), *Prehistoric Times* (1869, 7th ed, 1913). See e.g. B. Trigger, *A History of Archaeological Thought*, 2nd ed (Cambridge: Cambridge University Press, 2006). For uses of the term in private international law see B. Audit, *Droit international privé*, 4th ed (Paris: Economica, 2006), 58 ("prehistory of conflict of laws"); W. Posch, *Bürgerliches Recht VII: Internationales Privatrecht*, 3rd ed (Vienna: Springer, 2002), 7 ("Vorgeschichte"). Note P. Mayer, *Droit international privé*, 6th ed (Paris: Montchretien, 1998), 34 refers to the same period as "pre-doctrinal." Cf. Ancel, *Histoire*, 16–45 who refers to conflicts in Antiquity as *droit international privé anecdotique*.

[44] See N. Hatzimihail, "Pre-Historical Private International Law," paper presented at the Inaugural Conference of the European Society for Comparative Legal History, Valencia (July 2010).

1.5.2 *The Choice-of-Law Method, or: Classical Conflict of Laws*

The nineteenth-century break away from *statutist* theories has been registered in the historical consciousness as a paradigm shift. The early nineteenth century features in conflicts historiography as a time of transition. Friedrich Carl von Savigny (1779–1861) is presented as the emblematic figure of the new paradigm. Savigny was able to localize in space the legal relationship.[45]

Savigny's legacy has acquired mythical dimensions in conflicts literature. He is presented as having invented the multilateral, aprioristic choice-of-law rule – moreover, he is also said to have made the "international uniformity of result" the linchpin of his system.[46] At the same time, many have discovered in his work the roots of the unilateral, ex post devices of mandatory rules (*lois de police*) and public policy (*ordre public*), which are used to derogate from the multilateral aprioristic rules.[47] He articulated the concept of a *community of law* but he would allow states to maintain their legal particularities even in cases where he himself thought them egregious or moribund. He was – at least by the time he wrote on conflicts – a reactionary conservative.[48] Yet he gave conflicts doctrine its most lasting expression of political and economic liberalism.[49] Savigny is viewed as having premised his doctrinal system in the existence of state laws.[50] But he is also presented as the father, well ahead of his time, of the conception of conflict of laws as a conflict of private interests, as opposed to a conflict of state sovereignties.[51] Last but

45 See e.g. P. Picone, "Les méthodes de coordination entre ordres juridiques en droit international privé: cours général de droit international privé," *Recueil des cours*, 276 (1999), 9–296, 35ff.

46 T. C. Hartley, "Modern Approach," 26–27.

47 See e.g. P. Franceskakis, "Quelques précisions sur les 'lois d'application immédiate' et leurs rapports avec les règles de conflits de lois," *Revue critique*, 55 (1966), 1–18, 5 (suggesting that while Savingy may have mildly favored the classic choice-of-law rule, he recognized the *lois de police* as an equally valid process).

48 See e.g. J.-L. Halpérin, *Entre Nationalisme Juridique et Communauté du Droit* (Paris: Presses Universitaires de France (PUF), 1999), 47–48.

49 See A. Bucher, "Vers l'adoption de la méthode des intérêts? Réflections à la lumière des codifications récentes," *Travaux du Comité français*, 12 (1993–1995), 209–228, esp. 209–214. Cf. Bucher and Bonomi, *Droit international privé*, 89–90.

50 R. Michaels, "Globalizing Savigny? The State in Savigny's Conflict of Laws Theory, and the Challenge of Europeanization and Globalization" in M. Stolleis and W. Streeck (eds.), *Aktuelle Fragen politischer und rechtlicher Steuerung im Kontext der Globalisierung* (Baden-Baden: Nomos, 2007), 119–144.

51 Mayer, *Droit international privé*, 46–47.

not least, he is portrayed as the (grand-)father of legal formalism, but also the seed-sower of a functional analysis of conflicts rules.[52]

The kaleidoscope that is Savigny's place in our historical consciousness may be more telling about the faultlines and preoccupations of contemporary doctrine, than about Savigny's own work. It is apparent, nonetheless, that Savigny created an extremely sophisticated and nuanced doctrinal system, which was only fully appreciated much later.

A second stream of nineteenth-century conflict of laws, which may have been more popular than Savigny in the last third of the nineteenth century, but certainly enjoys less appreciation in the modern world is epitomized by the Italian statesman and academic Pasquale Stanislao Mancini.[53] Today, Mancini is remembered principally for his advocacy of nationality as the principal connecting factor in the choice of law (*nationality principle*), as an "Italian patriot" who "was very largely responsible [sic] for expressing in terms of private international law, the ideas and ideals of nationalism which swept Europe during the nineteenth century."[54] His principal contribution to conflicts literature, however, was an essay in 1874 "on the utility of making uniform for all States, in the form of one or more international treaties, a certain number of general rules of private international law, so as to assure the uniform decision [resolution] of conflicts between the different civil and criminal legislations."[55] The essay was a report presented to a new international academic institution designed with the intention of promoting such

[52] B. Audit, "A Continental Lawyer Looks at American Choice-of-law Principles," *American Journal of Comparative Law*, 27 (1979), 589–603.

[53] See E. Jayme, *Pasquale Stanislao Mancini: Internationales Privatrecht zwischen Risorgimento und Praktischer Jurisprudenz* (Ebelsbach: Verlag Rolf Gremer, 1980; also published in Italian as *Pasquale Stanislao Mancini: il diritto internazionale privato tra Risorgimento e attivita forense*, trans. Antonio Ruini (Padova: Edizioni CEDAM, 1988). Jayme has attempted to place Mancini in the ideological context of his time and emphasized his advocacy of party autonomy; Jayme's student, Yuko Nishitani, carried his work further. See Y. Nishitani, *Mancini und die Parteiautonomie im internationalen Privatrecht* (Heidelberg: Winter Verlag, 2000); Y. Nishitani, "Mancini e l'autonomia della volontà nel diritto internazionale private," *Rivista di diritto internazionale privato e processuale*, 37 (2001), 23–44.

[54] Forsyth, *Private International Law*, 50. Forsyth's section on Mancini is characteristically titled "P. S. Mancini, the rise of nationalism in Europe and the role of the *lex patriae*": ibid., 50–52.

[55] P. S. Mancini, "De l'utilité de rendre obligatoires pour tous les Etats, sous la forme d'un ou de plusieurs traités internationaux; un certain nombre des règles générales du Droit international privé pour assurer la décision uniforme des conflits entre les différentes législations civiles et criminelles," *Clunet*, 1 (1874), 221–239, 285–304.

projects, the Institute of International Law. It provided the impetus for a series of treaty projects which culminated in the first Hague Conventions on private international Law and the Hague Conference. The intellectual environment in which these initiatives took place saw an explosion in scholarly output and a new outlook: conflict of laws was linked to international law or even regarded as a branch of international law: the term *private international law* now acquired a true meaning.

The conflicts literature of the late nineteenth century includes many great works, far more sophisticated and eloquent than anything Mancini wrote. Mancini was a successful legislator, who achieved a model codification of conflicts rules in his own country, a spokesman both for the principle of nationality and an international codification; a statesman who almost succeeded in convening an international conference to achieve such codification. He was therefore a symbol for a collective ethos of jurists, who were called a "school" by adherents and detractors alike.[56] The term Italian or Latin school has been often used to describe them; I would propose the term *school of international law* (or international-law school), which better illustrates both their fundamental premises and broad geographical reach.

By the early twentieth century, the international-law school had lost its predominance – as a result of domestic and international politics, jurisprudential premises, developments in private law doctrine (as well as in international law), societal change, naïve methodology, and perhaps technical weakness. Opposing conceptions proliferated, and courts often went their own way.

The interwar and early postwar period saw a plethora of efforts at reconstruction. The doctrinal systems envisaged were more complex, more technical. The nascent discipline of comparative law increasingly provided a toolbox for bringing together private law and conflicts law, on the one hand, and different conflicts systems, on the other. Doctrinaire advocacy of a single grand connecting factor subsided, and efforts were made to bridge the divide between legal systems adhering to nationality and legal systems adhering to domicile. Legal issues, or devices, such as renvoi or the problem of legal characterization, which had in the past been used in attempts to derail the optimistic internationalist positivism

[56] See e.g. M. J. Farrely, "The New Italian School of Private International Law," *Juridical Review*, 5 (1893) 105–124, 197–211; G. de Vareilles-Sommières, *La synthèse du droit international privé*, vol. I (Paris: F. Pichon, 1897).

of the international-law school were now embraced as institutions helpful in achieving the field's mission.

1.5.3 Revolution, Crisis, Pluralism: Modern Conflict of Laws

For all the success of mature classical conflict of laws, another paradigm shift occurred in the mid-twentieth century. A few writers even seem to consider this shift as more important than the Copernican moment.[57] The majority, however, would regard change far subtler than in the mid-nineteenth century break: the traditional choice-of-law method with its jurisdiction-selecting rules has after all maintained its pivotal role.[58] On the other hand, it is no longer alone, having to coexist with other methods or even given way to them.

United States (US) law represents the clearest example of this shift – indeed, a veritable paradigm break as radical as the nineteenh-century shift. Influenced by developments in American legal theory, a "conflicts revolution" won against an inflexible version of the classical paradigm.[59] American conflict of laws subsequently embarked on its own path.[60] In many subjects (though by not means all) and in many states (though by no means all), the "jurisdiction-selecting" rules of the classical choice-of-law method were replaced by "approaches" – essentially, balancing exercises addressed to domestic-law substantive rules.[61]

The global consequences of this American conflicts revolution were not strong: in the rest of the world, the key word to describe develop-

[57] See e.g. A. Bucher and A. Bonomi, *Droit International Privé* (Basel: Helbing Lichtenhahn, 2001), 92ff who contrast to "classical" private international law "the emergence of methods inspired by the social goal of laws" – a notion comprising the American theories, the new unilateralism and the pluralism of methods. Celia Wasserstein Fassberg, "The Choice of Law Problem: Continuity and Change," unpublished S.J.D thesis, Harvard University (1982), 118ff, breaks the "world history" of the choice of law in three stages: antiquity, a traditional period bringing together preclassical and classical conflict of laws, and the modern period which signifies the rise of "substantivism."

[58] See e.g. H. Batiffol and P. Lagarde, *Droit international privé*, vol. I (Paris: LGDJ, 1993), 409 ("*La pensée européenne, si l'on peut employer ce terme génerique, est restée dans l'ensemble fidèle à l'inspiration de Savigny*").

[59] A. von Mehren, "Une esquisse de l'évolution du droit international privé aux Etats-Unis," *Clunet*, 100 (1973), 116–157; Audit, "American Choice of Law," 603.

[60] Cf. R. Michaels, "After the Revolution: Decline and Return of U.S. Conflict of Laws," *Yearbook of Private International Law*, 11 (2009), 11–30.

[61] For an overview, see S. Symeonides, *American Private International Law* (The Netherlands: Kluwer Law International, 2008).

ments appears to have been *evolution*, not revolution.[62] However, from the early postwar years concerns were voiced in Europe about a "crisis of the conflict of laws."[63] Eventually, a new paradigm did emerge: since the 1970s, we have come to think in terms of "pluralism of methods" within the conflict of laws discourse: traditional choice-of-law rules coexist with mandatory rules of immediate application, and escape devices.[64] Substantive policies are considered alongside – or through – "conflicts" policies.[65] The private international law regimes created in the European Union are certainly adding to this complexity.[66] On the other hand, EU private international law is clearly still reliant upon the choice-of-law method and in a way represents the fulfilment of the classical dream of a uniform system of conflicts rules.

At the same time, conflict of laws is no longer the only show in town: the postwar era has witnessed the growth first of international business law, and subsequently of uniform law, as autonomous fields – part kin, part rivals to the conflict of laws.[67] The so-called *lex mercatoria* and dreams of transnational law have captured the imaginations of many scholars. Accordingly, the *modern* paradigm of private international law might entail not just a pluralism of conflicts methods, and policies, but also a plurality of subdisciplines.

[62] K. Siehr, "Revolution and Evolution in Conflicts Law," *Louisiana Law Review*, 60 (2000), 1353–1660; S. Symeonides, "The American Revolution and the European Evolution in Choice of Law: Reciprocal Lessons," *Tulane Law Review*, 82 (2008), 1741–1799.

[63] See e.g. A. Miaja de la Muela, *Derecho internacional privado*, vol. I, 8th ed (Madrid: Atlas, 1979), 253 ("estamos en presencia de una profunda crisis del edificio siete veces secular de las doctrinas conflictuales"). The term "crisis" had became commonly known following G. Kegel, "The Crisis of Conflict of Laws," *Recueil des cours*, 112 (1964), 91–268. As Kegel, "Crisis," 95 n. 1 himself points out, the first written mentions of "crisis" appear in the late 1940s. See P. H. Neuhaus, "Die Krise im internationalen Privatrecht," *Deutsche Rechts-Zeitschrift*, 3 (1948), 86–87; and H. Kronstein, "Crisis of 'Conflict of Laws'," *Georgetown Law Journal*, 37 (1949), 483–513.

[64] See H. Batiffol, "Le pluralisme des méthodes en droit international privé," *Recueil des cours*, 139 (1977), 75–148. See also Batiffol and Lagarde, *Droit international privé*, 1:409 (speaking of "*approfontissement des méthodes*").

[65] M. Reimann, *Conflict of Laws in Western Europe: A Guide through the Jungle* (Irvington, NY: Transnational Publishers, 1995).

[66] R. Michaels, "The New European Choice-of-Law Revolution," *Tulane Law Review*, 82 (2008), 1607–1644.

[67] On uniform law, see e.g. P. Lalive, "Tendances et méthodes en droit international privé," *Recueil des cours*, 155 (1977), 3–424, 47–50; and C. Pamboukis, "Droit international privé holistique: droit uniforme et droit international privé," *Recueil des cours*, 330 (2007).

1.5.4 *Classical, Preclassical, and Modern*

To distinguish these three periods of historical conflict of laws, I have chosen to use the conceptual scheme of preclassical–classical–modern.[68] Effectively borrowed from art and cultural history, the conceptual scheme is rather new to private international law.[69] It is on the contrary used in intellectual and doctrinal legal history.[70]

In the history of artistic styles, classical has most often connoted a stylistic peak, a stage of development where the style is "at its fullest and most harmonious expression."[71] The classical thus conceived should be contrasted with something preclassical (or "archaic" or "primitive") on the one hand, and something "postclassical" or "modern" on the other – usually after a period in which the classical style "loses its original forcefulness and is sometimes meaninglessly elaborated."[72] Other qualities attributed to the Classical are harmony, clarity, restraint, universality, and idealism.[73] To legal classicism in specific is attributed the attempt to rationally order the whole legal universe.[74] It is characterized by a

[68] This scheme admittedly leaves out, for the time being, claims of an emerging "postmodern" paradigm. The argument for postmodern private international law has been most forcefully made by Eric Jayme. See notably E. Jayme, "Identité culturelle et intégration: le droit international privé postmoderne," *Recueil des cours*, 251 (1995), 9–268. L. Brilmayer, "Post-modernism in American Choice of Law" in J. Erauw et al. (eds.), *Liber Memorialis François Laurent* (Brussels: E. Story-Scientia, 1989), 695–705, who is also cited, argues for a "new, post-modern, generation" of US conflicts scholars to overcome the "tidy but misleading division of the world into two camps" between "old fashioned" territorialists and "modern" policy analysts (695).

[69] For an exception, see Bucher and Bonomi, *Droit international privé*, 89–92.

[70] In the context of US legal thought, see notably D. Kennedy, "The Rise and Fall of Classical Legal Thought," unpublished manuscript, 1975; reformatted 1998, published with a new preface by the author, "Thirty Years Later" (Washington, DC: Beard Books, 2006); W. M. Wiecek, *The Lost World of Classical Legal Thought: Law and Ideology in America, 1886–1937* (New York: Oxford University Press, 1998); D. Kennedy, "From the Will Theory to the Principle of Private Autonomy: Lon Fuller's 'Consideration And Form'," *Columbia Law Review*, 100 (2000), 94–175.

In English contract law, the distinction between classical and modern contract law is habitually asserted. See H. Collins, *The Law of Contract*, 4th ed (London: Butterworths, 2003), 3–7, for the statement of the historical consciousness; W. Swain, *The Law of Contract, 1670–1870* (Cambridge: Cambridge University Press, 2015), 172–230.

[71] See "Classicism and Neoclassicism," *Encyclopedia Britannica*, 3:355–356.

[72] Ibid.

[73] Ibid.

[74] Kennedy, *Rise and Fall*, 1ff ("Because this way of thinking amounted to a rationalistic ordering of the whole legal universe, I will call it Classical legal thought."); Collins, *Law of Contract*, 3 ("simultaneously sparse in content and imperialist in its ambitions of interpretation and regulation").

"coherent set of beliefs, values and assumptions,"[75] and a "relatively small set of fundamental principles."[76] These characteristics also presage its eventual decline, as these conceptual premises are challenged by reality or internal contradictions.

To use this conceptual scheme is to acknowledge that *classical* conflict of laws is at the center of the field's history. Classical doctrine serves as the yardstick with which subsequent developments and theories, no matter how respectful or rebellious, are to be measured. But, just like in art history, it is neither the end nor the beginning of the story.

A serious consideration in selecting a conceptual scheme was to avoid too strong a reference to specific doctrinal or conceptual battles, as well as any pejorative implication.[77] This is indeeed a "label that is as neutral as possible yet that retains some descriptive and suggestive content," and captures the essence of what was in effect "both an ideology and a structure of thought created by an intellectual community."[78] It also avoids too strong an allusion to the perceived primitiveness of what comes before the Copernican moment.[79]

But the principal objective in the choice of terms was to convey a general impression and the spirit of each era. When it comes to preclassical conflict of laws, we must set aside our fixation on "statutes" and to instead approach, in a comprehensive fashion and with an open mind, the thought of Medieval and Early Modern jurists.

1.5.5 Theory and Practice

Private international law has been characterized as "learned law" (*droit savant*) – a legal field largely made by scholars (and perhaps only appreciated by them).[80] We might envisage doctrinal evolution in terms

[75] Wiecek, *Lost World*, 4 ("Legal classicism was . . . a way of thinking . . . abstract, formal, conceptualistic, categorical and (sometimes) deductive.").

[76] Collins, *Law of Contract*, 3.

[77] Both are problems with other established terms: see Hatzimihail, "Conceptual Battlefield," 57–62.

[78] Wiecek, *Classical Legal Thought*, 3 (explaining his choice of "legal classicism" over "legal orthodoxy" or "legal formalism," both established terms in the history of US legal thought).

[79] I have been, however, influenced by D. Kennedy, "Primitive Legal Scholarship," *Harvard International Law Journal*, 27 (1986), 1–98 (a textual analysis of Grotius, Suarez, and Vittoria) and Bayly, *Birth of the Modern World* ("Archaic Globalisation").

[80] B. Oppetit, "Le droit international privé, droit savant," *Recueil des cours*, 234 (1992), 331–434. Cf. L. Brilmayer, *Conflict of Laws: Foundations and Future Directions*, 2nd ed

of an "anthill" being constructed by generation after generation of juristic writing, inspite of extrinsic adversities.[81] The history of the field, as usually told, tends to confirm this notion: historical literature emphasizes the role of scholarly writing, and theoretical ideas, in the creation and evolution of private international law.[82] Even the story told by this very book is fundamentally a history of legal scholarship: its difference lies in being conscious about the choice involved, mindful of context and nuances, and aware of the impact of the existing narratives.

It is remarkable that the predominance of legal scholarship is not frequntly acknowledged in express terms. In fact, when asserted it usually is a criticism, employed by those seeking to drastically alter, or demolish, the conflicts discourse. William Prosser famously called "the realm of the conflict of laws . . . a dismal swamp, filled with quaking quagmires, and inhabited by learned but eccentric professors who theorize about mysterious matters in a strange but incomprehensible jargon. The ordinary court, or lawyer, is quite lost when engulfed and entangled in it."[83] Having become an advocate of substantive-law solutions, Friedrich Juenger presented "scholars' predominance" as the cause of "our

(Boston: Little, Brown & Co., 1995), vii; In the Preface to the first edition of his treatise (1935), as reproduced in J. Fawcett and J. M. Carruthers, *Cheshire, North & Fawcett: Private International Law*, 14th ed (Oxford: Oxford University Press, 2008), vii, G.C. Cheshire wrote: "Of all the departments of English law, Private International Law offers the freest scope to the mere jurist. It is the perfect antithesis of such a topic as real property law. It is not overloaded with detailed rules; it has only been lightly touched by the paralyzing hand of the Parliamentary draftsman; it is perhaps the one considerable department in which the formation of a coherent body of law is in course of process; it is, at the moment, fluid not static, elusive not obvious; it repels any tendency to dogmatism; and, above all, the possible permutations of the questions that it raises are so numerous that the diligent investigator can seldom rest content with the solution that he proposes."

81 This metaphor is especially apt given that it was originally used to describe the collective consciousness of doctrinal writers. See P. Jestaz and C. Jamin, "The Entity of French Doctrine: Some Thoughts on the Community of French Legal Writers," *Legal Studies*, 18 (1998), 414–435, 426: "[D]octrine is like an ant-hill, where, in the end, each of the authors, even the most famous only carries out quite modest work. From time to time the legislator kicks over the ant-hill, but it is then built up once more. He never completely destroys it, as the existing doctrine is imposed on him to a certain extent." The article's original French version provoked an intense debate linked both to the politics of French private law and the theory of sources. See L. Aynès et al., "Antithèse de 'l'entité' (à propos d'une opinion sur la doctrine)," *Dalloz*, 1997, 229–230; P. Jestaz and C. Jamin, *La Doctrine* (Paris: Dalloz, 2004).

82 See Chapters 2 and 3 below.

83 W. C. Prosser, "Interstate Publication," *Michigan Law Review*, 51 (1953), 959–1000, 971 (immediately prior to enumerating "ten different and inconsistent theories . . . adopted by some court or suggested by learned writers").

discipline's obscurity and vexing nomenclature," and lamented the "speculative minds ... drawn into our discipline precisely because it offers a 'mental game with infinite complications.'"[84] Ironically, even Juenger himself tells the history of the field as a story of scholars and "learned law," while railing against a "a discipline whose hallmarks have been vacillation and uncertainty since it was discovered in the Middle Ages."[85]

Equal vigour has been employed in arguing the contrary view, i.e. that conflicts scholarship follows legal practice – notably courts and legislators. Concerns about courts' predominance are especially acute in systems with few or obsolete legislative rules, such as France, where the role of the case law has been traditionally very important. Some argue that the role of *la doctrine* is to explain, motivate and imbue some systematicity into *la pratique*.[86] The mainstream view accepts the role of courts in forming rules, but insists on their scholarly roots: especially prior to the nineteenth century, there had been only very few cases of little clarity, as contrasted to a doctrinal corpus, a "common fund," on which courts had to rely.[87]

84 Juenger, *Choice of Law*, 162–163.

85 Ibid., 151. See N. Hatzimihail, "Pages of History: Friedrich Juenger and the Historical Consciousness of Modern Private International Law" in L. Pereznieto Castro et al. (eds.), *Tradition and Innovation of Private International Law at the Beginning of the Third Millennium* (New York: Juris Publishing 2006), 81–123. In his advocacy of a third Restatement on Conflicts, Juenger came to attack case law as viciously than doctrine. See F. K. Juenger, "A Third Conflicts Restatement?," *Indiana Law Journal*, 75 (2000), 403–416, speaking e.g. of "gibberish" (403, 404), "judicial prose [having] an Alice-in-Wonderland kind of quality" (403), and "the unresteatable mixture of academic teachings and judicial fumbling" (415).

86 See e.g. M.-L. Niboyet and G. de Geouffre de La Pradelle, *Droit international privé* (Paris, 2007), 86 (at the conlusion of a short doctrinal history of conflicts law): "Cette présentation très sommaire de l'histoire des idées en droit international privé ne doit accréditer l'idée, qu'à la faveur d'un corps de textes, pendant longtemps embryonnaire en la matière, la doctrine a pu se substituer au législateur et forger les règles de notre droit international privé. En réalité, c'est toujours la pratique qui a fait apparaître les problèmes et leurs solutions. La doctrine s'est efforcée de les expliquer, voire de donner quelques impulsions et de les systématiser. Le dialogue entre la doctrine et les praticiens a toujours été particulièrement fructueux dans cette discipline, grâce à une écoute réciproque assez remarquable, sauf certains exemples de discorde, dans le plus célèbre est celui du phénomène du renvoi."

87 Audit, *Droit international privé*, 21 ("un corps de doctrine"); M. Simon-Depitre, *Droit international privé* (Paris: Librairie Armand Colin, 1964), 18 ("Ce rôle a été essentiellement celui des tribunaux, mais la jurisprudence n'a pas eu à créer de toutes pièces des règles, il existait un fonds commun coutumier dans lequel ella a pu puiser"), 18–20.

There is substantial truth in that statement, as well as a connection to the historical shifts outlined above. Scholarship is motivated by practical needs, but it is also needed to provide a new outlook to courts and practitioners. We will see Medieval and Early Modern jurists who elaborated doctrinal systems that were then carried in very different, distant jurisdictions. At the same time, the impact of established or emerging practice, is visible even in the scholarly works we shall consider. The Liberal internationalists who created the discipline in the mid to late nineteenth century (what we have called the *early classical period*) explicitly called for legal scholarship to assume a leading role in the construction of private international law: if public international law was to be constructed by statesmen and diplomats, private international law had to be the work of jurists.[88] A *science of private international law* had to be created, steering the middle ground between the extreme positivism of practice and the extreme idealism of natural lawyers.[89] Courts were to apply and enforce the rules of this private international law.[90] Things however did not go as smoothly as envisaged. Liberal internationalists were confronted not just by academic opposition but often by court resistance to classical models – due to ignorance of new ideas, politics, or in an effort to do justice in the individual case. At the same time, dissident scholars used these instances of judicial resistance to elaborate doctrinal opposition. Postwar reconstructive scholarship sought to integrate the major enclaves of court resistance into a doctrinal system.

The example of *renvoi* is characteristic.[91] In fact, the renvoi mechanism was "discovered" being used by certain courts in the late nineteenth century; it was presented as a threat to the project of unifying choice-of-law rules by national and eventually international legislation. It was certainly seen in those terms by scholars espousing diametrically opposed doctrinal approaches, but sharing in their pursuance of a uniform conflicts instrument and their conviction that the courts should follow

[88] Lainé, *Introduction*, 1:6: "Le droit international public sera donc surtout l'oeuvre des hommes d'Etat, le droit international privé celle des jurisconsultes."

[89] Laurent, *Droit civil international*, 1:65

[90] Lainé, *Introduction*, 1:6.

[91] The masterful examination by G. P. Romano, *Le Dilemma du Renvoi en Droit International Privé: La Thèse, l'Antithèse et la Recherche d'une Système* (Geneva: Schultess, 2014) of the underlying policies, theories, and epistemological assumptions of renvoi constitutes the definitive reference on the subject.

scholarship.[92] In countries where anti-renvoi scholarship did not prevail upon judges friendly to the institution,[93] a subsequent generation of scholars attempted to bridge the emerging gap between theory and practice, while still paying tribute to their predecessors, by integrating renvoi into a reconstructive conflicts paradigm of moderate internationalism.[94] Subsequent codifications, notably in the EU, have pushed back renvoi, but it keeps appearing in new instances and jurisdictions – to the chagrin of many students – and still incites considerable excitement to many scholars.[95]

1.5.6 On Conflict of Laws, Private International Law, and Other Names

At this point a note is needed about the employment of the terms *private international law* and *conflict of laws* throughout this book. The term *conflict of laws* is used in its Anglo-American conception, where it encompasses questions of applicable law, on the one hand (i.e. what the French call *conflits de lois*) and matters of international civil litigation such as especially civil jurisdiction, recognition and enforcement of judgments, even judicial cooperation, on the other hand (i.e. what the French call *conflits de jurisdictions*).[96] For the most part, I am using the

[92] According to H. Lewald, "La théorie du renvoi," *Recueil des cours*, 29 (1929), 519–620, 583: "presque partout la doctrine a protesté contre cette nouvelle conception du droit international privé; dans sa grande majorité, elle c'est prononcée contre l'admission du renvoi et il n'y a que peu de theoriciens de droit international privé qui ont cru *devoir accepter* la solution sanctionnée par la jurisprudence." (emphasis added).

[93] E. Rabel, *Conflict of Laws: A Comparative Study* vol. I (Ann Arbor, MI: University of Michigan Press, 1945), 75–76, speaking of "violently prejudiced literature confronting naively consistent practice."

[94] See notably H. Batiffol, *Traité élémentaire de droit international privé* (Paris: LGDJ, 1949), esp. 326–328; also P. Francescakis, *La théorie du renvoi et les conflits de systèmes en droit international privé* (Paris: Sirey, 1958); Rabel, *Conflict of Laws*, 1:82 ("If the world is split into two contradictory systems, there must be some modus vivendi. Renvoi is one of the best means to that end").

[95] In the words of J. G. Collier, *Conflict of Laws* (Cambridge: Cambridge University Press, 2001), 20: "[t]he topic is bedevilled by rather intemperate academic discussion; most writers are, in general, hostile to the renvoi, but courts in many states have adopted it." See Romano, *Dilemme du Renvoi*, 345–657 for a sweeping comparative survey.

[96] See e.g. Fawcett and Carruthers, *Cheshire, North & Fawcett: Private International Law*, 3–4. French private international law has traditionally also included the law of nationality and the status of aliens (*condition des étrangers*). For a modern explanation see Y. Loussouarn, P. Bourel, and P. de Vareilles-Sommières, *Droit international privé*, 8th ed (Paris: Dalloz, 2004), 5–15.

two terms interchangeably when it comes to contemporary doctrine. This is actually the state of affairs today, with "private international law" being the globally accepted term and conflict of laws being used in much of the Anglosphere.

Whether there is – or has been – any stake and signifance in the choice of either term is worth a separate study. Our literature is filled with examples of authors adopting one or the other name, some among them with a certain degree of – feigned or real – indignation.[97] In the past, so many names have been proposed – no other legal subject has ever had this privilege – that they could fill a "cabinet of curiosities."[98] As to the mainstream names, Joseph Story is credited by many for being the first to use – albeit very casually – the term "private international law," which however became common one to two generations later. As to the – older – term "conflict of laws," which we will not find in any of the Medieval writings on "conflicts," the attempt to provide a longer pedigree have reached as far as the 1st century Roman jurist Quintilianus.[99] But what do these names mean? As will be argued in this book, not much – and everything. The regular use of the term "conflict of laws," or its conceptual cousins, by authors in the Early Modern era, indicates the first stages of jurists understanding the specialty of the subject and beginning to deal in a systematic manner with what we are calling conflicts questions.[100] The adoption by a group of writers of the term "private international law," likewise indicated that they sought to place these conflicts questions within – or even, at the forefront – of what we would today call a normative project for global governance.[101] Another example is how the term *conflict of laws* prevailed over *private international law* in late nineteenth and early twentieth-century England. Presumably the fact that many of the conflicts considered were "internal" to the British Empire played its part, and the same rings especially true with regard to US scholarship. But for authors such as Dicey, the chosen term signified a choice or at least a

[97] See e.g. Forsyth, *Private International Law*, 5–6 (discussing mostly South African cases and authors ibid., n. 25; in in the end, as he regards both names "equally misleading," Forsyth chooses "for reasons of taste rather than logic" the former, because it sounds better in Afrikaans).

[98] See Chapter 6 n. 27 below.

[99] E. Spiro, *The General Principles of the Conflict of Laws* (Cape Town: Juta & Co., 1982), 2.

[100] See Chapters 14 and 15 below.

[101] See Chapter 6 below.

statement: affirmation of the common-law nature (and orientation) of the subject; commitment to the imperial (or federalist) project; last but not least, reluctance to follow the Continental "theoretical," aprioristic approaches and far-reaching normative projects.[102]

For the time being, however, two observations are all that is needed. First, we can only speak of *conflict of laws* for the period up the second half of the nineteenth century: the term "private international law" was only introduced in earnest in the mid-nineteenth century, and the *discipline* of private international law was constructed soon thereafter. Hence the book is entitled *Preclassical Conflict of Laws*. From that moment on until the postwar era, private international law *is* conflict of laws: both terms can only refer to the same material. In fact, in the second half of the nineteenth century, the term was even used in British and American treatises. Today, the equation of private international law with the conflict of laws is still the canon. In the light of the exposition above, about modern doctrine, it woul be more fruitful to think of the discipline of private international law as encompassing more than *modern* conflict of laws. Modern conflict of laws would thus be a subdiscipline. Even in that case, however, it is still the dominant private international law discourse.

This brings us to the second observation. To speak of "private international lawyers" is in principle the same as speaking of "conflicts lawyers," but the former term places a stronger emphasis on the multidimensional functions the field is called to perform, and better highlights the sense of forming part of a legal discipline – and its significance. To these concepts we must now turn.

1.6 Conceptual Premises

The essential theoretical premise of this book is that private international law is, today, an autonomous legal discipline.[103] This discipline has emerged out of the creative tension between private-law and international-law (or "multistate" or "multipolity") considerations. Even prior to the creation of an autonomous discipline, this creative

[102] A. V. Dicey, *A Digest of the Law of England with Reference to the Conflict of Laws* (London: Stevens and Sons, 1896), 15ff as discussed in Chapter 15 below.

[103] See in this sense notably Miaja de la Muela, *Derecho Internacional Privado*, 64–65 ("*el derecho internacional privado como disciplina científica*").

tension between what could be equated to private-law and international-law considerations had nourished a distinct legal discourse on conflicts issues. Yet the notion of an autonomous discipline matters: first, in order to first understand the present state of private international law and its provenance and to eventually outline an agenda for doctrinal renewal; and second, in order to eventually outline an agenda for doctrinal renewal.

1.6.1 The Discipline of Private International Law

A discipline, as defined in this book, is more than a *legal field*, and certainly much more than its subject matter. A discipline is a *socio-epistemological* construct. It is constituted by scholars, and practitioners, who identify – more or less consciously – as comprising a group with social functions and epistemological characteristics. A discipline involves one or more networks that foster communication among its members and lead to the consequent proliferation of academic production and discussion; it often involves a distinct agenda, and it certainly comes to claim its own methodology and general theory. Proliferation will lead to expansion and possibly tension. Tension as to methodology and general theory may lead to subdisciplines created or spun off.

What is today called *private international law* in most of the world and *the conflict of laws* in the rest is, presently a discipline in this sense. *Preclassical* conflicts doctrine was constituted by more or less isolated Medieval and Early Modern authors, who usually wrote of conflicts as part of general treatises on law. The *classical* paradigm took off decades after Savigny: once the first network was created and set an agenda, however, things moved fast. Institutions and journals proliferated and promoted a specific understanding of the method and premises of private international law. The next step was to integrate courses of private international law into the law school curriculum: for example, in France, the 1880 ministerial decree that created a specialized course in public universities led apparently to a veritable big bang of literature, from treatises to monographs to student outlines.

Today, there exists a cadre of specialized academics who: interact in professional associations; run law journals, monograph series, and specialized courses; marshal legions of research students; and identify other jurists as their peers. In fact, if we are to define private international law, following French textbooks, as "the special body of law that applies to private persons involved in international legal relations,"[104] we could distinguish new subdisciplines such as international business law, and possibly international uniform law, distinct from the "traditional" conflict of laws.

Considering private international law as a discipline will allow us to better understand its evolution and function. I would argue that the state of conflicts doctrine is directly related to the existence and operation of the social–professional networks described above. The means of producing and communicating knowledge are especially important. Journals are important for communicating ideas as well as for promoting common premises.[105] Courses are important both for recruiting students and disciples but especially for conveying to broader masses of lawyers the fundamental premises of the subject.[106]

1.6.2 The Governance Functions of Private International Law

In contemporary conflict of laws, both the private-law and international-law dimensions are taken as a given. In fact, private international law has a distinct impact on both subject matters. It could even be considered an instrument of, indeed a participant in, both international governance and private-law governance.

The term *governance* is used here in an effort to capture a phenomenon broader than positive law and systematic legal doctrine. Governance has been defined as "the complex of more or less formalized bundles of rules, roles and relationships that define the social practices of state and non-state actors interacting in various issue areas."[107] The

[104] I am taking the adjective *special* to imply a minimum of consciousness as to the distinctness of the subject matter, and probably the approach adopted to deal with.

[105] See in that sense, K. Nadelman, "*Internationales Privatrecht*: A Source Book on Conflicts Theory Analyzed and Reviewed," *Harvard International Law Journal*, 17 (1976), 657–677, both for the review of the book itself (a canon of approaches) and for the discussion of journals on private international law existing in the world. See ibid., 676: "Had there been an American journal specializing in private international law . . . this gap in intellectual exchange could not have developed. Attention to developments abroad would be automatic. Manuscripts would come from all sides."

[106] See e.g. Laurent, *Droit civil international*, 1:665, advocating the creation of specialized professorships on private international law in France and Belgium: "A mon avis, les travaux littéraires ne suffisent point; il faut agir sur les masses, et pour cela un enseignement oral vaut mieux que les livres."

[107] D. Kennedy, "New Approaches to Comparative Law: Comparativism and International Governance," *Utah Law Review*, (1997) 545–593, 549 n. 4.

process, however, by which the said bundles are produced, in the course of that interaction, is at least as important as the complex itself.[108]

1.6.2.1 International Governance and Private International Law

From the point of view of political science, private international law is a mechanism for the allocation of competences between the entities taking part in the international system – whether we are thinking in terms of a classic, horizontal *states system* with sovereign actors or of a more complex "international system." Even legal unification may, from such a perspective, be viewed as attempting to shift powers away from one level in the world system and toward another. The conflict of laws addresses, in a sense, the "existential" problems of these actors.[109]

At the same time, the conflict of laws is challenged, and nourished by the developments in the international system. It also becomes a battleground, a field for instrumentalist considerations. The nineteenth-century founders of the discipline thought of "private international law" as the branch of "international law" easier to construct. Fin-de-millénaire transnationalists viewed it as the part of the Westphalian firmament easier to demolish. Politics is, however, only part of the equation. For many authors, the international dimension serves principally as the doctrinal foundation of their conflicts system.[110]

Conflicts literature tends to minimize the extent to which private international law, and the choices made in it, help shape the world system. An author might envisage the world system as an "international society" of sovereign states, or as a nebula of spontaneous legal orders and diverse structures; she might aspire to a new world order, or simply to doctrinal cohesion. In all cases, the international system and its future prospects are presented to us as fixed.

In this regard, the study of preclassical conflict of laws poses new problems and offers new ideas. The Westphalian system of sovereign states is set up by the time the Dutch school blossoms in the late Seventeenth century, but what about the Medieval world? Can there be

108 See N. Hatzimihail, "Reflections on the International Dimension of Private International Law" in R. Jafferali et al. (eds.), *Liber amicorum Nadine Watté* (Brussels: Larcier, 2017), 287–302, 292.

109 See the very interesting work of Alex Mills in this regard: Mills, *Confluence*; and A. Mills, "Rethinking Jurisdiction in International Law," *British Yearbook of International Law*, 84 (2014), 187–239.

110 See Chapter 6 below.

a private international law without sovereign states, without sovereign legal systems? Were we to answer the question in the affirmative, what kind of a conflict of laws would that be? To answer this question, one has to go beyond the wording of isolated passages, to leave behind present-day concepts and aspirations. We have to consider a different political theory, to understand how the Medieval and Early Modern authors perceived the world-system of their day; we have to delve into their hierarchy of legal sources and ask ourselves how their theory of legal sources interacts with that world-system; we also have to consider their attitudes toward legal unity, legal diversity and the substantive stakes involved.

1.6.2.2 Private-Law Governance and Private International Law

Private international law also plays an important role with regard to the governance of private legal relations. These aspects of the discipline are only partly reflected in the discussion about whether, and how, to consider "substantive policies" and "substantive law." Obviously, even "substantive-law neutral" conflicts processes have an impact on the governance of private relations. Moreover, a decision on conflicts is likely to entail a choice between competing substantive policies.[111] Conflicts mechanisms may further or hinder the substantive policies pursued by the political-normative entities – be they Medieval Italian cities controlled by aristocrats and guilds, or complex modern nation-states. They also impact individuals and social actors seeking to materialize their own aspirations. Conversely, as private relations and individual strategies are undergoing continuous transformation, so are conflicts doctrines forever challenged and reshaped by material circumstances, and evasion.

The relationship between private international law and domestic private-law concerns is a delicate one. The conflict of laws is nourished by private-law concepts. Whether we are employing a theory of statutes, classic choice-of-law rules or interest analysis, private relations have to be grouped into legal categories using private-law concepts. Both the structure of a conflicts work, and the choice-of-law solutions it sponsors, are therefore affected by the private-law regime that informs and surrounds it.

[111] See e.g. J. W. Singer, "A Pragmatic Guide to Conflicts," *Boston University Law Review*, 70 (1990), 731–819.

At the same time, conflicts doctrine cannot be too closely affiliated with a certain private-law regime. Early classical conflict of laws had a rude awakening (with hindsight, one would say: surprisingly enough) when particularists pointed to the divergent scope – and use – of the same legal concepts in different legal systems. Private international law has sought to deal with the problem in two different ways. The first one was to give in to national legal systems and grant preference to one of the private-law regimes in question: the question, for example, of whether prescription of a contractual claim constitutes a matter of procedure or a substantive-law issue pertaining to contract law should thus be resolved by reference to the law of the forum (*lex fori*) or the law applicable on the merits (*lex causae*). A corollary remedy was to speak of systemic conflicts and employ devices such as renvoi to settle them. The second one was to create common, "autonomous" concepts, either by comparative research on national laws, or, in the case of international instruments containing uniform rules, by considering their text as an autonomous system.[112]

Preclassical conflicts doctrine was faced with similar problems. Medieval and Early Modern jurists who wrote on conflicts were part of a scholarly community which transcended the boundaries of local jurisdictions. They also had to draw on general scholarship in order to build their conceptual edifices and outline legal categories. At the same time, their thinking, and proposed rules, reflect the material world around them, as well as their efforts to achieve a better ordering of private affairs.

1.6.2.3 Autonomy

The simple consideration of the private and the international element does not suffice to understand private international law. For example, the quest for *decisional harmony*, which some regard as the primary mission of private international law, is a matter of both international governance (in the sense of harmony) and private-law governance (in the sense of legal certainty) tends not to be the primary concern in neither.

In general, while the theoretical and doctrinal choices made in the conflict of laws will impact both the "private law" and the "international

[112] On the former see Rabel, *Conflict of Laws*, 1:49–60 and the literature cited, including his own 1931 article. On the autonomous interpretation of EU instruments on private international law see e.g. M. Audit, "L'intérpretation autonome du droit international privé Communautaire," *Clunet*, 130 (2004), 789–816; U. Magnus, "Introduction" in U. Magnus and P. Mankowski (eds.), *Brussels I Regulation*, 2nd ed (Munich: Sellier, 2012), 32–34.

governance" milieux, conflicts discourse is still left with considerable leeway. We may hence talk of *private international governance* as a third type of governance done by private international law.[113] Alternatively, we could conclude that some questions are better first considered as conflicts questions, before we consider their "governance" impact.

The development of private international law is often described in terms of internal oppositions between territorial and personalist doctrines, unilateral and multilateral rules. The story is told in terms of conflicting worldviews, or in more technical terms. In recent times, we have seen a celebration of party autonomy as the pillar of private international law. We are also witnessing a reconfiguration of the division of labor between procedural and substantive conflict of laws: in commercial disputes, jurisdiction is becoming more important than choice of law.

1.6.3 A "Remarkable Trinity"

To understand the creation, and function, of private international law, one has to contemplate its triangular relation with private law and international law. Both terms are used here in a broad, functional sense.

The notion of "private law" would have been alien to the jurists prior to the nineteenth century – but clearly, Medieval and Early Modern jurists were contributing to what is today called private law (as indeed many have also contributed to what we today call public law).[114] International law is also a nineteenth-century concept, in fact a mid-nineteenth century term.[115] Even the term *law of nations* only acquired

[113] See N. Hatzimihail, Foundations of Party Autonomy and the Evolution of the Conflict of Laws. Unpublished LL.M. thesis, Harvard University (1997), 77.

[114] See C. Donahue, "Private Law without the State," *American Journal of Comparative Law*, 56 (2008), 541–565.

[115] See e.g. L. Renault, *Introduction au droit international* (Paris: L. Larose, 1879). The term international law is credited to Jeremy Bentham (1780), who did spoke of "international jurisprudence:" J. Bentham, *An Introduction to the Principles of Morals and Legislation*, (Oxford, 1879: reprint of the 1823 edition), § 17.25 esp. 326 n. 1: "The word international, it must be acknowledged, is a new one; though, it is hoped, sufficiently analogous and intelligible. It is calculated to express, in a more significant way, the branch of law which goes commonly under the name of the law of nations: an appellation so uncharacteristic, that, were it not for the force of custom, it would seem rather to refer to internal jurisprudence. The chancellor D'Aguesseau has already made, I find, a similar remark: he says that what is commonly called *droit des gens*, ought rather to be termed droit *entre les gens*." See also M. W. Janis, "Jeremy Bentham and the Fashioning of 'International Law'," *American Journal of International Law*, 74 (1984), 405–418;

its contemporary meaning in the late eighteenth century, after a long period in the shadow first of scholasticism and subsequently of natural law.[116]

The birth of the discipline of private international law, as a self-conscious discursive community with its internal dynamics was closely related to the creation of a discipline of international law, in the mid- to late nineteenth Century. However, the doctrinal core of the new discipline is due to the doctrinal writers of private law, from the twelfth-century glossators to the nineteenth-century legislative and academic positivists, who legated to the discipline much of its building materials. Subsequent developments in private international law were triggered by the movements in both parent disciplines, as well as by the internal dynamics of the conflicts discourse. Even the occasional suggestion that private international law is neither "private" nor "international" law is related to a specific understanding of both conflicts doctrine and the policies of private law and international law.[117]

This simple idea is often downplayed. Thus, Continental historiography presents a "particularist" assault on "universalist" private international law at the end of the nineteenth century.[118] The catalyst is supposed to have been either the growing fin-de-siècle nationalism or the increased sophistication of conflicts doctrine (with the discovery of devices such as *renvoi*, the *ordre public* exception, legal characterization). A more thoughtful explanation points to the equilibrium that needed to be restored between the private-law and international-law dimension of conflicts doctrine.[119] This may well be so. We should additionally consider the fact that the same period also saw the growth of comprehensive jurisprudential critiques of nineteenth-century legal formalism – what could be called the rise of *empirical conceptions* of law.[120] The twentieth century would subsequently bear witnesss to numerous efforts at

R. Domingo, *The New Global Law* (Cambridge: Cambridge University Press, 2010), 30–32.

116 E. de Vattel, *Le droit des gens, ou Principes de la loi naturelle* (Paris, 1758).

117 See notably J.-P. Niboyet, *Traité de droit international privé français*, vol. I, 2nd ed (Paris: Sirey, 1947), 1 ("c'est la branche appartenant, actuellement encore, en principe, au droit public national et, très exceptionnellement, au droit des gens"); I. Szászy, *Private International Law in the European People's Democracies* (Budapest: Akadémiai Kiado, 1964), 14–15 ("socialist private international law is neither international, nor private").

118 See e.g. Audit, *Droit international privé*, 74–75

119 See H. Batiffol, *Aspects philosophiques du droit international privé* (Paris: Dalloz, 1956), as discussed in Chapter 6 below.

120 Hatzimihail, "Conceptual Battlefield."

jurisprudential reconstruction and system-building, most of which by now are of interest only to the historian or the theorist. The most successful among them is the school of comparative private international law. It is interesting in that effect that the main use of the term *autonomy* regarding private international law is in describing the use of private-law terms 'autonomous' from national legal systems, through a comparative exercise (or, in more recent times, transnational lawmaking).[121]

1.7 Structure of the Book

This book consists of four parts. The first two parts lay out the doctrinal and historical framework for the case studies which constitute its second half.

Part I addresses the historiographical context for a study of preclassical conflict of laws. It concentrates on the review of the existing literature and a systematic exploration of the historical consciousness of private international lawyers. This is effected in two levels – first globally and then specifically with regard to preclassical conflict of laws.

Chapter 2 is a critical pesentation of the literature that has contributed to the formation of the modern historical consciousness. We shall begin by identifying – and categorizing – all sources of relevant material, before proceeding with a comprehensive taxonomy of historical narratives.The main body of the chapter tells a story: the account of how conflicts lawyers began addressing the history of the field, what ideas they sought to convey through historiography, and how the historiography of conflict of laws evolved, in direct relationship with the doctrinal evolution – and disciplinary identity – of private international law. At its core, this story is about how classical and modern doctrine perceived what preceded them. But the scope of the chapter is broader than preclassical conflict of laws.

121 Jayme, "Identité culturelle," 109, referring to Rabel. Cf. Kropholler, *Internationales Privatrecht*, 54–56 speaking of autonomy of the conflicts concepts (*Autonomie der kollisionsrechtlichen Begriffe*) of State, law, and nationality–citizenship compared to international law. For a notable exception, see A.-L. Calvo Caravaca and J. Carrascosa González, *Derecho Internacional Privado*, 6th ed (Granada: Comares, 2005), 4–5, who speak of "autonomía científica" and stress that private international law constitutes a veritable normative system, possesses its own object, different from the object of other legal fields ("'las situaciones privadas internacionales' presentan caracteres propios y distinctos, lo que hace preciso que sea una disciplina juridica independiente, autónoma . . . la que se encargue de su regulació juridical").

The place of preclassical conflict of laws in historical consciousness is addressed specifically in Chapter 3. The main body of the chapter attempts another taxonomy, this one of narratives about Medieval and Early Modern doctrine and the division of preclassical jurists, and doctrines, into "schools." The chapter begins with another story: the classical and modern quest for a Medieval foundational moment of conflicts doctrine, what it tells us about Medieval law and what inferences we may draw about present-day attitudes toward the role of scholarship in the conflict of laws. By this stage, the reader should possess the requisite knowledge about the historical context of the case studies in Parts III and IV, as well as an appreciation for the secondary literature and its debates.

Part II addresses modern conflicts doctrine in historical perspective: the aim is to identify our present-day problems and to prepare a set of questions which will be used in the historical case studies of Parts III and IV. To that effect, we shall examine the conceptions and images used to explain private international law and its evolution. The three chapters in this Part elaborate on the fundamental ideas explored in this Introduction, such as: the triangular relationship of private international law with the disciplines of private law and international law; the dialectic relation between theory and practice; and the aspirations of private international lawyers to impact their world and how these aspirations are paired with the need to provide *ex post* conceptual foundations for their doctrinal work.

Chapter 4 considers the principal conceptual oppositions – for example, territorialism–personalism, unilateralism–multilateralism – that have been used in doctrinal literature in efforts to "map" the evolution of the field and outline the principal dividing lines. Chapter 5 addresses the international-governance aspects of conflicts doctrine and proposes a framework for understanding the relationship between author and broader context. Chapter 6 addresses conflicts scholarship as a doctrinal exercise: how does conflicts doctrine deal with principles, rules, and the taxonomy of the legal subject matter; how are private-law institutions, such as the distinction between form and substance, or party autonomy, used into conflicts doctrine; and finally, what is the relationship between jurisdiction and choice of law and how truly important is uniformity of result, regarded by many as the paramount objective of the conflict of laws.

The next two parts consist of case studies in Medieval and Early Modern conflicts doctrine, each focused on the conflicts text by a canonical – but by no means generic – author. Part III (Chapters 7–10) is devoted to Bartolus of Sassoferrato, of the so-called Italian school, and Medieval conflict of laws. Part IV (Chapters 11–14) to Ulrich Huber, of the so-called Dutch school, and Early Modern conflict of laws.

Each study begins with a detailed presentation of the text examined.[122] Chapter 7 offers a critical presentation of the conflicts tract by Bartolus which has been included in his commentary on the glossed Code of Justinian. Chapter 11 discusses the conflicts tract contained in Huber's Latin-language treatise on the Digest. Both texts are examined in the light of – and in comparison to – earlier, lesser known versions of the same text.

The remaining three chapters in each case study correspond to the three chapters in Part II. The order however is here different than in Part II. We shall begin with the broader political context, following up on ideas outlined in Chapter 5, examining the author's political thought and theory of sources, in an attempt to understand the "world system" in which each of our authors operated. This is done in Chapter 8 for Bartolus and Chapter 12 for Huber. We shall then continue with examining each author's conflicts tract in the light of doctrinal questions not unique to the conflict of laws, following up on Chapter 6. This is done in Chapter 9 for Bartolus and Chapter 13 for Huber. The concluding chapter in each Part considers the author in the light of ideas and questions unique to the field, as elaborated on Chapter 4. This is done in Chapter 10 for Bartolus and Chapter 14 for Huber.[123]

This is a book written with the intention of being read from start to finish, but it is possible for readers who wish so, to read it vertically – for example, Chapter 5 with Chapters 8 and 12, Chapter 6 with Chapters 9 and 13, Chapter 4 with Chapters 10 and 14.

The book concludes with Chapter 15, which draws on the case studies to present a more complete, diverse – and accurate – picture of preclassical conflict of laws and to contemplate on the writing of history for private international law. Preclassical conflict of laws is defined internally

[122] I have made use of all English (and French, where available) translations of the texts, as well as the secondary tracts written on conflicts by each author. I have made corrections to the translations by having recourse to the original Latin text, including early print editions and, when needed manuscripts.

[123] The best-known – usually for the wrong reasons – fragment of each author's thought is discussed in these chapters. The so-called English question of Bartolus in Chapter 10 and the notion of comity in Chapter 14.

and externally – that is, in relation to what follows in conflicts scholarship. In fact, much of the value of preclassical doctrine to the conflict of laws has to do with our own sensibilities and aspirations. The exploration of Medieval and Early Modern doctrine thus becomes a journey of self-discovery for the private international lawyer of today.

PART I

History and Historiography in the Conflict of Laws

2

Uses of History in Private International Law

2.1 Introduction

Conflicts literature is ripe with aphorisms about the significance of history for our subject.[1] It has even been claimed that "in private international law, history is everything."[2] Others lament – or warn – that "everything worthy of trying has been tried before, under the same or other labels."[3]

Not unsurprisingly, there are also those in the other extreme, denying any use for history in conflicts doctrine, whether because they deem it irrelevant or because they are wary of its potential impact – as evidenced by the almost equally famous aphorism that "[t]his may be one of the rare legal subjects about which a page of history is worth less than a blank sheet."[4] This is a recurring – and subsiding – idea. For example, in the late 1990s, when globalization was thought by many to constitute a radically different paradigm and conflict of laws itself was treated as obsolete, a hindrance, a subject with an end-date, history was proclaimed

[1] See e.g. Juenger, *Choice of Law*, 6: "It has been said that the conflict of laws "may be one of the rare subjects about which a page of history is worth less than a blank sheet." That assessment is clearly wrong. The past has yielded an astonishingly rich accumulation of ideas, which still guide present theory and practice. Indeed, it seems fair to say that "everything worthy of trying has been tried before, under the same or other labels."

[2] "En droit international privé, l'histoire est tout:" The phrase comes from Max Gutzwiller (see Section 2.5.1 for its original context) and has been often quoted. See notably Fassberg, "Choice of Law Problem," 4 (opening epigram); Boggiano, *Derecho internacional privado*, 1:19 (opening sentence of the historical chapter).

[3] K. Nadelman, "Marginal Remarks on the New Trends in American Conflicts Law," *Law & Contemporary Problems*, 28 (1963), 860–869.

[4] W. Reese, M. Rosenberg, and P. Hay, *Cases and Materials on the Conflict of Laws*, 9th ed (Westbury, NY: Foundation Press, 1990), 3: "This may be one of the rare legal subjects about which a page of history is worth less than a blank sheet. That harsh judgment by some conflicts specialists flows from their impression that history – particicularly an exaggerated reverence for an ancient body of concepts and dogmas – may be in large part responsible for contemporary difficulties."

as irrelevant for the new age, or at least of little normative value. These antihistorical progress narratives were, of course, soon washed aside, along with the so-called irrational exuberance of those days. Today, the importance of both narratives and of actual lessons from the past, beginning with the Great Depression, for economic policy makers is widely acknowledged.[5] Globalization theorists have gravitated toward nonlinear and even cyclical narratives; past globalizations have been discovered, in an attempt to understand the forces at play or to create pedigree for ideas or groups. In fact, the allure of history – its lessons and the legitimation it can provide – has long proven too strong for globalists hostile to the conflict of laws. Proponents of a transnational substantive law present us utopic worlds of legal unity that preceded the world in which conflict of laws flourished, rejoicing in their conclusion that "choice-of-law rules in the modern sense are clearly not the only possible response to multistate problems."[6] Romantic genealogies of the law merchant constitute a literary subgenre: in fact, they are so resistant to historical evidence that they certainly merit study on their own.

In the end, we are all employing historical images, and images about history, in teaching ourselves and our students about present doctrine – and future directions. Contemporary private international law is deeply historical. One may or may not think in terms of "progress in science." One may believe the past matters a lot, somehow, or not at all. But, at the end of the day, we are all thinking in historical terms. Conflicts scholarship, and doctrines, of previous eras form part of our contemporary discussion: sometimes as *discursive participants* in a "unifying consciousness" sometimes as useful tales evocable "as pattern or warning," or as sources of an illustrious genealogy.

A systematic exploration of the historical consciousness of private international lawyers is therefore a prerequisite of any historical study – especially if one is revisiting the history of a period so distant and so extended in time. Such an exploration is not a literature review: on the one hand, it does not have to be as exhaustive of the material; on the other hand, it is not limited to historical literature strictly speaking;

[5] See e.g. H. James, *The Creation and Destruction of Value: The Globalization Cycle* (Cambridge, MA: Harvard University Press, 2009); R. Schiller, *Narrative Economics: How Stories Go Viral and Drive Major Economic Events* (Princeton, NJ: Princeton University Press, 2019).

[6] Juenger, *Choice of Law*, 10.

moreover, it approaches secondary literature as an object of study on its own right.

The first leg of this endeavor is to consider and categorise the various types of material that have contributed to the formation of historical consciousness. This is done in Section 2.2. The second leg is to identify the principal narratives, provide a typology and place them in – historical and doctrinal – context. This is done in the next four sections, one each for the period preceding the disciplinary moment ("2.3: Beginnings"), for early and mature classical conflict of laws ("2.4: Discipline Ascendant" and "2.5: Discipline Persists") and modern conflict of laws ("2.6: History as Pedigree"). The first three sections highlight specific authors, whereas the fourth one is structured more abstractly in terms of narratives. The sections on classical literature are more detailed: this is really the story of conflicts historiography, as well as a story about the creation and evolution of the discipline. The section on modern literature is more impressionistic and discusses the subject in terms of historical consciousness, rather than historical literature. This is easily explained: the grand classical historiographers of the late nineteenth and early twentieth centuries have bequeathed to us compelling narratives and detailed presentations of preclassical material, on which most of the modern literature has relied upon. At the same time, such influence is indirect; the classical authors are today read far less than the modern ones who have been building on their own narratives. The metaphor of a river culminating in an estuary, used below for the evolution of conflicts doctrine, also holds true with regard to the formation of our historical consciousness as well.

2.2 Materials

The literature dedicated – or containing references – to the history of private international law could be classified into four types of material: reference works, doctrinal studies, historical studies, and casual references.

Most *reference works* such as treatises and textbooks tend to include coherent historical narratives, of varied scope – and equally varied quality. A number of treatises contain especially insightful discussions of conflicts history. However, most simply rely on other reference works or the occasional historical study. Such "textbook histories" could obviously not claim a real contribution to historical research. However, treatises and textbooks constitute the principal means of shaping our historical consciousness: for the vast majority of lawyers, including most academic lawyers, these reference works may be the only thing they will read on the history of their subject. This phenomenon is even sharper in a field as separated from general legal history as private international law is.

Many *doctrinal studies* on a specific topic of interest to the contemporary doctrinal discussion also include historical narratives, usually by means of introduction to the subject.[7] Some of these accounts have played an important role in the formation of private international lawyers' historical consciousness and a few have contributed insights to the historical study of private international law.[8] However, whereas some historical accounts in doctrinal works are inspired by the actual reading of past texts, most rely on second- or third-hand readings.

Historical studies are works dedicated to the history of private international law. Their scope ranges widely – from comprehensive international histories of private international law, to studies of a certain period or legal system, to the study of a specific author or legal doctrine. Historical works involve direct contact with the object studied, usually old writings – in the original or translated text. A small number of historical works is also commonly cited in reference works.

Historical consciousness is also shaped by more "casual" historical references or invocations in doctrinal works. The invocation of a notion – or the dropping of a name – to corroborate the author's own position does not constitute an historical discussion properly speaking. Casual references are seldom cited and may not be considered as part of conflicts historiography properly speaking. However, in expressly assuming that the reader subscribes to the author's invocation, they reinforce specific historical images: for example, in likening modern American theories to the statutists, one affirms that fixation with the reach of statutes is the defining characteristic of preclassical conflict of laws and, more broadly,

[7] See e.g. with regard to contract choice-of-law and party autonomy, H. Batiffol, *Les conflits de lois en matière de contrats: étude de droit international privé comparé* (Paris, 1938), 8ff; O. Lando, "The Conflict of Laws of Contracts – General Principles," *Recueil des cours* 189 (1984) 225–446, 240ff; P. Nygh, *Autonomy in International Contracts* (Oxford: Clarendon Press, 1999), 4–8.

[8] For example, Batiffol's account – claiming that, at least until the late nineteenth century, the intention of the parties is only used to justify ex post – has been influential to historical work (including previous writings of the present author). See notably V. Ranouil, *L'Autonomie de la Volonté: Naissance et Évolution d'un Concept* (Paris: Presses Universitaires de France (PUF), 1980).

invites readers to attribute to the statutists whichever characteristics they tend to associate with American doctrines.

2.2.1 Conflicts History as Textbook History

No other legal field may claim such an abundance of historical sections in its textbooks, with such broad scope, as private international law does. A section on the *international* history of conflicts doctrine seems an essential part of any conflicts treatise.[9] In contrast to this, private-law treatises and textbooks contain only short histories of the evolution of the field in the author's country, with the emphasis given to its national legislation.[10] Legal history per se is entrusted to specialized courses: in most countries, it constitutes a distinct career track. The history of foreign law was traditionally left to the instructors of comparative law.[11] Comparative legal history is a relatively new subject. Works and courses on European legal history tend to tell either the story of a common learned law or a national legal history fitted in a broader European context.[12]

The only legal field comparable to private international law is public international law – an affinity that may relate to the common roots of the two disciplines especially in the late nineteenth century. The percentage

[9] It is obviously impossible to do justice to three quarters of late classical and modern scholarship that provide the bulk of references in this regard. Many other reference works are cited in this book. Among treatises that influenced me especially in an early stage see for example: in France, B. Audit, *Droit international privé*, 4th ed (Paris: Economica, 2006), 56–81; Y. Loussouarn, P. Bourel, and P. de Vareilles-Sommièeres, *Droit international privé*, 8th ed (Paris: Librairie Cotillon, 2004), 83–111; and P. Mayer, *Droit international privé*, 6th ed (Paris: Montchretien, 1998), 5–9 and 33–52. In Germany, G. Kegel and K. Schurig, *Internationales Privatrecht*, 8th ed (Munich: C. H. Beck, 2000), 144–181. Among discontinued treatises, see the French: J.-P. Niboyet, *Traité de droit international privé français*, vol. III (Paris: Librairie du Recueil Sirey, 1944), 37–196; the Spanish: Miaja de la Muela, *Derecho internacional privado*, 1:85–255; and the Greek George Maridakis: G. Maridakis, *Idiōtikon Diethnes Dikaion*, vol. I, 2nd ed (Athens: Ant. N. Sakkoulas, 1967), 116–196. In Argentina, see W. Goldschmidt, *Sistema y Filosofia del Derecho Internacional Privado*, vol. I, 2nd ed (Buenos Aires: Ediciones Jurídicas Europa-América, 1951), 143–186.

[10] See e.g. G. Cornu, *Droit civil: Introduction au droit*, 12th ed (Paris, 2005), 125–135.

[11] See e.g. K. Zweigert and H. Kötz, *An Introduction to Comparative Law*, trans. Tony Weir, 3rd ed (Oxford: Oxford University Press, 1998), esp. Chs. 6–17.

[12] See e.g. the masterful work by F. Wieacker, *A History of Private Law in Europe (with particular reference to Germany)*, trans. Tony Weir (Oxford: Clarendon Press, 1995). Cf. especially R. Lesaffer, *European Legal History: A Cultural and Political Perspective*, trans. Jan Arriens (Cambridge: Cambridge University Press, 2009).

of international-law textbooks containing an historical treatment is nonetheless significantly lower than in private international law.[13] This is remarkable: not only has there been a traditional bond, at least on the Continent, between public international law and diplomatic history, but in recent times a growing body of specialized literature on the history of public international law has emerged.[14] On the whole, if textbook history is paramount in private international law, it appears to be less so in public international law.

There are also differences in the narratives themselves: private international law tells a story of doctrinal ideas rooted in a local context; public international law has traditionally de-emphasized the local origins of its past intellectual contributors. Public international lawyers have also tended to insist more on the unitary identity of their discipline, as well as on a progress narrative, with emphasis placed on the growth of "positive law" sources.[15] Most of the specialized literature on the history of international law appears divorced from "domestic" legal history.[16]

[13] Among international law textbooks. K.-H. Ziegler, *Völkerrechtsgeschichte*, 2nd ed (Munich: C. H. Beck, 2007) is published in a textbook series. Arthur Wegner, *Geschichte des Völkerrechts* (Stuttgart: W. Kohlhammer, 1936) is announced as the third part of the first volume of a large treatise (*Handbuch*) edited by G. A. Walz.

[14] A specialized *Journal of the History of International Law* was launched in 1999 by R. McDonald and is now run by the Max Planck Institutes on international law (Heidelberg) and legal history (Frankfurt). The Frankfurt Max Planck also publishes a monograph series (*Studien zur Geschichte des Völkerrechts*), mostly theses under the supervision of Professor Michael Stolleis. Another journal (*Jus Gentium: Journal of International Legal History*) was very recently launched in 2016. There is no space to mention the several interesting monographs and collections of essays that have appeared over especially the past two decades, with the obvious exception of B. Fassbender and A. Peters (eds.), *Oxford Handbook of the History of International Law* (Oxford: Oxford University Press, 2012).

[15] See notably Wilhelm Georg Grewe – translated by Michael Byers, as *The Epochs of International Law* (Berlin: De Gruyter, 2000) – and other literature mentioned in M. Koskenniemi, *The Gentle Civilizer of Nations* (Cambridge: Cambridge University Press, 2002); and D. Bederman, *International Law in Antiquity* (Cambridge: Cambridge University Press, 2001). The point is best suggested and illustrated in the historical and historiographical work of David Kennedy. See especially D. Kennedy, "The Disciplines of International Law and Policy," *Leiden Journal of International Law*, 12 (1999), 9–135, 83–101; "International Law and the Nineteenth Century: History of an Illusion," *Quinnipiac Law Review*, 17 (1997), 99–138; and "Primitive Legal Scholarship," *Harvard International Law Journal*, 27 (1986), 1–98.

[16] See R. Lesaffer, "International Law and Its History" in M. Craven et al. (eds.), *Time, History and International Law* (Leiden: Brill, 2007), 27–41.

2.2.1.1 Structure and Narratives

This historical section will be found either within an extended Introduction, or at the beginning of the general part that follows it.[17] Historical sections included in the Introduction tend to compete for precedence with the section on sources of law; often, history comes second only to the definition of private international law.[18] Remarkably, the historical section appears in the very end of some works, as an appendix.[19]

The backbone of textbook narratives is a unitary intellectual history of the conflict of laws from the High Middle Ages (or earlier) until the nineteenth or twentieth centuries. The same writers and notions tend to appear in this mainstream or standard narrative, regardless of which is the author's own legal system. The standard narrative is usually supplemented by – and, in some works, distinguished from – a shorter account of more recent, especially local, developments. Conflicts textbook history is intellectual history. References to legislation – or, even less frequently, to landmark cases – are a rare phenomenon and always concern recent local developments. Occasionally, the narrative makes references to an ancient text or incident that highlights the antiquity of the conflict of laws approach. The past few generations have seen increased references to the prehistory of private international law.

Such single-mindedness is not absolute, however: the national legal system of the author often determines her emphasis, or even the structure of her narrative. For example, the idea of a German or a Spanish

[17] Examples of the former: Maridakēs, *Idiōtikon Diethnes Dikaion*, 1:116–196; Ballarino, *Diritto Intenazionale Privato*, 12–43 (Ch. 1.3, "Sviluppo storico degla discipline"). Examples of the latter: Miaja de la Muela, *Derecho Internacional Privado*, 1:85–255 (a historical discussion of "Doctrinal Systems" is the first chapter of General Part, following an extensive Introduction).

[18] E.g. Maridakes discusses Concept – Sources – History in his 200-page introduction. Kegel and Shurig's structure for their First Part is Concept – Interests – History – Sources – Literature; Kropholler treats sources alongside the definition in § 1, history in § 2 and only discusses issues of policy and foundations later.

[19] Most notable is J. H. Beale, *A Treatise on the Conflict of Laws*, vol. 3 (New York: Baker, Voorhis & Co., 1879–1975). See also E. L. Paras, *Philippine Conflict of Laws*, 7th ed (Manila: Rex Book Store, 1990), 438–444 (Ch. XXV, "A Brief History of Conflict of Laws"). Leo Raape discussed history in the last chapter (§ 21) of his general part. See L. Raape, *Internationales Privatrecht*, 5th ed (Berlin: Valen, 1961), 158–168. This became the last chapter in the first volume of L. Raape and F. Sturm, *Internationales Privatrecht*, 6th ed, vol. I (Munich: Valen, 1977), 401–413. Likewise in I. Schwander, *Einführung in das international Privatrecht*, 3rd ed, vol. I (St. Gallen/Lachen: Dike, 2000), 381–395 (chapter on "history and tendencies of private international law").

school of preclassical doctrine has been advocated primarily by German or Spanish authors respectively; in their turn, the French tend to insist on the importance of a distinct French school and, if they define that school more narrowly, to give emphasis on French participation in the so-called Italian school (thus turning it into a "Franco-Italian" one).[20] But such national claims have been fitted into the main narrative; reference works are on the whole reluctant to deviate from the traditional story. Starker contrasts are however to be found in the treatment of prehistory: if we take the leading postwar Greek and Spanish treatise, we will observe that the former dedicates eighteen pages to Graeco-Roman Antiquity (including six to Byzantium) and half a page (in small print) to the early Medieval West and the personality of laws regime.[21] On the contrary, the latter devotes less than a page to Greek and Roman antiquity but eleven pages to the early Medieval personality of laws.[22]

Another national pecularity is the division of the historical narrative, in certain French treatises, between an "external" and an "internal" history: the former emphasizes the status accorded or denied to aliens and is placed in the Introduction (between the "Object" and "Sources" sections), whereas the latter addresses the doctrinal evolution of the conflict of laws per se and is placed at the head of the *conflits de lois* part.[23] This division, which is not very common in more recent works, is related to the comprehensive scope of French private international law, which has traditionally covered much of nationality and alien law (*condition des étrangers*) alongside, or even preceding, choice of law (*conflits de lois*) and jurisdiction/enforcement (*conflits de juridictions*). It confirms the doctrinal character of conflicts history.

2.2.1.2 Historical Consciousness in the Common-Law World

The Anglo-American legal tradition maintains some degree of uniqueness with regard to textbook history in the conflict of laws.

Most English textbooks and treatises are not unlike those in the rest of the world, but the English tradition of the conflict of laws maintains its

[20] See Section 3.3.1.2.

[21] Maridakes, *Idiōtikon Diethnes Dikaion*, 1:101–118, 120–121.

[22] Miaja de la Muela, *Derecho internacional privado*, 1:85–86 and 86–96.

[23] See e.g. Batiffol and Lagarde, *Droit international privé*, 1:17–31 ("Notions historiques sur le développement historique du droit international privé)" that includes a short story of preclassical doctrine with emphasis on France and 371–410 ("Genèse historique de la théorie des conflits de lois"), a detailed historical treatment at the beginning of Part Two, which is devoted to the choice of law.

own peculiaries.[24] The two grand reference works, however, of Dicey and Morris and Cheshire and North, do not address the international history of the conflict of laws: emphasis is placed on the development of English conflict of laws as well as on immediate influences.[25] This is remarkable, considering that the early editions of both these works included historical narratives; the shift in focus can only be partly attributed to their present-day orientation toward legal practice.

United States literature reflects the exceptionalism – and preoccupations – of American conflict of laws. Only a few a few among US reference works – notably those authored by members of the American Society for Comparative Law – contain historical accounts about the international history of the field.[26] What makes this more remarkable is that the US conflicts discourse is profoundly historicist, albeit in the sense of attributing normative importance to the doctrinal evolution of US conflicts doctrine: in about every textbook and casebook, contemporary doctrine is described in terms of the replacement, in most, but not all, of the States, of the "traditional" conflict of laws by the new approaches.[27] A reason for this historicity probably lies in the fact that traditional doctrine still persists in a number of States, even with regard to those areas where it has long lost the battle of ideas, and in fact dominates

[24] See e.g. R. Mortensen et al., *Private International Law in Australia*, 4th ed (Melbourne: LexisNexis Australia, 2006), 7–15: the story of "scholarly development," which follows a paragraph on "ancient approaches," consist of paragraphs on the Italian, French, and Dutch schools, Story, English scholarship (especially Dicey), Beale, Savigny, and the American conflicts revolution. It is complemented by a brief section on "institutional writing as a source of law" (notably Dicey) and another on "judicial development in England" (during the same period as scholarly development).

[25] Thus, L. Collins (ed.), *Dicey, Morris and Collins on the Conflict of Laws*, 15th ed, vol. I (London: Sweet & Maxwell, 2012), 9–10 only includes a short account of the "late development in England" of the subject, with a footnote reference to major works on the history of private international law; the original outline of A. V. Dicey in the Digest, has been omitted. *Cheshire, North and Fawcett's Private International Law*, 14th ed (Oxford: Oxford University Press, 2008), 19ff devotes a separate chapter on "Historical Development and Current Theories." The first section is devoted to the beginnings of English conflicts law, while the second one to twentieth-century US theories. A notable exception is the textbook of D. McClean and K. Beevers, *Morris: The Conflict of Laws*, 7th ed (London: Sweet & Maxwell, 2009), 557ff: the last chapter on "theories and methods" includes a short consideration of Huber and Savigny, alongside Story, Dicey and the twentieth-century Americans.

[26] The main global historical treatments in Anglo-American textbooks/casebooks are Juenger, *Choice of Law*, 6–46; E. Scoles et al., *Conflict of Laws*, 3rd ed (St. Paul, MN: West, 2000), 9–18; and Symeonides et al., *Conflict of Laws*, 6–13.

[27] See e.g. Symeonides, *American Private International Law*, 63ff.

specific subjects.[28] Another reason has to do with the influence that developments in American legal thought have had on conflicts doctrine: the doctrinal upheaval in US intrastate conflict of laws is in part a consequence of the broader phenomenon in twentieth-century American law, where legal formalism or classicism gave ground to legal realism and eventually to the legal realists' intellectual progeny.

2.2.2 Historical Studies

In the late nineteenth century, conflicts historiography remained dominated by the historical treatments in ambitious treatise projects. In the French-speaking world, the sweeping discussion of preclassical authors by Francois Laurent and especially Armand Lainé, did not leave much space for individual studies on preclassical doctrine. Enrico Catellani dominated the Italian historiography.[29] Ludwig von Bar provided German-speaking scholarship with a very thoughtful and comprehensive history in his treatise.[30] The late nineteenth century saw the publication of classic texts of Medieval and Early Modern authors: in Scotland, William Guthrie appended to his translation of Savigny's work the texts of Bartolus, Dumoulin, Paul Voet, and Huber (1880).[31] The Swiss Ferdindand Meili repeated this exercise with regard to Bartolus and Baldus.[32] The trend continued in the Anglo-American world with the

[28] See the survey by S. Symeonides, *The American Choice-of-Law Revolution: Past, Present and Future* (Leiden: Brill, 2006), 51–62. See notably, and his annual survey of US cases, in the *American Journal of Comparative Law.*

[29] E. L. Catellani, *Il diritto internazionale privato e il suoi recenti progressi*, 2nd ed (Turin: Stamperia dell'Unione Tipografico-Editrice, 1895–1902). The first volume ("History of private international law") discusses at length the Antiquity (12–196) and Middle Ages.

[30] L. von Bar, *Theorie und praxis des internationalen privatrechts*, vol. I (Hannover, 1889), 32–146; see also the English translation of the treatise: L. von Bar, *Theory and Practice of Private International Law*, trans. G.R. Gillespie (Edinburgh, 1892).

[31] See F. C. von Savigny, *"Private international law, and the retrospective operation of statutes: a treatise on the conflict of laws, and the limits of their operation in respect of place and time by Friedrich Carl von Savigny;" trans (with notes) by William Guthrie; with an appendix containing the treatises of Bartolus, Molinaeus, Paul Voet, and Huber*, 2nd ed (revised) (Edinburgh: T. & T. Clark, 1880).

[32] F. Meili, "Die theoretischen Abhandlungen von Bartolus und Baldus über das internationale Privaat- und Strafrecht," *NiemeyersZ*, 4 (1894), 258–269, 340–346, 446–373; F. Meili, "Argentraeus und Molinaeus und ihre Bedeutung im internationalen Privat- und Strafrecht," *NiemeyersZ*, 5 (1895), 363–380, 452–472, 554–566; F. Meili, "Ein Specimen aus der holländischen Schule des IPR (Ulricus Huber 1636–1694)," *NiemeyersZ*, 8 (1898), 189–200.

early twentieth century translations of Bartolus and Huber by distinguished conflicts professors at Harvard and Yale.[33]

The first strictly historical works did finally appear by the early twentieth century. Karl Neumeyer (1869–1941) published a two-volume study on the development of international private (and criminal law) law in the *ius commune* until Bartolus.[34] E. M. Meijers researched early Medieval court practice in France and the Low Countries. Armand Lainé examined the legislative history of the Napoleonic Code.[35] Others presented studies of individual authors.[36]

The late interwar and postwar era was characterized by a proliferation of essays exploring the existence of private international law in Antiquity,[37] as well as explorations of roots and precedents outside Europe. The postwar era also saw a number of biographical monographs on preclassical and classical writers: some of them explored canonical figures and some lesser-known authors.[38] There have also been a few

[33] See Sections 1.4, 7.2.1, and 11.2.1.

[34] K. Neumeyer, *Die gemeinrechtliche Entwickelung des internationalen Privat- und Strafrechts bis Bartolus*, 2 vols (Munich: J. Schweitzer, 1901–1916); K. Neumeyer, "Zur Geschichte des internationalen Privatrechts in Frankreich und den Niederlanden," *Zeitschrift für Völkerrecht*, 11 (1920), 190–204.

[35] A. Lainé, "La rédaction du Code civil et le sens de ses dispositions en matière de droit international privé," *Revue de droit international privé*, 1 (1905), 21–60, 443–479.

[36] F. Surville, "La théorie des statutes d'après Bartole et Dumoulin," *Clunet*, 48 (1921), 1–15; P. Meylan, "Les statuts réels et personnels dans la doctrine de Du Moulin" in *Mélanges Paul Fournier* (Paris: Recueil Sirey, 1929), 511–526; J.-P. Niboyet, "Froland, les conflicts de qualification et la question du renvoi," *Revue de droit international privé*, 21 (1926), 1–25; C. Boucher, "La conférence des avocats et le droit international privé au XVIIIe siècle," *Clunet*, 63 (1935), 45–58.

[37] See notably W. Niederer, "Ceterum quaero de legum imperii romani conflictu," *Revue critique de droit international privé*, 49 (1960), 137–150; H. Lewald, "Conflits de lois dans le monde grec et romain," *Revue critique de droit international privé*, 57 (1968): 419–440, 615–639 [whch replaces earlier versions published in the Greek Αρχείον Ιδιωτικού Δικαίου (1946) and the Italian *Labeo* 1959]; G. S. Maridakis, "Introduction au droit international privé," *Recueil des cours*, 105 (1962), 375–515, 485–487 [summarizing an article he wrote in Greek on Isocrates's Aegeneticus in *Mélanges Georges Streit* (Athens, 1939)]; F. Sturm, "Comment l'Antiquité réglait-elle ses conflits de lois?," *Clunet*, 106 (1979), 259–273. On the Early Middle Ages in the West, see S. L. Guterman, "The Principle of the Personality of Law in the Early Middle Ages: A Chapter in the Evolution of Western Legal Institutions and Ideas." *University of Miami Law Review*, 21 (1966), 259–348. On Byzantium see G. S. Maridakis, "L'inapplicabilité du droit étranger à Byzance" in *Liber Amicorum Baron Louis Fredericq* (Ghent: Faculteit der Rechtsgeleerldheid te Gent, 1965), 719–735.

[38] F. Gamillsheg, *Der Einfluß Dumoulins auf die Entwicklung des Kollisionsrechts* (Berlin: De Gruyter, 1955) is commonly cited. See also G. Herrmann, *Johan Nikolaus Hert und die deutsche Statutenlehre* (Berlin: De Gruyter, 1963); G. Merzyn, *Der Beitrag Benedikt*

book-length attempts to provide a comprehensive history of private international law.[39]

2.3 Conflicts Historiography in the Beginnings

The first historical references in conflicts works appear near the end of the preclassical period. They appear in individual works and refer to the external world, in prehistoric times: Rome and the political breakdown that followed its decline. On the contrary, older doctrinal writers are never perceived in historical terms: they are either not mentioned at all or treated in the same manner as contemporaneous jurists, i.e. as if they still form part of an ongoing discourse. This state of affairs persists until the mid-nineteenth century.

2.3.1 Preclassical Historical Consciousness

Roman law remained, at least in theory, the starting point of conflicts systems until the nineteenth century and the promulgation of national legislation. Medieval jurists did not frequently profess their concern about the original context of the Roman legal rules they employed, but by the seventeenth century the willingness to admit that the geopolitical situation of the Roman Empire was different from the present-day world is evident, especially in those areas where Roman law was part of the law of the land but there was no formal affiliation to the Holy Roman Empire.

In the late seventeenth century, Ulrik Huber attempted to ground his principles on common practice ("accepted") and the Roman law ("the fundamental rules according to which this subject should be determined must be sought in the Roman law") and cited the Digest as authority for his axioms.[40] Anxious to assert the authority of Roman law, yet aware of

Carpzovs zur Entwicklung des Kollisionsrechts (Göttingen: O. Schwartz, 1963:); H. Richard, "La place du président Bouhier dans l'histoire du droit international privé" in *Mémoires de la Société pour l'histoire du droit et des institutions des anciens pays bourguignons, comtois et romands*, vol. 32 (1973–1974), 87–172; J. A. Clarence Smith, "Bartolo on the Conflict of Laws," *American Journal of Legal History*, 14 (1970), 157–183, 247–275.

39 R. D. Kollewijn, *Geschiedenis van de Nederlandse wetenschap van het internationaal privatrecht tot 1880* (Amsterdam: Noord-Hollandsche Uitgeversmij, 1937); Gutziller, *Geschichte*; Ancel, *Histoire* and now *Élements*.

40 Huber, *Praelectiones ad Pandectas*, 1.3.App.1. See Sections 11.3, 12.3.2, and 14.4.1.

the relative novelty of his ideas, he begins his treatment with a historical note: "since the sovereignty of Rome extended to all parts of the world and was regulated to a uniform law, it could hardly give rise to a conflict of different laws;" it is the "breaking up of the provinces of the Roman Empire" which led a division of Christendom "into almost innumerable nations (*populos*)."[41] In contrast to Huber, his contemporary Jan Voet – advocate of a less universalist approach – begins his conflicts treatment likening the world of his time to Gaul prior to Roman conquest.[42]

By the middle of the eighteenth century, French doctrine had long been under the dominance of territorialist ideas, both by d'Argentré and the Dutch territorialists. The political and material circumstances of the eighteenth-century kingdom may have led to nuances among a younger generation of jurists. Early in his treatment of conflicts questions in his treatise on the customs of Bourgogne, Jean Bouhier, President in the provincial High Court (Parliament) at Dijon linked the origins of conflicts doctrine to the ascendance of royal power: in earlier times, each province was ruled by princes at war with each other, very few contacts existed between even neighboring states, making each of the people "zealous of their proper laws" and reluctant to acknowledge any force of law to the rules of another. "Each wanted to remain absolute master in his own [territory] and this is the source of the colloquial axiom of our French law that all customs are real."[43]

This narrative lies at the roots of French conflicts historiography: of the four major historical accounts written in the classical period in the French language, three are reproducing this passage in its entirety.[44] His

[41] Ibid.

[42] Johannes Voet, *Commentarius ad Pandectas*, 1.4.App.1 (as translated by Percival Gane): "Julius Caesar once said of the Gauls that 'They are different in language, practice and laws.' That is still very true of the whole of the Netherlands, and, if you except language, of the federated Netherlands as well."

[43] J. Bouhier, *Les coutumes du duché de Bourgogne* (Dijon: Arnauld Jean-Baptiste Angé/ Pierre De Saint, 1742), 23.38 (454): "Ces raisons étoient anciennement fortifiées par la situation où se trouvoient alors les Provinces du Royaume. Comme elles étoient soumises à différens Princes, qui étoient souvent en guerre les uns avec les autres, il y avait peu de liaison entre les Etats voisins, et moins encore entre ceux, qui étoit plus éloignéz. Cela rendoit chacun de ces Peuples jaloux de ses propres Loix; en sorte qu'ils n'avoient garde d'admettre l'extension de la disposition d'un Statut dans les limites d'un autre. Chacun voulait demeurer maître absolu chez soi; et c'est la source de l'Axiome vulgaire de notre Droit François que *toutes coutumes sont réelles*, auquel Coquille a mal à propos voulu donner une autre origine."

[44] See Laurent, *Droit civil international*, 1:271; Lainé, *Introduction*, 1:277; Meijers, "Contribution," 15–16.

tale is an early indication of what twentieth-century French scholars would call the external history of private international law. The Napoleonic Code did grant certain rights to foreigners but also underlined the difference in status between aliens and nationals: in fact, the first historical work of private international law, by Demangeat, in 1844, almost a century after Bouhier, would be in this area.[45]

On the contrary, we shall find no sense of historicity regarding preceding legal scholarship in either eighteenth or early nineteenth-century literature. Joseph Story, for example, who noted that he consulted principally the writings of the leading writers of the so-called Dutch school (Rodenburgh, Huber, and the Voets) and the eighteenth-century French authors (Boullenois, Bouhier, and Froland) treats the "civilians of continental Europe" (including even Bartolus, who is derided and presented through the writings of his detractors) in synchronous terns.[46]

2.3.2 *Moments of Transition*

The 1840s and 1850s signaled the advent of a new era of conflicts doctrine. The work of Friedrich Carl von Savigny towers over several other interesting doctrinal contributions of the period, which were subsequently largely forgotten as the new classical paradigm took hold. The fact that the mid-nineteenth century constitutes a moment of transition for conflicts doctrine is reflected also in the limited historical consciousness of these works. Accordingly, lamentations about the inadequacy of past doctrine to deal with conflicts problems were a common occurence. This awareness about the need for something new was not matched by a strong self-consciousness, such as encountered in subsequent scholarship, where, on the one hand, historical narratives are employed in order to explain present problems and place past doctrines in perspective and,

[45] See Section 2.3.2.2. Bouhier, a minor figure of the French Enlightenment, is a pioneer in conflicts historiography in another sense as well: he is providing an alternative historical explanation for the strong French emphasis on territoriality to the one offered by Coquille (who had suggested that the axiom resulted from a misapplication of Italian statutist doctrine). See Lainé, *Introduction*, 1:300–301.

[46] See J. Story, *Commentaries on the Conflict of Laws* (Boston: Hilliard Gray & Co., 1835), 1–18 (§§ 1–16). C. G. von Wächter, "Über die Collision der Privatrechtsgesetze verschiedener Staaten," *Archiv für die Civilistiche Praxis*, 24 (1841), 230–311, 270–311 likewise discusses "the theory of personal, real and personal statutes" as the first part of his section on the "Representation and Critique of the Views of Others." See also ibid., 242–252 for a discussion of Roman law with a view to its contemporaneous legal significance.

on the other hand, it is argued that such problems necessitate the construction of distinct legal field.

2.3.2.1 Savigny

A towering figure in conflicts doctrine, as well as in legal history, Friedrich Carl von Savigny dedicated most of his energy to constructing a comprehensive system, and theory, of private law. Savigny's advocacy of a historical school was aimed primarily at providing private law with solid foundations.[47] His approach however led him to both elaborate a methodology for research on the history of law and to engage himself in thorough historical research relating to his primary source material, as epitomized by his seminal *History of Roman Law in the Middle Ages*.[48]

The limited role afforded history in Savigny's conflicts treatment is therefore remarkable. On the one hand, Savigny provides us early on with an example of his historical method: he quickly dismisses the contemporary relevance of the doctrines of ancient Roman law, namely the rules on *origo* and *domicilium*, invoked until that time by many scholars, by placing them into their proper context (i.e. "historicizing" them). On the other hand, we shall find no historical narrative regarding the evolution of conflicts doctrine in his work, and no historical distinction between past and present doctrine. Savigny is fully conscious of presenting a new method and he fits conflicts problems into his own

[47] In his programmatic statement (preface) to the inaugural issue of the *Review for Historical Legal Science* (1815), Savigny presented as fundamental the opposition between a *historical school* and a coalition of contradictory approaches which he called the "non-historical" school, and which he portrayed as suggesting "that each generation, free and independent in its sphere, lives for this school happy and brilliant or unhappy and obscure, in the measure of its ideas or forces." History thus serves only in providing us with moral fables. The historical approach on the contrary denies the possibility of an "absolutely individual" and "absolutely independent" human existence. See F. C. von Savigny, "Über den Zweck dieser Zeitschrift," *Zeitschrift für geschichtliche Rechtswissenschaft*, 1 (1815), 1–17. The article has been translated into French by Eduard Laboulaye and included in the introduction of his *Histoire du droit de propriété foncière* (Paris, 1839).

[48] F. C. von Savigny, *Geschichte des römischen Rechts im Mittelalter*, 2nd ed (Heidelberg: Mohr & Zimmer, 1834–1851). The first volumes of the first edition have been translated into French by Charles Guenoux as *Histoire du droit romain au moyen age*, 4 vols (1830–1839). Volume I was also translated into English: Carl [sic] von Savigny, *The History of the Roman Law during the Middle Ages*, trans. E. Cathcart (Edinburgh, 1829). The work has remained unsurpassed and the biographical information it provides on Medieval jurists remained the major reference until recently.

doctrinal scheme. Solutions proposed by statutist authors are considered within this scheme.[49]

2.3.2.2 Demangeat

The first work of conflicts history was a youthful work by Charles Demangeat (1820–1896), who was to become professor of Roman law at the Paris law faculty, and the editor of Foelix's conflicts treatise. In 1844, Demangeat published a study on the *History of the Civil Status of Foreigners in France in the Old and in the New Law.*[50]

Demangeat has a decidedly liberal perspective: he believes that foreigners must acquire exactly the same private-law rights (*droits civils*) as French citizens, and such full equality must extend over all kinds of property.[51] He criticizes French courts for insisting expansively on the legislative exceptions – a tendency he attributes to ancient ideas.[52] He wants case law to instead facilitate or lead the transition to the new legal regime that is needed.[53] The last third of this work is actually a doctrinal analysis of French law as it then stood.[54] The past is used in a decidedly normative way, in order to explain the origin of certain institutions, but also to convey a story of progression toward the desired state of the law: beginning with a brief consideration of Roman law, where the status of the alien *peregrine* gradually improves as needs and ideas change and the notion of human duality is abandoned;[55] moving to Germanic laws and the introduction of a personality of laws system with the Frankish "conquest;"[56] and then to the system (*droit d'aubaine*) established under the "feudal regime" of the French Kingdom until 1789 and subsequent developments.[57]

[49] The most characteristic case is his contextualization of the Roman doctrines of *origo* and *domicilium*. See Savigny, System, 8:38–109 (§§ 350–359).

[50] See C. Demangeat, *Histoire de la condition civile des étrangers en France dans l'ancien et dans le nouveau droit* (Paris, 1844).

[51] Ibid., v–vii and 419 ("Conclusion").

[52] Ibid., ix: "[L]a jurisprudence, qui du reste a souvent varié en ces matières, est encore tellement imbue des anciennes idées qu'elle laisse voir, en général, une certaine tendance à enchérir sur les rigueurs que nos lois ont cru devoir conserver à l'égard des étrangers. C'est là une pratique qu'est difficile de justifier au tribunal de la raison."

[53] Ibid., ix: "[U]ne jurisprudence en effet n'est intelligente et respectable qu'autant qu'elle est constamment le lien, la transition entre la loi en vigueur qu'on ne peut violer, et la loi future que sollicitent les besoins nouveaux et les moeurs nouvelles du people."

[54] Ibid., 293–418.

[55] Ibid., 3.

[56] Ibid., 34–71.

[57] Ibid., 72–234.

2.3.2.3 John Westlake in 1858

In 1858, a youthful John Westlake (1828–1913), Fellow at Trinity College, Cambridge, undertook to "furnish the profession with a volume at once compendious and useful," which treated of "private international jurisprudence, but regarded as a department of English law."[58]

A few years later, Westlake was to become a pivotal member of the international-law school that created the discipline of private international law: a co-founder of its flagship institutions, Westlake was the leading representative of the Anglo-American world in them for almost half a century.[59] But 1858 was still a transitional moment for Westlake. One might simply compare the structure of the – drastically revised – second edition of his Treatise in 1880, as well as subsequent editions, with the 1858 original. The revised treatise included a historical treatment in its Introduction, conjuring a progress narrative in the spirit of late nineteenth-century Liberal internationalists and clearly distinguished from a second chapter on the "Present State of the Subject on the Continent" and 16 doctrinal chapters.[60] In contrast, of the 14 chapters of the original 1858 treatise, three are of historical reference.

In Chapter II, "National Character," Westlake devotes one section to the "History of the Doctrine of Allegiance in England and France," and one to the "Present State of the Doctrine of National Character."[61] Westlake notes a "contest" between the "feudal" and the "Roman" principles, which determine allegiance based respectively on the place of birth and on the parents' condition:

> The feudal principle has progressively given away, but retains so much influence in England and some other countries, while in all it has so much the character of the groundwork into which the modifications arising from the other principles have been introduced, that the historical

[58] J. Westlake, *A Treatise on Private International law, or the Conflict of Laws, with Principal Reference to Its Practice in the English and Other Cognate Systems of Jurisprudence* (London: W. Maxwell, 1858).

[59] See Section 6.3. The collection of testimonies in *Memories of John Westlake* (London, 1914) covers all several aspects of his work.

[60] J. Westlake, *A Treatise on Private International Law with Principal Reference to Its Practice in England*, 3rd ed (London: Sweet & Maxwell, 1890), 8–23. See e.g. ibid., 23 ("The critical spirit of the nineteenth century has not been content with so barren a method").

[61] Westlake, *Private International Law* (1858), 5–15 and 15–27 respectively.

> method is best suited for describing the doctrines now current in different states.[62]

Westlake's statement is reminiscent of Savigny's historical school, in the idea of using "the historical method" so as to better comprehend present doctrines. But it also indicates another mentality, more characteristic of nineteenth-century Liberals than of Savigny: a progress narrative, a gradual move away from the "feudal" and toward the "Roman" principle. We will encounter many forms of a progress narrative among Westlake's brethren. Of course, the issue of the criterion for determining allegiance, even though that determination would also help determine the individual's personal law, is less important to Continental jurists.

After two chapters on "Domicile" and "Immovables," Westlake came to discuss extensively the "History and Principles" pertaining to "Jurisdiction and Obligations" (Chapter V).[63] What he did was to examine the "Roman rules of jurisdiction on obligations," again on historicist grounds: his examination was based on Savigny's own discussion, though Westlake differed with him, as "any opinion on the true interpretation of the Corpus Juris may, and at times does, become influential on the daily judgments of courts."[64]

It is only in the next chapter (Chapter VI), entitled characteristically *Principles of the International Obligation of Law* that Westlake finally discussed the "theories of the Reality and Personality of Statutes, and of the Comity of Nations," contrasting them with Engish and colonial practices and finally "Various Modern Theories," including Savigny but also Bartolus on contracts.[65]

2.4 The Discipline Ascendant: Progress Narratives in Classical Private International Law

Historical narratives begin appearing in earnest in the last third of the nineteenth century. The impact of the disciplinary awakening described in the Introduction – and especially of the proliferation of both published

[62] Ibid., 5.
[63] Ibid., 89–104.
[64] Ibid., 89.
[65] Ibid., 122–131, 131–147, and 147–158.

material and available readership – is obvious. By the 1880s, we encounter historical treatments even in student manuals.[66]

Much of classical historiography employed what is these days called *progress narratives*, where history is told in terms of the evolution or development of society or institutions toward a specific – and desired – ending. The term is a substitute for "Whig history."[67]

In his masterful account of late nineteenth-century public international law and its founding fathers – many of whom were also pivotal in the early classical private international law – Martii Koskenniemi characterizes their historical narratives as "progressive, or pedigree history," which "posited an early origin . . . and then described itself in terms of how the promise of that origin had been preserved or enhanced by later developments, and how the present could be seen as its highest (though always incomplete) stage of flourishing.[68] Koskenniemi is influenced by Raymond Geuss; in my opinion, however, the respective narratives of private international lawyers appear closer to what Geuss calls "genealogy."[69]

2.4.1 *François Laurent in 1880*

In 1880, François Laurent (1810–1887), prolific professor of civil law at the University of Ghent in Belgium, author of a much-cited treatise in 33 volumes on the Napoleonic Civil Code,[70] political activist and founding member of the Institute of International Law, begun the publication of an eight-volume treatise on International Civil Law.[71]

[66] See e.g. T. Vaquette, *Cours résumé de droit international privé* (Paris, 1884), 9–59, citing Laurent and especially the university lectures of Lainé.

[67] That term was coined by Herbert Butterfield: see H. Butterfield, *The Whig Interpretation of History* (1931).

[68] Koskenniemi, *Gentle Civilizer*, 102.

[69] R. Geuss, *Morality, Culture and History* (Cambridge: Cambridge University Press, 1999), 1–3.

[70] F. Laurent, *Principes de droit civil français*, 33 vols, 4th ed (Brussels: Bruylant-Christophe, 1887). In France, however, Laurent is largely forgotten: for example, J.-L. Halpérin, *Histoire du droit privé français depuis 1804* (Paris: PUF, 1996), 69 mentions Laurent among the "minor exegegists" of the French Civil Code. Halpérin views Laurent as an example of the contradictions inherent to the so-called exegetical method, given that he preached absolute adherence to the existing legislation at the same time that he advocated a full-scale revision of the Napoleonic Code for Belgium.

[71] See E. Nys, "François Laurent, sa vie et ses œuvres," *Revue de droit international et de legislation comparée*, 19 (1887), 408–423; R. Warlomont, *François Laurent, juriste, homme d'action et publiciste* (Brussels, 1948). See also the essays collected by the

Laurent is a remarkable example of a nineteenth-century Liberal noncomformist, in a prosperous middle-ranking European power divided politically between Catholics and Liberals.[72] A staunch legal positivist, he believed that the task of legal scholarship was to elaborate the general principles underlying statutory law: rather than subvert the will of the legislature, legal doctrine should propose amendments and campaign for the needed changes.[73] He was accordingly entrusted with drafting a proposal on the drastic revision of the Civil Code which was never adopted by the Belgian parliament.[74] The draft Code included a set of provisions on conflicts similar to those of the 1865 Italian Civil Code; indeed, Laurent's private international law treatise – elaborated in parallel with the draft Code – is dedicated to Mancini in acknowledgment both of his inspiration and of his political accomplishment.

History was important to Laurent, who had previously written an eighteen-volume series of *Studies on the History of Humanity*.[75] As has justly been noted of that work, "with the unflinching self-confidence of an eighteenth-century system-builder and in the restless, careless style of a preacher of the truth, Laurent indicated God's purpose in each development, in each great event in history."[76] This outlook is evident in Laurent's conflicts treatise: Part One of the work, which takes up the entire first volume bar the Introduction, is entitled "History of International Law."[77] Indeed, the preceding Introduction, essentially a

University Ghent on the centenary of Laurent's death in Erauw et al., *Liber memorialis François Laurent*, 3–199 and 663–678; and F. Dhont, "'L'histoire, Parole Vivante Du Droit?' François Laurent En Ernest Nys Als Historiografen Van Het Volkenrecht" in B. Debaenst (ed.), *De Belle Époque Van Het Belgisch Recht* (Brugges: Die Keure, 2016), 91–115.

72 See E. H. Kossmann, *The Low Countries: 1780–1940* (Oxford: Clarendon Press, 1978), 195–259; E. Witte, "The Battle for Monasteries, Cemeteries and Schools: Belgium" in C. Clark and W. Kaiser (eds.), *Culture Wars: Secular-Catholic Conflict in Nineteenth-Century Europe* (Cambridge: Cambridge University Press, 2003), 102–128.

73 See e.g. Laurent, *Principes de droit civil*, 1:322–366, esp. 346 ("si l'intepréte peut et doit même signaler au législateur les imperfections que l'application des lois découvre, il ne lui est pas permis de les corriger. Il n'est pas appelé à faire la loi.")

74 F. Laurent, *Avant-projet de révision du code civil*, 6 vols (Brussels, 1882–1885). See A. Lainé, "Etude sur le titre préliminaire du project de révision du Code Civil Belge," *Bulletin de la Société de législation comparée*, 19 (1890), 315–341, 383–413, 449–470, 525–567.

75 F. Laurent, *Études sur l'histoire de l'humanité*, 18 vols (Ghent: Hoste, 1855–1870). The first three volumes (on Antiquity) were previously published under the less ambitious title *Histoire du droit des gens et des relations internationals* (1850).

76 Kossmann, *Low Countries*, 229 (229–230).

77 Laurent, *Droit civil international*, 1:97–666.

long essay on the need for an international codification of private international law principles, conveys the same message: it includes a complete historical outline in 20 pages, with the expressive title "progressive development of private international law."[78]

To Laurent, *progress* is the fundamental law of "all that lives" and the importance of history therefore lies in "illuminating the past, explaining the present and revealing the future," making humanity conscious of the divine plan.[79] In the case of private international law, which Laurent described as still in quest of a fundamental principle, history would allow his readers to see through present-day incertitude and chaos and understand the progressive development inevitably leading to order and harmony.[80] Laurent would show how each stage in history led us closer to the moment in time – i.e. the present – when solid foundations of private international law were finally laid.

Laurent's history begins in Antiquity. Greeks and Romans could not have known of private international law (nor the law of nations) since they could not conceive the principle of human unity and did not grant legal status to foreigners.[81] Each city-state reserved rights and legal privileges to its citizens.[82] Romans only differed from Greeks in eventually establishing a sort of unity through domination.[83] It was Christianity that cultivated the respect of other peoples' dignity and contributed the notion of human unity – moving one step further from the theocratic tribalism of the ancient peoples but insisting on an absolute if fictitious unity that left no room for legal diversity.[84] The decisive step was taken in the Early Middle Ages, when the Germanic peoples, imbued with a strong sense of individualism, allowed foreigners to maintain their personal laws, thus bequeathing us with the principle of personality.[85] The next step was feudalism, which contributed the principle of territoriality to the mix.[86] The ground was then open for the "Italian spirit" to create

78 Ibid., 43–64.
79 Ibid., 43.
80 Ibid., 43–44.
81 Ibid., 44–45.
82 Ibid., 121–124.
83 Ibid., 134–179.
84 Ibid., 183ff.
85 Ibid., 219ff (talking of "absolute diversity").
86 Ibid., 248ff.

the first doctrinal edifices and inaugurate a long process until the present moment of creation of a private international law.[87]

2.4.2 Armand Lainé in 1888

Armand Lainé (1840–1908) became the first professor of private international law at the Paris Law Faculty, when a special course was created following the ministerial decree of 28 December 1880. Apart from his educational contribution and normative projects, his legacy includes some important doctrinal contributions, notably in French-language journals.[88] His crowing achievement would have been the systematic treatise on private international law he envisaged, spearheaded by a three-volume historical introduction to the subject. Unfortunately, he only published the first two volumes of his *Introduction to Private International Law* in 1888 and 1892.[89] His unfinished work could parallel, for the history of private international law, Savigny's history of Medieval law, which seems to have been a source of inspiration.[90]

Lainé certainly approaches history with more introspection than Laurent. He is interested in doctrine, not prehistory. The novelty of private international law does not negate the importance of past doctrines; indeed, he appears to appreciate Medieval and Early Modern writers more and will often find affinities (up to a point) with present-day ideas.[91] Lainé presents a doctrinal development in stages. The Italian school – including Dumoulin – was concerned with the pursuit of justice and experimented with several ideas and institutions.[92] He is more critical of the dogmatic pursuit of territorialism by d'Argentré and his

[87] Ibid., 273ff.

[88] A. Pillet, "L'oeuvre de M. Lainé," *Revue de Droit International Privé*, 5 (1909), 1–11.

[89] A. Lainé, *Introduction au droit international privé*, 2 vols (Paris, 1888 and 1892). For the outline of the complete treatise see ibid., 1:xx-xxi. An early version was published an earlier version in *Clunet*, between 1885 and 1887.

[90] The relationship between and influence of Savigny (both as a historian and as a conflicts writer) on Lainé is worth a separate examination.

[91] For example, Lainé, *Introduction* 1:184 observes that certain members of the Italian school seem to share the opinion gaining ground on his day of subjecting succession to the personal law of the defunct, "attributing a preponderant influence to the presumed will of the defunct, from the point of view of a family settlement and the idea of patrimonial unity:" "Eh bien, cette opinion, qui semple nouvelle, se trouve être en réalité une doctrine très ancienne, qui, avant de subir la longue eclipse après laquelle elle reparait, eut son heure, sinon de plein succès, au moins du lute et de célébrité." See e.g. Sections 9.2.2, 9.3.4, and 10.2.1.

[92] Lainé, *Introduction*, 1:93ff.

epigones in the Low Countries and Germany.[93] He argues that territorialist ideas captured ground in France only gradually, and never as strongly as suggested.[94] By the eighteenth century, the theory of statutes was evidently undergoing a new transformation that foreshadowed the ideas of nineteenth-century Liberal internationalists but had not yet reached maturity by the time of the French Revolution and failed to impact the conflicts provisions of the Napoleonic Code.[95] Lainé would attempt to answer why, near the end of his life, in a separate study on the influences and history and of these provisions.[96]

Underlying Lainé's approach is a convinction that the French positive law of his time can only be explained in historical terms. Even though initially developed to govern conflicts within the national territory, the theory of statutes had found its way to present-day France, both through the Civil Code and in parallel to the Civil Code.[97] The study of past doctrine is therefore necessary both in order to understand the "enigmatic terms" in which legislative intention was expressed and to see perhaps the original meaning of these terms.[98]

This brings us to a second, and most important, reason for Lainé's interest in history. Lainé is a forceful partisan of the school of international law and the new discipline of private international law, which, as he claims, had only begun to be constructed in the mid-nineteenth century and is undergoing growth pains.[99] His work's preface is an account of the efforts at the discipline's construction.[100] He admits that from the point of view of positive law, private international law appears as "multiple and diverse" as the number of existing domestic systems; but from a theoretical point of view, it is no less "unique and universal" than

93 Ibid., 310ff.

94 Ibid., 2:5ff. See also 1:341: "la démonstration d'un fait important et demeuré néanmois inaperçu, savoir que la division générale des lois en statuts réels et statuts personnels, inconnue avant d'Argentré, ne prit racine en France que fort longtemps après lui . . . que par conséquent elle n'y était acclimatée que depuis soixante-six ans environ lors de la rédaction du Code civil."

95 Ibid., 1:413ff, esp. 425 ("Dérivée de sources aussi diverses, la doctrine francaise du XVIIIe siècle présentera nécessairement des incohérences, mais elle aura aussi quelque chose de large, d'humain, de libéral, qui en vera vraiment l'introduction à notre Droit international privé et la préface de notre Code civil").

96 A. Lainé, "La rédaction du Code civil et le sens de ses dispositions en matière de droit international privé," *Revue de Droit International Privé*, 1 (1905), 21–60, 443–479.

97 Lainé, *Introduction*, 1:31–32.

98 Ibid., 45–46 ("Pour nous, en un mot, la théorie des statuts complète et éclaire la loi.")

99 Ibid., 38, 42, 44 ("né d'hier, il n'est pas encore formé").

100 Ibid., v–xxi.

public international law.[101] The progress of positive law will depend on mutual concessions as to the applicability of national laws and a common understanding (*entente*) leading to the establishment of common principles.[102] Lainé points at the disparity between Continental and Anglo-American law, the former drawing on a six-century tradition, the latter clinging on old borrowed ideas and a "feudal" spirit; this gap should however be reduced, chiefly by Anglo-American emulation of new Continental doctrines.[103]

A generation younger than Laurent and Mancini, Lainé appears more nuanced in both his doctrinal approach and his historical vision. His examination of preclassical texts remains unsurpassed to this day. In the spirit of his time, he presents us with a robust progress narrative but he also projects his own normative vision, and jurisprudence, on to the past.

2.4.3 A Lost Cause? de Vareilles-Sommières in 1897

Gabriel de Vareilles-Sommières (1846–1905) was professor of civil law and Dean of the Catholic Law Faculty of Lille. An ultramontane Catholic from a noble bloodline traceable all the way to Charlemagne, with personal animosity toward several of the French Liberal members of the Institute, Vareilles-Sommières wrote a treatise on private international law in which he defends territorialism and traditional doctrine, railing against what he calls "the School."[104]

The treatise of Vareilles-Sommières is intented as a restatement of the "theory of statutes," which he regards as both the law presently in force in France and the most appropriate doctrinal system for the solution of conflicts ("learned and rational, profound and judicious").[105] His historical narrative reflects his commitment: it is laid in Part One of his work ("The theory of statutes, the new theories and the theory of the Civil Code"). An extensive first chapter discusses the theory of statutes in a unified manner.[106] Most citations are to works of French and Dutch authors from the sixteenth century onward, but his list of authorities

101 Ibid., 43–44.

102 Ibid., 29–43.

103 Ibid., 40–42. Lainé's views on the primitiveness (and eventual integration) of Anglo-American conflicts law are reflected in his study of Dutch doctrine and especially Huber.

104 See G. de Vareilles-Sommières, *La synthèse du droit international privé*, vol. I (Paris: Librairie Cotillon, 1897), Vff, XIIIff.

105 Ibid., 8 ("savante et rationnelle, profonde et judicieuse").

106 Ibid., 1–97.

includes Accursius and Bartolus.[107] A second chapter discusses the "theory of personality,"[108] a third one the system of Savigny and a fourth one other modern systems (Wächter, Schäffner, Eichorn, and Pillet).[109] A fifth chapter demonstrates that the theory of statutes was unequivocally adopted in the Civil Code.[110]

This is certainly not a progress or evolutionary narrative. Traditional doctrine, as elaborated, is presented as being theoretically superior to modern ideas, as well as consecrated in the Civil Code.

2.4.4 Eugen Ehrlich in 1906

Austrian professor of civil law Eugen Ehrlich (1862–1922) is best known as one of the founders of legal sociology and father figure of the concepts of "living law" and legal pluralism.[111] This makes more remarkable a – largely forgotten – article on private international law he published in 1906.[112] The article is noteworthy less for its originality and more for conveying the spirit of the age. Despite Ehrlich's status as father of empirical sociology, his conflicts history is *doctrinal history* – of that type which presents the doctrine, sometimes, as responding to societal needs.[113] Its emphasis is on ideas, and it stretches the historical evidence in order to illustrate "how modern is the whole juridical edifice of private international law."[114]

Ehrlich saw two premises fundamental to the existence of private international law. The first one is sovereignty. "Each epoch has the private international law responding to the then-reigning conceptions

[107] Ibid., 7–8.
[108] Ibid., 97–129.
[109] Ibid., 97–129, 129–146, and 147–183 with a common conclusion (in addition to lengthy criticism of each system in the respective section) at 183–185.
[110] Ibid., 186–198.
[111] See M. Rehbinder, *Die Begründung der Rechtssoziologie durch Eugen Ehrlich*, 2nd ed (Berlin: Duncker & Humblot, 1986); and M. Hertogh (ed.), *Living Law: Reconsidering Eugen Ehrlich* (Oxford: Hart, 2008).
[112] See E. Ehrlich, "Les tendances actuelles du droit international privé," *Revue de Droit International Privé*, 4 (1908), 902–924. The article was originally published as "Internationales Privatrecht," *Deutsche Rundschau*, 126 (1906), 419–433 and subsequently translated in French by Robert Gaillemer).
[113] See e.g. ibid., 908.
[114] Ibid., 902. This claim is asserted categorically – and with some credence – regarding "antiquity and the German Middle Ages" (902–906). But then Ehrlich also regards the Italian cities as simple communities, members of the same State, the *Imperium Romanum* (907).

of the nature of State and on the nature of its law."[115] The second is the conceptual distinction between stranger (*Fremde*) who has no legal status, and foreigner (*Ausländer*) who does. Private international law could accordingly not exist in Ancient and Medieval times.[116]

Ehrlich viewed late nineteenth-century conflicts doctrine as characterized by an opposition between nationalist and internationalist doctrines. This antithesis has its antedecedents in the (Early Modern) beginnings of conflict of laws: d'Argentré was a partisan of absolute sovereignty, while the Dutch school was more mindful of internationalism. Ehrlich tells the story of this opposition as a progress narrative, where internationalist thought is gradually coming of age and gaining ground.[117] He claims inspiration from the doctrinal system of Ernst Zitelmann, which is hailed as taking the internationalist doctrine in new heights. But this is a *fighting* progress narrative: the success of Zitelmann's ideas will depend not on their "exactness" or "falseness" but "from a series of circumstances" that cannot be appreciated by a contemporary, unless one tries to connect it to past and future.[118]

2.5 The Discipline Persists: Interwar Progress Narratives

2.5.1 Scientific Optimism: Max Gutzwiller in 1929

Born to a family of Swiss bankers, statesmen, and charitable workers, Max Gutzwiller (1889–1989) was appointed to a professorship at the University of Fribourg, and then moved to Heidelberg for ten years; in 1936, refusing to comply with the Nazi "race laws" and divorce his wife, he resigned and returned to Fribourg.[119] Gutzwiller had begun his career as a professor of Roman law: indeed, almost 60 years separate his early work on Roman law from a systematic history of Medieval and Early Modern conflict of laws.[120]

115 Ibid., 915.

116 Ibid., 904, 907.

117 Ibid., 912–915, 916ff, 920.

118 Ibid., 924.

119 See e.g. *In memoriam Max Gutzwiller: Gedächtnisfeier der Juristischen Fakultät Heidelberg am 3. November 1989 im "Gutzwiller-Saal" des Instituts für Ausländisches und Internationales Privat-und Wirtschaftsrecht* (Heidelberg: Winter, 1990); M. Gutzwiller, *70 Jahre Jurisprudenz: Erinnerungen eines Neunzigjährigen. Neuauflage anlässlich des 100. Geburtstags von Max Gutzwiller* (Basel: Helbing & Lichtenhahn, 1989).

120 M. Gutzwiller, *Geschichte des internationales Privatrecht: Von den Anfangen bis zu den großen Kodifikationen* (Basle and Stuttgart: Helbing & Lichtenhahn, 1977).

Gutzwiller is best known in conflicts historiography for a relatively youthful work: his 1929 lecture series, at the newly established Hague Academy of International Law, on the historical development of private international law.[121] Gutzwiller presents us with a linear account of the progressive "development" of private international law. In the first period of doctrinal development, private international law consisted of a body of case law and scholarly writings (*droit international privé jurisprudentiel et scientifique*).[122] In the second period, which begun with the great codifications of civil law at the beginning of the nineteenth century and is still ongoing, the field has become grounded on legislation (*droit international privé légal*).[123] According to Gutzwiller, this second period can be further subdivided: originally, private international law norms were to be found in national legislations (*droit international privé individuel*), but the world circa 1929 appears to have moved to the next stage, where private international law norms are codified in international treaties (*droit international privé collectif*).[124]

Such optimism may appear remarkable to present-day readers: with hindsight, Gutzwiller wrote like a nineteenth-century Liberal at a time of nationalist reaction against liberal internationalist projects. But Gutzwiller's analysis was not just convenient or wishful thinking. Only recently, German and then Swiss civil law had been unified with considerable success – including the codification of conflicts rules. In 1929, new international institutions, governmental as well as academic, such as the League of Nations, Unidroit and the Hague Academy were still glowing with hope. And Gutzwiller was not expecting fast results: his famous aphorism on the special importance of history to private international law might be seen, in this light, as an effort to convince us about the "slow, but progressive and coherent (*conséquent*)" development of the field.[125]

[121] M. Gutzwiller, "Le développement historique du droit international privé," *Recueil des cours*, 29 (1929), 287–400.

[122] Gutzwiller, "Développement historique," 293–294, taking as point of departure the "confection de la célèbre glose accursienne."

[123] Ibid., 294.

[124] Ibid.

[125] See Gutzwiller, "Développement historique," 292: "Eh bien, la première et grand thèse que nous voudrions défendre au seuil de cette étude, c'est que: Parmi tous les domaines du Droit, aucun ne dépend à un tel degré de son histoire que le Droit international. En droit international privé, l'histoire est tout. Cela tient d'abord au développement lent, mais progressif et conséquent, de ce singulier problème et de ses principes directeurs."

2.5.2 Progress as Struggle: Meijers in 1934

Eduard Maurits Meijers (1880–1954) was professor of civil law, private international law and legal history at the University of Leiden, in the Netherlands. Quite a few of the people who wrote on the history of conflict of laws had some training in Roman law, but Meijers, who specialized in Medieval legal history, was the only one capable – and willing – to do archival research.[126] Meijers also had an important doctrinal contribution and a prominent place among the jurists of the interwar and immediate postwar period, who sought to construct a new doctrinal synthesis that reconciled doctrine with practice, and a spirit of moderate internationalism with the demands of national legal systems. In the aftermath of the Second World War, Meijers was also tasked with drafting a new Civil Code for the Netherlands.[127]

Meijers delivered his own Hague Academy course on the history of private international law in 1934, five years after Gutzwiller.[128] Meijers states as his objective to "explain how and why the principles of private international law were formed and developed since the Middle Ages until the modern codes."[129] Since the "opinions" of past authors have been well discussed, Meijers proposes to examine another aspect of conflicts history, "less studied, but equally interesting," namely "the tradition" as lived by the people or incoporated into case law.[130] This tradition is a powerful force, difficult to go up against.[131] It is however not an omnipotent force. Scholarship is still needed to explain rationally the origins of a rule that has persisted for centuries; moreover, traditions have often "died" as they became incompatible with new ideas introduced by legal

126 See Section 3.5.1.

127 See R. D. Chavannes, "E.M. Meijers and the Recodification of the Dutch Civil Code after World War II" (Oxford, 1997).

128 E. M. Meijers, "L'histoire des principes fondamentaux du droit international privé à partir du Moyen Age," *Recueil des cours*, 49 (1934), 542–686.

129 Ibid., 547.

130 Ibid., 547: "Ce ne sont pas seulement les auteurs qui ont fait l'histoire du droit international privé; il y a encore une autre force efficace. C'est la tradition, telle qu'elle vit dans un peuple ou est incorporée dans la jurisprudence."

131 Ibid., 547–548: "Surtout dans une société moins changeante que la nôtre, le droit privé n'est pas toujours consideré comme un moyen de réaliser des buts pratiques. Les règles de droit suivies fidèlement par les ancêtres et formant la base de toute la société sont vénérables par elles-mêmes. Celui qui s'oppose aux institutions existantes doit redouter des forces secrètes. Voice la force mystique ou religieuse des paroles qui ont crée l'ordre dans la société et le monde. C'est le λόγος des Grecs, le 'Au commencement était la Parole' de la Bible, c'est le *fas* – dérivé du verbe *fari* (dire) – des Romains."

scholarship.[132] The renaissance of Roman law thus led to the disappearance of the personality of laws regime.[133] For Meijers, tradition and legal doctrine abstractly defined (*la doctrine*) engage in a reciprocal action, where scholarship influences legal practice "consciously and uconsciously" but often has to submit to the dominant tradition.[134]

Meijers devoted a considerable part of his text to the Early Middle Ages. The nineteenth-century Liberal internationalists had viewed the personality of laws regime as something different from present-day private international law. Meijers reclaimed that tradition and refuted the idea that it was replaced by a regime of absolute territoriality. His own conclusion was that, in France and the Low Countries, an "international" or "intercustomary" law developed from the personality of laws regime, without any help from learned law – in fact, well in advance of learned-law developments.[135]

The central theme of Meijers history is the persistence of *tradition*, on the one hand against the stream of change, and on the other hand in spite – or ahead – of the legal doctrine. Whereas Gutzwiller's heroes are doctrinal writers, Meijers's *personae* are the doctrine abstractly defined, the case law, and the traditions.

2.5.3 *The Triumph of Comparative Law: Ernst Rabel in 1945*

Berlin professor Ernst Rabel (1874–1955) was the founding director of the Institute for Foreign and International Private Law and one of the most eminent jurists uprooted from Hitler's Germany. A private international lawyer trained in ancient Roman and Greek law, as well as an instrumental figure in efforts to produce an international law of sales, Rabel emigrated to the United States, where he produced a landmark four-volume treatise on comparative conflict of laws.[136]

Rabel's historical narrative reflects both his background and his preoccupation with bridging the gap between common law and the Continental tradition. He presents to us a community of learning and

[132] Ibid.
[133] Ibid., 506.
[134] Ibid.
[135] Ibid., 583–584.
[136] E. Rabel, *The Conflict of Laws: A Comparative Study*, 4 vols (Ann Arbor, MI: University of Michigan Press, 1945–1958).

purpose, which lasted from the Middle Ages until the late nineteenth century. By the time of the postglassators, this "branch of law" was "regarded as universally binding," due to its "artificial incorporation" to Roman law. The doctrines of the postglassators acquired a "territorial realm" that "exceeded even the boundaries within which the canon and Roman laws were received as 'written reason,' representing the law of all Christendom," and eventually – as "accepted and transformed by eminent scholars in France and Holland" – "gained recognition in England and in the United States."[137]

> The law of conflicts thus became one field, in which the common and civil laws had a common doctrinal basis and which could be thought of as a truly international law. This conception of a world community was still prevalent when in 1834 the great American, Joseph Story, merged the Dutch doctrine with the Anglo-American cases. His treatise acquired authority in both hemispheres and contributed to the continuation, in renewed form, of an internationally minded school on the European Continent. In particular, Germany's greatest jurist, Friedrich Carl von Savigny (1849), using Story's materials and rational method, established the fundamends of modern conflicts law. It was significant that his treatment of this subject formed the last part of the celebrated System of Modern Roman Law; for him, there was no doubt about the suprastate nature of the subject matter.[138]

The idea of a "world community," and the "international conception of 'international private law'," was adopted "by almost all outstanding authors until approximately 1890." They wrote on the topic "in a common atmosphere, among brethren of the same creed, envisaging its application to all countries" – even when they protested being classified as internationalists.[139]

Rabel treats as a single stream legal scholarship dealing with conflicts issues from the Medieval jurists to Savigny to international-law school champions such as Laurent and Westlake. There is no break, no fledgling novelty. So how is this paradise lost? Moreover, how should one account for the divide between common-law and continental jurists? Rabel's

[137] Ibid., 1:7.

[138] Ibid.

[139] Ibid., 8 ("[these] scholars . . . nevertheless thought that special studies, restricted to the positive laws of particular legal systems, unaided by general theory, narrow in perspective, are prone to choose improper premises or to misconceive the sphere of individual principles in the 'organism' of international private law").

explanation points back to to the nineteenth-century national codifications of private law and positivism:

> In time, the international community disintegrated. The common law lawyers, segregated from the civil law background, instinctively receded from naïve cosmopolitan attitudes. Absorbed in the judicial decisions of their countries, they gave slight attention to developments elsewhere. In the civil law countries on the other hand, from the end of the eighteenth century, there appeared an increasing number of national codifications of private law, which divided the European Continent into separate units, secluding them behind progressively higher barriers of national legislation.[140]

Such developments are, obviously, an early nineteenth-century phenomenon. So how do they account for the shift in late nineteenth-century conflict of laws?

> Relatively late, the impact of this process reached the conflicts law. The specialists in this branch of law, which seems always predestined to lag behind the currents of general jurisprudence, were tardily and rudely awakened by the discovery that the supposed international source of law did not exist. Former universalist conceptions gave way to the knowledge that conflicts rules no less than other rules of law must have their roots in the soil of some state and that international rules in the proper sense flow only from international custom or treaties, and at that in a very thin stream. Thus, the long-established international community of conflicts studies was dissolved, and the national conflicts rules succumbed to the same spirit of isolationism that permeated other fields of law. Against this background, the meager achievements of the Hague Conventions of 1902 and 1905 appeared like a little island of blossoming internationalism.[141]

The collapse was dealt with, first by new ideas of a few ingenious writers whose "deductive systems" were commonly rejected,[142] and finally by the new idea whose time had come: the comparative method.

> These three schools, the aprioristic internationalists, the faithful expositors of fragmentary statutes and cases, the propagandists of nationality as the standard of personal rights and duties, have had their time, and their time is over. A new epoch began about 1925. Previously, a few far-seeing scholars, Bar, Kahn, Anzilotti, Niemeyer, perceived that conflicts rules, though derived from a national source like other ordinary legal rules, have

[140] Ibid., 8–9.

[141] Ibid., 9.

[142] Ibid., 9–10 (summarizing the doctrines of Pillet, Zitelmann, and Frankenstein).

> special functions and purposes requiring a method of international scope. Kahn, one of the most acute advocates of positivism, went so far as to postulate that both the international and the positivistic methods should be integrated through the comparative method and so superseded.[143]

Rabel expects the comparative method to remedy the respective deficiencies of common-law and Continental approaches: "until about 1925, in the Anglo-American orbit, the theoretical approach and, in the Continental literature, the practical understanding, left very much to be desired," leading to a "deplorable state of this branch of law . . . worse than the experts would acknowledge."[144] After a worldwide survey of doctrinal contributions and legislative initatives, he concludes by noting "the immaturity of this branch of law . . . and its need of intensive prolonged cultivation."[145] The vision of a past international scholarly environment – moreover one uniting Anglo-American and Continental doctrine – serves as both an inspiration and a warning for the future of private international law.

2.6 History as Pedigree: Conflict and Eclecticism in Modern Private International Law

Modern consciousness is characterized by a variety in perspectives. Modern historical narratives reflect this pluralism. Optimistic narratives of progress and an eventual "end of history" for private international law have been replaced by darker evocations, of conflict between opposing conceptions and struggle against the perennial problems conflicts lawyers are called to resolve. The modern consciousness seems to adhere less to the notion of a linear conception, or a clear distinction between past and present. Modern doctrine, on the contrary, is more open to the idea of the present as the estuary of past doctrines and theories from different eras – or as a battleground of competing ideas from across time.[146]

143 Ibid., 10–11.
144 Ibid., 19.
145 Ibid., 41.
146 On the notion of a stream see e.g. Audit, *Droit international privé*, 57 (passage excerpted below at n. 170). On the notion of a battleground, see e.g. R. Quadri, "Quelques considérations sur la contribution du Professeur Wengler au progrès du droit international privé" in *Multitudo Legum Ius Unum: Festschrift für Wilhelm Wengler*, vol. II (1973), 2 (as translated by K. Nadelman, "Sourcebook"), 658 n. 3: "The various doctrinal currents of the history of [conflict of laws] have rendez-vous with each other for a

2.6.1 *Variations on a Theme*

The postwar period has seen an increase in the number of narratives presenting the history of conflicts doctrine as evolving variations on a theme. That theme might be the ongoing struggle to achieve a grand objective, or a dialectic antithesis between two opposing conceptions.

2.6.1.1 History as Quest

Narratives presenting the evolution of conflicts doctrine as an ongoing "quest" for the achievement of a purpose appear as the successor of late-classical narratives of progress. Their difference is a matter of perspective, and tone. In the modern narratives, the tone is somber; their emphasis is on the effort undertaken by generation after generation of jurists, rather than on the march toward the inevitable solution of conflicts problems. It might well be, in fact, that past generations had arrived closer than subsequent ones to the solution of problems. These modern narratives also suggest a stronger self-consciousness, a sense of taking part in a discourse with historical continuity.

We may find examples of "quest" narratives in two Hague Academy courses given in the mid-1960s by senior Italian academics: both courses use the adjective "historical" in their title.

Giuseppe Barile is preoccupied with the "historical function" of private international law.[147] His goal is to provide contemporary doctrine with a theoretical foundation possessing a historical pedigree. He was able to locate this *fonction historique* of private international law in the quest for the "uniform solution" of the same case. In Barile's story, the original, statutist principle of a "unique solution" is eventually – and as a result of the construction of sovereign-based legal systems (*ordres juridiques*) – "transformed" into the present idea of a "uniform solution."[148]

Rodolfo de Nova promises a "historical and comparative introduction."[149] His story was one of doctrinal writers trying, since the field's

confrontation which, even if not decisive, may well greatly contribute to the progress of science and practice."

[147] See G. Barile, "La fonction historique du droit international privé," *Recueil des cours*, 116 (1965), 305–376.

[148] Ibid., esp. 332–334.

[149] R. de Nova, "A Historical and Comparative Introduction to the Conflict of Laws (General Course)," *Recueil des cours*, 118 (1966), 443–622.

beginning, to establish a "set of rules having universal value and aiming at the solution of conflict of laws once and for all."[150]

2.6.1.2 History as Dialectics

In a modern French textbook, Pierre Mayer discusses the contemporary era (which covers the past two centuries) on the basis of the "essential points on which the authors oppose each other": conflict of sovereignties as opposed to conflict of interests; universalism as opposed to particularism; nationalism as opposed to internationalism; and personalism as opposed to territorialism.[151]

Such conceptual oppositions have been frequently used, especially in the last century, in order to illustrate the fault lines dividing contemporary doctrine. They are often projected onto preclassical conflict of laws: we will subsequently have the opportunity to examine the opposition between territorialism and personalism in this regard.[152]

Opposing nationalist to internationalist conceptions of conflicts doctrine has been a more recent phenomenon. We can locate such references in tun-of-century writers such as Eugen Ehrlich or Josephus Jitta, who presented the opposition in relatively neutral terms and certainly not as the basic theme of the narrative.[153] In the postwar era, Werner Goldschmidt drew an historical sketch of the fight (*lucha*) between legal cosmopolitanism and chauvinism.[154] But the opposition has recently acquired a more polemical tone, as would be expected at a time when the term "nationalist" has become almost a slander among intellectuals: at the turn of the millennium, French legal historian Jean-Louis Halpérin presented a history of conflict of laws in the past two centuries on the

[150] Ibid., 441 (441–477 are devoted to a historical treatment).

[151] See Mayer, *Droit international privé*, 45–52. Mayer divides his chapter on "the evolution of the law of conflicts" into the predoctrinal phase, the doctrinal phase, and the contemporary era: ibid., 33–52.

[152] See Section 4.2 on contemporary doctrine and Sections 10.2, 14.2, and 15.2 on preclassical doctrine.

[153] See D. J. Jitta, *La Méthode du Droit International Privé* (The Hague: Belinfante Frères, 1890), 14ff who sees a perennial opposition between a *tendance humanitaire* and a *tendance nationale*. While in temperament Jitta is compatible with the following generation of internationalists, his narrative could however still be classified as a liberal progress narrative. Jean-Paulin Niboyet, a political nationalist of the interwar years, opposes the universalism of Medieval jurists such as Bartolus and Dumoulin to the nationalism of Early Modern jurists such as d'Argentré, in a manner favoring the nationalists: see Niboyet,*Traité*, 3:54–55, 79.

[154] Goldschmidt, *Sistema y Filosofia*, 1:154–162.

singular axis of an opposition between "legal nationalism and community of law."[155]

2.6.1.3 History as Marxist Narrative

The postwar period saw the development of a regional system of Socialist countries, notably in Eastern Europe and Southeast Asia, which came to be considered a separate legal tradition.[156] In Socialist private international law we also encounter another kind of evolutionary narrative, combining echoes of the buoyant progress narratives of classical writers, a Marxian deterministic materialism, and the twentieth-century need to balance off different worlds.

The Marxist tradition at its purest has viewed legal doctrine as the legitimation of economic interests. Modern Marxist legal historians have tended to merge socioeconomic and legal history through the use of case studies and "field" research. A more traditional Marxist–Communist approach had put its emphasis instead on canonical doctrinal material, seeking to substantiate a big-picture progress narrative.

An illustration of that second Marxist approach as applied to the history of conflict of laws is offered by the Yugoslav Borislav Blagojević (1911–1985).[157] Private international law, in contrast "to all other fields of law and almost all other juridical disciplines ... appears as a completely new manifestation, a new category of the capitalist period."[158] The historical study of private international law provides "one of the best examples of application of the Marxist-dialectical views to law."[159] The particularities of each doctrinal school can be explained on the basis of economic interests: the Italian school advanced solutions conforming to the needs of the commercial aristocracy of Italian cities in the thirteenth and fourteenth centuries; Dumoulin and his successors expressed the interests of the French bourgeoisie struggling for a unitary national market and d'Argentré those of the feudal reaction; the Dutch school similarly expresses the ideology of Netherlands at the peak of its commercial power; Savigny supported the interests of the German

155 Halpérin, *Nationalisme Juridique.*

156 See e.g. I. Szászy, *Private International Law in the European People's Democracies* (Budapest: Akadémiai Kiadó, 1964).

157 B. Blagojević, "Théories des statuts à la lumière de l'histoire générale de l'évolution de la société" in *De Conflictu Legum: Essays Presented to Roeland Duco Kollewijn & Johannes Offerhaus at Their Seventieth Birthdays* (Leiden: A. W. Sijthoff, 1962): 67–81.

158 Blagojević, "Théories des statuts," 67–68.

159 Ibid., 68.

bourgeoisie "in the era of industrial capitalism," whereas Mancini "defended the restrained interests of the bourgeoisie only of the nations called of emigration and primarily of Italy."[160]

The approach provides an interesting counterweight to conventional doctrinal stories. At the same time, Blagojević restricts himself to doctrinal history, admittedly one tied to the context of a changing economy, even though case law could have provided him with better evidence of the linkages between law, economy and society than the thinking of legal academics.[161] In that sense as well, Blagojević is quite representative of Socialist legal scholars of Eastern and Central Europe in the Cold War era, especially in their interaction with Western lawyers. These scholars had to engage, especially when in contact with Western lawyers, in a balancing act between the bourgeois law they inherited and the anti-bourgeois ideological superstructure that had to form the foundation of their thinking. In private and public international law, this often led to a classic Marxist critique of the bourgeois legal tradition accompanied by an implicit acknowledgement of sharing that tradition.[162]

2.6.1.4 History in Circles

Narratives of a cyclical pattern, also visible in the genealogy of *lex mercatoria*, are an integral part of the modern consciousness of private international law.[163] Cyclical narratives tend to involve the preclassical period, which they portray as a time of cosmopolitanism, universal law, legal pluralism, the time when *ius gentium* and *lex mercatoria* reigned. In fact, it will often be a matter of intonation whether to characterize a specific narrative on conflicts history as being cyclical or of "progress with bumps on the road." As an example we may take Ernst Rabel's version of conflicts history. Rabel proposes a cautious progress narrative,

[160] Ibid., 69. The rest of the article is an elaboration of this thesis (until 1800).

[161] For an example of a materialist explanation of historical development making extensive use of case law see M. Horwitz, *The Transformation of American Law, 1780–1850* (Cambridge, MA: Harvard University Press, 1977).

[162] See also the Soviet narratve of L. A. Lunz, *Internationales Privatrecht: Allgemeiner Teil* (Berlin: Deutscher Zentralverlag, 1961), 82–116 (a chapter on conflicts history, from Ancient Rome to the early stirring of the US conflicts revolution, or, as the author puts it, a short history of prebourgeois, bourgeois, and imperialist doctrine). This is the German translation of the 1959 edition. On the Czech translation of the 1949 edition of the same treatise, see A. Drucker, "Soviet Views on Private International Law," *International and Comparative Law Quarterly*, 4 (1955), 384–389: "an unusual mixture of political propaganda and genuine learning" (ibid., 387).

[163] On *lex mercatoria* see Section 2.6.3.1.

where doctrine evolves and thus overcomes obstacles. He is concerned with bridging the Continental–Common Law dvide and his words are carefully chosen to convey a sense of continuity and optimism, as well as to identify a salient problem. However, the same story could also be rephrased as a "cyclical" narrative: either of doctrines being built, disintegrated, and reconstructed (with the cycle repeating itself), or in terms of cosmopolitanism giving way to nationalism–parochialism until an internationalist or cosmoplitan rebirth. Whereas in the former narrartives private international law scholars appear well-meaning, in the latter narrative the disintegration of the "international community" of scholars would be attributed in part to the biases of late nineteenth-century private international lawyers.[164]

A more interesting example of a cyclical narrative is provided by an essay in the early postwar period by French Jurist André Bonichon.[165] Preoccupied with the role of sovereignty in conflicts doctrine, Bonichon attempted to demonstrate that conflicts doctrine long preceded the idea of sovereignty – and that even that idea was considered and rejected in the past.[166] Bonichon distinguished three potential founding principles of conflicts systems: the *principe fonctionnel*, oriented toward "social justice and the necessity of legal commerce," which he ascribes to the Italian statutist school; the *principe essentiel*, oriented to the nature of the legal relations themselves, which he associates with the French statutist school and Savigny; and the *principe formel* which is oriented toward the "formal aspect" of the rules and their imperative nature as they emanate from a legislator.[167] In Bonichon's narrative, these principles are not mutually exclusive, but they had not been taken into simultaneous consideration – leading to a "narrowness of vision" as to the role of sovereignty, shifting from one extreme to the other.[168]

[164] See notably Halpérin, *Nationalisme juridique*.

[165] A. Bonnichon, "La notion de conflit des souverainetés dans la science des conflits des lois," *Revue critique*, 38(1949), 615–635 and 39 (1950), 11–32

[166] Ibid., esp. 620–622, 629.

[167] Ibid., 618–619. See also discussion in 620ff.

[168] Ibid., 619 ("L'histoire de droit international privé serait bien plutôt l'histoire des apparitions et des éclipses de ces trois aspects du problème, de ces trois principes de solution") and 620.

2.6.2 *Historicism and Pedigree History*

Whereas the abovedescribed narrative types inevitably recreate the past with the eyes of the present, another set of historical narratives appears more concerned in using the past to create or explain the present. We should distinguish further, between attempts to explain the present state of affairs and attempts to buttress specific contemporary doctrines or approaches with a historical pedigree. What these approaches share is an acknowledgement that history matters; that there is a certain degree of organic succession of developments; and that, at the same time, context and local conditions influence the results in a decisive way. We could in that sense speak of *historicist* narratives.[169]

2.6.2.1 Explanatory Historicism

Explanatory historicism might well be the prevalent state of mind today – at least in an unconcsious form. It is certainly a modern phenomenon in conflicts literature: The founders of the discipline shared many ideas with predisciplinary writers, but they regarded themselves as free to decide what to accept and what not. They may have been the ones who reconstituted the legacy of old writers, but they did not view themselves as inheritors, or trustees, of an estate. Modern consciousness, on the contrary, is more open to the idea of the present as the tributary stream – of past theories and doctines.[170]

This eclectic or linear version of explanatory historicism should be distinguished from a more cyclical (and preexisting) variety that shares affinities with normative historicism. This quasi-normative version still presents a story of geological evolution, but it tends to favor one of the stromata; it consequently has to explain or justify in historical terms the move away from it, and possibly make the argument for a restoration of sorts.[171]

[169] This is of course not the same as the determinist (mainly Hegelian and Marxist) historicism attacked e.g. by K. Popper, *The Poverty of Historicism* (New York: Basic Books, 1957–1960).

[170] See Audit, *Droit international privé*, 57: "La connaissance, même sommaire, de cet acquis présente un intérêt qui n'est pas simplement historique: d'une part, en effet, le droit positif est directement tributaire de certaines conceptions relativement anciennes; d'autre part, il est rare que des solutions qu'on serait tenté de proposer comme nouvelles n'aient pas déjà été suggérées ou ne connaissent quelque antécédent."

[171] For an example, see the general course of G. Sperdutti, "Théorie du droit international privé," *Recueil des cours*, 122 (1967), 173–336 (who expresses an affinity for the pre-

2.6.2.2 Normative Historicism

"Normative" historicism is concerned with providing a historical pedigree for a contemporary doctrine or theory. We could also speak of "genealogical" enterprises.

A visible modern example is the attempt of the proponents of party autonomy to establish an historical pedigree for that doctrine and to demonstrate that "the power of private parties to control the selection of a forum and the choice of applicable law is by no means a novel idea."[172] Unlike narratives of an ongoing quest, or of a dialectic opposition – both of which emphasize the persistence of the idea in the discourse across time – normative historicists aim at providing historical support, which may as well come only from specific periods, to a modern doctrine.

For a pointed example of normative historicism, which came to involve Ulrik Huber, we need look no further than the Supreme Court of the United States, and American conflicts and civil procedure specialists. For most of US history, the law on interstate jurisdiction appears to have followed the so-called *power theory* of jurisdiction.[173] The postwar era saw an increasing influence of US law by *fairness* theories.[174] A favorite target of fairness theories was the notion that service of process is *per se* sufficient to establish jurisdiction over an out-of-state defendant

sixteenth century eclectic doctrines of the Italian school): "Il faut alors se demander d'où vient qu'une très grande partie de la doctrine ne soit pas de cet avis ou s'exprime, de toute façon, de manière à faire croire qu'elle considère les règles de droit international privé comme se différenciant des principes de la théorie des statuts même en ce qui concerne l'objet de leur référence respective. Notre réponse est la suivante: il s'agit, à l'origine, d'un excès de réaction à des excès de synthèse conceptuelle dans lesquels s'était laissée entraîner la doctrine statutaire au cours des dernières siècles; par la suite, la diversité de l'objet de référence des règles de droit international privé a fini par être considerée comme un point acquis, voire comme le point de départ de l'analyse des éléments constitutifs de ces règles" (184). Another example of this tendency, with regard to the role of the concept of sovereignty in the conflict of laws (which also doubles as an illustration of the persistent dialectical relationship between the true constituent elements of conflicts doctrine) is Bonnichon, "Conflit de souverainetés." See also Section 4.6.1.

172 Juenger, *Choice of Law*, 8.

173 *Pennoyer* v. *Neff*, 95 US 714 (1878) epitomizes this approach.

174 For an early typology (and an historical account) in that sense see A. T. von Mehren, "Adjudicatory Jurisdiction: General Theories Compared and Evaluated," *Boston University Law Review*, 63 (1983), 279–340, esp. 282–311. More recently, A. Nuyts, *L'exception de forum non conveniens* (Brussels: Bruylant, 2003), 27–74. Cf. R. Michaels, "Two Paradigms of Jurisdiction," *Michigan Journal of International Law*, 27 (2006), 1003–1069.

who is just passing by – the so-called tag jurisdiction or transient jurisdiction.[175] The debate heated up once the US Supreme Court ruled unconstitutional the taking of jurisdiction over a nonresident defendant by sequestering property belonging to the nonresident.[176] In the end, a unanimous Supreme Court upheld, in principle, the constitutionality of transient jurisdiction in 1990.[177] Led by Justice Antonin Scalia, a plurality of the Court invoked the rule's historical pedigree to affirm its constitutionality.[178]

The genealogical battle around transient jurisdiction had begun a third of a century earlier. Those embracing a power theory of jurisdiction had argued that the rule's origins were lost in colonial America or the early Republic, whereas proponents of fairness theories counter-argued that the law had remained unsettled at least until *Pennoyer* v. *Neff* in 1877.[179] The reference of Joseph Story, in his 1834 treatise, to the service of process rule was accordingly seen as affirming established practice or an early elaboration of a rule whose time was yet to come.[180] By 1990, the revisionist position seemed accepted by a majority of writers but a new generation of advocates of the rule provided their own lists of early American cases where it been accepted.[181] The next step was to take the rule's pedigree even beyond Joseph Story into the Continental

[175] See e.g. A. A. Ehrenzweig, "The Transient Rule of Personal Jurisdiction: The "Power" Myth and *Forum Conveniens*," *Yale Law Journal*, 65 (1956), 289–314.

[176] *Shaffer* v. *Heitner*, 433 US 186 (1977).

[177] *Burnham* v. *Superior Court of California*, 495 US 604 (1990).

[178] Ibid., 610 Scalia, J., arguing that transient jurisdiction is "among the most firmly established principles of personal jurisdiction in American jurisdiction" (610) and providing a genealogy (611–618). While the decision of the Court was unanimous, Scalia was only joined by three other Justices. Brennan, J., joined by three others, wrote that "[a]lthough I agree that history is an important factor in establishing whether a jurisdictional rule satisfies due process requirements, I cannot agree that it is the only factor such that all traditional rules of jurisdiction are, ipso facto, forever constitutional" (629).

[179] See respectively Ehrenzweig, " Transient Rule," 300–309; G. Hazard, "A General Theory of State Court Jurisdiction," *Supreme Court Review*, 6 (1965), 241–288, 261.

[180] Justice Story is perceived by this camp as confirming their position. Cf. Story, *Commentaries*, 461 (§ 549).

[181] See J. Weinstein, "The Early American Origins of Territoriality in Judicial Jurisdiction," *St. Louis University Law Journal*, 37 (1992), 1–61, and T. Kogan, "A Neo-Federalist Tale of Personal Jurisdiction," *Southern California Law Review*, 63 (1990), 257–372 (with references to writers endorsing the revisionist position at 5 n. 17 and 258–259 respectively).

doctrines that influenced him.[182] Discussion at first revolved around Story's territorialist axioms and exposition, which are generally thought as inspired by Huber's axioms, but as opponents of the rule had argued that Huber's axioms had nothing to do with court jurisdiction, proponents went further into Huber's doctrine, reading him as adopting the serving of process as a necessary and sufficient requirement for obtaining interstate–international jurisdiction.[183]

We will come to the matter below, in our discussion of Huber's conflicts doctrine, sovereignty and jurisdiction. There is a lot to be learned in this regard, but it is at best unclear whether Huber and seventeenth-century Friesland could provide serious validation for such a jurisdictional basis in our age, or even his own.[184] What is remarkable is that a Supreme Court unanimous on the judgment split on the role the Court should grant to the historical pedigree of a rule – and on the historical facts. As often happens when history is put to use, the Justices on both sides seem to have misconstrued history. As was justly suggested by a writer who furnished historical validation for transient jurisdiction, Justice Scalia's plurality opinion overstated the historical case but so was Justice Brennan unjustifiably convinced by the historical argument of the "fairness" polemicists.[185] And neither appears to have understood how judicial jurisdiction really worked in the nineteenth-century United States.[186] This debate serves as a reminder of why professional legal historians, as well as an increasing number of doctrinal lawyers, have been so skeptical of normative historicism, and, by extension, often of historicism in general, leading to the other extreme.

2.6.2.3 Archaeological Historicism

Archaeological historicists are concerned with the source rather than the estuary: their cause is to liberate the historical past from the distortion of present-day looking glasses, to place past theories and doctrines in the context of their era. In doing so, the potential of past conflicts doctrine to

182 See especially J. Weinstein, "The Dutch Influence on the Conception of Judicial Jurisdiction in 19th century America," *American Journal of Comparative Law*, 38 (1990), 73–101.

183 See, respectively, Hazard, "General Theory," 260; and Weinstein, "Dutch Influence."

184 See Section 12.4. Ironically, Huber's Friesland may have been the only state in the area which did not practice transient jurisdiction; and Huber's own position, while admittedly a matter of interpretation, does not indicate much enthusiasm for such a principle.

185 See the critique of Weinstein, "Early American Origins," 42–61.

186 Ibid., 53–54.

influence contemporary doctrinal discussion is of course muted. Often professional legal historians, rather than doctrinal conflicts lawyers, archaelogical historicists may make significant contributions to our understanding of the historical context; they also tend to underestimate the doctrinal premises, as well as impact, of their work.

A case in point – which we will see in more detail in our study of Bartolus – is the contribution of Samuel E. Thorne (1907–1994), professor of Medieval English legal history at Harvard, to the sextentary commemoration of Bartolus's death.[187] A celebrated English legal historian, Thorne found Medieval "conflict of laws" rules strikingly similar to English rules about statutory interpretation.[188] He thus concluded that conflict of laws properly speaking appears when the Dutch school applies the theory of territorial sovereignty, which dates from the sixteenth century, to conflict of laws: "the appearance of the idea of sovereignty marks not a stage in its development, as is usually believed, but the beginning of it."[189]

A variation on the same theme emphasizes the role of the *ius commune* in Medieval conflict of laws: it is thus suggested that Bartolus deals with conflicts between the *ius commune* and the local law, rather than between the laws of different local entities.[190]

2.6.3 Historical Narratives as Opposition

In the modern world, conflict of laws is facing the sibling rivalry of international business law, spearheaded by the proponents of a *lex mercatoria*. This has also been reflected in the historical narratives of *lex mercatoria* apologists, but also in narratives of the history of the conflict of laws itself, produced by sympathizers of a transnational substantive law.[191]

[187] See S. E. Thorne, "Sovereignty and the Conflict of Laws" in *Bartolo da Sassoferrato: Studi e Documenti per il VI Centenario*, vol. II (Perugia: Universitá degli Studi di Perugia, 1962), 673–689.

[188] Ibid., 673–684.

[189] Ibid., 673.

[190] See A. Barry, Bartolus on the Conflict of Laws. Unpublished third-year paper, Harvard Law School (1998), esp. 26–28. The paper was written under the supervision – and influence – of Professor Charles Donahue, Jr. – Thorne's successor at Harvard Law School and a noted scholar in both English and Continental legal history and the *ius commune*.

[191] See for more N. Hatzimihail, "Genealogies of *lex mercatoria*," in *Studies in Memoriam of Professor Anthony M. Antapassis* (Athens: Ant.Sakkoulas, 2013) 311–351.

2.6.3.1 The Genealogies of *Lex Mercatoria*

The best example of a cyclical narrative comes from the discussion on the *lex mercatoria* and Berthold Goldman, in an article opened by the statement "*lex mercatoria* is a venerable old lady who has twice disappeared from the face of the earth and twice been resuscitated."[192]

We can notice a polemical element in this story: the word "resuscitated" implies a near or apparent death that in the end did not materialize, thanks to the – positive – action of someone.[193] Indeed, Goldman's *lex mercatoria*, unlike the mythical Phoenix, has not died and then been reborn on her own, but has almost died and been brought back to life through the intervention of others. Goldman's reader is invited to spot the villains who almost took the lady's life – i.e. the "legal nationalism" of especially the nineteenth century. The logical next step is to realize the struggle facing the friends and admirers of *lex mercatoria* in order to prevent the need for a new "resuscitation."

2.6.3.2 The End of History as Progress Narrative

Ironically, perhaps, claims that history is irrelevant to our era produce historical narratives of their own, since they are predicated on a specific interpretation of the past as well as the present. Such interpretation makes a sharp distinction between "past" and present/future, as to either the material context or the conceptual structures. Antihistorical narratives have found more resonance in recent times, and they reflect the parallel lines of argumentation in the discussion about globalization.[194]

One such argumentative pattern is the thesis that the conflict of laws was grounded upon the conception of sovereignty and the "Westphalian system" of sovereign states. The move away from sovereignty and the

[192] B. Goldman, "*Lex Mercatoria*," *Forum Internationale*, No. 3 (November 1983), 3. Goldman refers respectively to the *ius gentium* and the Medieval law merchant.

[193] The *Oxford English Dictionary*, 13.766 defines *resuscitate* as "to restore (a person) to life (physical or spiritual) or to consciousness."

[194] I have personally encountered this stance in certain scholarly settings, especially during the "irrational exuberance" of the late 1990s. Anthony Giddens, *The Consequences of Modernity* (Stanford, CA: Stanford University Press, 1991) is frequently alluded to as an expositor of such a thesis, but such a claim could more easily be made for his explanatory *Runaway World: How Globalization Is Reshaping Our Lives* (London: Routledge, 2002). Many international economic lawyers have hence subscribed to the so-called bicycle theory, which invokes the trauma of the Great Depression to suggest that an end to the progressive liberalization of international trade will lead to regression, just like stopping pedalling a bicycle while on a steep slope.

inter-national system and toward a global world signifies the end for private international law.[195]

Another "antihistorical" argumentative pattern attacks the "grand old men" of the field, either as having grounded their systems on these redundant conceptions,[196] or as having proposed schemes which are based on general principles too rigorous to find application in our complex, pragmatism-needing, world.[197]

2.7 Concluding Remarks

Aphorisms notwithstanding, the importance of history to the discipline of private international law is illustrated by the place historical sections occupy in conflicts textbooks, as well as in many doctrinal monographs or articles. The abundance – indeed predominance – of textbook histories in our field has had a definitive impact on the historical consciousness of contemporary private international lawyers. This impact has not been studied, however, until now. There has in fact never been a systematic examination of what material influences our contemporary historical consciousness. Nor has the subjective element in those accounts, especially the "tertiary" accounts of textbooks and doctrinal works, been considered.

The purpose of this chapter has been to at least raise awareness of these issues, before we embark on our actual historical exploration. As was stated on the outset, the secondary literature on conflict history must be reevaluated before we come to our primary material. Even though it certainly does not constitute a complete study of conflicts historiography,

195 Thus H. Patrick Glenn, "The Nationalist Heritage" in P. Legrand and R. Munday (eds.), *Comparative Legal Studies: Traditions and Transitions* (Cambridge: Cambridge University Press, 2003), 76–127 notes that "private international law is now systematically avoided by nearly all those with the knowledge and means of doing so, in favor or international arbitration" (98).

196 A good example, from the area of globalization theory, is Giddens's perspective on the relevance of the "grand men" (Marx, Weber) of social theory. For a critique – and defense of the vitality of studying "the classics" and of their complexity – see e.g. J. Rosenberg, *The Follies of Globalization Theory* (London: Verso, 2000).

197 See in that sense D. McLean, "*De Conflictu Legum*: Perspectives on Private International Law at the Turn of the Century," *Recueil des cours*, 184 (2000), 41–228. McLean pays his homage to the grand nineteenth-century figures: Savigny, Story, Dicey, and occasionally Huber, feature in the discussion of each topic. But he also emphasizes the creative role of today's judges (conflicts rules are "essentially directions to the legal personnel of a particular country:" 64) and suggests that we must look at a time before the "grand men" with their grand principles.

this chapter should at least help readers navigate through the existing literature; enable them to become mindful of the historicity and subjectivity of our "secondary" material, as well as to appreciate its richness; and, hopefully, invite them to contemplate on their own – our shared – historical consciousness.

A recurring theme in this book is that our historical consciousness is constituted by a shared narrative, at its core, with variations, giving rise to diverse perspectives and reinterpetations. This shared narrative is reflected in the *international* history of conflicts doctrine being told in almost any conflicts treatise and alluded to in many doctrinal works. At the same time, the history of the field tends to be told in ways which affirm the author's own doctrinal preoccupations. In fact, historical treatments appear as more neutral than the rest of the author's text, leading them to be reprised by subsequent writers unaware of the narrative's premises.[198] Historical narratives can often become an insidious argumentative weapon.[199]

Having noted the subjectivity – and instrumentalism – inherent in much of conflicts historiography, new questions arise: why this increased emphasis on history? What messages does it convey and how does it impact both historical research and present-day doctrine?

It would probably not do to suggest that conflicts lawyers are somehow endowed with superior historical erudition. A better reason may be the *quasi-international* nature of conflicts scholarship: just like public international law, our field has been constituted through an international discussion; but, unlike public international law, this international discourse was merged with an even stronger domestic, private-law discourse on the national level.

Another reason could well be the struggle between "theory" and "practice," exemplified by the contests of doctrinal writers (*la doctrine*)

[198] See e.g. G. Shreve, *A Conflict of Laws Anthology* (Cincinnati, OH: Anderson, 1997), 23. Shreve, a multilateralist suggests that Juenger (who had embraced substanstive-law approaches) is "careful to keep his own views on conflict of laws from obscuring his historical account." This is only partly true, as has been demonstrated in some length in Hatzimihail, "Pages of History." Shreve, however, uses Juenger's historical text as a corroboration of his own views and remarks with "wonder" that "conflicts movements as intractably opposed as multilateralism and unilateralism could be both so vital and regenerative" (Shreve, *Anthology*, 23).

[199] For the development of a similar argument see N. Hatzimihail, "The Many Lives – and Faces – of *Lex Mercatoria*: History as Genealogy in International Business Law," *Law & Contemporary Problems*, 71 (2008), 169–190.

and courts (*la jurisprudence*) as to who should set the guiding principles of private international law. History can provide arguments for either side.[200]

The strong, if not fully admitted, role of professionalization and of a disciplinary consciousness in the creation of private international law is also a factor. It was demonstrated in this chapter that interest in history developed in parallel with the disciplinary–professional growth of the field. Remarkably, the progressive development of doctrinal sophistication and professionalization was seldom, if ever, presented as the main point in the story. In fact, the opposite appears to have been the case: as private international law developed professional structures, its historical narratives increasingly tended to discover non-scholarly roots and to de-emphasize the role of scholarship in the creation of conflicts doctrine.[201] On the whole, however, the story of conflict of laws is principally a *doctrinal* story – including its beginnings in the Italy of the High Middle Ages, to which we shall now turn.

[200] Collins, *Dicey, Morris & Collins on the Conflict of Laws*, 14 (naming Huber, Story, and Savigny as the three "most influential foreign jurists" in English conflict of laws, while noting the judicial capacity of the first two).

[201] See Hatzimihail, "Pre-historical Private International Law."

3

Preclassical Conflict of Laws in the Historical Consciousness

3.1 Introduction

Modern historical consciousness is ambivalent toward Medieval and Early Modern conflict of laws. The key to these attitudes is found in classical conflict of laws, and our relationship with it. We – modern private international lawyers – identify as the descendants of the private international lawyers of the late nineteenth and early twentieth centuries. While remaining mindful of our own differences from these immediate ancestors, we also perceive them as having made a decisive break with their own Medieval and Early Modern ancestors. Which raises the question of how distant modern doctrine is from its preclassical counterpart: are we twice removed from our ancestors' ancestors, or has modern doctrine been moving in a circular pattern?

Before we proceed with our own historical examination of preclassical doctrine, it is vital to examine the existing literature and the narratives it projects. This is an examination of *historical consciousness*, in the sense that it extends not only to historical literature, properly speaking, but also to the narratives of textbooks and other doctrinal material that has been influential in shaping modern (and classical) perceptions about our subject.[1] This comprehensive approach is made more imperative by the fact that most of the first-hand scholarly work on preclassical doctrinal texts was done by a select group of classical jurists (whose own work we have been attempting to place in historical context, in order to make best use of it) and has remained influential through second- or thirdhand treatments in textbook histories.

This chapter is not a history of preclassical conflict of laws properly speaking. It should nonetheless provide readers with the requisite historical knowledge for what follows, as well as an understanding of the faultlines in the "maps" of the subject.

[1] See Section 2.2.

There are three principal themes explored in the chapter. First, the doctrinal mainstream treats the long period from approximately 1200 to 1800 as a single period, albeit one divided internally into schools or subperiods: dissecting these narratives, and evaluating their significance, constitutes the main thrust of the chapter. According to the historical literature available, the question must be asked: "Is there such a thing as a coherent 'preclassical' conflicts doctrine?" Which are the internal divisions, and which are the criteria with which lines are drawn? The term "school" is commonly used in these efforts at classification – but what does this term itself signify to its users?

Once these ideas have been discussed in the first two sections of the chapter, we shall turn to the second theme: conflicts literature posits a *foundational moment* in the High Middle Ages, but what is the significance of this preoccupation and of the narratives told? In responding to this question, we must undertake a historical reconstruction of High Medieval doctrine, which shall act as introduction to the larger-scale exploration of Part III.

Moreover, our discussion is connected to a third theme: the narrative(s) we have been exploring tell the story of conflicts doctrine as a story of learned law, more specifically of civil law – but is this all there is to it?

3.2 The Narrative

The period between the first scholarly writings touching on conflicts issues and the early to mid-nineteenth century is generally regarded in our historical consciousness as a single period, referred to as the *theory* or the *theories of statutes*.[2]

We could in fact speak of a single, central narrative about statutist doctrine (see Figure 3.1). In this narrative, the period in question is constituted by the doctrinal contributions of three "schools:"

(1) the Italian school, active in Italy and southern France between the thirteenth and the fifteenth (or early sixteenth) centuries;
(2) the French school, which flourishes in the sixteenth century (but may extend backward in time to the Late Middle Ages) and dominates French law up until the French Revolution or the promulgation of the Napoleonic Code; and

[2] Among the numerous examples of a standard narrative see e.g. P. Courbe, *Droit international privé* (Paris: Armand Colin, 2000), 27ff.

<table>
<tr><th><u>BEGINNING</u></th><th colspan="5">"Theories of Statutes"</th><th><u>ENDING(S)</u></th></tr>
<tr><td rowspan="5">[←pre-history]

Doctrine:
Ius civile
• *the solution:*
Gloss at C.1.1.1.
• *the question:*
Aldricus

Neglected influences:
-canon law
-court practice

law merchant?</td><td>**ITALIAN**
1200/1300 to 1500/1600</td><td colspan="2">**FRENCH**
1450/1550 to 1804/1880</td><td colspan="2">**DUTCH**
1600/1650 to 1700/1880</td><td rowspan="5">[classical →]

1800
National Codes
1830s:
treatises
1849:
Savignian method
1869-1873:
New discipline
1880
PIL courses & textbooks</td></tr>
<tr><td>•Doctrinal treatment of conflicts
•Basic (and classic?) theory of statutes</td><td colspan="2">•Classic theory of statutes
• Territorialism
• Characterization?
• party autonomy?</td><td colspan="2">• Territorialism
• Looking for foundation (for application of foreign laws)
• Comity</td></tr>
<tr><td>Commentaries on Digest, Code + consilia</td><td colspan="2">Commentaries on customs of French pays + consilia + [Commentaries on Dig./C.]</td><td colspan="2">Commentaries on Digest + "Institutes of National Law"</td></tr>
<tr><td>(post) glossators
Bartolus, Baldus
↓</td><td>Dumoulin
←
↓</td><td>d'Argentré
[+ XVIII c.]
↓</td><td>"French"
Rodenburg
←↓</td><td>Huber
Voet
↓</td></tr>
<tr><td colspan="2">**École des juristes**
- "Analytical"
- "Eclectic"
- "Universalist"</td><td colspan="3">**École politique**
- "Synthetic"
- "Dogmatic"
- "Nationalist"</td></tr>
</table>

Figure 3.1 Historical Narratives about Medieval and Early Modern Conflict of Laws

(3) the Dutch school which flourishes in the seventeenth century and continues to exercise its influence until the early to mid-nineteenth century.

The existence of these three schools is clearly engraved in the historical consciousness of modern private international lawyers.[3] Each of these schools has a different geographical focus but they are also spatially connected. Most importantly, they are generally presented in terms of a succession in time. However, when it comes to defining these schools and establishing their membership the diversity of opinion is such that we could speak of a profusion of internal variations to the central narrative.

The importance of eighteenth-century doctrine is diminished in this central narrative: a few authors have sought to find traces of subsequent approaches, but usually either that period is not considered at all, or – when it is considered – it is in terms of the theory of statutes running out

[3] On the contrary, efforts to highlight a German or a Spanish school of preclassical conflict of laws have not had much success.

of steam. In its turn, the early nineteenth century appears as a period of transition: the theory of statutes was already dead, but not yet replaced.[4]

3.2.1 *Mutations*

A few writers have produced notable narratives in which the preclassical period is cut in two by a single dividing line, drawn at some point of the sixteenth century. These narratives could be subdivided into two groups.

The first variety distinguishes early (Medieval) doctrine, which is presented as rudimentary, from more advanced forms of statutist doctrine, which correspond to an – expansively defined – French and a Dutch school. François Laurent, who distinguished *glossators* from *statutists*, is the most notable example: he places Medieval Italian jurists into the former category; and the rest, from Coquille in the fifteenth century to Bouhier in the eighteenth century, in the second.[5] Makarov follows a similar approach, distinguishing the Italian "origins" from the theory of statutes properly speaking.[6]

A second variety gives substantive content to the binary division: this dividing line cuts right through sixteenth-century French doctrine, with Dumoulin on one side and d'Argentré on the other. Doctrine in the first period appears more complex, more eclectic, perhaps more rudimentary; it furnishes rules but no grand principle. Doctrine in the second period has a clear territorialist orientation, and employs grand principles. Jean-Paulin Niboyet (1886–1952) is preoccupied with writing a history of French conflict of laws and its foreign influences.[7] Noting how ideas crossed borders and in a reflection of his own theoretical foundations and doctrinal preoccupations, he substitutes the traditional narrative (*opinion traditionnelle*) regarding the three schools with a story of opposition

[4] See e.g., Juenger, *Choice of Law*, 32–34 who emphasizes the role of Karl Georg von Wächter in that regard: "Wächter was an iconoclast. He debunked statutists learning, exposed the vested rights theory's circular reasoning and disparaged the comity doctrine . . . But the influence of Wächter's ideas on European conflict of laws proved to be minimal because his compatriot Savigny soon overshadowed him."

[5] See Laurent, *Droit civil international*, 1:273–335 ("Les Glossateurs"), on the one hand, and 335–521 ("Les légistes statutaires," with emphasis on sixteenth-century French jurists and distinct subsections on "Les réalistes Belges et Hollandais" and "Les statutaires Français du XVIIIe siècle").

[6] A. N. Makarov, *Précis de droit international privé d'après la législation et la doctrine russes*, trans. E. Nolde and P. Pereverweff (Paris: Marcel Giard, 1932), 74ff.

[7] Niboyet, *Traité*, 3:40 n. 2.

between a legal and a political "tendency."[8] The former characterizes *the school of jurists* exemplified by Bartolus and including Dumoulin; the latter characterizes *the political school* exemplified by d'Argentré and including the Dutch jurists as a subdivision.[9] Niboyet's narrative is reprised in a modern work distinguishing dogmatic and pragmatic doctrines.[10] Likewise, Bernard Audit distinguishes between *la théorie des statuts* (Italian school and French school except d'Argentré) and *les doctrines territorialistes* (from d'Argentré all the way to Story and Beale).[11]

Such mutations do not, however, depart from the central narrative in conflicts literature: even when different names are used, these authors are quick to affirm the unity of statutist doctrine and to espouse the distinction between the three schools. Laurent includes both his subdivisions in a chapter on the theory of statutes.[12] Audit distinguishes *la doctrine statutaire*, further subdivided between *l'école italienne* and *la doctrine statutaire en France*, from the *doctrines territorialistes*, subdivided into *territorialisme français* and *doctrine hollandaise* (the latter described as *territorialisme internationaliste*).[13] Niboyet subdivides the political school, with which he personally finds much resonance, into three periods: first, the creation of the school by d'Argentré in the sixteenth century;[14] second, the seventeenth-century transmission (*rayonnement*) of d'Argentré's doctrine by the Flemish and Dutch schools (all the way to Anglo-American territorialists);[15] and third, the school's reconquest of France through the evolving French doctrine of the late eighteenth century.[16]

8 Ibid., 42–44.

9 Ibid., 3:44ff, 60ff. This "school of jurists" which lasted from the thirteenth century to the sixteenth century, is also called by Niboyet the "Italian school" or "school of Bartolus" and includes Dumoulin. This "political school" ranged from the sixteenth century to the eighteenth century, and was divided into d'Argentré and "les Flammands, les Hollands."

10 M.-L. Niboyet and G. de Geouffre de La Pradelle, *Droit international privé* (Paris, 2007), 80–85: d'Argentré and the Dutch school are grouped together with Vareilles-Sommières, Niboyet, and Mancini as promoters of *doctrines dogmatiques*. The Italians and Dumoulin are grouped together with Savigny and Batiffol as promoters of *doctrines pragmatiques*.

11 See Audit, *Droit international privé*, 59ff, 63ff (Sections A and B of § 1 "La formation des grands doctrines").

12 Laurent, *Droit civil international*, 1:273–571.

13 Audit, *Droit international privé*, 60–62 (*école italo-française* in the third edition) and 63–65.

14 Niboyet, *Traité*, 3:60–79.

15 Ibid., 80–96

16 Ibid., 97–108.

3.3 The Division into Schools

The term *school* is ubiquitous in the literature on preclassical conflict of laws. The concept of a doctrinal *school* evokes connotations with general intellectual history, national legal histories, sociology of academic production, and European legal history. In conflicts literature, however, the term is taken for granted and never, even indirectly, defined. It is therefore imperative to examine how the term is used in conflicts historiography, and how the meaning conveyed reflects on our modern understanding of preclassical doctrine.

3.3.1 Schools as Paradigm

The principal approach in the history of legal ideas for identifying schools of thought has been to associate them with a paradigm or to credit them with a specific contribution to doctrine. The approach is not unlike general intellectual history, where the sociological element has traditionally been discounted, and *schools* have been commonly defined on the basis of one grand idea. Such an approach serves genealogical purposes but also, especially in textbook histories, educational objectives.

This is certainly the dominant approach in conflicts literature, and especially the historiography of preclassical conflict of laws: each school is defined in terms of contributing a new idea or doctrine. However, such an approach may work better for philosophy than for legal doctrine, where the thought process is often inductive and even abstract ideas have to be applied to insubordinately concrete situations.

In the case of preclassical conflict of laws, the opportunities for such an approach are as abundant as the problems inherent in it. Medieval and Early Modern conflicts treatments are considerably shorter than subsequent works and use more abstract terms: it should thus be easier to distill basic ideas and attempt a typology. But these writers certainly did not view themselves as engaged in a conflicts discourse: what especially the Medieval writers were doing, may be seen as one exercise of legal thinking among many, with an emphasis on the interpretation of statutes and customs. It is difficult to distinguish their thinking on conflicts from the rest of their work, because they themselves did not.

Preclassical writings are hence open to misinterpretation, especially when they are approached by doctrinal lawyers with normative visions of their own, as has often been the case in conflicts historiography. As a result, classical and modern authors have been engaged in a contest between "schools," as they undertake to assign to each school some among a number of specific ideas and doctrines (in the process, also sorting preclassical authors into the schools). The process is in effect circular: once an author decides to endow one of the schools with certain characteristics, doctrines (or jurists), the other two schools have to be defined accordingly so as to cover the remaining characteristics associated with Medieval and Early Modern conflict of laws.

3.3.1.1 Italian School

The Italian school comes first in these narratives: its beginnings are the beginnings of conflicts doctrine, but, as we shall see below, it is not clear where to draw the line – and what significance, if any, early "Italian" doctrine has in our understanding of the school. In historiography, the Italian school has been approached in two ways. The first is to present adherents of the school as preoccupied more with achieving justice than with finding a single way of characterizing statutes. Within the minority that supports this view, there are those who view the Italian school's doctrine with some sympathy.[17] Others however are hostile and regard it as simple primitivism.[18]

A strong majority of the literature, however, presents the Italian school in more formalist terms. In the very least, the Italians are supposed to have invented several choice-of-law rules with relevance to this day.[19] A few authors have even attributed to this school the invention of what

[17] Lainé, *Introduction*, 1:50. See also Niboyet, *Traité*, 3:53–55, characterizing the Italian school "eclectic and analytical" – as opposed to the subsequent systematicity and syntheticity of d'Argentré's "political school."

On his part, B. Ancel, *Les conflits de qualifications à l'épreuve de la donation entre époux* (Paris: Dalloz, 1977), 32–34 notes the dissonance between the Italians' theoretical positions and given solutions.

[18] See e.g. Makarov, *Droit international privé*, 77 ("il est difficile de trouver un système dans leur construction"), and especially E. Bartin, *Principes de droit international privé selon la loi et la jurisrpudence françaises*, vol. I (Paris: Editions Domat-Montchretien, 1930), 129 (("il n'y a ici ni théorie ni théoriciens") and 131 ("Aucun principe, aucune idée générale ... [L]e groupement ... est fait de façon aussi arbitraire que sommaire, sans que rien justifie l'idée générale à laquelle ils obéissent en le faisant, sans qu'aucune correspondance logique se laisse deviner entre les divers groupes de difficultés").

[19] See e.g. J.-G. Castel, *Droit international privé quebecois* (Toronto: Butterworths, 1980), 7ff. Even though influenced by Niboyet and Lainé, Castel presents the Italian school as coming up with concrete conflicts rules emanating from the territorial premises of of city legislation (7–8), associating Niboyet's concept of an *école des juristes* with Dumoulin (9).

we are calling in this book the *classic theory of statutes*, i.e. the classification of statutes as real, personal and mixed.[20] For most, however, the Italian school invented the strict division of statutes into real or personal (the *basic theory of statutes*), with the concept of mixed statutes coming subsequently.[21]

3.3.1.2 French School

A common theme regarding the place of the French school in historical narratives is that it must go one step further from the Italian school, in terms of doctrinal sophistication. Thus, if the basic theory of statutes is associated with the Italian school, the French school should be credited with the invention of the concept of mixed statutes. Dumoulin is the principal protagonist in these narratives, where he becomes the champion of both the classic theory of statutes and the French school.[22] Others, more skeptical of a break between Dumoulin and the jurists who preceded him, claim that the invention of mixed statutes happened as late as with d'Argentré.[23]

[20] While this is not the most prominent position in literature, it was adopted among others by the influential treatise of Tobias Asser. See T. M. C. Asser (translated and annotated by Alphonse Rivier), *Eléments de droit international privé ou du conflit de lois* (Paris, 1884), 9: "Ces docteurs, que l'on nomme généralement les Commentateurs ou Post-Glossateurs, divisent toutes les lois, tous les status, toutes les coutumes, toutes les sources du droit positif en vigueur dans un pays, en trois classes auxquelles on a donné les noms de statuts personnels, réels ou mixtes . . . Cette division tripartite se trouve déjà chez Bartole, Baldus, Abéric de Rosate et chez d'autres Commentateurs." Asser specifies in a footnote that the technical terminogy appears later (ibid., n. 1). But he is followed e.g. by P. Nygh, *Autonomy in International Contracts* (Oxford: Clarendon Press, 1999), 3 (with references to Bartolus). Among other examples see e.g. L. D. Wardle et al. (eds.), *Interstate and International Conflict of Laws: Cases and Materials* (Provo, UT: BYU Press, 1999), Ch. 2. A.3; Mänhardt and Posch, *Internationales Privatrecht*, 7; and H. Köhler, *Internationales Privatrecht*, 3rd ed (Vienna: Springer, 1966), 32.

[21] See e.g. J. Valéry, *Manuel de droit international privé* (Paris, 1914), 24; J. A. Martin, *Conflict of Laws* (Boston, MA: Little, Brown & Co., 1978), 1. Juan de Dios Trias y Giro and Jose Trias de Bes, *Estudios de Derecho internacional privado*, 112; F. Surville, "La théorie des statuts d'après Bartole et Dumoulin," *Clunet*, 48 (1921), 1–15, esp. 14–15; A. Anton, *Private International Law* (Edinburgh: W. Green & Son, 1967), 21; seemingly F. Despagnet, *Précis de droit international privé*, 5th ed. (Paris: Sirey, 1909), 294ff.

[22] See e.g. Meylan, "Status réels et personnels," esp. 513ff.

[23] See Lainé, *Introduction*, 1:316ff (including the suggestion that d'Argentré "pretends to borrow this classification from Italian doctrine," 322–323); R. Foignet, *Manuel élémentaire de droit international privé*, 2nd ed (Paris: Arthur Rousseau, 1909), esp. 78–79; Mortensen et al., *Private International Law*, 8.

Should the classic theory of statutes be credited to the Italian school, however, another grand idea defining the French school must be found. Such narratives became more common in the twentieth century, as scholars attempted to support doctrines, which have acquired increased importance in late classical and modern doctrine, by providing them with a reinforced pedigree and consolidating their place in the historical consciousness. Dumoulin and the French school are thus frequently credited with the invention or conceptualization of the principle of party autonomy in the choice-of-law.[24] As Dumoulin – long regarded among the greatest French jurists in general legal history – grew in stature also in the modern historical consciousness of conflicts, even the discovery of the problem of legal characterization (*qualification*) has been attributed to him.[25]

3.3.1.3 Dutch School

The conceptualization of the Dutch school is equally dependent on how the other two schools are defined.[26] In binary narratives with no intermediate French school, the Dutch school merges with – or is presented as following – d'Argentré: their adherents then include the French scholarship of especially the seventeenth and eighteenth centuries. In narratives where the French school is credited with the classic theory of statutes, or with the invention of some choice-of-law technique, the Dutch school can claim the elaboration of *territorialism* or even doctrinal systematicity as its defining mark/contribution to the field.[27] But in schemes where the French school is conceptualized around d'Argentré and territorialism,

[24] On Dumoulin as the godfather of party autonomy (i.e. he did not invent but was the first to emphasize) see e.g. Juenger, *Choice of Law*, 17. More skeptical but still affirmative F. Surville and F. Arthuys, *Cours élémentaire de droit international privé*, 2nd ed (Paris: Arthur Rousseau, 1895), 23. As examples of earlier works making no mention of parties' intention and allocating to Dumoulin only a fraction of the space they give to d'Argentré, see Valéry, *Manuel*, 27 or Trias y Giro and Trias de Bes, *Estudios*, 1:114.

[25] On Dumoulin and legal characterization see Loussouarn et al., *Droit international privé*, 90–91. Cf. Castel, *Droit international privé quebecois*, 9.

[26] South African jurists, for whom Roman-Dutch law, including the writings of jutists such Huber and Johanes Voet, remains living law have produced interesting and more nuanced work. See E. Kahn, "The 'Territorial School and Comity School' of the Conflict of Laws in the Roman-Dutch Era" in *Huldigingsbundel Aangebied aan Professor Daniel Pont* (Cape Town: A. A. Balkema, 1970), 219–239; C. Forsyth, "The Value of the Comparative Ethos to the Judicial Process in the Conflict of Laws" in C. Visser (ed.), *Essays in Honour of Ellison Kahn* (Cape Town: Juta, 1989), 151–172.

[27] See e.g. Valéry, *Manuel*, 29–31; S. Vrellēs, *Idiōtiko Diethnes Dikaio*, 3rd ed (Athens: Nomiki bibliothiki, 2001), 51; I. Getman-Pavlova, "The history of private international

jurists from the Low Countries dealing with conflicts issues in the Early Modern historical period are divided in two groups: the majority of them are presented as epigones of d'Argentré, whereas a select handful form a truly Dutch school, which is principally associated with the comity doctrine.[28]

3.3.1.4 A Comment

Most conflicts lawyers seem to have been, to some extent, conscious of the difficulty of writing the history of a legal field like a history of philosophy. The "grand idea" approach has thus been fitted into an historical consciousness possessing an "inventory" of specific doctrines or theories. The exercise of delimitation becomes an effort to allocate specific doctrines or theories among the schools. This effort reminds us of paleontology, trying to re-create the evolution of species by pinpointing them to geological periods, only that here sometimes the geological periods are redrawn in order to better fit the species.

This confusion cannot be fully blamed on the present-day agendas of classical and modern writers (though it is clearly an important factor). An equally strong reason may be that few of the preclassical writers approached these issues with the consciousness we are today, with hindsight, approaching them – the result being that their language invites us to such *ex post* attribution.

3.3.2 *National Schools*

Preclassical schools are almost always given national names. We thus have an Italian, a French, and a Dutch school, with occasional claims to a German or even a Spanish school. Even the few authors who use a different terminology do not diverge from this trend.[29] For each school, the respective nationality constitutes the core of its membership, but foreigners are also included. Lainé, for example, keeps the fifteenth- and sixteenth-century "successors of Bartolus in France" within the Italian school; but he then claims for the French school many more:

law: the theory of Belgian realism in the 16th century," *Sociology International Journal* 2 (2018), 431–437.

[28] See e.g. Lainé, *Introduction*, 1:395ff, 2:95ff. On the comity doctrine and its reception in historical consciousness see Section 14.4.

[29] The only real objection to this practice has been made by Niboyet, *Traité*, 3:42–44, but even he did not make a break. Same applies in part to Audit, *Droit international privé* and Laurent, *Droit civil international.*

most Dutch, Belgian and all Germans are classified as "successors of d'Argentré" in their respective countries.[30]

A certain national bias does exist in the historiography of preclassical conflict of laws, but it is remarkably limited. Undoubtedly, most classical and modern authors have tended to expand the membership and impact of "their" national school, or to gather together their fellow nationals of ages past. It must also be remembered that jurists from Italy, France and the Netherlands took part in good numbers in the creation of a discipline of private international law in the late nineteenth century, and wrote the principal works of conflicts historiography. And it was German and Spanish authors who made claims of a German or a Spanish school – claims that were never sponsored by the majority of their fellow nationals, however. It was the Frenchman Lainé who grouped the great French jurisconsult Dumoulin with the Italians, and the German Ludwig von Bar who was skeptical of the originality of Hert's contribution.

The process of claiming a national school is rather sophisticated: the first step is to identify a critical mass of jurists of a certain nationality or linguistic-cultural space (French, German) who wrote on conflicts topics. Once the group has been identified, it is often possible to discover some distinct ideas among them. For example, the claim of a German school emphasized references to the law of nations by eighteenth-century German jurists.[31] This dual process, where "native" conflicts ancestors are listed, with the innovation of a few among them shining upon the entire group, is frequent.[32] Even though this has often been formalistic and parochial, at its best it can allow for deeper historical research, and an emphasis on context often lost in pure "paradigm-seeking" definitions.

30 See Lainé, *Introduction*, 1:207–248 and 1:395–413 respectively.

31 See Gutzwiller, "Développement historique," 330–331 (for example: "Cocceji est le premier parmi les Allemands qui base sa théorie sur un Droit international étroitement lié au Droit naturel" – then comparing Cocceji with early twentieth-century writer Frankenstein: 330). See also Gutzwiller, *Geschichte*, 191ff. Cf. (with regard to Hert) Bar, *Theorie* 41 n. 4, 54. As to the Spanish school, emphasis is placed on the early Spanish authors and authorities that developed in parallel to the Italian. See Gutzwiller, *Geschichte*, 259–262 ("Excursus"); Miaja de la Muela, *Derecho internacional privado*, 1:126–131 (making a reference to "the Spanish statutists" but avoiding the term "school"); V.-L. Simó Santonja, *Aportación al estudio de los estatutarios españoles* (Valencia: Diputación provincial de Valencia, 1959). Cf. Despagnet, *Précis*, 294 n. 2 who allowed that "certain passages" of *Las Siete Partidas* may be regarded as *précedent de la théorie des Statuts*.

32 See the presentation of the "German school" by Gutzwiller, *Geschichte*, 177–217.

In general, the use of national names for "schools" implies a certain pride and some national bias.[33] But it also reflects the need for context and contacts between members, in order for a school to exist, while at the same time it can explain a certain degree of diversity of opinion within each school.

3.3.3 *A Sociological Approach*

Conflicts literature never alludes to the strict, sociological sense of the term *school*, which denotes either an organization, "a place where teaching takes place and authority and property are passed down through an explicit succession," or, at least, a nexus or "chains of personal relationships, of which the most important are relationships between teachers and their pupils; besides these vertical ties are horizontal links of personal contacts among contemporaries."[34]

A serious investigation of connections and influences between preclassical authors who wrote on conflicts would take substantial effort. It must also be an exercise in general legal history: even though several of the preclassical writers are today remembered principally for what they wrote on conflicts issues, they were "generalists," for whom this topic could only have been a minor concern. We can nonetheless draw conjectures with the help of general legal history and an examination of works cited and ideas shared between works.

The "Italian school" of glossators and commentators appers closest to a school in the sociological sense: a community of legal scholars, who interacted with each other in life and in writing, did exist in the later Middle Ages. Legal materials circulated between the various universities of central Italy and Southern France. Many of the professors demonstrated substantial mobility in their studies and career.[35] In the conflicts treatment of Bartolus alone, we count a good number of sholars from the generations immediately preceding him: the ideas of some are

[33] It is interesting in that sense that Italians, French, and Belgians/Dutch were the main founders of the discipline of private international law, and the nineteenth century is a period of revitalized interest in national legal history.

[34] R. Collins, *The Sociology of Philosophies: A Global Theory of Intellectual Change* (Cambridge, MA: Harvard University Press, 1998), 65.

[35] For example, Baldus held appointments in Perugia, Pisa, Florence, Perugia again, Padua, Perugia for a third time, and Pavia. See J. Canning, *The Political Thought of Baldus de Ubaldis* (Cambridge: Cambridge University Press, 1987), 2–6.

presented – and often refuted – in some detail.[36] In fact, almost all authors cited by Bartolus are connected with master-student ties (see Figure 3.2).[37] In this network of students, teachers and citations, the *ultramontani* postglossators of late-thirteenth and early fourteenth century Southern France feature as an integral part of the Italian school, even though they advocated positions suited to their own political environment. One gets the same feeling from a more casual examination of other Medieval writers. Along with his student Baldus, Bartolus is at the peak of Italian legal scholarship. Perhaps the fact that the Italian universities continued to flourish for another century and a half, building on the ideas and work of Bartolus, helped ensure his lasting legacy.

No such picture can be drawn with regard to the French school. Moreover, whereas the Medieval French jurists may have often ascended to high public or ecclesiastic offices but had tended to be university professors, almost none of the French jurists who are reported as having written on conflicts in the Early Modern period was a university professor; all had held high judicial or government office or were members of the Bar.[38] This reflects a general tendency in Early Modern French legal literature, where universities had limited influence compared to the Low Countries or Germany and most legal literature came from the bench or the bar.[39] This geographical and professional diversity must have privileged certain works over others. Literature with conflicts references appears divided between Paris and regional jurisdictions but Paris appears the hub through which these works circulated.

The Netherlands of the Golden Age sit somewhere in between. The United Provinces offered a small but vibrant academic environment, with

[36] See Bartolus ad C.1.1.1, esp. nus. 22, 28, 36–37, 41, and 47.

[37] The lines were drawn by J. A. Clarence Smith, in the "Introduction" to his translation of "Bartolo on the conflict of laws," drawing from his work on *Medieval Law Teachers and Writers, Civilians and Canonists* (Ottawa: University of Ottawa Press, 1975). The work of Savigny in his *Geschichte*, esp. Chs. 26ff is the major reference for anyone who wants to understand the "chains" of influence linking teachers to students and their contemporaries.

[38] Of the 28 names Lainé, *Introduction*, 1:207ff, 297ff, 342ff, 413ff, presents for the period between the mid-fifteenth and late eighteenth century, apart from Dumoulin (who taught in imperial universities for a considerable time following his exile) we have to get to the mid-eighteenth century in order to read of Prévot de la Jannés and Pothier, who were called to professorships at the University of Orleans, while they were also holding high judicial office there.

[39] J. P. Dawson, *The Oracles of the Law* (Ann Arbor: University of Michigan Law School, 1968), 263–373 (speaking of "The French Deviation").

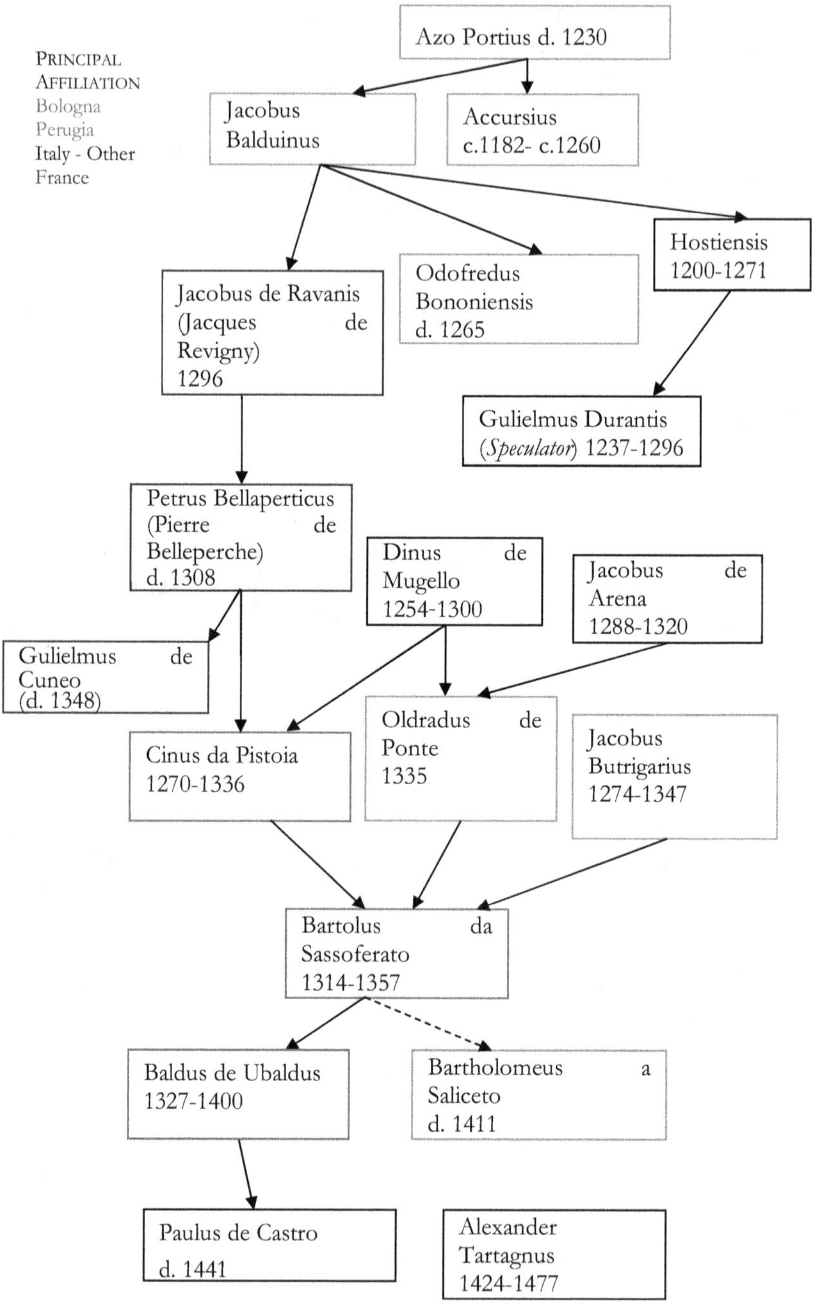

Figure 3.2 The "Italian School", 1200–1500: Teacher – Pupil Links and Bartolus ad C.1.1.1

a pivotal place in an international network.[40] Printed books facilitated the rapid circulation of ideas. Professors moved between universities, like Johannes Voet, or between the academia and the judiciary, like Huber. We will nonetheless see Huber citing as "recent" works written almost 40 years before his own.[41] It is telling that even the three principal writers of the so-called Dutch school fail to communicate with each other: Huber does not cite Paul Voet, who had published his treatise on statutes 20 years prior, and Johannes Voet reciprocates.[42] They are, however, not alone in this neglect.[43]

We have to get to mid-eighteenth century France, in order to find a group of (three) people – Louis Froland, Louis Boullenois, and Jean Bouhier – who appeared to have both worked consciously on conflicts issues and interacted with each other in the so-called *Conférence des Avocats*.[44] Their story was characteristically brought to broader attention by Armand Lainé, who was subsequently criticized for "inaccurate romanticism."[45] In any case, this venture was not continued further: the work produced by participants in the *Conférence* may have provided

[40] See e.g. J. I. Israel, *The Dutch Republic: Its Rise, Greatness and Fall* (Oxford: Oxford University Press, 1998), 899–902 (ibid., 899: "the three leading Dutch universitities – Leiden, Utrecht, and Franeker – collectively formed an academic forum which was international, and pan-European, at least within the Protestant sphere, to a greater extent than was found anywhere else"). The data provided for Israel as the numbers and provenance of foreign students are interesting (and indicating a decline in the importance of Dutch universities by the late seventeenth century).

[41] See Section 13.2.3.

[42] Ibid.

[43] In giving information about Rodenburgh, Lainé, *Introduction*, 1:404–405, remarks his surprise that he is not cited "a single time" by Stockmans, who wrote in 1670. Rodenburgh wrote in Utrecht and Stockmans in Brabant, which is not that far away but is still across the Protestant-Catholic border. The 1676 Brussels edition probably aimed at making Rodeburg's world more accessible across the border. What may be more interesting, and is also mentioned by Lainé, *Introduction*, 1:404 n. 2) is that Boullenois, who structured his *Traité de la personnalité et de la realité des lois* around Rodenburgh's principles, used the 1643 edition. See Boullenois's "Preface," XXI.

[44] See N. Hatzimihail, "Enlightenment, Identity and the Questions Mixtes in mid-18th century French legal literature," paper presented in the 15th International Conference on the Enlightenment (Edinburgh, 2019).

[45] Lainé, *Introduction*, 1:413–425; A. Pillet, *Principes de droit international privé* (Paris, 1903), v claims to "imitate the example of these illustrious ancestors" at the very beginning of the "Preface" to his treatise. For deeper investigation – and criticism of the classical jurists' romanticism – see esp. C. Boucher, "La conférence des avocats et le droit international privé au XVIIIe siècle," *Clunet*, 63 (1935), 45–58; and B. Lemarignier, *La conférence des avocats et les conflits des statuts concernant les effets du mariage au début du XVIIIe siècle* (Paris: Faculté de droit et sciences économiques de Paris, 1961).

useful material to Joseph Story, probably by means of Livermore, and probably others before him; however, as Lainé himself demonstrated, it did not influence the law reform ushered by the Revolution – nor did it register in the historical consciousness of private international lawyers.

It is of course possible, under the sociological definition of a school, to group together people dealing with the same issues in the same context. Such people would have been frequently taking account of each other, in support or in opposition, and were linked together in the writings of the next generation. At the end of the day, schools are constructed *ex post*, and preclassical conflict of laws is no exception. Still, it is remarkable that not even the Italians like Bartolus are talking of their generation's writers.

In any case, the historical narratives of private international lawyers have never taken account of a sociological definition of a school, especially in the more "institutional" sense that we spoke above with regard to the Medieval scholars. This may be because the sociology of intellectual work is a relative novelty in legal doctrine; or because legal academics have been reluctant to emphasize the role of "interaction rituals" in the production of legal ideas. But another reason may be that, in the one case where such a network exists, conflict of laws seems largely irrelevant to its existence.

3.3.4 A Contextual Definition

Conflicts historiography tends to make little reference to general legal history. In some cases – especially in earlier works – the requisite background knowledge is assumed of the reader, but quite often such knowledge is lost, as the history of conflicts doctrine is separated from the broader intellectual and doctrinal trends in legal evolution.

This is a matter of essential understanding, both of our subject and of the premises upon which our historical consciousness is being constructed. The history of European legal doctrine provides us with a conscious discursive community (one could dare speak of "disciplinary consciousness") spanning across the High and Late Middle Ages and the Early Modern period.[46] There is even memory of an Italian, French, Dutch school, "style" or "tradition" (*mos italicus*; *mos gallicus*; *mos hollandicus*) that seems to inform our own division into schools.

[46] See e.g. H. Lange, *Römisches Recht im Mittelalter*, vol. I (Munich: C. H. Beck, 1997), 151–191.

Without issuing any conclusions, it is true that the Italian school (whose foundations are laid, as we shall see immediately below, with the school of the Glossators) peaks with the school of Commentators: these jurists – who include Bartolus, Baldus, and their own influential successors – built on the work of the Glossators and shaped European private law, both through their strong influence on legal practice and through the disconcerted reactions they provoked to the legal humanists (i.e. those who created both the term *mos gallicus* for themselves and *mos italicus* for the predecessors they opposed).[47] The sixteenth-century French school is associated with the rejection of Bartolism, and its members are legal humanists and early Institutists; even the old debate as to whether Dumoulin should be placed with the Italian or the French school is in immediate correlation with Dumoulin's evolving contribution to legal doctrine.[48] As to the Dutch school, its members were Institutists and flirting with the early natural-law tradition.[49]

The distinction in schools also corresponds to the jurisprudence of each school. The Italian school seems more concerned with justice than coherence: it employs a plurality of authorities, a plurality of concepts and categories. The Dutch jurists have on the contrary embraced the vision of Reason, of a coherent exposition and a rational ordering in accordance with the minimum number of principles. The French are somewhere in the middle; the eighteenth-century French jurists try to make a rational system out of case law.

Beside the merits of such a contextual approach, it would appear that notions from the general history of legal ideas, and of private law, were in some previous stage transplanted into the historical conceptualization of the conflict of laws. The degree to which, for example, *mos gallicus* led to the construction of a distinct "French school" of statutist doctrine invites a separate examination and is only touched upon in this book. But we must in any case be mindful of the possibility that the ideas and knowledge held by the early historiographers of private international law has shaped their thinking – and consequently ours as well – about the conceptualization of preclassical doctrine and its schools.

[47] See e.g. O. F. Robinson et al., *European Legal History*, 3rd ed (Oxford: Oxford University Press, 2000), 42ff, 59ff; Lesaffer, *European Legal History*, 25–29; Wieacker, *History*, 28ff, 5ff; F. Calasso, *Medio Evo del diritto*, vol. I (Milano: Giuffré, 1954), 511ff, 563ff.

[48] See Robinson et al., *European Legal History*, 169ff; Lesaffer, *European Legal History*, 338ff.

[49] See Robinson et al., *European Legal History*, 213ff; Lesaffer, *European Legal History*, 438ff; Wieacker, *History*, 168ff, 199ff.

This observation makes even more salient the present-day separation of the history of conflict-of-laws doctrine from the general history of jurisprudence and private law. Such separation is impossible, as will be seen in our exploration of Medieval and Early Modern conflicts texts in the rest of the book. Its existence, however, is evident in the very way in which a story of doctrinal beginnings of conflicts doctrine is being told in our literature.

3.4 The Foundational Moment: "Si Bononiensis"

The foundational text for the doctrinal development of conflicts law, not unlike most of private law, is to be found in a gloss on the *Corpus Iuris Civilis*. Glosses were explanatory notes made on the margins of the authoritative main text.[50] Around 1220–1250, Bologna law professor Accursius (1185–1263) published a consolidation of glosses (*apparatus*) into the *Glossa ordinaria*.[51] His work became the starting point of subsequent scholarship and maintained its authoritative status up to the seventeenth century. In the process, most of the texts that Accursius based his own work on were lost to oblivion.[52]

The gloss in question is an annotation to the opening section of the first title of the Code (On The High Trinity (*De summa Trinitate*) and the Catholic Faith), known as *cunctos populos* (C.1.1.1). This is an Edict by the co-Emperors Gratian, Valentinian II, and Theodosius I, issued in 380 AD and known as the Edict of Thessalonica, which reaffirmed Nicene Christianity as the official religion of the Empire and laid the foundation for the suppression of all Christian heresies and polytheistic religions. The Edict begins by stating the Emperors' will that "all peoples" (*cunctos populos*) ruled by the temperance of imperial clemency

[50] See M. Bellomo, *The Common Legal Past of Europe*, trans. Lydia Cochrane (Washington, DC: Catholic University of America Press, 1995), 129–131.

[51] The traditional view held that a first edition of the Glossa (minus the Institutes), was published by 1228. It is now believed that the Gloss was constantly revised over a broader timeframe, such as 1220–1250. See e.g. R. Figueira, "Glossa Ordinaria: Roman Law" in C. Kleinherz (ed.), *Medieval Italy: An Encyclopedia*, vol. I (New York: Routledge, 2004), 437–439. See also Lesaffer, *European Legal History*, 256: "glossing of the Corpus iuris civilis was a cumulative undertaking, with the glosses being added from generation to generation."

[52] J. W. Wessels, *History of the Roman-Dutch Law* (Grahamstown: African Book Co., 1908), 116–117, quoting Savigny, *Geschichte*, 5:262ff.

(*quos clementiae nostrae regit temperamentum*) live in accordance to the religion passed to the Romans by the "Divine Apostle Peter."[53]

The Accursian gloss annotated *cunctos populos* as follows:

> Argument that if a Bolognese (*si Bononiensis*) is sued at Modena he ought not be judged according to the statutes of Modena to which he is not subject, because it says [i.e., the *lex*] 'which [the *imperium*] of our clemency [rules].[54]

This gloss invites two historical questions. First, was Accursius really the first "conflicts lawyer," at least in the sense of being the first to identify conflicts issues and elaborate a general doctrine to deal with them? Second, what we are to make of the position of this gloss within the broader *ius civile* system? Why was this *locus* chosen to ground this comment (a decision criticized across the ages)?

The answer to both these questions is inherently connected to another one: what relevance, if any, does this foundational moment have for present-day sensibilities? It will be argued that references to the gloss in conflicts literature can tell more about ourselves than about Accursius and his peers.[55]

3.4.1 *Of Founders*

Much of the literature has been preoccupied with naming the "actual founder" of conflicts doctrine. Accursius or even Bartolus have been

[53] C.1.1.1: "Emperors Gratian, Valentinian, and Theodosius Augusti to the People of Constantinople. Pr. We desire (*volumus*) that all people (*cunctos populos*) who are governed by the moderation of Our Clemency (*quos clementiae nostrae regit temperamentum*), shall practice that religion, which was handed down by the divine Apostle Peter to the Romans, as shown by the religion introduced by him and transmitted down to this day – the religion which, it is clear, is now followed by the Pontiff Damasus and by Peter, Bishop of Alexandria, a man of apostolic sanctity; that is, according to apostolic learning and the teaching of the evangelists, we shall believe in one deity of the Father and the Son and the Holy Spirit, in equal majesty and in a pious Trinity. 1. We order all who obey this law to embrace the name of Catholic Christians, and all others, whom We deem mad and insane, to suffer the infamy of heretical doctrine; they shall be stricken, first, by divine vengeance and, second, also by the vengeance of Our wrath, which We shall take in accordance with the judgment of Heaven."

[54] Accursius ad C.1.1.1 v° *quos* (Lyon, 1627), col. 13: "Argumentum quod si Bononiensis conveniatur Mutinae non debet iudicari secundum Statuta Mutinae quibus non subest, cum dicat: quos nostrae clementiae. »

[55] This Section is primarily concerned with historical consciousness of private international law doctrine. For the historical exploration see N. Hatzimihail, "On the Doctrinal Beginnings of Private International Law," *Yearbook of Private International Law*, 21 (2019/2020), 101–133.

named to that effect. Yet it is certain that Accursius was not the first to ground a jurisdiction-delimiting argument on *cunctos populos*, nor was he the first to put forward the argument of *Si Bononiensis*.[56] A generation before Accursius, another jurist of Bologna, Carolus de Tocco, had glossed *cunctos populos* as follows:

> Here note that he does not want to bind others than those who are subject to his *imperium*, and there is an argument [in this direction] below [C.3.1.14]. This is, however, contrary to the customs of the cities which also want to bind others with their statutes. And there is an argument that if a Modenese litigates against a Bolognese in this city [i.e., Bologna] that the statute not harm the Modenese. But some, however, say the contrary to this, [using the] argument that the Modenese here follows the forum by summoning the Bolognese [to the Bolognese court], and by this act (*unde*) he accepts all the laws of this forum.[57]

Ever since E. M. Meijers, following Neumeyer, brought him to the fore, Carolus has been the one most often – but still not always – given credit in name parades.[58] The contest, however, appears symbolic: the founder

[56] See Hatzimihail, "Doctrinal Beginnings," esp. 110ff.

[57] Ad C.1.1.1 MS Bibl. nat. 4546 v° *clementiae* fol. 2a.

> Hic nota quod alios noluit ligare nisi subditos imperio suo et est argumentum, infra, de iudiciis l. rem. primo responso (C.3.1.14 v° *quum igitur*, etc.). Est autem hoc contra consuetudines civitatum que etiam alios constringere volunt cum suis statutis. Et est argumentum si litigat Mutinensis contra Bononiensem in hac civitate, quod statutum non noceat Mutinensi. Sed quidam contra hoc autem dicunt, argumento illo quod Mutinensis hic forum sequitur conveniendo Bononiensem, unde omnes leges illius fori recipiat.

The text was transcribed by Neumeyer, *Gemeinrechtliche Entwickelung*, 2:75 and then Meijers, "Principes fondamentaux," 594. Neumeyer followed Savigny in attributing the manuscript to Rodofredus. See the contrary argument of Meijers, "Principes fondamentaux," 594 n. 1.

[58] See e.g. Loussouarn et al., *Droit international privé*, 87; Ballarino, *Diritto Internazionale Privato*, 16. Many textbooks do not associate any name with the gloss on *cunctos populos*, which is understandable, though Carolus seems a safe bet. The defining text was Meijers, "Principes fondamentaux," 594. In past days, others were proposed instead: for example, J. Krčmář, "Beiträge zur Geschichte des internationalen Privatrechts" in *Festschrift zur Jahrhundertfeier des Allgemeinen Bürgerlichen Gesetzbuches*, vol. II (Vienna, 1911), 133–161 credits Jacobus Balduinus. See A. Sack, "Conflicts of Laws in the History of the English Law" in *Law: A Century of Progress*, vol. 3 (New York, 1937), 342–447 credits Hugolinus with "formulat[ing] the general principle that the emperor imposed law only on his subjects" (342). More surprisingly, Yntema, "Historic Bases," 302 suggests, two decades after Meijers, that "Accursius himself is believed to have made [this "seemingly casual addition"] to the Glossa Cunctos Populos."

is simply a name. Carolus has become in our historical consciousness simply the author who first said what Accursius most famously formulated subsequently.[59] It is remarkable that few if any appear to have noticed the doctrinal differences between Carolus and Accursius – let alone to have understood what it might suggest for the state of legal practice in thirteenth-century Italy.[60]

Carolus' text is different from Accursius – and not simply because the latter switches the forum. To modern eyes, Carolus presents his readers with a fuller discussion, a clear indication of arguments on both sides, whereas Accursius presented one side as the dominant one. Viewed in historical terms, the contribution of Carolus lies in defining the issue in terms of a conflict between the law in place in two different city-states and seems to acknowledge the existence of political and jurisdictional elements. He also deploys legal arguments and authorities. But his response is more of a *quaestio*, where both sides of the argument are presented without the author taking himself a clear position.[61]

In his turn, Accursius is setting unequivocal limits on the city's ability to regulate its own territory, as should be expected of a Glossator: the city statutes represent a local derogation from the *ius commune* and may therefore only bind the city's own citizens.[62]

Carolus had left open the possibility that the claim of a Modenese being sued in Bologna would be adjudicated in accordance with Bolognese statutes. Accursius reverses the facts of the case, which would probably make his position more palatable to his immediate audience: the Bolognese is spared his subjection to Modenese statutes and customs. The reflective understanding of a modern lawyer would be to assume that the Bolognese facing the Modena court is, according to Accursius, subject to Bolognese law. This has led some to regard Accursius as an advocate of extreme personalism.[63] But it would appear highly unlikely for a

[59] See e.g. H. Gaudemet-Tallon, "Le pluralisme en droit international privé: richesses et faiblesses," *Recueil des cours*, 312 (2005), 9–488, 177.

[60] Meijers, "Principles fondamenteux," 595 ("cette glosse a été répétée avec quelque variante par Accurse"); Lalive, "Téndances," 56. Cf. Ancel, *Histoire*, 93–94.

[61] See Hatzimihai, "Doctrinal beginnings," 117–119.

[62] See ibid., 119–122.

[63] See e.g. Valéry, *Manuel*, 23: even though he initially hints at a conflict between city statutes and Roman law, he then places the Accursian rule in "formal opposition" to the territoriality principle. Valéry is not content with the absolute personalism of the gloss and suggests that Accursius may have had personal motives ("[la proposition ainsi formulée . . . était, assurement trop absolue; et il est permis de croire qu'elle fut inspirée à Accurse par le désir de servir les intérêts de quelque Bolonais de ses amis engagé dans

thirteenth-century Modena court to apply a particular Bolognese statute. The alternative to the law of Modena is the common Roman law. The same would be expected of another case not mentioned in the gloss: whether a Bologna statute might regulate the conduct of Bolognese outside the territory of their town. These are precisely the questions subsequently posed by Bartolus in his commentary on *cunctos populos* and the gloss. Bartolus and his contemparies, however, faced a very different political and legal landscape and approached the role of learned law and the relationship between Roman law and Italian society through another lens.

Even though very little effort has been made in conflicts literature to understand the gloss in historical terms, some writers have attempted to explain its importance for the subsequent development of the discipline, in ways that say more about their own preoccupations than about Medieval law itself. Many emphasize the discovery of a positive-law foundation for the conflict of laws – a point that will be examined immediately below. Others place emphasis on the problem having been identified: Hessel Yntema, for example, underlines the "rapid acceptance of the fruitful idea that a court should discriminate according to the nature of the case in the application of law to a foreigner."[64] Another view shifts emphasis to the approach adopted: E. M. Meijers, for example – who tells the history of early conflicts doctrine in terms of a move from a mostly "territorial" court practice to the development of a more general legal doctrine – places emphasis on the move away from an absolute reliance on the *lex fori*, which he presents as having been adopted even by eminent Glossators (including Accursius himself in earlier writings), with the elaboration of a distinction between procedure (ordinatoria litis) and substance (*decisoria litis*).[65] In short, the first viewpoint emphasizes a *foundation* relied upon, the second viewpoint a

une instance portée devant les juges de la ville voisine"). He obviously did not know about the preexisting glosses (but may have been aware of allegations of lax professional ethics by Accursius and especially members of his family).

[64] Yntema, "Historic Bases," 302.

[65] See e.g. Meijers, "Principes fondamentaux," 595–596, who credits Jacobus Balduinus with the distinction, regarding contracts (breaking with his teacher Azo who insisted on the *lex fori*; see Section 9.4.4). Noting the effort it took to make the distinction acceptable in Italy (as opposed to Southern France: 596–597), Meijers notes that "[a]vec cette distinction . . . la science moderne du droit international privé était née" (596). Meijers is followed by Lipstein, "General Principles," 111 and Forsyth, *Private International Law*, 36–37 who grants Jacobus right of first place. Lainé, *Intoduction*, 1:253 argues that the Italian school was founded upon this *distinction capitale* with which he credits Petrus Bellaperticus. See

problem approached, and the third one the development of *solutions*. In a sense, Yntema's take is more external to doctrinal development than Meijers. This can be explained. Yntema, a US scholar writing in an environment shaped by legal realism, and the early stages of the "conflicts revolution," does not privilege here such an approach: for him, it is enough that the conflict-of-laws problem has been identified and the domestic distinguished from the international. In contrast, Meijers was a leading light of mature classical conflict of laws – an emblematic figure of the reconstructive movement of European conflicts scholarship in the interwar and early postwar period, which sought to build a new synthesis overcoming both the naïve personalism of early classical internationalists and the doctrinaire territorialism of particularists. By emphasizing the substance/procedure distinction, Meijers illustrates the importance of the doctrinal art, telling a story of doctrinal development: doctrine also overcomes judicial prejudices. In normative terms, Meijers takes a middle position, dismissive of the excesses of both *lex fori* proponents and proponents of substantive considerations. At the same time, he denies to the personalists the legacy of the gloss, while telling the story of doctrinal development as a move away from *lex fori*.

3.4.2 Foundations

In historical terms, the contribution of Accursius to conflicts doctrine rests not on his originality but in the importance the *Glossa Ordinaria* carried for subsequent generations. By including this primitive argument about the conflict of laws in his authoritative work of general jurisprudence, Accursius bequathed a solid starting point. *Cunctos populos*, with the gloss, became the principal topos on which to ground a conflicts discussion, for as long as the principal means of legal reasoning was to work by appending comments or commentaries on passages of the Corpus Iuris.[66] We will see that, in the fourteenth century, the entire treatment of conflicts issues by Bartolus – and the same holds true of his contemporaries – comes as a commentary on the gloss *si Bononiensis*. Even in the sixteenth century, Charles Dumoulin would still ground his conflicts treatment on the *lex cunctos populos*.[67]

also M. Wolff, *Private International Law*, 2nd ed (Oxford: Clarendon Press, 1950), 24; Lalive, "Tendances," 57 and 375 (n. 85) speaking of "distinction radicale."

66 See e.g. Jacobus de Arena ad C.1.1.1, fol. 2[ra] (1541).

67 Molineaus ad C.1.1.1, 554a–557a.

Late Medieval writers also discussed what we would today call conflict of laws issues in other *loci*. The most notable example has been the *lex de quibus* of the Digest, which stated that "what ought to be held to in those cases where we have no applicable written law is "the practice established by customs and usage."[68] The best known case of anchoring such a treatment here is Bartolus, a century after Accursius.[69] But no other authoritative text ever provided an equally solid anchor. For example, Jacobus de Ravanis (Jacques de Révigny), a half century before Bartolus, discussed whether a custom (*consuetudo*) bound clerics and foreigners in *quaestiones* of his *repetitio* on the respective provision of the Institutes, but not on his *repetitio* on the "sister" *lex de quibus*.[70] We can also find some discussions appended to *omnes populi*, the opening passage of the Institutes of Gaius included in the first title in the Digest.[71]

The question is why was *cunctos populos* chosen over other topoi to ground this argument. There are two principal reasons. One has to do with the place of the Edict in the overall system of the *Corpus Iuris Civilis*. It has been located at the very beginning of the Code.[72] The other one has to do with Medieval reasoning. The imperial Edict provided a powerful argument by analogy. More precisely, an argument *a maiore ad minus* with allusions to an argument *a contrario*: if, in a matter as vital as religion, imperial Roman law would restrict its application to Roman subjects, it goes without saying that neither would Roman law apply beyond the territory of the Empire, nor could the local laws and customs

[68] D.1.3.32: "In those cases (*de quibus causis*) where we have no applicable written law, what ought to be held to is the practice established by customs and usage (*quod moribus et consuetudine inductum est*). And if this is in some way deficient, we should hold to what is most nearly analogical to and entailed by such a practice. If even this is obscure, then we ought to apply law as it in use in the City of Rome" (Julian, *Digest*, Bk 84).

[69] See Section 7.2. See C. Smith, "Bartolo," 157. Bartolus's commentary on *de quibus* is translated by C. Smith, "Bartolo," 163–174.

[70] Inst.1.2.9 (*ex non scripto*). See L. Waelkens, *La théorie de la coutume chez Jacques de Révigny: édition et analyse de sa répetition sur la loi De quibus* (Leiden: Brill, 1984), esp. 405ff.

[71] D.1.1.9: "All peoples who are governed under laws and customs observe in part their own special law and in part a law common to all men." See also Hatzimihail, "Doctrinal Beginnings," 107–108 with references to D.5.1.1 ("If people submit themselves and agree to someone's jurisdiction, any judge who is in charge of a seat of judgment or has other jurisdiction has jurisdiction over those agreeing"), C.8.52, C.8.48.1, and Meijers, "Principes fondamentaux," 593 n. 1.

[72] Lainé, *Introduction*, 1:106, quoting Petrus Bellaperticus as saying that *lex cunctos populos* may not have raised the same questions if it was found at the end of the book, "but is the first, and this place vests it with a solemn character" (*la revète d'un caractère solennel*).

of cities apply beyond the narrow confines allowed to them by Roman law, for example over a citizen of another city. Over time, this argument was weakened as cities begun to flex their legal muscles and the legal fiction of Empire subsided. But this was a gradual process, of which we witness a first step in Carolus (recording the argument that a noncitizen suing a citizen in the city has accepted city laws). Even then, however, *cunctos populos* held some appeal insofar it alluded to the matter being one of jurisdiction, not one of legal sources.

By the sixteenth century, legal education and the genres of legal literature had changed, along with the legal style. Most French writers published commentaries on the royally sanctioned collection of the customary law of a French province, including Dumoulin himself and his famous commentary on the Custom of Paris. Comments on the conflict of laws were appended in these works, as was notably the case with Bertrand is d'Argentré.[73] Indeed, the first criticism of the Medieval invocation of *lex cunctos populos* appeared at that time. Conflicts treatments continued to be principally a matter for learned law. By the seventeenth century, Roman law had become more of a language than a formal system of legal sources. *Usus modernus Pandectarum* had elevated the standing of the Institutes and the Digest, instead of the Code, and had encouraged commentaries in the form of systematic works, rather than as annotations to individual passages. Both Ulric Huber and Jan Voet, who placed their conflicts treatment in the introduction to their Commentaries on the Digest, offer characteristic examples.

The evolution in legal style gave also birth to a longstanding tradition of deriding the relationship between the *lex cunctos populos* and conflicts issues. Already in the sixteenth century, Guy de Coquille disparaged medieval writers: someone randomly chose the text, and the rest aped him.[74] In the late nineteenth century, François Laurent would question

[73] Bertrand d'Argentré, *Commentarii in Patrias Britonum Leges*, Art. 218, glossa 6, cols. 201–220. Article 218 states: "Toute personne pourvenue de sens, peut donner le tiers de son heritage à autre qu à ses hoirs, au cas qu'elle ne le feroit par fraude contre ses hoirs."

[74] See G. Coquille, *Questions et responses sur les articles des coutumes* (Paris 1644), 345, Quest. CXXXI (also quoted by Lainé, *Introduction*, 1:104): "Et comme ce domicile semble avoir été mal elleu et choisi, parce que le texte n'y est aucunement à propos, aussi la question y est traitée trop prolixement pour y être bien traitée. Mais le dessein du premier docteur qui a commencé a été suivy comme par singerie et indiscrette imitation par les autres suivants : tous lesquelles à la file ayans divisé chacun de trois volumes des Digestes, et le Code en deux parties, ont travaillé de tout leur pouvoir d'enrichir les premières

the link between *cunctos populos* and statutes, wondering "what relationship could possibly exist between an incomprehensible dogma and a legal doctrine."[75] A modern writer even called glossators' reasoning as "preposterous."[76] A more moderate voice has spoken of conflict of laws being "artificially incorporated" into Roman law.[77]

Early Modern viciousness, which lays at the roots of this derision, relates to broader jurisprudential ideas and the evolution in legal style: as the humanist *mos gallicus* replacing the scholastic *mos italicus*, legal humanists accused their medieval forefathers, especially the glossators, for their failure to understand the Roman world, and its language. Accursius himself was a prominent target of such attacks.[78] Modern reaction in the same mould has largely to do with our failure to understand the Medieval mind. Even Armand Lainé, who defended the choice made by Medieval jurists and explained their reasoning, conceded that they were "blinded by their faith" that the *Corpus Iuris* contained everything.[79]

lectures de cette partie, en y ramassant pêle mêle toutes les belles questions qu'ils sçavoient; et au milieu et à la fin de chacune desdites parties ont passé comme en courant disant peu, ou du tou n'y ont rien dict. Et selon mon advis ils eussent mieux fait de dire mediocrement à l'entrée, et suivre par tout avec la même mediocrité et style, pour enseigner par tout."

75 Laurent, *Droit civil international*, 1:297 (that passage is also quoted by Lainé, *Introduction*, 1:106), but also 298: "Les glossateurs fondent leur doctrine sur des textes mal interprétés, donc sur une base imaginaire. Ceci n'est pas un reproche. Les légistes du moyen âge étaient étrangers à tous études, littéraires, historiques et philosophiques; il faut s'étonner, non de leurs erreurs, mais de la subtilité de leur intelligence, digne de la race italienne."

76 See *in extremis* Juenger, *Choice of Law*, 11: "The reasoning is, of course, preposterous."

77 See Rabel, *Conflict of Laws*, 1:6–7.

78 See notably François Rabelais, *Pantagruel*, 2:5: "the books of the civil law were like unto a wonderfully precious, royal, and triumphant robe of cloth of gold edged with dirt; for in the world are no goodlier books to be seen, more ornate, nor more eloquent than the texts of the Pandects, but the bordering of them, that is to say, the gloss of Accursius, is so scurvy, vile, base, and unsavoury, that it is nothing but filthiness and villainy." The quotation is mentioned by Valéry, *Manuel*, 26.

79 Lainé, *Introduction*, 1:106–109. Cf. ibid., 109: "Ils s'imaginèrent à tort que le *Corpus juris* contenait tout, ne pouvait faire défaut à qui le scrutait bien. Aveuglés par leur foi, ils crurent sincèrement avoir trouver ce qu'ils cherchaient avec tant de confiance; ils donnèrent pour des règles concernant les conflict de lois des decisions qui son en rapport très indirect, très éloigné avec cet ordre d'idées, quand ells n'y sont pas entièrement étrangères." The Romanist Alan Watson, *Joseph Story and the Comity of Errors* (Athens: University of Georgia Press, 2002), 6 has a response to this as well (writing with regard to the references to Roman-law authorities *within* the text): "If Bartolus had been writing a treatise on Roman law, then his approach (and that of Huber) to the texts would be

There is another reason behind these modern attitudes. For many, what makes of the gloss *si Bononiensis* and its progeny a seminal moment for the discipline of private international law is the discovery of a doctrinal foundation. This is a moment signifying the linkage of the discipline with Roman law and thus with learned law and doctrinal sophistication.

Once we think in such terms, we can better understand Juenger's use of the term "preposterous" in the light of his hostility to scholarly insistence on the choice-of-law method. As to Laurent and Lainé, their own different attitudes (attributable in part to the different degree of each one's attentiveness to the subtleties of Medieval scholarship) can be associated to the evolving politics and aspirations of classical conflict of laws. Laurent was writing at the very beginnings of the school of international law (and near the end of his own life). Perceiving his mission as helping lay the groundwork for a new beginning, he does not look for validation of his views in Medieval or Early Modern doctrine. In Laurent's *Universalgeschichte*, "glossators" are supposed to have furnished to the subject the distinction between real and personal statutes, for which he found little basis on *cunctos populos*. In contrast, Lainé may have written only a few years later but represents another generation. His understanding of history was certainly less Hegelian. Lainé, who read more Medieval texts – and closer – than probably anyone before or since his time, also expressed considerable sympathy with the Italian school, which he identified with the pursuit of justice rather than a mechanical distinction between real and personal statutes. He was an instrumental figure of the School for decades, at the time when its original manifestos evolved into a web of doctrinal works, journals and academic

wrong. But that is not what Bartolus was doing. He was using Roman legal texts as the only authority he had (in the absence of local custom or statute) to build up a new area of law. By the canons of legal reasoning that were regarded as appropriate, he properly cited a Digest text out of context to get the result he favored." See also Baldus ad D.1.3.32 (fol. 18^r, Lyon 1498), as translated by J. Canning, *Ideas of Power in the Late Middle Ages 1296 – 1417* (Cambridge: Cambridge University Press, 2011) 137: "Our laws consider time and create their legal enactments in time. For time which has quite receded from human memory is for that reason thought of as if it had never been, because it has been destroyed and consumed by a different usage. What does it matter to us whether Caesar or Pompey ruled more justly? Certainly, it is nothing to us. For it was our ancestors who lived under Caesar. So let us get on with our own lives. Roots are not to be scrutinized, because man cannot find the cause of all God's works. Time which gives him life gives him law. But time which is always with us – that is what gives us custom, that is what gives us law. By time we live, are nourished and exist."

deliberations, and more of a pragmatist – less keen on a grand break with the past, more eager to keep what building materials and moral victories tradition could give him. As a result, Lainé was probably better able to understand the importance for a nascent subject of being anchored at the beginning of the Code, i.e. in a more visible place, than in the middle of the Digest or of a French provincial Custom. He thus notes that until the – recent – emergence of specialist treatises, the subject had been "always attached accessorily, in a more or less arbitrary fashion, to other subjects."[80] It is the word *always* that has the biggest importance: Coquille, d'Argentré, and Paul Voet have more in common with Bartolus and his predecessors than they claim. In this understanding, the decisive break happens when the subject has obtained its own foundations so as to achieve standalone doctrinal constructions. Grounding conflicts on *cunctos populos* could also be seen as more suggestive of the political aspect of delimiting jurisdiction.[81]

The modern stance is exemplified by Ernst Rabel, who emphasized the ambivalent relationship of conflict of laws with Roman law. In Rabel's story, conflict of laws was "artificially incorporated" into Roman law and thus became "universally binding," leading over time to "a truly international law."[82] In reading Rabel, one comes to think of early conflicts doctrine as a living thing trying to survive and conquer the world.[83] Moreover, the connection to Roman law eventually leads to a connection with a cosmopolitan learned-law world of the *ius commune* and its legacy.

A final point to be made has to do with the emphasis of different narratives on a positive-law foundation or the elaboration of a distinct

[80] Lainé, *Introduction*, 1:108: "Au surplus, est-ce que la matière des conflits de lois, jusqu'au jour où par son importance elle est devenue l'objet de traités spéciaux, n'a pas toujours été accessoirement rattachée de façon plus ou moins arbitraire à d'autres sujets?"

[81] See Rabel, *Conflict of Laws*, 1:6–7:

> It its generally accepted sense, the law of conflicts or private international law dates from the Medieval school of the postglossators ... Like the Roman law in which it was artificially incorporated, this branch of law was regarded as universally binding. The territorial realm of the doctrines of the postglossators exceeded even the boundaries within which the canon and Roman laws were received as "written reason," representing the law of all Christendom ... The law of conflicts thus became one field, in which the common and civil laws had a common doctrinal basis and which could be thought of as a truly international law.

[82] Ibid.

[83] See esp. ibid., 7–9.

conflicts doctrine, beginning with carving a distinction between substance and procedure. Both these ideas find some historical resonance, but neither has the key to the formation of conflicts doctrine. Indubitably they can and they do coexist in the thinking of many writers, but if we return to the two classic Hague courses, we see that the first one is adopted by Gutzwiller, who subordinated the role of courts and practice to that of the legal doctrine.[84] In his turn, Meijers who espoused the third, more technical, one, had envisioned a partnership of theory and practice and conducted more serious research into case law.

The personal element is also telling in that respect. Meijers was both a professional legal historian whose research was not limited to Latin doctrinal works, and a jurist involved in grand-scale legislative work. Furthermore, he had observed the clash between "theory" and "practice" in the early life of classical private international law. Gutzwiller and Rabel formed part of the first generation of lawyers to be trained under the German Civil Code (BGB), which influenced their – impressive but antiquarian – understanding of Roman law.[85] Eventually (especially after World War II), they came to rely on *ius commune*, the first modern incarnation of Roman law, as the foundation of a restored order and a bulwark against the horrors of their time (and nation).[86] But their

[84] See Gutzwiller, "Développement historique," 293–294:

> Les juges appliquent les règles de ce système statutaire non pas en vertu d'une autorisation supérieure, non parce qu'ils y sont obligés, mais simplement parce qu'ils obéissent à une autorité scientifique, parce qu'ils rangent le Droit international privé dans cet ensemble, dans ce système doctrinaire qu'on appelle le Droit commun d'origine romaine, qui le Droit privé par excellence, la raison écrite commune point de départ de ce Droit civilisée.

[85] On Rabel's historical training see R. Zimmermann: "'In der Schule von Ludwig Mitteis': Ernst Rabels rechtshistorische Ursprünge," *Rabels Zeitschrift*, 65 (2001), 1–38.

[86] The works of P. Koschaker, *Europa und das römisches Recht* (Munich, 1947) and F. Calasso, *Introduzione al diritto commune* (Milan, 1951) are the best examples of the postwar turn. See also F. Wieacker, *A History of Private Law in Europe*, trans. Tony Weir (Oxford: Clarendon Press, 1995), 5 n. 8 ("[t]he disastrous effects of German nationalism produced a radical revision after the Second World War" – leading toward "internationalism" and an increased study of the Medieval and Early Modern learned law, and away from the differentiation by German legal historians between "Roman" and "German" law and the general tendency to write national legal histories). From a different perspective, Wieacker also suggests with regard to twentieth-century law that "[o]n many points the courts are closer to the view of law entertained in Byzantium, in the Middle Ages, and the Age of Reason than to the jurists of classical Rome or to the Pandectists" (428).

conception of *ius commune* emphasized the constructive genius of Medieval jurists.

3.4.3 An Alternative Foundational Moment? Aldricus: "potior et utilior"

Master (*Magister*) Aldricus made his appearance in conflicts historiography a century ago, with the discovery of the following passage:

> It is asked: if men of different provinces which have different customs litigate before one and the same judge, which of them [the customs] ought the judge who undertakes to judge the case follow? I reply that [custom] which seems stronger and more useful (*potior et utilior*). For he ought to judge according to what has seemed better to him. According to Aldricus.[87]

Aldricus became very popular in the American conflicts discourse, where he is often regarded as an early proponent of the better-law approach.[88] Hessel Yntema even presented him as the first conflicts lawyer.[89] The reason for such warm reactions is self-evident: the better-law approach forms, at the very least, a legitimate part of modern conflicts discussion in the United States and may in fact have been subtly espoused by many

[87] Codex Chisiani Collectio § 46 (*An consuetudo legem vincat vel abrogare possit?*) in fine as published in G. Hänel (ed.), *Dissensiones dominorum* (Leipzig: Hinrichsii, 1834), 150–153, 153:

> Sed quaeritur, si homines diversarum provinciarum, quae diversas habent consuetudines, sub uno eodemque iudice litigant, utrum earum iudex qui iudicandum suscepit sequi debeat? Respondeo eam, quae potior et utilior videtur; debet enim iudicare secundum quod melius ei visum fuerit. Secundum Aldricum.

Neumeyer, *Gemeinrechtliche Entwickelung*, 2:67 was the first to point to this passage, which became better known by Gutzwiller, "Développement historique," 301.

[88] See esp. Juenger, *Choice of Law*, 12; also Symeonides et al., *Conflict of Laws*, 7 n. 2; McDougal, "Private International Law," 531. Cf. Sack, "Conflicts of Laws," 342, writing at a time prior to the US conflicts revolution ("Aldricus . . . clearly stated the problem of the conflict of laws and suggested the method for its solution").

[89] See Yntema, "Historic Bases," 301–302 ("esteemed," "had the genius to propose," "equitable conception"), 311 ("equitable conception") and 317 (Yntema's Postscript noting we have come full circle from the "equitable conception"). Yntema went as far as to invent a place for Aldricus to the pantheon of Medieval jurists. See Yntema, "Historic Bases," 301 who calls Aldricus "a younger and esteemed contemporary of the four celebrated 'doctores' of Bologna" (while he cites none to that claim, its source is Neumeyer, *Gemeinrechlitche Entwickelung*, 2:66).

American courts and writers.[90] Yntema himself did not go that far but he was one of the legal realists who revolted against Beale's American classical conflict of laws.

Continental European reactions were less enthusiastic. In his 1929 Hague Course, Max Gutzwiller became the first one to make Aldricus known to a broader audience, placing him "at the forefront of those distinguished by an independent and novel conception of the problem of application of laws."[91] Gutzwiller felt compelled to justify this by noting that in grand scientific problems, it is the question, not the solution that impresses the most.[92] Gutzwiller's take on Aldricus did find some supporters.[93] A few would even regard Aldricus as not just the "probable founder of conflicts law" but also an early proponent of a "multilateral approach," as opposed to the statutists' unilateral approach.[94]

Most, however, have remained skeptical or dismissive of his claim of fame. Meijers, for example, restricted his reference to Aldricus to one line in a footnote, characterizing him as a proponent of the "free choice of the judge"[95] and then immediately moving on to the beginning of the thirteenth century when "the science received a durable basis" in the principle *statutum non ligat nisi subditos*.[96] This has found resonance in much of the literature, which presents Aldricus as a jurist making a primitive effort to solve the conflict of laws problem without conceiving of it as a distinct problem.[97] Others present him as "partisan of the

[90] Lipstein, "General Principles," 157 presents David Cavers as "a new Aldricus." Cf. Forsyth, *Private International Law*, 64–65: even though he only mentions Aldricus by name in a footnote in his discussion of medieval conflict of laws, he uses his name in the title of his subsection discussing the doctrine of David Cavers.

[91] Gutzwiller, "Développement historique," 301; see also Neumeyer, *Gemeinrechlitche Entwickelung*, 2:66.

[92] Ibid., 301–302: "Comme dans tous les grands problèmes scientifiques, ce n'est pas la solution qui nous étonne le plus, mais bien la question."

[93] Notably Miaja de la Muela, *Derecho internacional privado*, 1:102; Maridakis, "Introduction," 486, 487.

[94] Mortensen et al., *Private International Law*, 8.

[95] Meijers, "Principes fondamentaux," 593 n. 2.

[96] Ibid., 594.

[97] See e.g. Audit, *Droit international privé*, 60; Kropholler, *Internationales Privatrecht*, 12. The Scottish Anton, *Private International Law*, 19 takes a middle position between Continental Europeans and Americans. Martin Wolff, *Private International Law*, 22 seems more appreciative but he makes his conclusion that Aldricus "was reffering to the quality of the law itself" seem like a fallback (Wolff apparently, and mistakenly, thinks

'better law.'"[98] Then there are those who shun Aldricus altogether.[99] In fact, by the end of his life, Gutzwiller came to conform to the dominant Continental approach by partly giving up on Aldricus.[100]

The relative neglect of Aldricus in many narratives may be due, in part, to his omission from the classic works of nineteenth-century writings (whose stories have been carried from one generation of writers to the other).[101] But this does not explain by itself either the dismissive references of Europeans or the references by Americans: this is not a matter of superior erudition and interest in preclassical conflict of laws. The real reason seems to be exactly that Aldricus did not conceptualize the conflict of laws as such or that, from the point of view of a modern conflicts lawyer, he sought to suppress the conflict of laws in its birth. If Aldricus had had his way, either there would have been no conflict of laws or, at the very least, learned law would have received stronger competition from the judge.[102]

3.5 Neglected Influences? Alternative Narratives about the Foundational Moment

3.5.1 A Role for Court Practice and Customary Law

The story of early conflict of laws is usually told as a doctrinal story. It is after all a move away from the *lex fori*, and judges have been, for good reason and throughout history, inclined to apply their own law. Judges are also notoriously averse to "grand scientific questions." Conflicts history has also been informed by specific conceptions of law and of

that Gutzwiller circa 1929 thought Aldricus a sponsor of the "most real connexion with the subject of litigation" approach).

[98] Lalive, "Tendances," 56–57; Forsyth, *Private International Law*, 36 n. 46, noting that "[t]he opinions of this ancient proponent of some very modern theories did not amount to much."

[99] No mention in Ballarino, *Diritto internazionale privato*, 17–19; Loussouarn et al., *Droit international privé*, 86–87.

[100] See Gutzwiller, *Geschichte*, 14–15. Gutzwiller went in fact as far as to raise the possibility of Aldricus never having existed. See Gutzwiller, *Geschichte*, 14 n. 20 (citing Savigny as noting that no manuscript exists the name "Aldricus."). But Aldricus appears separately from Albericus in the *Dissentiones dominorum* and Albericus himself refers to Aldricus. In short, there is clear evidence about Aldricus's existence dating between 1154 and 1177. See Lange, *Römisches Recht*, 1:202–204.

[101] Laurent, Lainé, and Catellani have made no reference to Aldricus, but then the text was apparently discovered by Neumeyer after they wrote.

[102] See also Hatzimihail, "Doctrinal Beginnings," 111–114 and 129–131.

legal evolution. The role of judges, in this story, should be to follow doctrinal constructs, to adhere to scholarly authority.[103]

Jurisprudential attitudes are combined with technical difficulties. It is not easy for a conflicts lawyer to reach beyond the published writings of Medieval scholars; especially before the advent of information technologies, archival research involving court records had resembled the proverbial search for a needle in the haystack. The pioneer in such research was E. M. Meijers, in the early twentieth century. Meijers studied early Medieval court records in both France and the Low Countries.[104] In the postwar period, Pierre-Clèment Timbal, a professor at the Law Faculty of Paris, produced and supervised interesting work in a similar direction, with emphasis in the late Medieval and Early Modern period.[105] Timbal also saw that Meijers's studies were translated into French.[106] Their work has been more recently continued by Bertrand Ancel, a student of Timbal and professor of private international law at the University of Paris.[107]

Meijers's contribution consisted not only in unearthing new texts, but also in the reevaluation of previously known evidence. He thus

[103] See Gutzwiller, "Développement historique," 293–294:

> Les juges appliquent les règles de ce système statutaire non pas en vertu d'une autorisation supérieure, non parce qu'ils y sont obligés, mais simplement parce qu'ils obéissent à une autorité scientifique, parce qu'ils rangent le Droit international privé dans cet ensemble, dans ce système doctrinaire qu'on appelle le Droit commun d'origine romaine, qui le Droit privé par excellence, la raison écrite commune point de départ de ce Droit civilisée.

[104] See E.M. Meijers's "Contribution à l'histoire du droit international privé et pénal en France et dans les Pays-Bas aux XIIIe et XIVe siècles" and "Nouvelle contribution à la formation du principe de réalité," translated into French by P.-C. Timbal and J. Metman E. M. Meijers, *Études d'histoire du droit international privé* (Paris: Éditions du Centre national de la recherche scientifique, 1967). The two studies were originally published in Dutch respectively as "Bijdrage tot de Geschiedenis van het internationaal privaat- en strafrecht in Frankrijk en de Nederlanden" in *Rechtshistorische opstellen aangeboden aan Mr. S.J. Fockema Andreae* (Haarlem: De Erven F. Bohn, 1914) and "Nieuwe Bijdrage tot het onstaan van het beginsel der realiteit," *Tijdschrift voor Rechtsgeschiedenis*, 3 (1922), 61–93.

[105] See P. C. Timbal, "La contribution des auteurs et de la pratique coutumière au droit international privé du moyen âge," *Revue critique*, 44 (1955), 17–32. See also S. Gruber-Magitot, *Les conflits de coutumes en matière de contrats dans la jurisprudence des Parlements: de Dumoulin au Code Civil* (Paris: Presses Universitaires de France (PUF), 1980).

[106] Se E. M. Meijers, *Études d'histoire du droit international privé* (Paris: Éditions du Centre national de la recherche scientifique, 1967).

[107] See Ancel, *Histoire*, 52ff; and *Élements*, esp. 81ff.

demonstrated that in instances which had been taken as an application of *lex fori*, the court was really thinking in terms of *locus rei sitae*. Meijers argued that the distinction between substance and procedure – which he regarded as fundamental to the birth of conflict of laws– had been made by French courts even before the Italian jurists.[108]

Other ideas promoted by Meijers are: first, the notion of an expanded conception of a *consuetudo* or *lex terrae* in French conflict of laws (even compared with the Low Countries), which Meijers attributed to the feudal influence on French property law; second, the importance of *conflits de jurisdictions* in the case of criminal offenses; third, the importance of a central power in facilitating extradition requests and other matters of cooperation among localities.[109]

The two objectives of Meijers and his historical work were to pull back the date of beginning of conflicts doctrine earlier in time and to claim a role for legal practice in it. With the exception of his Hague course, which summarized his previous research, he was not so much concerned with tracing the resistance of local lawyers to the introduction of learned law.[110] In presenting the results of his research, he also seems to have used anachronistically certain legal categories in order to drive better his point across.[111]

Meijers also unearthed the following text in a French manuscript of glosses to the Code and Institutes:

> Let us suppose that it is the custom in the city of Paris that if someone contracts marriage with some woman, the marriage having been dissolved by the death of the woman, the man (husband) ought to have half the goods given on account of the marriage (*donatio propter nuptias*) and it is the custom of Chartres, that if the marriage is dissolved by the death of the woman, the man has nothing. Let us suppose that someone contracts marriage in the city of Paris and afterwards goes to Chartres and stays there properly (*recte*) for a year and more and in that city the woman dies. The man seeks a half of the *donatio propter nuptias*. It is asked whether he can claim [to get it], bcause the heirs [of the woman] want to have the

[108] See Meijers, "Contribution," 23ff.

[109] See ibid., 64ff and 29ff.

[110] Resistance made famous by remarks such as the following: "Mark my words, Mr. Doctor, we Swiss pay no mind to your Bartolus and Baldus and your other doctors. We have special customs and liberties of our own here in this country." Quoted in Wieacker, *History*, 61 n. 29 (Schöffen of Frauenfeld). Cf. Bellomo, *Common Legal Past*, 78ff (esp. 81–83) who suggests a more integrated picture.

[111] As in his discussion of obligations: Meijers, "Contribution," 53ff.

> case decided by the customs of Chartres and not by the custom of Paris. But someone said in reply that he can properly claim.[112]

The case of a wife dying childless – triggering a conflict between the laws of the place where the marriage was celebrated (and the dowry contract executed), and the place where the couple subsequently made their home (the husband's domicile) – would have a long history to this day.[113] The example in this gloss is more interesting than others, because here each party seeks application of the custom (and jurisdiction of the courts) of the place of the other party's domicile. On the other hand, the author of the gloss takes no position here, except to refer to a *responsum* by a jurist who advocated the application of the custom of Paris. The case is thus a telling example of the increased practical interest in resolving conflicts problems, and of how it necessitated the creation of legal arguments in order to avail oneself of the most convenient court (and law). But we see no legal argument yet elaborated in this text.[114]

[112] Meijers, "Principes," 585, quoting from Manuscript 141 fol. 248^{v} Bibliotheque municipale d'Avranches:

> Hic ponitur quedam questio. Ponamus ut est de consuetudine in civitate Parisiensi quod si aliquis contrahat matrimonium cum aliqu[a] muliere, matrimonio soluto per mortem mulieris, vir debet habere medietatem rerum donatarum propter nuptias, et est de consuetudine in civitate Carnotensi, quod si matrimonium dissolvatur per mortem mulieris, quod vir nihil habebat. Ponamus quidam contrahit matrimonium in civitate Parisiensi et postea advenit ad civitatem Carnotensem et ibi moratur recte per annum et amplius et in illa civitate mulier decedit; ille vir petit medietatem donacionem propter nupcias. Queritur utrum potest, quia heredes volunt quod illa causa determinatur ex consuetudinibus Carnotensibus et non ex consuetudine Parisiensi. Sed quidam respondens dicebat quod bene potuit petere.

See A. Fliniaux, "Le manuscrit 141 de la Bibliothèque municipale d'Avranches et le problème de l'introduction en France au Moyen-âge de texte des compilations du justinien" in *Atti de Congresso Internazionale di diritto romano (Bologna et Roma, 17–28 Aprile 1934)* vol. I (Pavia, 1934), 313–327.

[113] See e.g. Bartolus ad C.1.1.1, nu. 19, as discussed in Sections 7.4.1 and 9.3.4.

[114] See also Hatzimihail, "Doctrinal beginnings," 114–116, where it is argued that the text which "looks more like a *quaestio*, with the facts balanced so as to best invite arguments on both sides, and readers left imagining what these arguments were," represents a moment of transition in Medieval thinking, as to the acknowledgment of the hard choices involved in choosing between "customary norms applicable to the same questions in different territories."

3.5.2 Law Merchant and the Conflict of Laws

Traditional conflics historiography has included references to merchant activity in the Italian cities of the later Middle Ages, with a view to explaining the cultural background of Italian jurists, as well as highlighting the practical needs for their work.[115] The movement of people was presented as having contributed conflicts beyond the scope of merchant and guild courts. Commercial disputes have also sometimes been presented as creating conflicts problems.[116]

But the broadened modern conception of private international law has also encouraged its own romance of the law merchant. Some writers have pushed the "cosmopolitan" claim that "the early scholars had the advantage of a broader intellectual perspective than today's conflicts experts, most of whom have been trained to believe that a choice among competing rules is the only way to deal with multistate problems."[117] And beyond this:

> [U]pper Italy was not only the birthplace of a continental European common law. Its flourishing trade and commerce also promoted the development of a law merchant, a process that has been described as a "rebirth of the old jus gentium of the Mediterranean." The *lex mercatoria*, which Maitland called the "'private international law' of the Middle Ages," offered supranational solutions to what have since become choice-of-law problems. In other words, when conflicts rules were first conceived, law was still cosmopolitan.[118]

What does this mean? In short range, this argument is used to suggest that "the particularistic tendencies implicit in such rules" were "more bearable than in our times of statism and positivism."[119] In long range, it presents conflict of laws as a functional alternative to the – more cosmopolitan – law merchant (which some imagine as having been less problematic in its application, since no complaints survive among the scant evidence of its practice).[120]

[115] See e.g. Blagojević, "Théories des statuts," 72–73; and Ehrlich, "Tendances actuelles," 908.

[116] See Meijers, "Contribution," 54–55 (treating the fair courts of Champagne as another instance of early Medieval conflict of laws).

[117] Juenger, *Choice of Law*, 15. The word "most," referring to today's scholars in the 1993 book, did not appear in Juenger's 1984 Hague text.

[118] Ibid., 16.

[119] Ibid.

[120] Indeed, Juenger himself moved to that direction over the next years. See Juenger, "*Lex Mercatoria*" (1136–1140 speak exactly of "the problems of private international law," meaning conflict of laws).

These ideas have drawn inspiration of historical – and especially genaological – explorations of a "cosmopolitan," "international," "transnational," or even "a-national" law of Medieval merchants. Such narratives can be dated back, in a more hybrid form, to nineteenth-century German romantic mercantilists pushing for legal unification and separation from Roman and civil law; to a group of English lawyers that have invoked "the romance of the law merchant" for similar purposes vis-à-vis the common law; and to the modern proponents of reviving the legendary *lex mercatoria*.[121] Their historical validation has been often discussed, even though they appear to persist in the modern consciousness.[122] For the purposes of this work, it suffices to quote a leading Medieval historian who notes that "the international commercial system, for all its glamour, was less significant in overall economic terms than the first level of the urban economy, the small-scale exchange of primary products and low-quality cloth and ironwork between towns and the countryside."[123] The increased economic complexity was a vital factor for the elaboration of legal doctrine, especially what we would today think of as private law, and it thus inevitably triggered conflicts issues and nourished preclassical doctrine. But we must think in terms of a virtuous circle of symbiosis rather than competing regimes.

3.5.3 *Canon Law and the Conflict of Laws*

To this day, canon law is barely mentioned in the historical literature of private international law.[124] This phenomenon goes back to the beginnings of conflicts historiography: the great nineteenth-century scholars who read and discussed tens of Medieval authors, such as Lainé, Laurent, and Catellani made no mention of canonists. We would have to reach the

[121] See J. Q. Whitman, "Commercial Law and the American Volk: A Note on Llewellyn's German Sources for the Uniform Commercial Code," *Yale Law Journal*, 97 (1987), 156; M. E. Basile et al., *Lex Mercatoria and Legal Pluralism: A Late Thirteenth Century Treatise and Its Afterlife* (1998), 123ff. See also Hatzimihail, "Genealogies of *Lex Mercatoria*."

[122] See e.g. C. Donahue, "Medieval and Early Modern *Lex Mercatoria*: An Attempt at the Probatio Diabolica," *Chicago Journal of International Law*, 5 (2004), 21–37; E. Kadens, "The Medieval Law Merchant: The Tyranny of a Construct," *Journal of Legal Analysis*, 7 (2015), 251–289; and "The Myth of the Customary Law Merchant," *Texas Law Review*, 90 (2012), 1153–1206. See also R. Michaels, "Legal Medievalism in *Lex Mercatoria* Scholarship," *Texas Law Review*, 90 (2012), 259–268.

[123] C. Wickham, *Medieval Europe* (New Haven CT: Yale University Press, 2016), 137.

[124] For an exception, see e.g. Mayer, *Droit international privé*, 40.

early twentieth century and Karl Neumeyer's all-encompassing inquiry into the Early and High Medieval roots of the conflict of laws to find some discussion.[125] Since Neumeyer, there have been some historical works on the canon-law contribution either to general conflicts doctrine or to specific rules and principles.[126] However, these works are seldom cited.

This book is concerned with the reasons behind this neglect – which, as we shall see, is reflected in how our historiography has paid little attention even to passages of canonical texts, including Bartolus, discussing "conflicts" involving ecclesiastical courts. On the contrary, this is not the place to appraise the possible contribution of Western canon law to early conflicts doctrine. Canon law nonetheless constitutes a major part of the Medieval legal heritage. It was developed academically and taught in the law faculties, in parallel as with well in conjunction with the *ius civile*: many of the commentators were trained "in both laws" (*utrumque ius*). Moreover, ecclesiastical courts fostered a vibrant legal practice and made significant contributions to the development of procedural law. It would appear that canon-law doctrine did help foster, or promote, certain ideas that found resonance with early conflicts doctrine.[127]

So why this reluctance to credit canon law with its due? Canonists may have been perceived as forming part of the learned-law tradition, but in fact the history – and historiography – of civil and canon law took

[125] See Neumeyer, *Gemeinrechtliche Entwickelung*, 2:107–149.

[126] See A. van Hove, "La territorialité et la personnalité des lois en droit canonique depuis Gratien (vers 1140) jusqu'à Jean Andre (1348)," *Tijdschrift voor Rechtsgeschiedenis*, 3 (1922), 277–322; L. Rigaud, "Contribution des canonistes aux plus anciens doctrines du droit international privé et influence de celui-ci sur le 'Codex juris canonici'" in *Actes du Congrès de droit canonique: livre du cinquantainnaire de la Faculté de droit canonique* (Paris: Letouzey & Ané, 1950), 376–386; K. Neumayer, "Das kanonische Recht und die Lehren der Kanonisten in ihrem Einfluß auf die Entwicklung des internationales Privatrechts (1250–1357)," *Tijdschrift voor Rechtsgeschiedenis*, 33 (1965), 177–197; D. E. Engdahl, "English Marriage Conflicts Law Before the Time of Bracton," *American Journal of Comparative Law*, 15 (1967), 109–135; D. E. Engdahl, "The Canonical and Metaphysical Background of the Classic Dutch Marriage Conflicts Rule," *Nederlands Tijdschrift voor International Recht*, 15 (1968), 42–67; W. Pakter, "Les origines canoniques de la règle forum regit actum dans le droit international privé," *Recueil des mémoires et travaux publié par la Société d'histoire et des institutions des anciens pays de droit écrit*, fasc. 11 (Université de Montpellier, 1980), 1–22.

[127] Meijers, "Principes fondamenteux," 593 n. 1 notes that civilian doctrine developed without canonist influence until the mid-fourteenth century and refers to Neumeyer's "very complete overview."

separate paths.[128] The intellectual and social history of canon law has suffered an appropriate fate.[129] By the mid-nineenth century, when the history of the conflict of laws was first written and most of the scrutiny of Medieval doctrinal texts undertaken, canon law had long been a specialized milieu and, quite frankly, not a popular intellectual pursuit among mainstream jurists. Nineteenth-century politics certainly did not help: the founding fathers of the international-law school tended to subscribe to political Liberalism and a certain degree of skepticism toward the authority of the Catholic Church. Inquiries into canon law and its literature were neither obvious nor useful to their genealogical projects. But even if they desired to engage into such an exercise, they would probably not know where to look. It is remarkable that the few twentieth-century studies on canon law and conflicts issues seem to cater more to legal historians than private international lawyers.

But this does not fully explain the persistence in omissions. Let us consider for example Niboyet, a conservative Catholic and one of the few twentieth-century writers making a passing reference to canon law: citing a "very detailed" study, he actually dismisses its significance, effectively calling canon-law ideas on conflicts "incompatible" with the organism of a territorial State.[130]

This can be explained both in terms of normative preoccupations, and doctrinal preferences. Classical conflict of laws revolved around a system of States – a horizontal system of sovereign entities, each with its own *ordre juridictionnel*. Canonical jurisdiction was something external to this system. Moreover, whereas the objective of classical conflict of laws was the management of legal diversity, canon law was viewed as having embraced full unity.[131] Especially over the

[128] Such identification has in modern times been stronger in England than in the Continent, where the history of civil and canon law took increasingly separate paths. See notably C. Donahue, "*Ius Commune*, Canon Law and Common Law in England," *Tulane Law Review*, 66 (1992), 1745–1780; and R. H. Helmolz, *The ius commune in England: Four Studies* (Oxford: Oxford University Press, 2001).

[129] See C. Donahue Jr., *Why the History of Canon Law Is Not Written* (London: Selden Society, 1986).

[130] Niboyet, *Traité*, 3:42 n. 1, along with the early Medieval personality of laws,ne peuvent s'adapter à l'organisme d'un Etat.

[131] Rigaux, "Contribution," 386:

> Jadis, dans l'Europe médiévale, et longtemps encore après le déclin des concepts d'empire et de chrétienté, l'universalisme juridique avait pu exister et persister grâce à la vogue de la doctrine romano-canonique et au prestige de Bartole. Cette tradition romano-canonique, vraiment

past few centuries, Catholic ecclesiastical law was unified, as its territorial and substantive scope shrinked.[132] It is interesting that the story of canon-law influences on the conflict of laws found more receptive ears as modern private international law toned down the classical vision of managed diversity among nations, and became more receptive to both the mentality of technicians and the ideal of complete unity.

The final explanation relates to the actual spirit of Medieval canon law. First, canon law was not simply learned law: it was inextricably linked to the court practice of a single jurisdictional system.[133] Second, we must go beyond standard genealogical exercises of claiming the parenthood of specific rules. We will then see that Medieval canon law was characterized by an expansive jurisdictional philosophy, which operated through a combination of personalist (with regard to *causae seculares*, i.e. matters that normally fell under the jurisdiction of secular courts) and territorialist (especially with regard to the allocation of jurisdiction between canonical courts) doctrines. The provision of equitable remedies seems to have been a major consideration.[134] Such an image of canon law probably confirms this work's conclusions on Medieval conflicts thinking. But it would appear as irrelevant or primitive to single-minded proponents of personalism (like Laurent) or territorialism (like Niboyet).

> internationale, est aujourd'hui à peine reconnaissable dans ce mirroir brisé que constituent les codifications nationales du droit international privé. Pas plus que la défunte Union de droit international privé de la Haye, pas plus que la précedente Société des Nations, l'Organization actuelle des Nations Unies ne paraît encore encore apte à modifier sensiblement cette regrettable anarchie juridique qui rend si décevante la science laïque contemporaine du droit international privé, science pourtant à tant d'égards si intéressante.
>
> Ici, comme en tant d'autres domaines, nous pouvons constater que l'Eglise est la seule société qui offre à nos yeux quelque vision de paix et d'harmonie, modeste anticipation de la Cité céleste.

132 The notion of divergent local interpretation of a single law was even less dear to nineteenth-century legal positivists (or their descendants) than to the Vatican.

133 Stein, *Roman law*, 50.

134 Thus, jurisdiction *ratione personae* was asserted on behalf of clergy, but also came to cover widows and orphans, where in the case of asserting jurisdiction *ratione peccati* (described by Wieacker, *History*, 52 as "where the subject matter involved confession") an important consideration was the unavailability of satisfactory secular remedies. Hence, murder jurisdiction was maintained by secular courts, but sins such as fornication and, in England, defamation were adjudicated by ecclesiastical courts.

3.6 Conclusion

The discussion in this chapter must have shed further light as to why Bartolus and Huber were selected as the subjects of our case studies in Parts III and IV. In any scheme, they are regarded as representatives of different "schools." By contrast, the differences of Dumoulin from Bartolus, and d'Argentré from Huber are less clearly emphasized: the principal idea seems to be that Dumoulin renovated Bartolan scholarship and came up with a few additional ideas, and that the Dutch carried d'Argentré's territorialist ideas to their fulfillment. The difference between Dumoulin and d'Argentré is also often overshadowed by their common environment, the effort to integrate them into a common school, and the genealogical politics of nineteenth- and twentieth-century French private international law: the strong territorialism of d'Argentré and the classical-era struggles between territorialism and personalism made writers evaluate differently both his intellect and his influence on French doctrine.[135]

But the principal purpose of the chapter was defined in the more ambitious terms of an examination of modern historical consciousness regarding preclassical conflict of laws, which entailed a critical presentation of existing literature. It was thus observed that a common thread runs through the various narratives about Medieval and Early Modern conflict of laws. We can of course observe a real diversity of perspective, which can tell us more about the authors of the narratives, and the evolution of classical and modern thought, than about the nuances of preclassical doctrine itself. There are also noticeable differences in the details of each story, which are equally telling of their authors' preoccupations and their sources and method. But all this cannot obscure the fact that the story of the beginnings of conflicts doctrine, and of the rise, transformation and decline of "statutes theory" is told in intrinsic terms, as a story of learned secular law.

The roots of conflicts doctrine are to be found in the High Middle Ages – a period of economic and cultural growth that also gave birth to academic and judicial institutions with resonance to this day. Medieval jurists, whose numbers expanded as their scholarly output flourished,

[135] Niboyet, *Traité*, 3:52 n. 2 proposed to distinguish between a "Parisian school" (Dumoulin) and a "Brittany school" (d'Argentré). Miaja de la Muela, *Derecho internacional privado*, 1:134–135 who speaks of a "second French school" with regard to the eighteenth-century French writers on conflicts, in effect asserts the unity of French conflicts thought.

found recourse to the *Corpus Juris Civilis*. Texts hastily compiled long ago, with the purpose of serving the needs – and ideological project – of an expanded despotic empire with a strong central bureaucracy were invoked as authority in resolving the legal – and political – problems of a very different world, which claimed to cling to the idea of imperial Roman continuity.

This is an epic story, and indeed the beginnings of conflicts doctrine in this environment are presented in most of the literature as a foundational moment for private international law. This foundational moment is however stripped of its historical context. This is moreover a story of secular legal doctrine. Scarcely any role is acknowledged to the other pillar of Medieval learned law, canon law. The story also has no curiosity for Medieval court practice and local customs.

In historical terms, such a narrative is not complete. A complete history of conflict of laws in the Middle Ages should consider evidence on legal practice and draw connections with canon-law scholarship. Likewise with the Early Modern period, where court records and notarial archives may yield even more results.[136] But such an endeavor falls well beyond the capabilities and ambition of this book project. For our purposes, what is probably more important is for us to understand the context of early conflicts writings – as well as how modern-day preoccupations tend to reflect on how we approach them. For example, the foundational moment of conflicts doctrine has been stripped of its historical context: the ways in which it is presented in conflicts historiography – at least that part of it which is not singularly concerned with naming the first conflicts writer – tend to indicate more about our concerns than about Medieval jurists. Putting Accursius back in his context is a first step toward understanding him and his peers. The contribution of the individual, and of the schools, has to do less with their actual originality (seldom easy to prove or disprove, and often meaningless) and more with the tools and edifices they constructed and the ones they enabled subsequent generations to construct or recreate.

The same holds true about the division of preclassical doctrine into schools. The traditional approach has been to insist on a grand idea or to create an inventory of notions and doctrines, as the defining characteristic of schools and of membership in them. One of the problems of this approach, aptly illustrated, is that it often attributes ideas ex post to

[136] See e.g. Section 13.6.

individual writers or eras. Even if attributions are correct, however, this does not settle the question of whether and how it matters to us. National or ethnic origins have also been an important criterion in the literature. Such approaches can claim at least some factual basis, but again not so much as might have been hoped or expected. A third approach relies on the sociological element in creating "schools" of thought. Such a criterion must not be discounted. However, unlike the nineteenth-century creation of a veritable, conscious "school" or even "schools," preclassical doctrine displays little evidence of either school consciousness or actual contact between school members. Which brings us back to general legal history as a fourth criterion: even though this is clearly not enough by itself or a panacea, writing the history of preclassical conflict of laws would certainly benefit from a good understanding of general European legal history.

On the whole, the story of the evolution of the conflict of laws is usually told in intrinsic terms, as a story of technical paradigms: conflict-of-laws "methods" replacing each other. This is a story usually isolated from developments in private law, the international system or legal theory. Occasionally, there appears the opposite tendency of telling the story in extrinsic terms: conflict of laws as dependent on the existence of sovereign states or specific philosophical ideas. The fact that most historical treatments focus on one or two key concepts or issues – namely the method, but occasionally also the role acknowledged to foreign law or (foreign) individuals – does not help. History is also often used to reinforce the author's contemporary agenda: a contemporary doctrine may thus be presented as transcending the boundaries of time and space to reach into antiquity or the Middle Ages; alternatively, it may be presented as a novel idea, resulting out of long intellectual fermentation.

Conflicts historiography is a fascinating object of study in its own right but as we conclude this Part we must address the feeling that history is irrelevant to present-day concerns. Superficiality has made the study or invocation of history lose its real meaning for private international law: in the parades of ancient names, our discursive ancestors appear obscure, if venerable, and somehow separated even from their own time, let alone ours. Why is it important whether it was a fourteenth-century Italian, a fifteenth or sixteenth-century French, or a seventeenth-century Dutch who invented the notion of a *mixed statute*? Did the inventor even mean what we attribute to him – and does this really matter? Why should we care as to which Medieval Italian scholar should be named "founder of private international law?" We cannot even be sure that

Bartolus – though certainly happy to be remembered seven hundred years after his birth – would feel that the obvious flattery of being called the "founder" of a subject he could not conceptualize outweights his being presented as a simpleton "grammarian." This is regrettable, because conflict of laws boasts of many brilliant texts that span the past eight centuries. These texts can tell us fascinating stories – about their authors, their time and place, but also about our own vocation. It is to that latter where we must now turn, before we examine the texts themselves.

PART II

Current Concerns

4

Conflict of Laws as a Conceptual Battlefield

4.1 Introduction

The history of private international law is frequently told in terms of a dialectical antithesis between opposing concepts or doctrinal approaches. Historical narratives are thus employed to address presentist concerns. Those supporting one of the embattled approaches often search for historical validation of their views: the history of the field is thus told in terms of the emergence, or persistence, of a dominant concept or approach. But those who seek to escape the constraints of binary oppositions also use history, either suggesting that the time has come to move beyond such antithetical schemes, or in espousing more complex schemes of their own. History can provide them as well with examples of how such polar approaches were tried and failed; or with material supporting notions of doctrinal complexity.

A common narrative in the literature of private international law has been to tell the story of conflicts doctrine in tersm of a long struggle between "territorialist" and "personalist" approaches to conflicts doctrine (Section 4.2). The opposition between "unilateral" and "multilateral" choice-of-law methods constitutes another conceptual pair employed in historical narratives (Section 4.3). In a third type of narrative, "universalist" aspirations toward a uniform conflict of laws system clash with the "particularist" assertion of national interests and sensitivities through a distinct national conflicts system (Section 4.4); variations on this story have contrasted an "internationalist" to a "nationalist" mode of legal reasoning (Section 4.5). Others have used the term "conflict of sovereignties" to describe either the actual state of play in dealing with conflicts or the notions underlying certain doctrinal approaches (Section 4.6): these images may today be less popular than the other four but they epitomize the ambiguous relationship and ambivalence of conflicts doctrine toward state sovereignty. Each of these five schemes is examined in a section of this chapter.

These conceptual schemes appear sometimes on their own in separate narratives, and sometimes in conjunction. One cannot examine the history of conflicts doctrine – let alone talk about the history of conflicts doctrine to an audience of modern private international lawyers – without at least considering them. Their most important contribution however is not toward history; rather it is the ideas they convey about conflicts doctrine, its evolution and prospects – and about what matters most in present-day discussions.

4.2 Territorialism and Personalism

In the words of a leading contemporary scholar, "[a]lthough it is no longer fashionable to speak in these terms, the history of private international law in general and the law of choice of law in particular is a story of clash and tension between two grand operating principles – territoriality and personality of the laws."[1]

The opposition between *territorialism* and *personalism* has been often used as the central axis for a history of private international law, as the primordial conceptual opposition cutting across the history – for some, even the prehistory – of conflict of laws.[2] In these narratives, territorialist doctrines are presented as having dominated most of the preclassical period – especially since the sixteenth century.[3] On the contrary, the internationalist fathers of the classical conflict of laws were strong proponents of personalism – and certainly were perceived as such.[4] Territorialism continued to dominate the Anglo-American world, from Joseph Story to A. V. Dicey in Great

[1] S. C. Symeonides, "Territoriality and Personality in Tort Conflicts" in T. Einhorn and K. Siehr (eds.), *Intercontinental Cooperation through Private International Law: Essays in Memory of Peter E. Nygh* (The Hague: TMC Asser Press, 2004), 401–433.

[2] See e.g. Elhoueiss, "Personnalité et territorialité."

[3] See e.g. Audit, *Droit international privé*, 63: "On peut voir dans la doctrine territorialiste d'origine un avatar de la théorie des statuts, bien qu'elle soit née en réaction contre cette théorie et qu'elle s'en démarque déjà par son caractère systématique. Elle reçut sa première expression en France dans le cadre des conflits de coutume; elle s'internationalisa au XVIe siècle aux Pays-Bas et connut par la suite une extension considérable du fait de sa réception dans les pays de *common law*." Audit indeed discusses d'Argentré (63-64), the Dutch school (64-65), moving immediately to the "Anglo-American" territorialism of Dicey and Beale (65-67), before moving back in time to discuss nineteenth-century personalism and Savigny.

[4] Ibid., 67–69.

Britain and Joseph Beale in the US, who employed the vested rights concept in its defense.[5]

According to the standard narrative, the stark contrast between territorialism and personalism lost much of its forcefulness at some point in the twentieth century.[6] Personalist approaches had their high day in the late nineteenth century; the attempts to use them as the engine of a near-universal regime, based on international conventions, only met with partial success, but their influence survived into the mid- to late twentieth century. In turn, the interwar and early postwar years did in fact see the dominance of two of the most sophisticated territorialist systems in conflicts doctrine: those epitomized by Joseph Beale in the US and Jean-Paulin Niboyet in France. Both came close to legislative adoption but in the end did not outlive their main creators.[7]

Since the early days of the discipline, and its historiography, the doctrinal approach favored by each author – whether identifying as territorialist, personalist, or eclectic/synthetic – has informed their historical narratives.[8] The nineteenth-century Liberal advocates of a strong personalist approach presented the territorial doctrines of their time as feudal remnants of a conflict within provincial jurisdictions.[9] They also sought to distinguish their approach from the early Medieval regime of personality of laws, which they compared instead with the tribal personal laws in the African and Asian colonies of their time.[10] Territorialists adopted the reverse approach: personalism was linked to such personal laws, or to feudal ideas of allegiance.[11] The creation of the

[5] Ibid., 65–67.

[6] See e.g. P. Louis-Lucas, "Conflits de méthodes en matière de conflits de lois = Conflicts of methods as regards conflicts of laws," *Clunet*, 83 (1956), 774–823: the "unitary method" of both territorialism and personalism has been overcome by pragmatism and eclecticism.

[7] On Beale and the criticism against his Restatement see S. C. Symeonides, "The First Conflicts Restatement through the Eyes of Old: As Bad As Its Reputation?," *Southern Illinois University Law Journal*, 32 (2008), 39–82. On Niboyet's influence in the 1955 Draft see Y. Loussouarn, "The French Draft on Private International Law and the French Conference on Codification of Private International Law," *International and Comparative Law Quarterly*, 5 (1956), 378–394.

[8] See Sections 2.3–2.6.

[9] See e.g. Laurent, *Droit civil international*, 1:270–271.

[10] See e.g. Lainé, *Introduction*, 1:60–69.

[11] Thus Savigny, *System*, 8:15-16 (§ 346), opposing "Race and Nationality" (*Volksabstammung – Nationalität*)) to "Country or Territoriality" (*Landgebiet – Territorialität*), associates the former with "wandering tribes, who have no fixed territory, as among the Germans in their nomadic era" the Ottoman Empire's system of personal

territorial State became for them the foundational moment for conflicts doctrine.[12]

A serious historical study of doctrinal systems will have to consider the extent to which personalism, territorialism and their opposition is central to a doctrinal system. It has been observed that a distinction must be made between those writers who make one concept the general rule, or even the foundation of their system, from those who refuse to commit *a priori* either way.[13] Such a distinction cannot be absolute, however. Even a strict unitary system will allow exceptions – openly or through the use of safeguard mechanisms. At the same time, even a self-proclaimed eclectic system is likely to end up favoring the one or the other approach in its reasoning or in the way it structures the subject-matter.

What is therefore needed is to examine in detail concrete doctrinal systems in order to understand what "terroriality" and "personality" mean in practice. Such examination therefore cannot be limited to the general principles declared by the author in question; it must consider his or her doctrinal systems as a whole. Moreover, it must be noted that, in legal doctrine, even when it appears that the doctrinal solutions emanate from the author's general theory or general principles, things may be in fact more complicated, with the general theory being constructed, configured, or reconstructed in order to provide a theoretical or doctrinal *foundation* to the doctrinal solutions provided.[14]

4.2.1 Definitions

But what exactly is personalism and territorialism? Let us first repudiate the tendency of equating personalism with the use of nationality as a connecting factor and territorialism with the respective use of domicile.

laws and draws analogies with the Roman division arising from the "political rank of certain classes of persons" into *cives, latini, peregrini*. See also W. Raeburn, "Dispensing with the Personal Law," *International and Comparative Law Quarterly*, 12 (1963), 125–147, esp. 127, tracing the whole concept of personal law back to Rome ("The citizen was there as of right. The alien was there on sufferance") and then the "abstract reasoning of the statutists." Nationality "arose out of the feudal doctrine of allegiance. In its most characteristic modern form it is the child of the French Revolution, adopted into its jurisprudence by the almost hysterical enthusiasm of Mancini and his followers."

12 Niboyet, *Traité*, 3:42 n.1 ("notre droit international privé ne commence qu'à partir du moment où a existé un Etat territorial. Les sources antérieures ne peuvent s'adapter à l'organisme d'un Etat").

13 See Section 5.2.2.

14 See Section 6.4.

Such a perception goes back to the late nineteenth and early twentieth centuries, when conflicts solutions tended to be linked to the person in the case rather than other material factors and the opposition between nationality and domicile dominated classical conflict of laws. At a time when a truly global agreement on a uniform conflicts system seemed feasible, opposition between nationality and domicile might indeed have been – and was certainly perceived as – the strongest obstacle to it. But the fact of the matter is that the contrast between nationality and domicile is but an internal opposition between personalist approaches, which arose relatively late in the overall history of conflict of laws.

It is therefore advisable to approach both terms in a broad sense, especially as we embark on an historical exploration. Let us first define as a *territorial approach* to the conflict of laws, the notion that a certain legal question should be attached to one or another normative community by means of the connection of one or another material element of the case with the territory of one community (e.g. *locus contractus*, *lex rei sitae*). Let us then define as a personal approach the notion that such attachment to a normative community should be made by means of the personal lien of one of the individuals involved to a certain community (e.g. *lex patriae*, *lex domicilii*).[15]

Once we follow these definitions, we are met with opposing conceptions within both the territorialist and the personalist camp. In the territorialist camp, we have the "*mild* or *transactional* territorialism" of the *lex loci actus* and the *real* territorialism of *lex rei sitae*. In the personalist camp, we have the well-known opposition between domicile and nationality.

Territoriality and territorialism, thus defined, should not be confused with the notion of extraterritoriality. The former concept forms part of the "multilateralist" discussion about constructing aprioristic choice-of-law rules. On the contrary, *extraterritoriality* properly speaking is a concept for unilateralist regimes. In multilateral territorialism, word is made of "extraterritorial effect," although normally the emphasis is less on the direct extraterritorial effect of legal rules, and more on their indirect effect, by means of the extraterritorial effect of acts validly made under these rules in question, in the territory where they apply.[16]

[15] See likewise Raeburn, "Personal Law," 125; and Rabel, *Conflict of Laws*, 1:101ff.

[16] See e.g. Niboyet, "Territoriality," 584–585. ("The [territoriality] system involes two propositions: first, that, in principle, the country best qualified to have its law applied to a given case is the country territorially interested in that case; and second, that a right

4.2.2 *Personalist Approaches: Domicile v. Nationality*

The conflict between domicile and nationality could be summarized as being about whether the personal lien between individual and normative community should be defined in terms of the formal adherence of the individual to one community (*nationality* as the connecting factor of the choice-of-law rule), or in terms of a real presence in a community's territory (*domicile* as the connecting factor of the choice-of-law rule).[17]

The conflict between domicile and nationality is a nineteenth-century creation: references made to "personal law" by preclassical writers concern domicile.[18] Savigny famously used domicile in his doctrinal system.[19] As to the common law, the adherence of common-law jurisdictions to domicile has continued unabated to this day.[20] It must be remarked, however, that especially the English definition of domicile came to espouse, in the nineeenth century a stronger emphasis on political and cultural attachment, especially through the institution of the *domicil of origin*.[21] It has been justly remarked that in the late

originating in a country in conformity with its law should be recognized in other countries, even if that law is 'territorial'.")

17 Cf. Bar, *Theorie*, 149 (§ 41): "Three grounds on which a person may be subjected to the law of any particular State are conceivable. These are actual residence, residence taken up with an intention that it shall be permanent, and, lastly, another kind of connection with the country, which has also a tract of time in view, a connection which originally may well have depended in every case upon ties of race, but subsequently could be established by means or other facts, e.g. birth in the territory. This connection we call nationality (Staatsangehorigkeit)."

18 See e.g. Parts III and IV, including 12.2.2.1. For an example of a more formal lien used in the early preclassical period see P. Dominguez Lozano, *Las circunstancias personales determinantes de la vinculación con el derecho local. Estudio sobre el derecho local altomedieval y el derecho local de Aragón, Navarra y Cataluña* (Madrid, 1988), reviewed by B. Ancel, *Revue critique*, 79 (1990), 238–241.

19 Savigny, *System*, 8:89ff (§§ 358–359).

20 See Story, *Commentaries*, 39–49; A. V. Dicey, *The Law of Domicil as a Branch of the Law of England Stated in the Form of Rules* (London: Stevens, 1879); Dicey, *Digest*, 79ff (noting the *animus manendi* alongside the physical presence); N. Bentwich, "Le développement récent du principe du domicile en droit anglais," *Recueil des cours*, 49 (1934), 377–465; and J. Foster, "La théorie anglaise du droit international privé," *Recueil des cours*, 65 (1938), 399–557. See also D. McClean, "A Common Inheritance? An examination of the private international law tradition of the Commonwealth," *Recueil des cours*, 260 (1997), 13–98, describing the process of making more territorialist the law of domicile within the British Commonwhealth.

21 *In extremis* see e.g. *In re Tootal's Trusts* (1893) 23 Ch D 532 (Chitty, L.J., ruling that testator maintained English domicile despite evidence that he had decided to reside permanently in Shangai and had no intention of returning to England). For stronger authority see the House of Lords decisions in *Winans* v. *Attorney-General* [1904] AC 287;

nineteenth century "intention replaced residence as the engine of domicile."[22] To this day, "every textbook confirms" that "the language of domicile is the language of intention," whose function however "is now more apparent than real."[23] The general trend, however, has been to move the law of domicile either toward taking "a long-term view of an individual's life"[24] or toward residence.

The term *nationality*, in its legal sense of belonging to a state, only appears in earnest in the early nineteenth century.[25] In the preclassical period, there is word of "subjects" – a term rejected as too feudal following the American and French Revolutions, in favor of "citizen."[26] The underlying concept of *allegiance* survived however, despite its feudal connotations, notably in English law: we have seen Westlake discussing "allegiance" in his 1858 treatise.[27]

Beginning with the Napoleonic Code and its interpretation by French courts,[28] the introduction of nationality as an alternative connecting factor gradually swept domicile, at least in Continental Europe. Mancini's lectures on the principle of nationality are regarded as a milestone, but the first great victory for nationality as a doctrinal tool was the Italian Civil Code of 1865.[29] Nationality became the personal-law connecting factor: a characteristic example is the case of personal property, where the traditional rule of *lex domicilii* was replaced by a rule

Ramsay v. *Liverpool Royal Infirmary* [1930] AC 588 (where respectively twenty-six and thirty-five years of residence in England were not enough to establish there a domicil of choice). For a characteristic recent case see *Cyganic* v. *Agulian* [2006] EWCA Civ 129 (the deceased, who had lived and worked in the United Kingdom for forty-three years but "retained a very strong sense of Greek Cypriot identity," had retained his domicile of origin in Cyprus).

22 R. Fentiman, "Domicile Revisited," *Cambridge Law Journal*, 50 (1991), 445–463, 463.

23 Ibid., indicating case law implies that someone's "substantial connection with a place is the best indication of their domiciliary intent."

24 P. McEleavy, "Regression and Reform in the Law of Domicile," *International and Comparative Law Quarterly*, 56 (2007), 453–462, 462.

25 M. Koessler, "'Subject,' 'Citizen,' 'National,' and 'Permanent Allegiance'," *Yale Law Journal*, 56 (1946), 58–76, 61 notes that it first appeared in 1835 of the Dictionnary of the French Academy.

26 Koessler, "'Subject'," 58–61.

27 Westlake, *Private International Law*, 5ff (also discussed at Section 2.3.2.3).

28 See notably Cour de Paris, 13 June 1814, S. 1814.2.393, as presented and commented in Ancel and Lequette, *Grands arrêts*, § 1 (2–6).

29 *Codice Civile del Regno d'Italia.* The conflicts provisions are found in the Code's Preliminary Provisions ("Disposizioni sulla publicazione, interpretazione ed applicazione delle leggi in generale"), which are separately numbered and often cited as *Dispozioni Preliminari.*

combining the *lex patriae* and mandatory rules of the *lex rei sitae*.[30] The "laws of the nation to which [the person] belongs" claimed not only questions of status and capacity, but also successions and all unilateral acts.[31] Even the applicability of the *lex loci conclusionis* in matters of formal validity and contractual obligations was preempted in the case of common nationality of the parties.[32] The principle of nationality had shown it could help achieve a successful codification of conflicts rules.[33]

Most proponents of the School of international law enthusiastically rallied to the cause of the *lex patriae*. To a great extent, this was the result of the spirit of the times and their own Liberal nationalism.[34] The move from domicile to nationality would reflect the then-recent achievement of political and legal unification in the European nation-states. German jurists came to espouse nationality once these conditions were satisfied in their own country.[35] The advocacy of nationality was further supported by the more holistic conception of statehood and citizenship as involving political rights and welfare policies.[36] But we must not

[30] Codice Civile, *Dispozioni Preliminari*, Art. 7(1).

[31] Ibid., Arts. 6, 8, and 9(2) al. 1.

[32] Ibid., Art. 9(1) and (2) al. 2

[33] Laurent, *Droit civil international*, 2.60–66 and 107: "On a dit dans la discussion du code italien que le principe de nationalité *fera le tour de monde*: Telle est aussi ma conviction."

[34] See e.g. Bar, *Theorie*, 266ff (§ 91). Lorimer, a Scottish member of the Institute, defended domicile on the basis of the distinction between political and private rights. Bar disagrees: "it seems to us to be anything but desirable to separate, as Lorimer proposes, for generations it may be, private and political rights in the same persons" (267).

[35] For the evolution in German law and scholarship see H.-P. Mansel, "L'adoption du principe de la nationalité par le EGBGB du 18 août 1896" in Erauw et al., *Liber memorialis François Laurent*, 869–879. For a contemporaneous account see Bar, *Theorie*, 226–274 (§§ 91–92), overviewing the evolution in German doctrine, and across Europe. Bar himself had originally (1862) advocated the principle of domicile. Bar, *Internationales Privat- und Strafrecht*, vol. I (Hannover, 1862), 90.

[36] T. Baty, *Polarized Law* (London: Stevens and Haynes, 1914), 19–20: "It will be seen how well this system of the solidarity of the nation, alike in public and private affairs, in politics and in business, fits in with the present-day conception of the bureaucratic State. The State is rapidly becoming . . . the universal provider for its population. Such measures as the Old Age Pensions Act and the Insurance Act, which limit or refuse their benefits in the case of persons of foreign nationality, exhibit the influence of the tendency even in Britain. They link up private relationship – such as the private law relationship of parent and child, and master and servant – with the conception of political nationality. The tendency of the State to depart from its public rôle, and to interfere in all business and private relationships – whether by protection of industry or by national insurance and education –is in thorough harmony with this system of determining private rights by the law of the political nationality. The nation forms a solid and coherent mass, in such a conception: it is not the elastic and loosely compacted federation of free individuals which

underestimate the impact of the positivist, formalist jurisprudence, which defined the School and its times. Nationality was a more formal legal construct than domicile, a creation par excellence of positive law and State power. It was stabler than domicile, easier to ascertain in law, as even its opponents would admit,[37] and more intelligible by the lay people.[38]

Seen together the political and jurisprudential dimension might best explain the preference expressed by nineteenth-century nationality proponents, for domicile of origin over domicile of choice, with regard to the rule applicable to composite systems, and their flirtation with a registration requirement in case domicile was to determine the applicable law.[39]

it seemed to be in the mid-nineteenth century. As long as government was obviously the preserve of the few, so olong its functions were equally obviously limited. A grand duke or a parliament might be technically autocratic, but it was implicitly recognized that that the sphere of their activity had a comparatively narrow range. But with the advent of comprehensive schemes of representation, the ruling authority asserts a right to speak with the united voice of the whole nation. The assumption, whether justified or not, enables it to interfere with details of private life which the old type of autocratic government could never under ordinary circumstances have ventured upon. Private rights present themselves as proper subjects for regulation by national law."

[37] Dicey, *Law of Domicil*, 365 acknowledges this as the principal argument in favor of nationality. The case of *Sottomayor* v. *De Barros* (also discussed in Baty, *Polarized Law*, 55–57) was characteristic. The litigants were Portuguese, who had come to England with their families in their infancy (1858). They married in a Registrar's Office in 1866 – at the time, Ms Sottomayor was fourteen-and-a-half and Mr De Barros sixteen – but did not consummate their marriage until 1872. In 1874, Sottomayor sought annulment since the spouses were first cousins and such a marriage would have required papal dispensation under Portuguese law; she alleged that she had consented to the marriage because she thought this was the only way to save her father from bankruptcy. At the High Court, Sir Robert Philimore refused to apply Portuguese law as the law of their domicile and maintained the validity of a "marriage contracted in England, and valid upon English law." His judgment was reversed on appeal and the marriage was diagnosed as null and void due to the spouses' "personal incapacity." See *Sottomayor* v. *De Barros* (1877) 2. P.D. 81, rev'd (1877) 3 P.D. 1 (C.A.). But the decree was for the High Court to make and when the case was retried, two years later, new evidence was presented as to the husband's father having actually settled permanently in England and the validity of the marriage upheld since one of the spouses was a British domiciliary. *Sottomayor* v. *De Barros (No. 2)* (1879) P.D. 94.

[38] Law Commission, "Report on Jurisdiction in Matrimonial Causes," (Law Com. No. 48, London, 1972), para. 20: "Most people know what their nationality is – which cannot always be said for domicile. It is one of the few legal concepts with which the man in the street is familiar and the only one of which he has or can easily obtain some documentary evidence – a passport."

[39] See the discussion in the 1880 Meeting of the Institute of International Law: *Annuaire de l'Institut de Droit International* 5 (1882), 45ff. A summary of the discussion appears in K. Nadelman, "Mancini's Nationality Rule," 428–432. A registration proposal made by

The principle of nationality would muliply cases of conflicts between laws.[40] Once generally accepted, however, it would also make an international codification of conflicts rules easier to achieve.

This was not to happen, however. The Institute came very close to adopting a Resolution in its 1880 Oxford Meeting, but a compromise solution with regard to composite legal systems was undermined by nationality proponents.[41] At the time, the general belief was that "the future will pronounce in favour of the principle of nationality."[42] In fact, the change in attitudes in this regard was one of the reasons why the pioneer Latin American attempts at regional codification of conflicts rules, with the 1889 Montevideo Conventions, did not have much success with adoption.[43] Indeed, the first Hague Conventions on family and succession matters adopted the nationality principle.[44] They were

Westlake, as a compromise, was rejected by both camps. Bar, *Theorie*, 271 retorts that "a new intermediate class of foreigners (or of citizens?) would be created" and points to practical problems.

40 An observation by Nadelman, "Mancini's Nationality Rule," 421.

41 See Nadelman, "Mancini's Nationality Rule," on the role of Augusto Pierrantoni (1840–1911), who had married Mancini's elder daughter and eventually succeeded him to his Rome professorship. As Mancini's ministerial duties and declining health kept him away from the Institute's deliberations, Pierrantoni came to be seen as his representative, although their views were not always in agreement, notably in the *Samama* litigation, where they were employed by the opposing sides (Caid Nissim Samama was a rich Tunisian Jew who left Tunisa first for Paris, where he made a will, and then Italy, where he died; his relatives challenged the validity of his will relying on Jewish law; Mancini argued that Samama had repudiated his Tunisian nationality by migrating to Italy; not possessing a nationality, his personal law should therefore be the *lex domicilii*, i.e. French law). Nadelman has woven a veritable detective story, which links the high financial stakes of the Samama litigation, the father-and-son-in-law collaborative as well as competitive relation and the debate regarding the personal law of nationals of multi-jurisdictional countries. While Nadelman is at least partly right, it is also true that Pierrantoni, a founding member of the Institute in his own right, represented the "younger" generation of the Institute's founders, who were often more militant than their elders, whether in the defense of the nationality principle or in seeking the establishment of international arbitration.

42 Bar, *Theorie*, 271 n.20, citing the 1880 Oxford Resolution, the 1878 "congress of the jurists of Spanish America" (in Lima) and Dicey, *Domicile*, 362ff, as well as Laurent. Ironically, Bar's text has the Institute pronouncing for domicile instead of nationality.

43 See N. Hatzimihail, "Latin America and Early Classical Private International Law" in J. M. Bareto and M. Packeiser (eds.), *Latin America and International Law* (forthcoming 2021).

44 See the Conventions of June 12, 1902 relating respectively to the "settlement" of "the conflict of the laws in matters of marriage," "the conflict of the laws and jurisdictions in matters of divorce and legal separation," and "the guardianship of minors" and the Convention of July 17, 1905 "concerning the conflicts of laws relating to the effects of

however doomed to failure.[45] By that time, it was no longer possible to bring the British or the Americans on board. Even in France, the waves of Southern and Eastern European immigration in the late nineteenth century had challenged the Liberal embrace of nationality, in favor of more territorial approaches.[46]

The conflict between nationality and domicile escalated in the interwar years. In the postwar period, nationality lost ground in some jurisdictions – and so did personalist approaches. Ironically, the modern connecting factor of *habitual residence*, first used in the Hague Conference on Private International Law to facilitate convergence between the nationality-minded Continentals and the domicile-minded Anglo-Americans, is farther away from nationality and personalism than domicile.[47]

4.2.3 Territorial Approaches: Actus *v.* Situs

The distinction between those territorialist rules/approaches concerned with the valid creation of legal acts and those concerned with the status of things is less talked about than the opposition between nationality and domicile.[48] This is understandable. Nationality and domicile were in direct competition where a choice had to be made between nationality and domicile as the relevant connecting factor for matters governed by personal law. Their coexistence would actually reduce legal certainty and

marriage on the rights and obligations of spouses in their personal relations and on the property of the spouses." On the "old" Conventions see e.g. M. Gutzwiller, "Das Internationalprivatrecht der Haager Konferenzen: Vergangenheit und Zukunft," *Annuaire suisse de droit international*, 2 (1945), 48–68.

45 In the long-run, making the nationality of the husband/father the deciding factor would make the Conventions run contrary to ideas about equality in the family.

46 The most emblematic may have been G. de Vareilles-Sommières, "Un Sedan juridique: Etude sur le droit des conflits successorales," *Revue de Lille* (n.s.), 5(13) (1902), 832–852.

47 See e.g. P. Stone, "The Concept of Habitual Residence in Private International Law," *Anglo-American Law Review*, 29 (2000), 342–367; M. Ní Shúilleabháin, *Cross-Border Divorce Law* (Oxford: Oxford University Press, 2010), 67–70; and T. Kruger, "Habitual Residence: The Factors that Courts Consider" in P. Beaumont et al. (eds.), *Cross-Border Litigation in Europe* (Oxford: Hart, 2017), 741–754.

48 See e.g. Loussouarn et al., *Droit international privé*, 107 ("Ces deux observations conduissent les doctrines de la territorialité à conclure que le commerce international doit s'adapter aux ordres juridiques avec lesquelles il entre en contact: là ou s'exerce son activité, il doit obéir au droit interne local"). Internal politics of the discipline constitute another reason for the lack of distinction: the most committed French territorialists of the classical period were nationalists. See ibid., 108–110 on Vareilles-Sommières and Niboyet.

especially uniformity of result and eventually gave rise to escape devices and even paradigm shifts. On the contrary, both kinds of territorialism could coexist. For example, a conflicts system could include both a rule to the effect that the validity of a contract will be governed by the law of the place where it has been concluded (*lex loci contractus*) and a rule stating that the acquisition of rights over immovables will be governed by the law of their place of situation (*lex rei sitae*).

These two territorialist conceptions – let us speak of an *actus territorialism* which brings the *locus actus* to the fore, and a *situs territorialism* revolving around the *lex rei sitae* – do nonetheless represent contrasting conceptions. Consider the example of the effects of a testamentary disposition, or of a contract disposing of rights over real property. Are we to follow an *actus*-centered rule, such as *locus regit actum*, or should we defend the prerogative of the *situs* to govern all matters of disposition of real property located in its territory? Ironically, a *lex actus* rule on testamentary succession would have an effect similar (namely, unity of succession) to a personalist rule, such as the applicability of *lex patriae* or *lex domicilii* (in fact, the act might likely have been concluded in the defunct's domicile).

The territorial dimension of the *lex loci actus* is most visible the more a conflicts system is expressly preoccupied with recognizing the foreign *actus*, once validly created. Let us consider for example two vocal proponents of actus territorialism. Joseph Story tends to put the conflict issue in terms of recognizing the effects of foreign acts; at the same time, these acts are *reified*.[49] Moreover, Story subjects both the formal and substantive validity of marriages to the *lex actus*.[50] Huber does likewise with the *lex actus* for all sorts of acts.[51]

The choice between *actus* and *situs* territorialism will depend on both material realities and the concepts prevailing in the given time and place. In the modern world, the concept of *actus* has given way to a number of different legal regimes; but the subject matter covered by the *lex rei sitae* has also lost much of its significance.[52] But let us compare, for example, two imaginary preindustrial societies: in the former, commerce matters

[49] Story, *Commentaries*, treating the respective subject in chapters on "foreign divorces" (168–192) and "foreign contracts" (193–307).

[50] Ibid., 101ff.

[51] For example, Huber, *Praelectiones ad Pandectas*, 1.3.App.8 made an exception with regard to fraudulent marriages whereas Story did not.

[52] See Section 5.3.

little but land is a very important asset, whether for economic or social purposes; in the latter, land is a settled commodity, commerce is paramount and many of its citizens spend much of their time abroad. In so-called territorialist preclassical doctrine, we might compare Bertrand d'Argentré with Huber in this regard. We will see below that Huber has to balance two "territorialist" rules: a general rule of *locus regit actum*, which covers the formal and substantive validity of contracts, testaments, and marriages, and a special rule regarding rights to immovables.[53]

Both these antagonistic territorial approaches are likely to coexist in any system. It is nonetheless interesting to see how they play out. For example, a doctrinal system may emphasize or de-emphasize the existence of *things*: some authors begin their systems with an enumeration of "real" statutes or a discussion of rights over land; on the contrary, the *locus actus*-minded Huber plays down property as a substantive category.[54] Moreover, a system promoting the *lex actus* rule will contain a *lex situs* exception. This "real" exception can be expansive, as in those systems which deny universal succession and let succession rights be determined for each thing in accordance with the law of the place of situation. Or it can be limited: for example, Huber's exception covers only the "incidents impressed" upon real property by the *lex rei sitae*.[55]

4.2.3.1 Public Policy Territorialism

We could also discern another territorialist approach, concerned with enforcing the policy of the forum. This is a decidedly modern approach, although its roots can be found in the public-policy (*ordre public*) exceptions contained both in personalist and *actus* territorialist regimes.[56]

Whereas the other two territorialist approaches are compatible with the "universal" conflicts system, often aim at its creation and certainly allow for application of foreign law, this later approach seems to pay less regard to decisional harmony and to lead to the application of the forum's law. But this is still "territorialism," albeit of a different kind, in the sense of a doctrine for preventing the application of personal law or foreign law.

[53] Huber, *Praelectiones ad Pandectas*, 1.3.App.3 and 15.
[54] Ibid., 14–15. See Sections 13.3.4 and 14.2.3.
[55] Ibid., 14.
[56] See e.g. Art. 12 of the Preliminary Provisions to the Italian Civil Code 1865; Huber, *Praelectiones ad Pandectas*, 1.3.App.8 and 13.

4.3 Unilateralism in the Conflict of Laws

Preclassical conflicts jurists are commonly presented as having had a "unilateralist" disposition.[57] There are of course those in the literature who remain more sanguine about the nature of preclassical unilateralism,[58] but one cannot examine conflict of laws in the Middle Ages and the Early Modern period without a consideration of how pervasive and conscious preclassical unilateralism truly was. Which brings us to the question: what do we mean by "unilateral" and "unilateralism" as it applies to preclassical doctrine?

The term *unilateralism* is common currency in private international law. A working definition would be to call unilateral those rules that only determine the scope of application of the forum's own law. This is contrasted to the *multilateral* or *bilateral* rules, which designate the applicable law in abstract terms regardless of whether it leads to the application of forum law or of another legal system.

The first statutory rules on conflicts, such as Article 3(1) of the Napoleonic Code on the status and capacity of French nationals, were – technically – unilateral. Invocations first of reciprocity and then of analogy were used to bilateralize the rule with regard to the status and capacity of foreigners in France. Scholarly defenses of unilateralism as a doctrinal approach to the conflict of laws only appeared at the very end of the nineteenth century.[59] These views received a significant boost by the adoption of unilateral conflicts rules in the imperial German codification of civil law (1896/1900).[60] Unilateralists have since remained in

[57] Among the doctrinal mainstream, see e.g. Symeonides et al., *Conflict of Laws*, 8–9. See also J. A. Pontier, *Conflictenrecht: grondslagen, methoden, beginselen en belangen* (Nijmegen: Ars Aequi Libri, 1997), 56–58; for an exception see the excursus of Mayer, *Droit international privé*, 88–89. Among scholars sympathetic to unilateralist doctrines see the classic study of P. Gothot, "Le renouveau de la tendance unilatéraliste en droit international privé," *Revue critique*, 60 (1971), 1–36, 209–243, 415–450, esp. 11–23 ("L'unilateralisme dans la tradition statutaire") to which references are made in this book.

[58] For example, Audit, *Droit international privé*, 88 argues that "unilateralism was spontaneously practiced for centuries," but dates the creation of the term at the end of the nineteenth century).

[59] See B. Audit, "Le droit international privé en quête d'universalité (cours général)," *Recueil des cours*, 305 (2001), 9–487, 231–266 who discusses "modern unilateralism" after his expositions of territorialism/personalism and localization.

[60] See M. Behn, *Die Entstehungsgeschichte der einseitigen Kollisionsnormen des EGBGB* (Frankfurt: Haag & Herchen, 1980). According to K. Siehr, "The Hague Conference on Private International Law and Germany," *Netherlands International Law Review*, 40 (1993), 129–142, 131 the unilateralism of the EGBGB, which overturned more advanced

the minority, in European conflict of laws, despite the failure of the turn-of-century internationalist projects for a uniform conflicts system. There has been an apparent shift in the theoretical foundations of unilateralist doctrine: the early unilateralists of the interwar period drew on a "public-law" approach grounded on the respect of sovereignty (the presumed "will" of the forum or the foreign country to have its law applied or not).[61] Postwar authors have tended to adopt a "private-law" approach emphasizing the need for continuity in the legal life of individuals.[62]

Unilateralism seems to have found more resonance across the Atlantic, among proponents of the US conflicts revolution, and especially among those sponsoring governmental-interest analysis.[63] It is therefore worth noting that in the American conflicts discourse the term *unilateralism* has been used more by those who oppose "unilateral" approaches.[64] On the contrary, the term is regularly used in US discussions of international law and policy. Such discussions in their turn are influencing American private international law.

In order to understand what meaning might "unilateralism" have when examining preclassical doctrine, we must first consider what unilateralism stands for today: an attribute of individual, substantive legal rules, a consistent conflicts method, or a "governance" ideology.[65]

earlier drafts, is due to the pressure of the German Foreign Office, which was at the time engaged in the negotiations of the Hague Conferences on Private International Law and "qualified private international law as being part of public international law." Siehr refers to the complete records of legislative history published by O. Hartwieg and F. Korkisch, *Die geheimen Materialen zur Kodifikation des deutschen Internationalen Privatrechts 1881–1896* (Tübingen: Mohr Siebeck, 1973).

61 See J. Schnell, "Über die Zuständingkeit zum Erlass von gesetzlichen Vorschriften über die räumliche Herrschaft der Rechtnormen," *Niemeyers Zeitschrift*, 5 (1895), 337–343; A. Niedner, *Das Einführungsgesetz vom 18 August 1896*, 2nd ed. (Berlin: Heymann, 1901), esp. 13ff.

62 Ronaldo Quadri is commonly regarded as the father of this new unilateralism. See R. Quadri, *Lezioni di Diritto internazionale privato*, 4th ed (Napoli, 1961), esp. 177ff. His theories became widely known and further expounded upon by Gothot, "Renouveau." See also De Nova, "Introduction," 570–590.

63 See Audit, "Cours général," 244ff.

64 See, subtly, Symeonides et al., *Conflict of Laws*, 8–9, 11 (but not invoking the concept in the main doctrinal discussion). In contrast, the multilateralism-unilateralism distinction is central to Shreve, *Anthology*, with the terms defined in Chapter 1.

65 As stated, the purpose of this section is to establish common terms of reference with the reader, who is referred for more to two sweeping explorations of the underlying theories, stakes, and nuances of modern uniliteralism: D. Boden, L'ordre public: limite et condition de la tolérance: Recherches sur le pluralisme juridique. Unpublished Doctoral Thesis,

4.3.1 *Doctrinal Unilateralism: The Choice-of-Law Process*

We shall begin with the mainstream conflicts discussion about unilateralism and *multilateralism* or *bilateralism*: the term *multilateral* carries more theoretical weight, and is used in most countries;[66] but *bilateral* is also an established term, especially in French-speaking private international law, in speaking of choice-of-law rules, in view of the fact that only one foreign law is selected.[67] The two sibling terms (bilateral–multilateral) also symbolize in that sense that the debate takes place in two levels: first, in opposing the unilateral choice-of-law rule to a bilateral one; second, in presenting a unilateralist method as something different than the "jurisdiction-delimiting," "multilateral" method of the "choice-of-law rule."

The "unilateral" method would take as the starting point of a conflicts problem the "law," determining its field of application, whereas the multilateral/bilateral would take as the starting point of a conflicts problem the "type of situation," and try to link it to one law or the other. We can envision "law" as the individual legal rule claiming applicability in this case, or as a comprehensive, gapless legal system. But what does this really mean?

4.3.1.1 Technically Unilateral Rules

One thing that easily becomes clear is that the wording of conflicts rules is not by itself enough to make them unilateral. Many of the early legislative rules on conflicts issues, notably the occasional provision in the Code Napoléon (especially Art. 3), but most famously most conflicts provisions in the Introductory Law to the 1896/1900 German Civil Code (EGBGB) were technically unilateral, in the sense that they were explicit only in prescribing the jurisdiction of French and German law, respectively.[68] But they were very soon *bilateralized* in practice and theory:

Université de Paris I, Paris (2002); G. P. Romano, *L'unilateralismo nel diritto internazionale privato moderno* (Zurich: Schulthess, 2014).

66 Especially Germany. Greek doctrine, for example, seems to have moved from "multilateral" (polymerēs) to "bilateral" (dimerēs) under the influence of French private international law.

67 See Audit, *Droit international privé*, 82–83.

68 Gothot, "Renouveau," 1 n. 1 distinguishes between technically "rigorously" unilateral rules of §§ 7.3, 8, 12, 13.2, 13.3, 14, 15, 16, 17.3, 18, 19, 20, 22, and 24 EBGB, the bilateral rules of §§ 7.1. 11, 17.1, 17.2, 21, and 23 EBGBG and "incompletely bilateral" rules such as § 25 EBGB (applying the *lex patriae* to the succession of a foreigner domiciled in Germany at the time of death).

whereas, for example, § 14.1 EGBGB prescribed that the legal relations of German spouses will continue to be governed by German law if the spouses are domiciled abroad, doctrine and courts came to read it as generally prescribing the application of the law of the spouses' common nationality.[69] This pattern of biliteralizing unilateral statutory conflicts rules has remained strong to this day.[70]

4.3.1.2 Determining Who Determines the Scope of Foreign Law

One could argue in reverse: what unilateral and bilateral conflicts rules have in common is that both delimit the legislative jurisdiction of the forum, and that, *ceteris paribus*, there is no *inherent* difference in the way they delimit it. Where the difference lies, at least in principle, is in how the scope of the foreign law is being delimited. Twentieth-century unilateralists, whether arguing on the basis of State sovereignty or raising jurisprudential issues, have suggested that the scope of the foreign law should best be determined by the foreign legal system itself.

For example, Ruritanian law states that the marital relations of Ruritanian spouses living abroad will be subjected to Ruritanian law. This is by itself a technically unilateral rule, which may be bilateralized if we deduce from it a rule that marital relations will be governed by the law of the spouses' nationality. It will be truly doctrinally unilateral if, when it comes to foreigners living in Ruritania, we look to their own law in order to determine which law should apply to them. Thus, relations of Zubrowkan spouses living in Ruritania would be governed by Zubrowkan law if Zubrowka also has a similar rule; if, however, Zubrowka follows *lex domicilii* rather than *lex patriae*, Ruritanian law should apply by operation of the *renvoi* doctrine. In such a case, the Ruritanian substantive law applies by virtue of Zubrowkan law. If, however, Ruritanian law stated that it should apply to married couples

69 See OLG Frankfurt, 7 August 1901 (and LG Frankfurt 29 October 1901), *Niemeyers Zeitschrift für internationals Recht*, 12 (1902): 611–614 is often cited by international authors (see e.g. Gothot, "Le renouveau," 2). See also Kammergericht, VII. C.S. 2.2.1901, *Niemeyers Zeitschrift für internationals Recht*, 11 (1901), 95–96; OLG Dresden, 10.5.1902, *Niemeyers Zeitschrift für internationals Recht*, 12 (1902), 466–468. See also Behn, *Enstehungsgeschichte*, who discusses the case law of the Hanseatisches Oberlandesgericht.

70 See for example the bilateralization by the courts of the Romanian conflicts rule on personal status and capacity as described by E. Jayme, "Codification," 41 with references to Romanian case law and doctrine. See e.g. Craiova First Instance Court, 10 November 1965, *Clunet*, 95 (1968), 417–419.

domiciled in Ruritania, that would have taken care of the Zubrowkan immigrants in Ruritania with no need of consulting Zubrowkan law, but we would need to look into Zubrowkan law for the Ruritanian couple living in Zubrowka (and again use renvoi to apply Ruritanian law if Zubrowka follows *lex patriae*).

The main benefit of such an approach is that it locates many "false conflicts," where one of the "conflicting" laws is discovered not to have any interest in its application. The main problem is that it leaves us open to the possibility of either two laws claiming application at the same time, or neither. Some of the problems may be addressed by the use of renvoi or modern approaches such as interest-analysis but it is not clear if a satisfactory solution can be provided in some among the commonest type of cases – that is, where both laws may have an "interest" in their application.

This problem also gives rise to two common perceptions about unilateralism, i.e. that it gives lower regard to the principle of legal certainty, and that it grants preference to the forum, since the law of the forum would have priority. On the other hand, a bilateral conflicts regime also creates similar problems, for example in the cases where the laws of different states characterize differently the legal relationship, or where their conflicts laws designate different foreign laws as applicable: these are the cases that inspired the twentieth-century unilateralist theories.

At this point a difference between Continental unilateralists and the US modern approaches must be noted. Both share the objective of reducing "false conflicts" and mistrust aprioristic bilateral rules, but Continental unilateralism tends to take the perspective of the forum as its starting point while seeking to establish equality between the two laws in their analysis and to bind the forum judge in a formal process of determination of the applicable law: the substantive law of the forum will most likely apply in the case of a "real" conflict but that would probably happen in most cases and it allows some certainty of result. Many American approaches start from a neutral point of view, endeavoring to guide the judge in a solution that is most appropriate in the specific case; but as more considerations are added to the equation, forum preference is strengthened.

4.3.1.3 Doctrinal Unilateralism as "International Governance"

Perhaps the answer lies somewhere else. Symeon Symeonides points to the right direction when he refers to a "system of a priori rules" as a defining characteristic of the bilateral method.[71] "Apriorism" had indeed been perceived, early on, as a defining characteristic of early classical conflict of laws. On the other hand, it is conceivable to have antiformalist "multilateral" systems and *a priori* "unilateral" approaches.

Those writers who suggest that the multilateral approach is "internationalist" are also pointing to the right direction, but not, as they suggest, because the multilateral approach treats equally the laws of forum and those of foreign states: this is of course a formal equality, and in practice the foreign state may have been better off with a "unilateralist" application of its own law.

What both these suggestions hint at is the "international governance" aspect of classical conflict of laws. It could be argued that a workable international conflicts system could only be constructed on the basis of the multilateral method. But maybe a global "unilateralist" system is possible. Maybe we should draw a distinction between, on the one hand, those unilateralist systems where the goal of conflicts uniformity is subordinated to the forum's other objectives (*aggressive unilateralism*), and, on the other hand, those which their authors try to make workable in a multilateral or global scale (*principled unilateralism*).

4.3.1.4 Jurisprudential Aspects of Doctrinal Unilateralism

Another perspective draws the line not between bilateral and unilateral conflicts rules, but rather between, on the one side, conflicts rules as a distinct, formal category of legal rules, and, on the other side, methods/ "rules" about interpreting formal legal rules. Conflicts norms by definition are about determing the scope of substantive norms. Living in the bilateral paradigm, we tend to view the choice-of-law process as a creation of "second-order" norms that determine the scope of these substantive norms. But a truly unilateral approach views the "first order" norms as capable of delimiting their own scope: hence the "second order" norms of truly unilateral approaches form part of the "first order" ones: in our first Ruritanian example, the marital relations of Ruritanian spouses living abroad will be subjected to Ruritanian law because that

[71] Symeonides et al., *Conflict of Laws*, 8: "The bilateral method postulates a system of a priori choice-of-law rules that designate the cases that fall within the scope of domestic and foreign law, respectively. In contrast, Bartolus' unilateral method approaches the matter from the other end. It focuses on the conflicting domestic and foreign laws themselves and tries to determine whether the case at hand falls within the intended scope of the one or the other law."

was the intention of the Ruritanian marital-relations legislation, or the Ruritanian governmental interest, or the interest of the Ruritanian couple themselves as Ruritanians, whereas the same applies to Zubrowkan spouses living in Ruritania, whether Zubrowkan or Ruritanian law applies to them by virtue of Zubrowka's own conflicts norm (which it does not not matter if it is unilateral or bilateral).

On the contrary, the rules created by a bilateral/multilateral approach tend to exist independently (autonomously?) from the "first-order" rules or system: the marital relations of Zubrowkan spouses located in Ruritania will be subjected to Zubrowkan law because Ruritania (and probably, but not necessarily, Zubrowka) thinks it is a good idea for spouses to be subjected to the law of their common nationality. This may be so for a variety of reasons – to maintain certainty, to avoid migration for evasion purposes, to maintain an emotional or practical link with the *patria*, in expectation of reciprocity or in the hope of helping establish *lex patriae* as an international rule in such matters.

4.3.2 Political Unilateralism: Extraterritorial Effects of Regulation

For the general public, unilateralism is strongly associated with international relations: an individual State trying to have it all *its* way – whether it is the actions unilateral actions, or in terms of interests weighted in. The concept of *unilateralism* – as well as its conceptual opposite, *multilateralism* – was carried over from international relations to public international law and international economic law.[72]

In modern private international law, the international-relations concept of unilateralism has influenced those areas in the periphery of traditional conflicts subject matter – notably regulatory law. In the fields of market regulation, data protection, or sanctions imposed to foreign individuals and companies, the question is to determine the extraterritorial effects of governmental action.

This is especially the case in the United States, where such issues arise under federal statutory law. Federal statutory law is to be applied and interpreted by US federal courts, which are unable under *Erie* to create "common law," including conflicts rules. The statute in question becomes

[72] See also e.g. the proceedings of a symposium on "Unilateralism in International Law: A United States – European Perspective," *European Journal of International Law*, 11 (2000), 1ff, 249ff; and, more recently, D. Wood "Extraterritorial Enforcement of Regulatory Laws," *Recueil des cours*, 401 (2019), 9–126.

thus the ground to decide the issue of extraterritoriality: discussions are more about statutory interpretation, with conflicts and multistate policy, especially comity, in cameo appearances.[73] In fact, the approaches on the doctrinal table range from strict territoriality to extreme extraterritoriality, and if we try to lay them across such a continuum,[74] we will observe at the territoriality extreme "conflicts-like" approaches,[75] on the – fertile – middle approaches which essentially adopt an expansive jurisdictional claim but seek to limit it through some "soft" invocation of comity and pragmatic considerations, and at the extraterritorial extreme an outspoken unilateralism that would apply US law whenever "the policies underlying the law would be advanced."[76] Unilateralism tends to be associated, at least more than multilateralism, with the pursuance of substantive interests or policies, but extreme unilateralism is also explicit in its hope of using this overextended jurisdiction to force foreign countries or enterprises into an agreement.[77]

Here we may note a second reason for the strength of unilateralist theories in the US: whereas conflicts lawyers have been unable to extend their discourse – which is already much more friendly to unilateralism than the Continental conflicts discourse – to these new areas, international-relations theory can claim both an indirect and, more recently, a direct influence on conflicts lawyers. Hence even jurists and statesmen ideologically committed to multilateralism view the unilateral exercise of jurisdiction as a weapon to push their vision; they are also likely to mask their "multilateral" approach in "unilateral" verbiage, in order to appeal to reluctant domestic constituencies.

[73] See e.g. *Hartford Fire Insurance Co.* v. *California*, 509 US 764 (1993), 798 (Justice Souter, writing for the majority finds comity does not intervene in a case where conduct abroad violating US antitrust law was lawful in the place of conduct).

[74] See R. J. Weintraub, *International Litigation and Arbitration*, 3rd ed (Durham, N.C.: Carolina Academic Press, 2001), esp. 346–347.

[75] See *American Banana Co.* v. *United Fruit Co.*, 213 US 347 (1909), where Holmes, J. expounds a strict territoriality doctrine in consonance with the conflicts doctrine dominant at the time (in fact Holmes seems to be invoking a vested-rights theory). A modern example is G. Born, "A Reappraisal of the Extraterritorial Reach of US Law," *Law & Policy in International Businesss*, 24 (1992), 1–100, who proposes the "most significant relationship" of the Second Conflicts Restatement (88–90).

[76] See W. S. Dodge, "Extraterritoriality and Conflict-of-Laws Theory: An Argument for Judicial Unilateralism," *Harvard International Law Journal*, 39 (1988), 101–169. Phrase taken from Weintraub, *International Litigation*, 346.

[77] See Dodge, "Extraterritoriality," 152–168 and 169 (such an approach "corrects for failures in the legislative process that lead to underregulation in areas like antitrust and . . . helps promote international cooperation").

We will call this breed of unilateralism, which is based on the systematic and expansive pursuance of substantive policies and interests of the forum, and which embraces the possibility of – or explicitly aims at – affecting the behavior of the foreign legislator or adjudicator, *political unilateralism*. This political unilateralism is to be opposed to the *doctrinal* unilateralism encountered in classical/modern conflicts doctrine in the strict sense of the term, but it affects the understanding of at least some conflicts lawyers and cannot be left out of our picture. It would also help to distinguish this political unilateralism from two peripheral visions of unilateralism explicitly addressed in the traditional conflict of laws discourse.

4.3.3 Limited Unilateralism

Modern conflict of laws has seen the proliferation of national rules that apply to international as well as domestic relations in preemption of the applicable conflicts rule.[78] Such rules have been called in turn *lois de police*,[79] "laws of necessary application," "laws of immediate application," "mandatory rules,"[80] or "overriding mandatory provisions."[81]

This is a different sort of unilateralism than the American-bred political unilateralism, which has the tendency to develop stand-alone legal regimes. On the contrary, the *lois de police* – whether they constitute single rules or form part of a comprehensive regulatory framework – are viewed as individualized exceptions to a general system. It is indicative that the *lois de police* phenomenon has been characterized, aptly, as *limited unilateralism*.[82] The application of foreign *lois de police*, a trend promoted in the European Union instruments and representing a "bilateralization" of sorts, may further illustrate how far the two conceptions diverge.[83]

[78] See P. Francescakis, "Quelques précisions sur les lois d'application immédiate et sur leurs rapports avec les règles de conflit de lois," *Revue critique*, 55 (1966), 1–18

[79] Following Art. 3(3) of the French Civil Code.

[80] 1980 Rome Convention, Art. 7

[81] Regulation 864/2007, Art. 16; Regulation 593/2008, Art. 9.

[82] The term is used by Loussouarn at the conclusion of his Hague General Course: see Y. Loussouarn, "Cours general de droit international privé," *Recueil des cours*, 139 (1973), 269–385, 380–383; See also Loussouarn et al., *Droit international privé*, 116–119.

[83] See 1980 Rome Convention, Art. 7(1); Regulation 593/2008, Art. 9(3). On the original provision of the Rome Convention see e.g. P. Mayer, "Les lois de police étrangères," *Clunet*, 108 (1981), 277–345; C. Tsouca, "Les règles étrangères d'application immédiate et

4.3.4 *Absolute Unilateralism*

Political unilateralism should also be distinguished from the so-called absolute unilateralism, where the forum will apply its law whenever it has jurisdiction, and dismiss the case if it does not have jurisdiction.[84]

The difference here lies in sensibility. The forum is more preoccupied with shielding itself from the rest of the world, whereas a politically unilateralist forum is more concerned with its interests, citizens and convenience not being slighted by the rest of the world. Jurisdiction in a regime of absolute unilateralism is more likely to be delineated on formal grounds (e.g. citizenship, territorial connection) than to be based on the explicit pursuance of substantive policies. It is not clear, of course, to what extent such a regime ever existed, even though the ancient world and the central royal courts of Medieval England are supposed to provide us with examples.[85] Another question is if such a model could survive for long: chances are that the judicial authorities will allow an equitable extension of their jurisdiction in cases where no adequate remedy would exist, and this could come to mean looking into other *fora* and their potential to grant remedies. Furthermore, absolute unilateralism would be inevitably undermined by the eventual recognition of rights acquired abroad, through the enforcement of judgments and contracts.

4.4 Universalism and Particularism

The distinction between the *universalist* aspiration toward a uniform conflict of laws system and the *particularist* assertion of national interests and sensitivities through a distinct national conflicts system was conceptualized a little over a century ago and remains a central theme in especially French-language historical narratives.[86]

Private international lawyers of especially the second half of the nineteenth century had aimed at an international system of conflict of laws rules: in fact, as this work argues, the *discipline* of *private*

leur impact sur la nature méthodologique du droit international privé,"*Koinodikaion*, 3 (1997), 227–269.

[84] Loussouarn, "Cours general," 376.

[85] See e.g. Sack, "Conflict of Laws," esp. 344ff. Sack's story (and generally narratives on the birth of English conflict of laws) are examined in detail in Hatzimihail, "Historiography."

[86] See e.g. Loussouarn et al., *Droit international privé*, 86ff; G. van Hecke, "Universalisme et particularisme des règles de conflit au XXe siècle" in *Mélanges en l'honneur de Jean Dabin*, vol. 2 (Brussels: Bruylant, 1963), 939–954, 941ff.

international law was created in the effort to achieve this goal. By the end of the nineteenth century, members of a new generation challenged the jurisprudential premises of that vision, suggesting that the intrinsic differences in the private-law regimes of different countries could not allow for a uniform system in these terms. Such challenges were not immune to the agendas of domestic and international politics – and the debates between scholars were often vicious with personal undertones. The opposition of "particularists" to "universalists" has been linked – and sometimes confused – with other conceptual oppositions dividing conflicts doctrine, such as the debates over unilateral as opposed to bilateral rules and between personalist as opposed to territorialist solutions.[87]

By the interwar period, the reconstructive approaches constituting we have been calling in this work "mature classical conflict of laws" sought to make the best of a bad situation. At the time, a universal system of conflict of laws appeared improbable to materialize in the immediate future, but small steps to that direction could be taken: subject- and area-specific international agreements; the use of the very devices – such as *renvoi* – initially brought into the picture by the particularists; and the emergence of the so-called comparative conflict of laws.[88] The school of comparative conflict of laws, also known as the "third school,"[89] sought not only to help the different conflicts regimes of different countries converge, but also to liberate private international law from the shackles of domestic private-law regimes.

The story opposing universalism to particularism is however mostly told in technical terms by the mainstream doctrinal literature. The discussion about the role of private law is not emphasized, although most people perceive its existence and take sides, usually implicitly. A universal conflict of laws system, and perhaps universal private-law regulation if practicable, still remains an objective for contemporary private international lawyers, who however have in the meanwhile to make the best of what they have.

In more recent times, the old particularists have even been attacked on a personal level, for nationalism or prejudices. A more interesting but less

[87] Loussouarn et al., *Droit international privé*, 107 ("l'histoire des doctrines révèle l'existence d'un lien constant entre ces deux tendances," namely particularism and territorialism).

[88] See e.g. Batiffol, *Aspects philosophiques*, 15ff; Rabel, Conflict of Laws, 1:28 and 49ff (advocating a "comparative method" for legal characterization).

[89] See K. Zweigert, "Die Dritte Schule Im Internationalen Privatrecht: Zur Neuren Wissenschaftsgeschichte Des Kollisionsrechts" in H.-P. Ipsen (ed.), *Festschrift für Leo Raape zu seinem Siebzigsten Geburtstag* (Hamburg, 1948), 35–52.

prevalent modern idea is the use of the terms universalism and particularism in order to illustrate the "fundamental antinomy" within private international law.[90]

4.5 Perspectives and Ideologies: Internationalism, Nationalism

Conceptualizing an opposition between a nationalist and an internationalist outlook in private international law has gained popularity in the past quarter century. Once again, these terms are employed diversely in the literature, and they project a variety of ideas. In some schemes, they identify an opposition in *doctrinal* terms. In others, the distinction is given a *formal*, source-based, character. In yet others, the emphasis is on the *ideological* or *psychological* dimension.

The *doctrinal* conception of the opposition tends to put its emphasis on the doctrinal foundation of private international law and/or the principle of State equality. "Nationalist" private international lawyers "attach more importance to the 'national interest' than to the ideal vision of a world where one's own State has to be treated on a strict footing of equality with the others."[91] Or they grant preference to one's own law over foreign laws, consenting with unease to the application of those latter.[92] Internationalism has been likewise defined in objective or subjective terms: in the former case, internationalists emphasize the "international obligation" of the State under general (customary) international law to apply foreign substantive law, whereas in the latter case, emphasis is placed in an "open," "non-parochial" attitude toward the application of foreign law in situations with a foreign element.[93] Subjective and objective criteria have been combined in a more expansive definition of doctrinal

[90] Audit, *Droit international privé*, 1ff.

[91] Mayer, *Droit international privé*, 50

[92] This definition also comes from Mayer, in previous editions of his textbook. See P. Mayer, *Droit international privé*, 4th ed (Paris: Montchretien, 1991), 58.

[93] F. Rigaux, "Rapport de synthèse: Pour une relecture de François Laurent en 1987" in Erauw et al., *Liber memorialis François Laurent*, 663–668 (668: "Ainsi conçu, l'internationalisme a deux faces: l'une est la conviction que l'adoption de solutions de conflit de lois nationales, impliquant que la règle de droit matériel interne doive parfois céder la place à une disposition étrangère, est la mise en œuvre d'une obligation internationale de l'Etat, qu'elle trouve son fondement dans le droit international général. L'autre face de l'ésprit internationaliste consiste à adopter en présence de situations ayant une attache avec un pays étranger une attitude ouverte, qualifiée de *non-parochial* dans la contribution d'un juriste de common law").

internationalism.[94] Again, others have used the nationalism–internationalism opposition in extensive doctrinal projects – by taking the political bite out of the definitions, on the one hand, while holding the opposing concepts as the spectrum in which the entire system can be judged.[95]

The *formalist* conception has focused on the "nationality" and "internationality" of the *sources* of conflicts law.[96] National conflicts rules "really were anything but international in nature; they were purely national, both in character and outlook, although they of course dealt with cases containing foreign components."[97] This purely national perspective is being replaced, "gradually, though not completely ... by an increasingly international orientation," hence turning "European conflicts rules ... from being purely national and mostly unilateral to being truly international and overwhelmingly multilateral."[98]

The formalist approach here fires at the "national" conflicts rules of the nineteenth century, most of which were drafted with a view to the unification of the conflict of laws. In its biased hostility to the national codifications of the nineteenth century, it constitutes the meeting point for two different schools of thought: the *antipositivists*, who long for a learned "common law," and the *neopositivists* seeking to re-legislate, on the international level or, increasingly, at the European Union level. In its formalism, this approach could be viewed as very different from the ideological approach. But the purism of an approach where a national source of law cannot be internationalist reveals its underlying ideology.

The *ideological* opposition is the one more closely related to the common-language use of the terms nationalist and internationalist and the psychological definition of nationalism. It also corresponds to recent doctrinal as well as political trends, both long-term and relating to debates "of the moment." The French legal historian Jean-Louis Halpérin thus presents the history of nineteenth- and twentieth-century private international lawyers caught "between community of law and legal nationalism."[99]

94 Ibid.

95 J. Meeusen, *Nationalisme en Internationalisme in het Internationaal Privaatrecht: Analyse van het Belgische Conflictenrecht* (Antwerp/Groningen: Intersentia, 1997).

96 Reimann, *Conflict of Laws*, 57–62 and esp. 57–58.

97 Ibid., 58.

98 Ibid.

99 Halpérin, *Nationalisme juridique*.

Work based on the ideological use of the terms has contributed to the history of ideas and to political discussion. But it has also served as a reminder, that, when the question arises of which one grand scheme could best capture the spirit of private international law debates in as large a scope as possible, terms such as nationalist and internationalist may not be the most effective. This is partly because terms such as "nationalist" and even "particularist" often carry a pejorative load, but especially because, even though the terms may account for twentieth-century Continental European private international law, they are not necessarily the best fit for the rest of the world and the rest of history.[100] They are nonetheless quite useful in showcasing both a real problem and a real conviction about that problem's existence.

4.6 Conflict of Laws as a "Conflict of Sovereignties"

Beginning in the late nineteenth century, a new generation of French academics identified the primary function of private international law in terms of arbitrating a conflict between state sovereignties.[101] The understanding of conflict of laws as a conflict of sovereignties (*conflit de*

[100] See in this regard Hatzimihail, "Conceptual Battlefield," 61–62, pointing to postwar American conflict of laws. In the pursuance of substantive policies and empowerment of the *forum*, US doctrine has come closer than any other conflicts discourse to fitting the ideal types projected by both terms, although the very "top hats" that have shaped it – located in "national" law schools, "forumless" in a way many cosmopolitan Europeans could never be, and for the most part convinced of the universal applicability of their theories – could be accused of neither particularism nor nationalism in the conventional sense (insofar at least as intrastate disputes are concerned). In theories such as Ehrenzweig's "proper law in a proper forum" or Brainerd Currie's opting for the *lex fori* in any "real conflict" in the choice of law in order to satisfy the – perceived – intentions of the forum legislature, there is no *substantive* bias against foreign law, only a certain appraisal of the practicalities of adjudication and/or a certain vision of the institutional division of legal labor within a state. Albert Ehrenzweig was much less a "nationalist" or a "patriot" in the general sense of the words than most members of the School of International Law. In their turn, these latter, who are also being sniped in our days alongside their nationalist detractors, definitely displayed doctrinal internationalism, which, interestingly enough, flowed through their adherence to the "principle of nationalities" as foundation of the world order.

[101] See notably E. Bartin, "Les conflits entre dispositions législatives de droit international privé: Théorie du renvoi," *Revue du droit international privé et de legislation compare*, 30 (1898), 129–187, 272–320, including ibid., 272–273: "Il est devenu banal de dire que le conflit de lois se ramène à un conflit de souverainetés. Depuis la démonstration décisive et très simple qu'on en a récemment donné [citing Pillet], cette assertion n'est plus contestée par personne."

souverainetés) was especially influential among French private international lawyers in the first half of the twentieth century.[102] It presented, in effect, the *conflict between a personal and a territorial conception of state sovereignty* as the fundamental problem for private international law.[103] The conflict came into focus by the mid-to late nineteenth century, when the emerging personalism of the school of international law clashed with entenched territorialism.[104]

This image of conflict of laws as a conflict of sovereignties lost its appeal in the postwar era. Niboyet's territorialism was dethroned by more internationalist reconstructive approaches, which placed more emphasis to comparative reasoning and the private-law dimension of conflicts rules. *Coordination* is the new key word.[105] Interestingly, the notion of a conflict of sovereignties remained in use. It now came to stand for the very image of a *world* of sovereign entities (*souverainetés*), in which the mission of the conflict of laws would be to allocate jurisdiction among them. In earlier times, this approach would have been considered as too broad or self-evident to have any bite.[106] At present, however, such a distinction aims at opposing a sovereignty-minded conception of the conflict of laws to a nonsovereignty minded one: namely, to the conception of conflict of laws as a conflict of interests. The purpose of this new imagery was not to challenge the idea of a states-system, but to move private international law away from international governance and into private-law jurisprudence.

Let us consider in this regard two definitions of the concept of a conflict of interests given by the French professor Pierre Mayer. In a theoretical essay, Mayer opposed to the conception of conflict of laws as a

[102] Writing in 1949 on the subject, Bonnichon, "Conflit des souverainetés," 615 singles out Arminjon, Lepaulle and Wigny as members of the minority who refuse to acknowledge the role of the idea of sovereignty "in the science of conflicts of laws" – and accuses them of a "summary negation."

[103] See e.g. H. Donnedieu de Vabres, *L'évolution de la jurisprudence française en matière de conflit des lois depuis le début du XXe siècle* (Paris: Recueil Sirey, 1938), 685 ("la solution de ces problèmes a-t-elle varié avec la notion de la souverainété elle-même").

[104] Thus Bonichon, "Conflit de souverainetés," 616. See a recent history of the notion in Banu, *Nineteenth-Century Perspectives*, 41ff.

[105] See e.g. Audit, *Droit international privé*, 74: "le conflit de lois a cessé d'être abordé en termes de délimitation des souverainetés et l'est davantage comme la recherche d'une coordination des ordres juridiques."

[106] Bonichon, "Conflit de souverainetés," 32: "Qu'on entende par souveraineté le simple domaine de la compétence ou l'attribut commun aux législateurs en présence, la notion s'avère dans les deux cas non pas fausse, mais stérile."

"conflict of sovereignties" the conception of conflict of laws as a "logically necessary choice of the applicable law to a relation between private persons."[107] Such a "conflict of interests" appeared in the form of a matrix, with state and private interests on the one hand and the consideration or not of the content of substantive rules on the other.[108]

In his treatise, however, Meyer adopted a narrower definition: "conflict of interests" now refered only to private interests – essentially, to private-law interests.[109] Once defined in so narrow terms, the opposition between conflict of sovereignties and conflict of interests becomes an opposition between "public-law" (*publicistes*) and "private-law" (*privatistes*) conceptions of the conflict of laws. This scheme could be seen as premised on a rather narrow conception of the theory and policies of private law, while also entailing a danger of understanding private international law as insisting on the conflict between sovereignties.

4.6.1 *The "Conflict of Sovereignties" in Historical Narratives*

All these perspectives have been translated in historical terms. For André Bonichon, who espoused the narrow definition of the "conflict of sovereignties" as a conflict between opposing conceptions of sovereignty, conflicts doctrine had preceded the idea of sovereignty – in fact, the idea of grounding conflict of laws on conceptions of sovereignty had been considered and rejected in the past.[110] He thus distinguished three potential founding principles of conflicts systems: the *principe fonctionnel*, oriented toward "social justice and the necessity of legal commerce," which he ascribes to the Italian school, the *principe essentiel*, oriented to the nature of the legal relations themselves, which he associates with the "statutists" (i.e. the French school) and Savigny, and the *principe formel* which is oriented toward the "formal aspect" of the rules and their imperative nature as they emanate from a legislator.[111] According to Bonnichon, even though these principles are not mutually exclusive, until his time they had not been taken into simultaneous consideration.

107 Mayer, "Le mouvement des idées dans le droit des conflits de lois," *Droits* 1985/2, 129ff.

108 Ibid., 129ff.

109 See Mayer, *Droit international privé*, 46–47 (modern conception "essentiellement privatiste:" 47).

110 See Bonnichon, "Conflit de souverainetés," esp. 620–622, 629.

111 Ibid., 618–619. See also discussion in 620ff.

The result was a "narrowness of vision" regarding sovereigny which moved from the one extreme to the other.[112]

In his turn, Pierre Mayer presented distinct narratives for each of his varying definitions of the conflict. In his short essay opposing an approach focused on sovereignty to an approach focused on interests, Mayer presented as examples of the "thesis assimilating the conflict of laws to a conflict of sovereignties" the universalist and particularist theories of the tun-of-century. As to the opposing conception, Mayer presented it via references to twentieth-century writings (with the addition of the Medieval writer Aldricus, reputed ancestor of the better-law approach).[113] Compared to Mayer's other effort, the emphasis is here less on an historical narrative; but his framework has similarities with the story of the evolution from *classical* to *modern* conflict of laws.

In his treatise, however, Mayer presents the opposition he describes as a story of *transition*, or a *shift of paradigms*, from the public-law "conflict of sovereignties" to the private-law "conflict of interests."[114] The former reigned supreme both in the preclassical period and the nineteenth century and continued well into the early twentieth century.[115] The latter paradigm was launched by Savigny but became dominant well after his time.[116]

4.6.2 *A Critique*

The conceptual opposition between "conflict of sovereignties" and "conflict of interests" throws some light on the dual, normative function of private international law at the level of relations between states and the

[112] Ibid., 619 ("L'histoire de droit international privé serait bien plutôt l'histoire des apparitions et des éclipses de ces trois aspects du problème, de ces trois principes de solution") and 620.

[113] See Mayer, "Le mouvement des idées," 131ff. On Aldricus see Section 3.4.3.

[114] See e.g. Mayer, *Droit international privé*, 46–47.

[115] Ibid., 46: "Non seulement la doctrine, mais les législateurs et la jurisprudence, avaient jusqu'au XVIIIe siècle conçu le conflit de lois et le conflit de juridictions comme des conflits des souverainetés. La soumission des personnes aux lois et aux juridictions d'une autorité politique est une manifestation du *pouvoir* de celle-ci. La même position est encore dominante durant tout le XIXe siècle et au début du XXe siecle. Qu'ils soient universalistes ou particularistes, internationalistes ou nationalistes, personnalistes ou territorialistes, c'est à partir d'une position commune sur ce point, position ressentie d'ailleurs comme évidente, que les auteurs se séparent."

[116] Ibid., 47 (Savigny as "une voix discordante . . . Savigny a fait jaillir la lumière de la vérité au sein d'une quasi-obscurité").

level of relations between individuals. If used properly – namely as a matrix of opposing tasks and interests – it could provide a fruitful combination of two other oppositions: on the one hand, the contrast between international/global and national/local; on the other hand, the contrast between the "domestic" jurisprudential modes of public law and private law. Such a scheme could also reckon with the normative or instrumental role of private international law, and the choices it has to make regarding both international and private-law governance.

Unfortunately, this conceptual pair has not fulfilled its potential. The conflict of sovereignties discourse has traditionally taken its constituent parts too seriously, forgetting they in fact represent ideal types. As a result, the dividing line has often been drawn too rigidly. We are told we have to make a choice between the one and the other; too often, we are told that the choice has already been made.

For example, both personalist and territorialist regimes appear to take the horizontal, State sovereignty structure as their basis, although they involve different conceptions of what really makes a State exercise jurisdiction: is it control over its territory, or the allegiance of its people?

At the same time, personal and territorial arguments could be made outside a conflict-of-sovereignties discourse. Even invocations of public law could be grounded on the prosperous human rights discourse or on the forum's Constitution.[117]

The *patria* and its judges will probably want the *lex patriae* applied, partly because of national pride and partly because of a genuine interest in the welfare of its citizens abroad, but they are bound to think of their prescriptive jurisdiction in some cases, while mistaking the forest for the trees in some others. But what about the host country applying the *lex patriae*? It may have a sovereignty-grounded interest in securing, through an indirect reciprocity, the application of its own law abroad. Or its sovereignty-minded regime may want to apply this foreign law out of courtesy. But it may well be that the forum's reason for applying the foreign personal law lies in its concerns as to the most effective administration of conflicts justice, or in

[117] See e.g., for such an analysis in the case of French law on foreign judgments, E. Guinchard, "La conception française de la territorialité de l'exécution en danger" (Mémoire D.E.A., Paris II, 1998) finding the foundation for French law's territorialist solution not in the general principles of public international law and "sovereignty," as commonly held, but in French constitutional law, which has consecrated territoriality of execution as a "fundamental principle recognized by the laws of the Republic."

the probability that the foreigners, whether migrants or tourists, have designed their daily life and social interactions on the basis of customs and legal convictions they have brought from home: the application of the local law would thus unsettle their arrangements and could even prove unfair in cases. Conversely, the forum may want to extent the application of its own law on the basis of efficiency in daily and commercial transnactions, by safeguarding the reasonable expectations of third persons,[118] or efficiency in the administration of justice, i.e. so that legal resources will not be wasted in translations and expert testimonies. On the battlefield of ideas, some intellectuals will view the application of foreign law as the most effective way to open up their legal system to foreign influences and an internationalist attitude; personal law could hence allow for the most extensive application of foreign law. On the contrary, other intellectuals will seek to subject the immigrants to local law in order to integrate them most effectively into the native population, or to avoid discrimination among or against the foreigners.

The reason for this narrowness of vision can only be that this "conflict of conflicts" was conceived in a specific context and inspired by the rhetoric of certain quarrels – territorialists against personalists, public lawyers against private lawyers, nationalists against internationalists, souverainistes against europhiles.[119] But once we look into the rhetoric (and beyond words, into the underlying considerations), we will then see that even writers who declare the conflict of laws to be effectively "a conflict of sovereignties" actually consider and engage in balancing of private-law "interests." This is even truer of writers, like our preclassical forefathers, which have been characterized *ex post* as subscribing to the "conflict of sovereignties" paradigm.[120]

[118] Baty, *Polarized Law*, 159–160: "France, so to speak, sends her son out into the world with one hand tied. What right, except on public grounds, has any other nation to untie it? Simply this, that all persons in England are entitled to place both their hands in his. If you throw a stone in the air, you depress the earth. If you regulate the legal status of a subject, you affect the position of everybody else. He is not living in a vacuum . . . There are many private interests involved in the application of any private law to a particular invidivual."

[119] This is a good example of conceptual oppositions not capturing what really is at stake: many of the French professors of private international law who signed the 2005 petition revolted not so much against the loss of French sovereignty but against what they view as a bureaucratic process that destroys their discipline and which they cannot control.

[120] See the discussion in Sections 10.4 and 14.5.

4.7 Conclusion

This chapter has explored the principal *conceptual oppositions* that are invoked in contemporary private international law, and which are often associated to historical narratives.

This exploration was primarily aimed at testing their usefulness for a study on the history of private international law and preclassical conflicts doctrine in particular, as envisaged. On the one hand, as potential themes of discussion or inquiry for our case studies. On the other hand, as terms and concepts, which can help establish a common vocabulary and reference framework between author, readers and the discursive community of private international lawyers. In the process, we had to engage with current concerns and ongoing doctrinal and theoretical discussions.

Considered together, these conceptual oppositions illustrate the long-standing efforts to capture the tensions most characteristic of the field: how are we to mediate the conflict between private law – the substantive policies pursued by the legal system in which we find ourselves located – and the international legal order, or whatever superimposes itself on the law of the forum.

To truly understand the history of the conflict of laws, we must not restrict our inquiry to questions such as whether Bartolus and Huber were unilateralists, or even what type of unilateralist they may have been. It is imperative to consider concrete aspects of their conflicts doctrine. It is also necessary to consider their epistemology. But first, we must place them within the context of their time and place.

5

Conflict of Laws as a Doctrinal Exercise

5.1 Introduction

For all the epistemological distinctness of private international law, a tract or treatise in our field is not unlike other doctrinal works, especially in private law, in the sense that it performs similar functions – and is built on similar premises. This chapter identifies six such themes and doctrinal tools and queries their significance for conflict-of-laws scholarship.

Section 5.2 addresses the mode of legal reasoning. Authors engaged in the construction of a doctrinal system often claim to ground it upon a few general principles. Should that be the case, what relation is there between such foundations and the structure of the doctrinal work, or the author's argumentation style?

Section 5.3 is concerned with the impact of substantive-law considerations on conflicts doctrine. Each doctrinal work addresses the legal subject matter, which is organized into legal categories (the term employed in a broad sense that encompasses not just legal fields or legal subjects, such as "contracts" and "testaments," but also legal concepts used for taxonomy purposes, such as "prohibitive statutes"). What is the relationship – and influences – between the categorization scheme employed by an author and the doctrinal principles elaborated in the work?

Section 5.4 pursues another line of inquiry connected to the process of categorization and classificiation of legal issues: namely, the distinction drawn, in the legal treatment of legal acts, between questions of form or formalities and substantive matters. The form/substance distinction is a doctrinal tool paramount in private law as well. Whereas, however, in a domestic legal setting, this is a matter of policy, in the conflict of laws a distinction drawn between formal and substantive validity may lead to different applicable laws and hence an additional layer of complexity – and often, two sets of contradicting policies. The form/substance distinction has strong affinities – and may share a similar function – with another distinction paramount for private international law, the one between procedural and substantive issues.

Section 5.5 then considers the role of jurisdictional considerations and jurisidictional rules in thinking about applicable law and the design of doctrinal conflicts systems. Section 5.6 examines the doctrine of party autonomy, and the role of individuals, in choice-of-law doctrine. Finally, Section 5.7 concerns what is regarded by many as the paramount objective of the conflict of laws – uniformity of result. This is also an objective unique to conflicts doctrine.

5.2 Legal Reasoning in Conflicts Works

5.2.1 On Rules and Formalism

Conflicts discourse has long been about rules. The unilateral rules of the statutists have been replaced by the Savignian paradigm of multilateral or "jurisdiction-selecting" choice-of-law rules. Such rules (known as conflicts rules, *règles de conflit*) have in their turn been challenged both empirically and philosophically.

Empirically, conflicts rules have been challenged in various ways. First, courts have often had their own mind when approaching conflicts issues – and real life has the tendency of providing us with ever more complex situations. Second, the escape devices – such as *renvoi*, *ordre public*, *lois de police* – which were invented or discovered in the attempt by courts and doctrine to balance conflicting objectives while adhering to the classical paradigm, have in a way undermined some of the classical claims to simplicity and uniformity. Third, the proliferation of choice-of-law *norms* (a term that includes both conflicts rules and the connecting factors used in these rules). For validation of these points, one might simply compare the classical systems of legislative conflicts rules, notably of the late nineteenth century, with modern international instruments or national codes on private international law.

The *philosophical* challenge against conflicts rules has come from European modern unilateralists, on the one hand, and the American conflicts revolution, on the other. The former challenged the reach of conflicts rules. The latter challenged their very utility.[1] The idea of

[1] See D. Cavers, "A Critique of the Choice-of-law Problem," *Harvard Law Review*, 47 (1933), 173–208.

replacing rules with an *approach*, in the sense of "a system which does no more than state what factor or factors should be considered at arriving at a conclusion" was also promoted.[2] The whole discussion about approaches is reminiscent of another discussion in American legal theory, as to the choice between rules and standards.[3]

Modern conflict of laws has opted principally for rules. This is a result, on the one hand, of the classical roots of much of contemporary doctrine and, on the other hand, of the fact that in the conflict of laws even the question who is to apply the standards is inderminate: the very subject negates the idea of a single Dworkinian Hercules. However, unlike the more abstract rules of the classical paradigm, the modern paradigm operates in constellations of special rules. For example, different rules today govern different aspects of tort liability. At the same time, standards were given an increased role. Modern choice-of-law rules such as the "proper law" of contract (and, occasionally, tort) have allowed judges considerable flexibility. The concept of subsidiary or "escape" choice-of-law rules (*clauses d'exception*) was also mooted.[4] Meanwhile, standard-producing escape mechanisms such as public policy (*ordre public*) were embraced by modern conflicts doctrine.

It has been argued that an opposition between rules and standards is a "false conflict," in the sense that, in practice, systems of rules will force the interpreter to generate standards in order to choose how to characterize the case and to determine whether the case is distinguishable from the cases clearly covered by the applicable rules, "whether to create a new exception or to modernize the law in order to comply with contemporary notions of social justice," or whether rigid application of the rule conforms to constitutional standards prohibiting fundamental unfairness.[5] On the other hand, "standards" will generate rules through consistent practice.[6] The story of the evolution of conflicts norms provides ample

[2] W. M. Reese, "Choice of Law: Rules or Approach," *Cornell Law Review*, 57 (1972), 315–334.

[3] See e.g. P. Schlag, "Rules and Standards," *UCLA Law Review*, 33 (1985), 379–430.

[4] See Art. 15 of the Swiss Federal Law.

[5] J. Singer, "Real Conflicts," *Boston University Law Review*, 69 (1989), 3–129, 19.

[6] Ibid. Singer rightly concludes that the "choice between rules and standards can only be made sensibly in the context of particular social conflicts and particular legal questions . . . [C]hoice of the best form for conflicts doctrine is inseparable from other choices about the appropriate substantive outcomes of conflicts cases" (ibid., 23). But to stop here would be to assume that the allocation of interpretive – and lawmaking – labor among legislators, academics and judges does not matter for its own sake. The choices made as to the form of conflicts norms are inseparable from choices made about the substantive outcome, but

evidence in validation of this statement. An interesting example in this regard concerns the default norms on the law applicable to contracts absent an express choice of the parties: by the late twentieth century, the "proper law of contract" approach had gained significant ground in both Continental and common-law jurisdictions. Yet the EU's "Rome I" Regulation has opted for a series of "mechanical" rules, each customized for one of the most typical transactions.[7] It would appear that standards have been relegated by the EU to the status of escape rules; it must be kept in mind however that the new hard rules have drawn on experience from actual transactional practice.

Suggestion of a "false conflict" rings true with regard to another debate that originated in the US: whether we should determine the applicable law by balancing "policies" and "interests" or by reference to the *material contacts* (connections) the case may have to each state – what the rest of the world has known as the "connecting factors" (*règles de rattachement*).[8] The distinction goes back to the interwar critique of the choice-of-law process.[9]

Policy-oriented approaches will still have to "localize" the reach of the various policies.[10] In their turn, selecting among material contacts is dependent upon substantive preferences. A non-US scholar could even remark that the sharp opposition between "policy" approaches and "contacts" approaches does not correspond to modern conflict of laws: not only are modern conflicts rules the result of extensive policy (*de lege*

they are also inseparable from the epistemology of private international lawyers, and the other actors involved in the process or the outcome.

7 Regulation (EC) 593/2008 on the law applicable to contractual obligations (Rome I), esp. Art. 4(1).

8 See Singer, "Real Conflicts," 23–32.

9 See e.g. Cavers, "Critique," 180: "The court is seeking a rule which, if it already has the pedigree of precedent, may have arisen in a case where the competiting domestic laws were, with relation to the facts of the transaction, the reverse of those now before it . . . Now, however pragmatic the considerations may be which move the court in its determination of the rule for choice of law, the fact remains that as to this case, and all subsequent cases in which that rule will be involved, the court is employing the divining rod, or, to use a more modern metaphor to symbolize fortuitous selection, it is engaging in a blindfold test. The court must blind itself to the content of the law to which its rule or principle of selection points and to the result which that law may work in the case before it."

10 See e.g. B. Currie, "Married Women's Contracts: A Study in Conflict-of-Laws Method," *University of Chicago Law Review*, 25 (1958), 227–268.

ferenda) discussions, but also the way in which they are interpreted *de lege lata* involves their teleological interpretation.[11]

But this "false conflict" is far from a useless conceptual pair. It highlights different approaches in legal theory, but also different visions of what the task of the conflict of laws is. "Policy" approaches embody a stronger perception of the role of the law in general, and conflict of laws in particular, as social engineering. At the same time, they seem to deny the autonomy or self-subsistence of the conflict of laws. "Material contacts" approaches, on the other hand, probably stand for a less "political" private law, and in particular a more neutral conflict of laws. But also these "material contacts" remind us of Batiffol's take on Savigny.[12] In differentiating the method and ideology of conflict of laws from both private law and international law, the "contacts" approaches did mark a decisive step toward the creation of classical conflict of laws and the discipline of private international law. For Batiffol, the next step was to think functionally, as well as comparatively, about rules.[13]

Such functionalism, however, is contrasted with the formalism prevalent in the field. We could speak of *rules formalism*, in the sense of taking our hard rules at face value, which must be distinguished from the *conceptual* or *interpretative formalism*, of attempting to ground the whole system on a number of general principles.[14] Modern European law has also shown a tendency to neoformalism, where judicial dicta, especially the reasoning of the European Court of Justice, is taken at face value as legislative

[11] See Audit, "American Choice of Law Principles," 590ff; B. Audit, "Le caractère fonctionnel de la règle de conflit," *Recueil des cours*, 186 (1984), 220–397.

[12] Batiffol, *Aspects philosophiques*, 14 (speaking of the threat of sterilization of philosophical reflection).

[13] Ibid., 15.

[14] D. Kennedy, "Legal Formalism" in N. J. Smelser and P. B. Baltes (eds.), *Encyclopedia of the Social & Behavioral Sciences*, vol. 13 (Amsterdam: Elsevier, 2001), 8634–8638, defines *rule formalism* as "a general preference for rules over standards," and *interpretive formalism* – i.e. what most legal academics think of when they speak of formalism, distinguished into *textual, conceptual* and *precedential varieties* – as encompassing "a range of techniques of legal interpretation based on the meaning of norms ... and refusing reference to the norms' purposes, the general policies underlying the legal order, or the extrajudicial preferences of the interpreter." These ideas are important to modern conflict of laws. "Rule formalism" corresponds to the debate as to whether rules or standards should be used; "interpretive formalism" pertains to the debate as to whether material ("territorial") contacts or policies should be used in the determination of the applicable law. Singer, "Real Conflicts," 6–33 discusses these two oppositions as "Two False Conflicts." But we are not going to find them in our examination of preclassical conflict of laws.

pronouncement. This is a normative and epistemic challenge, which, remarkably, also reflects in how we approach past scholarship.

5.2.2 *The Invocation of General Principles*

General principles are a vital instrument of rational, systematic, ordering of a legal subject or field. They have been associated with legal formalism and legal positism in classical doctrine. But how prevalent have they really been in conflicts doctrine across time?

Such an examination has already been attempted in the past, for example in the late classical French conflict of laws.

The French professor Pierre Louis-Lucas divided conflicts scholarship into three groupings – unitary, pragmatic, or eclectic – depending on the "method" followed (the term was used in the sense of a legal method, and not in the usual sense of a choice-of-law method).[15] Proponents of a *unitary method* include those seeking to ground a conflicts system on a single principle.[16] Louis-Lucas had in mind territoriality or personality, but a half century later we witness party autonomy being promoted by some as the primary principle.[17] We have also seen unitary systems grounded upon the distinct territorialist paradigms of *locus regit actum* or vested rights.[18] They would stand in opposition to the advocates of a *pragmatic method*. Hostile to aprioristic systems, these pragmatists could be subdivided into adherents either to a national pragmatism, exemplified by Etienne Bartin, or to an international pragmatism, exemplified by Henri Batiffol.[19] Louis-Lucas situated himself in the middle: the *eclectic method* appears "balanced and realistic" as it lays down guiding principles "in the light of various fundamental considerations which must be taken into account in a non-technical but careful approach."[20]

15 P. Louis-Lucas, "Conflits de méthodes en matière de conflits de lois = Conflicts of methods as regards conflicts of laws," *Clunet*, 83 (1956), 774–823.

16 Ibid., 780ff.

17 For an exploration in that direction see P. Nygh, "The Reasonable Expectations of the Parties as a Guide to the Choice of Law in Contract and Tort," *Recueil des cours*, 251 (1995), 271–400; and E. Jayme, "Le droit international privé du nouveau millénaire: la protection de la personne humaine face à la globalisation [conférence]," *Recueil des cours*, 282 (2000), 9–40.

18 See Barnich, *Actes juridiques*.

19 Louis-Lucas, "Conflits," 788ff.

20 Ibid., 801 (French version reads: "en fonction des diverses considérations fondamentales qui s'imposent à un esprit attentif et non prévenu;" 800). On the three methods see, respectively, 780ff, 788ff, 800ff.

Jean-Paulin Niboyet, a principal proponent of what Louis-Lucas defined as a unitary approach, employed in his historical narrative a scheme with three different pairs of "characters:" analytical as opposed to synthetic, eclectic as opposed to dogmatic, and universalist as opposed to nationalist. *Analytical* writers analyze situations, focusing on "clinical cases" whose number they expand or reduce but never below a certain minimum: the Italian preclassical school, and especially Bartolus, is his key example.[21] On the contrary, *synthetic* writers are imbued by "a spirit of synthesis or of system" and are wary of the dangers of losing direction through too much detail: Niboyet looks to the French school as the principal example.[22] *Eclectic* writers do not begin from a priori principles, and "abandon themselves" to whatever their analysis might lead them to.[23] *Dogmatic* writers proceed from one fundamental theme "which they affirm and around which everything revolves."[24] According to Niboyet, analytical writers tend to be eclectic and synthetic writers dogmatic.

These schemes of foxes and hedgehogs can better capture the nuance of doctrinal edifices but they can only take us up to a point. The story of doctrinal evolution in a legal field is told in terms of the fundamental ideas elaborated by a succession of scholars – or underpinning their work. The use of concrete examples may illuminate the authors' thought, or shed light on the implication of their doctrines, but it may not be enough to fully understand their doctrinal edifices. In this book, we shall attempt to take two extra steps. First, we shall acknowledge that the relationship between theoretical foundations and doctrinal solutions is not always one-way: often the theoretical foundations will be used to support the doctrinal solutions the author has decided upon.[25] Second, we shall look into the entirety of the edifice: the way in which the subject matter is organized, and the relative attention paid by the author in each subject.

[21] Niboyet, *Traité*, 3:53.

[22] Ibid., 70 (speaking of d'Argentré): "L'esprit français est essentiellement un esprit de synthèse ou de système parce qu'il répond à un besoin de clarté, de direction, tandis que trop de précision du détail dans l'analyse a pour rançon de faire perdre le sens de l'architecture de l'ensemble."

[23] Ibid., 54.

[24] Ibid., 73.

[25] This is a point discussed in Sections 6.1 and 6.4, using as an example another French postwar author (Batiffol).

5.3 The Classification of the Legal Subject Matter

The exercise of fitting legal subject matter into *legal categories* dates back to Roman law: obligations, things and persons, contracts, delicts, acts *inter vivos* and *mortis causa*. Categorization acts as a bridge – an intermediate level between abstract legal ideas and material circumstances.[26] It is a catalyst for the creation of doctrinal systems. It is also a major means of altering, and communicating, legal ideas. If successful, a novel categorization may actually impact the material world.

The history of legal doctrine has seen the legal subject matter being continuously structured and restructured into conceptual categories. There are periods in which such categories appear well-formed and categorization schemes orderly and comprehensive – but there are also periods of confusion. Across the Western world, mid- to late nineteenth-century legal thought embraced the so-called jurisprudence of concepts.[27] The edifices of legal formalism were challenged, even shattered, in the twentieth century – but the process of categorization remained, as did basic categories invented in the nineteenth century.[28]

We could in fact theorize about a *spiraling trend* or *pattern* with regard to the creation of legal categories and the division of legal issues into them. Egged on by worldy concerns, doctrinal discussion within a certain genre matures; broad categories such as "contract," "property" or "torts" consolidate and everything is fitted into one of them. Then a combination of material changes and jurisprudential criticism leads to a proliferation of "gray" areas which undermines these categories' empire. The circle then recommences: categories are redefined and boundaries are redrawn.

[26] One might even suggest that such categorization is necessary for the development of legal doctrine. See e.g. Donahue, "Private Law," 546, discussing why systematic discussion of private law is absent among the ancient Greeks but not the Romans: "For the Greeks there seems to have been no room between top-level generalizations of the philosophers and the specifics of the rhetoricians for the mid-level generalizations that characterize systems of private law. Nonliterate societies also seem to show the same dichotomy."

[27] See e.g. Wieacker, *History of Private Law*, 341–362.

[28] See e.g. G. E. White, *Tort Law in America: An Intellectual History*, expanded ed. (Oxford: Oxford University Press, 2003), for the story of the creation in the US of the concept of tort by the legal-science movement at the end of the nineteenth century, and its subsequent twentieth-century transformation. White remarks that Legal Realism "profoundly altered the intellectual foundations of tort law, but did not fundamentally change its conceptual apparatus" (ibid., 64).

The idea of studying the evolution in legal categories is a novel approach for conflicts literature, which tends to take the principal legal categories of the time for granted. Obviously, fitting the legal subject matter into the appropriate legal categories is "fundamental" to the conflicts process, but it is viewed in terms of "allocating an issue in dispute to the correct choice-of-law regime."[29] The question of how to classify a given legal issue has been around since the beginnings of conflicts doctrine, but the notion that the different classifications of legal issues in the various legal systems created latent conflicts was brought to the scholarly forefront by the essays of Bartin and Kahn at the end of the nineteenth century.[30] Tens of thousands of pages have been since spent on the problem of legal characterization.[31]

From the point of view of doctrinal legal history, however, examining the categories employed, and the borders drawn between them, in a work will help us better understand the legal thought of the writers we are studying. It will shed light, for example, on the relationship between their general theory and the specific rules purportedly emanating from it. For example, a plurality of opinions or a state of confusion as to the categorization of the subject matter is more likely to lead to a conflicts system with no singular general principle – what Niboyet called the analytical-eclectic model.[32] Conversely, a system in which the legal subject matter is orderly divided would better allow a clear division into a small number of legal rules or categories of the conflicts subject matter.[33] Examining the

[29] See e.g. R. Fentiman, *International Commercial Litigation*, 2nd ed. (Oxford: Oxford University Press, 2015), 176.

[30] On the issue of legal characterization see F. Kahn, "Gesetzeskollisionen: Ein Beitrag zur Lehre des internationalen Privatrecht," *Jherings Jahrbücher*, 30 (1891), 1–143; E. Bartin, "De l'impossibilité d'arriver à la suppression définitive des conflits de lois," *Clunet*, 25 (1897), 225–255, 466–495, 720–738, reprinted as "La théorie des qualifications en droit international privé" in *Etudes de droit international privé* (Lyon, 1899), 1–82. For a story of the concept see H. Weber, *Die Theorie der Qualifikation: Franz Kahn, Etienne Bartin und Entwicklung ihrer Lehre bis zur universalen Annerkerung der Qualifikation als allgemeines Problem des Internationales Privatrechts (1890–1945)* (Tübingen: Mohr Siebeck, 1986).

[31] See E. Lorenzen, "The Qualification, Classification or Characterization Problem in the Conflict of Laws," *Yale Law Journal*, 50 (1941), 743–761; and A. H. Robertson, *Characterization in the Conflict of Laws* (Cambridge, MA: Harvard University Press, 1940).

[32] This may be the case of Bartolus: see Section 9.3.

[33] This may be the case of Huber: see Section 13.3. Another example may be the division of the legal subject matter in French postwar conflicts textbooks into statut réel, statut personnel, actes et faits juridiques, and procedure.

organization of the legal subject matter into caregories will also allow us to better understand the author's general theory on conflicts.

Three examples of evolving conceptualization of legal subjects include property, tort, and family law.

First, property and the *lex rei sitae* rule. In the Early Modern era wealth was primarily associated with land – real property. The growth of commerce and industry led to increased significance and variety for movables – personal property – both for economic and social purposes. By the nineteenth century, material necessities, social attitudes and intellectual developments had led to a consolidated concept of property. These changes in conceptions – and in value – reflect in both the legal solutions given and their conceptualization (on which the adopted rule is grounded). Thus, in the Early Modern period, "territorialist" authors like Huber and Johannes Voet, or even d'Argentré, would subject personal property to the *lex domicilii* without much discussion; moreover, the matter is seen as arising only with regard to intestate succession (transfer of movable property by contract is simply a matter for the *lex actus).*[34] In contrast, in the 1865 Italian Civil Code, one of the first achievements of the school of international law and a flagship of personalist approaches, "movable goods" (*beni mobili*) are essentially subjected to the law of the place where they are found.[35] It is no accident that movable and immovable property are paired in the same Article (where, moreover, movable property is treated first).[36] At the same time, certain movables – vessels, aircraft – required special rules.

In recent times, the comparative importance of intangibles has risen, and this has posed its own challenges to the *lex rei sitae.*[37] All this has meant a proliferation of legal institutions with which to create and manage wealth – for example, business entities, trusts, and estates –

[34] Cf. Huber, *Heedendaegse Rechtsgeleleertheyt*, 1.3.51 ("movables form no portion of the country where they happen to be, but are carried from place to place and depend only on the good pleasure of the owner") discussed at 11.6, 13.3.4, and 14.2.

[35] Article 7(1) of the Preliminary Provisions to the 1865 Italian Civil Code: "The movable goods (*beni mobili*) are subject (*soggetti*) to the law of the nation of their owner, save for the contrary provisions of the law of the country where they are found (*del paese nel quale si trovano*)."

[36] Ibid., Art. 7(2): "immovable goods" (*beni immobili*) are subjected to "the laws of the place where they are are situated."

[37] On the challenge posed by intangibles on the *lex rei sitae* rule, see e.g. R. Fentiman, "Globalisation and Private International Law," Inaugural lecture of the Ganschoff-Van den Mensch 2000–2001 Chair at the *Université libre de Bruxelles.*

which in turn appear like a nexus of relations and certainly much more than simple contracts.

Second, torts. We will not see much of tort in conflicts works prior to the nineteenth century – on the contrary, we are going to find references to what is essentially criminal cases next to contracts and marriages.[38] Yet civil liability for wrongful acts was already developed in Roman law and was significant in the law of Medieval and Early Modern Europe.[39] It would appear that torts were principally approached in terms of remedies sought and thus tied to the *lex fori*.

In the nineteenth century, we witness a reconceptualization of delicts/torts.[40] Delicts and contracts were long considered as separate branches of the law of obligations, but in the nineteenth century the concept of obligation was further elaborated. Claims for delict became obligations and acquired stronger substantive characteristics. Torts were called "legal facts" (*faits juridiques*), in contrast to the legal acts (*actes juridiques*), and put together with them.

This conceptual shift led to a move away from *lex fori*, as the procedural law applicable to the remedy and the establishment of the *lex loci delicti* as the law of the place where the delictual obligation was created. The shift was gradual: the 1865 Italian Civil Code included no provision on torts. English law adopted the so-called double actionability rule (i.e. that the act must be a wrong both under lex fori and under the *lex loci delici commissi* for an action to brought in an English court), which was only recently abolished.[41] The conceptual and material expansion of the category was to the detriment initially of *lex fori*, but over time it signified a mutation of – and challenge to – *actus* (and even *situs*) territorialism: if we are to conceive of tort ("legal fact") as created in a certain place, lust like the legal act, can we talk of a tort's extraterritorial effects? The

[38] See e.g. Sections 7.4.2, 9.3.2, and 10.3.2 on Bartolus and Medieval conflicts writings.

[39] On Roman law and the *ius commune* with regard to delicts see R. Zimmermann, *The Law of Obligations: Roman Foundations of the Civilian Tradition* (Oxford: Clarendon Press, 1996), 902ff; on Medieval and Early Modern common law D. Ibbetson, *A Historical Introduction to the Law of Obligations* (Oxford: Oxford University Press, 1999), 39–70, 97–125, and 155–168.

[40] See M. Lobban, "The Development of Tort Law" in *Oxford History of the Laws of England*, vol. 12 (Oxford: Oxford University Press, 2010), 877–902; White, *Tort Law*, 3–19.

[41] See e.g. Westlake, *Treatise*, 221–222. In England the rule was abolished by the Private International Law (Miscellaneous Provisions) Act 1995. It persisted further in many jurisidctions following the common law: for example, Cyprus only repealed the common-law rule by L. 129(I)/2006, after accession to the EU.

alternative that has gained ground is to make applicable the law of the place of injury: this has often been the result of the modern American approaches, on the one hand, but also the consecration of *lex loci damni* as the default rule for tort conflicts in the EU.[42]

The third example is family law, which only appears as a unifying category of private law in the nineteenth century, effectively with Savigny.[43] Until that time, questions of paternal power (including emancipation), guardianship and parenthood (e.g. legitimation) are treated as part of the law of persons; in terms of conflict of laws, they are often regarded as personal statutes but discussions are raised as to their characterization and classification.[44] In the Middle Ages, the law of marriage is originally regarded as forming part of canon law but in the Early Modern period we find marriage being treated as part of the law of persons. At the same time, Early Modern conflicts treatments employ contractual analogies in dealing with the law applicable to marriage. But the patrimonial relations between spouses, the subject of much litigation, often arising in relation to succession cases, tend not to follow marriage into the law of persons and to be treated instead as part of the law of contracts.[45]

5.4 The Distinction between Formalities, Procedural, and Substantive Matters in the Conflict of Laws

The distinction between formal and substantive validity of legal acts – such as contracts, marriage, wills – is a staple of conflicts doctrine. In most legal systems there exists a general or default rule pertaining to legal acts in the abstract, and separate rules on special kinds of acts – marriage is the most common example, followed by testaments and special types of contracts which trigger stronger concerns (e.g. land conveyancing, consumer contracts).[46] Rules on form have become more liberal over time – from the simple localization of acts in the territory of their creation, we

[42] See Regulation (EC) 864/2007 on the law applicable to noncontractual obligations (Rome II), esp. Art. 4(1) and recitals (16)–(18).

[43] See Savigny, *System*, 1:345ff (§§ 54–55) and 8:324ff (§§ 379–380).

[44] See Sections 9.3.5 and 13.3.3.

[45] See Sections 9.3.6 and 13.3.3.2.

[46] See Rabel, *Conflict of Laws*, 1:223–262, 2:487–516, 3:154–172, 3:287–318 on the formal validity of marriages, contracts, bills and notes, and wills.

have moved to facultative choice-of-law rules which allow the act to stand as long as it is valid under any of the laws connected to the case.[47]

The conceptualization and structure of questions to form has also changed, in correspondence both with developments in private law and the increased complexity – and diversity – of conflicts situations. In the 1865 Italian Civil Code, a single rule governed all aspects of form in all cases.[48] The 1940/1946 Greek Civil Code introduced one general rule (governing both testaments and contracts) and two special rules (on land conveyancing and marriage).[49] The 1986 Swiss Federal Law of Private International Law, where specific provisions on the celebration of marriage and the form of marital agreements, wills, land conveyances, contracts (as well as arbitration agreements and acts for the recognition of paternity) are integrated into the respective sections.[50]

Discussion in the literature usually concerns the selection of the appropriate choice-of-law rules. The characterization of certain requirements as formal (or procedural) or substantive is also involved. It is accepted that "form" might have to be given a different meaning for conflicts purposes than under substantive forum law, in order to cover foreign institutions. However, we will seldom find a definition of what constitutes *form* and "substance." The reader is implicitly referred to the private-law treatises, or to common knowledge. From a theoretical point of view, this omission has two implications: first, it signifies a determination of what should fall under the domain of private international law – and conflicts discourse – and what does not. It also fosters an implicit understanding that the form/substance distinction is a natural idea and not a simple academic construct.

5.4.1 Form as a Private-Law Construct

To consider the role of the distinction between form and substance (and procedure) in the conflict of laws, we must begin with private law theory. As Duncan Kennedy has noted, this is "one of the dimensions along

[47] See e.g. Regulation 593/2008 (Rome I), Art. 11.

[48] See Art. 9(2) of the Preliminary Provisions to the 1865 Italian Civil Code: The form of all acts was subject to the laws of the place where concluded, unless the party or parties had followed the laws of their common nationality.

[49] See Greek Civil Code (Astikos Kōdikas), Arts. 11, 12, and, 13(1) respectively.

[50] See Arts. 44(3), 56, 93, 119(3), and 124 IPRG – but also arbitration agreements (Art. 178(1)), and recognition of paternity (Arts. 72–73). The result is a two-page study aid in K. Siehr, *Das Internationale Privatrecht der Schweiz* (Zurich: Schulthess, 2002), 322–323.

which we compare legal regimes and assess internal change, whether at the level of detail, of a large ensemble of rules, or of a system as a whole."[51] Such an examination should measure "the degree of insistence on compliance with formalities (what exceptions are permitted?) and the degree of absoluteness of the sanction of nullity for failure to comply (what remedies, if any, for a person who fails to comply?)."[52]

The aim and effect of formalities places them in opposition to legal institutions aimed at preventing people from particular activities deemed "morally wrong or otherwise flatly undesirable."[53] On the contrary, formalities are "legal institutions whose stated object is to facilitate private ordering ... Their purpose is to make sure, first, that the parties know what they are doing, and, second, that the judge will know what they did" – a cautionary and an evidentiary function.[54] Kennedy further distinguishes between the cases where the success of a substantive legal claim depends on following procedural rules (*procedural formalism*) and those where specific formalities are required for transactions such as contracts or marriages (*transactional formality*).[55] We could also further distinguish *administrative formalities*, involving the participation or sanction of public authorities.[56]

The ideas behind formalities operate in two different ways – one liberal and one restrictive.

5.4.1.1 Formalities as a Burden or Intervention

To the extent that the parties are allowed to shape their relationship on their own, the imposition of formalities from the outside comes to encroach on the autonomy of their will.[57] This is so despite the intentions of the lawmaker, which may be to make people take notice of their actions, or to protect the genuine will of one party.

In fact, even if the parties *themselves* have agreed on certain formalities to be observed in the future – for example procedural formalities as a

[51] Kennedy, "Legal Formalism," 8634.

[52] Ibid.

[53] Kennedy, "Form and Substance," 1691.

[54] Ibid.

[55] Kennedy, "Legal Formalism," 8634.

[56] Cf. Kennedy ibid., who – attempting a general study of form and formalism – characterizes as *administrative formalism* the procedural and transactional formalities surrounding the exercise of state power.

[57] The "autonomy" is here defined abstractly. After all, formalities indeed operate through the contradiction of private intentions. Cf. Kennedy, "Form and Substance," 1691.

mechanism for dealing with disputes arising under a contract they have concluded – this does, in effect, limit their future autonomy. For example, in the case of an arbitration clause which provides for a 60-day mediation period prior to having recourse to arbitration, a party could either stonewall for these 60 days even though it is clear no progress will be made toward a solution, or trade its right to insist on this formality.

An historical example of formalities as a burden is the transformation of Medieval and Early Modern marriage law. To the "substantive" requirements regarding consent were added formal requirements, regarding solemnity and especially publicity.[58] Remarkably, in some instances formalities pertaining to publicity were used to avoid evasion of substantive policies of the forum.[59]

5.4.1.2 Formalities as the Liberal Course of Action

On the other hand, considering the regulatory alternatives such as "prohibitive" institutions, formalities are the most liberal course of action once the lawmaker has decided to intervene. It has been remarked in this respect that formalities are "premised on the lawmaker's indifference as to which of a number of alternative relationships the parties decide to enter."[60]

Such purported indifference is reflected in the conflict of laws: formalities are easier to contextualize and to get rid of when crossing the border. Gretna Green flourished as a wedding venue because parental consent to a minor's marriage was consistently held to be a question of form.[61]

[58] E.g., Council of Trent, sess. 24 (11 Nov. 1563), Canones super reformatione circa matrimonium, c. 1 (*Tametsi*) in J. Alberigo et al. (eds.), *Concilium oecumenicorum decreta* (Bologna: Istituto per le Scienze Religiose, 1972), 755–7; cf. Lateran Council IV (1215), c. 51 (*Cum inhibito*), in ibid. at 258 (requiring publicity but its absence is not invalidating).

[59] See Section 13.3.3 on how the Dutch Province of Friesland, which followed a rigorous doctrine of paternal consent, dealt with its natives' marriages in East Frisia.

[60] Kennedy, "Form and Substance," 1691.

[61] *Ogden* v. *Ogden* [1908] P. 46; *Lodge* v. *Lodge* (1963) 107 Sol. Jo. 437. *Ogden* expanded the holding in *Simonic* v. *Mallac* (1860) ER 917, where the court characterized as a question of form the requirement to obtain the consent of their parents in marriage as "a respectful or formal act." See J. R. Gillis, *For Better, For Worse: British Marriages, 1600 to Present* (Oxford: Oxford University Press, 1985), 195 suggests that the "rich runaways enshrined in legend" were very few compared to the "ordinary folk who . . . wished a cheap, quick and private union."

On the whole, private international law uses formalities just like private law, but it tilts more heavily toward the liberal perspective. Of course, conflicts doctrine could be viewed as limiting party autonomy insofar the distinction made between form and substance of a contract subjects the latter to the law selected by the parties, while the former is governed by the *lex loci* – even if such limitation is viewed as acting to safeguard the "true" will.[62] But the modern general rule as to formalities ensures the formal validity of the contract, if valid under the *lex loci contractus* or the *lex causae* or even the law of their common nationality:[63] this means that the contract has three shots for formal validity compared to one for substantive validity.

In this sense, the story of conflicts doctrine involves the liberalization of certain transactions and relations by a means of transforming substantive requirements to formalities. Let us consider, for example, the requirement, in certain legal systems, that for a marriage to be valid it must be held before religious authorities.[64] At some point in the nineteenth century we find an argument that such a requirement is "substantive" and not "formal."[65] The argument itself lost ground over time: the trends toward the re-characterization of religious form as "form" rather than "substance" runs parallel to the trend of allowing for the possibility of a secular wedding.[66] The 1902 Hague Marriage Convention subjected all aspects of ceremony to the law of the country where the marriage was celebrated, allowing countries "by whose laws a religious ceremony is essential" to refuse to recognize as valid marriages contracted by their subjects abroad without the observance of this requirement.[67] It is interesting to remark how the "pro-substance" argument itself evolved:

[62] This is so in the case of a contract involving real property. See e.g. Art. 12 of the Greek Civil Code; and Art. 119(3) of the Swiss Federal Law.

[63] See e.g. Art. 11 of the Greek Civil Code; and Art. 124 of the Swiss Federal Law.

[64] See Rabel, *Conflict of Laws*, 1:213–216.

[65] See Savigny, *System*, 8:357 (§ 381.v, during his discussion of the rule *locus regit actum*): "[S]uch a law has a basis in religion and morality, and is therefore of a coercive nature (§ 349). For this reason I would hold the repetition of the ceremony in the country to which the parties belong to be necessary – not, however, because it must be presumed that the spouses had concluded their marriage abroad *in fraudem legis*, which purpose may not have existed at all, or at least may not be susceptible of proof."

[66] See the references in Donahue, "Private Law," 561 n. 68 on the German debate on the appropriate role for civil marriage.

[67] Convention of June 12, 1902 on the Validity of Marriage, Art. 5(1) and 5(2) respectively.

the initial defense on conceptual grounds was gradually substituted by "policy" arguments warning of evasion.[68]

Formalities also act as protection of the individuals and their relations from the intrusive examination of "substance." This is a matter of convenience for most and of principle for many of us, and a necessity for those trying to evade substantive prohibitions. In recent times, the issue has been pointedly brought to light in the case of "fraudulent" marriages aiming at helping the alien spouse with the granting of residence and work permissions. Accordingly, the formalities-based regime has been attacked by those most concerned with combating such phenomena, and defended by liberals (but also those concerned with the conceptual integrity of private international law).[69]

5.4.2 *Procedural Formalism and the Distinction between Substance and Procedure in Conflicts Doctrine*

The distinction between *procedural* and *substantive* law (*droit matériel*) is corollary but important in the conflict of laws – almost as much as in private law proper.[70] The distinction's importance in the conflict of laws lies principally because the category of procedural issues has been exclusively tied to the *lex fori*: Foreign law may not be applicable in procedural matters, and the choice-of-law process is dead in its tracks. This is important enough for the invention of the procedure–substance distinction to be regarded by many as the foundational moment of conflicts doctrine.[71] The characterization of a legal question as substantive or procedural acquires particular importance.

The textbook examples of disputed subjects include prescription and the burden of proof. Traditionally, the common law has viewed legal rules which affect the "rights and merits" as substantive and legal rules

[68] See e.g. Savigny, *System*, 8:356–357 (§ 381.v). Thus also, more defensively (postwar French conflict of laws was unwelcoming to the Greek rule which effectively held invalid civil marriages); and G. Maridakis, "Le marriage des Grecs orthodoxes hors de Grèce," *Revue critique*, 41 (1952), 661–671.

[69] See H. U. Jessurun d'Oliveira, "The Artifact of 'Sham Marriages'," *Yearbook of Private International Law*, 1 (1999), 49–83.

[70] See R. Garnett, *Substance and Procedure in Private International Law* (Oxford: Oxford University Press, 2012).

[71] See Meijers, "Principes fondamentaux," 595–596, as discussed in Chapter 3. For an example of how this is emphasized by doctrinal writers, see Loussouarn et al., *Droit international privé*, 74.

which affect the remedy only are procedural.[72] Consider the case of the English Statute of Frauds, which prevented certain contracts from being sued upon unless reduced to writing: English courts held that this rule pertained to evidence (and was hence a procedural rule) and not to form of contract.[73]

In that sense, the characterization of, for example, prescription as a procedural rather than substantive matter, leads to a stronger role for the *lex fori*.[74] Conversely, carving issues away from the procedural category has the potential to undermine the reach of the local law; at the very least, even the decision to apply forum law will necessitate some doctrinal discussion. There are of course conceptual issues involved as well: as we design a system for the resolution of cross-border disputes and the granting of relief, should primacy be given to the "core" of the legal relation, or should we think in terms of available remedies, enforceability and actions in law? What value is there to ideas such as the "sovereignty" of the contract? How important is uniformity of result?

5.5 Conflict of Jurisdictions and Conflict of Laws

In its traditional definition, the conflict of laws encompasses both matters concerning the law applicable to the case and matters concerning the determination of the country – or countries – whose courts have international jurisdiction over the case.[75] The French tradition of private international law uses in fact the term *conflict* or *conflicts of jurisdictions* to cover not only matters of jurisdiction but also the question of recognition and enforcement of foreign judgments, as well as the cross-border dimension of procedural issues, such as cross-border service of documents and the taking of evidence.[76]

Over time, the law of international civil jurisdiction has also tended to delve deeper into domestic – and comparative – procedural law.[77] Indeed, in certain legal traditions, civil proceduralists have claimed

[72] *Huber* v. *Steiner* (1835) 2 Bing NC 202 at 210, 132 ER 80, 88.

[73] *Leroux* v. *Brown* (1852) 12 CB 801.

[74] See Rabel, *Conflict of Laws*, 3:475ff.

[75] See e.g. Cheshire, North, and Fawcett, *Private International Law*, 7–9.

[76] See e.g. Audit, *Droit international privé*, 273–475.

[77] Compare for example Dicey, *Digest*, 206ff, who only discusses jurisdiction with Collins, *Dicey, Morris & Collins*, 203ff. with three chapters on procedure, including on "protective measures and judicial assistance" (as well as six additional chapters on jurisdiction and enforcement).

primacy over matters of "international procedural law" from private international lawyers. An important reason for this might be the increasing complexity in cross-border civil, and especially commercial, litigation. Many cases involve several litigants – joined in view of the economic connection between them, for purposes of risk allocation or forum shopping. Parallel proceedings in multiple countries may often arise, as would the need for preservation of evidence and assets abroad: this has created a market for injunctive relief measures, such as the antisuit and freezing injunctions.[78]

More recently, we have been observing an opposite tendency, The advent of international civil and commercial litigation as an autonomous subject creates both challenges and opportunities for the conflict of laws.[79] This is especially the case in the Anglo-American world, where of course the procedural focus was always stronger. In the US, we have witnessed a separation between a pragmatic, cosmopolitan "private international law" focused on commercial litigation (and, to a lesser extent, family and tort) and a theoretical, policy-driven conflict of laws mostly focused on interstate conflicts. The former has found much resonance with globalized law firms, and a number of academics; the latter, heir to the legal realist tradition, controls most of the US legal academia – and the bar of Middle America. In the UK, international commercial litigation has often become the new paradigm of a conflict of laws with stronger emphasis on the needs of transnational legal practice.[80]

This practical emphasis on litigation could conceivably reduce the conceptual, theoretical dimension of the conflicts discourse. It has certainly led to the discussion on choice-of-law losing some of its significance. The determination of jurisdiction to adjudicate comes before the

[78] See Fentiman, *International Commercial Litigation*, esp. 493ff, 543ff.

[79] The role of international commercial arbitration must also be considered in this regard, as it has become interconnected with both jurisdiction and judgments. Contracting parties trying to select a *forum* for their – prospective or actual – disputes shall consider the merits both of courts and of arbitral tribunals; thus, even allowing for the much stronger liberalism of arbitration law, policy objectives may be better served by jointly considering court judgments and arbitral sentences, and especially foreign-court clauses and arbitration agreements. International commercial arbitration has also challenged fundamental premises of classical private international law, through the notion of "a-national" awards and processes, and the practice of *ad hoc* choice of law; in fact, international commercial arbitration seems to be the main [real] driving force behind the creation of a distinct international business law.

[80] See e.g. Hartley, *International Commercial Litigation*; Fentiman, *International Commercial Litigation*.

determination of the applicable substantive law: if the former is dealt with satisfactorily, the latter might cease to be a problem; if it is not, all our choice-of-law efforts may yet come to waste. In that sense, the increased emphasis on procedural issues indicates not just pragmatism but also a loss of faith in the ability of choice-of-law to achieve its objective, i.e. harmonized solutions. Conversely, choice-of-law discussion flourished at periods when jurisdictional regimes were fixed, using few, if expansive, jurisdictional criteria. However, it may well be that this new phenomenon corresponds to a feeling that the discussion of "substantive" conflicts issues has reached a saturation point, whereas the procedural aspect had not been adequately dealt with. At the same time, the increased consideration of international procedural questions by academic private international lawyers has led to new theoretical concepts and increased doctrinal coherence.[81] Moreover, it was the success in the harmonization of civil jurisdiction among the EU Member States which encouraged its choice-of-law initiatives.

5.5.1 On the Relationship between Choice-of-Law and Jurisdiction Rules

The relationship between substantive-law and procedural conflicts has evolved over time. This book attempts a preliminary inquiry, which shall consider two aspects. First, the extent to which matters of jurisdiction (or other procedural matters, namely enforcement of judgments) were included in the conflicts treatments themselves (as contrasted to simply being discussed in other, unconnected parts of an author's broader doctrinal work). Second, the extent to which there was an effort to premise both choice-of-law and jurisdictional rules on common grounds: an example might be combining a rule about the jurisdiction of the place where real property is situated (*forum rei sitae*) with a rule about the law of the place being applicable (*lex rei sitae*); or the establishment of a jurisdictional basis for the place where a tort was committed (*forum loci delicti*) while making applicable the law of the same place (*lex loci delicti commissi*). We must distinguish further between those instances where such rules are intended to apply globally, and those where the jurisdictional rules of the forum are taken for granted.

[81] See notably Fentiman, *International Commercial Litigation*, 3–161 who builds a veritable system of English private international law, using the concept of *risk* ("transaction risk" and "litigation risk") and risk management as foundation.

Allowing for considerable oversimplification, a brief story of this interaction would be as follows: in the original state of affairs, prior to the development of the conflict of laws, judicial authorities in a territorial entity would only apply forum law.[82] In the preclassical period, courts were called to consider foreign rules in order to determine the existence and content of private rights. The exercise of court jurisdiction appears to have depended on the actual ability to exercise power over the defendant, primarily by means of his physical presence.

The nineteenth century witnessed a proliferation of regimes. Traditionalist systems continued to exist: Wächter, and his preference for forum law, is better understandable in such a context. We also have sophisticated efforts to coordinate judicial jurisdiction and applicable law, notably in the doctrinal system of Savigny, who tried to localize each case through the concept of the nature of the legal relationship. His specific rules also aimed at optimizing the coordination between *forum* and *lex*: for example, in contractual disputes, Savigny opted for the law of the place of performance (*lex loci solutionis*) as opposed to the traditional law of the place of conclusion (*lex loci conclusionis*); the law of the place of performance is a much more convenient, as well as neutral, forum for litigating the contractual dispute.

At the same time, we encounter novel expansive jurisdictional systems such as the one of Articles 14 and 15 of the Napoleonic Code, which allowed a Frenchman to sue or be sued by a foreigner in French courts for "engagements" abroad.[83] An expression of political unilateralism, nationalism and a possible desire to compel reciprocity, the impact of these provisions was gradually moderated by case law and legal

[82] See e.g. Sack, "Conflict of Laws," 344ff.

[83] *Code civil des Français*, Arts. 14-16 as translated by "a Barrister of the Inner Temple" (London: William Benning, 1827): "14. A foreigner, although not resident in France, may be cited before the French courts, to enforce the execution of engagements contracted by him in France with a Frenchman; he may be summoned before the tribunals of France, on account of engagements entered into by him with Frenchmen in a foreign country. 15. A Frenchman may be summoned before a French court, for engagements contracted by him in a foreign country, though with a foreigner. 16. In all causes, except commercial ones, in which a foreigner shall be plaintiff, he shall be required to give security for the payment of the costs and damages incident to the suit, unless he possess in France immoveable property of value sufficient to guarantee such payment." Article 16 (the so-called *cautio iudicatum solvi*) was not a jurisdictional basis but alludes to very old concerns about security being provided by the plaintiff.

scholarship.[84] Such a jurisdictional system would entail a lot of cases in which foreign law would have to apply, and this partly explains both the development of classical French conflicts doctrine and its relative intellectual separation from the law of jurisdiction.[85]

The twentieth century has seen reprisals of both the Napoleonic and the Savignian exercises. Long-arm jurisdiction in most US States created a dynamic environment necessitating new choice-of-law approaches. At the same time, the EU instruments envisage a partial coordination of special jurisdictional grounds and choice-of-law rules.

5.6 Individuals, Party Autonomy, and the Conflict of Laws

Party autonomy is today the most popular principle in the conflict of laws.[86] It has long been the established norm – at least since the nineteenth century – with regard to the choice-of-law for contracts.[87] Especially in the early to mid-twentieth century, its theoretical bases was contested by some of the leading late classical scholars.[88]

84 On the legislative history of the provisions see H. Gaudemet-Tallon, *Récherches sur les origines de l'article 14 du Code Civil* (Paris: PUF, 1964) as well as the foreword by Pierre-Clément Timbal. See also the book's review by Kurt Nadelman, *American Journal of Comparative Law*, 14 (1965), 348–350 who notes both the embarrassment of French academics for this jurisdictional privilege and its persistence. See also K. Clermont and J. Palmer, "French Article 14 Jurisdiction, Viewed from the United States," *Cornell Law Faculty Publications*, 13 (2004). On the evolution of French case law see especially the Court of Cassation rulings in Cass.Civ., October 19, 1959 (*Pellassa*), Dalloz 1960.37; and Cass.Civ., October 30, 1962 (*Scheffel*), *Revue critique* (1963), 387, reproduced with commentary in Ancel and Lequette, *Grands arrêts*, § 37.

85 See D. Holleaux, *Compétence du juge étranger et reconnaissance des jugements* (Paris: Dalloz, 1970), 241ff showing the effects of the dissociation between domicile and nationality on the French doctrine of judicial jurisdiction, especially the increased importance of *actor sequitur forum rei*. On the alleged intellectual separation see Pataut, *Principe de souveraineté*, 1ff. who begins his monograph by lamenting the "consensus" that conflit of laws and conflcit of jurisdictions are "independent" (it is however possible that Pataut is purposefully overemphasizing the strength of the conception he is critiquing).

86 A. Mills, *Party Autonomy in Private International Law* (Cambridge: Cambridge University Press, 2018); Nygh, *Autonomy*; G. Rühl, "Party Autonomy in the Private International Law of Contracts" in E. Gottschalk (ed.), *Conflict of Laws in a Globalized World* (Cambridge: Cambridge University Press, 2007), 153–183.

87 See e.g. the final sentence of Art. 9(2) of the Preliminary Provisions to the 1865 Italian Civil Code.

88 J.-P. Niboyet, "La théorie de l'autonomie de la volonté," *Recueil des cours*, 27 (1927), 5–116.

In modern doctrine, there is little contestation as to the primacy to be given to the intention of the parties as to the law applicable to their contract – discussions concern their freedom to select a legal system with no relation to the dispute, or to fully exclude state law in subjecting to their contract a non-state legal regime (often referred to as an "a-national" legal system).

At present, party autonomy has been promoted as a principle even in the areas of testamentary succession and noncontractual obligations. The EU Succession Regulation allows the testator to select the law of his or her nationality as applicable to his or her succession, instead of the law of the testator's habitual residence which is applicable as the Regulation's general rule.[89] The Rome II Regulation on the law applicable to torts and other extra-contractual obligations also makes provision for an agreement as to applicable law and mentions the need to respect "party autonomy."[90] Astonishingly, scholars and members of the European Parliament had attempted to make party autonomy the principal rule for EU tort conflicts law.[91]

This embrace of party autonomy has led to telling the story of the evolution of conflicts doctrine in terms of yet another progress narrative. The heroes in this narrative are the lay individuals and their right to self-determination. The "postmodern" era of private international law might rely on the selection by private parties of the law applicable to their contracts and other legal acts.[92]

[89] See recitals (38)–(40) and Arts. 22 and 21 Regulation (EU) 650/2012 on jurisdiction, applicable law, recognition and enforcement of decisions and acceptance of authentic instruments in matters of succession and on the creation of a European Certificate of Succession (Succession Regulation).

[90] Regulation 864/2007 ("Rome II"), Art. 14 and recital (31) (invoking the need to "respect the principle of party autonomy and to enhance legal certainty" in noncontractual obligations).

[91] See e.g. T. Kadner Graziano, *La responsabilité delictuelle en droit international privé européeen* (Basel: Helbing und Lichtenhahn, 2004), 27ff and 140: "selection of law" forms the first and default rule in his restatement of common European guiding principles. Most remarkably, see European Parliament, Report on the proposal for a regulation of regulation of the European Parliament and of the Council on the law applicable to non-contractual obligations ("Rome II"), A6-0211/2005: Amendment 3 added to then-recital (7) a sentence on the need to respect the intention of the parties, which survived into recital (31) of the adopted Regulation. Amendment 25 proposed a new Art. 2A entitled "Freedom of Choice."

[92] See E. Jayme, "Identité culturelle et intégration: le droit international privé postmoderne," *Recueil des cours*, 251 (1995), 9–268; Jayme, "Droit international privé." For works influenced from this approach (or, at least, adopting similar ideas and citing Jayme with

In fact, expression of parties' intention as to applicable law is a relatively recent phenomenon: prior to the twentieth century, few parties to a contract made an express selection of applicable law; in contrast to such express agreements, the courts were all too eager to discover a tacit agreement or implied intention, which not surprisingly led the court to apply either the forum's default choice-of-law rule or the forum's substantive law.

5.6.1 *On the Individual as the Epicenter of a Conflicts System*

Assuming preclassical conflict of laws is indeed a theory of statutes, individuals would play secondary role to *statutes* – or to legal acts. Questions would be posed in terms of whether the statute (or the act) had extraterritorial effect or not. On the other hand, most statutes producing extraterritorial effects actually concerned the individual.[93] But the difference of emphasis has been remarked upon by Liberal classical jurists in the nineteenth century.[94]

Classical conflict of laws in fact reversed the angle of the question: now the individual became the subject and the personality/territoriality question was rephrased: the question now was to determine under which terms individuals would continue to be bound by statutes after they have moved abroad.

The classical paradigm encompassed a diversity of perspectives. For the nineteenth-century Liberals of the international-law school, the application of personal law is justified on the presumed desire of the individual to carry "his" or "her" law abroad.[95] Mature classical – and, eventually, modern – conflict of laws emphasized instead the tendency of individuals to evade a country's law by triggering the application of a foreign law.[96] The extraterritorial effect of personal laws was justified by reference to the public policy of the forum rather than the migrants'

approbation) see M. de P. Diago Diago, *Pactos o Capitulaciones Matrimoniales en Derecho Internacional Privado* (Zaragosa, 1999); in its English summary: *Yearbook of Private International Law*, 2 (2000), 179–203, 180–182.

93 See Section 8.4.3 with regard to Bartolus.

94 See the critique of Lainé, *Introduction*, 2:116ff, esp. 121ff (who shows the contradiction in the territorialist rationale for the recognition of extraterritorial effect of personal statutes).

95 See Mancini, "De l'utilité," 230–231 (quoting from his 1851 course).

96 See B. Audit, *La fraude à la loi* (Paris: Dalloz, 1974).

national affections.[97] Another perspective adopted in mature classical and modern doctrine is the concept of individuals as generators of *choice-of-law* rules, or more precisely as an objective connecting factor: parties to a contract are enabled to select from among the competing legal systems, instead of making answers to the question of applicable law dependent on the forum called to determine the case. Party autonomy as "objective localization" is not the same concept as party autonomy in the sense of the individuals creating norms through contract. This perspective seems linked to a certain loss of faith in traditional choice-of-law norms, but also to the autonomy from "substantive law" regulation acknowledged to choice-of-law norms.

The latest modern or "postmodern" perspective would have individual autonomy become a theoretical foundation for the conflicts *system*: for example, Eric Jayme views respect for individual autonomy as the inevitable course of private international law faced with globalization.[98] Such a perspective is different from the pure "individualism" of those, especially in the field of international business law, who present individuals as the ultimate lawmakers. On the one hand, conflicts systems have to manage a variety of conflicting considerations, and they seldom manage to maintain, in the long run, the purity of their foundation. On the other hand, the foundation is often used to justify solutions previously arrived at. But then, even the idea of individual autonomy as the ultimate lawmaker, best expressed in some theories of the *lex mercatoria*, is not always as individualist as presumed. The concepts of *lex mercatoria* and of legal pluralism draw their origins from the interwar period and the quest for the "social" (a relationship lost in the partial discredit, after World War II, of many theorists of the period). We can thus discern in many images of the *lex mercatoria* corporatist ideas, where professional associations take over the role of the state legislator.

[97] See Batiffol, *Traité elémentaire*, 296–299. Batiffol begins with explaining that to do otherwise would defeat the very purpose of certain laws (297): "Il paraît preferable de partir de l'observation de fait que certaines lois sont manifestement tournées si elles ne s'appliquent pas avec quelque continuité. S'il suffit à un Français de demander le divorce à Genève pour l'obtenir dans les cas où la loi française le lui refuse, il est inutile de limiter les cas de divorce"). He then follows with references to preclassical authors who made the same observation; this passage is preceded and concluded by dissociating itself from Mancini's "temperament" rationale.

[98] Jayme, "Le droit international privé."

5.6.2 *On Party Autonomy*

The history of party autonomy has been told in two divergent narratives.

The main narrative has provided a pedigree for party autonomy reaching back to antiquity and certainly Dumoulin.[99] Some have even located the principle of party autonomy in both Bartolus and Huber, as well as other preclassical writers.[100] This narrative is especially dominant in the English language. Friedrich Juenger's historical treatment inspired many casual references to Dumoulin as the discoverer of party autonomy in American law review articles. In his seminal study of party autonomy doctrine, Peter Nygh is more circumspect.[101]

A counter-narrative does not deny the historical fact of Dumoulin invoking the intention of the parties in arguing for the determination of the law applicable, but notes that, in this case and in many that followed until the late nineteenth century, such invocations were always used ex post by reading into the parties' agreement a presumed intention to apply the desired law (usually *lex fori*). This narrative is stronger in the French literature, following Henri Battifol's study on the history of contractual choice-of-law.[102]

Why this divergence in narratives? Admittedly, the second narrative relies on closer examination of doctrinal sources.[103] In fact, both narratives have their own politics. The former, more emphatic narrative certainly serves as genealogy to those who view party autonomy as a source of transnational substantive norms. It was also promoted by more moderate scholars who espoused a moderate position in favor of party autonomy; this might be best explained considering the opposition to party autonomy of US conflict-of-laws theorists in the mid-twentieth century.[104] The latter narrative corresponds to the "objective

[99] See e.g. Juenger, *Choice of Law*, 17.

[100] See Yntema, "Comity," 15 (Bartolus), 27 (Huber), as well as 24 (J. Voet).

[101] See Nygh, *Autonomy*, 4–8.

[102] See Batiffol, *Conflits de lois*; V. Ranouil, *L'autonomie de la volonté: naissance et évolution d'un concept* (Paris: Presses Universitaires de France (PUF), 1980).

[103] My first venture into the history of private international law led me from Juenger to Batiffol: N. Hatzimihail, Foundations of Party Autonomy and the Evolution of the Conflict of Laws. Unpublished LL.M. thesis, Harvard University (1997).

[104] The Restatement had adopted a strict *lex loci contractus* rule. See Beale, *Treatise*, 2:1079–1080. Uniform Commercial Code § 1–105, adopted a party autonomy rule but subjected it to a reasonable relation requirement. On the persisting hostility to party autonomy among American conflicts theorists see the open letters exchanged between Professors Friedrich Juenger and Larry Kramer with regard to the possible revision of Art. 1, appended in P. Borchers, "The Internationalization of Contractual Conflicts

localization" theory of party autonomy. Theoretical opposition to the concept of party autonomy may have been even more vivid in interwar France, but case law had already accepted the principle of party autonomy.[105] The question now was to distinguish the express intention of the parties from "implied intentions."

I would argue that it was the will theories of contract – and probably a growing sense of the irrelevance of the *locus contractus* – that led to the emergence of party autonomy as a choice-of-law principle in classical doctrine. It is true that the "intention of the parties" was invoked in preclassical times; but it appears to have been so in order to validate the application of either the *lex loci contractus*, or the law of the place of performance. Huber and Story give characteristic examples in their references to the "intention of parties." In classical times, a similar function was performed by the "implied intention" of the parties (which was indeed more frequent than express intention until the early twentieth century). But the early classical rhetoric is different: even if the judge would in the end use the "implied intention" to apply the law of the place of performance, he was at least making an effort to examine that intention.

5.7 Decisional Harmony

The expressions *harmony of solutions*, *decisional harmony*, *uniformity of decision*, *international uniformity of result*, or even *uniform solution*, have been used to portray the ideal situation where the same concrete case would be treated in the same manner, and produce similar effects, irrespective of which country will end up as the forum. Many regard the achievement of this ideal situation as the primary mission, the "historical function," of private international law – "its grand objective, an objective so important that all other objectives are merely secondary."[106]

Law," *Vanderbilt Journal of Transnational Law*, 28 (1995), 421–443, 434–436, as well as the appended, with regard to the initial work of the ABA Article 1 Task Force: ibid., 444–486.

105 Cass.civ., December 5, 1910, S.Jur. 1911, I,129 (*American Trading Co.* v. *Quebec Steamship Co.*), reprinted in Ancel and Lequête, *Grands arrêts*, § 11.

106 Hartley, "Modern Approach," 26 – claiming that this attitude characterizes "some theorists." Hartley – who argues that procedural aspects could never allow a full uniformity of result – is partly creating a strawman, here (he cites only Savigny in favor of the need for the international uniformity of result to predominate). Among more

However, we all know that we are far from achieving this function. For generations, many conflicts teachers have alluded to the lady who, when asked by her co-passenger in a train if she is married or not, looks outside the window to see over which state the train is passing before responding. We could call that state of affairs *decisional dissonance.*

As a concept, decisional harmony is narrower than legal certainty and broader than uniform law. Compared to the former, decisional harmony provides harder dictates as to legal norms. Compared to legal uniformity, its effects are softer. We may have legal certainty as long as we know in which states our contract would produce its effects, and in which it would not.[107] On the other hand, it would be more efficient, let alone reassuring, if we could know that our contract would produce its effects everywhere. The greater the divergence between choice-of-law systems is, the more difficult it becomes to divine the outcome of a case in a foreign jurisdiction.

As to its relationship to the idea of uniform law, decisional harmony can be achieved even while states maintain distinct and diverse private law regimes, as long as the conflict of laws does its job. It is conceivable that even if each legal system were to have its own conflicts norms, these norms could allow for harmonious results. On the other hand, experience has proven that the weaker the communication between the different legal systems, the bigger the possibility of decisional dissonance. This experience has militated in favor of a unified or uniform conflicts system. Many would go even further, and suggest that only the uniformization or at least convergence of private-law regimes can lead to decisional harmony.

forceful proponents see Barile, "Fonction historique," 305ff; and Barnich, *Actes juridiques*, esp. 56–61 (but also the preceding chapters which lead to this conclusion by considering and playing down other possible central objectives) and the references therein. On the other hand, see e.g. Batiffol, *Aspects philosophiques*, 195ff who views *harmonie internationale des solutions* as one of three objectives (he actually considers it second: 212–221), along with the protection of the person which amounts to protecting the community (*collectivité*) and private utility, that need to be considered together to explain private international law.

107 See e.g. Fentiman, *International Commercial Litigation*, 4–5: "Legal risk invariable takes two forms – the risk of an unfavourable outcome, and the risk of an uncertain outcome. But an unfavourable outcome which is certain may be preferable to uncertainty. The risk is then clear, and be costed. This does not mean, however, that legal institutions which provide for an element of discretion are invariable unwelcome – not if the market can rely on the exercise of discretion to ameliorate risk."

A final observation about decisional harmony has to do with the way in which it is presented in the literature. Just like legal certainty, one gets the impression that the individuals with whose activities we are dealing strongly desire this ideal state. However, experience teaches us that many individuals would prefer even deafening dissonance in their concrete case, if that would serve them better. It is thus up to the lawyers – in particular, scholars, judges and legislators among them – to achieve such decisional harmony.[108] Of course, the main reason for this is that only they – that is, we – seem to be focused on the long term and the general interest. But we should perhaps also contemplate the role of our world-view in it. It is this world view which suggests that to have dissonant solutions in the same case indicates a failure in our mission, and perhaps a failure of our legal concepts and method.[109]

[108] Batiffol, *Aspects philosophiques*, 212ff.

[109] Kahn-Freund, "General Problems," 469–470: "The ideal of 'harmony' or (better) uniformity is not an aesthetic caprice of academics: it is … a requirement of justice. The ideal is unattainable. All ideals are … This does not mean that we should give up pursuing the ideal, following a road leading to its direction – but this, too, is no more than a 'guding line,' not a 'policy' to be adhered à *outrance* … The pursuit of harmony is the principal task of those who make it their concern to think about private international law. Yet it will always clash with what I have called 'realism' – the 'homeward trend' is the negation of international harmony. An immense intellectual effort has been invested in this discipline for many centuries. If any result commensurate with this effort is ever to be achieved, a clear vision of the ideal of harmony must be combined with an equally clear insight into the social facts which ever prevent it from being attained. Only those advance society … who combine the qualities of Don Quixote with those of Sancho Panza. Many will never be able to see more than a tilt at windmills … Sometimes they may even be right. But one hopes that there will always at least be some who can see that these hazards are giants of injustice, and who will, as best they can, try to overcome them."

6

Conflict of Laws as a World System

6.1 Introduction

In 1949, the French Professor Henri Batiffol published the first edition of a treatise on private international law that was to have a long history.[1] The 800-page work begins with a section on the "Object of private international law":

> **International Society. International Order.** Domestic law envisions the juridically constituted society in the form of a State: French domestic law, public and private, is established in order to regulate the relations that constitute Franch society, as if there were no other. Bur relations are established by the force of things between the different groupings constituted into States. These relations are established under different modes: on the one hand, the individuals form relations with each other, a French, for example, marries an Italian, enters into a contract with an Englishman, on the other hand, the States enter into relations the ones with the others, France for example concludes a treaty with England, discusses with Italy about a border.
>
> This complex (*ensemble*) of relations constitutes what we call the international society. Experience shows that every society invokes rules to in order to coordinate the relations that constitute it: *ubi societas ibi ius*; absent such rules, the individual intelligence, raised in its appropriate lights, or the individual will with its weaknesses would not be capable of discerning or following practical ways and of avoiding those leading to conflicts, that is, absent sanction, to the disintegration of society.
>
> There is thus place to inquire in accordance with which directives ought the constitutive relations of the international society to be established, in order for that one to be able to subsist and procure to its members the good that they expect from its existence. These directives constitute the international order ("l'ordre international"), the rules expressing them [constitute] the international law.[2]

[1] Batiffol, *Traité élémentaire.*
[2] Ibid., 1.

Batiffol begins with a positive definition of the "international" (society, order, law). This definition is connected to a dual distinction. On the one hand, between the domestic and the international legal domain. On the other hand, between the "international" relations involving States themselves and those involving their citizens. It follows as a logical next step that a different set of rules corresponds to each of the two relationship modes. Public international law is that branch of international law constituted by the rules addressed to States, while private international law contains those rules addressed directly to individuals. The "general object" of private international law is defined as "the complex (*ensemble*) of rules applicable only to individuals in the relations of the international society." It must be noted that the object concerns the rules rather than the relations themselves. From a jurisprudential point of view, this could be related to the author's ideas about the objectives of private international law. But as far as his present argument is concerned, the emphasis on rules relates to his sociological observation: *ubi societas ibi ius* – international society must have rules, for both States and individuals, else it will be disintegrated. The "intelligence" and "will" of the "individual" (State or person) does not suffice to avoid conflicts.

The next step is for Batiffol to point to the similarity of sources – and the authority from which they emanate – between the two branches of international law. As noted, in order to be imposed to their addressees, rules must emanate from an authority that assures their observance. But the international society possesses no such authority, which could formulate and enforce these rules: it is the States and their conduct which affirm the existence of rules, whose application is often facilitated by treaties. This holds true for public but also private international law, whose rules also emanate from the conduct of States, as expressed through their domestic legislation and courts. It does not matter that there exist substantial differences between national legislations: in both fields, each State determines – to a great extent freely – what it considers as forming part of the "international order." The difference lies in effectivity: whereas in public international law effectiveness is dependent on the relative power of a State (consider, for example, an isolated State opposed by a much stronger neighbor), the rules of private international law are applied (*une sanction effective*) by a State's domestic courts.[3]

[3] Ibid., 1–2 (§ 2).

Batiffol's balancing exercise comes near the end of the classical period. It is a good example of the complexities involved in the doctrinal work of private international lawyers, especially when system building is concerned. Public international lawyers have had to steer between apology and utopia.[4] But conflicts doctrine has its own navigational challenges.

There are four distinct aspects to consider in this regard, in the four Sections that follow:

First, the tension created by the inevitable need of conflicts doctrine to shift or mediate between *perspectives*. In Batiffol's case, such perspectives are provided certainly by French domestic law, to some extent also by foreign domestic law and of course the "international order."

Second, the normative aspect of conflicts doctrine. Private international law is an active participant in *international governance*. For example, the imagery of "international society" and "international order" is supporting the liberal vision of a world of states organized in a community governed by "international law."

Third, the need to ground the doctrinal system to *foundations*. These foundations help explain the choices made in the doctrinal system – choices as to the norms and solutions given, as well as to the sources used and concepts developed. Batiffol is a good example, as will be discussed below, but this tends to hold generally true of systematic doctrinal edifices.

Last, but not least, each author is situated in a certain world and perceives that world in a certain way. Their works are likewise situated, whether they provide an express description or they simply assume a world view.

6.2 Mediating between Perspectives

From a doctrinal point of view, conflict of laws as a legal field exists because of the need to manage the tension between the "public" international structure and the domestic "private" law governance. Since the beginnings of a conflicts discourse in the High Middle Ages, long before there actually *was* a *private international law* properly speaking, conflicts lawyers found themselves – or at least their subject matter – situated *within* individual legal systems.[5] At the same time, rules different from

[4] M. Koskenniemi, *From Apology to Utopia: The Structure of International Legal Argument* (Cambridge: Cambridge University Press, 2006).

[5] See e.g. the discussion about the gloss on *cunctos populos* and its contemporaries in Chapter 3 above.

our own and coming from "foreign" legal systems inevitably challenge this domesticity. To deal with this foreign or transnational element, private international lawyers have felt the need to have recourse, as a foundation for their doctrines, to something "external" to and transcending those systems.

Lea Brilmayer has captured this tension by presenting it in terms of opposing an *internal* to an *external* perspective. The former treats conflicts as a matter of interpretation of the forum's own positive law. The latter locates itself with reference to a normative system external to – and considered as more important than – the authority of the forum.[6] Much of the tension arises because, on the one hand, it is difficult to explain the legitimacy of the external normative system being invoked, and, even more so, to locate pertinent and authoritative norms within such external system. On the other hand, the forum might have the norms or at least the capacity to generate them, but it still has problems justifying the exercise of its authority vis-à-vis the other states – problems that pertain both to the fact of this authority being exercised and its actual impact.

In the process of achieving this, private international law works conjure visions for the structuring of what is today commonly called the *international society* and for the role of private international law in it – a simultaneous claim of passive neutrality and active participation. In short, the "international" or "external" dimension of the conflict of laws has both a *normative* and a *foundational* function, each of which will be explored in the following Sections.

6.3 International Law as a Governance Project

In 1869, three jurists and statesmen met in Ghent, Belgium and decided upon the creation of a French-language *Review of International Law and Comparative Legislation*: the Belgian Gustav Rolin-Jaequemyns (1835–1902), the Dutchman Tobias Asser (1838–1913), and the Englishman John Westlake.[7] The three jurists were also instrumental, along with the Swiss German Johan Gaspar Bluntschli and the Italian Pasquale Mancini, in the creation, again in Ghent, of the *Institute of*

[6] L. Brilmayer, *Conflict of Laws*, 2nd ed (Boston: Little Brown, 1995), 1ff.

[7] See Koskenniemi, *Gentle Civilizer*, 39–41; A. Stille, "Asser et Rolin-Jaequemyns. Compte-rendu de quelques contacts personnels entre deux contemporains de Laurent" in Erauw et al., *Liber memorialis François Laurent*, 1089–1097.

International Law in 1873.[8] A month later, the *Association for the Reform and Codification of the Law of Nations* (renamed the International Law Association in 1895) held its own inaugural congress in Brussels. The two collective bodies were supposed to complement each other. The Institute was conceived as a *corps permanent ou académique*, which would study international law and formulate its fundamental principles. Its membership was selective and self-perpetuating. A maximum was set on the number of its Members. National quotas were also established, in order to assure a balance in representation. As to the Association, its role was to reach – and mobilize – a broader audience.[9]

The Institute devoted its next meeting to the discussion of elaborating a set of general principles of conflicts rules, so as to make possible an international codification.[10] This new private *international* law was hence further distinguished from "private law" properly speaking, which would remain administered on the domestic level.[11] The members of the Institute began the lobbying of the major European powers on an international treaty conference to that effect. Mancini led initiatives to bring together European (and American) countries on the treaty table in both his stints as a member of the Italian cabinet (1867 and 1881–1885); the Kingdom of the Netherlands had in the meantime made a concrete proposal for a conference on the enforcement of foreign judgments in 1875.[12] These initiatives received a lukewarm response: if 1867 was probably too early to ignite serious interest on such a project of international lawmaking, the subsequent initiatives were hampered by the Franco-German rivalry, on the one hand, and the increased isolationism of Britain and the United States, on the other. It took the concerted efforts of two generations of lawyers and diplomats to get to the first

8 A. Rolin, *Les origines de l'Institut de droit international, 1873–1923* (Brussels, 1873), 5–23; E. Nys, "La science du droit des gens" in *Memories of John Westlake* (London, 1914), 43–58.

9 Rolin, *Les origines*, 22: "Vulgariser, répandre, réaliser, tel sera son rôle essentiel, tandis que l'Institut restera dans les régions élevées et sereines de la science."

10 P.-S. Mancini, "De l'utilité de rendre obligatoires pour tous les Etats, sous la forme d'un ou de plusieurs traités internationaux, un certain nombre des règles générales du Droit international privé pour assurer la décision uniforme des conflits entre les différentes législations civiles et criminelles," *Clunet*, 1 (1874), 221–39, 285–304 (essentially the first report presented to the Institute of International Law).

11 T. M. C. Asser, 'Droit international privé et droit uniforme,' *Revue de droit international et de législation comparée*, 12 (1880), 5–22.

12 See e.g. K. Lipstein, "One Hundred Years of Hague Conferences on Private International Law," *International and Comparative Law Quarterly*, 42 (1993), 553–653, 554–557.

treaty Conference on private international law, hosted by the Kingdom of the Netherlands at The Hague in September 1893, with 13 countries attending – all of them from Europe.[13] A total of four conferences between 1893 and 1904 led to six treaties on matters of civil procedure and family law. Latin American countries had in the meantime embarked upon their own process of international treaty-making. The United Kingdom and the United States would not join until 1955 and 1964. But Mancini's vision of making at least the essential conflicts rules "mandatory for all States, in the form of one or more international treaties . . . in order to assure the uniform decision of conflicts" between their laws, has persisted.

Conflict of laws did not have much association with the law of nations prior to the mid-nineteenth century. Jurists in the Early Modern period, such as Ulric Huber, might have alluded to the "law of nations" (*ius gentium*) but they appear to have viewed it as part of their "domestic" law and not as a distinct legal system.[14] It is also certain that this "law of nations" was viewed more as an empirical phenomenon (i.e. practice shows nations act out of comity), than as a legal principle imposing its way from above. In short, any reference to such "law of nations" served as further validation of their maxims and rules. Even that function, however, was better served by the *ius commune*. Things gradually changed in the eighteenth and early nineteenth centuries, as the intellectual foundations of the law of nations were transformed and the first international institutions were created. These changes, however, are only marginally reflected in the perceptions of conflicts doctrine. Probably the clearest example of such influence was Carl Georg von Wächter, whose answer to the changing environment was the embrace of legislative positivism and a forum-centric approach.[15] Savigny himself famously promoted the

[13] On the history of the early Hague Conference see J. H. A. van Loon, "Quelques réflexions sur l'unification progressive du droit international privé dans le cadre de la Conférence de la Haye" in J. Erauw et al. (eds.), *Liber memorialis François Laurent* (Brussels: E. Story – Scientia, 1989), 1133–1149, esp. 1134–1140.

[14] See e.g. in this sense – regarding Huber – Watson, *Comity of Errors*, 7 (Huber viewed *ius gentium* as being part of Roman law and thus Frisian law). Cf. Sections 12.3.1 and 14.4.

[15] C. G. von Wächter, "Über die Collision der Privatrechtsgesetze verschiedener Staaten," *Archiv für die Civilistiche Praxis*, 24 (1841), 230–311 and 25 (1842), 1–60, 161–200, 361–419. See K. Nadelman, "Wächter's Essay on the Collision of Private Laws of Different States," *American Journal of Comparative Law*, 13 (1964), 414–428, 417–428 for a translation of critical passages and R. Michaels, "Carl Georg von Wächter" in J. Basedow et al. (eds.), *Encyclopedia of Private International Law* (Cheltenham: Edward Elgar, 2017) on the role of forum in Wächter.

notion of a "community of law" or of "legal feeling" (*Rechtsgemeinschaft*), which constituted the "foundation of the universal customary law (*algemeine Gewonheitsrecht*) so often appealed to in inquiries of this kind" and deriving "from the (constantly progressing) concurrence of writers and judicial decisions." Whereas he notes the advantages of a common system of rules in dealing with conflicts between territorial laws, including treaties between neighboring states, such norms are rare and regarded as an "expression" of this community.[16]

This state of affairs was altered drastically by the group of people who have been called the Italian or Latin school or, in this work, the international-law school. The adherents of the school were political Liberals, espousing liberal nationalism at home and international cooperation abroad. Many of them had held parliamentary seats, and Mancini had repeatedly held cabinet jobs. Both their politics and their theoretical outlook pushed them toward a jurisprudence of strong legislative positivism.

Thus, a few years after the creation of the Institute, François Laurent sought to merge the "positive" science of history and the "theoretical" science of philosophy in constructing the *science* of – private and public – international law. "There is no science without an ideal, just as there is no science without facts serving as basis to the idea," concluded Laurent.[17] In the name of Principles and Justice, he dismissed the invocation of 'utility' and 'interests' (*l'intérêt n'est pas un principe*), and by consequence comity and diplomacy.[18] In their turn, his more pragmatic peers sought to combine the "practical element" of international practice to the theoretical one of science.[19] The distinction made by these same people between collective and individual science, emphasizing the potential of the legal scholar's collective action to have impact (and to reduce their fallibility), also moves in the same direction.[20] Again and again, the

[16] Savigny, *System*, 8:23–39 (§§ 348–349), with references also to *algemeine Rechtsgemeinschaft* or *völkerrechtliche Gemeinschaft*. The expression "community of legal feeling" in used by Guthrie to translate *Rechtsgemeinschaft* in one occasion. Savigny, *Private International Law*, 72 in fine.

[17] Laurent, *Droit civil international*, 1:73.

[18] Ibid., esp. 70–71.

[19] Rolin, *Origines*, 21–22.

[20] G. Rolin-Jaequemyns, "De la nécessité d'organiser une institution scientifique permanente pour favoriser l'étude et les progress du droit international," *Revue de droit international et de législation comparée*, 5 (1873), 463–491, 464–465.

normative role for scholarship is emphasized in the school's texts. Private international law is often presented there as the branch of international law which is easier to construct.[21] In a reversal from Wächter's position as to the role of the judge in interpreting the spirit of his State's (domestic) legislation, the school sees the lack of legislative intervention in conflicts matters as an opportunity (and responsibility) for scholarship to construct the subject on proper grounds (with a view to an eventual legislative codification).[22]

Many historical references to late nineteenth-century private international law do not even mention the word "international law," emphasizing instead the "common doctrinal basis," the insistence on fundamental principles or the advocacy of the nationality principle.[23] In contrast – in his advocacy of a systematic approach and awareness of the distinctness and connections of private international law – Henri Batiffol argued that Mancini and his school subordinated philosophically private to public international law. This philosophical subordination – and the relative disregard of historical realities and court practice – was the cause of their decline.[24]

By the end of the nineteenth century, these deficiencies had led to a reaction by a new generation of scholars oriented toward private-law doctrine who suggested, in their turn, that the connection between domestic private law and private international law was unbreakable. The most characteristic example was the issue of legal characterization which was "discovered" (or perhaps more accurately brought to the spotlight) by Etienne A. Bartin and Franz Kahn.[25] But the increased attention paid to issues such as *renvoi*, and even the emphasis on the elaboration of *fraus legis* doctrine, are also examples of this approach.[26]

[21] See e.g. Laurent, *Droit civil international*, 1:80–81.

[22] See e.g. R. Philimore, *Commentaries upon International Law*, vol. 4 (London: William Benning & Son, 1861), 11: "It is a matter for rejoicing that [this branch of jurisprudence] has escaped the Procrustean treatment of positive legislation, and has been allowed to grow to its fair proportions under the influencec of that science which works out of conscience, reason and expression, the great problem of Law or Civil Justice."

[23] See e.g. Rabel, *Conflict of Laws*, 1:xv, 8–10.

[24] Ibid., 10–12, esp. 12: "C'est sans doute l'écart excessif entre le système de Mancini et le donné historique et jurisprudentiel qui explique son déclin, aussi rapide et complet que son ascension avait été immédiate et brilliante."

[25] See Chapter 5, fn 30 above.

[26] See in this regard two other essays by E. Bartin, both republished in his *Études*: E. Bartin, "Les conflits entre dispositions législatives de droit international privé: Théorie du renvoi," *Revue de droit international privé et de legislation comparée*, 30 (1898),

The same holds true of the various attempts to propose new names for the legal field, which placed less emphasis on the international-law connection.[27] Critics attacked both the political and jurisprudential premises of the school of international law, leading to the erosion of government support for international codification projects.[28] One of the arguments they could draw upon was the nonexistence of "positive" international law in the sphere of private law and conflict of laws.[29] In his turn, Batiffol argued that this led to the other extreme, i.e. the subordination of private international law to (domestic) private law, which led to a narrow perception and failure to appreciate the originality of private international law.[30]

Over time, the number of approaches to the conflict of laws increased in proportion to the number of people working in the field. Projects for international legislation also proliferated – with variable success. What begun as a common normative project became a complex relationship between two different legal disciplines, each with their own baggage. The

129–187, 272–320; and "Les dispositions d'ordre public. La théorie de la fraude à la loi, et l'idée de la communauté internationale," *Revue de droit international privé et de legislation comparée*, 29 (1897), 385–427, 613–658.

27 For example, Frederic Harrison proposed the term *intermunicipal law*. See F. Harrison, "Le droit international privé ou le conflit des lois au point de vue analytique, particulièrement en Angleterre," *Clunet*, 7 (1880), 533–551 (the second of two essays on the "Conflict of Laws," first published in 1879 and subsequently reprised as F. Harrison, *On Jurisprudence and the Conflict of Laws* (Oxford: Clarendon Press, 1919), 130. A. V. Dicey, *A Digest of the Law of England with Reference to the Conflict of Laws* (London: Stevens & Sons, 1896), 12–15 proposed the term "extraterritorial effect of law" but regarded as even better the term "extra-territorial recognition of rights" proposed by Holland (15). Baty, *Polarized Law*, vi proposes "what many will consider a fanciful name" in his attempt to find "a really descriptive title for this branch of the law" (dismissing other "descriptive names" such as "interlocking laws," "harmonizations of law," "correlations of law"). For a veritable parade of names, see E. Zitelmann, "Der Name 'internationales Privatrecht'," *NiemZ*, 27 (1918), 177–196 (esp. 193ff, where he is proposing "zwischenprivatrecht," as an alternative to "zwischenstaatliches Privatrecht"); E. Frankenstein, *Internationales Privatrecht (Grenzrecht)*, vol. I (Berlin: Rothschild, 1926) uses the term *Grenzrecht* throughout his treatise (see e.g. 31ff, and his defense of the term at 262–263); A. Schnitzer "Aussenprivatrecht" (as quoted by Kurt Siehr, *Internationales Privatrecht*, 8). Max Gutzwiller, "International Privatrecht," in Rudolf Stammler (ed.), *Das gesamte Deutsche Recht*, vol. I (1931), 1511–1661, 1549–1551, offers the most comprehensive overview but remarks nonetheless that "*wer eine heitere Stunde genießen will, der durchgehe die Literatur zur Namensfrage*" (1549).

28 See also Hatzimihail, "Conceptual Battlefield," 59–61; Mills, "Confluence," 66–70.

29 Holland, *Jurisprudence*; and A. V. Dicey, e.g. *Digest*, 17–19 are the main examples.

30 Batiffol, *Aspects philosophiques*, 14–15.

new thinking has been aptly summarized in the evolutionary terms of a move from positivism to constitutionalism.[31]

6.4 International Law as Doctrinal Foundation

In Brilmayer's scheme, the external perspective is employed as a doctrinal foundation for the conflict of laws. This is indeed a common pattern in conflicts doctrine. We have already seen, and will examine in detail below, how Medieval jurists used the *ius commune* and the fiction of a "universal" Roman empire in order to explain the legal authority of their material and to ground their systems of norms.[32] Perhaps a more telling example is the illustration of how Ulric Huber, mostly known for his invocation of comity as a fundamental axiom of his conflicts tract, essentially uses these axioms as a foundation for his three actual rules – which consecrate the *lex loci actus* as the predominant conflicts rule.[33] The most famous example in the history of private international law is, however, Friedrich Carl von Savigny, and his concept of *community of law*.

We have chosen to focus on Batiffol, because he comes after the normative drive of early classical conflicts lawyers. Batiffol is a mature classical lawyer, an heir to the Liberal internationalists who succeeded to the disciplinary institutions they created (specialized publications, courses and associations) but also of their critics.[34] Mid-century conflicts lawyers have had to cope with the normative and theoretical failure of the previous generations and elaborate ("reconstruct") doctrinal systems that took into account both aspirations and realities. We have seen Batiffol's views on the school of international law and its critics; in the same narrative, Savigny is presented as having sought a way out of this perilous antithesis by "materializing" (or perhaps better by *reifying*) the legal relations.[35] Batiffol in his turn espoused the comparative method: an

[31] Mills, *Confluence*, 74ff.

[32] See Sections 3.4, 8.2.1, and 8.4.

[33] See Sections 13.2.2 and 14.4.

[34] On Batiffol, see principally P. Gothot, "La place d'Henri Batiffol dans le doctrine," *Travaux du comité français de droit international privé*, 11 (1991–1992), 21–31; and Y. Lequette, "L'influence de l'œuvre d'Henri Batiffol sur la jurisprudence française," *Travaux du comité français de droit international privé*, 11 (1991–1992), 32–48.

[35] Batiffol, *Aspects philosophiques*, 10, 12–14.

approach intermediate like Savigny's but more legalistic like his epigones.[36]

One could be tempted to notice the affinities in the imagery of Batiffol's *Traité Élémentaire* with the *school of international law* from almost a century before. Private international law is international law, only more effective: an international law with domestic sanctions.[37] In this way, Batiffol managed to reverse the sources-based argument of those stressing the domestic character of private international law (i.e. that no positive international law exists on conflicts issues). He used the idea of *dédoublement fonctionnel*, under which the same organs operate in the domestic and the international level.[38]

Batiffol's imagery is consonant with a project of international governance, which grants central role to the States; but he is clearly interested less in the normative implications of his theory for the international system and more in outlining a solid foundation for his conception of *the conflict of laws as the law of the coordination of legal systems*.[39] This was the foundation for the "reconstructive" doctrinal solutions that Batiffol gave to salient problems of the time, such as legal characterization and *renvoi*, reconciling scholarship and case law in France.[40]

6.5 World Views and World Systems

Each work, like its author, is situated in a time and a place. They come from a certain world and especially from a certain perception of that world. They express, more or less clearly, a certain world view. At the

[36] Ibid., 15ff.

[37] It must be remembered that the world talked about is not that of the contemporary activists engaging in human-rights and environmental litigation by way of effective "international governance."

[38] See e.g. G. Scelle, *Manuel de droit international public* (Paris, 1948), 15–24. The theory dates back to the early 1930s. See the references in A. Cassesse, "Remarks on Scelle's Theory of 'Role Splitting' (*dédoublement fonctionnel*) in International Law," *European Journal of International Law*, 1 (1990), 210–231, 210 n. 2. Batiffol makes express reference to Scelle and his doctrine in *Aspects philosophiques*, esp. 103 n. 1, 135 n. 1, and 185 n. 1.

[39] See Batiffol, *Aspects philosophiques*, esp. 102ff. See also E. Jayme, *Internationales Privatrecht: Ideengeschichte von Mancini und Ehrenzweig zum Europäischen Kollisionsrecht* (Heidelberg: C. F. Müller, 2009).

[40] See Batiffol, *Traité élémentaire*, 309ff, chapter entitled *Relations des systèmes de solution* dealing with the so-called *conflit des qualifications* (310ff) and especially with the problem of renvoi or *conflit des rattachements* (320ff).

same time, the most successful works across time have been the ones that can rise above the circumstances of the time and place of their creation.

Works of conflicts doctrine are by definition connected to an image of a world, indeed often an image of the entire world. We saw, for example, how Batiffol grounds his doctrinal system upon the image of a world – an "international society" – consisting of States. Batiffol's States possess all atrributes of State sovereigny. Indeed, it is these States that provide the norms and institutions that govern private international relations. They do so, obviously, by entering into agreements with one another but also in functional terms: States together constitute the international community and their individual actions and directves create an "international order."[41]

This imagery presents a political theory that is evidently underlying Batiffol's doctrine – or used to provide legitimacy. It is also connected with his theory of legal sources and their hierarchy.

In the case studies that follow, we shall consider these three, interconnected, aspects of the author's thought as they appear in, or influence, the work examined.

First: how are the sources of law identified, approached and organized into a hierarchy. Most preclassical conflicts texts are about Roman law – but there is a fundamental difference between Medieval Italian jurists and seventeenth-century Dutch jurists. The former present a direct line of authority between Late Antiquity and Medieval emperors; they approach the jurisdiction of polities as emanating from imperial consent and adopt a complex, even pluralistic perspective. The latter are strongly grounded in their own polity; Rome is seen as an historical example, not a political reality; Roman law is a valuable source of law, which has been made part of the law of the land by decision of their own polity. The question of sources is a core legal question, but it is inherently linked, for both Medieval and Early Modern jurists, to their political thought and political action.

Second: the fundamental bases of the author's political thought. For example, how did Bartolus perceive the legal status of Medieval, especially Italian, polities? How did he reconcile the political realities that surrounded him with the texts and fictions of Roman law, including the glossators' pro-imperial legacy? What role is there for notions such as "sovereignty" or "jurisdiction"? What about Huber, who lived in the immediate post-Westphalian world?

[41] Batiffol, *Traité élémentaire*, 1–2.

This is linked to a third aspect: the author's political context. What politics underlie the author's world view and how do they matter for a history of conflicts doctrine? What ongoing struggles was the author involved in and what was their relevance to this work?

We have already seen that conflicts writers may approach or at least present the world surrounding them in an instrumentalist fashion. Conflicts treatments by their nature allow this. They also invite us to consider the comprehensive system in which the authors imagine themselves – and probably want us to imagine them – as participating.

In approaching these questions, we can draw from other disciplines concepts that may allow us to analyze both actual operation and perceptions.

The concept of *world systems* originated in economic and global history.[42] It has found resonance in international relations, as well as other social sciences, where the concept of an *international* or a *world system* seeks to explain – and underline – the interaction between different levels of political entities, or *units.*[43] I have chosen it over the more established term of a *state* or *states system*, which may account for the post-Westphalian world but not for the complexity of Medieval Europe.[44]

A comprehensive approach to world/international systems, would list five levels: systems, subsystems, units, subunits, and individuals.[45] These levels may be moved up and down. In the Bartolan world system, for

42 The concept originated with I. Wallerstein, *The Modern World System I: Capitalist Agriculture and the Origins of the European World-Economy in the Sixteenth Century* (Berkeley: University of California Press, 2011 reprint of 1974), esp. 347: "A world-system is a social system, one that has boundaries, structures, member groups, rules of legitimation, and coherence. Its life is made up of the conflicting forces which hold it together by tension and tear it apart as each group seeks eternally to remold it to its advantage. It has the characteristics of an organism, in that it has a life-span over which its characteristics change in some respects and remain stable in others. One can define its structures as being at different times strong or weak in terms of the internal logic of its functioning. What characterizes a social system in my view is the fact that life within it is largely self-contained, and that the dynamics of its development are largely internal."

43 See notably B. Buzan and R. Little, *International Systems in World History* (Oxford: Oxford University Press, 2000). Buzan and Little opt for the term "international system" because some international systems are not world ones, while others are, and to avoid too close an association with the theories of Immanuel Wallerstein: ibid., 32–33.

44 Bederman, *International law in Antiquity*, 16ff uses the concept of a state system as defined by Hedley Bull, for his study of the Ancient Near East, Greek city states, and the period of Roman expansion.

45 Buzan and Little, *International Systems*, 69.

example, we may view as units the cities, like Perugia, which recognize no superior; as subsystems the regional alliances between cities (and other localities) or the area of Central Italian papal territories; depending on the context, the system could be the Roman Empire in its fictive legal form, or the cultural–geographic area of Italy as a whole.

Interdisciplinarity, however, can only help us up to a point. Functionalist and realist approaches predominate in international relations theory over so-called ideational approaches (which might have more affinity with intellectual and doctrinal legal history). This is seen in the debates as to who is the pivotal force in a world system: behavioural approaches point to the individual entities ("subsystems") interacting with each other and thus creating/transforming the system above; neorealists believe that the structure of the system dictates the behavior of the entities; constructivists would suggest that it is really both things at the same time.[46] International-relations theorists examine the world system in terms of one or more "sectors:" military, political, economic, sociocultural, or environmental.[47] At best, law is viewed as a subordinate tool in each sector.[48]

We could, however, draw on these ideas to contemplate a *legal* world system, as expressed in the hierarchy of legal sources: consider the role granted to international law as opposed to municipal law, federal as opposed to state law, state law as opposed to local law, contractual freedom and individual autonomy as opposed to "state" law, but also to natural law, divine law, and so forth. This role is determined through notions of subordinate bodies of law, of "residual" or "common" law and of "legal systems" which are more comprehensive than other bodies of law.[49]

This book is concerned with achieving a better understanding of the world in which the subjects of our study *lived*. Even more so, we should be interested in the subjective understanding of how they experienced, and sought to influence, this world.

Such an exercise requires a balancing act between the use of outside sources – primary as well as secondary – and the work of our authors; but

[46] See for a summary Buzan and Little, *International Systems*, 35ff (citing for each of the three conceptions mentioned in our text Singer, Wald, and Wendt).

[47] Buzan and Little, *International Systems*, 73–74.

[48] It might perhaps be possible to employ these international-relations constructs and examine the circulation of legal ideas and doctrines and the roles of lawyers in terms of a legal sector in a world system.

[49] See, in this sense, Sections 8.4 and 12.3.

also, within their work, between their conflicts treatment and the rest of their work. In examining what is essentially the political foundations of doctrinal edifices, we must also be mindful of the extent to which our authors may present a picture of their world which they themselves know not to be true: for example, Bartolus regarding the power of the Roman Emperor (and the Pope), and Huber regarding the practice of nations to apply each other's law.

6.6 Conclusion

The international or external order might operate in two ways in conflicts doctrine. We could call the persistent effort to harmonize law on the international plane – whether with regard to conflicts rules or private-law regimes themselves – the *mobilization of the "international" as governance.*[50] But the history of private international law in the twentieth century (as well as of doctrinal systems prior to that) is also the history of what we could call *the mobilization of the "international" as doctrinal foundation.* The former dimension aims at achieving a normative goal – for example, a unified and codified conflict of laws – while the latter is primarily concerned with providing a doctrinal/theoretical foundation to a doctrinal system whose existence may have preceded that of its foundation.

The intrinsic dynamics of private international law doctrine are a central theme of this book. Private international law is created through the tension between the private/internal and the international/external – indeed the *coexistence* of the two domains/perspectives – and the different approach taken by different theories. It has to respond to external pressures and stimuli while maintaining some degree of internal coherence. A system without solid foundations is destined to collapse. However, legal doctrines have often survived the collapse of the philosophical premises they were built upon.[51] It could be argued that theoretical foundations are often employed ex post in legal argument, in order to explain or coordinate existing structures or edifices already under

[50] For this use of the abstract-noun concept of "the international" (spelled by many with a capital I and without quotation marks) see D. Kennedy, "Receiving the International," *Connecticut Journal of International Law*, 10 (1990), 1–26.

[51] See e.g. J. Gordley, *The Philosophical Origins of Modern Contract Doctrine* (Oxford: Oxford University Press, 1991).

construction. On the other hand, it is impossible to isolate a structure from its foundations.

Which brings us to a second theme: the instrumentalism involved in invocations of fixed images of the "international" – whether sovereign states, or the runaway world of globalization – in private international law discourse. Private international law is an active participant in international governance: it may support one or another vision of globalization, it may help reconcile, or strongly privilege, conflicting sets of public policies and individual desires. On the other hand, this does not mean that conflicts doctrine is subordinated to this dimension. We certainly cannot understand past or present conflicts theories, principles and norms, and potential alternatives, without an appreciation of the world in which they originated and where they are asked to operate. At the same time, so much of conflicts doctrine has shown remarkable resilience across time and space. Context is vital, yet it is clearly not everything.

PART III

Bartolus da Sassoferrato and the Conflict of Laws in the Middle Ages

7

"*Nunc veniamus ad glossam*": Bartolus on the Conflict of Laws

7.1 Introduction

Bartolus (or Bartolo in the vernacular) was born in either 1313 or 1314, in a village near the small town of Sassoferrato, in the March of Ancona – a territory forming part of the Papal States. He first studied law at the University of Perugia, where his most notable teacher was Cinus da Pistoia, a founding figure of the so-called School of Commentators.[1] He then obtained his doctorate from Bologna in 1334, where his teachers included Oldradus da Ponte, Jacobus Buttrigarius, and Ranierus de Forlivio. After a brief judicial career in Todi and possibly Pisa, Bartolus begun teaching at Pisa in 1339 and finally joined the law faculty of Perugia in either 1342 or 1343 until his death in 1357.[2] His students there included the other great Commentator Baldus de Ubaldis (1327–1400).

Bartolus was especially prolific.[3] His "monumental" commentary on the entire *Corpus Iuris Civilis* "had an authority in succeeding generations unmatched even by the Gloss."[4] He also wrote a number of

[1] Cinus (1270–1336/1337) was educated in Bologna but his work – especially his influential commentary (*Lectura*) on the Code – drew substantially from the work of the *ultramontanus* Petrus Bellaperticus. See Savigny, *Geschichte*, 6:71ff; Lainé, *Introduction*, 1:122.

[2] See F. Calasso, "Bartolo da Sassoferrato," *Annali di storia del diritto*, 9 (1965), 472–520. Among the literature on Bartolus, see C. N. S. Woolf, *Bartolus of Sassoferrato: His Position in the History of Medieval Political Thought* (Cambridge: Cambridge University Press, 1913); P. Franzina in J. Basedow et al. (eds.), *Elgar Encyclopedia of Private International Law* (Cheltenham: Edward Elgar, 2017), 158–163, the contributions in Centro Italiano di Studi sul Basso Medioevo, *Bartolo da Sassoferrato nel VII Centenario della Nascita: Diritto, Politica, Società* (Spoleto: Fondazione Centro Italiano di Studi sull'Alto Medioevo, 2014).

[3] Citations in this work are from Bartolus de Sassoferrato, *Opera Omnia*, 5 vols. (Basel, 1562) in facsmimile (Frankfurt: Vico Verlag, 2007). I have additionally consulted the Venice 1602 and Lyon 1533 editions.

[4] Robinson et al., *European Legal History*, 65.

monographs and smaller tracts and hundreds of *consilia* (legal opinions).[5]

7.2 The Commentary on *cunctos populos*

The principal treatment, by Bartolus, of subjects that today would be regarded as falling within the province of conflicts doctrine is to be found within his commentary on *cunctos populos* (C.1.1.1).[6] The greater part of Bartolus's commentary on that *lex* is a comment on the gloss *si Bononiensis* itself: in the reorganization by subsequent editors into numbered sections, the relevant text corresponds to nus. 13–51.[7] The 12 preceding sections of the commentary on *cunctos populos* refer to general matters of statutory interpretation, religious doctrine as law, the legal treatment of heretics, and certain types of personal incapacity.[8]

Much of the commentary on the gloss *si Bononiensis* is also replicated in the discussion by Bartolus "on the effect of custom," in his *repetitio* to an early passage of the Digest (D.1.3.32 princ., *de quibus*), which discusses the role allowed for customs and usage in the absence of "written law."[9] It has

[5] In the 1562 Basel edition, the fifth and final volume includes 38 *tractati* (253–758), of which the first two consist of 264+117 *consilia* and 22 *quaestiones*.

[6] Bartolus ad C.1.1.1, 5b–12a, vol. IV (Basel, 1562).

[7] Ibid., 7a–12a.

[8] The "marrows" (*medullae*) of nus. 1–12, as listed by subsequent editors are as follows: 1. *Relativum, quis ponitur declarative, augmentative et restrictive* (the relative pronoun "who" is [sometimes] put in a declarative manner, [sometimes] in an argumentative, and [sometimes] restrictively). 2. *Lex non debet esse ludibrio* (the law should not be made a matter of mockery). 3. *Verbum, volo, quandoque inducit dispositionem* (the word "I will" sometimes introduces the dispositive [part of the law]). 4. *Relativum, Quis vel Qui, est relativum substantiae* (the relative pronoun "who?" or "who" is a relative of substance [not of quality]. 5. *Religio quomodo summatur, et quid nobis afferat* ("religion" how is it considered and what it contributes to us). 6., 8. *Usurae, quando possunt de mente et voluntate iuris civilis exigi, et ut interesse peti* ("usury," when it can be required according to the mind and will of the civil law and [when it can] be sought as damages). 7. *Minus malum permittur ut evitetur maius* (the lesser evil is permitted in order to avoid the greater). 9. *Dementia alia vera, alia ficta* (some insanity is real and some is made up). 10. *Argumentum de periuro ad haereticum quando procedat* (when an argument on the ground of perjury is suitable against a heretic). 11. *Haeretici hodie infames et repelluntur a testimonio* (heretics today are infamous and repelled from testifying). 12. *Infames de facto quando possunt testifiari* (those who are infamous, when can they testify about a fact). 13. *Haeretici qua poena puniantur* (heretics, by what penalty they are punished).

[9] Bartolus ad D.1.3.32, nus. 25–31, 44b–45b, vol. I (Basel, 1562). Bartolus's commentary on *de quibus* is translated by Clarence Smith, "Bartolo," 163–174. See also Section 8.2.1. For the actual passage in the Digest see Section 3.4.1.

been suggested that Bartolus wrote first the commentary on the *lex de quibus*.[10] In fact, if we compare the two texts, the commentary on *cunctos populos* seems as a reprisal and further elaboration of the ideas outlined in the commentary on *de quibus*: only a smart part of that latter commentary is devoted to "conflicts" issues, which take up considerably less space than in the commentary on *cunctos populos*; the distinction between "conflicts" and other issues is less clear and some major aspects of Bartolan conflicts doctrine are only hinted upon. We shall accordingly occupy ourselves with – and refer to – that text, as has generally been the case since the Middle Ages. The commentary on *de quibus* will be considered only for purposes of verification and better understanding the development of Bartolan doctrine.[11]

The Bartolan text treats what we would today regard as conflicts questions in a manner comprehensive and sophisticated – if not always systematic. Evidence suggests that Bartolus presented the entire commentary on *De summa Trinitate* in a separate evening lecture, as a *repetitio*.[12] In this book, we are accordingly referring to the Bartolan commentary on *cunctos populos* (ad C.1.1.1) as a *repetitio*; moreover, for convenience purposes we are treating nus. 13–51 as a standalone text, as if they were not preceded by nus. 1–12. But readers should beware. We must especially not rush to draw conclusions from the text's relative autonomy. The term *conflictus legum* – or any term that could be seen as covering the entire subject of conflicts questions – is nowhere to be found in Bartolus. Nor did he deem the subject worthy of a stand-alone "treatise" (*tractatus*), a genre with which he was quite familiar.[13] We would in fact search in vain for a separate publication of the conflicts treatment, or the entire *repetitio*, prior to the late nineteenth century.

[10] Thus Clarence Smith, "Introduction," 157. Among other arguments, Clarence Smith notes that the gloss on *de quibus* formed in fact part of the first-year curriculum, whereas the beginning of the Code was taught on the fourth year. It is however difficult to generalize about "Medieval law schools." Some of the statutes we have put the *Digestum vetus* first, others place the *Codex* first. The commentary on de quibus remains in relative neglect, with the exception of M. Köpcke, *A Short History of Legal Validity and Invalidity* (Cambridge: Intersentia, 2019), 73ff.

[11] See Sections 9.4.4 and 10.2.2.

[12] See also Vatican City, Bibliotheca Apostolica Vaticana, MS Vat. Lat. 2589, fol. 68v. The commentary on *de quibus* is titled *repetitio* in the 1562 Basel edition. See also Calasso, "Bartolo," 518 and 519 for other manuscripts of both *repetitiones*.

[13] The word *tractatus* is actually mentioned once in the text: Bartolus ad C.1.1.1, nu. 47, referring to the commentary of Cinus.

7.2.1 *Establishing the Text*

We have no original text by Bartolus himself, or an author-approved version. The Bartolan text made its way for centuries through copying by hand. Despite the exemplary diligence of Medieval scribes, copying mistakes must have been unavoidable: the shortform used by the scribes certainly did not help in the long run.

The invention of the printing presses proved helpful only up to a point. Errors might still occur during the typesetting process. A lot depended on the editor's diligence, and the quality of the manuscripts he consulted. Shortform was also used – and this has created problems for transcriptions still persisting to this day.

The Bartolan text was made more widely accessible in the late nineteenth century, when the conflicts treatment (i.e. nus. 13–57) were published, independent from the rest of Bartolus's work. The first reprint appeared in Edinburgh in 1880, when William Guthrie appended the text (alongside other major texts of preclassical jurists) to his translation of Savigny's book on the conflict of laws.[14] The second was attempted in 1894 by Ferdinand Meili.[15] Legal historians have been, justly, critical of both transcriptions.[16] This does not however diminish their contribution in getting people to actually read the Bartolan text, which evidently few had done since the Middle Ages. But a new transcription of the text into longform Latin was necessary for any textual analysis.[17]

14 See Savigny, *Private International Law*, 433–452. This was the Latin text used by Beale in his translation. Guthrie seems to have used the 1588–1589 Basel edition of Bartolus' works, also used by Clarence Smith for his own translation.

15 F. Meili, "Die theoretischen Abhandlungen von Bartolus und Baldus über das internationale Privaat- und Strafrecht," *Niemeyers Zeitschrift*, 4 (1894), 260–269, 340–346, 446–465. Meili used the Turin edition of 1574.

16 See Clarence Smith, "Introduction," 160 n. (e): "[a] rough count shows about forty new misprints in Guthrie's text, all but two of single letters, excluding mistakes in the references." Meili is in his turn charged with "a fair sprinkling of errors, including, mirabile dictu, some of Guthrie's, but mainly in extending abbreviations and in translating the references into yet another system."

17 For this book, as well as for my earlier research, I have relied upon the transcription into digital form prepared by Andrew Barry under the supervision of Professor Charles Donahue, Jr. at Harvard Law School (1998). That transcription, as subsequently revised by Prof. Donahue, including corrections noted in this and my earlier work, is now available online and constitutes a valuable resource. For the – often neglected – passages on clerics (nus. 28–31), a better transcription can be found in O. Condorelli, "Bartolo e il diritto canonico" in *Bartolo da Sassoferrato nel VII Centenario della Nascita: Diritto, Politica, Società* (Spoleto: Fondazione Centro Italiano di Studi sull'Alto Medioevo, 2014), 463–457, 489 (n. 45). Barry relied on the 1602 edition of Bartolus's works, which was also

Two English translations of the text are available today: the most popular one was made by Harvard law professor Joseph Henry Beale.[18] A second, partial translation was made by Canadian legal historian Clarence Smith as a supplement to his translation of the commentary on the *lex de quibus*.[19] Beale's translation – which is used here with modifications – has been vividly criticized.[20] It nonetheless provided the basis for a Portuguese edition by Haroldo Valladão.[21] In French, Armand Lainé's extensive presentation was standard reference (and effectively a partial translation), until the recent publication of an excellent translation by Bertrand Ancel.[22]

generously made available to myself by Prof. Donahue, who also decisively helped me with obtaining and reading the manuscript Vat. Lat. 2589 (originally consulted by Clarence Smith). Consulting manuscripts is necessary given the many problems in the transcription from manuscript to the Early Modern printed texts (a result of unclear words and abbreviations) but since a new edition of the text is not an objective of this book, these materials, along with my own facsimile of the 1562 Basel edition were sufficient for present purposes. In the discussion of the text that follows, the use of two daggers (††) signifies that a word or phrase was erased from the text, after consulting the manuscript. A phrase between single daggers suggests that the phrase has been re-written following our consultation of the manuscript. This Chapter improves upon – and replaces – an earlier publication on Bartolus ad C.1.1.1: N. Hatzimihail, "Bartolus and the Conflict of Laws," *Revue hellénique de droit international*, 60 (2007), 11–79.

18 *Bartolus on the Conflict of Laws*, trans. Joseph Henry Beale (Cambridge, MA: Harvard University Press, 1914).

19 Clarence Smith, "Bartolo," 174–183, 247–275.

20 See A. Ehrenzweig, "Beale's translation of Bartolus," *American Journal of Comparative Law*, 12 (1963), 384–385. The better qualified Clarence Smith, "Introduction," 157 alleges "continual errors, some of them truly monumental … not worthy treatment of a text nearly every paragraph of which was cited time and time again for three hundred years." The remark is not fundamentally unjust: Beale omits the "not" from the Accursian gloss (17), translates *mutuavit* as "borrowed" rather than "lent" (20), repeats the error of the printed edition in distinguishing between prohibitive, permissive and "prohibitory" (*prohibitoria*) in § 32 (30), and makes Jacques de Révigny (*Jacobus de Ravanis*) hail from Ravenna (44). More confusing is Beale's translation of nus. 25–26 (… *An autem tale testamentum porrigatur ad bona alibi exsistentia ubi non est talis consuetudo, infra dicemus / Sed circa hoc dubitatur quid si statutum disponit circa personam* …") as "we now come to the question whether such a will extends to goods which are elsewhere, where there is no such custom. But as to this, doubt is raised whether, if the statute disposes with regard to a person" (27), instead of "We shall see below [nus. 36–37; *trans.*] as to the question … But doubt is raised …" A few other serious errors are noted in the course of this chapter. And, of course, Beale tends to translate Bartolan concepts in contemporary legal terms (e.g. *solemnitas* becomes "form," *dispositio* "substance") and Bartolus is presented as if he had espoused the idea of vested rights.

21 Bartolo, *Conflito de leis* (Rio de Janeiro: Canton & Reile, 1938).

22 Lainé, *Introduction*, 1:133–163; B. Ancel, "Le commentaire de Bartole ad legem Cunctos populos sur la glosse Quod si Bononiensis mis en français" in B. d'Alteroche et al. (eds.),

7.2.2 Basic Structure

The commentary is divided into nine sections, which themselves are grouped into two parts. Each part corresponds to one of the two questions into which Bartolus divides the issue posed in the gloss:

> Now let us come to the gloss which says "if a Bolognese makes a contract at Modena, he shall not be judged by the statute of Modena." As to this, two things are to be noticed: first, whether a statute extends †† to those not subject (non-subjects); second, whether the effect of a statute extends beyond the territory of those who set it down (the legislator).[23]

In the first part of his Commentary Bartolus examines consecutively the question with regard to contracts (nus. 13–19), delicts or more precisely wrongs (nu. 20), testaments (nus. 21–26) and "those things that are neither contracts nor delicts nor last wills," where he apparently deals with real property (nu. 27). A fifth section examines "whether statutes and customs of the laity bind the clergy" (nus. 28–31). In the second part, Bartolus examines "whether statutes or customs may extend their effect outside the territory."[24] The issue "must be examined by many lines of questions" (nu. 32): some statutes are "prohibitive not by reason of a penalty but by reason of some solemnity" (*statuta prohibitoria*; nus. 32–33), other are permissive (*statuta permissoria*; nus. 34–43), and other "punitory" or punitive (*statuta punitoria*; nus. 44–49). The Commentary's final section examines the (extraterritorial) effect of punitive judgments (*effectum sententiae punientis*; nus. 50–51).

The first four sections all begin with a hypothetical case in which a foreigner takes a broadly described action with legal consequences under the laws of the local jurisdiction, triggering the question "of what place should the statutes be observed or looked?"[25] The last four ones do not begin with hypothetical cases, but instead refer to statutes and cases as illustrations of the doctrinal arguments already made.

Mélanges en l'honneur d'Anne Lefebvre-Teillard (Paris: Editions Panthéon-Assas, 2009), 53–74, now reprinted in Ancel, *Éléments*, 165–187.

[23] Bartolus ad C.1.1.1, nu. 13: "Nunc veniamus ad glossam quae dicit quod si Bononiensis conveniatur Mutinae, non debet iudicari secundum statuta Mutinae, quibus non subest cuis occasione videnda sunt duo et primo utrum statutum porrigat †extra territorium† ad non subditos, secundo utrum effectus statuti porrigat extra territorium statuentium."

[24] Ibid., nu. 32.

[25] Ibid., nu. 13.

7.3 "*Cujus occasione videnda sunt duo* ..."

The potential for misunderstanding is evident already in the opening distinction. The text that has made its way into all printed copies of Bartolus' works (the oldest of which dates from 1471 or earlier), indeed inquires "whether a statute extends beyond its territory (*extra territorium*) to those not subject (*nisi subditos*)." Such a phrase however makes little sense – and does not in fact correspond to the wording of manuscripts.[26] In any case, the additional *extra territorium* did not overshadow the fact that Bartolus made the distinction of a territorial and a personal question the starting point of his conflicts analysis.[27] In fact, the opposite problem has arisen. Most writers have given so much emphasis on the division of the original question as to the sway of local laws into the reach of local laws – over foreigners within the locality, on the one hand, and the reach of the same local laws over citizens beyond that locality, on the other – that it is today rather common to read Bartolus, and the Italian or Franco-Italian school along with him, as preoccupied with the *unilateralist* examination of the reach of the forum's statutes, on the one hand, and the rigorous division of statutes into personal and real, on the other hand. These common assumptions and their validity will be addressed in detail in a subsequent chapter.[28] The reader should, however, begin forming a personal opinion as we proceed through the text in the next few pages.

7.4 "... *utrum statuta porrigantur ad non subditos*"

7.4.1 Contracts (nus. 13–19)

Bartolus begins his treatment with a substantial section on contracts:

> And first, I ask, what about contracts? Suppose a contract celebrated by a foreigner in this city: a contest arises, and suit is brought in the place

[26] The manuscript in the Bibliothèque Nationale (Paris, Bibliothèque Nationale MS Lat. 4591) reads: "Nunc venio ad glossam qui dicit "Si Bononiensis" cujus occasione videnda sint duo, primo utrum statuta porrigantur ad non subditos, secundo utrum effectus statutorum ... statuentium." See Gamillscheg, *Einfluss Dumoulins*, 54 n. 2 and more extensively F. Gamillscheg, "Überlegungen zum Text und zur kollisionsrechtslichen Methode bei Bartolus" in *Festschrift für Franz Wieacker zum 70. Geburtstag* (Göttingen: Vandenhoeck und Ruprecht, 1978), 235ff. The omission is corroborated by the Bibliotheca Apostolica Vaticana manuscript first consulted by Clarence Smith, "Bartolo," 160–161 and then verified by myself: MS Vat. Lat. 2589, fol. 70r.

[27] For a writer who has actually observed the second *extra territorium* in the sources see Fassberg, "Choice of Law Problem," 193–194 n. 6.

[28] See Sections 10.2 and 10.3.

> where the contract was made: of what place should the statutes be observed or looked at? Since these questions are much discussed, let us omit other distinctions, and examine the questions more fully than the doctors have done. We either speak of statute or custom with respect to the solemnity of the contract itself (*quae respicuit ipsius contractus solemnitatem*), or the manner of conducting the case, or with respect to jurisdiction over the performance provided for in the contract itself.[29]

According to Bartolus, "the place of the contract is looked to (*inspicitur locus contractus*)" regarding the first case (solemnity or, as commonly translated, "form").[30] As for matters pertaining to "the manner of conducting the case" (*ad litis ordinationem*), "the place of trial will be looked to" (*inspicitur locus iudicii*).

With regard now to matters that concern the decision of the case itself (*ad ipsius litis decisionem*), Bartolus draws a further distinction between matters arising from the nature of the contract itself at the time it is made (*secundum ipsius contractus naturam tempore contractus*) and matters arising *ex post facto* due to neglect or delay (*aut de his quae oriuntur ex postfacto propter negligentiam aut moram*).[31] As to the former, the place of celebration of the contract (*locus contractus*) will be "looked to."[32] This is so even with regard to contracts for the sale of land located elsewhere: for matters pertaining to the contract itself the place where the contract was concluded (*locus celebrati pactus*) must still be looked to.[33]

As to the latter group of cases, however, the place of performance will be looked to, because this is where the neglect or delay has taken place.[34] Bartolus draws here a further distinction, depending on whether a place

[29] Bartolus, ad C.1.1.1 nu. 13. Cf. MS Vat. Lat. 2589, fol. 70r. Clarence Smith, "Bartolo," 174 omits *ad litis ordinationem*, in the light of Bartolus ad D.1.3.32, nu. 27 (on which see Sections 9.3.1 and 9.4.4).

[30] Bartolus ad C.1.1.1 nu. 14. On the translation of the word solemnitas as "form" or "solemnities" see Section 9.4.1.

[31] Bartolus ad C.1.1.1, nu. 15: "Secundo casu aut quaeris de his quae pertinent ad litis ordinationem et inspicitur locus iudicii. [D.22.5.3 *in fine*] Aut de his quae pertinent ad ipsius litis decisionem et tunc aut de his quae oriuntur secundum ipsius contractus naturam tempore contractus, aut de his quae oriuntur ex post facto propter neglegentiam vel moram." Most transcriptions (including Guthrie and Barry) spell *oriunt* rather than *oriuntur*, presumably having used printed texts with hook symbols for the suffix -ur. This is, however, both gramatically inaccurate and does not conform to the original printed text. See e.g. Venice 1602, fol. 4ra (using hook symbols); Lyon 1533, fol. 5rb, Basel 1562, 7a (spelling the entire word).

[32] Bartolus ad C.1.1.1, nu. 16.

[33] Ibid., invoking D.21.2.6, the gloss on it as well as Dinus ad D.44.7.21.

[34] Ibid., nu. 18 (*ibi est contracta negligentia seu mora*).

(or places) of performance has been designated or not. If performance has been fixed in a single place (*solutio est collata in locum certum*), the custom of that place applies. If more than one place have been designated, giving claimant the option to elect the place of performance, or if no place has been fixed (leading to the same result), the place where the claim is made (*inspicitur locus ubi petitur*).[35]

Bartolus then applies his proposed rule to two fully developed examples, both of which involve problems that have persisted for centuries. First, dowry contracts, which he has from the outset distinguished from his general rule.[36] Bartolus brings the case of the wife dying childless.[37] The marriage was celebrated at Assizi, where the dowry contract was moreover executed (presumably this is the place of domicile of the wife's family). The husband comes from Perugia. The husband may enjoy a third of the dowry, according to an Assizi statute, or half, according to a Perugia statute. Bartolus argues that the law of Perugia shall apply ("certainly the law of the husband's domicile"), invoking the Digest as authority.[38]

Second, prescription. A Florentine borrowed money in the Roman court (*in curia Romae*), with the promise to repay the money in Perugia. Perugia however has a statute prescribing actions on debt after ten years. Bartolus is of the opinion that if the claimant has "slept for ten years," the local statute shall apply because this is where neglect was committed.[39] Bartolus at this point breaks with the Gloss, which states that the matter will be determined by the law of the place of trial (*non inspicitur locus contractus, sed judicii*).[40] Gulielmus de Cuneo had, in the meantime, drawn his own distinction between "matters of common concern according to the contract of the defendant, and by provision of the contracting parties" and those arising unexpectedly (*ex improviso*), such

[35] Ibid. This further distinction is not found in Bartolus ad D.1.1.32, nu. 27. See Clarence Smith, "Bartolo," 166.

[36] Bartolus ad C.1.1.1, nu. 17.

[37] Ibid., nu. 19.

[38] D.5.1.65: "A wife should lay claim to her dowry in the place where her husband had his home, not where the dowry agreement was drawn up; for it is not the sort of contract in which the place where the dowry agreement was made has also to be considered rather than the man to whose home the wife herself was due to go under the conditions of the marriage" (Ulpian, *Edict*, book 34).

[39] Bartolus ad C.1.1.1, nu. 19 (*erit ibi locus statuto, quia est contracta in illo negligentia*).

[40] Ibid. Beale, *Bartolus*, 21, 22 translates "place of the judgment." The term l*ex fori* is nowhere in the text and hence avoided in this presentation.

as an action to set aside the contract (*ad resolvendum contractum*).[41] Gulielmus argued that the place of trial should be looked to in these latter cases, a position with which Bartolus vehemently disagrees ("his words have not the savor of truth"), repeating instead his own criterion. The [law of] the place of contracting will be looked to for relief from prejudice (restutione ex laesione) arising out of the contract itself at the time of the contract (*tempore contractus*).[42] But for relief from prejudice arising, after the contract (*post contractum*), from neglect, such as delay, the [law of] the place where such delay occurred (that is, the place of performance). This place may or not be the place of the trial.[43]

7.4.2 Wrongs (nu. 20)

The second question is about wrongs (*de delictis*).[44] "[I]f a foreigner does a wrong here shall he be punished according to the statutes of this city?" The issue is easily settled if the *ius commune* characterizes the foreigner's act as wrong.[45] If it is not, however, then the act will be punished under the local law if either "the foreigner must have lived so long in the city that he really ought to know the statute," or the act is "commonly prohibited by all cities." An example of such a wrong is "carry[ing] grain outside the territory without license from the government, which is

[41] Thus Clarence Smith, "Bartolo," 176. Beale, *Bartolus*, 21–22 speaks of "matters in connection with the performance of the contract."

[42] Bartolus ad C.1.1.1, nu. 19. Beale, *Bartolus*, 22 translates "at the time of contracting."

[43] Bartolus ad C.1.1.1, nu. 19 ("in that case the gloss tells the truth, else it is false").

[44] Bartolus ad C.1.1.1, nu. 20. This section is placed first in the commentary on *de quibus*: Bartolus ad D.1.1.32, nu. 26. See the discussion at Sections 8.3.3.3, 9.3.2, and 10.3.2. Strictly speaking, this is more about criminal offenses than civil claims, but connections can be drawn (see Chapter 8). As to the translation of the term, Clarence Smith, "Bartolo," 161 notes the following: "'Delictum,' however, does not become 'delict,' which is not English. For this word, which indicates both a crime and a tort, one has the choice between 'offense' which looks more like crime, and 'wrong' which looks more like tort: since Bartolo was (from the context) clearly referring to crime I have chosen 'offense'." This section is indeed more about criminal offenses than civil claims, but connections can be drawn so I have sought a neutral term. Beale, *Bartolus*, 23 translates as "delicts," and I did likewise previously in Hatzimihail, "Bartolus," 19. Unlike Clarence Smith, I do regard the term *delict* as appropriate in legal English; however, in today's legal vocabulary, the term is more neutral than "tort" but still refers directly to Roman law of obligations. In this book I have chosen the term "wrong," following W. Blackstone, *Commentaries on the Laws of England*, vol. 3 (Oxford: Clarendon Press, 1768), 2 distinguishing between "private" and "public wrongs." The distinction found its way onto Pollock and the term "civil wrong" as equivalent of "tort."

[45] Bartolus ad C.1.1.1, nu. 20: this position is followed by Dinus, Jacobus and "all."

commonly prohibited throughout all Italy."[46] If the act is "not so generally prohibited," he is not held responsible unless he knew of the prohibition.[47]

7.4.3 *Testaments (nus. 21–26)*

The section on testaments develops around the issue of the validity and reach of a hypothetical "statute or custom" of Venice "that a testament shall be valid [if made] before two or three witnesses." Would a testatment made by a foreigner under the local law be valid?[48] This is a recurring – one could say textbook – case in preclassical conflicts: Roman law had insisted on increased formality with seven witnesses – the rule for most formal legal acts – and, in some occasions, five, but an increasing number of polities had begun to adopt more liberal regimes, requiring fewer witnesses and making use of notaries.[49]

Bartolus does not evidently begin his discussion from a conflicts perspective, addressing instead the validity of such a statute under Roman law.[50] This probably best explains his choice of Venice, which had from early on claimed to be exempt from imperial authority. Jacobus de Arena had reportedly argued that such a statute or custom would be "bad and imprudent" (as it was the fear of forgery that led to the requirement of seven witnesses and to a minimum of five even in places where there is knowledge of the law); it could only be valid if it had the consent of the *princeps*.[51] Bartolus takes a different view: the local statute is valid even if the *princeps* does not know of it. He proposes several arguments. First, publication is required for the written testament to have validity but the solemnities of publication can be reduced and altered by statute and customs.[52] Second, just like the father (*pater*) may dispose between his children with only two witnesses, the *patria* can dispose between subjects. Third, there is no prohibition of such legislation in the

[46] The example invoked by Bartolus is that of "carry[ing] grain outside the territory without license from the government, which is commonly prohibited throughout all Italy."

[47] Bartolus cites Sext.1.2.2 and the gloss ("an ignorant man is not held unless his ignorance was gross and supine").

[48] Bartolus ad C.1.1.1, nu. 21.

[49] See Sections 9.3.3 and 9.4.2.

[50] This part of the text is omitted by Beale, *Bartolus*, 26, but not by Clarence Smith, "Bartolo," 167–169.

[51] Bartolus ad C.1.1.1, nu. 22.

[52] Ibid.

Roman law and it must therefore be allowed: the requirement of five witnesses restricted existing custom and did not prohibit future custom or statute. Fourth, such custom is not imprudent but useful, good, and benevolent (*favorabilis*), for all involved: testator, legatees, and witnesses.[53]

This opposition carries over to the question of testaments made in the city by foreigners. Can they be validly made under the local statute or custom? Jacobus simply answers in the negative: "as a statute is called the law proper to the city (*ius proprium civitatis*) it does not extend to foreigners."[54] On the contrary, Bartolus draws distinctions depending on the wording (*dicendum*) of the statute. If the statute limits its effect to citizens, it does not extend to foreigners: Bartolus offers the example of a statute relaxing solemnities with regard to countryfolk (*rusticis*), which should not be taken to extend to everyone.[55] But if the wording of the statute is general and unqualified (*statutum loquitur simpliciter et indefinite*) the statute extends to all testators.[56]

Bartolus then continues by arguing that, in matters of voluntary (i.e. noncontentious) jurisdiction, "a statute binds foreigners, just like with contracts."[57] As to the matter of the effects of such a testament to the ownership of goods located elsewhere, he refers us to his subsequent discussion on permissive statutes.[58]

This brings him to other questions pertaining to the law of persons and connected to the doctrinal treatment of testaments in Roman law, namely legitimation and emancipation.[59] Statutes "cannot legitimate a

[53] Bartolus ad C.1.1.1, nu. 23. Arguments involve the examples of reduced formalities as to the testament of military men and for disposal between children; as to witnesses, not to take them away from their business. See also Bartolus ad. D.1.1.32, nu. 28: "in the city of Venice, on account of the claims of business, witnesses are almost impossible to find and it is the same in other cities for many reasons best known to the citizens living there" (as translated by Clarence Smith, "Bartolo," 169).

[54] Jacobus ad D.1.1.9, as cited by Bartolus ad C.1.1.1, nu. 24.

[55] Bartolus ad C.1.1.1, nu. 24, invoking C.6.23.31 together with D.29.7.8.2. In the former, Justinian allowed country folk in places where men with knowledge of letters were hard to come by to maintain their custom, instead of his seven-witness requirement for testaments. Jacobus had used the same provisions to deny that the statutory derogation could extend to foreigners in all cases. Bartolus limits the effect of this authority.

[56] Bartolus ad C.1.1.1, nu. 24.

[57] Bartolus ad C.1.1.1, nu. 25. See also Bartolus ad. D.1.1.32, nu. 27: "And the argument from contracts to testaments holds good."

[58] See Bartolus ad C.1.1.1, nus. 36–37 (in the section on permissive statutes) as to the extraterritorial effects.

[59] Ibid., nu. 26.

person not subject to them, nor can they make any disposition about such a person."[60] Things are different and statutes extend to foreigners only insofar as they have to do with formalities, "[f]or the solemnity of an act pertains to the jurisdiction of the city in whose territory it is done; so it varies according to the difference in places; but whenever there is a difference of person, a statute cannot dispose, except about a person subject to it."[61] The example that Bartolus uses is the case of a statute prohibiting a man from making his wife an heir (*vir non potest instituere uxorem suam*), which cannot prevent a foreigner from doing exactly that.[62]

7.4.4 *Rights over Real Property (nus. 27)*

Only one question is asked in the fourth section: "Suppose one has a house here, and it is a question whether he can raise it higher. Briefly, when there is a question of any right growing out of a thing itself, the custom or statute of the place where the thing is should be observed."[63]

The passage has been taken to imply the application of *lex rei sitae* across the board as to rights over real property. The example that Bartolus uses does evoke the servitude *altius non tollendi*.[64] But the wording of the phrase seems to make mention of "regulatory" statutes where the city authority restricts the height, bulk or type of a citizen's building. Such statutes did exist in Italian cities at the time.

7.4.5 *Clerical Privileges (nus. 28–31)*

In the fifth section, Bartolus examines whether secular statutes and customs bind the clergy and ought to be observed in the bishop's court.[65] The section has been usually discarded in discusions or even

60 Ibid.

61 Ibid.

62 Ibid., citing Gulielmus Durantis, *Speculum Juris* (*de sententiae*, § 5 v.3).

63 Bartolus ad C.1.1.1, nu. 27: "Quarto quaero quod in his quae non sunt contractus neque delicta neque ultimae voluntates. pone quidam habet domum hic et est quaestio an possit altius elevare. breve cum est quaestio de aliquo iure descendente ex re ipsa, debet servari consuetudo aut statutum loci ubi est res."

64 Inst.2.3.1.

65 Bartolus ad C.1.1., nu. 28 (*Quinto quero utrum statuta et consuetudines laicorum ligent clericos et debeant servari in curia episcopi*).

translations,[66] as irrelevant to the conflict of laws.[67]This is understandable if anachronistic: we would do better to ask ourselves instead why this section is there. I would argue that the section helps us understand how Bartolus thought about, and organized, the subject matter we are concerned with.[68]

Bartolus starts by considering the scope and purpose of clerical privileges granted by the Pope or the *princeps*. Cinus had answered our question in the negative, referring to decretals by Innocent III requiring church approval for any lay statute affecting churches, whether favorably or unfavorably.[69] Bartolus is in his turn relying on a *constitutio* by Emperor Frederick II, which only disallowed statutes running contrary to privileges granted to church or clergy, in order to make an argument *a contrario* and draw distinctions.[70] It is clear that statutes that directly regulate church or ecclesiastical matters are invalid, since the legislating authority lacks jurisdiction. As to statutes however that deal with regular matters (*facta simpliciter*), Bartolus draws a distinction between statutes that touch upon ecclesiastical privileges and are invalid, whereas statutes that affect "not an [ecclesiastical] privilege but anyone" bind clergy and must be observed in bishop's court provided they are "honorable."[71]

To illustrate his approach, Bartolus uses the example of two Perugian statutes. The first statute allowed the execution of an authentic instrument (*instrumentum publicum*) without the need of a petition (*sine libello*), i.e. a contested process. Bartolus examines whether the episcopal court should apply, in proceedings brought by a layman against a cleric, the city statute and allow for execution *sine libello*. Contrary to

[66] Both Beale and Clarence Smith omit nus. 28–31 from their translations. Lainé, *Introduction*, 1:144 does the same thing. It is, however, included in Ancel, *Éléments*, 171–173.

[67] As Barry, "Bartolus," 11, observes, "though it does not clearly belong with the first four sections, it clearly does not belong with the latter four." Cf. Ancel, *Éléments*, 152: "De nouveau, Bartole s'éloigne de l'approache conflictuelle et raisonne en termes de compétence normative."

[68] See Sections 8.2.2.2 and 9.2.18.

[69] Bartolus ad C.1.1.1, nu. 28, with reference to X. 1.2.7 (*Que in ecclesiarum*) and X. 1.2.10 (*Ecclesiae Sanctae Mariae*).

[70] Bartolus ad C.1.1.1, nu. 28, with reference to C.1.2.12. Auth. *Cassa et Irrita*.

[71] Bartolus ad C.1.1.1, nu. 29: "aut statuta sunt directo super ecclesiis vel rebus ecclesiasticis et non valent, quia non pertinent ad iurisdictionem concedentis; aut statuta sunt facta simpliciter et tunc aut redundant contra ea quae sunt concessa ecclesiis vel clericis in privilegium, et non valent; aut contra ea quae conpetunt ecclesiis vel clericis non in privilegium sed ut cuilibet et tunc ligant clericos et sunt servanda in foro episcopali, dum tamen sint honesta."

Hostiensis, Bartolus answers to the affirmative.[72] The second statute held invalid testaments that are not opened in public (*quod not valeant testamenta propter omissam insinuationem*): if this requirement is not observed (*non fuit insinuatum*), the cleric's last will is only valid to the extent that it confers property to pious causes, since the pope has specifically dispensed with formal requirements in those cases.[73]

7.5 "... *utrum effectus statuti porrigat extra territorium statuentium*"

Bartolus now comes to the question of extraterritorial effect of city law ("whether statutes or customs may extend their effect outside the territory"). This issue "must be examined by many lines of questions," at the heart of which lies the distintion between prohibitive, permissive, and punitive statutes. The difference between prohibiting and permitting a certain action is easy to understand; in contrast, Bartolus feels compelled to explain the carving of a category of *statuta prohibitoria*, distinct from *statuta punitoria*: "certain statutes are prohibitive not by reason of penalty, but by reason of another solemnity" (*non ratione poenae sed ratione alterius solemnitatis*).[74]

7.5.1 Prohibitive Statutes (nus. 32–33)

Having distinguished prohibitive statutes from statutes imposing a punishment, Bartolus draws an internal distinction between statutes prohibitive by means of solemnity (*ratione solemnitatis*); statutes whose prohibition concerns a thing (*in re[m] et respectu rei*); and statutes whose prohibition concerns a person (*in personam*).[75]

The example given of a *statutum prohibitivum ratione solemnitatis* is a statute requiring the testament or instrument to be made before two notaries. Such a statute will not have extraterritorial effect: "in matters of

[72] Ibid., nu. 30.

[73] Ibid.

[74] Ibid., nu. 32. Printed editions tend to include the word *prohibitiva* in lieu of *punitoria*. See e.g. Venice 1602, fol. 5va; Lyon 1533, fol. 6vb; Basel 1582, 8b. This is reflected in the translation of Beale, "Bartolus," 30. The manuscript has confirmed this is an error: MS. Vat. Lat. 2589, fol. 72r.

[75] Ibid., nu. 32.

solemnity we always look to the place where the thing is done" (*in solemnitatibus semper inspicitur locus ubi res agitur*).[76]

The example given of a *statutum prohibitivum in re[m] et respectu rei* is a statute prohibiting a joint-property owner from alienating his or her own share to a third person (*extra consortes*).[77] Bartolus comes here to the opposite conclusion: "[t]hen wherever a disposition of such a thing is made it is not valid, because such a provision affects the thing and prevents the title from passing."[78]

Statutes prohibitive *in personam* require a further distinction between those containing a "favorable" or "benevolent" provision (*statuta favorabilia*) and those containing a "burdensome" or "malignant" provision (*statuta odiosa*). For further authority on this "distinction between a prohibition which is reasonable and benevolent and [one which is] malignant," Bartolus refers to canon law (a decretal of Boniface VIII, according to which it is right to construe malignant provisions strictly and benevolent provisions widely).[79]

Bartolus offers three examples of *statuta favorabilia*, explaining the rationale in each case. First, a statute prohibiting minors – for example, those under twenty years of age – from making a testament ("in order that young persons shall not be deceived in the making of testaments").[80]

[76] Ibid., with reference to the earlier discussions regarding contracts and testaments.

[77] Ibid., nu. 32. Beale, "Bartolus," 30 translates the *extra consortes* passage as "where it prohibits the title of property to be passed between husband and wife." He is followed by Barry, "Bartolus," 13–14. "Between" is an evidently wrong translation of *extra*, but also the word *consors* is principally used in Latin to denote those whose share, e.g. an inheritance, and only rarely a "wife." See the *Oxford Latin Dictionary*, "consors." My translation concurs with Clarence Smith, "Bartolo," 181, and Lainé, *Introduction*, 1:146.

[78] Bartolus ad C.1.1.1, nu. 32.

[79] Ibid., nu. 33 in fine (*de ista distinctione, de prohibitione rationali, favorabili, et odiosa*), with reference to Sext 5.13.15 (*odia*). I am following Clarence Smith, "Bartolo," 183 in this regard. On the contrary, printed editions of Bartolus refer to VI 5.11.26 (*si sententia*), according to which no individual member of a people placed under an interdict may anywhere take part in worship and receive the sacraments of the church. This is followed by Beale, "Bartolus," 32 n 5.

[80] Bartolus ad C.1.1.1, nu. 32. There is a question as to the age stated. The printed editions I have consulted state the Latin numeral for 25 ("XXV"), which resonates with classical Roman law. See e.g. Basel 1582, 8b (*minor XXV. annis*). This is followed in Andrew Barry's transcription and in the translation of Ancel, *Éléments*, 173. Beale, *Bartolus*, 31, has it as "fifteen." See also Ancel, *Éléments*, 154. On the contrary, printed editions of Bartolus ad D.1.3.32, nu. 31 speak of "twenty years" in letter form. See e.g. Basel 1582, 45b (*minor uiginti annis*). This has prompted Clarence Smith, "Bartolo," to corrected the reference in the Code commentary as well into "twenty." This is corroborated by Vat. Lat. 2589 (*XX annos*), and that should weigh in favor of that reading.

Second, a statute providing "that a man may not bequath (*legare*) to his wife and the opposite, lest by reason of their mutual love they may despoil or deceive one another."[81] Third, a statute interdicting a person from disposing of his property (*in suo iudicio bonis interdicitur*), the inderdict on property being "so that his goods shall not be wasted" (*ne sua bona pereant*).[82] The effects of such a prohibition or interdiction would extend everywhere the person, or respectively the property, may be found.[83]

The example given of a statute containing a "burdensome" or "malignant" prohibition (*prohibitionem odiosam*), is of a statute prohibiting the daughter from succeeding to an inheritance: such a statute, being prohibitive and burdensome, cannot have effect over property situated elsewhere.[84]

7.5.2 Permissive Statutes (nus. 34–43)

The section on permissive statutes is by far the longest in the *repetitio*. This is after all the largest, and most diverse, group of statutes derogating from the *ius commune*. Bartolus does indeed distinguish between several types of cases: statutes granting authority to someone; cases of dispensing with solemnity requirements; and cases of affecting personal quality; among this last category, statutes addressing the status of property form a distinct sub-category.

At the heart of Bartolus's treatment of permissive statutes lies the distinction he draws between the two questions involved: On the one hand, the extraterritorial effect of the statute itself, i.e. the validity of an act executed in conformity to the permissive statute, outside the city's territory ("whether a permissive act may be done outside the territory of the permitting law"). On the other hand, the extraterritorial effect of a

[81] Bartolus ad C.1.1.1, nu. 32. The phrase is *pone statutum est quod vir non posit legare uxori suae, vel econtra, et hoc est factum ne mutuo amore se ad invicem spoliet vel decipiant*. The phrase of justification (which is not included in Bartolus ad D.1.3.32, nu. 31) comes from D.24.1.1, where it however refers to donations *inter vivos* between husband and wife.

[82] Bartolus ad C.1.1.1, nu. 32.

[83] Ibid.

[84] Ibid., nu. 33. The printed text refers to *filia foemina*. See e.g. Basel 1582, 9a. Clarence Smith, "Bartolo," 183 translated as "female child." Beale, *Bartolus*, 32 as "daughter as a woman." Ancel, *Éléments*, 174 simply as *fille*. We should at least consider the possibility that the reference was originally to *filia familiae*, i.e. an as yet unemancipated daughter-in-power. See Section 9.3.6.

legal act, i.e. the effects that may be produced outside the city's territory by an act executed in conformity to the pemissive statute in that city's territory ("if it is exercised in this very way or place which the law permits, whether it takes effect outside the territory.")

7.5.2.1 Statutes Conferring a Privilege

The first type of permissive statutes are those which "concede and permit something which by reason belongs only to those to whom a special privilege is granted" (*aliquando nam statutum concedit et permittit id quod rationabiliter non conpetit nisi in his in quibus specialiter privilegium est concessum*).[85] The cases alluded to here concern notarial acts and acts of emancipation.

A notary appointed under the laws of a city (*per statutum civitatis aliquis est effectus notarius*) may not draw legal documents (*conficere instrumentum*) outside the territory of that city, and the same holds for similar matters that can only be done within the territory.[86] This is because acts of voluntary jurisdiction under power granted by authorities lower than the princeps cannot be executed outside the territory.[87]

On the contrary, "instruments drawn by such a notary within his territory shall have effect (*faciant fidem*) everywhere outside the territory."[88] The same holds for an act of emancipation executed before the authority having jurisdiction under the city laws, "because it is a matter of solemnity rather than of disposition (*ad dispositionem*)."[89]

7.5.2.2 Statutes Facilitating Permissible Acts

The second group of statutes are those statutes which "allow what is already permitted by the *ius commune*, but they remove some requirement of the *ius commune*" (*quandoque statuta sunt permissiva permittendo id quod de iure permittitur, sed per statutum tollitur obstaculum*

[85] Bartolus ad C.1.1.1, nu. 34. Beale, *Bartolus*, 33, has translated this as "for always a statute allows and permits what it does not reasonably forbid, excepting those things in which a privilege is specially granted." Lainé, *Introduction*, 1:148 omits the passage. Clarence Smith, "Bartolo," 247, translates: "sometimes then local legislation grants and permits something which in nature could be within no one's power, but only by franchise particularly granted, and in matters to which it extends." See also Ancel, *Éléments*, 174: "Parfois, en effet, le statut confère un pouvoir qui, raisonnablement, n'est pas offert à tous, mais seulement à ceux qui le reçoivent spécialement par privilège."

[86] Bartolus ad C.1.1.1, nu. 34.

[87] Ibid., nu. 35 with reference to Sext. 2.2.1 in fine.

[88] Bartolus ad C.1.1.1, nu. 36.

[89] Ibid. (*hoc est magis ad solemnitatem quam ad dispositionem*).

quod erat de iure communi). They are further distinguished, depending on whether they remove a solemnity requirement (*obstaculum solemnitatis*) or a limitation on personal capacity.[90]

7.5.2.2.1 Solemnity Bartolus now returns to the *ius commune* rule requiring seven witnesses for a valid testament. In the third section of our text, we saw Bartolus not only affirming the city's power to pass a statute reducing the solemnity requirement to, for example, four witnesses, but also holding that such a rule can be availed by all within the city's territory. His position was contrasted to earlier jurists, such as Jacobus de Arena, who had sought to limit the scope of city derogation from the *ius commune*, notably by denying the extension of such a statute over non-subjects of the city.[91] Whereas Bartolus's reasoning in the third section conformed to his concept of a permissive statute, he did not use that term, not even in his vague cross-reference to "below" regarding the salient question of whether the effects of a a testament drawn under such a statute would extend to the testator's property outside the territory for later.[92]

Bartolus once again begins with an extensive discussion of the opinions of past jurists.[93] However, this time the emphasis appears to be less on legislative jurisdiction or the hierarchy of legal sources and more on the practical consequences, including the danger of having such a testament produce effects only in some territory and with regard to some property. Succession of non-subjects (who would be more likely to have property outside the city territory), would, in that sense, not only create questions of political and legal power but also be likelier to create more legal problems as to the establishment of sucession rights over property.

Jacobus de Arena, and presumably most glossators before him, would have solved the problem by application of the *ius commune* rule across the board. But, as local legislation proliferated and its scope expanded, such a solution was becoming increasingly unrealistic and unable to effectively deal with the problem. This reflects in Bartolus stating that the late glosslators, such as Hubertus de Bobio and the "older Ultramontani," reported by the Speculator do not come to clear conclusions.[94] Things

[90] Bartolus ad C.1.1.1, nus. 36–37 and 38–41 respectively.
[91] Ibid., nus. 22–23.
[92] Ibid., nu. 25 in fine.
[93] Ibid., nus. 36–37.
[94] Ibid., nu. 36, citing *Speculum Iuris*, 12.16.

apparently changed with Jacobus de Ravanis (*Jacques de Révigny*), who found no inherent problem if succession to property located within the city's territory would take place in accordance with the testatement, while the rules of intestate succession would govern succession over property located outside the city's territory. Jacobus is not deterred by the Digest passage *ius nostrum* stating that "our law" does not allow the same person to die both testate and intestate,[95] since this is the result of the plurality of customs (*diversitas consuetudinum*), just like it could have been the result of a "plurality of estates" (*diversitas patrimonii*).[96]

Jacobus found some adherents, including, originally, Cinus, the teacher of Bartolus in Perugia.[97] But he was in his turn refuted by Gulielmus de Cuneo, who provided extensive argumentation in favor of the testament's universal validity ("the testament was valid without distinction, and extended to property everywhere, even outside the territory").[98] Gulielmus was followed by both Cinus, who changed his position and added a passage in his treatment, and Jacobus Buttrigarius, Bartolus's teacher in Bologna.[99] Bartolus himself agrees with Gulielmus's conclusion but not with all his arguments.

The primary argument of Gulielmus was that "the statute operates upon the testament itself" (*statutum operat circa testamentum*).[100] If therefore the testament was valid initially, the statute's effect "extends from the testament itself to all the property by consequence" and accordingly "although the statute cannot dispose of the property directly, it may

[95] D.50.17.7: "Our law (*ius nostrum*) does not allow the same person among civilians to die both testate and intestate; for there is a natural conflict between these states, 'testate' and 'intestate.'"

[96] Jacobus ad C.1.1.1, as reported by Bartolus ad C.1.1.1, nu. 36, with reference to D.1.7.22.

[97] Bartolus ad C.1.1.1, nu. 36 in fine. Lainé, *Introduction*, 1:123–124 translates a pertinent passage of Cinus, who presents at length the position of Jacobus de Ravanis, noting that Petrus Bellaperticus agreed insofar as the laws were really contrary but not when both cities followed the *ius commune*, and then remarking that more modern writers think that the *héritier institué* is entitled to all goods, by reference to the place where the testament was made. It must be reminded that Petrus was Cinus's teacher and Jacobus the teacher of Petrus (or the teacher of Petrus's teacher). The two writers omitted by Cinus and mentioned by Bartolus are contemporaries of Cinus (see Figure 3.2).

[98] Bartolus ad C.1.1.1, nu. 36 in fine (*indistincte testamentum valere et porrigi ad bona ubicumque et si sint extra territorium*).

[99] Cinus ad C.1.1.1, nu. 18 (as cited by Clarence Smith, "Bartolo," 250); Jacobus ad C.1.1.1, fol. 4vb (Paris, 1516).

[100] Ibid., nu. 37.

do so by consequence."[101] Bartolus does not agree with this argument. He acknowledges that what is not permitted directly may be permitted by consequence, but only when this is a necessary consequence (*quod non licet directo habet necessariam consequentiam*).[102] The fact that a testament is valid, however, does not make it a necessary consequence that the testament would cover all property (*si testamentum fuerit validum non sequitur necessario quod hebeat omnia bona*): Bartolus invokes a Digest passage regarding special arrangements for a soldier's testamentary disposition,[103] in support of his position that it is possible, "by the force of law" (*ex legis potestate*), for a person to die in part testate and in part intestate.[104]

Gulielmus's other line of argument involved analogies with judicial proceedings. Just like an action may be brought properly in a place other than where the land is located, so a disposition may be made elsewhere, where the thing (*res*) is.[105] Acts made in the court of one judge (i.e. the record) will be given credit (*faciunt fidem*) in the court of another.[106] Moreover, a testament validly made before a judge in a place where less solemnity is required will produce effect everywhere.[107] Bartolus adds in support of this argument the cases of testaments made in the countryside (before five witnesses), testaments made by servicemen in the field: in both cases, testaments made under reduced solemnity produce effects everywhere.[108] And the custom of the area in which will be

[101] Ibid., nu. 37 (*si fuerit validum ab initio tamen ex ipso testamento porriget ad omnia bona per quemdam consequentiam. Licet non possit disponere de bonis directo, sed per consequentiam*), with reference to D.26.4.3.1.

[102] Ibdi, nu. 37 in fine, citing Dinus ad D.26.8.1.

[103] D.29.1.6 ("If a soldier has appointed someone heir in respect of a farm it is accepted that he died intestate with respect to the remainder of his estate; for a soldier can die partly testate and partly intestate").

[104] Bartolus ad C.1.1.1, nu. 37. Reference is also made to D.29.41 (also regarding soldiers' succession) and C.5.9.1 with its commentary (see e.g. Basel 1562, 465b) This latter provision restricted the succession rights of a woman who hastened to contract a second marriage without the observance of proper mourning, including the effective cancellation of anything bestowed upon her by her first husband's testament (with no prejudice to its validity otherwise).

[105] Ibid. (*sicut actio competens potest praeponi alibi quam ubi sit fundus, sic disponens alibi potest fieri, quo ubi sit res*), with reference to C.7.33.12.

[106] Ibid., with references to C.2.1.2 and other passages.

[107] Ibid., with reference to C.6.23.19.

[108] C.6.23.31.3.

looked to in matters of solemnity regarding any act about which a question is raised.[109]

7.5.2.2.2 Personal Status Bartolus takes a stricter stance when it comes to the extraterritorial effect of statutes removing limitations on personal status (*obstaculum qualitatis personae*).[110] The examples he uses concern, first, statutes allowing an unemancipated son (*filius familias*) "or some other person forbidden by law" to make a testament and, second, statutes allowing a *spurius* to be appointed heir.[111] Bartolus states that, for the purposes of this discussion, he assumes that such legislation is valid (i.e. a city has the power to enact such statutes under the *ius commune*), promising to discuss the issue "elsewhere."[112]

Bartolus treats differently those cases in which the act has taken place in a territory other than where the person is to become an heir, from those where the act has taken place in that territory.

As to the former cases, Bartolus holds that such a person may not make a testament, or be apppointed heir, outside the city's territory and then enter into inheritance there: "since this is a grant by an authority lower than the Emperor, although it is concerned with a voluntary act of the granting authority, it still cannot be performed outside the

[109] Bartolus ad C.1.1.1, nu. 37, with reference to D.25.4.1.

[110] Clarence Smith, "Bartolo," 252 uses the term "personal capacity" both in this instance and for most references in this section to *legitimare*, including translating *legitimatio facta per statutum civitatis* as "grant of capacity by the local legislation of the city." Beale, *Bartolus*, 39 and 40 translates more literally as "limitation of personal quality" and "legitimacy created by the statute of the city" respectively, whereas more recently Ancel, *Éléments*, 176 translates "empêchement lié à l'état de la personne" and "capacité accordée par le statut de la cité." I have chosen to translate the former instance as "personal status" and not "capacity" in view of the distinction between capacity and status that often appears, especially in conflicts doctrine (for example, it is an important distinction for Huber as discussed in Sections 11.5 and 14.2.2). As to the latter, I have kept the term "legitimation" but readers should be mindful of its broader meaning in these passages.

[111] Bartolus ad C.1.1.1, nu. 38. The law distinguished between legitimate and illegitimate children, which were in turn further distinguished between natural (*filii naturales*) if their parents' union would have been allowed by law (concubinage) and spurious (*filii spurii*) if their paternity was uncertain, or they were children of "thoroughly illicit unions," including incest, adultery and clerical concubinage. See Section 9.3.6.

[112] Bartolus ad C.1.1.1, nu. 38. See Bartolus ad D.1.10.12 and ad C.5.12. For an example of such a discussion in our text see Bartolus ad C.1.1.1, nus. 22–23 (discussed at Sections 7.4.3 and 8.3.3.1).

jurisdiction of the granting authority."[113] Legitimation by city statute can only have effect in that city's territory, in the same manner that a father legitimating his son by an offering (to enroll him as a member) to the municipal council (*legitimatio filii per oblationem curiae civitatis*) only produces effect as to the father and the son.[114]

Bartolus is more concerned with the latter case, which is very difficult and "constantly recurring" (*insurgit forte dubium et quotidianum tale*). If such a person makes his will or enters into inheritance in the same city where the act removing the limitation has been executed, do the effects of such an act extend to property located in another city?[115]

An affirmative response could rely on the arguments made as to statutes relaxing solemnities.[116] Moreover, an emancipation thus made should produce effect everywhere, just like an act by notary produces effects everywhere;[117] a testament should extend to property located elsewhere, just like a court judgment must be enforced by a judge in another territory and over property located elsewhere.[118]

Bartolus however sides with the negative position. He first notes that "a provision in general terms can only be understood as referring to property in the territory of the providing authority" (*simplex dispositio non intellegitur nisi de bonis quae sunt in territorio disponentis*).[119] Invoking authorities construing strictly the effects of legitimation, he notes that even legitimation by the Pope does not extend to matters not under his jurisdiction, such inheritance and other temporal matters, which fall in the imperial territory.[120]

113 Bartolus ad C.1.1.1, nu. 39 (*Quaeritur an talis persona extra territorium possit institui et heriditatem adire. dico quod non, cum hoc concedatur ab alio inferiori a principe licet spectet ad actum voluntarium, tamen non possunt exerceri ex iurisditione concedentis*), with reference to D.1.16.15.

114 Ibid., drawing the example from C.5.27.8 and N.89.c.4. Bartolus means that this institution did not make the son agnate or cognate of his father's relatives. On the *oblatio curiae* see e.g. W. W. Buckland, *A Text-Book of Roman Law*, 3rd ed. (Cambridge: Cambridge University Press, 1963), 129–130. Beale, *Bartolus*, 40 speaks of "legitimation by a grant of a city court." Clarence Smith, "Bartolo," 252 of "offer to the city council." Ancel, *Éléments*, 176 of *oblation à la curie*.

115 Bartolus ad C.1.1.1, nu. 40.

116 Ibid., nu. 40, referring presumably to the discussion in nu. 37.

117 Ibid., nu. 41, referring to nu. 35.

118 Ibid., nu. 41, with references to D.5.1.45.1, D.42.1.15, and C.3.1.13.3 as to judgments and to D.28.1.1 as to the testament being like a judgment (*quasi sententia*).

119 Bartolus ad C.1.1.1, nu. 41.

120 Ibid. (*legitimatio facta per Papam non trahitur ad ea quae non sunt suae iurisdictionis ut ad heriditatem et alia temporalia quae sunt in territorio imperato*), with references to

Bartolus insists on distinguishing solemnity and status: "a provision as to the solemnity of an act is another thing from legitimating a person to make the act."[121] The reason he gives is that "when there is a difference of place, different reasons exist for different results."[122] For example, a military testament requires fewer witnesses because fewer people can be available due to the military occupation; likewise, if a city has more *homines legales* than another, their respective statutes will require a different number of witnesses. This being the reason for of the solemnity (*ratio solemnitatis*), it also extends to testaments made by foreigners (*testamentum forensis*) in the city and therefore a rule as solemnity lawfully produces its effect everywhere, without prejudice to another city, "for that act could be done elsewhere, even though not with that solemnity."[123]

On the contrary, a provision about legitimating a person so that he can make an act is "not of that nature." "I cannot legitimate except in so far I have the power to make such disposition, nor can [such power] extend outside my territory without causing prejudice to another."[124] Bartolus dismisses arguments based on the discussion regarding notarial acts and the provision of the Code about a father born elsewhere being able to emancipate his son if munipical law conferred such power to the local magistrates: "the statute does not emancipate the son, which it could not do to foreigners, but the father emancipates the son, with the solemnity provided by the statute."[125] Likewise, the notary has no power to make a disposition, but to solemnize the act making the disposition.[126] Bartolus then deals with analogies to the effects of court judgments, as discussed above:

D.42.5.12.1, Auth. 7.1.4 (*filium vero*), Nov. 89.4, as well as to Gulielmus on the gloss. Beale, *Bartolus*, apparently omits the phrase (*sed contra videtur quod non porrigat*) with which this argument is introduced in opposition to the former view.

121 Bartolus ad C.1.1.1, nu. 41 (*aliud est in dispositione circa solemnitatem actus quam circa legitimationem personae ad actum*).

122 Ibid. (*ratio: quia factam diversitatem locorum diversificantur rationes solemntitatis*).

123 Ibid. (*ideo ista ratio solemnitatis habet locum in testamento forensis sicut in civitate. ideo ius voluit quod quantum ad solemnitatem inspiciat effectus eius ad omnem locum. non nam per hoc alteri civitati praeiudicat, cum ille actus ubicumque poterit celebrari, licet non cum illa solemnitate*).

124 Ibid. (*ideo non possum legitimare nisi quantum ad me ipsum disponentem pertinet, nec porrigitur extra meum territorium quia facerem alteri praeiudicium*).

125 Ibid. (*non nam statutum emancipat filium quia tunc non porrigeretur ad forenses sed pater filium emancipat cum solemnitate statuti*), referring to C.8.48.1.

126 Bartolus ad C.1.1.1, nu. 41 (*idem in notario, non nam adhibet ipse ad disponendum, sed ad solemnizandum circa actum ab alio dispositum*).

> [T]he judge deals with rights already grounded and defined, rights which accompany the person everywhere, as when he gives judgment against someone, regarding an obligation already existing, which binds the defendant in everyplace: hence execution can be requested of another judge. But when the judge himself creates a new right, by judgment within the territory, this does not extend beyond the territory, as has been proved above.[127]

7.5.2.3 The English Question: Primogeniture and Effects as to Property

The section on permissive statutes moves now to its final leg, with a discussion about the potential conflict between legal regimes allowing several heirs and legal regimes restricting the right to succession to the first-born son (the primogeniture system). Primogeniture is also a matter of personal status but the problems it raises have particular significance with regard to acquisition and transfer of rights over property: as a result, it is treated immediately subsequently but separately to questions of status and capacity, with Bartolus using the case to treat effects as to property (as he had already promised in his original discussion of testaments in the third section). This is one reason why, even though the actual practical significance of the so-called English question in Italian courts of the *trecento* must have been limited, Bartolus's take on the case took a life of its own in the centuries that followed:[128]

> It is the custom of England that the eldest son succeeds to all the goods. Now one having goods in England and in Italy dies. What is the law (*quaeritur quod iuris*). Jacobus de Ravanis and Gulielmus de Cuneo hold that as to goods in England judgment is given according to the custom of that place; while as to those in Italy, they are distributed under the *ius commune* and divided between the brothers. Though a certain form (*forma*) is given for goods situated there, it does not extend everywhere. Cinus holds the same here. Others say that the place where inheritance vests should be looked to, just as if a contract were made there, since in contracts we look to the place of contracting.[129]

[127] Ibid., nu. 41 in fine: "non obstat quod supra dictum est de sententia quia ibi iudex disponit super iure iam fundato et formato quod ius respiciebat persona ubicumque. ut puta condemnat aliquem occasione [praecedentiso bolonis], qui ligat reum obligatum in omni loco, ideo mandatur executioni per alium iudicem. sed quando ipse iudex de novo inducit ius faciendo intra territorium tunc non porrigit extra territorium, ut supra probatum est."

[128] See especially Section 10.2.3.

[129] Bartolus ad C.1.1.1, nu. 42.

What follows is one of the most frequently alluded-to – and probably the most misunderstood – of Bartolus passages:

> It seems to me that the words of the statute or of the custom are diligently to be examined. For either the provision is made about a *res*, as by these words: *the possessions (goods) of decedents shall pass to the first-born (bona decedentium veniant in primogenitum)*, and in that case I should adjudge all the possessions according to the custom and statute of the place where the things are situated, for the law affects the things themselves, whether they are possessed by a citizen or a foreigner (D.50.4.6, C.8.10.3); or the words of the statute or of the custom make provision about a person, as by these words: *the first-born shall be heir (primogenitus succcedat)*, and then either such decedent was not from England (*erat de Anglia*), though he had possessions there, in which case such a statute does not affect him and his sons, because a provision about persons does not affect foreigners, as was said above in the second [meaning third, in nu. 26; *trans.*] question; or such decedent was English and then the first-born succeeds to the goods which are in England, and to the other ones he succeeds at *ius commune*, according to what the said doctors say; because this may either be said to be a statute depriving the younger sons, in which case it is odious and does not extend to goods situated abroad, as was proven above in the sixth question [nu. 33; *trans.*], or you can say that the statute is permissive, in removing an obstacle so that the younger sons may not interfere with the first-born, and that is the same with what was said above [nu. 40 or 41; *trans.*]. [On this point, that one should examine if the provision is in rem or personam, see D.18.1.81.][130]

Bartolus concludes with a brief refutation of the position of those who look to the place where the inheritance vests: reference to such a place can only be made in case of devolution of the inheritance, which cannot occur until after the question is resolved. He is equally unconvinced about analogies with contracts.[131]

7.5.3 *Punitive Statutes (nus. 44–49)*

Bartolus now comes to punitive statutes. The discussion in this section does not concern criminal acts committed within the city's territory, a

[130] Bartolus ad C.1.1.1, nu. 42.

[131] Ibid., nu. 43. We do not know whom Bartolus is referring to. Clarence Smith, "Bartolo," 256 notes that later writers credited Jacobus Butrigarius, citing Bartolus here, but he was himself unable to corroborate this. He suggests that "it seems rather to echo a reductio ad absurdum" by Jacobus de Ravanis "of a suggestion by his master" Jacobus Balduinus. Such arguments did find resonance in subsequent eras.

subject treated in the second section of our text. Bartolus declares that our examination must proceed "along many lines of question," but he essentially distinguishes between those punitive statutes which expressly forbid acts outside the city's territory, and those stated in general terms.[132]

7.5.3.1 Statutes with Explicit Extraterritorial Effect

Regarding the former category, Bartolus first examines the case where both the offender (*delinquens*) and the victim (*ille in quem delinquitur*) are foreigners: "then the rule is that the statute, though it expressly forbids the act, does not extend to those persons who are outside the territory etc., because the statutes are law peculiar to the city (*ius proprium civitatis*)."[133] But the opposite is true in the case of confederated and allied cities ("as if a statute in Perugia provided that an offender at Assizi might be punished here"), or if the state in whose territory the offense was committed had consented to the making of the statute.[134]

Bartolus is also skeptical regarding the effects of statutes punishing a wrong perpetrated by a foreigner against a citizen outside the city's territory ("if a statute provides that the foreigner should be punished here, would this be valid?"). Bartolus notes, as arguments in favor of acknowledging such effect to the statute, the analogy to the jurisdiction that ecclesiastical courts acquire over a layman injuring a cleric, and the suggestion that the person of the injured citizen constitutes a place subject to the city and thus the act fell within the city's territory. But he dismisses them. The true reason for church jurisdiction is that the layman "commits sacrilege, which is an ecclesiastical crime, and therefore pertains to the church."[135] He is even more dismissive of the latter argument: the place of the offense has to refer to something immovable, like territory, not to a movable or self-moving thing.[136]

Bartolus acknowledges two exceptions (in addition to the one already noted, with regard to confederated cities, which is affirmed here as well). The first one concerns those stealing from a shipwreck, who may be

[132] Bartolus ad C.1.1.1, nus. 44–46 and 47–49.

[133] Ibid., nu. 44. The phrase *ius proprium civitatis* is taken from D.1.1.9.

[134] Bartolus ad C.1.1.1, nu. 44.

[135] Ibid., nu. 45.

[136] Ibid.: "Such a statute is not valid, because a city cannot legislate beyond its territory upon persons not subject to it."

punished by the injured person's judge.[137] The second addresses the inaction of the judge of the place where the citizen was injured (whether because the judge does not want to act or because he cannot).[138]

In contrast, Bartolus accepts the extraterritorial effects of a statute expressly punishing delinquent conduct by a citizen abroad ("by reason of his origin he may be punished for a crime committed anywhere; therefore, since such an offense is within the jurisdiction, a statute about it may be made").[139]

Bartolus would also allow the chief authority (*podestà*) of a city whose army occupies the territory of another to punish, for example, the murder of one foreign soldier by another. He does not see a contradiction with the more general rule. "Territory is so-called from 'terrify' (*terrendo*). But while the army of this city is there, terrifying and coercing that place, properly an offense there committed may be punished by the *podestà* although committed in that territory."[140]

[137] Ibid., with reference to D.47.9.7. This is a rule with a long tradition behind it, even though Cinus is noted by Bartolus as having opposed this extension.

[138] The passage could also be interpreted in the opposite fashion. The Latin text used by Guthrie and hence Beale, but also Barry's transcription read as follows: "Item fallit si iudex loci ubi civis meus *offendit*, offensam non vindicat (ut quia non vult, vel quia non potest) tunc poterit fieri statutum contra offendentem civem extra territorium" (emphasis added). Beale, *Bartolus*, 51 translates this as follows: "Another exception, where my fellow citizen offends and the judge of the place does not punish the offense . . . then a statute against the offending citizen may be made outside the territory." If the translation is not very convincing, a bigger problem is to view the text in context. The jurisdiction of the city with regard to the offenses of its citizens abroad is dealt immediately below. Indeed, a re-inspection of the original 1602 book showed a small hook next to the verb *offendit*: the symbol, in the early age of printing, for the passive-voice ending *-ur*. [Lyon, 1533, 8ra actually omits the hook, but this edition is generally less reliable than Venice 1602] The existence of the hook was corroborated by the inspection of the manuscript MS Vat.Lat. 2589, 74r. Once it has been established that the forum's citizen *offenditur* rather than *offendit*, the active participle *offendentem* is read not as an adjective to *civem*, but as a verbal participle, with *civem* its object.

[139] Bartolus ad C.1.1.1, nu. 45 (or 46). Beale's text has this part under an extended nu. 45. This is corroborated in Venice 1602, fol. 6va, which Barry, "Bartolus" has followed: nu. 46 begins with *Sed iuxta praedicta potest*. The same holds with the Lyon, 1533 (fol. 8ra) and Basel, 1562 editions (10b). Guthrie's text jumps from nu. 45 to nu. 47 in paragraph numbering. On the contrary, Clarence Smith, "Bartolo," 260 marks the beginning of nu. 46 at *aliquando civis delinquit extra territorium*. Our manuscript, which is the same that Clarence Smith used, does have a change of paragraph sign at that point. This would also make sense in the light of the *offenditur* correction proposed by Clarence Smith and myself.

[140] Bartolus ad C.1.1.1, nu. 46, with reference to D.1.16.239.8 (as to territory) and Nicolas Matarellus and Jacobus Buttrigarius (in support of his position).

7.5.3.2 Statutes Expressed in General Terms

The second category of issues concerns the extraterritoriality of statutes expressed in general terms (*non cavetur expresse sed simpliciter*). For example:

> [I]t is provided by the statute of the city of Perugia that the *podestà* may enquire of any homicide whatever, or proceed by accusation or by inquisition. It is provided in another statute that a certain penalty shall be imposed for homicide.[141]

Should the *podestà*, in the case of a homicide committed outside the territory of Perugia by one of its citizens, follow these statutes or the *ius commune*? A criminal proceeding under the *ius commune* would normally require accusation, i.e. the bringing of a complaint by someone; the proceeding could only be commenced at the initiative of the public authority in cases of public vengeance, and so that offenses could be punished and not covered up.

Past jurists engaged in a long debate, with Odofredus arguing against the extraterritoriality of the local legislation, and Cinus for it.[142] Their arguments, reproduced at length by Bartolus, offer an interesting perspective on Medieval political thought. Odofredus with Albertus argued that any public harm can only exist in the place where the offense was committed, and not in the offender's place of origin (*ius commune* did allow for inquisition *ad vindictam publicam*), and that the rulers of cities are called in the *Authentica* fathers of their subjects, and accordingly not of foreigners who have a different father. Cinus counter-argued that jurisdiction already exists; that a *civitas* has an interest in having good citizens, and men are made good by punishing (their) offenses; that this is demanded by "public policy and morality" (*ratio publicae disciplinae*)."[143]

[141] Ibid., nu. 47.

[142] Bartolus tells us that the case was first discussed by Odofredus, who answered in favor of the *ius commune* on both counts: his views were preserved by Albertus Gandinus. Bartolus' teacher, Cinus, came to the opposite conclusion. Bartolus remarks that Cinus, who used Sienna in the hypothetical, failed to credit Odofredus (*iura Odofredi licet de eis nulla fiat mentio*).

[143] Bartolus ad C.1.1.1, nu. 47 (translation of the last phrase by Clarence Smith, "Bartolo," 263, who also consulted M.S. Vat. Lat. 2589) compared the printed text to a manuscript). Other arguments involved the drawing of analogies between contracts and wrongs, as well as between statutes and judgments: one may bind one's subjects by a judgment, and hence it follows they can be bound by a law.

Bartolus tries to avoid philosophical speculation and proposes instead "that the words of the statute should be more diligently examined."[144] He first repeats that if the statute refers to "what a citizen does, even outside the territory," it can be used for his prosecution and punishment, whereas the opposite holds true if the statute is expressly limited to what happens inside the territory. If now the statute is expressed in general terms, Bartolus distinguishes between "statutes addressing the process or the institution of litigation" (*statuta quae respiciunt processum seu litis ordinationem*) and statutes addressing the substance of the case (*statuta quae respiciunt litis decisionem*).[145] The former shall govern any proceedings instituted in that city, as was noted above with regard to contracts, and therefore the podestà may proceed by inquisition.[146] As to the latter, however, where the manner of punishment is concerned, the accused must be punished under either the *ius commune* or the law of the place where the offense was committed (*secundum statutum loci, ubi delinquit*), because such statutes "do not have effect over those [things] that were committed beyond the [city's] territory, but the place where the thing is situated should be looked to, as stated above, both for contracts and for wrongs."[147]

7.5.4 *Effects of Judgments (nus. 50–51)*

The last section concerns the effects of a punitive judgment (*effectum sententiae punientis*). Bartolus differentiates between judgments regarding persons and judgments regarding property (*bona*).[148]

7.5.4.1 Judgments as to Persons (in personam)

Judgments as to persons (*sententiae quae respicit personam*) are subdivided between judgments interdicting/banishing the person from a certain

[144] Bartolus ad C.1.1.1., nu. 48.

[145] Ibid.

[146] Ibid., referring to nu. 15 and declaring agreement with Cinus.

[147] Ibid. (*quia statuta quae respiciunt litis decisionem non porriguntur ad ea quae extra territorium sunt commissa, sed debet inspici locus ubi res est situata, ut supra dictum est tam circa contractus quam circa delicta*) with reference to Sext 1.2.2 (*ut animarum*), § 1 and declaring his agreement with Odofredus and Albericus. Clarence Smith, "Bartolo," 265 substitutes "the transaction occurred" in lieu of the literal "the thing is situated" and translates "as much for an offense as for a contract," referring to Bartolus ad C.1.1.1, nu. 16. I have chosen to follow Beale on this point, having concluded that Bartolus also alludes to his discussion on wrongs (ibid., nu. 20).

[148] Ibid., nu. 50.

place (*interdictio certi loci*), judgments interdicting the person from a certain occupation (*interdictio certae artis*), and judgments diminishing the person's status (*diminutio status*).[149]

The effects of the two types of *interdictiones* are limited to the territory of the interdict (though banishment may extend to some other places "by consequence and disposition of the law").

On the contrary, diminution of status "has its effect everywhere." The classic example of such diminution is a person rendered *infamus*. But Bartolus is more concerned with "penal slavery" (*servi poenae*): thus, a woman sentenced to death by burning but then rescued by her family, remains slave of her punishment, incapable of making a testament or a contract or doing other such things. Just like the case of excommunication, "those penalties ... are inflicted upon the person and follow the person as leprosy does the leper."[150]

7.5.4.2 Judgments as to Property (in rem)

Bartolus now comes to judgments where the punishment regards property (*poena respicit bona*): if a person has been sentenced in a city to the forfeiture of his property, does such forfeiture (*publicatio*) also extend to his property located elsewhere?

Gulielmus de Cuneo had argued that the possessions of the condemned, being *bona vacantia*, escheat to each city to the extent that they are in its territory.[151] Nicolas Matarellus distinguished between those cases where the forfeiting judge both exercised his jurisdiction and issued the judgment under the *ius commune*, and those cases where he proceeds, in one or both respects, under "municipal law" (*a lege municipali*). In the

149 Ibid. Regarding the second sub-category (*interdictio certae artis*), D.3.1.9, to which reference is made, speaks of *pro alio postulare*, i.e. of the right to make an application to the magistrate on another's behalf (the term includes both setting out the claim and opposing the claim of another: D.3.1.1.2). Beale, *Bartolus*, 62 translates *interdictio certae artis* as interdiction "of a certain kind," which makes no sense (Beale's translation of the eighth section is generally problematic, but then Lainé, *Introduction*, 1:163, is right when he remarks that "la matière est traité d'une manière vague et obscure"). Clarence Smith, "Bartolo," speaks of "occupation" in the introductory outline (163) and translates as "calling" (268). Ancel, *Éléments*, 184 speaks of "profession." Barry, "Bartolus," 24 translates *artes* as "skills." Barry may be reading too much into the rule – while reducing its scope – in noting that Bartolus "seems to refer in particular to skills practiced in connection with the courts. As such, it is consistent with Bartolus' rule that procedural issues are determined by the law of the forum" (ibid.).

150 Bartolus ad C.1.1.1 nu. 50.

151 Ibid., referring to Gulielmus ad C.1.1.1 and ad D.4.5.2, drawing especially on D.7.2.3 and C.1.3.20.

former cases, the judgment reaches all property, but each judge will forfeit property located in his own territory. The reason is apparently that the judges are seen as operating under a single *fiscus*. In the latter cases, the forfeiture can have effect only in the territory of the judge passing the judgment.[152]

Bartolus follows a different approach. He begins by considering the fiscal powers of the cities. A city cannot forfeit goods to itself on account of a wrong punishable under the *ius commune*; nor does it possess *merum imperium* and jurisdiction over the most serious crimes. An exception exists for those cities which either have been granted such privilege by the emperor, or can claim an ancient custom ("which has the force of a constituted privilege") to that purpose. Interestingly, Bartolus claims that cities which possess a fiscal chamber (*camera fiscalis*), exercise the rights of the *princeps* over the property on their own behalf, by virtue of the – tacit or express – imperial grant.[153]

He then goes on to distinguish between those cases where the *iurisdictiones* are separate, but the "fiscal purse" (*bursa fiscalis*) is in effect common, and those where there also exist separate *bursae fiscales*.[154]

Within the first group of cases, a distinction is further made as to whether the forfeiture takes place under the *ius commune* or "under some ordinance or special laws" (*secundum constitionem vel leges speciales*). In the former case, the forfeiture will take place everywhere, carried out by the official of the place where the possessions are located. For example, a forfeiture ordered by the papal representative (*pro curia Romana*) in the March of Ancona under the *ius commune* will extend to the man's possessions in the Duchy of Spoleto, but the execution in the Duchy will be carried out by its *procurator fiscus*. In the latter case, however, the special legislation under which the forfeiture is taking place must also be in force in each place where property is located. Bartolus gives two examples. In the first, a single king appoints several judges for various territories of his kingdom. Forfeiture under a royal ordinance allows the forfeiture to be carried over in all territories of that kingdom. In the second, a forfeiture taking place in the March under an ordinance valid there but not in force in the Duchy will have no effect on property located in the Duchy.[155]

152 Bartolus ad C.1.1.1, nu. 50 (Nicolas is reported "by others").
153 Ibid., nu. 50 in fine.
154 Ibid., nu. 51.
155 Ibid.

In the second group of cases, where each territory is a separate *bursa fiscalis*, forfeiture will have effect beyond the judge's territory only if it takes place under the *ius commune*, but in each place each fiscal authority (*procurator fisci*) will take for its own purse the possessions situated on its territory. The reason for this is that the city exercises, for its own benefit, the fiscal powers of the Emperor, which include forfeiture under the *ius commune*.

Bartolus concludes the *repetitio* by noting, in contrast to Nicolas, that he does not regard as pertinent whether the judge has jurisdiction (*iurisdictionem*) under the *ius commune* or under the municipal law. What really matters is if he is enforcing a right created de iure communi, or if he creates one *de novo*.[156]

[156] Ibid., nu. 51 in fine.

8

The Political Context of Bartolan Conflict of Laws

8.1 Introduction

It is impossible to separate Bartolus from the complex political environment in which he lived. In this world of *institutional pluralism*, legal scholars of his caliber were important players but they also had to constantly engage in balancing acts between competiting – and concurrent – sources of political authority and power.[1] Law was not just an important tool for the exercise of power and *buon governo*, but an equally important currency for the legitimacy of polities and institutions.[2] The fact that law was itself a plural, multidimensional stream of norms and ideas added to both its potential and the challenges faced by jurists.

Viewed in this light, Bartolus thought – and certainly argued – in terms of a *world* system, albeit not one necessarily identical with the actual "world system" in which he lived. From a certain legal (and political) point of view, the work of Bartolus is about the foundations, structures and operation of a veritable (if fictive) world empire. From another point of view, however, his work is about the governance of the polities he was intimately connected with, i.e. "those parts of Italy which he knew and whose problems were actually before him – Lombardy, Tuscany, the March and central Italy generally."[3]

1 See the essays in L. Armstrong and J. Kirshner (eds.), *The Politics of Law in Late Medieval and Renaissance Italy* (Toronto: Toronto University Press, 2011), as well as Sbriccoli, *Interpretazione dello statuto* and L. Martines, *Lawyers and Statecraft in Renaissuance Florence* (Princeton: Princeton University Press, 1968).

2 In addition to works cited below see J. Watts, *The Making of Polities: Europe 1300–1500* (Cambridge: Cambridge University Press, 2009), esp. 73ff, 254ff; K. Pennington, *The Prince and the Law, 1200–1600* (Berkeley: University of California Press, 1993); F. Maiolo, *Medieval Sovereignty: Marsilius of Padua and Bartolus of Saxoferrato* (Delft: Eburon, 2007).

3 C. N. S. Woolf, *Bartolus of Sassoferrato: His Position in the History of Medieval Political Thought* (Cambridge: Cambridge University Press, 1913), 108.

This tension is reflected both in the work of Bartolus itself, and in how it has been approached in our historical consciousness. Conflicts lawyers have long taken for granted the continuity between the ideas expressed by Bartolus in our text and subsequent thinking on what seem to be the same issues. But the opposite has also been argued, namely that what Bartolus is doing has more affinities with statutory interpretation than with private international law; that instead of the horizontal conflicts between the laws of same-level states or polities, Bartolus and Medieval jurists are dealing with vertical conflicts between *ius commune* and *iura propria*, exploring the scope of local derogations from a hierarchically superior body of law.

This chapter is also an exploration of – and response to – these ideas. It is organized in two sections. Section 8.2 addresses political hierarchies and their legal vocabulary: Empire and local entities, universal and territorial "sovereignty," *iurisdictio*. The bulk of the section considers in this light the main political actor in everyday legal life, and the *repetitio* itself: the Italian city. Section 8.3 then examines the hierarchy of bodies of law (*iura*), from natural law and *ius gentium* to city law – our statutes. *Ius commune*, in the sense of the Roman law as elaborated by Medieval scholars, permeates the chapter – just as it permeated the legal and political discussions of Bartolus.

8.2 Polities and Hierarchies

8.2.1 A World Empire (with Its Common Law)

In his work, Bartolus presents us with a veritable "world system" structured around a *world empire* – the Roman empire, constituted by the *populus Romanus*, under the secular scepter of the emperor and the religious scepter of the pope. This world is defined both internally and externally.

As to its internal definition. Bartolus's *populus Romanus* consists of all who obey the Roman Church (*populus Christianus*), and hence recognize the Emperor as *dominus omnium*: this includes not only those who obey the *imperium Romanum* fully or partially (e.g. the Tuscan and Lombard cities), but also those who claim an exemption based on imperial privilege (e.g. Venice). Included, too, are those upon which the Church exercises the *imperium* (the territories of the Donation and clerics), and even the kings (e.g. of France and England) who deny any subjection to the *rex romanorum*: they have to acknowledge the emperor as *dominus omnium* in order to claim their independence *de iure.*[4]

The external definition is shown, notably, in how Bartolus approaches the entire world surrounding the Empire, on the one hand, and the entire history of the world, on the other.

Whereas the gloss on D.49.15.24 presented humanity as divided into five *genera gentium* – Romans, Greeks, Tartars, Saracens, and Jews – Bartolus suggested that *principaliter* there are two: *populus Romanus* and *populi extranei.*[5] He thus grouped together all those who did not recognize the Roman Emperor as *dominus universalis*, believing instead their own ruler to be lord of the world. With hindsight, these perspectives would probably appear to us more tolerant than those Medieval and Early Modern writers who declared the whole world as subordinate to Western Christianity, or remained wilfully ignorant of a Eurasian world from which much of the Italian prosperity did derive. But what really motivates him is to define and discuss the *populus Romanus.*[6] By suggesting that all *populi extranei* believe their ruler to be lord of the world, Bartolus strengthens the imperial party's claim that universal *dominium* is the natural order of things.[7]

This is also reflected in how Bartolus uses the eschatological narrative of the four great kingdoms preceding the end of time and the Kingdom of God.[8] Bartolus's own scheme is of a succession of four world Empires – Babylonian, Mede-Persian, Greek, and Roman. With the advent of Christ, the Roman Empire became His. He then transmitted it to His

[4] Bartolus ad D.49.15.24, nus. 3–7 (Basel, 1562), vol. 3, 983b. See also N. Figgis, "Bartolus and European Political Ideas," *Transactions of the Royal Historical Society*, 2d ser., 19 (1905), 147–168, 156 n. 1; Woolf, *Bartolus*, 25–27 quoting a substantial part of the text.

[5] Bartolus ad D.49.15.24, nus. 2 and 8.

[6] Indeed, Bartolus's two principal references to *populi extranei* pertain to the conduct of public war by the Emperor against them. See however C. Storti, *"Early "Italian" Scholars of Ius Gentium* in G. Bartolini (ed.), *A History of International Law in Italy* (Oxford: Oxford University Press, 2020), 19–46, 29ff.

[7] J. Baszkiewicz, "Quelques remarques sur la conception de dominium mundi dans l'oeuvre de Bartolus" in *Bartolo da Sassoferrato: Studi e Documenti per il VI Centenario*, vol. II (Milan: Giuffrè, 1962), 9–25, 9.

[8] The story comes from the Book of Daniel in the Old Testament. See Daniel 2 and 7. In some narratives from the Later Antiquity, Rome was the fifth empire. See e.g. D. Mendels, "The Five Empires: A Note on a Propagandistic Topos," *American Journal of Philology*, 102 (1981), 330–337. For the Medieval political context see M. Ryan, "Political Thought" in D. Johnson (ed.), *Cambridge Companion to Roman Law* (Cambridge: Cambridge University Press, 2015), 423–451, 432–431.

vicar, who, in his turn, transmitted it to the Emperor.[9] Bartolus manages in this way to defend simultaneously, on the one hand, certain papal claims and, on the other, the universal Roman *dominium* against those who argued that they could not in their turn be accused of usurping from the Romans the territories the Romans had themselves usurped by force.[10]

In short, Bartolus is primarily concerned with defending the nominal authority of the emperor and the unity of Western Christianity under emperor and pope. At the time, the imperialist aspirations of the early glossators are gone along with the Hohenstaufen, but the Roman Empire is not dead in legal terms. Bartolus is probably all too aware of the world – Western and non-Western alike – surrounding the Italian peninsula. He knows the limits of the real power of both Emperor and Pope, having lived almost his entire life during the exile of the popes in Avignon. Effective papal power in Middle Italy was restored only near the end of his life, but it was nonetheless restored. This was also the time when cities acknowledged the emperor's nominal jurisdiction, paying him a tribute in exchange for his legitimating their exercise of powers – an exercise that in the future would often be repeated by the emperors and popes who named as their "vicars" the city tyrants they could not depose.

In this environment, it is not Law being invoked in the service of Empire, as much as Empire being invoked to provide political legitimacy and doctrinal foundations to Law. What clearly interests Bartolus is to lay the foundations for a doctrinal system reconciling timeless ideals and present-day realities. Hence, Bartolus's emperor was *dominus universalis* without hindering the existence of *domini particulariter*.[11] Furthermore, Bartolus in his commentaries repeatedly drew a distinction between the imperial power *de iure* and the partial or complete disobedience of many peoples (*gentes*) *de facto*.[12] Our own *repetitio* contains several characteristic examples of such distinctions and doctrinal subtleties.

[9] Bartolus, *Tractatus super constitutione* Ad reprimendum vo *totius orbis*, nus. 9–10 (Basel 1562), vol. 5, 532b–533a

[10] See Woolf, *Bartolus*, 346ff.

[11] See Bartolus ad D.6.1.1 (as quoted in M. Ryan, "Bartolus of Sassoferrato and Free Cities," *Transactions of the Royal Historical Society*, 6th ser., 10 (2000), 65–89, 71): "I say that the Emperor is Lord of the entire world in a true sense. Nor does it conflict with this that others are lords in a particular sense, for the world is a sort of *universitas*. Hence someone can possess the said *universitas* without owning the particular rights within it."

[12] For a list see e.g. F. Ercole, "Impero universale e Stati particolari: la 'civitas sibi princeps' e lo Stato moderno" in *Da Bartolo all'Althusio: Saggi sulla storia del pensiero pubblicistico del rinascimento Italiano* (Florence: Vallechi, 1932), 49–156, 72 n. 1.

8.2.2 *Cities (and the Power to Make Law)*

The nature and scope of the Italian cities' power to make and enforce laws is a recurrent theme in the work of Bartolus, including our own *repetitio*. Bartolus treated only casually the kingdoms (*regna*) of France, England or even Naples and Sicily, but *regna* and *civitates* posed many of the same problems regarding their political status and governance and Bartolus himself drew substantially from arguments about the independence of *regna*.[13]

8.2.2.1 The Legislative Jurisdiction of Cities

It would be an obvious anachronism to speak of "sovereignty" in Bartolus. Yet the delimitation (and allocation) of the power of offices constitutes the cornernstone of his political and legal thought. Bartolus espouses a *disaggregated* and *hierarchical* model of "sovereignty," at the heart of which is the concept of jurisdiction (*iurisdictio*). Power abstractly defined (*imperium*), is broken down into numerous concrete powers to take specific actions. The jurisdiction required for an official to exercise such powers is allocated by, ranked and operating within a hierarchical system. In this environment, the issue of validity of local statutes vis-à-vis the *ius commune* (as opposed to divine law and natural law) becomes an issue of jurisdiction.

Bartolus, building on the Gloss, defined *iurisdictio* as "the power granted by public law requiring the rendering of judgment according to law and of laying down equity, as by public person."[14] He divided it into two species, *imperium*, which pertains to the *officium nobile* of the judge and is further divided into *merum* and *mixtum*, and *iurisdictio simplex*, which belongs to the *officium mercenarium* of the judge.[15] The distinction between *imperium* and *iurisdictio simplex* seems to correspond to

[13] On Bartolus and *regna* see Woolf, *Bartolus*, 107–112 (noting that Bartolus, who is credited with the notion of *civitas sibi princeps* did not use the phrase *rex in regno suo est Imperator regni sui*, because "the problems, which made the solution necessary, rarely presented themselves to him except in connection with the Civitas:" 109). See also Francesco Ercole; "L'origine francese della formola Bartoliana 'civitas superiorem non recognoscens est sibi princeps'," in *Da Bartolo all'Althusio: Saggi sulla storia del pensiero pubblicistico del rinascimento Italiano* (Florence: Vallechi, 1932), 157–217.

[14] Bartolus ad D.2.1.1, nu. 3 (107b): "*Iurisdictio est potestas de iure publico introducta cum necessitate ius dicendi et aequitatis tamquam a persona publica statuendae.*" Bartolus is here adding *tamquam a persona publica* to the definition of *iurisdictio* by the Gloss, in order, he says, to distinguish *iurisdictio* from the power given to fathers and tutors.

[15] Bartolus ad D.2.1.3, nus. 4ff.

Table 8.1 *Grades of* Iurisdictio *in Bartolus (Bartolus ad D.2.1)*

Iurisdictio			
	Officium iudicis nobile		Officium iudicis mercenarium
	Imperium		**iurisdictio simplex**
	Merum imperium	Mixtum imperium	
Maximum, -a	Legislation (*potestas contendi legem*) (reserved to princeps and the Senate)	Can be exercised only by the *princeps*, e.g. granting of adulthood status (*venia aetatis*), legitimation	Cases of great prejudice, e.g. causes involving liberty (cause liberales)
Maius, -or	Punishment of criminals (*potestas animadvertendi in facinotous homines*)	Hearing a case following *supplicatio* (power reserved to the *princeps* and provincial prefect)	Cases where a judgment may give rise to torture (*cruciatio*)
Magnum, -a	Power to remove someone's civic status (i.e. *exilium*)	Power to grant *restitutio in integrum*	Value of over 300 gold coins
Parvum, -a	Power to relegate someone outside the city (*relegatio*)	Power to grant possession of property	Value of below 300 gold coins
Minus, -or	Modest corporeal punishment (imprisonment) (*modica coercitatio corporis*)	Matters appropriate to the *officium nobile* and requiring summary *cognitio* (e.g. *cognitio* on the possession of property)	[no description or example]
Minimum, -a	fine (*levis mulcta*)	Matters appropriate to the *officium nobile* and required by the *cognitio* of the case (e.g. manumission, emancipation)	Below 100 gold coins
	Utilitas publica	Utilitas privata	

the ancient Roman distinction between the part of the magistrate's power in which he had discretion and the part in which he was bound by the law. In their turn, *merum imperium* is exercised for the public utility while *mixtum imperium* is exercised for private utility (as is *iurisdictio simplex*).[16] Each of the three species is divided into six grades:[17] the lowest grades define powers widely available to magistrates, whereas the highest ones, such as the power to make laws (*potestas condendi legem*) which is characterized as *maximum merum imperium*, are reserved to the Prince and Senate (see Table 8.1).[18]

[16] Ibid., nus. 7, 15, 23.

[17] Ibid., nus. 8ff, 17ff, and 24ff.

[18] This hierarchical taxonomy, which integrates functions from the Roman constitution and contemporaneous practice, avoids a stark contrast between the *imperium* of the Prince and that of lesser magistrates. In this, Bartolus is contrasted to both the glossators' pro-imperial approach, but also Baldus who, thinking also of independent cities, spoke

Bartolus held that a statute will be valid if it does not run contrary to the law (*lex non resistit statuto*), and provided it conforms to *bonos mores* and public utility.[19] As to customs, they are valid if they go beyond the law (*praeter legem*), but not if they are *contra legem*, unless the custom is subsequent to the *ius civile* rule and has been induced *ex certa scientia*.[20] But what about a city's jurisdiction to make such statutes? Some – Bartolus mentions Gulielmus de Cuneo – would allow cities the right to make statutes regarding private utility (*in his quaem privatam utilatem respiciunt*), but not public utility.[21] Bartolus himself draws a distinction depending on the degree of jurisdiction each city possesses.[22] Cities with no jurisdiction (principally *villae* and *castra*) can make statutes that "concern the administration of property that the people own collectively" (*pertinens ad administrationem rerum ipsius populi*) on their own, but they can legislate on the hearing and deciding of cases (*statutum pertinens ad causarum decisionem*) only by authority of their superior.[23] Such cities could not for example take any action for forfeiture of property.[24] Cities with limited jurisdiction are similarly limited.[25] On the contrary, a *populus liber* with full jurisdiction, like the *populus Romanus*, can make laws and statutes as it pleases. But the peoples that do not have jurisdiction *de iure communi*, as well the provinces, which possess *merum imperium* but are also subject to a superior, need confirmation by the superior for their statutes to be valid.

Bartolus's example of entities needing such confirmation of their statutes is characteristic: the cities of the March (of Ancona) and the Duchy (of Spoletto), which were subject to the pope but remained outside effective papal control until near the end of Bartolus' life. According to Bartolus, in the papal territories the Church has substituted for the emperor in his temporal powers. Additionally, many cities are granted a *de iure* claim to self-governance by imperial concession or by

of *merum imperium absolutum*. See e.g. M. P. Gilmore, *Argument from Roman Law in Political Thought* (Cambridge, MA: Harvard University Press, 1941), 42–43 and esp. Woolf, *Bartolus*, 165–166.

[19] Bartolus ad D.1.1.9, nu. 26 (Basel 1562), vol. 1, 19b.

[20] Bartolus ad C.8.53.2, nu. 45 (Basel 1562), vol. 4, 815a.

[21] Bartolus ad C.10.63.5, nu. 4 (Basel 1562), vol. 4, 892b.

[22] Ibid., referring to Bartolus ad D.1.1.9.

[23] Bartolus ad D.1.1.9, nu. 3.

[24] Bartolus ad C.1.1.1, nu. 50.

[25] Bartolus ad D.1.1.9, nu. 4 (*quando habet iurisdictionem limitatam, in his in quibus habent administrationem, seu iurisdictionem, possunt facere statuta, in aliis non, sine superioris autoritate*).

proving the ancient exercise of their power.[26] But Bartolus goes further: in the course of his commentaries, we will see him repeatedly suggesting that legislative powers thus reserved to the Emperor can be validly exercised by the king, prince or people not recognizing the Emperor as superior, often using the famous phrase *quia ipsamet civitas sibi princeps est.*[27]

The notion of *civitas sibi princeps*, as well as the elaboration of the *de iure – de facto* distinction are regarded as the main contributions of Bartolus to political theory.[28] Again and again, Bartolus ends up by upholding the core of the cities' external and internal sovereignty, while still trying to keep them under a nominal leash.

An illuminating example, from the discussion of punitive judgments in the last section of the *repetitio*, concerns the forfeiture of property in other territories.[29] Bartolus appears to restrict a city's power to forfeit goods *to itself* only in its territory and on account of minor wrongs for which it is allowed jurisdiction (not even serious crimes).[30] But he then expands this power: starting with the obvious case of an express imperial grant or an "ancient custom," he introduces the legal construct that cities with a fiscal chamber (*camera fiscalis*) can claim a tacit or express imperial grant to exercise imperial power to their own benefit. He then allows the city issuing the judgment to forfeit itself goods in other territories, where the "fiscal purse" (*bursa fiscalis*) is common, as for example in the Papal States or in a kingdom, provided it takes place under the *ius commune* or some common special legislation, with the help of the local authority in each place. The next step is to accept that each city where property is located can forfeit to its own purse property covered by the judgment, not only if forfeiture has been ordered under the *ius commune* – as suggested by others – but also if ordered even under "municipal law" (*ius municipale*), as long as the *right* being enforced is acknowledged by the *ius commune.*[31]

[26] Bartolus ad C.2.3.28, nus. 4–5 (Basel, 1562), vol. I, 141a.

[27] Examples include the restitution of fame to someone declared infamous (D.3.1.1), granting to a minor the administration of his property (D.4.4.3), etc. See the list in Woolf, *Bartolus*, 155–160. In our text see e.g. Bartolus ad C.1.1.1, nu. 51.

[28] Cf. Ryan, "Bartolus and Free Cities."

[29] Bartolus ad C.1.1.1, nus. 50–51 as discussed at Section 7.5.4.2. See also Woolf, *Bartolus*, 119–122.

[30] Ibid., nu. 50.

[31] Ibid., nu. 51.

8.2.2.2 The "Internal Sovereignty" of Cities

The internal workings of *iurisdictio* offer us a characteristic example of Bartolan thinking in action, which connects to our *repetitio*. The fourteenth century saw the consolidation of what could be, again somewhat anachronistically, called the Italian cities' "internal sovereignty."[32] Bartolus was at the forefront of these attempts.[33] Guilds were allowed their own judges and officials, and they could make special statutes differing from the general law of the city, "concerning the affairs of that guild or profession, but not about other things, for example inheritances."[34] But guilds, their members and their officials remained subject to the jurisdiction of the *podestà*.[35]

On the contrary, most jurists were inclined to allow ecclesiastical jurisdiction to stand independent from that of the city. Like foreigners, local clergy were regarded as *non subditi* to the laws of the city.[36] Cinus had even argued that clergy and laity were two *populi*.[37] Even Baldus had to argue that clerics were "part of the people insofar as this is to their advantage, but not insofar as it is to the church's detriment."[38]

If we now look at our own *repetitio*, we see Bartolus himself going further than Baldus in his language: there is no allusion to a *populus* or *populi*, with discussion being framed in terms of ecclesiastical privileges and intented reach of the legislation.[39] We must actually draw a distinction between adjudicative and legislative jurisdiction. Clerics were subjected to ecclesiastical courts, falling under the Holy See, not secular courts run by lay authorities; so the real question is about the instances when ecclesiastical courts should apply city law, in derogation from the

[32] See e.g. P. Jones, *The Italian City-State: From Commune to Signoria* (Oxford: Clarendon Press, 1997).

[33] Ryan, "Bartolus and Free Cities," 78ff, esp. 79, suggesting that "the *civitas sibi princeps* is aimed first and foremost at those who denied the right of their fellows to govern them within the city itself," and 84 ("The tensions in Bartolus' ideas about the interaction between free cities and wider sovereign bodies such as the empire are real and important, but they are only so crassly obvious because these matters were not Bartolus' primary concern. It was more urgent to decide what happened within a city once the jurisdiction of the emperor had been denied. If he did not have disciplinary powers, who did?").

[34] Baldus ad D.1.1.9 (quoted in Canning, *Baldus*, 152–153). Cf. Bartolus ad D.1.1.9, nu. 6.

[35] Baldus ad C.3.13.57 (quoted in Canning, *Baldus*, 152).

[36] Se K. Kim, *Aliens in Medieval Law* (Cambridge: Cambridge University Press, 2000), 60–88, using Medieval England as an example.

[37] Cinus at C.8.52.2, nu. 27 (excerpted in Canning, *Baldus*, 138). See also the reference to Cinus of Bartolus ad C.1.1.1, nu. 28.

[38] Baldus ad X.1.2.7 n. 7 and in general see Canning, *Baldus*, 131ff.

[39] Bartolus ad C.1.1.1, nus. 28–30 (presented at Section 7.4.5).

ius commune.[40] Bartolus allows this to happen provided certain conditions are met. First, the city statute must not run contrary to actual privileges granted to the clergy by Pope or Emperor – that is, it can only preempt the default rules of Roman (or canon) law as constructed by the jurists. Second, if that condition is met, the city statute must be "honorable."[41] Third, if the statute does apply, its effects must not contradict privileges granted. For example: Perugia law imposing certain publicity requirements on the opening of testaments will apply to clerics' testaments (in Perugia); so dispositions of property in a cleric's testament made in violation of the statute will be invalid with the exception of dispositions pertaining to "pious causes," because these latter are covered by an express canon-law rule on solemnity.[42]

8.3 Laws and Their Hierarchies

The work of Bartolus is first and foremost about the *ius commune* – the law common to the *populus Romanus.* This includes therefore not simply Roman or imperial law (*ius civile*) but also the law of the Church: Canon law authorities are thus invoked along with the Roman ones.[43]

But what is the role of *ius commune* according to Bartolus? Is it a legal system – a "sovereign," all-encompassing *ordre juridique* in the way nineteenth and twentieth-century scholars came to conceive of national law, whose scope must be determined? A functional equivalent to the modern international law – a superior, or at least common, body of law acknowledged by diverse polities and invoked in their relations? A body of learned law (*droit savant*) aiming at the elaboration of common legal principles and the management, or reduction, of legal diversity? Is it simply a formidable apparatus containing tools and doctrines to be used in order to achieve the sought-after results? Or – as the discussion in conflicts literature on the use of *cunctos populos* would seem to indicate – a convenient if fictive foundation to ground a doctrinal system?

40 Ironically, given how often that the passage has been omitted from presentations of the *repetitio*, this is a choice-of-law question: the court (*forum*) considers the application of the law of another jurisdiction, albeit one in which the court itself is physically located.

41 Bartolus ad C.1.1.1, nu. 29.

42 Ibid., 30.

43 See G. Le Bras, "Bartole et le droit canon" in *Bartolo da Sassoferrato: Studi e Documenti per il VI Centenario*, vol. II (Milan: Giuffrè, 1962), 297–308. More serious consideration of canon law is supposed to have been one the characteristics of commentators, in comparison with the glossators.

Ius commune is for Bartolus more, and all, of these things. We have seen *ius commune* being defined as the law of the *populus Romanus*, but in reality the *populus Romanus* is the political foundation of the *ius commune*. It has in fact been argued, and for good reason, that it is the *ius commune* Bartolus is thinking about when he tries to keep Western Christianity together as *populus Romanus*, or when he speaks of the emperor.[44]

Bartolus and the other Medieval academic lawyers approached and reshaped *ius commune* in scholarly terms (with Commentators, including Bartolus integrating canon-law authorities together with Roman-law ones). But they regarded – or at least presented – *ius commune* as emanating from a political authority, and this idea did find validation in their authorities, notably Justinian's pronouncements.[45] If we take our own *repetitio* as an example: the commentary of Bartolus is usually examined by itself, but one cannot fully understand his legal arguments without examining the authorities cited (and, if one is to go further, how these authorities were perceived by his audience).

Bartolus conceives of law – *ius commune* and local law – as a whole. From a "positivistic" point of view, *iura propria* are the result of the *iurisdictio* with which the imperial power, and imperial law, have vested lesser authorities. At the same time, it has been justly remarked that "a random glance at any page of Bartolus would show the large part played by both statute and custom, not merely as illustrations, but in the actual elaboration of a law which, while Roman in basis, was to be practically effectual for the Italy of his day."[46]

Ius commune permeats the discussion that follows in this section. We shall first look at the bodies of law that could possibly be regarded as hierarchically superior to the law of the Empire. We will then consider *iura propria*: first, how city laws are approached in jurisprudential terms; then, how the effective interaction of city law and *ius commune* as illustrated in the *repetitio*.

8.3.1 Of Ius Gentium *and the Law Common to All Peoples*

Bartolus envisages a hierarchy of laws in which divine law, natural law, and the *ius gentium* are all, in some sense, higher than the law of the

[44] Woolf, *Bartolus*, 198, 207.
[45] Ryan, "Political Thought," 423–431.
[46] Woolf, *Bartolus*, 147.

emperor.[47] It must first be noted that it is difficult to understand what Bartolus precisely means with each of these concepts. His Roman law sources were not clear on this matter, and concepts such as natural law and *ius gentium* have had substantially different meanings over time.[48] But what is of actual interest to us here is the role these higher *iura* perform in his argumentation.

For Medieval jurists, such *iura* constituted a structure of axiomatic higher norms, within the context of which the power of the emperor to create positive law had to operate.[49] They were therefore binding even on the emperor – and of course, they are at least as binding on all other polities nominally or formerly subordinate to him. For example, Bartolus views natural law as setting limits to what could be done to change procedural systems.[50] He also argues that the Emperor cannot just take away individual property (*dominium*) without cause because it derives *de iure gentium.*[51] This is a hierarchical function internal to the legal system.

On the other hand, these higher *iura* also provide common legal rules for the interactions between *populus Romanus* and *populi extranei.* That is, they operate externally to the Roman legal system. As long as the *ius commune* may be invoked to mediate between two polities, there is no need for *ius gentium* or natural law. Two examples are characteristic in this regard.

The first comes from Bartolus's tract on reprisals.[52] Bartolus tried both to limit the instances of reprisals, and to subject reprisals to due process. When it came to relations between *populus Romanus* and *populi extranei,*

47 Bartolus ad D.1.1.9, nu. 2. Cf. Baskiewitz, "La conception de *dominium mundi,*" 15 (suggesting Bartolus confuses *ius gentium* with natural law).

48 See A. P. d'Entrèves, *Natural Law: An Introduction to Legal Philosophy* (New Brunswick, NJ: Transaction, 1994). Romans conceived of natural law as providing a legal standard uniting humanity into a universal community. Medieval canonists and especially scholastic philosophers elaborated the idea of natural law as grounded on God's will. Medieval Roman lawyers, including Bartolus, mostly adhere to the former idea, which is expressed in their authorities, but they are not shut to the theology and philosophy of their era. As to *ius gentium*, the ambiguity of the term in Roman sources is notorious.

49 Canning, *Baldus*, 76: "[T]he constitutive element of law was not the ruler's command or the people's consent alone, but that will exercised in accordance with moral, religious and rational criteria."

50 Bartolus, *Tractatus Ad reprimendum*, v° *figura*, 542b, after making the *ius civile* — *ius naturale* distinction.

51 Bartolus ad C.1.22.2 nu. 3 (*quaedam de iure civili, ut actiones, et istae possunt auferri per principem. Quaedam de iure gentium, ut dominium, et istud non potest auferri*).

52 Bartolus, *Tractatus de repraesaliis* (Basel 1562), 592b–605a. The argument in this paragraph draws from Woolf, *Bartolus*, 195ff, esp. 203ff.

Bartolus equated reprisals with war (*concedere repraesalias est indicere bellum*). A just war requires that neither party has a superior – as well as a just cause. Bartolus classifies reprisals (with war) under the *manus regia seu potestas regia* instead of the *officium judicis*: hence they are *de iure gentium* and not *de iure communi*. But, having made this classification, then Bartolus comes to reprisals between Italian cities – and he finds recourse to the *ius commune* to "establish [their] orderly working."[53]

The second example comes from his first *quaestio disputata*. Bartolus is disputing the validity of the city statute that makes a *bannitus* (roughly, an outlaw) subject to being killed by anyone: if it is city law that led to his condition, the *bannitus* maintains his rights under the *ius commune* (*iura civitatis Romanae*), but if the punishment is under the *ius commune*, the *bannitus* maintains his rights under the *ius gentium* (*iura gentium*).[54] Here again, *ius gentium* is invoked when the subject of rights has been cast out of the legal community of the *populus Romanus* (and the scope of its law).

If natural law appears to be for Bartolus a kind of substratum on which other law was built, *ius gentium* appears to come into play in the very limited cases falling outside the legal complex constituted by *ius commune* and all law emanating, in reality or by fiction, from its authority. We are still away from the *ius gentium* developing into the law of nations of subsequent eras.[55]

8.3.2 From City Laws to City Law

At the heart of Medieval thinking about the nature – and position within the legal hierarchy – of city laws lies the need to reconcile an evolving reality on the ground with the theory of the sources of law in the Roman texts, as received.

Roman law was effectively revived in early high Medieval Italy, in territories where customary practices already held considerable sway. It soon acquired considerable authority for political and practical reasons – namely, it provided an adequate, common vocabulary and solutions appropriate to an economy and society undergoing radical

[53] Woolf, *Bartolus*, 207.

[54] Bartolus, *Quaestio I*, nu. 20 (Basel, 1562), vol. 5, 76b.

[55] Cf. Baldus (as discussed at Section 8.4.2). In the late thirteenth century, *ius gentium* had been invoked by jurists, notably in the Kingdom of Sicily, arguing against the legitimacy of the Roman Empire. See Ryan, "Political Thought," 436–437.

transformation and growth in the High Middle Ages. By the Late Middle Ages, as new structures were consolidated in city-states (and kingdoms) and city authorities acquired legitimacy to regulate the city's population at large, special legislation proliferated (and surviving customs were codified), raising a new challenge to the *ius commune*. This is, in a nutshell, the difference in context between glossators and commentators.

Glossators espoused a theory of legal sources closer to their – laconic – Roman texts, which privileged (general) written law but acknowledged custom as a source in the absence of written law.[56] Glossators therefore treated statutes as "written customs" (*consuetudo scripta*). Taken together with the other local customs, such written customs constituted the *ius municipale*, which was subordinate to the general law and subject to the consent of the superior. A certain normative role was also acknowledged to *collegia licita* or *approbata* – a term covering not only territorial entities but also other corporations, such as guilds – could regulate their own affairs and members.[57] But, by the fourteenth century this notion of subordinate jurisdiction could not justify the expanded aims – and scope – of city legislation. Bartolus and the other commentators had to work out a more sophisticated theory of legal sources and contribute toward the consolidation of internal and external sovereignty.

If we now look at the writings of Baldus, Bartolus's most important student, in the second half of the fourteenth century, we will get a sense of the direction of both political ideas and the shape of polities. Baldus stands for the consolidation of the cities' legislative power and places emphasis on popular consent as basis of legislative power.[58] In a telling reversal of the glossators' doctrine about statute being a "written custom," *consuetudo scripta*, Baldus called custom a "tacit statute," *tacitum statutum*.[59] Like Bartolus, Baldus also uses a scheme of grades of jurisdictional power, in order to explain the cities' legislative power while maintaining in some form the established hierarchy: he thus

[56] See notably D.1.3.32 (Ulpian), C.8.52.2 (Constantine, to the effect that customs may prevail against neither reason nor legislation).

[57] Bartolus ad D.1.1.9, nu. 6: "*Secundo quaero utrum collegia possint facere statuta: videtur dicendum, quod collegia licita et approbata in his in quibus habent iurisdictionem, et quo ad ea quae ad ipsos collegiatos pertinent, possunt facere statuta.*"

[58] Canning, *Baldus*, 102: "Bartolus' achievement had been to establish the legislative autonomy of populi by arguing essentially *from* the independence involved in the formation of custom *to* independence in statute-making. Baldus writes when the full legislative power of the people has already been established."

[59] Baldus ad Auth. *Et qui iurat*, ad C.7.72.9 (quoted by Canning, *Baldus*, 102 n. 31).

distinguishes between "people" with no jurisdiction (like the places "subjected to some city"), full jurisdiction ("conceded by the emperor or prescriped by custom"), and limited jurisdiction.[60] But he then takes a novel step: the power of a people to make statutes without the consent of its superior is said to exist *de iure gentium* provided the statutes are "good ones bearing in mind the requirements of the place in question and the preservation of its public good."[61] We have here two steps that look familiar to the thinking of subsequent eras but Bartolus was unwilling to make: on the on hand, Baldus is ready to dispense with the fiction of imperial "tacit" consent, or even ex post approval; on the other hand, *ius gentium* is invoked in order to allocate jurisdiction – albeit vertically – beween political authorities emanating from the *populus Romanus* but no longer pretending to be bound by it.

8.3.3 Iura propria

We now come to our own *repetitio* and its place within Bartolan political and legal thought. Bartolus is here clearly concerned with the power of cities to bind with their laws those "not subject" within their territory, on the one hand, and those "subject" but outside their territory on the other. The first part is concerned with the former question. The second part is concerned with the latter: it examines, in parallel, not just the reach of the city's jurisdiction beyond its territory, but also the extend to which the city's exercise of its legislative and adjudicative power inside its own territory – through notarial acts, testaments, acts altering personal status – may produce effect elsewhere. The move from the first to the second part is in a sense a move from the core of the city's legal system – if we are allowed to use such a term for that kind of legal environment – toward its circumference.

[60] Baldus ad Inst.1.2.1 (translated excerpt in Canning, *Baldus*, 98–99).

[61] Baldus ad D.1.1.9. See Canning, *Baldus*, 104ff. The excerpt, translated in Canning, *Baldus*, 106 is as follows: "And if [a people] rules itself well a superior cannot stand in its way, because prohibitory laws were not made for those living good lives but for those who stray; for if they naturally do what the law demands, they are a law unto themselves. And the healthy need no medicine from without . . . If therefore statutes are good ones bearing in mind the requirements of the place in question and the preservation of its public good, they do not need anyone else's direction, because they have been confirmed by their own natural justice."

8.3.3.1 Citizens at Home

Bartolus essentially assumes in the *repetitio* the power of cities to bind their lay subjects in their own territory.[62] That much was accepted, in principle, even by glossators trying to reduce derogation from the *ius commune* to a minimum.[63] But then we see him providing an expansive justification of the statutory relaxation of the Roman-law requirement as to the number of witnesses required for testaments, where he combines legal, political and practical arguments in order to deny that imperial consent or even tacit approval of the statute is needed.[64] That position might be viewed as another small step in the assertion of city legislative jurisdiction; it also contributes to legal certainty in a manner as important as the validity of testaments, which may have effects beyond the city's territory.

8.3.3.2 Foreigners Abroad

At the opposite end, Bartolus would only allow the city in extreme cases jurisdiction over non-subjects acting beyond its territory. The issue is brought up with regard to the extraterritorial effect of punitive statutes.[65] The case when both offender and victim are foreigners is easily disposed of prior to any discussion.[66] The real debate involved instances where the victim is the city's subject. Bartolus would still only allow foreigners to be prosecuted under city law *in extremis* – namely, if the judge of the *locus delicti* does not act to punish the offense, or if they have stolen from a shipwreck – and provided that the statute is worded as to govern such conduct abroad.[67] This is still more than his teacher Cinus did

62 Bartolus ad C.1.1.1, nus. 13, 22–23, and 38.

63 See Section 3.4.1 as to Accursius ad C.1.1.1 and the gloss *si Bononiensis*, and more broadly Hatzimihail, "Doctrinal Beginnings."

64 Bartolus ad C.1.1.1, nus. 22–23, in refutation of the position of Jacobus de Arena that such a rule cannot be valid without imperial consent. It is interesting that Venice is used as an example: Bartolus recognizes its claim not to be subjected to imperial power but nontetheless chooses to elaborate a broader set of rules.

65 Ibid., 44–49. See Section 7.5.3.

66 Bartolus ad C.1.1.1, nu. 44. The "exception" acknowledged as to associated or allied cities, or cities that had consented to the enactment of the punitive statute essentially confirms the principle: ibid., nus. 44, 45. The same is also true as to the jurisdiction of the *podestà* over a wrong inflicted by one foreigner to another in a territory as to military occupation (contested by others and acknowledged by Bartolus): ibid., nu. 46.

67 Bartolus ad C.1.1.1, nu. 45. The former case brings to mind the so-called passive nationality basis of jurisdiction. The latter, considering the universal condemnation of stealing from shiprecks for fear of inducing piracy, has affinities with our universal jurisdiction.

accept.[68] But it is far less than what was advocated by those who made the sweeping arguments in favor of city jurisdiction (analogies from the assertion of ecclesiastical jurisdiction over lay offenders injuring clerics; equating the city's subject with its territory), which Bartolus considers and dismisses.

8.3.3.3 Foreigners in the City

Bartolus seems inclined to accept, as a matter of principle, that a city statute may extend to citizens and non citizens alike.[69] But he proposes no general rule and indeed treats differently the various subjects in the first part of the *repetitio*.[70] First, even though the section on contracts begins with the case of "a contract celebrated by a foreigner in this city," no allusion is made – let alone distinction drawn – anywhere in the section. Testaments are more interesting in this regard: past jurists had argued against the possibility of foreigners to avail themselves of more permissive statutes as to testamentary formalities, but Bartolus dismisses their argument that "as a statute is called the law proper to the city (*ius proprium civitatis*) it does not extend to foreigners."[71] He proposes instead to look to the wording of the statute, which should extend to all testators unless it expressly limits its effects to citizens.

Even more interesting is Bartolus's discussion about the effects of penal laws (*wrongs*) over the conduct of foreigners in the city.[72] The statute definitely applies if the wrong is also punishable under the *ius commune*. Even if it is not however, the statute also applies if the foreigner knew or ought to have known about the prohibition (namely, if he lived in the city for so long, or the punishable act is "commonly

[68] Cinus ad 3.15.2a, as reported by Bartolus ad C.1.1.1, nu. 45.

[69] Bartolus speaks of "foreigners" rather than "non subjects." The word *forenses* is used 21 times, in the opening (1) and in the sections on wrongs (2), testaments (8), permissive statutes (3), and punitive statutes (7). The term *subditus* is used 10 times, namely in the opening (1) and in the sections on testaments (4) and on punitive statutes (5); and the world *subiectus* another 4, on punitive statutes (3) and on judgments (1). But these references are about someone (or even something) being "subject" or not being subject (and, in the discussion on punitive statutes, where most of them come from, to describe the arguments of other jurists). The term *non subditus* is only used in the opening. The word *cives* is only used once, in a reference to imperial Rome: Bartolus ad C.1.1.1, nu. 25. Clarence Smith, "Bartolo," translates *forenses* as "outsider."

[70] We assume that the question regarding buildings in Bartolus ad C.1.1.1, nu. 27 has foreigners in mind; the city statute is held to apply to all. The fifth section is discussed at Section 8.2.2.2.

[71] Ibid., nu. 24 (citing Jacobus de Arena).

[72] Ibid., nu. 20.

prohibited" by cities that he ought to have known it) but not if, cumulatively, he did know about it and the act is not so generally prohibited.

8.3.3.4 Subjects Abroad

So far, we have seen Bartolus answer each of our first three cases with a single principle (albeit with exceptions). But when it comes to the fourth – and most salient – case he draws a more complicated scheme. Whether city law follows citizens – and more broadly its residents – abroad depends on the subject and the purpose of the law.[73]

To return to our example of the punitive statutes, Bartolus is in no doubt that a city's punitive statutes that *expressly* address its citizens' conduct abroad apply to such conduct.[74] His statement that "by reason of his origin he may be punished for a crime committed anywhere" is a defense of the city's legislative power under the *ius commune*, in response to the old glossators' attemtps to treat city law as *ius municipale* that can only produce effects in the city's territory.

But Bartolus does not go as far as his teacher Cinus, who would apply city law in all such cases. Moreover, wheras Odofredus and Cinus presented abstract arguments to support positions in either extreme, Bartolus places emphasis on the wording and the purpose of the statute: "the words of the statute must be more diligently examined."[75] So a statute that expressly addresses only conduct in the city's territory cannot apply to conduct outside, but when it comes to statutes "expressed in general terms," Bartolus advocates a distinction between procedural and substantive matters: statutes addressing the process or the commencement of litigation shall govern all proceedings instituted in the city, but as to those statutes addressing the substance of the case (including punishment) Bartolus would have city law give way to either the *ius commune* or the law of the place where the wrong was committed.[76]

Both these solutions merit closer inspection. As to the law applicable to proceedings, the case presented as an actual example by Bartolus (inquisition, i.e. the city authorities brining criminal proceedings of their own motion) constituted a serious derogation from the *ius commune*,

[73] Thus, of the punitive judgments as to persons, those diminishing the person's status have effect elsewhere, whereas the effects of interdictions are only limited to the territory of the interdict. Bartolus ad C.1.1.1, nu. 50.

[74] Bartolus ad C.1.1.1, nu. 46 (and again nu. 48).

[75] Ibid., nu. 48.

[76] Ibid.

which required accusation for the initiation of criminal proceedings.[77] The power moreover to initiate such proceedings would fall under the second higher grade of jurisdiction (*merum imperium majus*) in Bartolus's scheme (see Figure 8.1).[78] As to the law applicable to the substance and punishment, such "legislative" jurisdiction fell under the highest grade, *merum imperium maximum* in the scheme, so Bartolus's restraint conformed to ideas of political power and jurisdiction.[79] But the facultative reference to the law of the place where the wrong was committed made it more likely that the citizen would be punished, i.e. in the case that the *ius commune* did not provide for punishment but the other city's law did.[80]

8.3.3.5 Legal Acts and Legal Rights

Contrary to punitive statutes, Bartolus does not appear to distinguish between citizens and foreigners when it comes to permissive and prohibitive statutes. Most of the cases he has in mind are about succession, or about questions of personal status that are connected to succession. They appear to involve someone who lives or lived in the city and has property elsewhere; in some cases, the person in question has travelled or subsequently moved out of the city; in others, someone from outside the city has property in the city.

We can of course see the expression of the territorial dimension of all polities within the populus Romanus, in the rule that an act made before a notary or other city authority is only valid if made in the territory of that city.[81] But the scheme Bartolus draws principally relies on substantive considerations, beginning with the very distinction between permissive and prohibitive statutes. Thus, the effects of a prohibitive statute in personam extend everywhere the person may be found if the statute is "favorable" (*statutum favorabilium*) but not if it is "burdensome"

[77] This explains the vigorous disagreement between jurists such as Odofredus (a glossator, fighting against the derogation from the *ius commune*) and Cinus (a commentator), as extensively reported by Bartolus. Ibid., nu. 47.

[78] Bartolus ad D.2.1.3, nu. 8.

[79] Ibid. See also Bartolus ad C.1.1.1, nu. 47, noting that Cinus conceded that the city cannot create "a new essence of obligation (*novam obligationis substantiam*) outside its territory but could add a new quality (*novam qualitatem*) to a wrong existing under the *ius commune*, for it is easier to add a quality than an essence."

[80] See also Section 10.3.2.

[81] Bartolus ad C.1.1.1, nus. 34–36.

(*statutum odiosum*).[82] As to permissive statutes, the principal distinction is between statutes reducing or removing solemnity requirements, on the one hand, and those reducing or removing limitations on personal capacity (status) on the other.

Acts made in accordance with permissive city laws dealing with solemnity requirements will thus produce effect everywhere. This was apparently not as obvious in the High Middle Ages as in subsequent eras.[83] Originally, glossators had argued against the very application of city law derogating from the *ius commune* in such cases, raising the specter of different persons becoming the heir in different lands in contradiction of the Roman axiom *nemo parte*. Subsequent jurists such as Jacobus de Ravanis defended the application of city law in the city's territory, but still found themselves acknowledging that its effects could not extend elsewhere: an heir may thus be installed and property disposed in the *locus celebrationis* in accordance with a testament made under the local rules as to witnesses; but the same defunct would be succeeded intestate *de iure communis* for property located elsewhere. The next step was taken by Gulielmus de Cuneo, who argued in favor of the testatment (and thus the local permissive statute) having effects everywhere. If we would go back to our scheme of the three governance aspects of private international law,[84] we could say that, in asserting absolute priority on the uniformity of result, Gulielmus took the same approach as to "private international law governance" as the glossators (and their Roman sources), but the exact opposite approach as to whether primacy should be given to *ius commune* or *ius proprium*, i.e. as to "international governance." The third dimension, "private law governance" is not addressed explicitly, although it could be argued that the local statutes in question tended to reduce formalities and were thus more favorable to the validity of testaments. Moreover, Gulielmus uses a jurisprudential argument about the statute operating to the testament itself and thus having the power to dispose of the property "by consequence" (*per consequentiam*).

Let us now consider the position of Bartolus in this light. He agrees with Gulielmus as to the result but insists on a different rationale. Whereas Gulielmus could be seen as arguing, on jurisprudential grounds,

[82] Ibid., nu. 33.

[83] See the discussion in Bartolus ad C.1.1.1, nus. 21–25 and 35–38, as presented at Sections 7.4.3 and 7.5.2.2.1.

[84] See Section 1.6.2.

to the effect that a testament, once validly made in a certain place, will produce effects everywhere, Bartolus is more circumspect in his jurisprudential outlook and he would still acknowledge a role for the *ius commune* in such cases as superior law, even if this led to the testament being held valid in some but not all territories.

Bartolus's stance is better understood once we consider the case that follows in the *repetitio*, namely whether extraterritorial effects should be acknowledged to permissive statutes reducing or removing a limitation as to personal status – for example by enabling a person prohibited by law to make a will or to be named an heir. To better understand the issues in question, let us think in terms of two distinct legal actions, which may result from a single legal act, but not necessarily. First, we have the *legal act* by which the limitation of personal status has been removed, in accordance with the permissive statute: such an act, which may be the testament itself, involves a notary or other city authority and can only take place in the territory of that city, as already stated. Second, we have the legal result of the person benefiting from the permissive statute: this would happen by him coming into the inheritance under that first legal act, or under a subsequent legal act (testament), or even by intestate succession – always provided that the first legal act is valid. Bartolus here draws a distinction depending on where the main effect of the permissive statute's disposition is going to be: the legal act removing the status limitation can only have effect if made in the same place where the person in question is to become heir. The city has no jurisdiction to change someone's status simply in order for that person to enter into inheritance elsewhere.[85] But the really difficult and "constantly recurring" question is what happens when both the change in the person's status and his appointment as heir have occured in the same place: would the person in question have claims over property located elsewhere? Bartolus here answers in the negative: it would appear that he regards such statutes as too strong a derogation from the *ius commune*.

The same could be said as to the solution Bartolus provides to the so-called English case, where someone dies intestate leaving property both in territories where primogeniture applies and in territories where all male heirs of the same degree equally inherit, in accordance with the *ius commune*: the solution that Bartolus proposes favors examining the purpose and wording of the rule in question, but its result would

[85] Ibid., nu. 39.

effectively exclude the application of primogeniture in any property located in *ius commune* territories and only allow it to apply to property in England in some cases.[86]

The *repetitio* concludes with a section on punitive judgments, including judgments as to persons: Bartolus holds that those diminishing the person's status have effect elsewhere, whereas the effects of interdictions are only limited to the territory of the interdict.[87] This is a telling example because it could be explained in several ways: first, it appears to conform to the ideas of Roman law, and indeed Bartolus only cites Roman authorities on this point. But it could also be seen as conforming to substantive-law ideas, namely legal certainly as to the status of a person and her ability to conclude contracts or make a testament. Yet another approach would be to consider this in the light of Bartolus's acceptance of the legality of "tyrannical" measures taken by the city, such as expulsion and his stance on factional politics in Italian cities.[88]

8.4 Bartolus, *Ius Commune*, and the Conflict of Laws

In this chapter, we explored the political/institutional framework within which Bartolan doctrine on conflicts issues was conceived and supposed to operate. We also attempted a detailed examination of the solutions given in the *repetitio*, in order to ascertain, on the one hand, how far would Bartolus be willing to allow the legislative power of the city to extend – directly and indirectly – and, on the other, how much would this power, thus extended, chip away at the *ius commune*. The underlying question was of course: is this conflict of laws? Is it not more akin to statutory interpretation? Moreover, in the latter case, should we be thinking principally in terms of the interpretation of the cities' statutory law? Or in terms of the interpretation of a superior, default body (or system?) of law in its interaction with a subordinate system (or body) of law.

This is a question in which we shall also return in the next two chapters, but a tentative answer is in order.

86 Bartolus ad C.1.1.1, nu. 42. See Section 7.5.2.3 for the text and Section 10.2.3 for discussion.

87 Thus, of the punitive judgments as to persons, those diminishing the person's status have effect elsewhere, whereas the effects of interdictions are only limited to the territory of the interdict. Bartolus ad C.1.1.1, nu. 50.

88 Ryan, "Free Cities," 85–87.

First of all, Bartolan doctrine strikes a balance between city and empire, and more to the point, between *ius commune* and *ius proprium civitatis* – moreover, between preserving legal unity and best serving his conception of substantive justice. There is an undeniable political ("governance") element in his work. Bartolus is no glossator, but he does seek to limit the jurisdiction of Italian cities in certain cases – certainly more than his immediate successsors – at the same time as he is defending their core powers.

Bartolus does not appear as an apologist of either imperial or city power. He seems instead more concerned is with providing a doctrinal system that could work, ideally across time and space but especially in early and mid-fourteenth century Italy. The jurist's instinct is to secure a harmony of solutions (similar cases treated similarly), and to minimize legal diversity, if possible. At the same time, most jurists would accept divergence and even decisional dissonance as a necessary side effect, or price, in the cases when it would allow their strong substantive preferences to survive. We can find various examples of this state of mind in our *repetitio*, especially in the way in which Bartolus makes arguments for denying or acknowledging extraterritorial effect to local statutes, where the *ius commune* is used less as a positive *system* of rules restricting the application of local law, and more as an invaluable apparatus in the pursuance of justice. This is especially so with regard to certain references to the Digest and the Code, which represent extreme cases of "arguing by analogy."

In this regard, we may take note of the two cases in which Bartolus denied extraterritorial effect to actual Perugian statutes derogating from the common law: the first made it less easy for spurious children to inherit everything instead of those who would otherwise be heirs and the second required more witnesses than the *ius commune*.[89] Both rules might have been regarded as unfair. They might have also been less easily recognized in other cities.

Beyond that, we have examples where the emphasis shifts to the statute's literal meaning: Bartolus should be seen as attempting to breathe soul and motives into statutes, instead of simply superimposing an external rule. We have just such an example with regard to the extraterritorial effect of punitive sttutes.[90] We shall examine an even more pointed example, the so-called English case in Chapter 10.[91]

[89] Bartolus ad C.1.1.1, nus. 39 and 41.

[90] Ibid., nus. 48–49. See discussion in Sections 7.5.3 and 8.3.3.4.

[91] Bartolus ad C.1.1.1, nu. 42. See discussion at Section 10.2.3.

But this is certainly not an author, who. like Baldus, views Roman law as "supplement[ing] the provisions of local customs and statutes and provid[ing] a generally acceptable standard of law for their interpretation."[92]

The role of *ius commune* in Bartolus – and Baldus – is not only instrumental: it serves as the *interface* needed to connect the local polities – an operating system for local statutes. The concepts that Bartolus uses are taken from the *ius commune* in the broader sense (including, often, the canon-law additions from the previous century).[93] An interface is necessary, and the better it works the better everything goes. But it can be replaced by another interface, even a very different one, as long as certain features are in place. The *ius commune* may have been a very effective interface in this regard.

To summarize from a conflict of laws perspective, the Bartolan doctrine on the conflict of laws is certainly not a purely horizontal one; but the center of attention is nonetheless the city statute and its reach. This is so even though in most of the cases examined in the *repetitio* the opposing laws are the *ius commune* and the local statute: the opposition between *ius commune* and local statute is made explicit only in a few cases, and the fact that so many people have still thought of the Bartolan world as one of horizontal conflicts suggests there was something in it.[94]

In fact, most conflicts in the world of Bartolus indeed involved one city whose law derogated from the *ius commune*, and one which followed the *ius commune* in the case at hand. We could hence speak of a *triangulation*, in which Bartolus invokes the *ius commune* as an arbiter between the jurisdictional claims of two states. This triangulation however is not absolute. We can observe instances, notably with regard to punitive statutes, where "foreign" law is used in order to enable derogation from the *ius commune*: first, in the case of a foreign resident whose offense is "commonly prohibited" by city statutes, and then, in the case of a citizen

92 Canning, *Baldus*, 149.

93 See e.g. references to the Sext (*Liber Sextus*, the collection of decretals publised by Boniface VIII to supplement the five books of the early thirteenth-century *Liber Extravagantium Decretalium* or Extra) in Bartolus ad C.1.1.1, nu. 20 (regarding the punishment of foreigners under local legislation) and 33 (distinction of prohibitive statutes into *statuta favorabilia* and *statuta odiosa*).

94 See Ancel, *Conflits de qualification*, 34 speaking of a "décalage entre la position théorique de la question et sa solution . . . habituel aux statutaires italiens" in explaining the change in the meaning of the doctrine nisi subditos.

punished under the law of the place where the wrong was commited.[95] All things considered, Bartolan conflict of laws could be seen as an exercise in delimiting the scope of statutes derogating from the *ius commune*. But, if this may have been the end of the story as far as the original gloss on *cunctos populos* is concerned, where the emphasis is given in shielding the Bolognese from the statutes of Modena, it is certainly not the end of the story with Bartolus. We may be still away from "traditional" conflict of laws, but the critical steps have been made. This reflects on the fascinating complexity of the text and its multiple layers of reading it invites.

[95] Bartolus ad C.1.1.1, nu. 20 and 48. For a discussion see also Section 10.3.2.

9

Doctrinal Aspects of Bartolan Conflict of Laws

9.1 Introduction

J. A. Clarence Smith once defined the influence of Bartolus on the jurists who succeeded him in the following terms:

> Not everyone agreed with all that he said, but he could be called their spiritual domicile in the sense that it was from him that they set out on their journey, and to him that at the end of the day they returned. He expressed thoroughly and completely, with a touch as light as it was sure, the law as it had come to be lived, but in the terminology and according to the concepts that Justinian had caused to be written down.[1]

This remark holds true about our *repetitio* as well. Many of the underlying ideas and even some of the doctrinal tools Bartolus used in that text have had a long life, often up to the present. Yet many of his doctrines and concepts can only be understood – or even make sense – in the material and intellectual context in which they were written. We may be reading the *repetitio* as a stand-alone text, but we cannot forget that it is premised upon Medieval doctrines about lawmaking authority and the scope of legal rules. Moreover, for all the complex thinking the text reveals, its orality is also evident. Nor has the practice of our text's principal commentators–translators, to omit those "peculiar" passages which could help tie the Bartolan conflicts doctrine properly speaking to the rest of his doctrine, helped.[2]

In this chapter, we shall examine certain aspects of the *repetitio* that shed light on its doctrinal character. Section 9.2 examines the mode of legal reasoning with an emphasis on the structure followed by Bartolus.

[1] Clarence Smith, *Medieval Law Teachers*, 82.

[2] See especially the omission of nus. 22–23 (authority to make statute) by Beale, *Bartolus*, 25 (Lainé, *Introduction*, 1:139–140, seems on the contrary to have understood the relevance); the omission of the fifth section by Beale, *Bartolus*, 29, Clarence Smith, "Bartolo," 173, 180 and Lainé, *Introduction*, 1:144; and the playing down of the forfeiture discussion by Lainé, *Introduction*, 1:163.

In Section 9.3 we shall examine the kind of substantive-law issues treated by Bartolus and the way in which substantive law is organized into categories. Section 9.4 examines the use of a distinction between form, procedure, and substance in Bartolan conflicts doctrine. The next three sections examine respectively the role of adjudicative jurisdiction (Section 9.5), party autonomy (Section 9.6) and decisional harmony (Section 9.7) in Bartolan choice-of-law system.

9.2 Legal Style

In much of conflicts literature, Bartolus is credited with introducing new ideas, even as his doctrine is presented as rigid or mechanical.[3] An opposite tendency would on the contrary emphasize the "eclectic" or "analytical" character of Bartolan thinking: it is even suggested that Bartolus, and more generally the Italian school, placed more emphasis on considerations of substantive justice than on formal legal principles.[4] To answer this question, we shall first inspect the structure of the Bartolan commentary and then discuss the modes of legal reasoning employed.

9.2.1 Structure of the Text

The structure of the *repetitio* is remarkable but rather strange to modern eyes. Across the ages, even writers with strong territorialist or personalist views have tended to structure their subject matter in a way that corresponded to discernible legal categories which took account of contemporaneous notions, but which they also tried to shape in accordance with their own territorialist or personalist preferences. In contrast, the *repetitio* only partly adheres to an organization of substantive-law matters into categories, such as contract or testaments. Nor does it correspond to a categorization in terms of the adopted conflicts solution – as we should expect if Bartolus did make a clear distinction between "real" and "personal" statutes. We cannot even at first blush discern the normative preferences of Bartolus.

The very opening of the text provides us with the first evidence as to how remarkable it is: the original question, as to the sway of local laws, is divided into two separate questions: on the one hand, the reach of local

[3] See Section 10.2.1.

[4] See Sections 2.4.2 and 3.3.1.1.

laws over "non-subjects" within the locality; on the other hand, the effects of local laws – and notably acts done under them – beyond the locality. In his – probably earlier – commentary on *de quibus*, Bartolus comes to the question of the effect of a custom (*effectus consuetudinis*), where he identifies three lines of inquiry: having already dealt with the first two – on the power of the custom to contradict a law and on whether it can be interpreted and its force extended – he asks "to what persons and to what places does its force extend?"[5] When discussing persons, Bartolus equates customs and statutes and begins by addressing, with a cross-reference, their effects over minors and lunatics.[6] He then comes to foreigners (*forenses*), where he draws the distinction between different subjects, beginning with wrongs ("the answer is that it depends on whether we are considering wrongs"), then treating contracts, testaments, matters that are neither contracts, nor testaments, nor wrongs and he concludes with clerics.[7] The substance of these discussions largely corresponds to the one in our *repetitio*. In contrast, the second leg of the question ("what places are bound by custom") consists of a statement of the distinction between prohibitive, permissive, and punitive statutes and a discussion on prohibite statutes, similar to the sixth section of the *repetitio* on *cunctos populos*.[8]

It would appear that as Bartolus developed further his thought, he excised cross-references to matters truly unrelated to our subject and rephrased his opening question in a more satisfactory manner. I would argue that we should see the underlying logic behind this division as an exploration moving from the *core* of the city's jurisdiction and the statute's intended effects toward the periphery. Moreover, in a world where local law constitutes an – increasingly frequent – derogation from the *ius commune*, it could be argued that only after ascertaining what effects can local legislation have within the city's territory can we consider the effects it may have outside its territory. This also explains why, in critical points of the *repetitio*, Bartolus begins discussing whether – and under which circumstances – specific local statutes are valid to begin with (that is, whether they may produce effect even with regard to

[5] Bartolus ad D.1.3.32, nu. 25: "Tertio potest intelligi, ad quas personas, et ad quae loca suam virtutem extendat et de hoc agendum est primo de personis; et omnia quae dicam in consuetudine, intelliguntur in statutis, et econverso."

[6] Ibid.

[7] Ibid., nus. 26, 27, 28, 29, and 30 respectively.

[8] Ibid., nu. 31 (*quos liget consuetudo locorum*).

citizens acting within the city's territory).[9] This is neither a personalist nor a territorialist logic.

The unique character of our text is even more apparent in the very different manner in which each of its two parts is divided. In the first part, the first four sections correspond to substantive legal categories: contracts, wrongs, testaments, and land. In the second part, the three first sections correspond to a classification of statutes into three classes: prohibitive, permissive, and punitive. The fifth and final section of the first part is about a distinct category of persons and their subjection to local law: clerics. The final section of the second part examines the effects of judgments, rather than statutes properly speaking.

The internal subdivisions of each section are even more interesting. The distinction between solemnity and substantive disposition, or between either of them and procedural matters, is a recurring tool in the text.[10] In the second part of the *repetitio*, we also observe repeatedly a distinction depending on whether the effects of a statute or judgment operate in personam or in rem.[11] In other instances, we observe qualitative distinctions as to the "benevolent" or "burdensome" effect of the statute in question.[12] In yet other cases, the criterion employed to determine the scope of a statute relates to its wording.[13]

The structure of the *repetitio* is moreover not watertight: there are cross-references and repetitions. Section three is about the validity of local legislation regarding testaments, over both citizens and foreign residents, but the section concludes with a discussion of statutes regarding legitimation or emancipation.[14] The discussion of the English rule forms part of the section on permissive statutes – more specifically it concludes the section, following statutes dealing with personal status. But if we are to follow Bartolus's own logic, the English derogation from the *ius commune*, which prevents the younger sons from becoming heirs, is prohibitive.[15] There is a rationale for both cases: the former involves matters often arising in relation to testamentary succession, as in the example used by Bartolus (a statute prohibiting the designation of a wife as heir); its inclusion thus not only makes sense in terms of subject but

9 Bartolus ad C.1.1.1, nus. 22–23.
10 Ibid., nus. 13–14, 24–26, 30, 32, 36–41, 48.
11 Ibid., nus. 32–33, 42, 50–51.
12 Ibid., nus. 32–33, 42.
13 Ibid., nus. 24, 42, 44, 45, 48.
14 Ibid., nu. 26.
15 Ibid., nu. 42.

also makes it easier for Bartolus to reduce the scope of such legislation even within the city's territory. The latter comes as the culmination of a long discussion, in several sections, of the effects of statutes regarding capacity and personal status with regard to succession; it also serves Bartolus's own emphasis on the Italian rule, which could be regarded as "permissive" compared to the English one. In both cases, therefore, their placing reflects the normative objectives of Bartolus.

At this point, it would be useful to compare Bartolus with the respective commentaries of his two immediate successors, Baldus and Bartholomeus de Saliceto.[16] Bartholomaeus would examine if the Bolognese is sued in contract or for a wrong or a last will (*si convenitur ex contractu quam si ex delicto vel ultima voluntate*).[17] His treatment is accordingly divided into three respective parts: the first one on contracts is easily comparable with Bartolus;[18] the second section considers wrongs committed both in the city's territory and abroad (thus corresponding to the second and eight section of Bartolus);[19] the third section discusses at length succession, corresponding to the sections on prohibitive and permissive statutes and including a more serious discussion of intestate succession.[20] In his own, more extensive, commentary, Baldus also makes a distinction into three parts invoking the Roman-law division "every statute either deals with persons, or with things, or with actions."[21] Following the order of this scheme, Baldus first discusses the law of persons (*de iure personae*): his fundamental distinction is between statutes giving capacity to those not having (*habilitando inhabiles*), taking capacity away from those having (*inhabilitando habilem*), or giving form (*habilitando servata certa forma, et inhabilitando ea cessante*). The bulk of his treatment is devoted to these questions, corresponding to the third, sixth, and seventh sections of Bartolus.[22] Contracts are dealt more briefly in the next – and smallest – section.[23] The third section deals with misdeeds (*circa maleficum*), beginning with outsider offenders (*nunquid*

[16] Baldus de Ubalids ad C.1.1.1, nus. 57–103, fol 8ra–10ra (Torino, 1576); Bartholomeus de Saliceto ad C.1.1.1., nus. 4–18, fol. 5ra–5vb (Lyon, 1560). For a summary see Lainé, *Introduction*, 1:166–178 and 178–188 respectively).

[17] Bartholomeus ad C.1.1.1., nu. 4.

[18] Ibid., nus. 4–6.

[19] Ibid., nus. 7–8.

[20] Ibid., nus. 8–18.

[21] Baldus ad C.1.1.1, nu. 57, referring to D.1.5.1.

[22] Ibid., nus. 57–92.

[23] Ibid., nus. 93–94.

statutum civitatis liget extraneum delinquentem), and then moving to punishments of acts and sentences, corresponding to the second, eighth, and ninth sections of Bartolus.[24] Baldus has dealt with the question of whether city legislation produces effects over clerics just above his "conflicts" treatment.[25]

The structure of the Bartolan text appears more experimental than either of these treatments.[26] For a modern doctrinal lawyer, it may even require more of an effort in order to reconstruct Bartolus' system of doctrinal solutions. At the same time, it could be said that our *repetitio* contains the prototype for several different structures, from those of his epigones to subsequent statutist systems. It moreover seems that his structure best corresponds to his thought and the normative choices he makes. Bartolus thought that the substantive category made a difference in deciding whether a foreigner would be subject to a city's statutes when the foreigner was in the city's courts, and hence in its territory. When it came to determining the extraterritorial reach of the statutes, however, Bartolus seems to have thought that the type of statute was more important than whether it primarily addressed a person or a thing – a distinction not always clear to begin with. Even the inclusion of a section on clerics at the culmination of the first part – a subject not always included or moved to the sidelines even in contemporaneous treatments – fits his doctrinal scheme. The same applies with regard to punitive judgments, which are treated last.

9.2.2 *Mode of Reasoning*

As Lainé notes in his presentation of the Italian school, Medieval jurists employed the "scholastic method," which has been "vividly criticized ... for the divisions and subdivisions, distinctions and sub-distinctions, deductions and limitations, for the incessant and minutious controversy" and the "continuous recourse to Roman laws and preceding authors," but

[24] Ibid., nus. 95–103.

[25] Ibid., nus. 54–55.

[26] See also the neglected *repetitio* of Baldus on C.1.1.1 ["*Tractatus de vi et potestate statutorum ratione personarum, territorii et rerum*," transcribed and published by E. M. Meijers: *Tractatus duo de vi et potestate statutorum* (Haarlem: H. D. Tjeenk Willink & zoon n. v., 1939), 1ff], Baldus treats separately statutes which command, prohibit, permit, and punish (examining in each case their reach on citizens and foreigners, in and out of the city's territory).

which Lainé deems "fecund" and "marvelously appropriate" for establishing a doctrine in conflicts matters.[27]

Bartolus, the most famous member of the Italian school, epitomizes the method, its pitfalls, and the rewards it promises. We can find in the *repetitio* arcane concepts and distinctions but also traces or the roots of a multitude of doctrines, tools, and ideas that subsequently found use in the conflict of laws or were even elevated to cornerstones of entire doctrinal systems. This will become even more apparent in the discussion that follows in this and the following chapter, where terms and doctrines that look familiar will be placed in context and the functional relevance of more obscure concepts will be revealed. Yet no general principle or axiom is apparent in the *repetitio*: Bartolus neither begins with *a priori* principles nor deduces such principles from his analysis. In that sense, Niboyet is right in his characterization of Bartolus as analytical and eclectic.[28] Bartolus dissects his subject using a number of "clinical cases," including the basic cases discussed by the preceding generation of jurists, and lets himself get carried over by his analysis, but he does not attempt to be exhaustive of the subject let alone to organize it into a coherent scheme.

The idea of Bartolus as an analytical and eclectic author is also corroborated if we examine his text in terms of the employment of rules and standards.[29] Especially in the first part, Bartolus uses *a priori* second-order rules that look very much like our own multilateral choice-of-law norms as well as technically unilateral norms that are effectively multilateral. His discussion of categories of statutes in the second part appears to embrace the unilateral method but combines norms as to the classification of statutes that are a prioristic in the sense of not discriminating between rules of the same subject depending on the substantive result of the rule; norms that actually make the classification and scope of the rule dependent upon its substantive result but invoke an "external" standard (*ius commune* and the learned law); and norms that directly call for the interpretation of legislative intent as to scope. Throughout the text, standards are invoked: from the easy one of an action "commonly

[27] Lainé, Introduction, 1:114–115: "En cette matière, il faut nécessairement distinguer et sous-distinguer; car les conflits doivent recevoir une solution différente suivant la nature des rapports de droit au sujet desquels ils s'élèvent. En cette matière, il faut nécessairement discuter les opinions en presence; car il s'agit d'établir une doctrine."

[28] See Section 5.2.2.

[29] See Section 10.3.

prohibited in all cities" to the definition of what constitutes a prohibitive statute *favorabilium* or *odiusum*. Lainé remarked that jurists of the Italian school followed their *inspiration individuelle* in this regard, and indeed Bartolus himself offers several examples and no definition, Baldus invokes *bonos mores* until we get to Dumoulin who reaches the same result invoking the universal good and harmony with natural justice.[30]

This character was both a point of strength and a weakness in the Italian school, and certainly for Bartolan doctrine. It allowed the combination of a variety of ideas that gave rise to long-standing doctrinal discussion. But it also created uncertainly, especially as the discursive and interpretative community expanded and became more diverse. This often resulted in many of the nuances in Bartolan doctrine getting lost, giving way to a memory of scholastic formulas and hard, even "mechanical" rules.[31]

9.3 Organization of the Legal Subject Matter

In Chapter 5, it was suggested that conflicts doctrine has over time followed a spiraling trend of formal categorization of the legal subject-matter.[32] Viewed in such terms, Bartolus could be placed in a middle point of the ascending part of the spiral. His categories are a harbinger of much doctrinal work on taxonomy in the centuries that followed but the elaborate structure of our conflicts treatment is only partly based on categories of the legal subject matter. The correlation therefore between substantive-law categories and choice-of-law solutions is more difficult with Bartolus than with subsequent writers.

The bulk of the *repetitio* is devoted to two major legal subjects: contracts and acts *mortis causa*. This is more apparent with regard to the first part of the *repetitio*, but a substantial part of the cases discussed in the second part also revolves around matters of succession and legal acts somehow related to succession. Bartolus does not even pretend to follow the tripartite division of the legal subject-matter according to Roman law.[33] We will try to expore below the relation of especially the

[30] Bartolus ad C.1.1.1, nus. 32–33; Baldus ad C.1.1.1, nu. 87; Molinaeus ad C.1.1.1, 556b.

[31] See Section 10.2.

[32] See Section 5.3.

[33] Inst. 1.2.12 "All our law is about persons, things or actions. We turn to persons first. There is little point in knowing the law if one knows nothing about the persons for whom it exists." The first two sentences go back to Gaius Institutes, 1.8, from which the axiom itself – the first sentence – made it to D.1.5.1.

second part to the law of persons. But it is noted that of the Justinian law of things only subcategories are treated: the law of contracts is only a part of the Roman law of obligations, the law on testaments is only a part of the Roman law of succession and of the law of single things the only thing that remains is a servitude – or is it a public-law statute?[34] The third grand category, the law of actions, is, in the Bartolan *repetitio*, absorbed into the individual subcategories (namely contracts). Also missing from the *repetitio* is any distinction between private and public law, which is consecrated in the opening of Justinian's Institutes.[35] At the same time, very few preclassical jurists – even in the Early Modern period – did actually emulate the structure of the Institutes in their treatment of conflicts questions.

9.3.1 *Contracts*

Bartolus begins his discussion with contracts. The section is built around an abstract case: a foreigner concludes a contract in Perugia, a dispute arises; suit is brought therein. But Bartolus also includes two concrete cases with a richer factual setting, both of which had apparently been – and certainly continued to be – persistent problem cases in conflicts scholarship: dowry contracts and prescription.

Bartolus's analysis of the conflict of contract laws is the most modern of his entire commentary – and apparentrly remained unmatched for some time. It is also the most complete. Not only does he treat differently matters of solemnity, and procedural matters, from matters of substance, but he also draws internal distinctions within that latter that go to the heart of contracting. Matters of interpretation, validity, and ascertainment of the content of the contract ("matters arising out of the nature of the contract itself at the time it was made," or, in the words of Gulielmus, "matters of common concern according to the contract and by provision of the contracting parties") will be governed by the law of the place where the contract was concluded (*locus celebrati contractus).* Matters regarding the possible breach of the contract and remedies sought ("matters arising ex post facto due to neglect or delay," or, in the words of Gulielmus,

[34] See Inst. 3.13.2 (obligations distinguished between contractual, quasi-contractual, delictual and quasi-delictual; the elaboration of the law of obligations is structured accordingly); and Inst. 2.9.6 (distinction made between testate and instestate succession, and each mode treated separately).

[35] Inst. 1.1.4.

unexpectedly, *ex improviso*) will be dealt with by the law of the place of the performance.

This scheme has a triple function. First and foremost, it confirms the primacy of the place of contracting – whose law will apply to solemnity and in most substantive matters. Second, it reduces the role of the law of the place of the trial, which will apply as such in procedural matters. Third, it creates a second, auxiliary category of substantive matters that cuts further into the scope of the law of the place of the trial.

We can better understand this scheme if we compare Bartolus with existing – and subsequent – doctrine and consider the three particular cases he discusses: warranties provided for the performance of a contract for the sale of land; claims of the deceased wife's husband under the dowry contract; and prescription of a money debt.

We should begin with the two most relevant passages from the Digest. *Contraxisse* states: "Every person is considered to have concluded a contract in the place where he had bound himself to pay."[36] *Si fundus* states: "[W]hen land is sold, the transaction should be in accordance with the custom of the region, and the undertaking in respect of eviction should be adapted accordingly."[37] This was glossed as follows:

> Although the land may be elsewhere, for there may be a sale of land translated elsewhere ... It follows that whether the vendor is bound to refund double the purchase price, or simply the purchase price, or furnish a surety or not, it is the custom of the place of contracting that is looked to.[38]

Two centuries after Bartolus, Dumoulin will invoke the (presumed) will of the contracting parties to give the opposite solution in exactly the case raised by the Gloss: Italian custom could not apply in the case of a man from Tübingen who sold, from Italy, his house in Tübingen, providing guarantees in case of nonperformance (eviction).[39] But Bartolus is in agreement with the Gloss.[40]

[36] D.44.7.21 (Julian): "Contraxisse unusquisque in eo loco intellegitur, in quo ut solveret se obligavit."

[37] D.21.2.6 (Gaius): "Si fundus venierit, ex consuetudine eius regionis in qua negotium gestum est pro evictione caveri oportet."

[38] Accursius ad D.21.2.6, v° *oportet*, col. 1981. Translation by Clarence Smith, "Bartolo," 166 n. 11.

[39] Molinaeus ad C.1.1.1, 554a.

[40] Bartolus ad C.1.1.1, nu. 16: "For though a sale of land is to be carried out where the land is, yet the place of conclusion of the contract will be looked to."

The solution given with regard to the dowry contract is of course different: it is the law of the husband's domicile that will be looked to, and not that of the domicile of his wife's family (where, in all probability, the dowry contract was concluded), and this must have been the common position. But, unlike Dumoulin who again invoked the presumed intention of the parties, Bartolus grounded his answer on another, pertinent, Digest passage (*exigere*).[41] The case of dowry contracts is treated as a specific exception to the place-of-contracting rule.[42]

The place that Bartolus grants to the law of the place of performance is obviously nothing like the *lex loci solutionis* of Savigny.[43] It is even more limited than the "mode and incidents" of performance.[44] It is really limited to matters arising *ex post facto*, "out of neglect or delay," and indeed all the Digest passages cited by Bartolus refer to costs incurred due to – or in the course of – overdue performance.[45] The example that Bartolus brings up is the prescription of a money debt, in a case where it is clear that the place of contracting is different from the place of performance.[46] The Gloss would subject prescription to the law of the place of trial (*locus judicii*).[47] But even Gulielmus, who had previously drawn up a scheme similar to that of Bartolus, would look to the law of the place of the trial for matters arising unexpectedly.[48] By pointing to the place of performance, therefore, Bartolus breaks with both. In the actual case he discusses – where the suit has been brought at the place where the money was to be paid – this would not lead to a different solution. But the scheme proposed by Bartolus would be critical in contractual disputes and could better accommodate commercial realities. The same holds true as to the further distinction he makes depending on

41 D.5.1.65 (Ulpian): "A wife should lay claim to her dowry in the place where her husband had his home, not where the dowry agreement was drawn up; for it is not the sort of contract in which the place where the dowry agreement was made has also to be considered rather than the man to whose home the wife herself was due to go under the conditions of the marriage."

42 Bartolus ad D.1.3.32, nu. 27.

43 Savigny, *System*, 205ff (§ 370).

44 Rabel, *Conflict of Laws*, 2:464–466.

45 D.12.1.22; D.13.3.3; D.22.1.1.pr.

46 Bartolus ad C.1.1.1, nu. 19. Cf. Bartolus ad D.1.3.32, nu. 27.

47 Accursius ad D. 13.4.2., v° *arbitraria actio utriusque.*, col. 1352. See translation by Clarence Smith, "Bartolo," 176 n. 57.

48 Bartolus ad C.1.1.1, nu. 18. This is not found in Bartolus ad C.1.1.1, nu. 27.

whether a single place of performance has been fixed in the contract or not.[49]

9.3.2 *Delicts, Wrongs, and Crimes*

Bartolus was obviously aware of the Roman-law concept of obligation, including delicts. Yet we do not find much that looks like a tort in our *repetitio*. When Bartolus does speak of *delicta*, in the second section, he appears concerned with penal offenses and not with any liability incurred toward another party. The eighth section (on punitive statutes) essentially continues the discussion of the second section: having examined there the reach of punitive statutes within the city's territory, Bartolus moves to examine the extension of such statutes outside the territory.[50] The absence of a third (private) party is noticeable in both.

This is not uncommon in Medieval conflicts writings.[51] We have already noted that in his earlier commentary, such wrongs are the first thing that pops up as soon as Bartolus asks if a custom or statute binds a foreigner.[52] The solutions of Bartolus bear some resemblance to modern doctrines of criminal and international law.[53] In conflicts literature, they have been regarded by some as an early example of the *lex loci delicti commissi* rule. This is an exaggeration, although it must be admitted that what Bartolus lays down could be converted into a choice-of-law system for torts. If we however compare these passages to the rest of the *repetitio*, we could regard them as representing an earlier stage in the gradual development of conflicts thought: Bartolus approaches the question of the scope of penal/punitive legislation as one of the attributes of a statute or custom: the conceptual distinction between this and other questions does not appear so sharp. Yet in order to answer questions as to whether local legislation would apply over a certain kind of situation involving contracts, testaments, or over a certain group of – permissive or prohibitive – statutes, Bartolus employs a variety of concepts and tools and draws distinction upon distinction, but – in the end – his answer for each abstractly defined category is a straightforward one: usually a yes or a no,

49 Bartolus ad C.1.1.1, nu. 18. Bartolus ad D.1.3.32, nu. 27 only mentions the case where performance has been fixed in one place.

50 See Section 10.3.2.

51 See e.g. Jacobus de Arena ad C.1.1.1; Baldus ad C.1.1.1, nus. 93–103.

52 Bartolus ad D.1.3.32, nu. 26.

53 See Section 10.3.2.

sometimes something looking like a choice-of-law rule, but in all these cases we come near a second-order norm. In that sense, the decision of Bartolus to expand and move his treatment of contracts first, in lieu of his treatment of wrongs that is now sandwiched between contacts and testaments, is evidence not just of an awareness of the growing importance of the former subject but also of a budding awareness that these issues should require distinct consideration.

9.3.3 *Succession*

Testaments and legal acts somehow related to succession constitute the most discussed subject in the *repetitio*: they take up the entire third section, i.e. the longest of the first part, as well as the bulk of especially the seventh section, i.e. by far the longest in the entire *repetitio*, and they also come up in other sections as well. This observation seems to hold true with regard to other fourteenth-century treatments as well.

Succession is not however treated as a unified category. The *repetitio* seems primarily concerned with testamentary succession, or at least agreements *mortis causa*.[54] This emphasis may be attributed to the "horror" of intestacy evident in the Roman-law sources; it may also indicate a preponderance of testamentary succession in Medieval Italy.[55] The only passage which could be dealing with intestate succession is the so-called English case, which is probably an example of French, not Italian, provenance.[56] Bartolus makes no explicit mention of succession being *ab intestam*, but the solution given refers to statutory rules as to the division of property and nothing seems to imply the existence of a testament allocating the property in a different manner. Furthermore, under English law land could not be transferred by testaments.[57] Baldus deals with an equivalent case – involving a French feudal lord – drawing

[54] For example, the *statutum odiosum* in Bartolus ad C.1.1.1, nu. 33, prohibiting a daughter from inheriting could be concerning a legal act by which she would renounce future claims to intestate succession. See Section 9.3.6.

[55] See T. Kuehn, *Heirs, Kin, and Creditors in Renaissance Florence* (Cambridge: Cambridge University Press, 2008), 9–13, on the discussions as to whether the actual records we have do indicate the "primacy of testaments," and the notion that "the revival of Roman law in the Middle Ages created a similar renewed loathing of intestacy."

[56] Bartolus ad C.1.1.1, nu. 42.

[57] J. H. Baker, *An Introduction to English Legal History*, 5th ed (Oxford: Oxford University Press, 2019), 285–286.

a distinction between the cases where a testament exists and those when it does not.[58]

Moreover, the effects of succession to property are dealt with indirectly. In both parts of his work, Bartolus is preoccupied with either the formalities required for a valid testament or the capacity of certain types of persons to inherit or to make a testament.[59] This has an impact on the substantive choices made.

We could rephrase the way in which Bartolus approaches succession-related questions as follows. First, can a testament be made validly under the formalities imposed by a local statute, rather than under the requirements of the *ius commune*? If yes, is the answer the same for foreigners (and clerics) based in the city's territories? Moreover, does such a testament also produce effects outside the city's territory? Second, what effects may local jurisdiction have over the determination of heirship? Can local law alter the *ius commune* rules as to who can become an heir, either by removing the right to be installed as heir from *a class of persons* that possessed it (for example, a wife or a daughter) or by conferring the right to such a status to a class that did not (for example, a spurius)? Additionally, by removing (for example, from persons under a certain age) or by conferring (for example, to sons-in-power) the right to make a testament? What effects would that have for foreigners in the city's territory and what effects would it produce outside the city's territory? On a second level, what effect would attempts by the local law to alter the rules of the *ius commune* as to who has the power to change the status of *a certain person*, such as by emancipation or legitimation, produce outside its territory?

This outline shows how fundamental is the distinction between formalities and "substantive" dispositions to the system of solutions Bartolus gives. It allows him to answer with relative ease the first set of questions in the affirmative, with the qualifications we have seen, but it also provides him with arguments in other matters. The second set of questions calls for more circumspection: this is indeed the part of the

[58] See Baldus ad C.1.1.1, nus. 84–86 (Lyon, 1585, fol. 8vb–9ra). See also the translation by Lainé, *Introduction*, 1:175–176.

[59] Regarding formalities, see ibid., nus. 21–25 (derogation from the seven-witness rule of the *ius commune*). Regarding capacity to inherit, see ibid., nu. 26 (wife), nu. 33 (daughter), nus. 38ff (spurious)). Regarding capacity to make a testament, see ibid., nu. 32 (minor), nus. 38ff (unemancipated son or generally anyone forbidden by the law). On repudiation (*repudio*) see Bartolus ad. D.29.2.1 (reprised by Paulus de Castro ad D.29.2.1), discussed in Kuehn, *Heirs, Kin and Creditors*, 27–29.

repetitio where all the tools usually associated with statutist doctrine are employed. To begin with, such statutes in derogation of the *ius commune* do not bind foreigners in the city's territory (except with regard to solemnity).[60] When it comes to their extraterritorial effects, the answer is different for prohibitive and permissive statutes. Prohibitive statutes are divided into "favorable," such as prohibiting a minor from making a testament, and "burdensome," such as prohibiting a daughter from inheriting: the former produce effect everywhere but the latter do not.[61] Permissive statutes evoke more problems. After a long discussion, Bartolus takes a negative position as to the effects of such laws, including valid legal acts based on them, over property situated outside the territory.[62]

9.3.4 *Property*

We will search in vain for *ius rerum*, i.e. property law, in the section headings: what has been taken to constitute a discussion of the *lex rei sitae rule* is the smallest section in the treatment, dealing with matters "than are neither contracts nor wrongs nor testaments" in a total of 46 words. In fact, the hypothetical of raising a house higher, which Bartolus is using, could be regarded as involving a servitude (*altius non tollendi*) but might as easily be handled as *ius publicum* under the *Corpus Iuris* and would in much of the modern world be dealt with as a matter of administrative rather than private ("property") law.[63] Furthermore, we can only assume that when Bartolus speaks of *bona*, as in his discussion of the English case, he means movables as well as immovables: we should be led to think so, but then the English rule of primogeniture was only concerned with succession to land (primogeniture rules in France also concerned only feudal property).[64]

[60] Bartolus ad C.1.1.1, nu. 26.

[61] Ibid., nus. 32–33.

[62] Ibid., nus. 37–41.

[63] The relationship of the servitude *altius non tollendi* to the Roman public law on the same topic is problematical. See W. W. Buckland, *A Text-Book of Roman Law*, 3rd ed (Cambridge: Cambridge University Press, 1963), 264 and references. For the Roman public-law sources on the general topic, see O. F. Robinson, *Ancient Rome: City Planning and Administration* (London: Routledge, 1992), esp. 38–42.

[64] For the English law, see Baker, *English Legal History*, 287; F. Pollock and F. W. Maitland, *The History of English Law before the Time of Edward I*, 2nd ed reissue (Cambridge: Cambridge University Press, 1968), 2:268–278, 292–294, 309. For the French law, see P. Ourliac and J.-L. Gazzaniga, *Histoire du droit privé français de l'an mil au Code civil*

This is not uncommon in Medieval writings, all the way to Dumoulin, whose own contribution comes at the end of his own treatment, where he states that as to statutes dealing with ownership by prescription or *usucaptio* of "corporeal things, either mobile or immobile . . . without distinction the law of the place where the thing is will be looked to."[65] Lainé regards this as evidence of the unimportance of a clear distinction between real and personal statutes for the Italian school.[66] This may well be so. What is certaintly observable is that the essential questions about the effects of legal acts over property are treated in a separate context from the question regarding the essence of property rights once acquired. The latter question does not appear to require much discussion. It is the treatment of the former that merits more attention.

We have already seen above that, in dealing with the effects of testaments, Bartolus is reluctant to allow the *lex loci celebrationis* to govern the distribution of property in foreign places that presumably – though not necessarily – follow the *ius commune*. On the other hand, he would look to the *lex loci conclusionis* for a contract for the sale of land elsewhere. There are further nuances to explore at this point. For both prohibitive and permissive statutes, Bartolus draws a distinction between statutes having effects *in rem* and *in personam*: the former do not produce extraterritorial effects whereas things are more complicated as to the latter, as we have seen above. The distinction between in rem and in personam is stated in the very beginning of the section on prohibitive statutes: Bartolus discusses *statuta prohibitiva in re[m] et respectu rei* before he goes into *statuta prohibitiva in personam*, bringing up the example of a statute prohibiting a joint-property owner from alienating his or her share to a third person (*extra consortes*): "such a provision affects the thing and prevents the title from passing."[67] When it comes to permissive statutes, however, we have to wait under the very end and the discussion of the English case in order to discover an allusion to the distinction, which is only thinly veiled but has been misunderstood for centuries.[68]

(Paris: A. Michel, 1985), 324–328. For a comparison of English and French law in this respect, see C. Donahue Jr., "What Causes Fundamental Legal Ideas," *Michigan Law Review*, 78 (1979), 59–88.

65 Molinaeus ad C.1.1.1, "De Praescriptionibus sive exceptionibus," 557a.

66 Lainé, *Introduction*, 1:154–155, 252–253.

67 Bartolus ad C.1.1.1, nu. 32.

68 Ibid., nu. 42. See Sections 10.2.1 and 10.2.3.

9.3.5 *Bartolus and the Law of Persons*

Bartolus, unlike Baldus, makes no mention of the law of persons (*de jure personae*): even his original reference to "persons" in his commentary on *de quibus* signified something else. On the other hand, like Baldus, a substantial part of his treatment is dedicated to matters of personal status and personal capacity, both general and specific (e.g. capacity to make testaments). These issues dominate especially the second part of his *repetitio*. To begin with, the statutes that may attempt to regulate (effectively: to limit) the activity of the forum's citizen abroad will for the most part have to do with the citizen's personal capacity or status: we thus have statutes regulating legitimation, emancipation, the capacity of a minor to make a testament, the capacity or non-capacity of a daughter to inherit, the ability of spouses to make presents to one another – even joint ownership is treated in terms of capacity to contract on one's own with third parties.[69] His discussion of punitive statutes revolves around the fate of the alleged offender.[70] Capacity issues are moreover treated in the section on punitive judgments, as in the case of penal slavery. The third section on testaments also concludes with matters of status – in fact, the example of a prohibitive statute disallowing the institution of a man's wife as his heir.[71] Even the issue of the validity of a notary's acts is phrased by Bartolus as a question of the extraterritorial effects of the appointment of a notary under the laws of the city.[72] Moreover, in distinguishing between "favorable" and "burdensome" prohibitive statutes, Bartolus's criterion is whether the statute's aim is to the benefit of the person to which the prohibition is aimed: prohibiting donations to one's spouse is thus favorable, whereas prohibiting someone from inheriting is burdensome.[73]

Yet – unlike subsequent authors – the *repetitio* is not organized in such substantive-law terms. Sections six to eight are distinguished from each other and subdivided internally on the basis of the characteristics and intended reach of statutes and not on the basis of their legal subject-matter. We thus find together – among permissive statutes – solemnity requirements and issues of emancipation and legitimation.[74] On the

[69] Bartolus ad C.1.1.1, nus. 32–33.
[70] Ibid., nus. 20, 44–48.
[71] Ibid., nu. 26.
[72] Ibid., nus. 34–36.
[73] Ibid., nus. 32–33.
[74] Ibid., nus. 34–41.

other hand, a statute prohibiting the daughter from inheriting is prohibitive and a statute allowing an illegitimate son to inherit is permissive.[75] Moreover, it is unclear if the primogeniture rule is prohibitive or permissive.[76] The discussion of the English rule forms the final part of the section on permissive statutes, but, if we are to follow Bartolus's own logic, the English derogation from the *ius commune*, which prevents the younger sons from becoming heirs, is prohibitive. Besides, aren't these sections considering the extraterritorial effects of all types of statutes that can make such claims?

9.3.6 Marriage and the Family

We have found in our *repetitio* only scattered references to the relations between husband and wife, or to the emancipation and legitimation of children. We must in fact remember that family law is a nineteenth-century doctrinal construct: in the Middle Ages, the social relationships that would eventually come together in order to constitute this field of private law either fell under canon law or were not conceptualized as such. This lack of conceptualization of social relationships as *relationships* made it easier to deal with conflicts issues as a matter of extraterritoriality of statutes. We need to think in the abstract and reified terms of a "legal relationship" in order to provide an abstract choice-of-law rule for it; conversely, once we think in terms of a legal relationship we cannot examine ad hoc the reach of the individual legal rules seeking to regulate it.

At the same time, family constituted the fundamental economic, social and political unit in Medieval Italy, with law playing a very important part.[77] A powerful model for the organization of the family was provided by Roman law – whose sources already provided evidence of significant changes over time, from the second century to the sixth century. Social needs and political decisions led city states to a proliferation of statutes altering the rules of the *ius commune*. One common example, alluded in our text, concerned statutes that sanctioned the *exclusio propter dotem*: in

[75] Ibid., nus. 33 and 38 respectively.

[76] Ibid., nu. 42.

[77] See T. Kuehn, *Law, Family and Women: Toward a Legal Anthropology of Renaissance Italy* (Chicago: University of Chicago Press, 1991); the classic study of M. Bellomo, *Ricerche sui rapporti patrimoniali tra coniugi* (Milan: Giuffrè, 1961); and the essays in J. Kirshner, *Marriage, Dowry, and Citizenship in Late Medieval and Renaissance Italy* (Toronto: University of Toronto Press, 2015).

the presence of male heirs and in consideration of her dowry, the as yet unemancipated daughter-in-power (*filia familiae*) agreed to renounce any future claim (sometimes any claim of her own descendants as well) to the intestate succession of her father and his ascendants, or occasionally of her mother as well.[78] Such agreements were contrary to Roman law but were nonetheless widely recognized by the time of Bartolus.[79]

Another example concerns the status of illegitimate children.[80] By the time of Justinian, for example, children born in concubinage (a permanent, non-adulterous relation not constituting marriage) were legitimated by the subsequent marriage of their parents, even when there were other legitimate children and could be included in their father's testament.[81] Canon law extended this to all *natural* children. On the contrary, children born out of an adulterous or incestuous union were treated as if they were of uncertain fatherhood, i.e. as *spurii*. Legitimation could therefore only take place by imperial rescript or an act of the governing body of a city.[82] Clerical celibacy led to a new problematic category: children born to an ordained cleric who were, in most cases, viewed by the Church as *spurii* rather than natural, even though the practice of bequeathing property to them appears to have been widespread.[83] On the whole, we observe a noticeable diversity of rules as to the capacity of the illegitimate and the legitimated child to inherit, to make testaments and to dispose of property, especially in Italy and France.[84] Some cities attempted to provide for such children, including by making legitimation easier,

[78] See L. Garlati, "Women's Succession from the Middle Ages to the Modern Era" in M. G. di Renzo Villata (ed.), *Succession Law, Practice and Society in Europe Across the Centuries* (Cham: Springer, 2018) 207–230, 210–213.

[79] Ibid., with reference also to F. Ercole, "L'istituto dotale nella pratica e nella legislazione statutaria dell'Italia superiore," *Rivista italiana per le scienze giuridiche*, 45–46 (1908), 191–302, 212 and Bartolus ad C.2.3.30 and C.6.20.3.

[80] See T. Kuehn, *Illegitimacy in Renaissance Florence* (Ann Arbor: University of Michigan Press, 2002), 34–38, with references to Dinus de Mugello; A. T. Sheedy, *Bartolus on Social Conditions in the Fourteenth Century* (New York: Columbia University Press, 1942), 72.

[81] See e.g. Buckland, *Roman Law*, 128–130.

[82] A famous decretal of pope Innocent III, *Per venerabilem* (X 4.17.13) deals with the issue *in fine*. The power to legitimate children was one of the privileges Emperor Charles IV conferred on Bartolus (and his descendants who were doctors of law).

[83] S. T. Salvi, "A Difficult Legacy. Initial Comments on the Inheritance Rights of Filii Clericorum in the Middle Ages and Early Modern Period" in M. G. di Renzo Villata (ed.), *Succession Law, Practice and Society in Europe Across the Centuries* (Cham: Springer, 2018) 381–416, esp. 382–397.

[84] J. Brundage, *Law, Sex and Christian Society in Medieval Europe* (Chicago: University of Chicago Press, 1987), 543–544.

whereas other polities attempted to be even more restrictive than the *ius commune*, for example by restricting the right of a *spurius* to make a testament.[85] Canon law had adopted the most liberal position on both legitimation and legitimacy, but the canonists' early attempts to extend the jurisdiction of their courts over the inheritance aspects of legitimation were rebuffed.[86] English law even refused to recognize legitimation under canon law.[87]

Unlike the Early Modern texts, there is no mention of issues regarding marriage. The reason is twofold. First, marriage is treated as a sacrament, and thus falls under the ecclesiastical jurisdiction of the Church. This phenomenon is at its most intense in the High and Late Middle Ages, when the Church is the sole legislator on the formation and validity of marriages.[88] Second, despite divergent local practices, marriage law is considered as unitary, just as it was supposed to be.

Medieval conflict of laws did however come into play with regard to the patrimonial consequences of marriage. The Roman law had established a separate-property system that was followed across Italy but the administration of the wife's property as well the needs of household made things more complicated. We have both to appreciate local diversity and to approach marital property together with succession in order to really understand the state of affairs.[89] The *ius commune* distinguished between three categories of the wife's property.[90] The wife brought to the household her dowry, which constituted her contribution "to the burdens of marriage" and was under her husband's control: he enjoyed the *fructus* and had no need for her consent during the duration of the marriage. She

[85] Perugia itself had passed the statute like the one mentioned in Bartolus ad C.1.1.1, nu. 38. In other cases, canon law required the father to provide for the support of his spurious son, and Bartolus in other passages suggests that the father can leave in his testament a certain amount for the support of his spurious son and of his own sons after his death. See Sheedy, *Bartolus*, 75–76.

[86] Brundage, *Law, Sex and Christian Society*, 543.

[87] Baker, *English Legal History*, 528–529.

[88] C. Donahue Jr., *Law, Marriage, and Society in the Later Middle Ages* (Cambridge: Cambridge University Press, 2009), 1–43.

[89] For an overview of potential issues see T. Kuehn, "Property of Spouses in Law in Renaissance Florence" in M. G. di Renzo Villata (ed.), *Family Law and Society in Europe from the Middle Ages to the Contemporary Era* (Cham: Springer, 2016), 109–133; J. Kirshner, "Materials for a Gilded Cage: Nondotal Assets in Florence, 1300–1500" in *Marriage, Dowry, and Citizenship in Late Medieval and Renaissance Europe* (Toronto: University of Toronto Press, 2015), 74–93

[90] See J. Kirshner and J. Pluss, "Two Fourteenth-Century Opinions on Dowries, Paraphernalia and Non-Dotal Goods," *Bulletin of Medieval Canon Law*, 9 (1979), 65–78.

also brought into the household other things (*parapherna*), which were administered by her husband for her and the family's benefit but subject to her – usually tacit – consent. Finally, things (*res extra dotem*) that remained in the wife's ownership and control: any use of them had to be returned to her. The wife's proprietary interests had to be restituted in case the marriage ended by ecclesiastically sanctioned separation or – more frequently – by death. It was, however, not always very clear what fell into which category, nor what precisely were the rights and duties of each marriage partner. Legislative intervention also often complicated things, especially when the case involved more than one jurisdictions. In his discussion on contracts, Bartolus brings up such a case: a man from Perugia married a woman in Assizi – which was in all probability her family home as well as the place where the dowry contract was executed – and presumably brought her back to Perugia.[91] When the wife died childless, the husband claimed half of the dowry under a Perugia statute, whereas an Assizi statute provided for a claim to a third. This is a recurring case in the history of the conflict of laws, which prompted Dumoulin's *Consilium 53* and gave Bartin an example in his criticism of early classical formalism.[92] But Bartolus holds that dowry contracts constitute an exception from the general rule that the law of the place of contracting should be looked to with regard to matters arising from the nature of the contract. This position, grounded on the Digest, survived into the sixteenth century, when Dumoulin invoked the presumed intention of the parties to reach the same conclusion. As the idea of a common law superimposed over local customs and customs lost ground, it had to face challenges from both *situs* and *actus* territorialism, until the reconceptualization of marital property and the law of the family in the modern era.[93]

Two other cases, involving prohibitive statutes, are examined subsequently in the *repetitio*. In the third section, Bartolus mentions statutes prohibiting the institution of a man's wife as his heir.[94] A number of Italian cities had passed legislation that restricted the rights of the widow over her husband's property, placed conditions on the proprietary

[91] Bartolus ad C.1.1.1, nu. 19.

[92] Molinaeus, *Consilium 53* (Paris, 1681), vol. 2, 953–956b; Bartin, "Conflits des qualifications."

[93] See e.g. Huber, *Praelectiones ad Pandectas*, 1.3.App.10 and discussion at Sections 13.3.3 and 13.6.

[94] Bartolus ad C.1.1.1, nu. 26.

interests legated to the widow, or obliged her to guarantee the handing over of the dowry to her sons (or even the first-born son).[95] Bartolus holds that such a statute will not extend to foreigners located in the city's territory, but he apparently does so because the city does not have the power to achieve such derogation from the *ius commune*. The statute is clearly prohibitive – but does it constitute a *statutum favorabilium* or a *statutum odiosum*?

In the sixth section, Bartolus considers a statute prohibiting a man from leaving a legacy (*vir non posit legare*) to his wife and the opposite, "lest by reason of their mutual love they may despoil or deceive one another."[96] That phrase is from the Digest where it refers to donations *inter vivos* between husband and wife.[97] This touches upon an important aspect of Medieval and Early Modern marital-property regimes: alienation of a spouse's proprietory interest as a result of the use of some legal or emotional power by the other spouse. Indeed, a similar preoccupation led to the rule of customary law of Normandy, discussed by Dumoulin, which allowed the wife to rescind any transactions by which her deceased husband sold her heritage.[98] Dumoulin held that, given its rationale, both natural justice and the reason of the *ius commune* concur that such a prohibition should extend everywhere.[99] Bartolus agrees and thus treats the statute as *favorabilium*, whose effects extend everywhere. Seen in conjunction with the characterization of a statute prohibiting the daughter from inheriting as *odiusum*, we could conclude that a statute removing or restricting rights available to the surviving spouse under the *ius commune* would be *odiosum*, whereas a statute preventing him or her from acquiring property by a donation or legacy of his/her spouse would be *favorabilium*.

9.4 Form, Substance, and Procedure

Bartolus begins his discussion of conflicts issues, and specifically of the question whether contracts concluded by a foreigner in a city must

95 Garlati, "Women's Succession," 214–218.

96 Bartolus ad C.1.1.1, nu. 32.

97 D.24.1.1.

98 Molinaeus ad C.1.1.1, 556b: "*Consuetudo Neustriae: quod uxor vendens hearedium viro authore, vel cum eo possit post mortem viri revocare.*" This rule survived into the late eighteenth century, giving rise to conflicts issues and legal literature, including Louis Froland, *Mémoires concernant l'observation du Senatusconsulte velléien dans le Duché de Normandie et diverses questions mixtes qui en dependent* (Paris, 1722).

99 Molinaeus ad C.1.1.1, 556b.

conform to local legislation, with a distinction between statutes pertaining to the solemnity of the contract (*contractus solemnitatem*), statutes dealing with procedure, and those affecting the decision of the case itself (*ad ipsius litis decisionem*).[100] From a modern perspective, it would appear that the twin distinction between formalities and substance of the contract, on the one hand, and between substantive and procedural matters, on the other, permeates Bartolan conflicts doctrine. But we will find no such general principle being announced, in contrast for example with Dumoulin who begins his own commentary with a rule as to solemnity extending to all legal instruments.[101] We will have to examine the *repetitio* in detail to consider how Bartolus approaches – and employs – such concepts.

It was suggested in Chapter 5 that the legal construct of formalities can serve diverse private-law functions when employed in the conflict of laws. Any conflicts treatment has the difficult task of setting out rules for the regulation and circulation of legal acts in an environment where different jurisdictions have different rules that possibly serve different policies, but in the case of Bartolus, such diversity of purpose is attenuated because, on top of the effective, "horizontal" conflict of local jurisdictions, he also has to deal with the hierarchical relation between the local law and the *ius commune*. After a brief excurcus into terms and concepts, we shall therefore examine the use of formalities first in terms of the validity of legal acts and then in terms of managing the reach of local law.

9.4.1 *Form, Solemnitas, and Formalities*

Embodied in the rule *locus regit actum*, the concept of form has been traditionally used in conflict of laws to secure the validity of acts as well as to uphold certain standards of public policy and certainty. Bartolus is even regarded by many as having been the first to draw clear lines distinguishing the form of a contract from issues pertaining to

[100] Bartolus ad C.1.1.1, nu. 13. Cf. ibid., nu. 14, which has led Clarence Smith, "Bartolo," 173 to translate this passage similarly to Bartolus ad D.1.3.32, nu. 27.

[101] Molinaeus ad C.1.1.1, 555a: "*Aut statutum loquitur de his quae concernunt nudam ordinationem vel solemnitem actus, et semper inspicitur statutum vel consuetudo loci, ubi actus celebrator sive in contractibus, sive in iudiciis, sive in testamentis, sive in instrumentis aut aliis conficiendis.*"

substance.[102] What makes Bartolan thought appear even more similar to our own is that the term *form* has been consistently employed to translate the word *solemnitas* that Bartolus is using.[103] Medieval legal historians, however, are skeptical.[104] They point to the fact that Bartolus uses the term *forma* only sparingly, and in a different sense than we present him as doing.[105] Where conflicts lawyers translate him as speaking of "form," Bartolus writes *solemnitas.*[106] Furthermore, he seems to be contrasting *solemnitas* with *dispositio*, the meaning of which has more to do with the "effects" of the act or statute than with its "substance."[107] A sharp contrast between "form" and "substance" would have been quite incomprehensible to someone familiar with the vocabulary of Medieval philosophy (as Bartolus almost certainly was).[108] In Medieval philosophy, at least the philosophy that employed Aristotelian terminology, "substance" was contrasted not with "form" but with "accidents" or "attributes." That this distinction is one that Bartolus has in mind can be seen in the one place in the *repetitio* where he uses the word *substantia*, contrasting it with *qualitas* (one of the "accidents").[109] "Form" in Medieval philosophical language is most often found paired not with "substance" but with

102 See e.g. W. S. Johnson, "Exctinctive Prescription—Conflict of Laws—Sources of Quebec Rules," *University of Toronto Law Journal*, 4 (1941), 109–130, 110.

103 See e.g. Lainé, *Introduction*, 1:135, 142, 149, 151, and especially Beale, *Bartolus*, 18, 34, 40, 42–43. Clarence Smith, "Bartolo," 174, 179, 180, 181, 248, 252, 254, 255, has opted for "formalities."

104 The argument in this paragraph is the child of a long-standing discussion with Professor Charles Donahue.

105 The word *forma* appears in four places in the *repetitio* coupled with the word *statuti* or *statutorum*. Bartolus ad C.1.1.1, nus. 26, 47, 49, 50. In one of these places (nu. 26), it corresponds to what elsewhere Bartolus calls *solemnitas* (it is the "form" that one uses to legitimate), but even here the meaning seems to be broader. In all the other cases, and to a certain extent in this one, the meaning is broader: it is the statute that gives *form* to the otherwise inchoate *matter* (admittedly not a term that he uses) that is its subject. Finally, in yet another case, the use of *forma* is quite dramatic: the English rule gives "form" to the goods that are in England (*certa forma est data bonis ibi positis*), i.e. changes their nature from being inheritable by all the children. Ibid., nu. 42.

106 Bartolus ad C.1.1.1, nus. 13, 22, 26, 32, 36, 37, 40, and 41.

107 See e.g. ibid., nu. 36.

108 See Gordley, *Philosophical Origins*, 39–40; D. Caglioni, "'Regnativa prudentia.' Diritto e teologia nel 'Tractatus testimoniorum' bartoliano" in *Théologie et droit dans la science politique de l'État modern* (Rome: École française de Rome, 1991), 155–170.

109 Bartolus ad C.1.1.1, nu. 47. Bartolus is reporting the opinion of Cinus that a citizen may be punished for a crime committed outside the territory under a statute, so long as the statute is punishing something that was already a crime under the *ius commune*: the statute cannot extraterritorially create a *novam obligationis substantiam*, though it may change the *qualitatem* of that *substantia*.

"matter," with "form" added to prime matter to make something that exists (a "substance"). There are hints of this usage in the way that Bartolus uses the word "form" in the *repetitio*.[110] "Solemnity" was not a technical term in Medieval philosophy, and while Bartolus's use of the term sometimes suggests that he is thinking of an "accident," it is probably significant that he does not use the latter term.

All this must be taken into account. If anything, it requires a closer, more cautious examination of the entire *repetitio*, without limiting ourselves to the first section. We shall then see that Bartolus uses *solemnitas* in a manner that would be familiar to the many subsequent conflicts lawyers who used the form/substance distinction to achieve doctrinal goals. Moreover, this appears to have been the case with subsequent jurists as well.[111] Accordingly, an intermediate approach is being followed in this book: *solemnitas* has been translated as "solemnity," rather than form, in our presentation of the *repetitio*.[112] Yet the Bartolan *solemnitas* is not the same as what we would *today* call solemnity: it appears as a singular abstract noun, as a concept encompassing all the individual solemnities or formalities. In that sense it is closer to the present-day "form," and it is certainly understable why it has been approached as such in conflicts literature.

9.4.2 *Formalities and the Validity of Legal Acts*

Whether he defines formalities as matters of *solemnitas* or as maters "concerning the making of the contract itself" (*respiciunt ipsius contractus ordinationem*), Bartolus distinguishes such matters from those "pertaining to rights arising out of the contract" (*quae pertinent ad ius ex ipso contractu oriente*) – a category in which he included both matters as to the manner of conducting the case and the decision itself – and would look to the place of contracting (*inspicitur locus contractus*) for such

110 For a relatively straightforward introduction to these topics, see R. H. Popkin (ed.), *The Columbia History of Western Philosophy* (New York: Columbia University Press, 1999), index, s.v. *accidents, attributes, form and matter, hylomorphism, matter, substance*. For a more complex discussion, see N. Kretzmann et al. (ed.), *The Cambridge History of Later Medieval Philosophy* (Cambridge: Cambridge University Press, 1982), under the same catchwords.

111 See e.g. Baldus ad C.1.1.1, nu. 57 (*de iure solemnitatis vel formae*); Molinaeus ad C.1.1.1, 554a.

112 In the three chapters discussing the actual text, however, the term "solemnities" or even "formalities" has also been used depending on the context of the discussion.

matters: this would make local law applicable as to the formalities of all contracts concluded in that city.[113]

The rules that Bartolus states is an important reason why the section on contracts feels familiar to us. Another reason however is that the cases in this section seem to involve actual conflict between local legislation on both sides, whereas in most instances conflicts in the world of Bartolus are between a polity following the *ius commune* and another one whose local legislation has derogated from the *ius commune*. But the distinction between form/solemnity and substantive disposition plays an important role in how Bartolus treats testaments and other legal acts that affect succession or more general. We will have to reconstruct a principle of *locus regit actum* by putting together a series of rules, beginning with the third section. Bartolus's flagship example in discussing testaments would be today regarded as a classic case of formalities: the number of witnesses required to make a valid testament.[114] This is a recurring – one could say textbook – case in preclassical conflicts: in the Early Modern era, similar conflicts arose as northern polities adopted or "received" the Roman law on this point as well.[115] Roman law had insisted on increased formality and the *ius commune* inherited a rule of seven witnesses (the rule for most formal legal acts), and on some occasions, five.[116] An increasing number of polities had begun to adopt a more liberal regime, especially as testamentary succession grew in importance and notarial practice became more sophisticated.[117] Hence Bartolus's hypothetical example of a Venice statute requiring only two or three witnesses. Bartolus first has to address the question of the very validity of such a statute, before he can consider whether it can extend to foreigners within the territory: he answers that question in the affirmative, as long as the wording of the

113 Bartolus ad C.1.1.1, nu. 14.

114 Bartolus ad C.1.1.1, nu. 21.

115 See Sections 13.3.4 and 13.4.1.

116 C.6.11.2 and C.6.23.31. Buckland, *Roman Law*, 282–288; C. Sánchez-Moreno Ellart, "The Late Roman Law of Inheritance: The Testament of Five or Seven Witnesses" in B. Caseau and S. Huebner (eds.), *Inheritance, Law and Religions in the Ancient and Mediaeval Worlds* (Paris: CHCByz, 2014), 229–257.

117 See e.g. Kuehn, *Heirs, Kin, and Creditors*, 89–95 and references therein. For an overview of the evolution in form and importance of notarial deeds at the time see D. Herlihy, *Pisa in the Early Renaisance: A Study of Urban Growth* (New Haven, CT: Yale University Press, 1958), 1ff (chapter on "Notarial Chartularies") with further references to A. de Boüard, *Manuel de diplomatie française et pontificale*, vol. II: Actes privés (Paris: Picard, 1948).

statute is "general and unqualified," i.e. unless the city has expressly limited its scope to citizens.[118]

The mirror image of this statute would be customs or statutes imposing stricter formality than the *ius commune*, such as that the testament be made before two notaries.[119] Bartolus draws a distinction between statutes prohibitive *ratione solemnitatis*, *in rem*, and *in personam*: the former will not have extraterritorial effect, since "in matters of solemnity we always look to the place where the thing is done."[120]

Bartolus returns to statutes relaxing solemnity requirements in the seventh section, where he discusses the extraterritorial effects of *permissive statutes*. He has already stated, with regard to prohibitive statutes, that statutes concerning solemnity may not govern a legal act made outside the city's territory. The question is about the extraterritorial effects of legal acts made validly, in the city's territory under such permissive statute. Bartolus puts himself in the middle of the debate: the glossators who would deny any effect to such a statute derogating from the *ius commune* had long lost; some *ultramontani* and early Commentators argued for the recognition of the validity of the testament inside the city's territory but not outside; others, beginning with Gulielmus de Cuneo, argued that the legal act, created validly in the *locus celebrati* should be held valid everywhere and that the effects of the statute extended "from the testament itself to all the property by consequence," including property located *extra territorium.*[121] Bartolus agrees with Gulielmus as to the result but not as to his rationale. He argues that it is not a *necessary* consequence of the fact that the testament is valid that its effects should cover all property everywhere. Unlike actus territorialists who would argue that the legal act, made validly under the *lex loci celebrationis*, will produce effects everywhere regardless of the law in these places, Bartolus holds that, if the legal act was made in accordance with the formalities provided under the *lex loci celebrationis*, we should be satisfied as to its formal validity, regardless of our own rules on formalities.

From the point of view of conflicts doctrine, these solutions appear to derive from the *locus regit actum* principle: they serve the goal of

[118] Ibid., nu. 24. For the discussion see ibid., nus. 22–23 and 36–37.

[119] Bartolus ad C.1.1.1, nu. 32. Cinus ad C.1.1.1 and others mention a Bologna statute requiring ten witnesses.

[120] Ibid.

[121] Bartolus ad C.1.1.1, nu. 22–23, 36–37, discussed in Sections 7.4.3 and 7.5.2.2.1.

certainty but do not show any pro-validity bias. Once we consider their context, however, we see that Bartolus has managed to serve his substantive objectives while minimizing the scope of derogations from the *ius commune* rules on testamentary formalities.

9.4.3 "Form," "Substance," and the Limits on the Reach of Local Law

The second aspect of the Bartolan doctrine on *solemnitas* is the use of the concept in order to distinguish cases where the effects of a statute or an act may extend to foreigners or foreign places, from cases where they do not. The distinction between "form" and "substance" is thus emphasized in order to manage or minimize the scope of local derogation from the *ius commune*.

Bartolus begins his discussion on permissive statutes with an odd category: statutes granting authority to someone. In effect, this is about the legal foundation for the validity and extraterritoriality of notarial acts.[122] The solution adopted in these passages is pretty much our own.[123] The notary cannot draw legal instruments outside the territory of his appointing authority, but deeds drawn within his territory "have force everywhere ... because it is a matter of solemnity rather than of substance."[124] The Bartolan characterization leads to "modern" results but also suggests the conceptual differences across time, which will become evident almost immediately below.

This does not however mean that every notarial act, or other legal instrument, which has been made in accordance with the rules of the *locus celebrationis* or *conclusionis*, will produce its effects everywhere. In discussing the effects of local legislation regarding legitimation or emancipation over foreigners in the city's territory, Bartolus states that the effects of such a statute may only extend to foreigners making acts in the city whenever and only when they have to do with form:

> [F]or the solemnity of an act pertains to the jurisdiction of the city in whose territory it is done; so it varies according to the difference in places; but whenever there is a difference of person, a statute cannot dispose, except about a person subject to it.[125]

[122] Bartolus ad C.1.1.1, nus. 34–36.

[123] See e.g. C. Pamboukis, *L'acte public étranger en droit international privé* (Paris: L.G.D.J., 1993); P. Callé, *L'acte public en droit international privé* (Paris: Economica, 2004).

[124] Bartolus ad C.1.1.1, nu. 36.

[125] Ibid., nu. 26.

Bartolus returns to this idea when discussing the extraterritorial effect of permissive statutes removing *ius commune* limitations on personal status (personal qualities), bringing up two examples.[126] First, statutes allowing an unemancipated son or another person prohibited by law to make a testament. Second, a statute allowing a *spurius* to be appointed as heir. Bartolus assumes for the sake of argument that such statutes constitute a valid derogation from the *ius commune*, but he is negative as to the ability of someone being appointed as heir – or making a testament – under this statute in a different place than the one in which the entry into inheritance (*aditio*) must occur.[127] Bartolus invokes here the argument about *iurisidictio*: this power (of appointment as heir, of making a testament) has been granted by an authority lower than the princeps and cannot therefore produce effect outside the authority's territory. But the connection with the earlier discussion regarding the lack of extraterritorial effects of statutes conferring a special privilege and the resulting inability of a notary to draw legal instruments outside the territory of his appointing authority is evident.

But what about the effects of *aditio* outside the territory in the "very difficult and constantly recurring" case where both the appointment of the spurius as heir and the entry into inheritance occur in the same territory?[128] Bartolus cannot outright invoke the same argument about the lack of *iurisdictio*. Other jurists had argued in favor of allowing the succession to produce its effects everywhere, arguing among other things by analogy to court judgments and an act of emancipation, which under Roman law was effective everywhere: are not these legitimation statutes the same with those making an act such as a testament or emancipation possible?

Bartolus is opposed to this argument. He argues that allowing the *spurius* to be heir grants him status/capacity to do an act (*aditio*), as opposed to specifying the solemnities required for the act. In support of his argument, he elaborates on the distinction between solemnity and substantive disposition: "a provision as to the solemnity of an act is another thing from legitimating a person to make an act."[129] Solemnity requirements are different in different places – "when there is a

[126] Ibid., nu. 38.
[127] Ibid., nu. 39.
[128] Ibid., nu. 40.
[129] Ibid., nu. 41.

difference of place, different reasons exist for different results" – but the same act could be done elsewhere, even with different solemnity, since there would be prejudice to the city where the effects of that act will be recognized.[130] The notary is here Bartolus's model with regard to the role of solemnity: "for he takes no part in the disposition itself, but in solemnizing an act done by another."[131] Likewise, in the Roman case of a father emancipating his son before local magistrates to whom such power was conferred by *ius municipium* it is not the statute that emancipates the son, but the father, "using the solemnity specified by the statute."[132] Bartolus continues his argument onto the effects of court judgments: the judge disposes, in his judgment, of rights already created and defined, which follow the person everywhere, and this is why another judge can be requested to execute the judgment, but when the judge himself creates a new right (i.e. one that could not arise under the *ius commune*) in his territory, that right does not extend outside the territory.[133]

This Bartolan analysis could be viewed as containing the roots of both the public–private distinction and the vested rights doctrine. But it is not necessarily convincing, especially when one considers the thin line between legitimation and emancipation.[134] This would not suggest that Bartolus fell victim to hair-splitting conceptualism. Legitimation of children was still, at the time of Bartolus, a point of political, legal, and social contention, which also challenged both the limits of ecclesiastical jurisdiction and the powers of local political entities.[135]

9.4.4 Substance and Procedure

The distinction between substantive and procedural matters has been regarded by many as a foundational moment for private international law, in the sense that, by allowing substantive matters to be liberated from the *lex fori*, Medieval jurists enabled the choice of law process itself.[136] Bartolus himself distinguishes at every opportunity between

[130] Ibid.
[131] Ibid.
[132] Ibid.
[133] Ibid.
[134] See T. Kuehn, *Emancipation in Late Medieval Florence* (Rutgers: Rutgers University Press, 1982).
[135] See esp. Kuehn, *Illegitimacy*.
[136] See Section 3.4.2.

matters concerning the manner of conducting the case (*ad ordinatoria litis*) and matters concerning the decision itself (*ad litis decisionem*), making clear that when it comes to the former matters we ought to look to the place of the trial (*locus iudicii*) and statutes governing them have effect over all trials initiated in the city.[137] In most subjects treated in the *repetitio*, Bartolus deals with issues we would be calling substantive, with the exception of the sections on contracts and punitive statutes.

In his eighth section, Bartolus considers the circumstances under which city legislation will extend to wrongs committed by a citizen outside its territory. If, as is likely, the statute does not expressly govern – or exclude from its scope – such actions, then Bartolus distinguishes between statutes concerning procedure ("the process or manner of conducting the case"), which shall govern all proceedings instituted in the city and statutes concerning substance ("the decision itself"), including punishment, which do not apply.[138] The actual example that Bartolus gives – whether the *podestà* may inquire about an offense absent the accusation required under the *ius commune* but not city law – falls into the first category.[139]

The first section shows the development of Bartolan and Medieval thought in this regard. In his earlier commentary on *de quibus*, Bartolus contrasted customs or statutes "concerning the making of the contract itself" (*respiciunt ipsius contractus ordinationem*) with those "pertaining to rights arising out of the contract" (*quae pertinent ad ius ex ipso contractu oriente*) – a category in which he included both matters as to the manner of conducting the case and the decision itself.[140] The *repetitio* on *cunctos populos* begins with the tripartite distinction, but the immediately subsequent paragraph seems to consider *litis ordinationem* and *litis decisionem* together. Whether this change is the result of further evolution in the thinking of Bartolus himself, or the subsequent work of an editor from another generation, it is interesting that Bartolus does not draw too sharp a line between *litis ordinatio* and *decisio*, especially contrasted with *solemnitas*. A reason for this may be that it is easier to separate matters of "making" the contract from the judicial venue and probably easier to ascertain the formal requirements for their making: some of the most important contracts involved notaries and other

[137] Bartolus ad C.1.1.1, nus. 15, 19 and 48.
[138] Ibid., nu. 47.
[139] See Section 10.3.2.
[140] Bartolus ad D.1.3.32, nu. 27.

authorities. In contrast, when it comes to actual litigation a lot of critical matters are inherently related to the forum, including the remedies to be requested and possibly granted, what needs to be proved and how. "Substantive" maters would have required more of an effort to ascertain foreign customs or statutes than matters of solemnity. In this regard, the separation of solemnity was the first step in reducing the role of *lex fori* in contract disputes. The next step was the elaboration of a strong substartive category of matters falling under the *lex loci contractus*, defined in terms of matters arising from the nature of the contract itself, leaving only matters arising *expostfacto* for the smaller substantive category. Having thus established the doctrinal autonomy of contract, which is largely localized in the place of contracting, Bartolus can pull this last category away from the *lex fori*, at least in conceptual terms, by distinguishing the place of performance from the place of the trial, even if in most cases the place would have been the same. The characterization – contrary to the Gloss but also to subsequent jurists, including Huber – of prescription as a matter for the law of the place of performance, rather than the *lex fori*, serves as a very good example in this regard.

9.5 Conflicts of Jurisdictions and Conflicts of Laws

There is little discussion in the *repetitio* either of adjudicative jurisdiction or of the connection between jurisdiction and applicable law. There are in fact three instances where adjudicative jurisdiction is discussed – all of them dealing with matters commonly regarded as peripheral to the conflict of laws – in addition to several more mainstream instances where it is implied.

The first comes in the discussion on punitive statutes and the extension of the jurisdiction of the city's *podestà* over offenses committed abroad: the examples concern his power to punish offenses between foreign soldiers (presumably mercenaries) committed in a territory occupied by the city, and whether he can exercise procedural powers available under city legislation but not under the *ius commune* in order to investigate offenses committed abroad by citizens.[141] The second, in the final section on punitive judgments, concerns the power of local jurisdictions to forfeit property located in their territory, subsequent to a forfeiture sentence in another jurisdiction (presumably where the person is located

[141] Bartolus ad C.1.1.1, nu. 44–48. See also Section 10.3.2.

or is closely connected with), and which *bursa fiscalis* will benefit from it.[142] In both cases, Bartolus explores the reach of the city's adjudicative jurisdiction as allowed by the *ius commune*. In the former, he begins from a local vantage point: city authorities apply local law insofar as allowed by the *ius commune*. In the latter, he adopts a more elevated, imperial one: city authorities exercise jurisdiction by authority of the *ius commune* (even if they benefit themselves in most instances). Only in the end is the horizontal case where each jurisdiction is a separate *bursa fiscalis* considered – and the result is similar to the discussion about categories of statutes in the previous sections.

The third instance concerns the application of city statutes or customs in proceedings before the ecclesiastical courts of the city.[143] Bartolus defines why and the cases in which this will happen. From a more modern point of view, one may argue that this is a matter of "internal sovereignty" but we must be mindful of the context and the arguments employed. Royal courts, *podestà*, and ecclesiastical courts may in fact serve different masters but *de jure* they all form part of – and derive jurisdiction from – an imperial legal system. Especially Italian polities exercised their civil and criminal jurisdiction within the operating system created by the *ius commune*. In this environment, adjudicative jurisdiction mattered less for the elaboration of a system allocating legislative jurisdiction. It would appear that it would be relatively easy for a strong city to claim longarm civil jurisdiction, at least over residents and property situated in its territory: learned law could provide the justification, with the concept of *territorium* and the system of *iurisdictio* under the *ius commune* used to limit the exorbitant use of such jurisdiction. But when it came to legislative jurisdiction, i.e. the scope of local legislation, even though from a certain point of view statutes and customs represent an effort at a similar extension, their scope could only be determined in accordance with the *ius commune* and by means of learned law.[144] It is moreover easier to simply interpret restrictively the scope of statutes, and application of *ius commune* or even foreign law could serve as a

142 Ibid., nu. 51. See also Section 8.2.2.2.

143 Ibid., nus. 28–31. See also Section 8.2.2.2.

144 For an illustration – albeit a century after Bartolus – see e.g. J. Kirshner, "Pisa's Long-Arm" Gabella Dotis (1420–1525): Issues, Cases, Legal Opinions" in *Marriage, Dowry and Citizenship in Late Medieval and Renaissance Italy* (Toronto: University of Toronto Press, 2015), 197–214.

way of making more equitable any longarm exercise of adjudicative jurisdiction.

The *podestà* himself had sworn, in taking his office, to observe the city's laws. This has been interpreted as an oath to uphold the rule of law but, given that the *podestà* – and many of the young lawyers working under him – came from another city, the oath may have intended to prevent the subversion of the local laws by making them binding on the *podestà*.[145]

We thus find many instances where the city court is expected to apply the *ius commune* rule rather than the local custom or statute. We also find several instances where the court is called to look to another city's law: notably in the discussion of contract in the first section, but also in the case of a citizen being punished for conduct abroad –the local statute being expressed in general terms as to its scope – under either the *ius commune* or the law of the place where the wrong took place.[146] In fact, most "foreign law" instances have to do with what today could be called the consideration of foreign law as a *fact*. An example is the punishment of a foreigner for a wrong committed in the city, when the act is "commonly prohibited by all cities."[147] Another example is found in the numerous cases where the extraterritorial effects of legal acts (notarial acts, contracts, testaments, judgments) are contemplated, and the occasional extraterritoriality with regard to the disposition of goods. On the contrary, Bartolus is skeptical of the extraterritorial effect of "new" rights, such as bestowing by statute upon a *spurius* the capacity to be heir.

Conflict of laws at the time of Bartolus still shows a medium corelation between jurisdiction and applicable law. Both are approached with similar motivation, and a common conceptual basis. Yet Bartolus does not seem to think in terms of fixed *ordres juridiques* which can exclude or include "foreign law": he is concerned at least as much with achieving equitable results than with providing a clear delimitation of "legislative" and "adjudicative" jurisdiction. We could say he assumes the existence of adjudicative jurisdiction and looks into the reach of city legislation – or,

[145] See also ibid., nu. 49 (the conclusion of the eight section) containing a formula which Bartolus invites the judge to use at the conclusion of his inquisition: "Upon these things all and singular I intend to proceed and inquire according to the form of the statutes (*secundum formam statutorum*) of this city, and to punish and condemn the [accused if] guilty according to the form of law (*secundum formam iuris*)." Bartolus comments "and so in procedure he refers himself to the statute and in condemning to the *ius commune*."

[146] Ibid., nu. 48.

[147] Ibid., nu. 21.

with hindsight, that *repetitio* is concerned with defining the law applicable by the court.

All this serves as a reminder that a conflict of laws system was still-emerging in the Late Middle Ages. Questions that we today regard as essential for the conflict of laws were not treated as such until the subject was conceptualized as a distinct field and was able to draw "peripheral" subject matter into its constitution.

9.6 Individual Autonomy and Bartolan Conflict of Laws

A modern writer has remarked that Bartolan conflict of laws:

> [R]ested on three conceptions; the sovereign power of legislation, the existence of a common law, and the autonomy of the will of the parties, the relative consideration of which has ever since been of concern in this field of law.[148]

What could we mean by "autonomy of the will of the parties" in Bartolan doctrine? Something close to what today is called party autonomy in the choice of law? Or, simply an acknowledgement that individuals have considerable freedom to enter into contracts and make testaments?

There is little evidence in our text of a role for party autonomy in the choice of law – not even to their implied intentions as an argument in support of another choice-of-law rule. We should distinguish here contracts and succession.

Bartolan rules on contracts might appear familiar to modern eyes. Parties exercise what we would call their autonomy in classic private-law fashion: that is, by entering into agreements and stipulating terms. They also enjoy a certain degree of autonomy in selecting where to perform, and where to sue: Bartolus acknowledges this, especially when making a distinction between the place of performance and the place of trial: if the parties have agreed about the place of performance, then the law of that place will be looked to with regard to matters of breach.[149] The division that he makes, for purposes of applicable law, between "matters arising out of the nature of the contract itself at the time it was made" and "maters arising ex post due to neglect or delay" is also important, but in his wording Bartolus gives less emphasis to party autonomy than Gulielmus, who first espoused such a distinction but worded it in terms

[148] Yntema, "Comity," 15, citing Meijers, "Principes fondamentaux," 635.
[149] Ibid., nu. 18.

of the parties' intentions rather than the nature of the contract ("matters of common concern according to the contract and by provision of the contracting parties" as opposed to matters *ex improviso*).

Bartolus does eventually state, with reference to his discussion of contracts, that "contracts extend as far as the will of the contracting party goes; which is presumed to have been according to the custom of the place where the thing is done."[150] It must be noted however that Bartolus makes this statement, in his discussion of the English case, in order to dismiss the contractual analogies made by advocates of subjecting succession to the law of the place where the inheritance is vested (*aditio*). We may contrast, in this regard, Bartolus with Baldus, who deals with the same case by suggesting that someone dying intestate has tacitly accepted (*tacite testari*) that his succession will be subjected to the law of the place where the property will be acquired. The contrast is even stronger with subsequent jurists such as Rochus Curtius, who would suggest that the parties tacitly agreed to be subjected to the law of the place of contracting, or especially Dumoulin, who called for an examination of the circumstances surrounding the expression of the parties' will.[151] Like Bartolus, Dumoulin used the parties' presumed intention to remove primarily issues of contract performance, breach, and termination from the customs of the place of contracting. The will of the parties also enabled Dumoulin to break from the Roman authorities. In the case of a man from Tübingen who sold his house there, while in Italy, providing guarantees in case of nonperformance (eviction), Dumoulin uses his presumed intention to part with both Bartolus and the Gloss and disallow the application of the Italian law.[152] Dumoulin and Bartolus would apply the law of the husband's domicile in a dotal contract, but only Dumoulin invokes the parties and their (presumed) intention.[153] We will not find in Bartolus the invocation of the parties' will neither as a doctrinal foundation nor as an actual principle.

Bartolus's treatment of legal acts *mortis causa* is even more telling of his primary concerns and the role of the individual and individual autonomy in his doctrinal system. The seventh section on permissive

[150] Ibid., nu. 43 (*contractus se extendunt quatenus voluntas contrahentis fuit quae fuisse praesumitur secundum consuetudinem loci ubi res agitur*).

[151] Molinaeus ad C.1.1.1, fol. 554a (*inspicitur circumstantiae voluntatis, quarum una est Statutum loci, in quo contrahitur; et domicilii contrahentium antiqui vel recentis, et similes circumstantiae*), 554b (*ius est in tacita et verisimiliter mente contrahentium*).

[152] Ibid., 555a. For both cases, see Section 9.3.1.

[153] Ibid., 555a.

contracts contains an actual doctrinal discussion of legal acts, more specifically notarial acts: yet instead of discussing legal acts, the issues are phrased in terms of a statute conceding or permitting something which "by reason belongs only to those to whom a special privilege is granted."[154] The substantive solutions that Bartolus arrives are not very unsimilar to our doctrines of *locus regit actum*. But someone who starts from a modern private-law perspective and considerations of "individual autonomy," will observe a different, almost reverse, picture in Bartolus and preclassical doctrine more generally.[155] In modern doctrine, with the emphasis on the individual, the "territorial" conception of laws allows the individual to travel away from the local restrictions – for example, in obtaining a divorce or in doing away with the formality requirements of an act. A "personalist" rule, on the contrary, is a rule that accompanies the individual everywhere, making sure, for example, that a citizen of a Catholic country could not obtain a divorce elsewhere. On the contrary, in preclassical doctrine the "subject" is the statute and its capacity to produce extraterritorial results.

9.7 Harmony of Solutions

The *harmony of solutions* or *decisional harmony*, which ensures that a single legal relation is not treated differently in different jurisdictions (i.e. the same marriage is valid in some countries but not others) has been to this day a constant preoccupation in conflicts thinking. Many contemporary lawyers will find resonance with Gulielmus de Cuneo's expressions of horror about a man dying in part testate and in part intestate, when his testament has been made in accordance with the laxer requirements of a local statute.[156] Gulielmus is of course alluding to a famous axiom in the *ius commune* that however concerned succession under a single law.[157] The axiom itself must be moreover seen in its context.[158]

154 Bartolus ad C.1.1.1, nu. 34.

155 See Section 5.6.

156 Bartolus ad C.1.1.1, nus. 36–37: statute requiring only four witness, instead of the seven of the *ius commune*.

157 D.50.17.7 (Pomponius): "Our law does not allow the same person among civilians to die both testate and intestate; for there is a natural conflict between these states, 'testate' and 'intestate.'"

158 See e.g. P. Meylan, "Nemo pro parte testatus pro parte intestatus decedere potest" in *Zum Schweizerischen Erbrecht: Festschrift zum 70. Geburtstag von Peter Tuor* (Zürich: Polygraphischer Verlag, 1946), 179–200; G. Copolla, "Nascita e declino dell'adagio

A modern will is essentially a postmortem conveyance; it is hence perfectly natural for the property mentioned in the will to pass according to the will while the property not mentioned in the will passes according to the rules of intestacy. The principal function of a Roman testament, however, is to make an *heir*, a universal successor who steps into the shoes of the deceased, gets all property (excepting the legacies), assumes all debts, and gets all credits. The same held true with regard to the intestate heir(s). Under these circumstances, a case of partial testacy and partial intestacy would certainly raise problems. But Gulielmus also seems disturbed by the same thing that has disturbed later conflicts lawyers: the validity of the testament is dependent on the fortuity of where the property lies, leading to two different results in the *same* case. At the same time, it is noticeable that notable Medieval jurists such as Jacobus de Ravanis (and Cinus, for a while) were willing to allow such a result. We could regard this stance as evidence of a territorialist attitude or view it as somehow foreboding of the late nineteenth century, "particularist" acceptance that the same legal case will be treated differently in different fora; We could also interpret it in a long line of Medieval jurists' attempts to reduce the scope of application of the "particular" rule derogating from the *ius commune*. In this regard, we could consider the change of Cinus's position, seen by Lainé as a move from the *lex rei sitae* to the *lex loci actus*, as evidence of a growing realization of the complications of managing private rights in a world of legal diversity.

In either case, Bartolus seems the closest among this group to contemporary mentality. On the one hand, he grants extraterritorial effect to the will and – generally – his system seems concerned with ensuring that acts validly executed have effect everywhere. On the other hand, he would not subordinate to this objective the hierarchies and objectives of laws. As a result, even though he agrees with the result reached by Gulielmus and the mature Cinus and does not need such an argument to reach his conclusion in the given case, Bartolus wishes to make clear that it is possible "by force of law" for one to die testate in part and intestate in part. In arguing that it is possible, and perhaps advisable, for a testament to have partial effect, Bartolus appears less conceptualistic and more of a legislative positivist.

This is characteristic of the general attitude that Bartolus has with regard to the effects of legal acts. He supports the universal effects of acts

'nemo pro parte testatus pro paret intestatus decedere potest'," *Teoría e Storia del Diritto Privato*, 5 (2012), 1–172.

validly made in their territory, insofar as they do not cause prejudice to the foreign city. But he seems to be drawing the line of "prejudice" broadly enough. The distinction made with regard to judgments enforcing preexisting obligations and rights created *de novo* by the judge also works in a similar manner.[159] On the other hand, the "divergence" effect of such reservations is mitigated by the existence of a common "general" law.

In fact, the instances where Bartolus sees "prejudice" occur wherever the statute achieves a substantive effect that could not be achieved by the law of the other city or the *ius commune*. Testaments can be made everywhere. How one makes them is up to the jurisdiction where one makes them. But *spurii* can be legitimated only by the emperor or the pope. If a city purports to legitimate a *spurius*, that is prejudicial. Interestingly, Bartolus does not see it as prejudicial to the intestate heir, but to the city which doesn't recognize the rule.

9.8 Conclusion

Bartolus is providing us with a complex and sophisticated doctrinal system. Upon close inspection, many private international lawyers across time are likely to find some resonance with some of his ideas (not necessarily the same). At the same time, Bartolan doctrine bears the distinct marks the time and place in which it was elaborated and can only be understood in that context.

Bartolus has been justly described as an analytical and eclectic writer, but his work also has the markings of an attempted, if incomplete, synthesis. He is also constructing a veritable doctrinal system, but it requires much effort to comprehend. In fact, many today would not consider Bartolus a *systematic* writer. He is certainly not one in the sense often used in the conflicts discourse, i.e. that systematic writers are those possessing a clearly articulated theory or approach that accounts for their entire conflicts work or "system." He is also not evidently systematic if we consider the structure of the *repetitio*, at least at first blush. Even if we compare his text with those of his immediate predecessors and successors, we find the *repetitio* as more ambitious in scope as well as more "raw," as if Bartolus was more interested in sketching-opening paths than in providing a model of systematicity. The *repetitio* sounds indeed like an

159 See Bartolus ad C.1.1.1, nu. 41 *in fine*.

oral presentation, where the teacher starts with the details and then works his way up to generality – issues first and theory later. General rules are assumed or simply alluded to. The discussion of some issues departs from where the discussion of other points had previously stopped. In other cases, important points are repeated in an effort to underline basic tenets. At the same time, Bartolus stops short of pronouncing principles in the manner of subsequent preclassical jurists. We could contrast him not only with someone like Huber, from whose neatly stated axioms everything springs, but also Dumoulin, who represents the culmination of Bartolist doctrine, often dealing with the same cases, but is nonetheless more systematic in his structure and outlines general rules and doctrinal foundations. There is also little evidence in Bartolus of either the basic let alone the classic theory of statutes, with their neat classification of statutes into real, personal, and (eventually) mixed.

We can conclude that Bartolus does not wholeheartedly espouse any of the "aprioristic" theories which rose to prominence in subsequent times. This reluctance to make an *a priori* commitment to a grand principle reflects on the choice-of-law solutions that Bartolus gives to specific doctrinal problems. There is no clear preference for personal law, the *lex situs,* or the *lex actus* – indeed, even the subject matter treated is not categorized on the basis of such rules. Notions of territoriality and extraterritoriality are central to this work, yet large chunks of it evade them. *Locus regit actum* is also important, but is very far from being a "paradigm," and the idea of vested rights exists, at best, in hybrid form. In either case, such doctrines seem to have been developed by Bartolus as a way of certain doctrinal solutions to practical problems (e.g. how emancipation can have universal effects, but not the legitimation of a *spurius*).

In fact, the structure of the Bartolan conflicts treatment appears not like a Cartesian treatment of the subject in two opposing parts but more like a double helix. Which leads us to the next leg of our examination.

10

Bartolan Conflict of Laws in the Conceptual Battlefield

10.1 Introduction

In the historical consciousness of private international lawyers, Bartolus is one of us – an illustrious ancestor. This is almost regardless of what present-day relevance his contribution is perceived to have. Occasionally, however, it has been argued that what Bartolus was doing in this text was an exercise not in the conflict of laws properly speaking, but in statutory interpretation or in the modernization of a superior body of law.

We could in fact position opinions as to the relevance of Bartolan conflicts to private international law across an inverted triangle (see Figure 10.1). The top side is populated by the mainstream conflicts literature (and at least some legal historians). At the first corner are those who emphasize the connection between the *basic theory of statutes* (i.e. the distinction between real and personal statutes) and sovereignty – and have located both in Bartolus.[1] At the second top corner, Bartolan conflicts doctrine is perceived as a distinctly "private law," often technical, enterprise – usually by authors who think of conflict of laws in these terms.[2] From this perspective, Bartolus is affirmed as an integral

[1] See e.g. Despagnet, *Précis*, 295 (the theory of personal statutes presupposes terrirorial sovereignty and imposes to it limits; it combines individuality and territoriality; the distinction between personal and real statutes reflects the distinction between Roman and local law (statutes)); Pontier, *Conflictenrecht*, 57. Many writers, less explicit, simply seem to take this idea of a horizontal conflict between polities as a premise: see e.g. Jayme, "Identité culturelle," 40. See also E. M. Meijers, "Introduction à la publication d'oeuvres inédites de Balde et de Van der Keesel," *Revue critique*, 35 (1946), 203–219: "Ce qu'on nomme aujourd'hui la science du droit international privé se réduit pour Balde à la recherche des limites de la souverainété des villes." The main effort to refute this idea from the point of view of the history of political ideas is A. Checchini, "Presupposti giuridici dell'evoluzione storica dalla 'Bartoliana' teoria degli statuti al moderno diritto internazionale privato," in *Bartolo da Sassoferrato: Studi e Documenti per il VI Centenario* vol. II (Perugia, 1962), 61–105. Checchini presents in detail the arguments affirming the existence of "sovereignty" or "ordre juridique," especially by Catellani and Calasso.

[2] See e.g. Bonnichon, "Conflit de souverainetés."

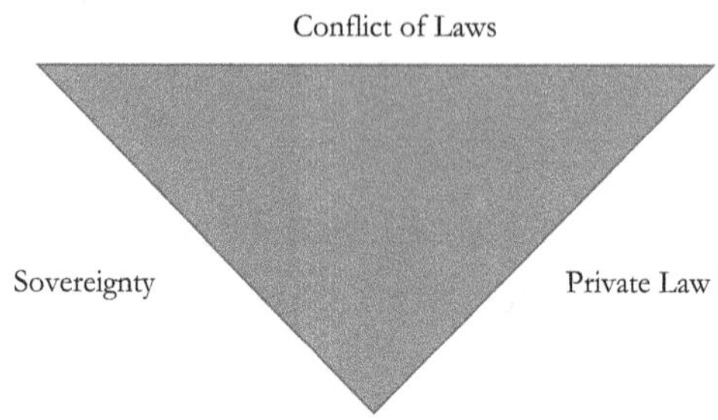

Figure 10.1 Bartolus and the Conflict of Laws in Historiography and Historical Consciousness

part of conflicts doctrine, while sovereignty is presented as less important both for him and for the conflict of laws more generally.

The bottom corner is populated by those – essentially Medieval historians and modern globalists in an uneasy coexistence – who question whether we should place Bartolus and his contemporaries into the conflict of laws tradition. There are two aspects to the skeptical perspective. First, that the Medieval "world system" is such that it cannot give rise to conflict of laws as we mean it. Second, that Bartolus himself has different preoccupations (and sensibilities) from those of conflicts lawyers properly speaking.[3] It is also argued by some that the adherence of Bartolus and his contemporaries to the *ius commune* was such as to make Bartolan doctrine fundamentally different from the modern conflict of laws.[4]

Modern conflict of laws has embraced, for the most part, the idea of an historical move in conflicts doctrine, away from a sovereignty-centric discourse, in its earlier history and toward a more sophisticated body of legal doctrine with stronger private-law sensibilities. Such perceptions are exemplified by narratives of a transition from a "conflict of sovereignties" toward the "conflict of interests" but they are widely held in the doctrinal mainstream. It is therefore interesting that those skeptical of Bartolus forming part of a conflict-of-laws discourse adopt a reverse narrative, in which state sovereignty is the true foundation, the high ground

[3] Thorne, "Sovereignty" could be seen as providing arguments in this regard. Thorne himself does not manage – and probably did not seriously intend – to shake off the connection between Bartolus and conflict of laws properly speaking. By showing the similarities between rules, on the one hand, and the drastically different theory/world view on the other hand, he provides material for the conceptions noted above.

[4] Barry, "Bartolus," 27–28.

of – classical and perhaps also modern – conflict of laws, just as they argue that the pre-Westphalian, or at least the pre-Reformation writers lack this grounding. Such an understanding may be less anachronistic than the doctrinal mainstream's narrative but not necessarily less subjective.

Moreover, skeptical perspectives raise three issues. First, a rigid definition of conflict of laws can identify it with one stream of thought: hence, in his essay, Thorne describes contemporary conflict of laws with reference to Huber, Story, and Beale and an emphasis on the Anglo-American tradition of vested rights.[5] Second, a reading of Bartolus as "working wholly within a private law scheme" may lead to a general understanding of private international law as essentially a "private law" affair and hence to playing down its international-governance dimension.[6] Third, painting a picture of "a complete change in theory" but little change in rules, without accounting for this process, may be contributing to the perception of conflict of laws as a "technocratic," isolated subject.

It is now time to turn to the upper part of our inverted triangle and explore the basic ideas and preconceptions about Bartolan doctrine in the doctrinal mainstream. The two most common notions are, on the one hand, that Bartolus thought in terms of a division of statutes into real and personal and, on the other hand, that he espoused or invented the unilateral method in the choice-of-law. They will be considered in Sections 10.2 and 10.3 respectively. Section 10.4 briefly considers what relation if any the conflict of sovereignties concept could have with Bartolus.

10.2 Bartolus and the Basic Theory of Statutes

A modern conflicts lawyer first approaching Bartolus's conflicts treatment may quickly deduce from its very opening that it is founded upon ideas of territoriality and extraterritoriality commonly expressed in the division between real and personal statutes. As we have seen, even the Accursian Gloss, upon which our text is supposed to comment, has been

[5] See Thorne, "Sovereignty," 685ff.

[6] Thorne, "Sovereignty," 684: "Working wholly within a private law scheme, it was on principles of what is right and just that Bartolus established his rules, which have lasted from his day to our own despite the advent of territorial sovereignty and a complete change in outlook."

perceived in these terms.[7] Our examination in the previous chapters has already shown that things are much more complex and nuanced. Yet the appreciation of such complexity has failed to take root in the historical consciousness of private international law.

10.2.1 *Bartolus, the Basic Theory, and the Modern Historical Consciousness*

The following excerpt, in a leading conflicts work, is characteristic of how the conflicts doctrine of Bartolus is being perceived today – and indeed for quite some time:

> Bartolus's method of resolving conflicts was based on a simplistic classification of local laws into two categories: real or personal. Real statutes were those that operated only within the territory of the enacting state but not beyond. In contrast, personal statutes operated beyond the territory of the enacting state and bound all persons that owed allegiance to it. Bartolus thought that this classification could resolve all potential conflicts because all statutes, both domestic and foreign, belonged to either the one or the other category, leaving neither gaps nor doubts.
>
> Obviously, this was naively optimistic, but worse than that was the fact that Bartolus' criteria for classifying a statute into real or personal were completely mechanical in that they were based solely on the statute's wording. For example, he argued that if the statute's words referred to a person, such as saying that "the first-born son shall succeed to the property," then the statute was personal. If the words referred to a thing, such as by saying that "the property shall pass to the first-born son," then the statute was real. It is therefore not surprising that Bartolus was ridiculed by subsequent authors. This criticism was justified to the extent it referred to Bartolus's mechanical classification of statutes. However, such criticism should not obscure Bartolus's impact, positive or negative, on the future direction of private international law.[8]

This view of Bartolan doctrine is a caricature.[9] It is nonetheless very common to make fun of "the absurdity of this grammatical approach."[10]

[7] See Section 3.4.1.

[8] Symeonides et al., *Conflict of Laws*, 8.

[9] For a more eloquent expression of frustration, a century before the quoted text, see Lainé, *Introduction*, 1:131–133, 334–335.

[10] As to how entrenched in popular culture this caricature has become, see Bisping, "Statutist Trap," 44 (n. 65): the author makes a reference to "Bartolus' famous quaestio Anglica" as an example of "the absurdity of this grammatical approach," without citing his source (presumably one of the textbooks), at the same time as noting how "extraordinary authority" Bartolus held with later generations of lawyers (citing S. Vogenauer).

Kurt Lipstein remarked that "[n]o distinction could be more fortuitous, no result could be more arbitrary."[11] Wolff called the rule a "very crude literal interpretation."[12] Anton concluded that "the verbalism of this approach hardly commends it . . . and it is hard to believe that such a canon of interpretation was generally applied."[13] Loussouarn, who held Bartolus even less in high regard, characterized this as primitive, shallow dialectic.[14] Even Despagnet, who displays a better understanding of Bartolan thought, appears to have believed that the rule in the English case was Bartolus's basic criterion for distinguishing between personal and real statutes and became accepted by most of his disciples, with the exception of Baldus, until Dumoulin.[15]

This caricature is also very ancient. In the sixteenth century, Dumoulin indeed expressed his disagreement.[16] D'Argentré appears to have made this supposed rule the epitome of the "sophistry" for which he viciously attacked Bartolus, calling the rule "futile," "childish," akin to "playing jacks."[17] In the seventeenth century, Paul Voet declared that the Bartolan solution "fully merited to be rejected *in totum*."[18] In the eighteenth century, Jean Bouhier presented the distinction as widely accepted by earlier jurists but also called it "frivolous."[19] Froland criticized the "blind

[11] Lipstein, "General Principles," 117, quoted approvingly by Forsyth, *Private International Law*, 38 who also calls the solution "arbitrary."

[12] Wolff, *Private International Law*, 25, nonetheless taking issue with d'Argentré for "condemning a scholar greater than himself merely for not having broken away from the narrow methods of his epoch."

[13] Anton, *Private International Law*, 20.

[14] Loussouarn et al., *Droit international privé*, 89 ("dialectique primitive et sans profondeur").

[15] Despagnet, *Précis*, 295–296.

[16] Molinaeus ad C.1.1.1, 556a (Paris 1680); also, in the same edition, his annotations on the consilia of Alexander Tartagnus: V.44 (fol. 959ra), VII.41 (fol. 1000va).

[17] Laurent, *Droit civil international*, 1:299–300 quoting a poignant passage from d'Argéntré without citation. See Argentraeus, *Commentariis*, CCXVIII (De Donationibus), gl. 6.14, 16, and 24. One is reminded at this point of Clarence Smith, *Medieval Law Teachers*, 116: "If the *mos italicus* (Italian style) continued to be precise and calm despite its more literary expression, it was otherwise with the *mos gallicus* in France. Here a lively contempt was fashionable, spieced with invective which to us seems merely vulgar, and directed both at contemporary rivals and above all at the past."

[18] See Section 10.2.2.

[19] Bouhier, *Coutumes*, 23.46 ("la plus ancienne, et qui a eu le plus communément cours parmi les Interprètes, est celle que proposa autrefois Bartole") and 47 ("Il est surprenant qu'une distinction aussi frivole entre deux Statuts, qui, dans le fond, prononcent la meme chose, ait pu trouver des partisans; sur tout après que Balde en eut fait voir le ridicule").

veneration" of those who could adopt such foreign opinions.[20] Boullenois marveled at how much authority Bartolus must have had to have charmed all these jurists into following a rule so scarcely reasonable.[21] Yet none of them cited Bartolus, and neither did Joseph Story, who drew most of his authorities from them.[22] Story thus presented Bartolus as providing "a memorable example of these niceties" associating him with "subtilities" that "have so perplexed the subject that it is difficult to venture even an explanation."[23] Even the usually insightful Ludwig von Bar made simple mention of the "verbal rule" – again, with no actual evidence of him having read the text.[24] It will take François Laurent, and especially Armand Lainé, for someone just to suggest that this was an individual rule with perhaps some rationale behind it.[25]

Lainé also provided evidence that the rule may have not been adopted as widely – and as mechanistically – as suggested. Any Medieval authorities mentioned to that effect by the eighteenth-century French jurists come from Dumoulin (and d'Argentré).[26] It seems that only Boullenois apparently took the effort to look into an actual authority mentioned by Dumoulin: a legal opinion (*consilium*) by Alexander Tartagnus

[20] Froland, *Mémoires*, 30 and 29 ("la règle . . . ne me paroît pas bien solide, ni facile à faire valoir . . . on a pareillement accusé [Bartole] d'avoir raisonné quelquefois en Sophiste, plutôt qu'en Jurisconsulte, qui ne doit s'attacher qu'à la solidité & au bon sens").

[21] Boullenois, *Traité*, 1:16: "La règle que Barthole a imaginée pour distinguer les Statuts personnels et les status réels, avoit de son temps, j'ose le dire, séduit tous les ésprits. Elle se trouve dans tous les Auteurs qui lui sont contemporains, & dans beaucoup qui sont venus après lui. Il est incomprehensible comment un règle aussi peu raisonnable a pu faire un aussi grand progrès; & je ne trouve rin qui marque plus de quel poids & de quelle autorité étoient dans ces temps-là, les décisions de cet Auteur, & le grand nom qu'il s'étoit fait parmi les Jurisconsultes. Aussi est-il appellé, Lucerna Juris, & quelques Autuers, comme Jason, ont été jusqu'à dire que jamais Barthole n'avoit erré, *Barthole semper dicit veritatem.*"

[22] Story, *Commentaries*, 16 n. 1 (citing Boullenois and Livermore in stating the Bartolan rule) and n. 2 (citing the same two, plus Froland, Martin, and Bouhier as to the "civilians" that have "justly exploded" the distinction). Same in *Saul v. His Creditors*, 5 Mart. (n.s.) 569, 591 (La. 1827). Cf. S. Livermore, *Dissertations on the Questions which arise from the Contrariety of the Positive Laws* (New Orleans, 1828), 62ff.

[23] Story, *Commentaries*, 14–15 (quoting a more general statement by Hert) and also 16: "This distinction has been justly exploded by other civilians, as the mere order and construction of the words of the statute, and not its objects, would otherwise decide its character."

[24] Bar, *Theorie*, 39 (§ 18). Bar does make a general reference to Bartolus ad C.1.1.1 in-text, but this in marked contrast with him citing specific paragraphs from the works of other Medieval jurists in his footnotes.

[25] See Laurent, *Droit civil international*, 1:298–301; Lainé, *Introduction*, 1:154–161.

[26] See Froland, *Mémoires*, 30–31; P. Dumouchet du Bac, *Traité sur les questions mixtes* (Paris, 1787), 54 refers to Froland in his turn.

(1423–1477).[27] In his annotations of Alexander's *consilia*, Dumoulin was critical of the result Alexander reached – and the rule he used in this and another *consilium* – but also pointed to other *consilia* where Alexander allegedly took a contrary position, presumably rejecting the rule.[28] Lainé himself examined several of Alexander's *consilia* in more detail: he concluded that they were proof of the "definite" acceptance of Bartolan doctrine in fifteenth-century Italy and its practical application over a variety of situations and saw no contradiction between them.[29] What Dumoulin failed to realize was how seriously Bartolan conflicts doctrine was altered by Alexander in order to serve his own ends.[30]

By the time of Dumoulin and d'Argentré, *mos gallicus* had made Bartolus "the archcommentaror and easily the lawyer most detested by the humanist community," even though, in the process of the German *Rezeption* of Roman law, a measure of respect for Bartolus was restored.[31] It is true that the division in legal doctrine between Commentators and legal humanists was not as extensive as their rhetoric might suggest.[32] But in many areas, including apparently the conflict of laws, all that did effectively remain of Bartolan doctrine was practical rules devised by subsequent generations of "Bartolists" – and a caricature of such rules. The emergence of the territorial state further sealed the decline of Bartolus's influence in this regard. Insofar as conflicts doctrine is concerned, from the sixteenth century onward the actual text of

27 Boullenois, Traité, 1:16ff, esp. 16–18 where he is discussing Alexander, *Consilium* V.44. See the original in Alexander Tartagnus, Consilium 44, *Consilia et Responsa*, vol. 5 fol. 54va–56rb (Venice, 1610).

28 See Molinaeus ad Alex. cons. 5.44, 959b, with references to *consilia* I.16, I.128, VI.19; for a summary see Boullenois, *Traité*, 1:18–19 (discussing *consilium* I.16).

29 Lainé, *Introduction*, 1:191–200, especially 199 ("Ces trois consultations appliquent deux règles distinctes de la théorie de Bartole").

30 Lainé, *Introduction*, 1:193, 195 ("La doctrine de Bartole est donc en partie dénaturée. Alexandre, d'ailleurs, sans convener que, sur ce point, il est en désaccord avec Bartole, se rend très bien compte de la portée de son proper système"), and 197 ("Dumoulin ne remarque pas la modification que la doctrine de Bartole a subie et qui l'éloigne bien plus encore de la règle admise en France").

31 The quotation comes from J. Whitman, *The Legacy of Roman Law in the German Romantic Era* (Princeton: Princeton University Press, 1990), 27 who discusses Melanchton's change of heart and 1537 oration in praise of Irnerius and Bartolus.

32 See also, among recent works, the essays in P. du Plessis and J. Cairns (eds.), *Reassessing Legal Humanism and Its Claims: Petere Fontes?* (Edinburgh: Edinburgh University Press, 2015).

Bartolus on conflicts is rarely quoted and read even less.[33] His caricature is acquiring mythic proportions.

Despite its long history, this common understanding of Bartolus is a considerable exaggeration. After three chapters, it is becoming apparent that Bartolus certainly did not think that "all potential conflicts" could be resolved by simply classifying statutes into real or personal. The organization of his treatment certainly suggests that much; the actual doctrinal solutions he proposes appear more nuanced. We will find no mention of "real" or "personal" statutes, or even a distinction between *in rem* and *in personam* effects of legal acts, until the sixth section. It is possible, however, that our modern quotation points to a deeper reality. It may be that a distinction between real and personal is underlying the fundamental division of the *repetitio*. And it is certainly true that Bartolus's resolution of the "English case" employs a distinction between *in rem* and *personam* and looks, at first blush, mechanical. It is to these topics that we must now turn.

10.2.2 Territorialism, Personalism, and the Bartolan Doctrine

The opening statement of the *repetitio* is held by some as affirmation of the paramount importance of the territorialism-personalism distinction in Bartolus.[34] If that opening statement is to be taken at face value, the first part of the Commentary deals with the territorial reach of statutes ("whether a statute extends to those not subject") and the second part with the personal or extraterritorial reach ("whether the effect of the statute extends beyond the territory of those who set it down"). Bartolus even seems to state the question in terms not unlike some classical-era territorialists.[35]

We should probably be cautious. The passage does not use the terms we are looking for. The "territorialist" first leg of Bartolus's distinction uses the "personalist" notion of "not subject."[36] The "personalist" second leg speaks in terms of the effects of a statute with no reference to persons and its development in the second part includes "territorial" topics such

[33] There is for example no reference in Voet, *Commentarius ad Pandectas*, 1.4.App.

[34] See e.g Surville and Arthuys, *Cours*, 21–22.

[35] See e.g. de Vareilles-Sommières, *Synthèse*, 1:VI and XXX.

[36] Compare for example with the territorialist second axiom of Huber, *Praelectiones ad Pandectas*, 1.3.App.2: "Those are held to be subject to a sovereign authority who are found within its boundaries, whether they be there permanently or temporarily."

as the lack of effect of rules as to formalities abroad or intestate succession to land. This is corroborated by the opening statement of the – earlier – commentary on *de quibus*: Bartolus asks "to what persons and to what places does [the force of a custom/statute] extend?"[37] Bartolus essentially follows the same structure as in the commentary on *cunctos populos*, with the difference that, as to the scope of local law regarding persons, he discusses minors and lunatics together with foreigners, whereas as to places, his treatment is limited to prohibitive statutes.

The opening statement does not therefore provide us with a grand principle underlying Bartolus' system. It exists for analytical and educational purposes. Bartolus states that he is charting new paths.[38] His opening paragraph seems more concerned with the simple-mindedness of the Accursian gloss and its emphasis on the "personalist" dimension. To the declaration of the gloss that the Bolognese will not be "subject" to the statutes of Modena, Bartolus counters that the issue of the reach of statutes actually consists of two questions, first as to the effects of the statute on foreigners in the legislator's territory, and then on its effects on both citizens and foreigners beyond the territory.

We could go even further: while the opening distinction does allude to a potential contrast between personal and territorial, Bartolus presents them not as opposing perspectives, but as different parts of a coherent whole: in fact, he evokes a unitary image of a "statute" and inquires into its reach, vertically and horizontally.

Things are not markedly different for subsequent Medieval jurists, at least as far as their systematic treatments are concerned. But the contrast is sharper if we compare Bartolus with an Early Modern scholar of learned law writing on statutes three centuries later, the Dutch professor Paul Voet.[39] Voet begins his chapter on conflicts issues enumerating – and dismissing – all the different ways in which statutes might be classified – including all distinctions used by Bartolus – only to conclude with his choice: "Statutes are commonly divided into real, personal and mixed."[40] The rest of the first section is dedicated to the denouncement

[37] Bartolus ad D.1.3.32, nu. 25: "*Tertio potest intelligi, ad quas personas, et ad quae loca suam virtutem extendat? De hoc agendum est primo de personis; et omnia quae dicam in consuetudine, intelliguntur in statutis, et econverso.*"

[38] See also, a little further down, Bartolus ad C.1.1.1, nu. 13: "Since these questions are much discussed, let us omit other distinctions, and examine the questions more fully than the doctors have done."

[39] P. Voetius, *De statutis eorum concursu* (Amsterdam, 1661).

[40] Ibid., 4.2.1.

of the idea – attributed to Bartolus – that a statute is real if the discussion starts from the thing (*a re orditur oratio*) and personal if it starts from the person.[41] In the next three sections, Voet dismisses previously proposed definitions of what constitutes mixed, as well as real and personal statutes until he finally proposes his own criterion for the tripartite distinction: their effects.[42] The doctrinal treatment that follows is structured in accordance with this scheme: structure, arguments, and solution clearly show Voet's preference for a territorialist approach, which became – especially as further elaborated by his son, Johannes – the doctrine associated with the Dutch school.[43]

Paul Voet expresses a clear preference for an approach – a territorial approach – and the solutions he proposes clearly reflect this approach (or his approach reflect his normative preferences). Voet acknowledges that what we have been calling the classic theory of statutes is the dominant paradigm for these matters and proposes his own set of definitions after a long examination of the ideas of past jurists. At the same time, the beginning of his work shows that the Medieval distinctions between statutes prohibitive and permissive, *favorabilia* and *odiosa* may be unpopular but not forgotten in Paul Voet's time, all while Bartolus is associated with a rudimentary – one is tempted to say "mechanistic" – version of the distinction between real and personal statutes.

Bartolus, on the contrary, is disinclined to commit *a priori* to either "territorialism" or "personalism," even defined in broad functional terms. He does make substantive choices as he goes along but again his emphasis seems to be on solving the specific questions while using the generic tools (and framework) provided to him by the *Corpus Iuris* and learned law, including the rest of the *ius commune*. In order to determine the scope of statutes, he principally uses the concepts derided by Voet. He does not even define what a *statutum realium* or a *statutum personalium* is – in fact, he does not even use these terms: he only speaks of a statute providing with respect to things or persons and only on two occasions. The first one is in distinguishing between prohibitive statutes whose prohibition concerns a thing (*in re[m] et respectu rei*) and statutes whose

[41] Ibid., with an actual citation to Bartolus ad C.1.1.1, nu. 42 and using a quotation from Donneaux (*Quod non verbis sed rebus leges sint impositae; adeoque nec verba captanda*) that goes back to D.1.3.17.

[42] Ibid., 2, 3–4, and 5.

[43] Ibid., 5–17.

prohibition concerns a person (*in personam*).[44] In the commentary on *de quibus*, Bartolus states the two terms slightly differently, with a reference to the prohibition "regarding a person or act of a person."[45]

The second one is in the English case, where in the actual discussion of the case, it is the pair of terms *circa rem* and *circa personam* that is used. The discussion concludes with a reference, "as to the point that it should be examined whether a provision is *in rem* or *in personam*," to D. 18.1.81 ("intention" will determine if the guarantor, who pays, shall have the land also pledged to the creditors as conditional purchase or as security).[46]

The fact of the matter is that the triangular nature of conflicts especially in Medieval Italy would make it even more difficult for Bartolus to think in binary terms of territorialism or personalism. The horizontal conflict between cities' laws is often played out in terms of a conflict or deviation of local law from the *ius commune*, which also works as a superstructure for the whole system. A striking example is the discussion of whether a foreigner should be punished under the local law for a local delict: if the act is wrong under the *ius commune* as well, he ought to be punished; if not, the assertion of territoriality gives way to a restrictive notion of foreigner's criminal awareness measured by objective standards, while the personal law of the foreigner is not even mentioned.[47] Anachronistic comparisons to the double actionability rule could be made, but the Medieval discussion on ignorance of law appears more relevant.[48]

All this is not to deny that the *repetitio* takes account of a territorial and a personal dimension of statutes and their effects. It could even be argued that we can find in Bartolus the roots of many such subsequent distinctions and concepts. To begin with, the conceptual clarification of the opening serves as a reminder of the dual nature of sovereignty. The subject matter treated in the second part deals with issues pertaining to the person and rather disconnected to the territory. The statutes in the first part are more capable of territorial localization. We could even see the *repetitio* as a distant forerunner of the distinction between the legal categories of *statut réel* and *statut personnel* as used by early classical

44 Bartolus ad C.1.1.1, nu. 32.

45 Bartolus ad D.1.3.32, nu. 31: *Aut [statutum] est prohibitivum in rem, id est respectu rei. . . . Aut prohibitio respicit personam seu actum personam.*

46 Bartolus ad C.1.1.1, nu. 42.

47 Ibid., nu. 20.

48 F. Roumy, "L'ignorance du droit dans la doctrine civiliste des XIIe-XIIIe siècles," *Cahiers de recherches médiévales et humanistes*, 7 (2007), 1–20.

French doctrine. What is certain is that the story is far more complicated that the grammatical characterization of statutes into real and personal, as is frequently thought.

10.2.3 Bartolus and the English Case

The so-called English case in all likelihood originated in France: Bartolus himself refers to the *ultramontani* Jacobus de Ravanis and Gulielmus de Cuneo as well as Cinus, who was probably the one who brought the example in Italian universities.[49] These three jurists espoused a "territorial" solution ("as to goods in England judgment be given according to the custom"), but Bartolus notes that others argued that the place where inheritance was vested should be looked to instead.[50] That position must have had very little support whereas we know from other sources contemporaneous to Bartolus –addressing the whole issue but not referring to the English case – that there was some support for the place of origin of the defunct.[51]

All these solutions appear familiar to classical and modern jurists. This is more than can be said about the solution of Bartolus, who could even be said to be taking a step backward. In lieu of the proto-multilateral rules of his peers, Bartolus calls for "the words of the statute or custom to be diligently considered (*diligenter intuenda*)."[52] He then invokes the

[49] Bartolus ad C.1.1.1, nu. 43. Lainé, *Introduction*, 1:122–123 comments that Cinus essentially replicates the conflicts treatment of Petrus Bellaperticus, dealing with the questions in the same order, "simply substituting in the appropriate spaces the names of Italian cities for the names of the French cities."

[50] Bartolus ad C.1.1.1, nu. 43. We cannot know whom Bartolus is referring to, but Baldus ad C.1.1.1, nu. 85 mentions Jacobus Butrigarius. Clarence Smith, "Bartolo," 256 notes that later writers credited Jacobus, citing Bartolus on this passage, but he was himself unable to corroborate this. He suggests that "it seems rather to echo a reductio ad absurdum" by Jacobus de Ravanis "of a suggestion by his master" Jacobus Balduinus.

[51] Albericus de Rosate ad. C.1.1.1, nu. 25, fol. 8va (Venice, 1586), presents as the two opposing solutions the law of the place where the property is situated and the law of the place of the defunct's origin, which he supports himself (*Aliquis uno loco originarius habens bona in diversis locis morit. Quaeritur an de haeriditate sua iudicare debeamus secundum statutum originis, an locorum patrimoniorum*). He also mentions a third, "singular" opinion in favor of the law of the place where the defunct died on the basis that intestate succession constitutes a tacit testament concluded there. His passage is translated by Lainé, *Introduction*, 1:127–128. Bartolus does not mention Albericus, which is less notable than the fact that he makes no reference of the "personal-law" approach which seems to have had more adherents than the place of death.

[52] Bartolus ad C.1.1.1, nu. 42. Beale, *Bartolus*, 45 translates "diligently examined." Clarence Smith, "Bartolo," 256 "carefully scrutinized."

distinction between provisions dealing with things (in rem) or persons (in personam).[53]As an example of a statute providing about things, Bartolus offers us the wording "let the goods of the decedents go to the firstborn" (*bona decedentium veniant in primogenitum*). As an example of a statute providing about persons, we have the wording "let the first-born succeed" (*primogenitus succedat*).[54]

This solution has been presented as offering a mechanical method for determining whether the statute is real or personal. A common reading of the passage is to suggest that the important criterion is the first word or the *subject* of the sentence: if the "goods" are the subject, the statute is real; if the person is the subject, the statute is personal.[55] *Prima facie*, this would indeed be a "mechanical" standard.

The characterization of the statute as mechanical would imply two things. First, that the determination of territorial reach is based on something – such as syntactic structure – which could be fortuitous. As a result, either the legislators could not have been thinking of this matter when they phrased the precise sentences of their statutes, or it is not reasonable for us to expect them to have thought thus, or, even if they did, no interpreter could be expected to easily understand and act upon such intention. Second, that there is no substantive ground for treating such two rules/sentences differently: to do so would therefore be more like relying on the legislator's whim in lieu of the "external" rule – or at least of the external criteria – expected of a conflict-of-laws approach.

We should probably know more about the wording of the statutes before we pass such a judgment: maybe the drafting techniques *in the specific time and place* were such that the placement of the words signified something to most members of the interpretive community. In any case, the first criticism is trumped once a substantive difference may be shown between the two rules – and it is to this and we will now turn.

Many have been misled by the fact that the word *primogenitus* appears in both the statutes of the example – and indeed the substantive result

[53] Ibid. *in fine*, with reference to D.18.1.81.

[54] Bartolus ad C.1.1.1, nu. 42.

[55] The common reading actually tends not to even mention syntax. For example, Despagnet, *Précis*, 295 speaks of "first word" in the sentence. Cf. P. Voet, *De statutis*, 4.2.1 (*à re orditur oratio*). To his credit, Despagnet does suggest that criticism is exaggerated, and that "the substance of [Bartolus's] thinking is that we must appreciate the real or personal character of law according to its dominant idea, and that this idea may be revealed by the terms in which it was conceived" (296).

concerns precisely the effects of primogeniture. But the key to the passage lies in the sentences as a whole – not syntax, nor the order of words. We now see that the "real" statute speaks of the fate of the goods of the deceased (*bona decedentium*). Instead, the "personal" statute talks about "being heir" (*succedat*). The difference is not simply grammatical. The *in rem* statute appears concerned only with the disposal of property. But being *the* "heir" also means being the universal successor, inheriting not only the property but also the active and the passive of the obligations. Indeed, in Roman law, the heir would also inherit the *sacra familiaria*.

Bartolus speaks in terms of the wording of the statute or custom. He was operating in a world in which local law was, for the most part, contained in written statutes or codified customs: this was even more the case with the Italian cities of his day, than it was in France of one or two generations prior, although even there the process of writing down customs was ongoing in earnest.[56] But English law in his day, and on the very topic that he covers, was not to be found in such a source. It is possible that Bartolus was aware of this. If so, we must either assume that he could think of no way of dealing with unwritten customary law or conclude – and this seems more likely – that he is speaking not only of the wording of the statute, but also of the substantive import of the legal rule.

Once we take this latter approach, Bartolus's criterion makes sense and has immediate application to the actual case. English law in the fourteenth century did not practice universal succession. Primogeniture was a rule about land; in fact, only certain kinds of land. We may locate hints of this where Bartolus describes the rule as that "a certain form is given for goods situated there."

Viewed from this perspective, what Bartolus has achieved with his solution to the English case is to minimize the actual "hard" conflicts in such cases: in a likely scenario of someone who left behind him property in Italy and feudal holdings in England, English law would apply to the latter but *ius commune* would apply to the former.

Bartolus allows no extraterritorial effect to the English rule. If the custom (or statute) provides for the property (*in rem*), its effects extend to property located in that land only, regardless of whether the deceased or heirs are "citizens" or "foreigners." If the custom is regarded as providing for persons, then we have three distinct cases. The obvious

[56] Dawson, *Oracles of the Law*, 266–273.

one is that the rule produces effects with regard to the succession of citizens in the polity (i.e. English persons in England). The second case involves foreigners who died while possessing property in the polity's territory: it is implied that the rule is about personal status and it was already stated that there can be no derogation from the *ius commune* in such a case. It is obvious that this settles the matter even more for the succession of such persons to assets abroad. The third case involves the effects of such an heirship rule abroad: Bartolus here comes to his distinction between prohibitive and permissive statutes. Viewed from the point of view of the younger sons, the custom/statute is prohibitive, but viewed from the point of view of the firstborn the statute is permissive, because it removes an impediment to his own heirship. This argument appears scholastic but it actually helps Bartolus drive home his result: in either case, the English rule can have no application outside England. If it is a prohibitive statute, it is an obviously *statutum odiosum*, of which it was already said that they have no effect outside the territorium.[57] But what about the case when the statute is permissive? Bartolus here has recourse to a different line of argument: his distinction between statutes permissive of relaxing solemnity requirements and statutes permissive as to personal status. The case at hand fits with the second group of cases: the local law has done something not permitted by the *ius commune*.

On the contrary, the Italian rule could find its way to Italians in England, since it is the *ius commune* rule and the English rule is only concerned with English *subditi*. This confirms our understanding that Bartolus presents the rule as an exception from the *ius commune*: he does not treat on an equal basis the two opposing rules (primogeniture and division), but makes the English one a subsidiary rule.

Our analysis is confirmed if we now view the solution proposed by Bartolus in more abstract terms: its effects are illustrated in Table 10.1. There are eight different variations of the case, depending on whether the decedent is English or not, the disputed property is located in Italy or in England, and the statute or custom is *in rem* or *in personam*. The Italian/*ius commune* rule will apply in five of these eight cases, including four of the six principal variations. Furthermore, the Italian rule will apply to property in Italy under any circumstances.[58]

[57] Bartolus ad C.1.1.1, nu. 42 with reference to nu. 33.

[58] On the socioeconomic rationale for the Italian rule see e.g. C. K. Zuber, "Plague and Family Life" in M. Jones (ed.), *New Cambridge Medieval History*, vol. VI (Cambridge: Cambridge University Press, 2008), 124–154, 152–153.

Table 10.1 *Territoriality, personality and the English Case (Bartolus ad C.1.1.1, nu. 42)*

	Property in England	**Property in Italy**
Statute *in rem*		
Statute *in personam*	Defunct is English	
	Defunct is not English	

Primogeniture rules applies (English law)

Property divided among sons (*Ius commune* / Italian law)

In fact, the only additional case that Bartolus could have conceivably chipped away from the primogeniture rule concerns the instance in which a foreign (non-English) decedent had left English property and the English statute was *in rem*. It would not be very realistic for someone like Bartolus to expect that *ius commune* could apply over this kind of cases, given that they were likely to involve feudal lands and thus be of direct interest to the English polity. One possibility would be to limit derogation from the *ius commune* to only English subjects: this would however be a reduction of local autonomy that would fly in the face of actual practice and the entire discussion about the reach of statutes and customs (and it would not be very effective, anyway, given that by definition a feudal vassal was a subject of his liege with regard to his feudal holdings). The second possibility would be to assert a proto-bilateral personalist rule, something like "the rights of heirs will be determined under the law of the place of origin." This was actually proposed by Albericus, although with no reference to primogeniture or allusion to feudal lands. Such a solution however would by itself create more problems in Italy than it would solve. It should thus have been accompanied by an argument that the primogeniture rule violated Italian *ordre public* with regard to property in Italy. Such a technique clearly does not exist in the world of Bartolus, who may have been occasionally using "bilateral" rules but did not conceptualize them as such (not, in any case, when he forms the question as opposing *ius commune* to local law). Bartolus did not possess the doctrinal consciousness of a conflicts lawyer that would be necessary to attempt what we have come to think of as legal characterization and *ordre public.*

Be that as it may, what Bartolus is doing does serve functions similar to both legal characterization and the *ordre public.* We have shown how beneath his distinction between *circa rem* and *circa personam* lies a very rudimentary – but still substance-based – exercise in legal characterization. Moreover, the results reached are not unlike the effects of a modern-day invocation of the *ordre public* exception to the application of foreign law.

While on the surface this may appear different from conflicts doctrine, it operates in a similar way. Aside from the – conscious or unconscious – bias of many conflicts lawyers vis-à-vis the policies of their homeland, it is reminiscent of the way in which governmental interest-analysis sought to reduce conflicts by narrowly defining what kind of cases the foreign state wanted to regulate. The way in which Bartolus instantly kills the question of extraterritoriality in the many cases when the statute may be *in rem* also reminds us of the "false conflicts" doctrine and the legitimation of forum law's application.

We could thus interpret the Bartolan rule as a way to mitigate the effect of the primogeniture rule, especially with regard to Italy. It is clear that Bartolus does not like the rule, and, in fact, this seems to have been the majority opinion in his time. But Bartolus's solution manages to limit the effect of the primogeniture rule more than either of the existing solutions that Bartolus mentions: the solution favored by the *ultramontani* would have also prevented the application of the English rule in France/Italy but would acknowledge that English law would apply over a deceased Italian's property in England. It would moreover lead to different succession arrangements in all situations where property was situated in both places, whereas the solution that Bartolus advocated would spare such a decisional dissonance in at least some of the instances where an Italian also has property in England. The other proposed solutions – which were advanced generically for succession cases – appear at first to be providing a unitary solution for all property but would probably fail upon closer inspection: it is not even certain that the *origo* of the defunct, or the place of *aditio* could be easily established without contestation in all cases. Their application across the board would create practical and possibly political problems.

The Bartolan solution should also be contrasted with the one by his student Baldus, who in his discussion of permissive statutes brings up the similar case of a baron dying leaving "many castles" in both France and

Lombardy.[59] Baldus distinguishes depending on whether or not there has been a testament by which the baron named his first-born as sole heir. If such a testament was made validly under the *ius commune*, the first-born will inherit all castles in both France and Lombardy.[60] If the testament was made validly under French law, then it will produce effects as to property in France but not in Lombardy, which means that the first-born will inherit all castles in France and all brothers will share equally in the Lombardian castles.[61] If now there was no testament, Baldus, after briefly considering the solutions discussed by Bartolus, would still argue for the same solution on the grounds of a tacit testament and this being a matter of acquiring property and not regarding a person: primogeniture for the property in France, according to customary law and equality of succession in Lombardy under the *ius commune*.[62]

Bartolus, of course, makes no mention of testaments but given Roman law such a testament would be valid.[63] So the real questions regard intestate succession. Baldus presents to us a concrete case – case, which might actually have happened: he speaks of "castles" in both France and Lombardy. Baldus states that this matter concerns the acquisition of property, not persons, and, in all probability, the French custom would be regarded as *in rem* under Bartolan doctrine. Moreover, Baldus does not allow the French customary rule of primogeniture to govern succession into the Lombardy castles. So Baldus and Bartolus appear to be reaching the same solutions on this specific case and its variations.[64] Their difference lies in that, even if we can safely assume that Bartolus has in mind feudal lands in the Western kingdoms, Bartolus is addressing a more general situation that could involve any kind of property in either England or Italy. The real question would be whether Baldus would have his solution also apply in a different, for example non-feudal, factual setting. Both Bartolus and Baldus would apply the local rule over a

[59] Baldus ad C.1.1.1, nus. 84–86.

[60] Ibid., nu. 85.

[61] Ibid.

[62] Ibid., nu. 86: "*Venio ad secundum, scilicet ad successionem intestate. Et videtur quod idem quod in testament, nam qui non testatur expresse, videtur tacite testari. In contrarium, quia hic non agitur de persona, sed de acquisitione: ideo debet inspici locus rerum acquirendarum.*"

[63] Baldus actually discusses the validity of a statute permitting the first born to inherit excluding all others: ibid., nu. 84.

[64] Ibid., noting that on this point his opinion is shared (*hanc partem tenant*) by Gulielmus, Cinus, and Bartolus.

foreigner on the basis of that rule being *in rem*, but Bartolus seems to require further examination, whereas Baldus seems to have settled the matter more completely: acquisition of property is a matter to be dealt with under the law of the place where such acquisition takes place. The fiction of intestate succession being a tacit testament further supports this notion.

In his discussion on the English case, Bartolus himself is more skeptical of analogies to contracts, for example dismissing the idea that to look to the law of the place where inheritance is vested is similar to looking to the law of the place of contracting.[65] In a way, Bartolus's invocation of the words of the statute is a way to turn the legislator against those who advocated extraterritoriality by analogy to *locus regit actum*, by turning the legislator against them.

Bartolus's solution was perhaps too modern for its time. It was not much followed by his immediate successors, as we saw, and it had its own share of inherent potential problems.[66] It was eventually reduced to the literalist mutation subsequent conflicts lawyers came to know and abhor. But the notion of legislative positivism Bartolus articulated did survive. It seems that the Bartolan primogeniture rule played right in the middle of a neglected tension among preclassical conflicts lawyers. The tension pitted, on the one hand, a "scholarly" sensibility which tried to come up with abstract criteria to divide types of statutes on the basis of the subject matter they treated, against, on the other hand, a "positivist" sensibility which paid closer attention to the word of the statutes and the intention of the lawmaker. The first tendency is represented by most famous preclassical writers, including Huber. We may see the second tendency reflect in Johannes Voet, but it must have been most prominent among precisely those people who decided – or wrote upon – conflicts cases without developed ideas.[67]

Bartolus uses a textual positivist argument most clearly in two instances. First, during his discussion of whether a statute making a *spurius* an heir has extraterritorial effects.[68] This and the subsequent

[65] Bartolus ad C.1.1.1, nu. 43.

[66] Forsyth, *Private International Law*, 38 points to this as the "deeper [flaw]" in Bartolus's "arbitrary" solution: "If . . . the legislator, who fixed the word order, could decide whether a statute was real, personal, or mixed . . . then there was nothing inherent in the nature of the statute which determined which category it fell into; it was a matter of the legislator's whim, i.e. the very basis of the theory came tumbling down."

[67] See Section 14.4.

[68] Bartolus ad C.1.1.1, nu. 41.

discussion of the primogeniture rule are the two legs of the Bartolan discussion of the extraterritorial effects of permissive statutes pertaining to a person's capacity (with a view principally to inheritance). Bartolus goes at great lengths to deny such extraterritoriality (e.g. when he claims that emancipation pertains to "form" and legitimation to "substance"), but first he tries to limit the number of "conflicts" by noting that "[a] provision in general terms can only be understood as referring to possessions in the territory of the providing authority."[69]

Second, when he urges that the words of the punitive statute be more "diligently examined."[70] Bartolus essentially lets the citizen be punished under a statute that refers to his conduct "even outside the territory" and points to the possibility of the statute limiting itself to conduct inside the territory. In the likely case when the statute is in general terms, Bartolus in effect denies the statute extraterritorial effect (he allows it for procedural issues, but that was essential and does not include sentencing). We shall return to this case in Section 10.3.

10.3 Bartolus and the Limits of Unilateralism

Bartolus and the Italian school are widely credited with the introduction of the so-called unilateral conflictual method or perhaps better the unilateral approach to the conflict of laws. Parallels are often drawn between the "unilateralism" of preclassical doctrine and the unilateral approaches, or instincts, of modern conflicts approaches. A few authors conversely credit Bartolus with using the division of statutes "multilaterally to determine whether a foreign statute would be applied within the forum."[71] But the image of Bartolan doctrine that has registered into historical consciousness is best captured in the following passage:

> Bartolus introduced the "unilateral" conflictual method, as distinguished from the "bilateral" conflictual method which was developed later in history.
>
> The bilateral method postulates a system of *a priori* choice-of-law rules that designate the cases that fall within the scope of domestic and foreign law, respectively. In contrast, Bartolus' unilateral method approaches the matter from the other end. It focuses on the conflicting domestic and

[69] Ibid.

[70] Ibid., nu. 48.

[71] Forsyth, *Private International Law*, 37 who regards this as "Bartolus's greatest contribution to private international law."

> foreign laws themselves and tries to determine whether the case at hand falls within the intended scope of the one or the other law.[72]

The careful examination of the *repetitio* has unveiled elements and even norms that could be claimed as evidence of a "unilateral" or a "multilateral" approach but it has also revealed a much more complicated doctrinal edifice to which we must return.

The very opening of our text seems to lead us to an easy answer. On the face of it, both questions into which the original has been divided are phrased in unilateral terms of looking into the scope of legislation: on the one hand, "whether the statute extends to non-subjects" and, on the other, "whether the effect of the statute extends beyond the territory of those who set it down."[73] From a modern point of view, this would indeed appear a unilateralist approach. Yet on the very same page, once Bartolus starts examining his subject matter, he proposes what would to modern eyes appear as a multilateral system of rules. Especially his first section, on contracts, presents us with a veritable system of aprioristic and multilateral rules, but in fact, the first four sections all begin with a hypothetical case in which a foreigner acts in a way that has legal consequences under the laws of the local jurisdiction, triggering the question "of what place should the statutes be observed or looked to?"[74] The question is asked primarily from the perspective of the local jurisdiction.[75] Yet the answer sought aims at designating the applicable law in all cases.[76] We must look to the second part, which addresses extraterritoriality properly speaking, for an actual "unilateralist" discussion with little evidence of *a priori* multilateral rules: whereas sections in the first part were organized on the basis of legal subject matter, in the second part sections were organized on the basis of a typology of the effects of statutes.

Things are more complicated once we examine more carefully the entire text. To begin with, we cannot view the second part in isolation from the first, or vice versa: there is an evident *interaction* between them, with the perspective and some of the issues discussed in the second part

[72] Symeonides et al., *Conflict of Laws*, 8.

[73] Bartolus ad C.1.1.1, nu. 13.

[74] Ibid.

[75] See e.g. ibid., nu. 21 ("Second, I ask what about delicts. If a foreigner does a wrong here, shall he be punished according to the statutes of this city?").

[76] Cf. Barry, "Bartolus," 2: ". . . and asks whether the laws of that jurisdiction govern the case."

complementing those of the first part. We will thus examine as a whole, first (at 10.3.1), the discussion of succession, which involves prohibitive and permissive statutes, in the third, fifth and sixth section and, second (at 10.3.2), the discussion of wrongs, which involves punitive statutes, in the second and eighth section.

Our last preliminary consideration concerns the vantage point of Bartolus. Whom is he addressing himself to? Are we supposed to think of him as writing from the point of view of his adopted homeland, Perugia? From the point of view of another, generic Italian city-state or even more generally any Medieval polity? Or is he discussing things from a higher altitude – from the point of view of the legal fiction that is the Roman Empire of the *ius commune*?

There can be no simple answer. Bartolus makes multiple references to Perugia, as well as nearby localities, and draws several examples from Perugian legislation. But this could well be nothing more than a teacher's use of "local" examples in order to make the topic under discussion more understandable and more accessible to students. Medieval law professors faced the task of proving their practical relevancy to their world – including students from all over Western Europe – and frequently used local examples to that purpose: given where Accursius taught, it is no accident that it is a Bolognese who is spared the application of Modenese law in the Accursian gloss. Commentators like Bartolus were even more explicit about the importance of their local settings; this was, after all, one of the major things that differentiates them from the glossators. On the other hand, a quick comparison of Bartolus with Huber regarding the geographical localization of cases and examples contained in each, can be revealing as to what truly constitutes a localist sensibility. Huber's native province of Frisia is the *forum* in almost all eighteen cases mentioned in his text. In contrast, Bartolus includes several cases in which Perugia plays no role, but which are of practical interest not only to his students or to Perugian statesmen, but also to his broader audience.[77] Several hypotheticals have no apparent local connection to a specific city. In some, we know from other sources that legislation in Perugia may provide the background for the example, but similar legislation had been passed in many other cities. Even in many of the cases where there

[77] See e.g. Bartolus ad C.1.1.1, nu. 22 (number of witnesses required for a testament to be valid under Venice law; and validity of that latter under the *ius commune*) and nu. 51 (forfeiture of goods by the papal representative in the March of Ancona and its effects in the Duchy of Spoleto (neighboring to Perugia, see Map 2).

appears to be some connection to Perugia, it can only be assumed that these cases are supposed to end up in the courts of Perugia. The English case would probably have little practical interest for Italian lawyers but should present significant interest for those embarking upon a career in France, England, or Northern Europe.

I would suggest that Bartolan thought can be characterized as *hierarchical* and *pragmatic*. Bartolus addressed himself to the magistrates, in order to explain to them a system put in place from above, by a higher authority.

10.3.1 Permissive and Punitive Statutes

The complex system of Bartolus is most evident in his discussion of prohibitive and permissive statutes, in the sixth and seventh sections from the second part of the *repetitio*. These sections – which regard primarily statutes pertaining to succession and personal status, of relevance to succession – must be read together with the third section from the first part. As already noted, there was a proliferation of statutes (as well as customs) in Italian city-states that derogated from the *ius commune*: some restricted and some granted rights or status to classes of persons; some removed and some imposed additional formalities.[78] Beyond Italy, legal divergence was even more noticeable: the English primogeniture rule is very telling in this regard.

Bartolus approaches the entire matter primarily in terms of derogation from the *ius commune*. This is especially evident in the beginning of the third section, when the very validity of such a statute is debated at length.[79] The conclusion that Bartolus reaches, i.e. that such statutes apply to citizens in the city's territory, holds for all such statutes. It must nonetheless be noted that this a statute about solemnity requirements, indeed about *relaxing* solemnity requirements: of all kinds of statutes to be examined in these sections, these are the ones that will merit the most favorable treatment. Bartolus can now consider whether such statutes extend to foreigners. The answer is that statutes pertaining to the solemnity of testaments shall apply, unless they expressly exclude foreigners from their scope – a logical exception and the first referral to legislative intent or wording. As to statutes pertaining to status – Bartolus mentions here legitimation, emancipation, and excluding a man's wife from

[78] See Section 9.3.

[79] Ibid., nus. 22–23. See Section 7.4.3.

heirship – they shall apply only if they are dealing with solemnities.[80] In the end, everyone in the city may make testaments, emancipate, or legitimate their children under the same solemnity requirements but the *ius commune* continues to govern the status and heirship rights of *forenses*.

Once we move outside the city's territory, Bartolus employs the concept of prohibitive and permissive statutes to deal with the extraterritorial effects of these statutes. Again, in both cases, we begin with solemnities. It is clear than in both the case of the city imposing an additional solemnity requirement (*prohibitive statute*) and the case of the city removing a solemnity requirement (*permissive statute*) the local law shall apply to legal acts made inside the city's territory but shall not apply to legal acts made outside the city's territory. It is also expressly stated that legal acts made inside the city's *territorium* in the solemnity allowed by its permissive statute shall have effect everywhere: this appears like a multilateral rule.[81] But what about legal acts made inside the city's territorium in conformity to the solemnity required by the *ius commune* but not the city's prohibitive statute? This is obviously a far less likely eventuality than the former case, in which Bartolus is evidently interested. A doctrine that takes *locus regit actum* seriously would answer that such an act may not produce effect anywhere, but some would acknowledge legal effect to legal acts made by their forum's citizens abroad in conformity with the forum's formality requirements even if not in conformity with the requirements of the place where such an act was made.[82]

If we now move to statutes dealing with "substantive" provisions, we see Bartolus employing another distinction that cuts across both permissive and prohibitive statutes, i.e. the distinction between statutes providing as to the property (*in rem, circa rem*) and statutes providing as to the person (*in personam, circa personam*). Statutes *in rem* cannot have extraterritorial effect. As to statutes in *personam*, Bartolus denies extraterritorial effect both to permissive statutes *circa personam* and to "burdensome" (*odiosa*) prohibitive statutes *in personam*. The only exception concerns "favorable" (*favorablia*) prohibitive statutes in personam. That is, the only local law with extraterritorial effect would be those statutes or customs preventing a class of persons from taking actions that could be

[80] Ibid., nu. 26.

[81] Ibid., nu. 37.

[82] See Section 14.2 for an example of such debate within the Dutch school.

to their detriment: Minors under a certain age from making a testament, spouses from making donations or legacies to each other.

In his discussion of permissive statutes under the English case, Bartolus makes another referral to legislative intent. In all other instances of referral to the words of the statute, we are meant to consider if the legislators had set themselves the scope of their statute, similarly to instances of limited unilateralism: the words would perform a choice-of-law function without going into substance. In the English case, Bartolus's referral calls us to interpret the substantive rule in order to determine whether it should be classified as in rem or in personam.

From the point of view of modern conflicts doctrine, we could even argue that Bartolus seems to weigh the foreign law and its claims to applicability: the scope of the English rule will be determined by the intention of the rule itself. This is reminiscent of modern unilateralism in the sense of Quadri and Gothot, where the foreign law is let to determine the applicability of its own law as a way of reducing the number of real conflicts.[83] The difference is that the Bartolan conflicts are triangular, of sorts: the *ius commune* is the law of the one of the two cities, but also a common vocabulary and the source of the residual substantive rules.

10.3.2 Punitive Statutes and Unilateralism

Another interesting case involves the second section, on delicts/wrongs, taken together with the eighth, on punitive statutes. Both sections address criminal offenses, and thus matters that would today fall outside the conflict of laws and be in any case treated by a unilateral "conflicts" approach. Many of the solutions that Bartolus gives evoke comparisons with modern international-law doctrines of prescriptive jurisdiction, which by definition have a strong unilateralist dimension.[84]

In fact, the second section seems to be deviating from the "multilateral" approach of the first part and to follow modern ideas about the criminal liability of foreign residents. The discussion here is not unlike discussions in modern criminal law as to when a foreigner is criminally

[83] See Gothot, "Le renouveau," 3; see also Section 4.3.1.

[84] One may compare, for example, the limited instances in which a foreigner may be punished for conduct abroad against a citizen as well as the city's power over its own citizens abroad in Bartolus ad C.1.1.1, nu. 35 with *Restatement (Fourth) on Foreign Relations Law*, §§ 410–412 (active/passive personality, protective principle) and possibly § 413 (the prosecution of shipwreck has echoes of universal jurisdiction).

liable or excused the ignorance of law. The decisive factor seems to be the foreigner's awareness, as measured against objective standards: prohibition by the *ius commune*, long stay in the city, prohibition common in many cities. It is noted that the personal law of the foreigner does not come into the equation. More remarkable is that, rather than the superior law we have seen in previous discussions, the *ius commune* is here reduced to a standard. On the other hand, Bartolus is less forum-minded than modern "unilateral" approaches to criminal jurisdiction over foreigners: local law operates within a common legal environment shared with other cities as well as the *ius commune*. The matter continues in the eighth section and the case of a – possibly capital – offense allegedly committed by a citizen outside the city's territory. Bartolus seemingly takes a middle-of-the-road approach that allows the application of city law to some but not all cases and combines unilateral and multilateral norms.[85] At the first stage, he calls for the "words of the statute" to be "more diligently examined," in order to see if the statute was actually intended to cover (or *not* to cover) such conduct by the citizen – this is a unilateral approach, but, in a way, it is similar to the limited unilateralism of *lois de police*. What is more interesting is what happens if the statute is expressed "in general terms," in which case Bartolus would refer, as to the "manner of punishment," to either the *ius commune* or the law of the place where the offense was committed. The second possibility looks like a multilateral rule: encouraged by Bartolus's justification of it, some may even be tempted to see in this an early example of the *lex loci delicti commissi* rule.[86]

Tempting as such an anachronism would be, it would be more fruitful to consider the case in context. It would appear that the issue had been the subject of a heated debate among jurists, as it went to the heart – and involved the very foundations – of a city's political power: Bartolus indeed devotes considerable space to presenting the arguments of both sides.[87] His own solution would enable the city law to apply in most cases. In fact, the city legislation derogating from the *ius commune* would produce effects only in three out of the six possible cases distinguished by Bartolus (see Table 10.2). In two more cases – i.e. when the statute

[85] See Bartolus ad C.1.1.1, nu. 48: if local statute expresses itself in general terms, either the *ius commune* or the law of the place where the offense took place (*lex loci delicti commissi* in modern terms) will be applied.

[86] Ibid.

[87] Ibid., nu. 47 and discussion in Sections 7.5.3 and 8.4.3.4.

Table 10.2 *Effects of punitive statutes over wrongs committed outside the city's territory (Bartolus ad C.1.1.1, nu. 48)*

Object of the Statute	Statute expressly covering the case	Statute expressed in general terms	Statute expressly limited to what happens inside the territory
"the process or the institution of litigation" (*statuta quae respiciunt processum seu litis ordinationem*)			
"the substance of the case" (*statuta quae respiciunt litis decisionem*)			

Statute applies

by consent of local legislation

by default

by default, unless city applies the *ius proprium* in the place of the offense

Ius commune applies

expressly limited its scope to wrongs committed inside the territory – *ius commune* will apply because the city statute expressly allows it to apply. This appears like a remarkable reversal of the Medieval hierarchy of laws, where it is the *ius commune* that allows or empowers local legislation and sets its limits. In modern conflicts doctrine, this could be regarded as an example of a unilateral conflicts norm (and, as suggested, the same could be said about the two cases on the left-hand column where the city has defined more expansively the scope of its own statute). From yet another point of view, however, what Bartolus is actually doing here is to identify a "false conflict." This allows him to limit controversy to the middle-column cases where the statute is expressed "in general terms." Having reached this point, Bartolus employs the tool of distinguishing procedural from substantive matters: as a result, city law would apply in the fifth case, which includes his actual example of a statute granting the *podestà* the power to inquire without requiring an accusation. In the sixth and final case, – which concerns a matter pertaining to the substance of the case – we also observe a conditional application of the *ius commune*: presumably, if the law of the place where the offense was committed is more similar to the city's own legislation than the *ius commune* (for example, both make a criminal offense out of an action not punishable under the *ius commune*), that law will be looked to, which would in effect allow the city to punish the act in a manner possibly similar to what is prescribed in its own inapplicable legislation.

10.3.3 An a priori Unilateralism?

The "unilateralism" of Bartolus is one that seeks to limit the unilateral expansion of the forum's law. Just like proponents of interest-analysis, Bartolus seeks to locate "false conflicts," but unlike them, he is not concerned with expanding thus the jurisdiction of the forum: the result is the return of the residual law, the *ius commune*.[88] Bartolus has, moreover, no concept of "false conflicts," partly for epistemological and partly for practical reasons, including the existence of this "residual" and superior body of law.

One of the underlying concerns of unilateralism is to prevent evasion of local legislation. In the examination of Huber that follows, we will see his effort to manage such concerns within his multilateralist system of actus territorialism.[89] In contrast, we can only identify one such case in the *repetitio*: the possibility of someone acquiring personal status in a more liberal city and then returning to the forum to inherit. That case is

[88] In several instances – notably the statute allowing a *spurius* to inherit – Bartolus does not acknowledge extraterritorial effects to statutes we know his adopted city to have promulgated, which derogate from the *ius commune*.

[89] See Chapter 14.

dealt with not by creating an escape mechanism from the general rule, but by not granting any extraterritorial effect to statutes enabling this change in status.[90]

We still have to deal with the first part's aprioristic consideration of the possibility of foreign law to govern an action that occurred within the forum's territory. The approach in itself is not surprising: it is justifiable to distinguish between the two questions as a matter of conceptualization, but to address the former one has also to consider the latter. This is especially so when the author is as mindful of the *ius commune* and preoccupied with assigning one and only solution to each case as Bartolus in this instance. Nonetheless, a unilateralist's job could be quite well done by discussing the limitations that the *ius commune* imposes to the reach of Perugia's statutes.

Even though Bartolus is, for the most part, still quite far from the paradigm of bilateral *a priori* choice-of-law rules, he does not seem to offer a good example of a unilateralist. He seems, on the contrary, both committed to "universal" jurisprudence and quite reliant on a methodological eclecticism so as to carry out his commitment. Moreover, the "interface" we referred to above makes it difficult to determine what is aprioristic and multilateral and what is unilateral.

We would in any case talk of *principled unilateralism*: it is possible for all cities to apply the choice-of-law rules that Bartolus indicates, leading to legal harmony; it could even be suggested that Bartolus writes with a view to all cities applying his rules.

10.4 Bartolus and the Conflict of Sovereignties

Medieval scholarship has been a recurring presence in classical and modern attempts to conceptualize private international law in terms of either a conflict between opposing conceptions of sovereignty, or of a paradigm shift from public-law considerations ("conflict of sovereignties") to private-law ones ("conflict of interests"). In these narratives, Bartolus and the Italian school have been presented alternatively as epitomizing the focus of early conflicts doctrine toward sovereignty and the political discussion, or as early examples of a less formalist approach to conflicts issues focusing on substantive justice.[91] Our own extensive

[90] Bartolus ad C.1.1.1, nu. 39.

[91] See Chapter 4.

examination has found evidence to support both perspectives but also shown the limits of such conceptions.

It must be noted that the term sovereignty does not exist in Bartolus's world, but it is also true that the concept of *iurisdictio* was employed in a manner foreboding the discussions on sovereignty of subsequent centuries. Much of Bartolan conflicts doctrine is laid out in terms of territorial competences allocated, and occasionally wrested, from above; it could even be argued that both in advocating the universal respect of acts made validly within the city's territory and in refusing to recognize extraterritorial effect in certain other statutes, especially the ones altering personal status, Bartolus outlines notions of territorial sovereignty. The roots of sovereignty over persons are also to be found in his text, where the terms *subditus* (subject), *cives* (citizen), and *forenses* (foreigner) appear frequently. However, we are far away from the Romantic notions of nineteenth-century personalism.[92] The way in which Bartolus draws the distinction between form and substance has to do less with sovereignty and more with the pursuance of justice. Bartolus is indeed mindful of the territorial competences of polities, but a close examination of his doctrinal discussion and rules must have shown that his decisions as to the scope of statutes are often motivated by substantive considerations and value choices.

For an example of how Bartolus combines both political/hierarchical and "private-law" arguments we need look no further than the discussion, notably with regard to the number of witnesses to a testament, about when can a local statute derogate from the *ius commune* have effect: having established the power of at least some cities to enact such legislation on the basis of a tacit consent by the Emperor, Bartolus argues that the statute should stand even if the Emperor did not know anything about it, "for many reasons best known to the citizens living there."[93] This is the proverbial *privatiste* argument for legal diversity: the local rule addresses better local needs and should be let to stand. A similar argument is also employed when Bartolus explains why it is in principle

[92] One would be tempted to contrast the romantic nineteenth-century allusions to the biological links between the individual temperament and national laws to the Bartolan metaphor of the punishment following the person everywhere like leprosy. See Bartolus ad C.1.1.1, nu. 50.

[93] Bartolus ad D.1.3.32, nu. 28 (expanded version of Bartolus ad C.1.1.1, nu. 22), as translated in Clarence Smith, "Bartolo," 169. Bartolus is here arguing against the suggestion that the said custom is "impudent and bad."

possible for someone to die testate in some places and intestate in other places.[94]

Another set of examples comes from those cases where Bartolus directs us to look to the wording of the statute so as to determine its scope. On the face of it, this would appear as an example of legislative positivism and a defense – or acknowledgment – of the "sovereignty" of the forum's legislator, but the effect of Bartolus's solution in both cases is to reduce the number of "real" conflicts.[95]

In conclusion, the skepticism expressed almost from the outset as to the applicability of such schemes to Medieval doctrine is corroborated by our historical examination. Bartolus, for example, could be *prima facie* classified under either paradigm; but a closer look makes it difficult, if not useless, to classify him as such. Allowing for the little that such distinctions meant to him, he seems to be giving emphasis to the "private law" character of the legal subject matter but he is also mindful of the political impact of his solutions. In the end, Bartolan conflicts doctrine is about "sovereignty" – the external as well as internal sovereignty of the cities, the "sovereignty" of the empire, or at least its law – just as it is about private law. It is impossible to separate political and substantive argument pragmatic considerations in the argumentation of his text.

10.5 Conclusion

Bartolus emerges from our examination as a very complex doctrinal writer, whose legacy has been misjudged. In modern historical consciousness, he is often credited with the contributions of others to conflicts doctrine: he is presented as having been the first to anchor the doctrinal treatment of conflicts issues onto *cunctos populos* (considering the criticism this choice has received by some, this was not always a compliment!). Subsequent ideas have also been read into his text. At the same time, we have seen that his own doctrine is often presented in unfair or simplistic terms. On the whole, these misreadings have obscured the true genius of Bartolus, which lay in exploration, analysis, and synthesis.

Three notable cases of misreading stand out. First, the belief that Bartolus invented the division between real and personal statutes does not hold. Second, Bartolus has been unjustly condemned on his treatment of the primogeniture case. These two misconceptions are

[94] Bartolus ad C.1.1.1, nu. 41.
[95] See Sections 10.2.3 and 10.3.2.

connected: Subsequent writers understood what Bartolus wrote as a *mechanical* rule and then many presented that mechanical rule as a key, or even the general, idea of Bartolan system. Third, Bartolus was not the unilateralist commonly alleged.

Our inspection of the *repetitio* has shown Bartolus pursuing the art of distinction between statutes, including the distinction between statutes *circa rem* and statutes *circa personam*. But these terms are not the same as *statuta realia* and *statuta personalia*: they consider the object of the statute, toward which its immediate effects are directed. Classification of a statute as real or as personal would be a subsequent step, even if Bartolus lays its foundations. In any case, this classification does not constitute the general principle of Bartolan conflicts doctrine and the suggestion that the structure of the *repetitio* can be explained on the basis of a territorial/personal division has not withstood scrutiny.

We noted above that Bartolus makes no clear distinction between real/territorial and personal/extraterritorial statutes – unlike the classic "statutists," who provided their readers with some introduction elaborating a definition of "personal," "real," and "mixed" statutes and expressing their preferences or presumptions. Such an introduction is nowhere to be found in Bartolus, who never gives a definition, or a simple criterion, as to what would make a statute "real" or "personal," including his misunderstood solution in the English case. In fact, rather than establishing a mechanical rule, the proper interpretation of Bartolus on the English case shows him concerned with the function of the norms in question and their normative impact across territories. Bartolus emerges from our inspection too preoccupied with identifying problems and elaborating a system of solutions that could satisfy both private needs and the governance of polities for him to propound a "theory of statutes" in the style of d'Argentré or the Voets.

In the end, Bartolus is still a "theoretical" writer, in the sense used by Dicey: he believes that there is a "common law" defining the reach of statutes and he tries to clarify it.[96] But he is a different sort of "theoretical" writer: his system is a pluralist one, and it still relies on the statutes themselves. This last aspect of his work allows his system to be used by positive jurists. Bartolus himself did use positivist arguments upon occasion, in order to achieve what he regarded as the proper solution to certain problems.

[96] Dicey, *Digest*, 15 ff (discussed at Section 15.6).

This brings us to the question of Bartolus's unilateralism. This is a complicated question, not least because it imports anachronistic terms into a discourse different than the classical/modern ones.

Most of the cases discussed in the *repetitio* are phrased in terms of city statutes introducing additions or modifications to the *ius commune*, such as making punishable an act not heretofore punished, imposing a different penalty, and imposing or softening a requirement of form/solemnity (e.g. the number of witnesses required for a testament). The answer given to these questions resembles a "unilateralist" technique – except that the *unum latus* also appears as a subordinate entity, and that the "unilateralist" answer usually pits local law against the *ius commune*, and very seldom local law against foreign local law.

At the same time, Bartolus also uses bilateral techniques, especially in his section on contracts – tellingly, the area of subject matter with the most sophisticated treatment. To some, this could indicate an evolutionary narrative, in which increased sophistication leads to bilateralization. Without rejecting this, a more compelling reason may be that the conflicts of the first section pit local law divergent from the *ius commune* against local law – a law that is also divergent from the *ius commune.*

The "bilateral" part of the Bartolan conflicts treatment, and especially its seamless connection to the "unilateral" part, tends to corroborate the argument made above: the conflicts of the *ius commune* with the local law are to Bartolus more than just a conflict between the national or imperial and the local. We spoke of a "triangulation" between the *ius commune* and the legal systems of the two cities. In the bilateral conflicts, the triangle is obvious. In "unilateral" conflicts, one of the two local laws aligns with the *ius commune*, although on occasion – notably with regard to punitive statutes – two or more local laws may align with each other in opposition to the *ius commune.*

In sum, Bartolus is unilateralist when the conflict can be phrased in terms of derogation from the "common law," and bilateralist when the conflict can be phrased in terms of selecting one of two rules, both derogating from the *ius commune.* In both cases, the reach of the local rules is judged from above, the "external" system of the *ius commune.* In the former case, the *ius commune* intervenes directly, opposing or permitting the extension of the local rule – it is both a rival to the local rule and a meta-system, an imperfect meta-system. In the latter case, the *ius commune* acts the part proper to a meta-system.

All this makes Bartolus more exotic, but also closer to contemporary conflicts lawyers than we normally imagine. His conflicts "system" uses premises alien to the modern lawyer (such as the *ius commune*), as well as principles and approaches that even our eclectic, "modern" plain disciplinary consciousness tends to regard as contradictory: these and other considerations may make us doubt if Bartolus is really talking about the same things that we do, and which we want him to talk about. On the other hand, we do share a certain affinity with Bartolus, and we cannot fail to observe that he engaged in patterns and processes of construction and justification which many others have since repeated.

PART IV

Ulrik Huber and Conflict of Laws in the Early Modern Period

11

"*Saepe fit, ut negotia*": Huber on the Conflict of Laws

11.1 Introduction

Ulric Huber or *Ulricus Huberus* (1636–1694) was a scholar, judge, and statesman of the Dutch "Golden Age" who published widely on law and on politics, in both Latin and the vernacular.[1] His work on private law has lived through in South African Roman-Dutch law, whereas his contribution to constitutional theory and public law is noted by legal historians.[2] A modern authority on Roman-Dutch law even claims that "[n]ext to Hugo Grotius [Huber] was probably the greatest, as he was certainly the most prolific Dutch jurist."[3]

Huber is however best remembered today for his relative short treatment of conflict of laws issues, included within his broader systematic work on the Roman law as applied in the United Provinces. In the words of Armand Lainé, these "ten pages" of Huber's conflicts treatment "have had as much weight as ten volumes."[4] *Dicey & Morrris* present him to

[1] On Huber see M. Hewett, *Ulric Huber (1636–1694): De ratione juris docendi & discendi diatribe per modum dialogi* (Nijmegen: Gerard Noodt Instituut, 2010), 79–99; T. J. Veen, *Recht en nut: Studien over en naar aanleiding van Ulrik Huber (1636–1694)* (Zwolle: Tjeenk Willink, 1976), also containing "Historia Vitae Mea vernacule scripta ob certam rationem," the short memoirs by Huber on his deathbed.

[2] See e.g. C. Link, *Herrschaftsordnung und bürgerliche Freiheit* (Vienna: Böhlau, 1979), 44; H. Mohnhaupt, "Von den 'leges fundamentales' zur modernen Verfassung in Europa: Zum begriffs- und dogmengeschichtlichen Befund (16.-18. Jahrhundert)" in H. Mohnhaupt (ed.), *Historische Vergleichung im Bereich vom Staat und Recht* (Frankfurt: Vittorio Klostermann, 2000), 35–72, 41, 62; A. W. G. Raath, "Aspects of Ulrich Huber's Theory of Universal Public Law and Post-Constitutional Contracting," *Tydskrif vir Hedendaagse Romeins-Hollandse Reg*, 75 (2012), 206–222 (and works cited therein, especially in n. 4).

[3] Percival Gane, "Note on the Author," xix, in his translation of Huber's *Heedensdaegse Rechtsgeleertheyt*.

[4] Lainé, *Introduction*, 2:96.

have been as influential to English law as Savigny and Story.[5] Symeon Symeonides goes as far as to credit him with being the first to use the term "conflict of laws."[6] Some modern scholars have even claimed to trace Huber's influence on Latin American law.[7] That may not be very likely (any such affinities must be through the impact of the work of subsequent scholars such as Joseph Story who were themselves influenced by Huber). What is clear is that Huber certainly found resonance, first with Lord Mansfield and other eighteenth-century British jurists, and then with the lawyers in the North American British colonies, which became independent soon thereafter but maintained the English common law they had inherited.[8] Huber thus became connected to the construction of Anglo-American conflict of laws on both sides of the Atlantic Ocean. A half-century later, Joseph Story would – justly – proclaim that Huber had "hitherto possessed an undisputed preference on this subject over other continental jurists, as well in England as in America."[9]

Important as the legacy of Huber has been for Anglo-American conflict of laws, there appears to be little evidence of Huber's influence on the European Continent, with regard either to the late preclassical conflicts doctrine of the eighteenth and early nineteenth century or, especially, to the classical conflicts doctrine that emerged in the second half of the nineteenth century and completed the transformation of our field from a method of legal interpretation to an autonomous discipline. Story himself admitted that in Continental Europe Huber "is not so often spoken of, except by jurists belonging to the Dutch school."[10] Even in the

[5] Collins, *Dicey, Morris & Collins on the Conflict of Laws*, 14. Cf Maeb Harding, *Conflict of Laws*, 4th ed (2014), 10: "Ulricus Huber, a seventeenth-century jurist, laid down three principles which came to be regarded as the basis for the English system of the conflict of laws."

[6] Symeonides, *American Private International Law*, 15.

[7] See H. Grigera Náon, "Huber and Contractual Choice-of-Law in the Argentine Civil Code," *Netherlands International Law Review*, 39 (1992), 195–207; V. Matteo et al., "Dutch Threads in a Uruguayan Tapestry," *Netherlands International Law Review*, 39 (1992), 209–227.

[8] See in this regard Watson, *Comity of Errors*. Watson regards as the principal reason for Huber's appeal to British judges the familiarity with his work of the foreign (especially Scottish) students at Franeker and other Dutch universities.

[9] Story, *Commentaries*, 32.

[10] Ibid. This is clearly evidenced in the books of eighteenth-century French jurists that Story himself consulted.

Netherlands, Huber appears to be sparsely cited on this topic near the twilight of Roman-Dutch law.[11] Lainé himself not only devotes less than two pages to Huber, as contrasted to over eight for Johannes Voet, but also presents first the latter, thus reversing their chronological order.[12] The same holds true of the other classical scholars who wrote extensive histories of earlier conflicts doctrine.[13] Even nineteenth-century writers whose theories are very close to Huber's actual doctrine fail to mention him.[14]

Huber lived in the northern Dutch province of Friesland, a place with a distinct political organization and identity.[15] The son of a village notary, Huber studied at the Academy of Franeker, obtained his doctorate from Heidelberg and was immediately (1657) appointed to the chair of eloquence, history and politics at Franeker, gradually (1662–1665) moving over to the Faculty of Law, where he was to spend the rest of his life. Huber refused twice offers of a professorship at Leiden, but he did take the "major step up the social ladder" of becoming a councilor-judge at the province's supreme court, the Court of Friesland (*Hof van Friesland*) and thus a member of the Frisian patriciate.[16]

Whereas Johannes Voet directed his principal effort toward his commentary of the Digest,[17] Huber's own literary output was more diversified – including some recycling of his material.[18] He worked a lot of his

[11] For example, he is not cited by J. van der Linden, *Regtsgeleerd, practicaal en koopmans handbook* (Amsterdam: Johannes Allart, 1806), 1.1.5. Whereas van der Linden includes Huber's vernacular treatise and other works – but not his *Praelectiones* – in his extensive bibliography, he only cites Paul and Johannes Voet at the end of his brief discussion on conflicts issues.

[12] Lainé, *Introduction*, 2:96, 99–107, 107–108.

[13] See e.g. Laurent, *Droit civil international*, 1:457–484; Catellani, *Diritto internazionale privato*, 1:52–56.

[14] See Vareilles-Sommières, *Synthèse*, 1:8 (only Paul and Jan Voet are mentioned as Dutch statutists).

[15] See Section 12.2.1.

[16] Expression by Hewett, *Ulric Huber*, 81.

[17] See J. Voet, *Commentarius ad Pandectas*, 2 vols. (The Hague, 1698–1704): at over 2,200 pages of main text and hundreds of supplementary material, Voet's work is more than twice as big as Huber's equivalent. References to Johannes Voet in this book are to that edition. Quotes to Voet in this work come from the annonated translation by Percival Gane, *The selective Voet; being the Commentary on the Pandects, Paris edition of 1829, and the Supplement to that work by Johannes van der Linden*, 8 vols. (Durban: Butterworths, 1955–1958).

[18] On Huber's publishing strategy see Hewett, *Ulric Huber*, 85 referring to R. Feenstra, *Bibliografie van hoogleraren in de rechten aan de Franeker Universiteit tot 1811* (Amsterdam: Koninklijke Nederlandse akademie van wetenschappen, 2003), 47–98. See

lectures, disputations, and pamphlets into his systematic works – written in Latin and Dutch – which continued to be updated into new editions until the late eighteenth century.

Huber's main contribution to the *usus modernus pandectarum* was a three-volume systematic work on Roman law, entitled *Introductory Lectures* (*Praelectiones*). The work – which is organized in chapters corresponding to each title in each book of the respective work of the Corpus Juris – consists of two parts: a first volume on the Institutes (1677) and two subsequent volumes on the Digest (1689).[19] In between, Huber published a two-volume practical treatise in Dutch, in the genre of "Institutes of national law," entitled *Contemporary Jurisprudence as applied elsewhere and in Friesland* a practical treatise on Roman law as applied in Friesland.[20]

With the exception of the Anglo-Scottish connection, the longterm international outreach of Huber's learned work was not much helped by his location in the Dutch periphery. Its practical spirit however did find resonance among Dutch practitioners even beyond Friesland, despite the differences in law with Holland (and the relative self-absorption of Holland's legal literature), and Huber's work eventually found a new home in South Africa, where Roman-Dutch law has persisted to this day.[21]

Section 11.2.1 and esp. Section 14.4.1, where Huber's third axiom is shown as an example both of such recycling – in both languages – and of the evolution in Huber's thought and style.

[19] U. Huberus, *Praelectionum Juris Civilis Pars Prior, Quae est secundum Institutiones Justinianaeas*, 2nd ed (Franeker, 1687); U. Huberus, *Praelectionum Juris Romani et Hodierni Pars II*, 2nd ed. (Franeker, 1700), covering the first twenty-one books of the Digest and followed by *Pars III* (Franeker, 1701). All parts were published together in the annotated 1735 edition: U. Huberus, *Praelectionum Juris Civilis Tomi III* (Leipzig, 1735). In this book, references are made to the 1700 edition unless otherwise indicated.

[20] U. Huber, *Heedensdaegse Rechtsgeleertheyt, soo elders, als in Frieslandt gebruikelijk*, 2 vols. (Leuwarden, 1686). The fifth edition (published in Amsterdam, in 1768, by son Zacharias Huber) was translated by Percival Gane as *The Jurisprudence of My Time* (Durban: Butterworth & Co. Africa Ltd, 1939). In the discussion of the vernacular text in this book and in earlier work, I have relied upon Gane's translation cross-referenced, in addition to the first, with the third edition in Dutch (Amsterdam, 1726), the first published after his death and edited by Zacharias Huber.

[21] For the story of the circulation of *Heedendaegse Rechtsgeleleertheyt* in South-Africa see M. Hewett, "Quae Legentem Fefellissent, Transferentem Fugere non Possunt" in *Ex Justa Causa Traditum: Essays in Honour of Eric H. Pool* (Pretoria: UNISA, 2005), 163–171.

11.2 *De Conflictu Legum Diversarum*

11.2.1 The Text

Huber became famous for his treatment of conflict of laws, in Latin, titled "On the Conflict of Different Laws in Different States" (*De Conflictu Legum Diversarum in Diversis Imperiis*), which is appended as a distinct second part to Huber's discussion of Book One Title Three ("Statutes, Senatusconsulta and long-standing customs") of the Digest.[22] This is the only standalone chapter of the entire work, as well as the only chapter with its own title: *Praelectiones* otherwise faithfully follows the structure, and titles, of the Books and Titles of the Digest (and the Institutes, as far as the first part is concerned).

The conflicts treatment has been published separately, along with translations in English, three times. In 1798, a translation in English was appended by A. J. Dallas to his report of a US Supreme Court judgment on a debt enforcement case: Dallas had prepared the translation in the course of pleading the case.[23] The Latin text was published, without translation, as an appendix to an annotated translation of Savigny's volume on the conflict of laws in 1880.[24] Two new translations, accompanied by the original text, appeared in the interwar period: one in the US, by Ernest Lorenzen, and one in England, by D. J. Llewellyn Davies.[25] These appear to have inspired, and influenced, a translation to Portuguese by Professor Haroldo Valladão, which appeared in Brazil

[22] Huber, *Praelectiones ad Pandectas*, 1.3.App. (30–36 in the 1700 edition; 538–543 in the 1735 edition).

[23] *Emory* v. *Grenough*, 3 US (3 Dal.) 369 (1797): a debt was contracted in Massachusetts, where both parties were domiciled, but the defendant moved to Pennsylvania, availing himself of its bankruptcy laws: the plaintiff won at the trial level and the writ of error was removed on a technicality. Dallas, the Court's first reporter of decisions was co-counsel for plaintiff; his translation is appended in a massive footnote at the end of the reported case: ibid., 370–377.

[24] Savigny, *Private International Law*, 508–516.

[25] E. Lorenzen, "Huber's De Conflictu Legum," *Illinois Law Review*, 13 (1919), 401, reprinted in his *Selected Articles on the Conflict of Laws* 162–165 (1947). See D. J. Llewellyn Davies, appended to his article "The Influence of Huber's *De Conflictu Legum* on English Private International Law," *British Yearbook of International Law*, 18 (1937), 49–63, 64–78. Lorenzen's translation is better known in the US, but in this book, unless otherwise indicated, I am making use of Llewellyn Davies's translation, which gives a better image of the original language. This chapter revises and expands N. Hatzimihail, "Huber on the Conflict of Laws" in *Dignatio rerum Professor Elias Krispis* (Thessaloniki: Sakkoulas, 2018), 239–264.

soon after World War II.[26] A French translation was published very recently by Professors Betrand Ancel and Horatia Muir Watt.[27]

A similar conflicts treatment, in Dutch, is incuded in Huber's treatise *Contemporary Jurisprudence*, which appeared shortly prior to his treatise on the Digest: bearing the title "On the Observance of Frisian laws in other countries and of those of other countries in Friesland," it constitutes the third chapter of the first book of the work.[28] An English translation of the text is available thanks to a 1939 translation of the entire treatise by the South African jurist Percival Gane.[29]

This vernacular text tends to follow the Latin one. Whereas the Latin text is better organized and presents Huber's thought in more developed form, the Dutch text has a slightly more practical orientation and is somewhat longer, including more examples. It will thus be examined, in this chapter, in parallel to the better known Latin one, making references notably to examples and further thoughts included in the former. We shall moreover return to it in the subsequent discussions of Huber's political thought and jurisprudence.[30]

These two texts have eclipsed any other contribution by Huber on the subject.[31] Huber had previously treated conflicts matters in his treatise *On the Law of the State (De Jure Civitatis)*, within the first chapter of the fourth section of the third and final book, concerning the law of the

[26] See U. Huber, *Conflito de leis: Tradução portuguêse no Seminário de Direito Internacional Privado da Faculdade de Direito, dirigido pelo Professor Haroldo Valladão* (Rio de Janeiro: Pontifícia Universidade Católica do Rio de Janeiro, 1951).

[27] B. Ancel and H. Muir Watt, "Du conflit des lois différentes dans des Etats différents" in *Mélanges Jacques Héron* (Paris: LGDJ, 2009), 1–22, and now Ancel, *Éléments*, 340–351.

[28] U. Huber, *Heedensdaegse Rechtsgeleertheyt* (Franeker, 1686), 1.3 ("Van't gebruik der Friesche rechten in andere landen, en die van andere landen in Friesland." I have used the pages 11–17 in the 1742 edition).

[29] Huber, *Jurisprudence of My Time*, 11–17.

[30] *Heedensdaegse Rechtsgeleertheyt* has been previously discussed, notably by J. Weinstein, "The Dutch Influence on the Conception of Judicial Jurisdiction in 19th century America," *American Journal of Comparative Law*, 38 (1990), 73–101 with a view to the contemporary discussion on the constitutionality and historical roots of transient jurisdiction.

[31] See in addition U. Huber, *Beginselen der Rechtskunde gebruikelijk in Friesland* (Leeuwarden, 1696), 567–578. This work, which originally appeared in 1684 and was effectively replaced by *Contemporary Jurisprudence*, two years later, includes in its very end a "last chapter" on the subject. The only difference with Contemporary Jurisprudence is that Huber uses here the word "power" (*kracht*) rather than the subsequent "observance" (*gebruik*).

administration of the State.[32] "De Conflictu Legum" largely reprises the content of the – largely forgotten – text, with some differences noted in the wording of the opening part.[33] The earlier text also treated issues of civil jurisdiction, which have been omitted from "De Conflictu Legum."[34]

11.2.2 Structure of the Text

The conflicts treatment, like each chapter in the *Praelectiones*, begins with a summary of contents – essentially the title of each of the fifteen sections it is divided into.

In the text itself, Huber begins by first defining his subject and then explaining where its fundamental rules are to be found. Huber then states the fundamental principles (axioms), "which being conceded as they should be everywhere will smooth our way for the solution of the remaining questions."[35]

Once the axioms have been given, the rules governing specific legal issues can be derived from them. Section 3 derives from them the "proposition" that all "acts *inter vivos* and *mortis causa* are valid everywhere according to the law of the place where they are done." Sections 4–8 explain the application of the proposition with regard to testaments, contracts, *res judicata*, the bringing of actions, and marriage. Section 9 explains that the rule extends "to the effect of the above transactions, even as regards immovables" (i.e. that the law of the place where the act was held applies, in principle, over the acquisition of property rights abroad). Sections 10–11 point to the "limitations" (and "amplification") of the rule, in the cases where the parties had a place other than the place of conclusion in mind (primarily with regard to performance) or when the *lex loci contractus* causes "prejudice . . . to the citizens of the other state with respect to rights acquired by them." Sections 12–13 examine "the rule that personal qualities impressed in a particular place have force everywhere" and its limitations. Section 14 declares that "as regards immovables the law of the place where they are situated [is] to be observed" in apparent derogation from the general proposition of

32 U. Huberus, *De jure civitatis*, 4th ed (Franeker, 1698), 3.4.1.11–47 ("*De his quae exteri sibi invicem debent*").

33 In its turn, "Observance" reprises the earlier text of *Beginselen*.

34 Huber, *De jure civitatis*, 3.4.1.32–47.

35 Huber, *Praelectiones ad Pandectas*, 1.3.App.1 in fine.

Section 3, and this point is further "explained in the case of testaments, contracts and interstate succession" (§ 15).

11.3 Foundations

Most scholarly attention paid to Huber's conflict of laws – whether it has emphasized comity or played Huber up as an early theoretician of territorial sovereignty – has focused on his axioms. The axioms have indeed acquired almost iconic status in conflicts literature, especially English-language works. Many have made reference to them, or even reproduced the axioms in their treatises (some have even reproduced Huber's citations to the Digest!), yet few appear to have considered even Huber's discussion of them.[36] Yet Huber devotes his first two sections in explaining his approach (§ 1) and his axioms (§ 2). In order however, to place them into context, as well as to connect them to Huber's doctrinal system, such an exercise is vital.

11.3.1 Foregrounding (§ 1)

Huber's opening is worth quoting in full:

> It often happens that transactions (*negotia*) entered into one place have force and effect in the territories of a different state, or have to be adjudicated upon in another place. Moreover it is well known that the laws of every nation differ in many respects, for since the breaking up of the provinces of the Roman Empire, Christendom has been divided into almost innumerable nations (*populi*), not subject to one another and not sharing the same system of government. It is not surprising that there is nothing on the subject in Roman law, for since the sovereignty of Rome extended to all parts of the world and was regulated by a uniform law (*aequabili jure gubernatum imperium*), it could hardly give rise to a conflict of different laws. Nevertheless the fundamental rules according to which this subject should be determined must be sought in the Roman law, although the subject itself pertains more to the law of nations (*ius gentium*) than to the civil law (*ius civile*) since that which different nations (*populi*) should observe among themselves clearly pertains to the law of nations. For the purpose of unfolding the difficulty of this particularly intricate subject we shall formulate three axioms, which being accepted as undoubtedly it appears they should be, seemed to clear the way for us for

[36] See e.g. Anton, *Private International Law*, 22–23; Wolff, *Private International Law*, 29; Harding, *Conflict of Laws*, 10.

the solution of the remaining questions (*viam nobis ad reliqua planam redditura videntur*).[37]

11.3.2 Statement and Justification (§ 2)

In Section 2, Huber states the axioms. He cites passages in the Digest in support of axioms One and Two. But it is Axioms Two and Three that he elaborates on.

11.3.2.1 Axioms

Huber's three axioms are:

1. The laws of every sovereign authority have force within the boundaries of its state, and bind all subject to it, but not beyond. [D.2.1.20]
2. Those are held to be subject to a sovereign authority who are found within its boundaries, whether they be there permanently or temporarily. [D.48.22.7.10 in fine]
3. Those who exercise sovereign authority so act from comity that the laws (*iura*) of each nation having been applied within each own boundaries should retain their effect everywhere so far as they do not prejudice the power or rights of another government or its subjects.[38]

11.3.2.2 Citing the Digest

The first axiom refers to D.2.1.20, which states the following:

> One who administers justice beyond the limits of his territory may be disobeyed with impunity. The same applies where he purports to administer justice in a case exceeding the amount established for his jurisdiction.[39]

[37] Huber, *Praelectiones ad Pandectas*, 1.3.App.1.

[38] Ibid., 1.3.App.2: "*I. Leges cuijusque imperii vim habent intra terminos ejusdem Reip[ublicae] omnesque ei subjectos obligant, nec ultra, per l. ult. ff. de Jurisdict. II. Pro subjectis imperio habendi sunt omnes, qui intra terminos ejusdem reperiuntur, sive in perpetuum, sive ad tempus ibi commorentur, per l. 7, s. 10 in fin. de interd.et releg. III. Rectores imperiorum id comiter agunt, ut jura cujusque populi intra terminos ejus excercita, teneant ubique suam vim, quatenus nihil potestati aut juri alterius imperantis ejusque civium praejudicetur.*"

[39] D.2.1.20 (Paulus): "*Extra territorium ius dicenti impune non paretur. idem est, et si supra iurisdictionem suam velit ius dicere.*"

The second axiom refers to D.48.22.7.10 in fine. We quote the entire paasage, emphasizing the final sentence, on which reference is made:

> The governor can bar someone from the province which he himself rules, but not from another; and the deified brothers wrote in a rescript to this effect. The consequence of this was that a person who had been relegated from the province in which he had his domicile could remain in the place from which he originated. However, our emperor and his deified father have provided for this. For they wrote in a rescript to Maecius Probus, governor of the province of Spain, that a person could also be barred from the province from which he originated by the governor of the province where he had his domicile. *It is also proper that persons who, though not residents of a province, commit an offense there, should come under the force of [this] rescript.*[40]

We are not concerned here with the relationship between the seventeenth-century use of the Roman texts and the text's original purpose and context. Authorities from Roman law have been invoked to different effect than what was originally intended ever since the Medieval renaissance of legal scholarship, a point aptly demonstrated in Medieval conflicts texts.

A more useful exercise is to look up the role of these same *loci* in Bartolus. Bartolus cites D.2.1.20 only twice.[41] First in support of the statement that a local punitive statute does not extend over a case where both parties are outside the territory.[42] And subsequently in his argument where Bartolus argues that if forfeiture takes place under law derogating from the *ius commune* and peculiar to that locality, it cannot extend its effects to other localities.[43]

The Medieval treatment of D.48.22.7.10 is more interesting. Bartolus reportedly cites to D.48.22.7.9,[44] but, given the fact that he talks about the rule that an offender may be punished under the laws of his place of origin for an offense committed elsewhere, the reference seems to be to D.48.22.7.10. It must be noted that our *locus* is used here to substantiate

[40] D.48.22.7.10 in fine (Ulpian).

[41] Additionally, Bartolus ad C.1.1.1, nu. 47 in fine refers to the commentary on D.2.1.20 of either Cinus or Petrus Bellaperticus, who argue that the city's magistrate can punish a citizen for an offense committed abroad (the printed text refers to Cinus, but Clarence Smith, "Bartolo," 265–266 notes that it is Petrus, whom his student Cinus is quoting).

[42] Bartolus ad C.1.1.1, nu. 44.

[43] Ibid., nu. 51.

[44] "However, I know that governors generally relegate to those parts of a province which are more deserted."

not Huber's kind of territoriality, but a "personalist" rule. The gloss is more explicit in that direction: *ad rescripti auctoritatem pertinere* is glossed "they may be banned from the province of their origin by the governor of the province which they inhabit… And so observe that a man may be charged with an offense in the province of his inhabitance, although he offended elsewhere [reference to C. 3.15.1]."[45]

In the end, the Medieval authors and Huber emphasize different aspects of the Roman text: the glossators emphasize the extraterritorial effects of the decision to ban someone, while Huber emphasizes the extended definition of that someone.

A comparison with Johannes Voet may help us illuminate things further: Voet quotes in his main text for his statement that "strictly speaking, all statutes have territorial effect only."[46] We also find him placing D.48.22.7.10 as authority used by "some" to argue for the extraterritorial effect of personal statutes – a position he then refutes.[47]

11.3.2.3 Discussing the Axioms

Huber's axioms are followed by a brief explanatory discussion, beginning with the third axiom:

> From this we conclude that this matter should be pursued according not to a single civil law, but the common weal and the tacit consent of the nations, for although the laws of one nation cannot apply directly to another, yet nothing could be more inconvenient to the intercourse and various practices of nations than that which is valid by the law of one place should be rendered invalid elsewhere owing to a difference in the law.[48]

Huber then notes that the third axiom has been generally accepted ("no one hitherto seems to have entertained any doubt") and where doubt seems to appear instead is the second axiom: "some persons seem to be of a different opinion and deny that foreigners are subject to the laws of the

45 Accursius ad D.48.22.7.10, s.v. *ad rescripti*, col. 1582, vol. III (Lyon, 1604), as translated by Clarence Smith, "Bartolo," 262 n. 48.

46 Voet, *Commentarius ad Pandectas*, 1.4.App.5.

47 Ibid., 8.

48 Ibid., 2: "*Ex quo liquet, hanc rem non ex simplici jure Civili, sed ex commodis et tacito populorum consensu esse petendam: quia sicut leges alterius populi apud alium directe valere non possunt, ita commerciis et usu gentium promiscuo nihil foret magis incommodum, quam si res jure certi loci validae, mox alibi diversitate Juris infirmarentur, quae est ratio tertii axiomatis: quod, uti nec prius, nullum videtur habere dubium.*" See Section 14.4.1 where the translation by Llewyllyn Davies is discussed.

place in which they act." Huber himself, he tells us, will admit this in some cases:

> But the proposition that all within the boundaries of a government are to be deemed subjects thereof is nevertheless perfectly correct, for it is in conformity not only with the nature of a state and the custom of subjecting all found therein to its sovereignty (*mos subigendi imperio cunctos in civitate repertos*), but also with the doctrine accepted by almost all nations concerning personal arrest.

In support of the former argument, Huber cites Grotius who suggested "he who contracts in any particular place is subjected as a temporary subject to the laws of that place."[49] As to the second argument, he notes that the notion that "the sovereignty is deemed to extend over all found within its territory" is the only plausible ground why "foreigners are compelled to submit to mesne arrest, for no other reason than that they are found in a place."[50]

11.4 Primary Rule: *locus regit actum*

Section 3 makes the rule *locus regit actum* (the phrase itself is not used), the fundamental doctrinal principle of Huber's system:

> The following proposition follows from the above: all transactions (*negotia*) and acts both in Court and out of Court, whether *mortis causa* or *inter vivos*, properly executed according to the law of a particular place are valid even where a different law prevails, and where if done in like manner, they would not be valid. On the other hand, transactions and acts executed in any place contrary to the law of that place, as they are in their origin invalid, cannot be valid anywhere. And this applies not only to persons who have their domicil in the place of the contract but also to those who are there for the time being. But there is this exception: that if the rulers of another people would suffer a serious inconvenience thereby, they would not be bound to give effect to such acts and transactions in accordance with the limitation of the third axiom. The matter is sufficiently important to be explained by examples.[51]

[49] H. Grotius, *De Jure Belli ac Pacis* (Paris, 1625), 2.11.5: "These, however, are the special effects of municipal law, and they therefore have nothing in common with the law of nature or the law of nations, except that it is natural that they should be observed in the places where they are in force. In consequence, if a foreigner makes an agreement with a citizen, you will be bound by the laws of the latter's country, for the reason that a person who makes a contract in any place is under the law of that place as a temporary subject."

[50] Huber, *Praelectiones ad Pandectas*, 1.3.App.2.

[51] Huber, *Praelectiones ad Pandectas*, 1.3.App.3.

11.4.1 Acts inter vivos and mortis causa

Huber takes a very broad view of what constitutes a legal act: not just contracts and acts *mortis causa*, but also procedural acts and marriages themselves. The first category he deals with, however, i.e. testaments and contracts, has had the longest story of treatment by conflicts writers and probably the biggest practical implications in Huber's time as well.[52]

11.4.1.1 Testaments (§ 4)

Section 4 then gives examples of validity as to form, concerning the different number of witnesses required for a valid testament: two (and a notary) in Holland, seven in Friesland.[53] A testament made by a Hollander (Batavian) in Holland under the more liberal local law will still have effect to goods located in Frisia, pursuant to the third axiom (but not the first). A testament made thus in Holland by a Frisian who then returns to Friesland will be valid under the second axiom. Generally, "an act valid from the beginning, should be valid in accordance with the third axiom, and this applies without any distinction between movable and immovable property, and this is the law as it is applied."[54] The reverse also holds: the testament that a Frisian, or a Hollander, makes in Friesland, conforming to the laxer requirements of Holland law (two witnesses) but not of Frisian law (seven witnesses) will have no effect in Holland, because it was invalid from the beginning.[55]

In his vernacular text, however, Huber mentions an 1683 decision in which the Court of Friesland held valid the testament made by a Frisian in Overijssel in accordance with Frisian law (seven witnesses) but not in conformity with the law of Overijssel:

> This conflicting decision appears to be founded on the ground, that there was no reason to nullify and reject in Friesland a testament made elsewhere by a Frisian, if it was legal and regular according to Frisian law, even though it could not have held good at the place where it was made.[56]

The fact that Huber sandwiches this reference between assertions of the position that such testaments "neither ought nor could have held good"

[52] Bartolus's text is a case in point.
[53] This was the original rule in Roman law, which Friesland had not at the time preempted with more liberal local legislation. See Section 13.3.4.
[54] Ibid., 5.
[55] Ibid.
[56] Huber, *Heedensdaegse Rechtsgeleertheyt*, 1.3.15.

in the deceased's homeland (Friesland in § 15, Holland in § 16), must be interpreted as an indication that Huber does not approve the decision's result but recognizes it as the *lex vigens* in Friesland.

11.4.1.2 Contracts (§ 5)

Section 5 (acts *inter vivos*) seems to extend the rule *locus regit actum* to substantive requirements: the main example is the prohibition of the sale of a good. A sale made where the prohibition holds is void. A sale made where the prohibition does not hold is valid and will make the buyer liable in the place of the prohibition. But the buyer will not be liable if the goods sold are to be delivered – or were delivered secretly – to a place where their sale is prohibited ("it would be repugnant to the law and interest of the state").[57]

In *Contemporary Jurisprudence*, Huber's discussion of contracts revolves even more clearly around the case of a sale in prohibited goods (sale of "brandy or certain other commodities" "may be forbidden in certain places, as it formerly was here").[58] Accordingly, he takes a stronger position on this case:

> According to law he cannot bring an action anywhere on such a scale, not even outside the Province, should he find the purchaser there; certainly no action would arise on the sale, because they both did what they were forbidden to do; unless equity on account of special circumstances might provide some extraordinary remedy against the avaricious purchaser.[59]

He then continues with more examples. On the one hand, the case of citizens of a locality prohibiting brandy who go and drink brandy outside its jurisdiction (no claim in the locality, but elsewhere a claim arises).[60] On the other hand, the case of a locality prohibiting exactly the consumption by its citizens just outside its territory "in order not to lessen its duties, an enactment of which instances are known" (the citizens are

[57] Huber, *Praelectiones ad Pandectas*, 1.3.App.5. See also ibid.: "On the other hand, if the merchandise should be sold secretly, in the place where such sale is prohibited, the sale will not be valid from the beginning and no action we lie no matter where it may be brought not even to compel the delivery; For every purchaser should refuse to pay the price after delivery she will be bound not so much by virtue of the agreement asked by the delivery of the thing insofar as he would enrich himself at the expense of another.

[58] Huber, *Heedensdaegse Rechtsgeleertheyt*, 1.3.19–23.

[59] Ibid., 21.

[60] Ibid., 22.

"punishable in their own town for this act; but the trade is legitimate and therefore gives a claim everywhere except in that town").[61]

11.4.2 Res judicata and Actions

The focus next moves to what could be called procedural issues not unlike what is today grouped under recognition and enforcement of foreign judgments, but the perspective adopted is different and all issues are presented as falling under the *locus regit actum* rule. Huber's emphasis is on the effects granted to other states' judgments, including default judgments, and the subsequent limits posed on the forum's jurisdiction, but also the mode of such judgments' enforcement.

11.4.2.1 Res judicata (§ 6)

Section 6 extends the *lex loci actus* rule to *res judicata*:

> A sentence pronounced in any place, or a pardon of a crime granted by one having that jurisdiction has effect everywhere, nor is it proper for the magistrates of another state to prosecute or to permit to be charged again a party who has been acquitted or pardoned in another place, even without adequate reason.[62]

The only exception holds in the case of "evident danger or prejudice" to the forum.[63] Huber provides two such examples.

The first example, drawn "from [his] memory," concerns a person who, having struck someone in Frisian territory, fled to Overijssel and rendered himself to the authorities there; they in turn acquitted the man and requested Frisians to grant him freedom from punishment.[64] For Huber, even if acquittal was the right decision, to give effect to the judgment from Overijssel would "open the way too much for the evasion of the Frisian jurisdiction."[65]

[61] Ibid., 23.

[62] Huber, *Praelectiones ad Pandectas*, 1.3.App.6. Huber, *Heedensdaegse Rechtsgeleertheyt*, 1.3.24 adds "everywhere recognized and enforced without inquiry into the reason for it" *(Een sententie by eenige Rechter wettelijk uitgesprooken, of ook Pardon gegeven by den geenen, die macht heeft om het te geven ter plaetse daer't is voorgevallen, wordt overal erkent en effect gegunt, sonder ondersoek op de reeden van dien)*. He claims this is so "in virtue of rule 3."

[63] Huber, *Praelectiones ad Pandectas*, 1.3.App.6.

[64] See Map 3. Overijssel (Overyssel in old spelling) is given as *Transisulania*. Lorenzen, "Huber's De Conflictu Legum," 168, 169 has it mistakenly translated as Transylvania.

[65] Huber, *Praelectiones ad Pandectas*, 1.3.App.6.

The second example concerns a civil judgment that came to involve three provinces: a citizen of Haarlem (Holland) made a contract with a citizen of the province of Groningen, in which he "submitted himself to the judges of Groningen." When he was summoned, he did not appear, and was hence condemned as contumacious. The enforcement of the Groningen judgment was sought – and debated – in Friesland: enforcement was granted "at that time," "some of the judges being of the opinion that it was not open to the Frisians to inquire into the grounds on which the judgment was given, but merely whether it was valid according to the law of the place" and others noting that a Haarlem magistrate had allowed the proceeding. Huber notes that the Haarlem magistrate ought not to have done this, and points to a similar case where the magistrates in Amsterdam declined to enforce a default judgment rendered by a Frisian court in similar circumstances. Huber's own position, grounded on the exception to the third axiom, seems to be that "if a defendant cannot be found in the territory of the judge to whom he had submitted, he cannot by reason of the submission be proceeded against by contumacy . . . nor can effect be given to such judgments without detriment to our own jurisdiction and prejudice to our own citizens."[66]

11.4.2.2 Actions (§ 7)

The next question is which law should apply to an action "brought here on a contract made elsewhere," when the action would have been denied under one law and granted under another. Huber's rule is that "in matters of procedure the practice of the place where the action is brought is observed, even as regards transactions concluded elsewhere."[67]

Huber's first case raises the age-old question of prescription: the real-life example of a Frisian who became "indebted in Holland on account of goods sold there by retail" and is subsequently sued in Friesland after two years. The action at that time is prescribed in Friesland, but not in Holland, where the contract was entered into (and whose law therefore applies to the contract itself). The Frisian Court held for the defendant in two cases.[68]

[66] Ibid.

[67] Ibid., 2.3.7, with reference to J. van den Sande, *Decisiones Frisicae sive rerum in Suprema Frisiorum Curia Iudicatarum* (Leeuwarden, 1635), 1.12.5.

[68] Huber, *Praelectiones ad Pandectas*, 1.3.App.7, with references to the cases of Justus Blenkenfield and Johannes Jomoliin, tailor to the Prince of Orange, both decided "before the great fair of 1680."

Another example concerns an action in Friesland "on an instrument executed before magistrates in Holland which is entitled there to summary execution, but not by the general law." Huber argues that such action will "require trial and judgment" in Friesland. He then proceeds with the general rule: "prescription and execution do not pertain to the validity of the contract, but to the time and mode of bringing the action, which in itself constitutes as it were a contract, and a separate transaction."[69]

Huber reiterates this rule in *Contemporary Jurisprudence*, where he notes than in cases where "the mode and the law of the place where the execution takes place" is different from those of the tribunal "before which judgment was pronounced," the former shall apply, on grounds of convenience but also because "execution is of itself a separate transaction, and ought to be governed by the law of its own place."[70] And he continues:

> Indeed, everything belonging to the administration of justice, even prior to execution, is regulated by the place where action was instituted, and not according to the customs of the place where the transaction which is the subject of the suit took place; for legal process is of itself like a contract, and therefore also involves its own observances.[71]

11.4.3 Marriage

Whereas contracts, testaments, prescription and the effects of judgments are matters that we have also seen discussed in Medieval conflicts treatments, conflict of laws pertaining to marriage itself was a more novel issue, which rose to prominence in the aftermath of growing secularization of marriage law following the Protestant Reformation and the Tridentine reforms – and leading an increasing number of polities to impose stronger degrees of formality as a condition for validity, on the one hand, and to reduce marriage prohibitions, again in varying degrees, on the other hand. Huber treats marriage as a sui generis contract. We also see marital property issues such as dowry contracts being dealt with within the marriage concept, as *effects* of the *act* of marriage, separate from other contracts of § 5.

[69] Ibid.
[70] Huber, *Heedensdaegse Rechtsgeleertheyt*, 1.3.27.
[71] Ibid., 28 (continuing with examples of prescription and summary judgment in §§ 29–30).

11.4.3.1 Validity (§ 8)

"Marriage also falls under the same rules."[72] Huber here uses examples of substantive requirements as well as solemnities. As to solemnities, Friesland, but not Holland, considered the exchange of mutual consent between man and woman as husband and wife to constitute a valid marriage, even without a religious form. Holland would nonetheless have to grant to Frisians married thus all rights pertaining to a married couple. In the same manner, Frisia will recognize the marriage of a man from Brabant, who married there by papal dispensation within the prohibited degree (his niece) and then migrated to Friesland.[73] But the opposite will hold true in the case of a Frisian who goes to Brabant so as to marry his niece, "since our law would thereby be evaded by the worse precedents."[74] Huber admits his special concern with the instances of young Frisians running off to East Frisia or another place where the consent of the guardian is not required, celebrating their marriage there and then instantly returning back.[75]

> I consider that this obviously involves the subversion of our own law, and that, therefore, our magistrates are not bound by the law of nations to recognize and give effect to such marriages here. And still more should it be held that those persons appear to act contrary to the law of nations who by means of their slipperiness (*facilitas*), knowingly and intentionally share with the citizens of another state a right contrary to the laws of their own country.[76]

[72] Huber, *Praelectiones ad Pandectas*, 1.3.App.8.

[73] Ibid. This case must have been a purely hypothetical one. See Section 12.2.3.2.

[74] In speaking of Brabant, Huber is referring to the province in the Spanish Netherlands. The northernmost part of the historical province of Brabant had come *into* Dutch hands by 1529, as States Brabant (today the Dutch province of North Brabant). The States Brabant, together with States Flanders and the enclave around Maastricht (States Limburg) were administered by the United Provinces as a buffer zone – known as the "Generality Lands." The population in States Brabant had remained mostly Catholic, but public practice of the Catholic faith was not permitted. See Israel, *Dutch Republic*, 658–660. It would be impossible, therefore, to have a valid marriage under Catholic rules.

[75] Huber, *Praelectiones ad Pandectas*, 1.3.App.8. East Frisia was an independent principality in Huber's time (1654–1744; seat with right to vote in the Reichstag since 1677). A County since 1454, it became part of Prussia and then Hanover (today part of Lower Saxony).

[76] Huber, *Praelectiones ad Pandectas*, 1.3.App.8. Lorenzen, "Huber's," 172, and Davies, "Influence," 72, translate *facilitas* as "facility," but the word is best translated as "slipperiness" with connotations of "guile."

In his vernacular text, Huber devotes all his attention regarding the validity of marriages to the Brabant and East Friesland cases.[77] He concludes in an even stronger tone:

> The marriage is however illegal here and can at once be obstructed and nullified by the guardians. For it obviously tends to undermine and stultify our laws. Rather one might remark that the Church and the administration of those countries ought not to have received such young persons to their undoing in this manner.[78]

11.4.3.2 Effects (§ 9)

Huber then extends the *locus actus* rule to "the rights and effects attached" to contracts and marriages. Holland (and most of the United Provinces) had a regime of total community property, whereas Friesland maintained a regime of "community of profit and loss, and not of the property itself" (i.e. the property of spouses remained separate, but the income and other earnings generated from it were in common).[79] The arrangement of Hollander spouses will extend to their Frisian property, and Frisian spouses will remain the separate owners of property situated in Holland.

In fact, Huber provides for a *conflit mobile*: property acquired after a change in the matrimonial domicile will be subjected to the law of the new domicile:

> But when the [Frisian] spouses remove from one province to another, property which afterwards comes to either of them, ceases to be in community and remains in separate ownership, just as property previously owned in community remains in that legal status which it had acquired.[80]

But what about the notion (which Huber himself accepts in the final part of his treatment), that "the laws of another state cannot affect integral parts of another territory," such as immovables? Huber provides a "dual" answer:

> The first is that it is not by virtue of the immediate force of a foreign law, but in consequence of the consent of the supreme power in the other state that effect is given to foreign laws where they have been applied within its

77 Huber, *Heedensdaegse Rechtsgeleertheyt*, 1.3.31–32.
78 Ibid., 32 in fine.
79 See Section 13.3.3.2.
80 Huber, *Praelectiones ad Pandectas*, 1.3.App.9.

> territory, in consideration of the mutual convenience of nations, provided no prejudice results to itself or its citizens, which is the basis of the whole of this subject. The second answer is, that this is not so much the operation of the law as the agreement of the parties to share their property with one another, by which means a transfer of property may be effected by marriage no less than by other contracts.[81]

11.4.4 Limitations

Huber concludes his exposé on his primary rule by demarcating the limits of its effects.[82] He proceeds in two steps. The first is to reconfigure the *locus* itself in some cases, by invoking the intentions of the parties themselves, so as to avoid any need to have recourse to the prejudice exception (§ 10). The second step is to elaborate on his exception mechanism (§ 11).

11.4.4.1 Intention of the Parties (§ 10)

> But the place where the contract was entered into should not be too strictly regarded, for if the parties in contracting had another place in mind, the former should not prevail. "Everyone is deemed to have contracted in that place in which he is bound to perform." D.44.7.21. Hence the place of the marriage is not so much the place where the marriage contract is entered into, as the place where the contracting parties intended to make their home.[83]

Huber applies this "intention of the parties" rule to the case of Frisians who marry in Holland and then bring their wives to Friesland: "if at the time of marriage they had such an intention, there will be no community

[81] Ibid., 9 in fine: "*sed responsio est duplex. Prima, non fieri hoc vi Legis alienae immediata, sed accedente consensu Potestatis summae in altera Civitate, quae legibus alienis in loco suo exercitis praebet effectum; sine suo suorumque praejudicio, mutuae populorum utilitatis respectu, quod est fundamentum omnis hujus doctrinae. Altera responsio est, non tantum hane esse vim Legis, sed etiam consensum partium bona sua invicem communicantium, cujus vi mutatio dominii non minus per matrimonium quam per alios contractus fieri potest.*"

[82] Huber, *Praelectiones ad Pandectas*, 1.3.App.10–11. In his *Contemporary Jurisprudence*, Huber placed the respective sections, which essentially discuss the limitations to *locus regit actum*, at the end of the entire chapter: see Huber, *Heedensdaegse Rechtsgeleertheyt*, 1.3.52–54. The content is the same, the pertinent text more condensed, and the idea of a limitation of *locus regit actum* less explicit. As a result of this structure, Huber makes two references to the intention of the parties, one as part of his discussion on limitations and one in discussing contracts and juridical acts: ibid., 34.

[83] Huber, *Praelectiones ad Pandectas*, 1.3.App.10.

of property . . . for in this case the law of Friesland is the law of the place of the contract" (*ius loci Contractus*).[84] In his vernacular treatment, Huber goes a bit further, noting that the primary rule regarding marital property (*lex loci celebrationis*):

> [I]s founded on the tacit wish of the contracting parties, which, however, ceases to exist if the marriage has been contracted and celebrated in Holland, but the spouses intend to reside in Friesland . . . In that case they cannot be presumed to desire to be governed by the law of Holland, but rather by that of Friesland, which they have in contemplation, and where they intend to live.[85]

11.4.4.2 The Prejudice Exception (§ 11)

A potentially more far-reaching limitation follows below:

> The effects of contracts entered into in a certain place are recognized elsewhere according to the law of the former place provided *no prejudice is caused to the citizens of the other state with respect to the rights acquired by them*, and the sovereign of the other place is not bound to extend, *nor can it extend*, the law of another territory that far.[86]

The emphasis placed in the original text is not unimportant: it indicates the author's concern with the implications of his advocated rule being fully adopted.[87]

Both examples given concern third-party rights.[88]

The first one is about rights over property. Under Roman – and hence Frisian – law, the prior hypothecation of movable property by agreement gives a right of priority (πρωτοπραξία) even against a third-party possessor; but the rights of the third party in Holland, where the rule is not admitted, "cannot be taken away by the law of another territory."[89]

[84] Ibid.

[85] Huber, *Heedensdaegse Rechtsgeleertheyt*, 1.3.34. Unlike "De Conflictu Legum," in the vernacular the case of a change of domicile is discussed subsequently: Huber, *Heedensdaegse Rechtsgeleertheyt*, 1.3.35.

[86] Huber, *Praelectiones ad Pandectas*, 1.3.App.11: "*Effecta contractuum certo loco initorum, pro iure loci illius alibi quoque observantur, si nullum inde civibus alienis creatur praejudicium, in iure sibi quaesito, ad quod Potestas alterius loci non tenetur neque potest extendere ius diversi territorii.*"

[87] Italics in the original. Both Lorenzen, "Huber's," 174–175, and Llewelyn Davies, "Influence," 73 have kept the italics in their transcription but not in their translation.

[88] For the underlying substantive law in both cases see Section 13.3.2.

[89] Huber, *Praelectiones ad Pandectas*, 1.3.App.11.

The second example involves patrimonial effects of the relations between spouses. In Holland the spouses can agree by private contract that the wife shall not be liable for debts contracted by the husband alone; in Friesland such agreements require publication, "nor do they affect those who have reasonable grounds of being ignorant of them:" a wife from Holland will thus still be liable in Friesland for a debt contracted in Friesland – but not for a debt contracted in Holland, "because here one law only, and not two, namely the law of the place of contracting comes into consideration."[90]

Huber's argument leads him to reconceptualize the conflict between two contracts as a veritable conflict between two laws and "enlarge this rule" as follows:

> If the law of the place [of contracting] in another state should conflict (*pugnet*) with the law of our state, where a contract was also entered into, which is inconsistent with the contract which was concluded elsewhere, it is more reasonable that we should follow our own law than the foreign law.[91]

11.5 Second Rule: Personal Status and Capacity

The second principle of Huber's system is a complicated personality rule, or "axiom," which is supposed to derive from the "rules laid down at the beginning."

[90] Ibid. Huber mentions here (11 in fine) *Batavia*. Davies, "Influence," 74, translates *lapsu calami* as Brabant. Other possibilities considered and rejected in my translation were the use of the terms either to denote all non-Frisian Dutch or to refer to the East Indies settlement of Batavia (present-day Jakarta). By Huber's time, the colony of Batavia had a substantial population but no "economically independent Dutch burgher class." See Israel, *Dutch Republic*, 323–325. The careful examination of the text itself, as well as the context in which the terms "Batavia" and "Batavians" – above in the sumare used in the Latin text leads to the conclusion that Huber is referring to the province of Holland – which retained and nurtured the strongest association with the ancient Batavians. See generally I. Schöffer, "The Batavian Myth during the sixteenth and seventeeth century" in J.S. Bromley and E.H. Kossmann (eds.), *Britain and the Netherlands V: Some political mythologies* (The Hague: Martinus Nijhoff, 1975), 78–101. Sande, *Decisiones*, 4.8.7 begins his report with *Albertus à Loo Batavus Lugduni Batavorum condidit testamentum* and continues with references to Holland.

[91] Huber, *Praelectiones ad Pandectas*, 1.3.App.11.

11.5.1 The Rule: Personality (§ 12)

> Personal qualities impressed upon a person by the law in any place are carried with him and accompany his person everywhere, with this effect, that everywhere persons enjoy and are subject to that law which persons of the same class enjoy and are subject to in such other place. Therefore, those who with us are under tutelage or guardianship, such as minors, unemancipated sons, prodigals, and married women, are regarded everywhere as persons subject to guardianship, and possess and enjoy the rights which guardianship confers in any particular place.[92]

What Huber does here is to distinguish the *classification* of an individual as being of a certain status, as, for example, being under tutelage or guardianship, from the rights (and capacity limitations) coming from that status: this has been called a distinction between status and capacity.[93] A person coming from a province where the age of majority is twenty-one will have the "rights of majority" even in provinces where the age of majority is twenty-five.[94]

The rest of § 12 presents examples of the universal effects of one's status characterization.[95] In *Contemporary Jurisprudence*, Huber also makes an exception to protect third parties:

> He who has been interdicted from managing his own affairs can nowhere be bound by contracts nor sued upon them, unless for reasons of equity, such as that persons elsewhere had been kept in ignorance of the fact, or some such reason.[96]

11.5.2 The Rule Does Not Create Personal Statutes (§§ 13–14)

Having laid the rule, Huber devotes the next section of his treatment to draw a line distinguishing himself and his rule from those who argued for the full personality of laws on capacity. He remarks that such a doctrine "does not appear to [him] well-founded, as it would produce too great a confusion of laws, and too great a burden upon neighboring states from the laws of other states."[97] In his vernacular treatment, Huber provides clarification:

[92] Ibid.

[93] See Lorenzen, "Huber's De Conflictu Legum," 139; Davies, "Huber's De Conflictu Legum."

[94] Huber, *Praelectiones ad Pandectas*, 1.3.App.12.

[95] Ibid. See also Huber, *Heedensdaegse Rechtsgeleertheyt*, 1.3.37–40.

[96] Ibid., § 39 in fine.

[97] Huber, *Praelectiones ad Pandectas*, 1.3.App.13.

> Some would have it that whatever a person cannot on account of personal incapacity do in his native country, he can do nowhere, not even in places where such persons are allowed to do it; but it would cause too great inconvenience if in respect of persons who do business among us we had to be guided to such an extent by the law of another country.[98]

Huber's first example is of a Frisian unemancipated son, who cannot make a testament in Friesland but makes one in Holland, where the Roman-law doctrine of parental power is not in force. The testament should be valid in Holland pursuant to the first two axioms, "because the laws bind all those who are within its territory, nor is it proper that as regards transactions concluded in their own country the Batavians should ignore their own law and ignore the case according to foreign law."[99] It will have no validity in Friesland pursuant to the third axiom, "because in that way nothing would be easier than for our citizens to evade our laws, as they could be evaded every day."[100] What follows is even more interesting:

> But elsewhere such a testament would be valid, even where an unemancipated son cannot make a testament, for in such a case the principle of the evasion of the laws of their country by their own citizens does not apply, for here no evasion would be perpetrated.[101]

Huber's second example covers the other aspect of the territorial rule on capacity: a seventeen-year-old Frisian studying in Groningen made a testament there. However, Groningen, unlike Friesland, did not allow minors under twenty years of age to make a testament. The court in Groningen held the will invalid "consistently to what we have said," but after debate and with some judges dissenting.[102]

11.6 Third Rule: The *lex rei sitae* Exception (§ 15)

11.6.1 The Rule as to Immovables

The conclusion of the tract provides an exception to what had been stated as "the basis of the whole of the subject (*fundamentum universae*

[98] Huber, *Heedensdaegse Rechtsgeleertheyt*, 1.3.44.
[99] Huber, *Praelectiones ad Pandectas*, 1.3.App.13.
[100] Ibid.
[101] Ibid.
[102] Ibid., 14 referring to a decision of 27 October 1643, reported by Nauta, M.S. 134 (Gaius Nauta was councilor to the Court of Friesland).

huius doctrinae) . . . the subjection of persons to the laws of any country so long as they act therein, whence it follows that an act which is valid or invalid from the beginning is also valid or invalid elsewhere."[103]

> But this principle does not apply to immovables, when regulated not as depending upon the free disposition of their owners, but as impressed with certain incidents (*notae*) by the law of the particular country where they are situated. Such incidents remain unchangeable in that state no matter what the laws of other states or individual dispositions may provide to the contrary, for the laws enacted relating to such property could not be varied by such dispositions without general confusion and prejudice to the state where the immovable is situated.[104]

The examples Huber uses explain what he means by incidents (*notae*).

First, the disposal of immovables by testament is prohibited in Groningen. Given that "Frisian law does not operate so as to affect that which constitutes integral parts of another territory," a Frisian cannot bequeath his land and houses situated in Groningen by a testament.[105] Huber sees no contradiction of this result with his general rule that "if a testament is validly made according to the law of the place (*jure loci*) it operates on property situated elsewhere where it is lawful to dispose thereof by testament" but different formalities are required:

> There is no inconsistency, since the diversity of laws in this case does not affect immovable property, nor does it refer to it, but regulates the act of making a testament, and the will having been properly made, the law of the country does not prohibit that act from being valid in respect of immovable property so far as no quality (character) impressed upon it by the law of the place is injured or diminished.[106]

Huber's other two examples concern the acquisition of immovable property by contract, namely "Frisian immovable property sold to persons in Holland in a manner prohibited in Friesland, but valid where the sale

[103] Huber, *Praelectiones ad Pandectas*, 1.3.App.15.

[104] Ibid.

[105] Ibid. Huber, *Heedensdaegse Rechtsgeleertheyt*, 1.3.46 mentions instead of "Groningen" the Ommelands (*Ommelanden*). The Province of Groningen was effectively divided, for administrative purposes, between the city of Groningen (and its dependent territories to the south and west) and the rural heartland of the province, known as the Ommeland quarters, which were situated between the rivers Eeems and Lauwers (and once formed part of historical Frisia). City and Ommelands had one vote each in the provincial States. See Israel, *Dutch Republic*, 248–250.

[106] Huber, *Praelectiones ad Pandectas*, 1.3.App.14; Huber, *Heedensdaegse Rechtsgeleertheyt*, 1.3.47.

takes place."[107] In "Observance," Huber elaborates that such a sale fulfills the requirements of Frisian law regarding publicity ("notices") and official approval ("consents").[108] The rule extends over "things which although not immovable are attached to the land:" a contract in Holland for the sale "by the lasts" (*secundum lastas*) of corn still growing in Friesland, where such a sale is prohibited, would thus be invalid.[109]

11.6.2 Intestate Succession and a Reference to Movable Property

The last issue touched ("the same rule applies") is the intestate succession of the *paterfamilias*, when property is situated in different places. As to immovables, the *lex rei sitae* will be followed. But as to movables, Huber applies the law of the deceased's last domicile,[110] referring to Johan van der Sande (*Sandius*) for more.[111] To quote from *Contemporary Jurisprudence*:

> But as regards movable property the law of the place where the deceased resided is followed, for movables form no portion of the country where they happen to be, but are carried from place to place and depend only on the good pleasure of the owner, so that in relation to them we can only regard the place where the man or woman was last resident; just as we are accustomed, both in affairs of death and in transactions between living persons, to follow the custom of the place where we are at the time.[112]

11.7 Concluding

Both the Latin and vernacular texts end with a conclusion of sorts.

"On the Observance of Frisian Laws" concludes with the following words: "We believe that we have now explained this subtle and confused subject simply and thoroughly, according to the treatment of great

[107] Huber, *Praelectiones ad Pandectas*, 1.3.App.15. Unfortunately, a printing error has led the text reading "is deemed to be duly sold" (*recte venditae intelliguntur*) which goes against the section's logic as corroborated in *Contemporary Jurisprudence*.

[108] Huber, *Heedensdaegse Rechtsgeleertheyt*, 1.3.48. See Section 13.3.2.

[109] Ibid., 49. Huber, *Praelectiones ad Pandectas*, 1.3.App.15. See Section 13.3.2.

[110] The Latin text actually speaks of "testator" (*ubi testator habuit domicilium*), but since we are talking about intestate succession "deceased" is a more appropriate term.

[111] Sandius, *Decisiones frisicae*, 4.8.7.

[112] Huber, *Heedensdaegse Rechtsgeleertheyt*, 1.3.51.

jurists."[113] "On the Conflict of Different Laws," which came later and is more well-rounded theoretically and doctrinally, ends on a slightly more modest tone: "These principles are such as would be capable of a fuller explanation, since there are writers on the Statutes who think differently on several matters."[114]

Given the future development of the subject, including how much controversy the interpretation of Huber has generated in the ensuing centuries, this remark appears prescient.

[113] Huber, *Heedensdaegse Rechtsgeleertheyt*, 1.3.55 ("Dus meinen wy dese subtyle ende verwerde Materie, gelyk sy van groote Rechtgeleerden wordt behandelt, eenvoudiglyk ende grondelyk oopen gelegt te hebben"). In the foonote, in Latin, Huber cites "post *Argentraeum et Burgundum*" Christian Rodenburgh, "*De jure quod oritur ex statututorum vel consuetudinum discreptantium conflictus.*"

[114] Huber, *Praelectiones ad Pandectas*, 1.3.App.15: "*Sunt hae definitiones eiusmodi, ut a latiori explicatione non abohorreant, quando Statutarii Scriptores non desunt, qui de nonnnullis aliter existimaverint.*" Huber here refers to Sandius, *Decisiones frisicae*, for these jurists and adds a reference to "recent work" of Rodenburgh (the same chapter, but this time he mentions that it is included in Rodenburgh's Tractatus de Jure Conjugum).

12

The Political Context of Huber's Conflict of Laws

12.1 Introduction

Huber did not write in a vacuum. A close inspection of his conflicts treatments is demonstrating that we cannot limit ourselves to his axioms, as well as the relevance of political (and social) context and Huber's jurisprudential world view in understanding his doctrine. Such an exploration is even more vital in the case of someone who has been associated, in the modern consciousness, with the transition into the Westphalian world of sovereignty and state systems, and especially with comity and territorialism. Whereas preclassical jurists tend to be decontextualized in conflicts literature, Huber has been contextualized in some narratives, in a manner that must be considered before we proceed with our own examination. One of the most vivid images of this kind is drawn by a distinguished American jurist:

> As a Protestant and an officeholder, Huber's views were likely to be suspicious and resentful of Catholic Spain's prior dominance of the Low Countries. Thus it may be understood that Huber's principles represent the triumph of the national power over the Church: the ascendancy of territorial, exclusive, provincial and local authority over the universal. Under Huber's formulation, there is no power outside or above the state compelling it to recognize foreign law. In this sense, Huber rejected a law-of-nations approach in favor of the forum's law. Finally, Huber was rejecting the intellectual tradition of the Catholic Church embedded in statutism. His principles suggest the artificiality of the categories constructed by the statutists, who theorized that the inherent power of legislation somehow could bind the court of another country. Huber recognized that courts exercise discretion in determining the applicable law, and that the determination of the applicable law could shift from the law makers to judges. Behind the carefully constructed categories of the statutists lay a tradition of Catholic scholasticism and essentialism in which ideas were composed of absolute essences that could be known

> through reason. Huber rejected essentialism for judge-made law, moral absolutes for humanism, scholastic law for incipient positivism.[1]

This is an elaborate narrative, whose normative implications – soliciting Huber as an authority for a more vigorous pursuit of public policy – will be discussed further below.[2] For the time being, it suffices to note that such allusions may tell us more about the modern preoccupations of their authors, than about Huber himself, his world, and his politics – or about how he perceived and exploited the various groups or bodies of norms (Roman law, provincial statutes, *ius gentium*) constituting the law of his jurisdiction.

This chapter is divided into three sections. Section 12.2 considers Huber – a political actor and theorist, situated in a unique time and place – and his ideas about State, States, and sovereignty. Section 12.3 addresses Huber's theory of legal sources and their hierarchy. Section 12.4 examines Huber's doctrine on cross-border civil litigation in the light of these ideas.

12.2 Ulrik Huber in Political Context

Huber lived during the so-called Golden Age of the United Provinces of the Netherlands – a loose federation of seven former provinces of the Holy Roman Empire, each of which regarded itself as a sovereign state and was in turn governed in a more or less decentralized manner.[3] At the heart of the Dutch polity lay the tension between, on the one hand, the republican bodies that exercised sovereign powers – namely the provincial States (*Staten*) and, at the confederal level, the States General (*Staten-Generaal*) that were comprised of provincial representatives – and, on the one other hand, the Stadholders ("stewards," *stadhouderen*) of the provinces who came from the House of Orange and were commanders-in-chief of the armed forces. This tension has led to the apt characterization of the United Provinces as a "monarchical republic."[4]

[1] J. Paul, "Comity in International Law," *Harvard International Law Journal*, 32 (1991), 1–96, 16.

[2] See Section 14.4.

[3] On the United Provinces of the Netherlands see Israel, *Dutch Republic*; M. Prak, *The Dutch Republic in the Seventeenth Century* (Cambridge: Cambridge University Press, 2005); J. de Vries and A. van der Woude, *The First Modern Economy: Success, Failure, and Perseverance of the Dutch Economy, 1500–1815* (Cambridge: Cambridge University Press, 1997).

[4] Lesaffer, *European Legal History*, 336–338.

12.2.1 A Commercial Republic (or Republics)

Even more apt – and more commonly used – has been the term "Commercial Republic." The Dutch relied on their maritime strength and global trading networks for survival as well as prosperity.[5] It could be argued that this entrepreneurial and progressive spirit is reflected in the strong emphasis that Huber's conflicts doctrine puts on legal certainty and on facilitating the making and enforcement of legal acts.

At the same time, even during their Golden Age the Netherlands were under constant threat from the great monarchic powers of Europe. It was only in 1648 that the – intermittent – Eighty Years' War with the Spanish Empire came to its end and Dutch independence from the Habsburgs was formally recognized by all. But the history of the United Provinces is complete with wars, all the way to the late eighteenth century and their demise. In his lifetime, Huber witnessed three Anglo-Dutch Wars, but also a Dutch King in the British Isles; numerous colonial conflicts; and Dutch involvement in several European wars as part of broader alliances. The Dutch were for long able to at least hold their own, but the events of the "year of disaster" (*rampjaar*), 1672 – when the Republic was invaded by France, in concert with England, and only managed to come back from the brink following violent political conflict and what was effectively a coup d'Etat – traumatized Huber and his compatriots and served as a reminder of precariousness.[6] This state of affairs may be seen as reflecting on the pragmatic internationalist outlook of Huber and his contemporary Dutch statesmen, with their insistence on mutual respect of sovereignty.

These attitudes also relate to Huber's particular provenance: Friesland, the northernmost Dutch province. In the loose federation that was the United Provinces in the "Golden Age," Friesland came a distant but very proud second to Holland.[7] Friesland's economy was turned to agriculture

[5] See e.g. D. Ormrod, *The Rise of Commercial Empires: England and the Netherlands in the Age of Mercantilism, 1650–1770* (Cambridge: Cambridge University Press, 2003).

[6] The French land invasion was supported by French and English naval action, as well as by additional forces from German Catholic principalities. With most of the country's interior under French occupation, political strife – pitting the Calvinist populace supporting the Orange party against the more moderate aristocratic establishment associated with the States party – escalated, leading to the violent murder of Grand Pensionary Johan de Witt and the ascent into power of Stadholder William IV. See Israel, *Dutch Republic*, 796–806.

[7] In Huber's time, Holland contributed 58.3 percent of the Union's budget and Friesland 11.6 percent, followed by Zeeland at a little over 9 percent (the other provinces were

(particularly cattle-raising), fishing, and trading in the North Sea.[8] Frisians were a distinct linguistic-ethnic group, whose language was closer to Old English than any other continental language.[9] Middle Frisia, which became the Dutch province of Friesland, had only fallen under imperial control and become part of the Netherlands rather late (1521), whereas the easternmost part of historical Frisia remained a German principality.[10] With few Catholics and an historical resentment of centralized government, the revolt won ground quickly and Friesland was effectively independent by 1578, even though the Province only joined the 1579 Union of Utrecht several months after the treaty's conclusion, with many Frisians opposed to a union with the other provinces.[11] Friesland also had a different stadholder (*stadhouder*) than Holland, albeit one from a junior branch of the House of Orange. The question therefore of who possessed "sovereignty" acquired additional importance for a Frisian statesman like Huber.

Frisian location – and identity – also played a part in Huber's stronger exposure to Northwestern Germany, as well as to a relative detachment, compared to authors based in Amsterdam, Leiden, and Utrecht, from what was going on at the heart of the United Provinces (let alone the border territories near Brabant and Flanders). One could speculate further that the respective locations of Huber and Johannes Voet in the periphery and the center of the Dutch microcosm have something to do with their different approaches to comity.[12] Friesland, and Huber, was

charged with a little over 5 percent each). See Prak, Dutch Republic, 77; Israel, *Dutch Republic*, 286.

8 Friesland was by far the most agricultural of the United Provinces: only a fifth of the population lived in one of the 11 recognized towns but was dwarfed in terms of population even by minor provinces such as Gelderland. See the figures mentioned in Israel, *Dutch Republic*, 15, 113–114, 332.

9 Dutch was however spoken by the governing elites, especially since a large number of non-Frisian Dutch and non-Dutch took offices since Charles V (Huber himself was a third-generation Frisian with Swiss origins). On the use of Dutch in sixteenth-century Friesland, see Israel, *Dutch Republic*, 73 with reference to J. M. M. Hermans, "Wat lazen Friezen aan het einde van de Middeleeuwen," *De Vrije Fries*, 70 (1970), 7–38, 20–21.

10 Friesland became part of the Kingdom of Burgundy under Charles V (1521). Historic Middle Frisia also extended over the heartland of the Groningen Province (*Ommelanden*). West Frisia, across the South Sea, formed part of the Province of Holland. As to East Frisia see Section 11.4.3.1.

11 See Israel, *Dutch Republic*, 189–192, 201. Unlike the south and east (three of the seven provinces had to be readmitted into the Union after the French occupation), Friesland remained unconquered during the Franco-Dutch war of 1672–1678.

12 See Section 14.3.

primarily concerned with conflicts among the United Provinces (and East Frisia), and this is apparent if we examine the actual and hypothetical cases discussed in Huber's conflicts treatment.[13] In contrast, Holland was the center of Dutch international trade and had constant interaction with the Spanish Netherlands, France, and England. Whereas Huber wanted to ensure Frisian laws were "observed" in the other provinces, Holland could afford some degree of unilateral action vis-à-vis both the eastern Provinces and the outside world.

12.2.2 Sovereignty and the State

The jurists–statesmen of the Dutch Golden Age had to defend their republican model from both external and internal challengers, in word as well as in deed. They had to come up with definitions of statehood and sovereignty that could apply to the various forms of polities, from "aristocratic democracies" to absolute monarchies, in Europe and beyond; externally, promote a normative vision of a system of states mutually respecting each other's sovereignty; internally, account for the complex allocations of institutional power both between and within each Province. Huber is motivated by all this in his own definition:

> By a "state" we here understand simply a body of citizens (*Burgerschap*) under a fixed government. Thus the two component parts of a state must be noted, namely the citizens and the government. By "body of citizens" is understood a people (*Volk*) united under a sovereignty for the enjoyment of common rights and a happy existence. By "people" we understand a complete collection of a number of households.[14]

This definition is missing the third requirement of statehood in classical and modern international law: territory. It does not suffice to explain this as omitting the obvious. Hugo Grotius had given the same definition of sovereignty (*summa potestas*) just over a half-century earlier, in his

[13] All 18 cases mentioned in "De Conflictu Legum" involve Friesland, usually as the forum but only one simly as the forum. As to the other jurisdiction, sixteen involve the neighbouring Dutch provinces: 13 involve Holland, 3 Groningen, and 1 Overijsel (one case is a conflict of jurisdiction between Holland against Groningen, with Friesland as the enforcement forum). Another involves the neighboring German principality of East Frisia. Only the – purely hypothetical – eighteenth case involves Brabant in the Spanish Netherlands: that was necessary for the example of Catholic dispensation that Huber wanted to give.

[14] Huber, *Heedensdaegse Rechtsgeleertheyt*, 4.2.1.

seminal natural-law treatise *On the Law of War and Peace.*[15] Emer de Vattel would do the same, almost a century later.[16] But neither does this indicate that Early Modern jurists espoused an a-territorial conception of sovereignty: already in Medieval political and legal thought, *territorium* was inherently linked to the idea of jurisdiction and provided the foundation for the idea of sovereignty.[17] Huber himself defines sovereignty in "De Conflictu Legum" as exercised within the polity's boundaries (*intra terminos [populi]*) and we will see several examples of how "boundaries" are used for the allocation of jurisdiction between sovereigns, or even within the magistrates in Friesland itself.

What these definitions do indicate is that Early Modern jurists appear less interested in defining statehood per se and more in determining where ultimate authority lies within a polity – or with legitimating such authority. For them, "this question of sovereignty . . . lies at the very basis of civic peace."[18] This ties in with the whole idea of political theory providing the foundation for legal doctrines.

This is certainly the case of Huber, who is concerned with defending the "sovereign" status and power of government in the Dutch provinces. In the very beginning of *Contemporary Jurisprudence*, Huber explains the prominence of Roman law in Friesland "in a purer and more downright form" than anywhere else by a narrative about how the anarchy that reigned in the country during the factional wars of the High Middle Ages let the ancient local laws sink into oblivion: the new princes (reference to 1521), having "found the country almost at a state of anarchy and without any recognized system of law . . . at once introduced the Roman law here."[19]

Equally telling is the fact that, having, in the first volume, announced his intention to follow the tripartite scheme of the Institutes, Huber actually began his second volume with a book on "the things which are necessary to the foreknowledge and the prosecution of actions."[20] Aptly

[15] Grotius, *De Jure Belli ac Pacis* 1.3.7: "That [power] is called supreme/sovereign (*summa*) whose actions are not subject to the legal control of another, so that they cannot be rendered void by the operations of the human will."

[16] E. de Vattel, *Le droit des gens*, vol. 1 (London, 1758), 17 (§ 1.1.1).

[17] See Magnus Ryan, "Territory in the Political Thought of the Medieval Lawyers."

[18] Huber, *Heedensdaegse Rechtsgeleertheyt*, 4.5.1

[19] Huber, *Heedensdaegse Rechtsgeleertheyt*, 1.2.46. Cf. Whitman, *Roman Law*, 17–28 on the political motivations behind Luther and Melanchton's eventual embrace of the *ius commune*.

[20] Ibid., 4.1.2.

given by its translator the title "Of the State and its Officers of Justice," Book IV is essentially a manual on the powers of Frisian officials and especially judges that covers the full range from political theory to practical advice on court proceedings. Huber explains his choice as follows:

> It is necessary that we should dispose of this subject first and in this place partly because the fountain of justice is the superior magistracy, and the power behind it is derived from the sovereign; and also because it is really necessary that people should be able to have a reasonable knowledge or the mutual powers and duties of magistrates and subjects, ignorance of which has heretofore occasioned very dangerous movements and still may any day produce them.[21]

This statement is followed by a Hobbesian narrative about the creation of political institutions to overcome men's innate disposition to rule those over whom they have power and a perpetual state of war.[22] Huber locates himself in the middle, opposing all those covenant-based theories regarding sovereigns as inferior to those who granted them that power, those who make obeyance dependent on whether the sovereign governed well, as well as the other extreme, which he associates with Hobbes, those that would regard the sovereigns as absolute in their power, once granted.[23] According to Huber, the minority maintains its "popular right" even after the majority has been ascertained (and power assumed by the few or the single ruler), but subjects do owe obedience, regardless of the good or bad government of the sovereigns, unless the sovereign orders something "which God has expressly forbidden, or which conflicts with the limitations which ... apply to all governments."[24] Law is therefore Huber's tool for ensuring civic peace. But also political theory is used as a foundation of legal doctrines and the exercise of jurisdiction. For Huber, "sovereign" is the body or the person in whom this power vests:

> Sovereignty (*Oppermacht*) is simply the power to govern a people in such a way that actions of the sovereign cannot be altered by the will of any other person.[25]

[21] Ibid., 4.1.3.
[22] Ibid., 4.1.4–21.
[23] Ibid., 4.5.1–19.
[24] Ibid., 4.5. See also T. Wittman, *Das Goldene Zeitalter der Niederlande* (Leipzig: Koehler & Amelang, 1975), 223.
[25] Ibid., 4.6.1.

Huber is a republican statesman who emphasized the rule of law and favored a regime of representation, an "aristocratic democracy."[26] He declares that, in the case of a people ruled "communally," "the decision of the majority must be taken to be the decision of each and all individually," and bind everyone, but the rights of the minority must also be guaranteed.[27] However, "when the sovereignty resides with the multitude" chaos ensues, so that almost all peoples have preferred to transfer sovereignty to "one person or an assembly of a fixed and limited number of citizens."[28] Hence, the "nobles and landed proprietors in Friesland, endowed like the kings and princes with sovereignty in general terms, have the same sovereignty as is possessed by the majority in a communal government" and are "masters of themselves and the people together, without dependence on or subjection to the multitude."[29] The dedication of his vernacular work is as telling.[30]

[26] In 1672 Huber published anonymously a pamphlet (*Spiegel van doleancie en reformatie, nae den tegenwoordigen toestant des vaderlandts*), reprinted in J. J. Kalma and K. de Vries (eds.), *Friesland in het rampjaar 1672* (Leeuwarden: Fryske Akademy, 1972), 120–136. See Israel, *Dutch Republic*, 807 (Huber proclaimed that "the politics, and constitution, of Friesland were different from those of Holland and that disaster would ensue, if the disorder and disrespect for authority, gripping Holland, should spread to Friesland") and 809 (Huber and Grotius were "[v]eteran observers .. deeply attached to the institutional forms of the Republic and "convinced of the rightness, and advantages, of rule by a narrow, wealthy, entrenched oligarchy and detested popular pressure in politics as a menace to the Republic they extolled [and] perceived . . . to be a benefit for all").

[27] See generally Huber, *Heedensdaegse Rechtsgeleertheyt*, 4.3. (quoted excerpt is in 4.3.11).

[28] Ibid., 4.4.2–3.

[29] Ibid., 4.4.16.

Friesland was historically divided into four quarters. Politically, into eleven cities and thirty ridings (*grietenijen*), each with two representative and one vote in the States of Friesland – the deliberative body in which sovereigny vested according to Huber. Voting franchise was conditional upon certain property requirements. This was the most representative democracy among the Provinces. To compare with the other two Dutch provinces including areas of historic Frisia: the States in the – much more powerful and urban – Holland were composed of eighteen cities and the college of nobles; the Province of Groningen was founded on a parity between the city of Groningen and countryside (Ommelands).

[30] The treatise is dedicated "To the nobility, landed gentry, and other true lovers of pristine freedom and integrity in Friesland – wishing them God's blessings upon the land, and peace in our time, this work is respectfully dedicated" (*Aen myne heeren de eedelen, eigenerfden en de andere ware liefhebberks van de aloude vryheyt en oprechtheyt in Frieslandt, word dit werk, met towenschinge van Godes zeegen over den lande, en vreede in onse dagen*).

In a sense, for Huber sovereignty equals the state:

> [T]he government differs from the civic body (body of citizens) as intellect from the human frame, or, as some put it, as harmony from a set of strings.[31]

And this leads to Huber's criterion as to what constitutes a state:

> Where, then, such regulating power is one and the same, there is one civic body and republic or state; where the regulating powers are different, there are different republics and states.[32]

This means there can be only one sovereign in each state, as well as one state for each sovereign – a position finds immediate application in his own environment:

> The Helvetians, therefore, and the United Netherlands do not constitute one republic, but as many in number as there are cantons or provinces, since each in themselves have their special regulating sovereignties, with their derivative magistrates and laws, notwithstanding that by a close bond, which the Helvetians call "League," and the Netherlands "Union" they are, as it were, united into one republic or state.[33]

Huber also regards the "High German Empire" as a case of a Union of republics ("each principality and free city has its own sovereign and laws").[34] The Spanish Empire is a case of many civic bodies having one head, and hence consists of "almost as many republics or states as it comprises kingdoms and territories."[35]

Huber has a homogenized – or homogenizing – view of states. Having noted that the term republic is used for "free peoples," he decides to employ the term as coterminous to "state" and "civic body."[36] To Huber, sovereignty is the same, whether exercised over a city-state or over an empire.[37] What matters is the effectiveness of power, which requires a population minimum and a finality in the state's decisions.[38]

[31] Huber, *Heedensdaegse Rechtsgeleertheyt*, 3.2.9.

[32] Ibid.

[33] Ibid., 4.2.10. On the attraction that the Swiss example held see Israel, *Dutch Republic*, 608.

[34] Huber, *Heedensdaegse Rechtsgeleertheyt*, 4.2.11.

[35] Ibid., 4.2.12.

[36] Ibid., 4.2.7–8.

[37] Ibid., 4.2.3: "The great Turkish Empire is simply a state with citizens, and the tiny city of Ragusa has the same constituents. We must say that to make a state the civic body must suffice in numbers and stability for protection against robbers and assassins."

[38] Ibid., 4.6.8: "[T]he States of Friesland have the sovereignty over their province just as much as a king or emperor would have over his widely extended lands and peoples, since the decisions of the former are as little subject to alteration as those of the latter."

12.2.2.1 Citizens, Foreigners, and Domicile

This brings us back to Huber's "body of citizens" as a requirement for the existence of a State. Huber distinguishes between two different uses of the term citizen:

> Citizens are those who have their fixed dwelling place in the Province whether in some town or in the country; on the contrary those who sojourn in the land for a time only, intending before long to depart, are foreigners. Those however who live in the towns are also called citizens in a special sense, meaning those who are accepted among and registered as citizens by the authorities of the towns and have paid the dues owing by them as such.[39]

The former use is directly relevant for law and our own discussion: "citizens" is here contrasted to "foreigner," in the model of Roman law. It is largely devoid however of its political content and essentially equated with domicile in the Province (*general domicile*).[40] The latter use of the term was important for Dutch, and Frisian, politics, where cities constituted the main political unit for purposes of representative democracy and administered citizenship. But it bore no jurisdictional significance: the so-called *particular domicile* ("in reference to a certain town or bailiwick") extended to both "residents" and "citizens."[41]

It is important to note that Huber draws no distinction between domicile and residence, in the modern sense. There is also no discussion of origin (*origo*).[42] He tends to use the words *domicilium*, in Latin, and *wooninge*, as well as *woonpaets*, in Dutch, almost interchangeably. A (particular) domicile is "where a person has made his domestic circle and the seat of his fortune."[43] The critical distinction for jurisdictional purposes is between citizens and residents, on the one hand, and visitors, who "sojourn in a place without any intention of establishing their settled

[39] Huber, *Heedensdaegse Rechtsgeleertheyt*, 1.4.36–37.

[40] Ibid., 4.22.2

[41] Ibid., 4.22.2, 5 and 4 ("residents are those who have their domicile and occupation in the town but have not been enrolled in the list of citizens").

[42] Cf. Voet, *Commentarius ad Pandectas*, 5.1.93.

[43] Huber, *Heedensdaegse Rechtsgeleertheyt*, 4.22.2 ("if he has divided this between two places or has obtained citizenship at two places then he is and remains subject to legal process at both of them").

home there but with the idea of stopping temporarily at certain places," on the other.[44] All residents have general domicile in Friesland.[45]

12.2.3 Religion

In his discussion "Of the Rights of the Sovereign Regarding Religion," Huber presents us with a continuum, where one end is taken by the Catholic position of "ascribing to the Popes the whole right of regulating church matters," followed by the Presbyterians who grant this right to the consistories or the clerical councils "and entirely exclude the supreme powers or sovereigns therefrom, if they are unbelievers; if believers, they merely recognize them as protectors of the church and executors of what the clericals happen to resolve or enact in regard to."[46] At the other end, we have "those who ascribe to the church no more than the bare confession of belief" and finally Hobbes, who treats all doctrines other the "fundamental principle that Christ is our Savior" as matters "not . . . of belief, but of allegiance" to the sovereign, who has "direction and control both of religion and of ritual."[47] Huber himself supports the middle position that relies on a distinction between "religion" and "ritual" to state his position:

> [R]eligion is independent of the jurisdiction of the higher powers, but the ritual is dependent upon and ought to be subject to them [. . .] sovereignty embraces a jurisdiction over all matters and transactions of the subjects excepting only what has not been assigned to it but tacitly or expressly withdrawn from it; and secondly, excepting all that God our Lord has clearly enjoined or forbidden humankind to do. Now no one will deny that the essential details of ritual, as observed among us or in other countries are not so prescribed by God our Lord. This is perfectly clear from the fact that this same ritual is observed quite differently in different places, though they may confess the same beliefs as ourselves, and not

[44] Ibid., 6. Visitors include "domestics, salesman and others who hired themselves out for a time in towns or villages and have their parents, guardians or households elsewhere" as well those appointed to a temporary office, such as assemblies, are visitors to a place, even if they have moved there with their families; but those appointed to permanent offices are considered as residents. Married women obtain their husbands' domicile. Ibid., 7. See also Section 14.2.2.

[45] Ibid., 9. The notion of general domicile is additionally used to establish trial jurisdiction of the Court of Friesland over certain residents superior to the ordinary condition of citizens and yeomen (including nobility, pastors and university professors). Ibid., 9–17.

[46] Ibid., 4.10.8–9.

[47] Ibid., 11–12.

> merely without detriment to unity and fraternity but in many matters with mutual assent and approval. This being duly premised we must point out what the things are which God our Lord necessarily demands, and which are subject to his degree alone; and secondly what things pertained to ritual as being variable and consequently subject to the sovereign.[48]

Huber's position is consonant with the political theory of Calvinism – his own church and the principal Dutch denomination.[49] These distinctions impacted the regulation of marriage, as well as the conflicts of marriage laws, as we shall see immediately below. We will also return to his definition of these "necessary commands of God . . . natural or revealed" in examing Huber's theory of legal sources. But we must first consider the theological context of Huber's writings, including his alleged anti-Catholicism and its possible impact on his conflicts work.

12.2.3.1 Protestantism, Catholicism, and Conflicts in Huber's Friesland

Calvinism was the dominant religion in the United Provinces, with increasing toleration shown toward especially other Protestant denominations.[50] Huber's Friesland was predominantly Calvinist, more than other provinces, but the structure was the same: there was an established denomination, the Reformed Church, whose members had the right to "attend and take part in public worship in the State Churches," as well as various heterodox groups who were tolerated in different degrees.[51] Yet none of these groups had the right to public ("legalized") meetings for worship.[52] Moreover, the publicity requirements of marriages of "parties of some other persuasion" were handled by a magistrate, unlike

48 Ibid., 15–16.

49 See e.g. C. Zwierlein, "Resisting the Thomist Temptation: A Good Political Order According to Calvin" in A. Hujgen and K. Maag (eds.), *Calvinus Frater in Domino: Papers of the Twelfth International Congress on Calvin Research* (Göttingen: Vandenhoeck & Ruprecht, 2000), 125–148.

50 Israel, *Dutch Republic*, tellingly entitles his respective chapters for the early Golden Age 1588–1647), later Golden Age (1647–1702) and the eighteenth-century Age of Decline as "Protestantization, Catholization, Confessionalization" (361–398), including a section on "The Rejection of Toleration"), "Confessionalization, 1647–1702" (637–676, including a first section on "The Rise of Toleration"), and "The Churches" (1019–1037, including a section on "The Loosening of Internal Confesion Barriers").

51 Huber, *Heedensdaegse Rechtsgeleertheyt*, 1.4.47.

52 Ibid., 1.4.49–50 (the meetings of Mennonites, who have been singled out by Huber as enjoying longstanding protection, "are not legalized, but merely regarded with tolerance, unless a long and uniform tolerance of more than one hundred years could be construed into a vested right of recognition.")

marriages of members of the Reformed Church, where banns were simply called in Church.[53]

Catholicism, in particular, had retained a small foothold among old Frisian nobility and Catholic minorities survived in the cities, reaching its peak at 10% of the Province's population around 1640 (significantly more than in the neighboring inland Provinces), but the provincial authorities were very hostile, especially in the countryside, and anti-Catholic sentiment was re-ignited following 1672.[54] Huber himself, writing a few years later, mentions Catholics ("Papists") first among the heterodox groups but notes that:

> Papists are under more restraint from the laws, because, having previously had the upper hand, and now seeing their party the most powerful in Europe, and being bound to the Pope by a very close tie, and emboldened on that account, they are supposed to be dangerous to the State.[55]

It would be wrong, however, to read too much into Huber's anti-Catholicism while explaining his conflicts doctrine. We will indeed find little love for the Catholic Church in his work, but also little attention: references to Catholic practices are used for illustrative purposes, or to explain the origins of certain doctrines. For example, in discussing kinship impediments to marriage, Huber makes two references to "Papal law." The first one concerns the different way in which it defined the degrees of blood relationship: rather than the Roman-law rule of counting one degree for each birth between the two persons, the papal rule – used in determining whether Frisian judges had to be excused in a case involving their relatives – counted only their distance from the common ancestor.[56] Given that under the papal rule one would have the same distance with one's uncle/aunt and his/her children, Huber concludes that the "imperial" rule is "more reasonable" with regard to the former cases.[57]

The second reference, which brings us to the Brabant case of "De Conflictu Legum," concerns marriage within the prohibited degrees. Huber regards the prohibition of marriages between uncles and nieces as sanctioned by both Roman law and divine law, being part of "the law

[53] Ibid., 1.5.22.

[54] See Israel, *Dutch Republic*, esp. 383–384, 642ff and the tables in 389 and 1022.

[55] Huber, *Heedensdaegse Rechtsgeleertheyt*, 1.4.48.

[56] Ibid., 1.5.67–82.

[57] Ibid., 82.

of nature innate to mankind."[58] In Frisia "such marriages, however long they may have been in existence, are declared null and void and the parties put asunder ... the punishment of banishment is inflicted ... so far as the man is concerned, for the woman is excused on the ground of ignorance of law."[59] On the contrary, he is critical of the Catholic extension of the impediment so far that "even the children of second cousins are forbidden to marry," which he attributes to the papal desire to "make money out of dispensations or indulgences ... even in the degrees forbidden by God, as they frequently do between uncles and the children of brothers or sisters, and in many other cases."[60]

Huber is here expressing the anti-Catholicism of Dutch Protestants of his time. Catholic canon law had indeed retained the extensive late-Medieval prohibition on intermarriages up to third cousins. This led to a practice of dispensations – easy to obtain for second- and third-cousin marriages, and hard but possible for first-cousin marriages. Protestants denounced both legs of this system. Most Protestant states would allow marriage between first cousins.[61] It was moreover acknowledged that a sovereign could grant dispensation for marriages forbidden only by Civil Law but not for marriages forbidden by Divine Law, such as this one.[62]

The case is hypothetical: no dispensation appears to have been granted for an uncle-niece marriage, any more than for a brother-sister marriage. The Roman Catholic Church in fact also regarded uncle-niece marriages as contrary to divine law until recently. Yet what is remarkable is that Huber, guided by the mistaken notion that such a marriage – contrary to natural or even divine law – could be valid in the Habsburg Netherlands, is only concerned with the possibility of Frisians evading the prohibition laid by natural law and Frisian law. He would however acknowledge, even in Frisia, the effects of a marriage held between "Brabanters" in Brabant (and seemingly tolerate the effects, in Brabant, of such a marriage held in Brabant between Frisian Catholics who had moved there), in application of the rules derived from the law of nations, in spite of his and his province's strong moral position and the conviction that this is contrary to divine law. This seems far not just from virulent anti-

[58] Huber, *Heedensdaegse Rechtsgeleertheyt*, 1.5.87 and 1.5.90.

[59] Ibid., 87 citing cases from 1636 (a man had married the daughter of his deceased wife's half-sister) and 1683.

[60] Ibid., 91.

[61] See additionally Voet, *Commentarius ad Pandectas*, 23.2.32.

[62] Ibid., 37–38.

Catholicism but also from "reject[ing] a law-of-nations approach in favor of the forum's law," but we will have the opportunity for a more reasoned assessment in this regard later.[63]

12.2.3.2 Religion and Early Modern Marriage

If we are to understand the treatment of foreign marriages in Huber, we need to consider the theological dimension of Early Modern marriage law. In the Middle Ages, marriage was defined in strictly theological terms, as a sacrament. At the same time, Medieval canon law of marriage contained many contractual ideas to deal with de facto situations, such as a "present consent" marriage.[64] Protestants viewed this sacramental conception of marriage, and the jurisdiction that the Church derived from it, as contrary to biblical teaching and a usurpation of the magistrate's authority.[65] The Reformation actually ushered in a variety of new theological perspectives on marriage.[66] Protestants may have differed on the appropriate rules and the degree of secularization of marriage.[67] But they shared a strong awareness of both its importance and the need for legislative reform: the rationalization of marriage impediments (as well as the attempt to limit the power of Church or State to dispense with particularly egregious impediments) is an obvious example. But there was also an increased emphasis on parental consent – which led to a reassertion of Roman rules on this matter in many states – and an insistence on ecclesiastical consecration.[68] As a result of the coexistence

[63] See Sections 13.4.2 and 14.4.4.

[64] See e.g. Donahue, *Law, Marriage and Society*, 16ff.

[65] J. Witte, *Law and Protestantism: The Legal Teachings of the Lutheran Reformation* (Cambridge: Cambridge University Press, 2002), 199.

[66] See J. Witte, *From Sacrament to Contract: Marriage, Religion and Law in the Western Tradition* (Lousville, KY: Westminister John Knox Press, 1999). Witte discerns a Lutheran conception of marriage as "social estate," a Calvinist conception of marriage as "covenant," and an Anglican conception of marriage as "commonwealth" (on the contrary, a conception of "marriage as contract," which Witte traces back to Enlightenment theology, did not take hold in law until the twentieth century).

[67] According to Witte, *Sacrament to Contract*, 216 the Lutheran model was the one which gave the most complete jurisdiction to the territorial authority, the Calvinists "assigned interlocking marital roles to local consistories and city councils," while the Anglican model kept ecclesiastical courts, under the supervision of the political power (216).

[68] In the words of Witte, *Law and Protestantism*, 199: "That a child could enter marriage without parental permission or church consecration betrayed . . . basic responsibilities of family church and state to children." The respective attitudes of Protestant denominations reflected on the approach to such issues, with Calvin more insistent than Luther. See Witte, *Sacrament to contract*, 57–58 and 83–84.

of several denominations and the territorial diversity of marriage laws, these ideas were embodied in an increased transactional formalism, which is attested to in Huber's work.[69]

A similar process is observable in Catholic countries. The canon-law conception of marriage had been moving toward stronger formalization of marriage laws for some time before Reformation and this was enshrined in the legislative reforms of the Catholic Council of Trent (1545–1563). By the time of the *tametsi* decree (1563), most Protestant states had already reduced marriage impediments and increased formality and publicity requirements.[70] The Tridentine reforms did not apply uniformly across Catholic Europe, however: France, for example, promulgated its own marriage laws, which in some cases went further than the Council itself.[71] In conclusion, the divergence of Early Modern marriage laws has to do with both theological pluralism and the plurality of would-be legislators, as well as with an increased societal interest in the regulation of marriage that prompted all sides to action.

12.3 Legal Sources and Their Hierarchies

Huber's theory of legal sources is expressly brought up, as we have seen, in discussions about comity and his conflict of laws doctrine. It has been suggested that Huber rejected "a law-of-nations approach in favor of the forum's law," "scholastic law for incipient positivism," accepted the role of "judge-made law" and the assertion of discretionary power by judges over legislators as regards to applicable law.[72] Others have on the contrary suggested that Huber viewed *ius gentium*, the law of nations, as part of domestic law and hence as binding on the judge. Before we begin our examination of Huber's conflicts doctrine, it is therefore imperative to

[69] See Section 13.4.2.

[70] Engdahl, "Canonical and Metaphysical Background," 43–48 suggests on the contrary that the Council of Trent brought the first major blow to legal unity. The argument may be inspired by the eventual return of English marriage law to the Medieval canon-law rules (see Witte, *Sacrament to Contract*, 159–163). Chronologically, given when Protestant legislative reforms took place, the argument could stand only if we were to transpose the 1563 rules back to 1545 (something Engdahl correctly does not do; but he may have underestimated the legal change in Protestant Europe). In any case, Trent seems to have been only one stream in the tide of legal reform, though admittedly a stream trying to stop the others.

[71] For example, the Ordonnance de Blois required publication of the marriage banns. See more generally Donahue, *Law, Marriage, and Society*, 633ff.

[72] Paul, "Comity," 16.

better understand how he approached legal authorities and sources of law, again examining his vernacular work, which is addressed to judges and legal practitioners.

Huber begins his work with the custom definitions of jurisprudence and justice, relying upon Roman-law sources and – by way of Grotius – Aristotle.[73] He defines Equity as the agreement that laws must have with the rules of Justice ("so far at least, that they do not conflict with them"), distinguishing between natural equity (which "looks at cases in their universal simplicity") and civil equity (which "includes also the consideration of what is useful and profitable for a nation").[74] Civil equity emanates from natural equity; in adding national considerations to what is universally established, civil equity is broader than natural equity but also allows for derogations – or special doctrines – integrated into civil law. Huber's characteristic example concerns protecting women from undertaking suretyships on behalf of other's debts: whereas "it is generally equitable that the word of a woman who binds herself for another person's debt should hold good," the "law . . . rendering null and void bonds entered into by women on behalf of other persons" is "civilly equitable."[75]

Huber's distinction between natural and civil equity has parallels with his distinction between the "civil law" particular to a polity (but, including, the learned essentially Roman law) and universal law, such as natural law and the law of nations. It also illustrates his attitudes toward the role of judges. The remainder of this section is organized along these three topics.

12.3.1 Natural Law and the Law of Nations

Huber's definition and typology of law is also Grotian. *Law* (*Wet*) is thus defined as "a rule for the transactions of mankind, binding them to what is right and honorable."[76] Grotius distinguished between intuitive law

[73] Huber, *Heedensdaegse Rechtsgeleertheyt*, 1.1.1–11. Unlike his Latin works, Huber only cites Grotius and genrally avoids citations to the clsssics or even modern philosophers in *Contemporary Jurisprudence*.

[74] Ibid., 12–15.

[75] Ibid., 16.

[76] Ibid., 1.2.2.

(*aengebore[ne] Wet*) and derivative law (*gegeve[ne] Wet*).[77] Huber makes the same distinction:[78]

> Intuitive law – or the law (*recht*) of nature – is the judgment of the intellect, informing us what things, by their own nature, are honorable or dishonorable, with Divine obligations to do or not to do them. And the essence of this kind of law is to command or to forbid. . . . [I]n its proper sense intuitive law is immutable, so long as circumstances remain the same. Every kind of virtue belongs to it, and every kind of vice is in conflict with it."[79]

This *intuitive law* encompasses "only what must be done or avoided of necessity."[80] The narrower definition endorsed by Huber and Grotius is contrasted to the expanded scholastic definition of natural law as including also "things which are indeed allowed, but which, even apart from such permission, may nevertheless be done without committing a crime," such as the right of "a man to protect himself against violence and to live in freedom" ("permissive natural law," *Toelaetende Recht der Nature*) or things which are "better done than not done, but in regard to which we have never been prohibited from acting otherwise," such as to leave one's property to the next of kin ("directory natural law," *Aenraedende Recht der Nature*).[81] In contrast also to the Roman conception of *ius naturale* as what nature has taught to all animals (which is characterized as "natural instinct"), the Early Modern conception of natural law requires a "sense of justice" and reasoning.[82] This is as far as Huber goes in this

[77] Grotius, *Inleiding*, 1.2.4. This is often translated as natural law and positive law respectively. See e.g. C. Herbert, *The Introduction to Dutch Jurisprudence of Hugo Grotius* (London: John Van Voorst, 1845), 5. Grotius, *De jure belli ac pacis*, 1.1.9 uses to the same effect the terms "natural law"(*ius naturale*) and "volitional law" (*ius voluntarium*), claiming to follow Aristotle, who however – as correctly pointed e.g. by Neff, *Grotius*, 28 (n. 25) – discusses justice and equity. See Aristotle, *Nicomachean Ethics*, 5.10. Huber, who had discussed Aristotelian ideas about justice in the preceding chapter, makes no such mistake.

[78] Huber, *Heedensdaegse Rechtsgeleertheyt*, 1.2.3.

[79] Ibid., 1.2.4 (citing Grotius, *Inleiding*, 1.2.8) and 1.2.7. Thus also Grotius, *De jure belli ac pacis*, 1.1.10 princ ("The law of nature is a dictate of right reason, which points out that an act, according as it is or is not in conformity with rational nature, has in it a quality or moral baseness or moral necessity; and that, in consequence, such an act is either forbidden or enjoined by the author of nature, God").

[80] Ibid., 1.2.5.

[81] Ibid., 5–6 (citing Grotius, *De Jure belli ac pacis*, 1.1.10).

[82] D.1.1.1.3 (Ulpian): "Jus naturale is what which nature has taught to all animals; for it is not a law specific to mankind but is common to all animals – land animals, sea animals, and the birds as well. Out of this comes the union of man and woman which we call

text regarding the law of nature, but if we look to Grotius, whom Huber follows closely in this regard, he suggests there are two "lines of proof" of the content of the law of nature: either "demonstrating the necessary agreement or disagreement of anything with a rational and social nature" (*a priori*), or "concluding, if not with absolute assurance, at least with every probability, that that is according to the law of nature which is believed to be such among all nations, or among all those that are more advanced in civilization" (*a posteriori*).[83]

Derivative law is *divine* or *human*.[84] Divine law is further divided into the old divine law given by Moses to the Jewish people and the new divine law given by Christ to all peoples.[85] Of the old divine law some – moral or ethical law – is also common to all nations, whereas the rest – political and ceremonial law – is peculiar to the Jewish people, albeit those of its norms "founded on essential principles of virtue and honor" may be binding as an expression of intuitive law.[86]

Human law is divided into the *law of nations* and the *civil law*:[87]

> The Law of Nations (*wet der volkeren*) is the name given to that law which has acquired binding force through being observed by the whole human race or the greater part of it. To this belong the law of war, the law of the common weal, property in goods and almost all obligations and agreements (or contracts), together with the laws of marriage, last wills and other such things.[88]

For Huber, just like Grotius, this Law of Nations is different from the Law of Nature.[89] The latter is, as we have seen, defined narrowly as

marriage, and the procreation of children, and their rearing. So we can see that the other animals, wild beasts included, are rightly understood to be acquainted with that law." Grotius, *De jure belli ac pacis*, 1.1.11 suggests that the Roman distinction is "of hardly any value; for strictly speaking, only a being that applies general principles is capable of law."

83 Grotius, *De jure belli ac pacis*, 1.1.11 in fine: "For an effect that is universal demands a universal cause; and the cause of such an opinion can hardly be anything else than the feeling which is called the common sense of mankind."

84 Huber, *Heedensdaegse Rechtsgeleertheyt*, 1.2.9.

85 Ibid., 10.

86 Ibid., 11–19, and 17 ("Nevertheless, so far as the municipal laws are, we are bound substantially to observe them").

87 Ibid., 1.2.20–21.

88 Ibid., 1.2.22, citing D.1.1.5.

89 In subsequent editions, the following was appended to Huber, *Heedensdaegse Rechtsgeleertheyt* (1734) 1.2.22 in fine: "Some authorities prefer, it is true, to make no distinction between the Law of Nature and of Nations, but I find no reason for diverging from the old distinction."

"intuitive law" consisting only of positive commands or prohibitions and its rules are imminent and immutable.[90] Grotius wrote that the Law of Nations "received its obligatory force from the will of all or many Nations" (*Gentium omnium aut multarum voluntate vim obligandi accepit*).[91] He explained his reference to "many" by noting that "outside of the sphere of the law of nature . . . there is hardly any law common to all nations. Not infrequently, in fact, in one part of the world, there is a law of nations which is not such elsewhere."[92] The reference to parts of the world indicates what is meant by "most" or "greater part of the human race." We saw that in Bartolus, *ius commune* was supposed to provide a common law, for war and peace, between all polities of Western Christendom (the *populus Romanus*); *ius gentium* was to do the same between them and the *populus extraneos* of the Eastern Mediterranean and Eurasia; but there was no fundamental difference between the ones and the others. By the seventeenth century, *ius gentium* had to provide the common norms for the relations between the Western European polities as well; at the same time, the world had expanded to the entire globe – including *gentes* that appeared much more alien than Bartolus's Greeks and Saracens – and even ancient literary sources were being used as authority to establish the content of this law of nations. Indeed, both examples Grotius refers to, captivity and postliminy, concern rights under the law of war no longer enforced among Christians.[93]

There are subtle differences in perspective between Huber and Grotius. Huber essentially reverses the order of Grotius, who treats human law first and divine law second, and indeed civil law, very briefly, prior to the law of nations.[94] Huber is also more laconic with regard to the law of nations, which he presents as "acquiring" its binding force through observance "by the human race." In contrast, Grotius has the law of nations "receiving" its binding force "from the will" of nations or being "adopted" by them.[95] Huber makes no mention of ascertaining the content of the law of nations, so we must again look to Grotius:

> The proof for the law of nations is similar to that for unwritten municipal law; it is found in unbroken custom and the testimony of those who are

[90] Thus Grotius, *De jure belli ac pacis*, 1.1.10.
[91] Ibid., 14.
[92] Ibid.
[93] Ibid., 3.7.9 and 3.9.19.
[94] Ibid., 1.1.14–15.
[95] Ibid., 14 and Grotius, *Inleiding*, 1.2.11.

> skilled in it. And to this purpose eminent Historians are of excellent use of to us.[96]

12.3.2 Civil Law

Huber defines civil law as essentially the domestic, positive law of each state but also takes account of the role of Roman law:

> Civil Law is that which has its immediate origin in the will of the sovereign power of a free people. But because the laws of the State of Rome spread with her ancient empire through the whole of Europe, and because they surpass all other known systems of law in sagacity and justice, Roman law kept its force among almost all Christian peoples, so much so that it has been adopted by many of them; not, however, without every free nation taking away or adding what seemed to it good. Among some nations also it has no binding power, but rather serves as a pattern of wisdom and legality, without the judges being actually bound by it.[97]

Huber's rationale for the validity of Roman law is much different than Bartolus's. Medieval doctrine was grounded on Roman law and a notion of legal unity. In Huber's age, not only had Roman law persisted but the geographical scope of its influence had in fact expanded, notably through its Reception in German and even Nordic lands. Whereas, however, the Medieval *populus Romanus* was a creature of – or a fiction supported only by – Roman law, in the Early Modern Era Roman law derived its authority from its "reception" by these innumerable *populi.*[98] By the seventeenth century, however, even if the actual number of territorially organized political entities with effective autonomy (*populi*) may have decreased, compared to the Middle Ages, the weak, nominal, or even fictional links superimposing on Medieval polities were gone. It is now by the will of the sovereign power of each free people that Roman law forms part of their law – and it forms part only insofar the sovereign power has allowed. Whereas Bartolus viewed the territorial entities of his time as under the umbrella of a continuous Roman empire blessed by Christ, and hence under the scepter of Roman law, Huber keeps from the old empire only the fact that its power helped Roman law travel through Christianity.[99]

[96] Grotius, *De Jure Belli ac Pacis*, 1.1.14 in fine.

[97] Huber, *Heedensdaegse Rechtsgeleertheyt*, 1.2.23–24.

[98] See Section 12.3.2.

[99] Thus also Huber, *Praelectiones ad Pandectas*, 1.3.App.1. See also Huber, *Heedensdaegse Rechtsgeleertheyt*, 4.15.14–15: "The Roman law again consists of two parts: the one has regard to the circumstances of the old Roman republic; the other is general, applying also

This holds true in Friesland, which adopted Roman law in the sixteenth century but had apparently derogated less from it than any other Dutch province.[100] Roman law is "only respected . . . in so far it has been adopted by the Frisians" and "only applies in cases for which the Frisian law does not provide."[101] We will see that Huber essentially reverses this presumption to make Frisian law apply only in cases for which it expressly provides. He is certainly dismissive of the continuing usefulness – indeed survival – of pre-Reception Frisian customary law.[102] In his own words, "the confusions of our ancestors have brought us this advantage, that the Roman law is maintained here in a purer and more downright form than in any other region, country or state of Christendom."[103]

The Reception theory which Huber espouses is coupled with his holistic approach as to what constitutes civil law (*Burgerlijk Recht*). Huber objects to the "usage" which "ordains that the Roman law should be called par excellence Civil Law and the special laws of each free people Territorial or Local law."[104] To him, they are both "as much civil" and they together constitute the Civil law of each people's fatherland.[105] Thus, in his exposé of Frisian law, he will call Roman law "Universal" or "Imperial law" and the laws of Frisia "Territorial Law" or "Ordinances of Friesland."[106] Taken together with his historical narrative of Roman law in Friesland, Huber's equation of local law with Frisian legislation is indicative of Huber's emphasis on learned and positive law to the detriment of old Frisian custom and usages.

to our own time. This last part is really enough for a Judge to know, but since the whole Roman law is linked together, and the one part serves to explain the other, a Judge cannot get a firm knowledge of the latter part without making the first also, and thus the whole science of law his own."

100 As examples from our own text see e.g. Huber, *Praelectiones ad Pandectas*, 1.3.App.4, 9, and 11. Of course, derogations of Frisian law from the *ius commune* were also numerous, as reading especially Huber's vernacular treatise might suggest. See for more J. H. A. Lokin et al., *Roman-Frisian Law of the 17th and 18th Century* (Berlin: Duncker & Humblot, 2003), esp. 31ff; T. J. Veen, "Een Transformatie Van Het Begrip Fries Recht," *Tijdschrift voor Rechtsgeschiedenis*, 38 (1970), 565–570.

101 Huber, *Heedensdaegse Rechtsgeleertheyt*, 1.2.30 and 28 respectively.

102 Ibid., 43–46.

103 Ibid., 47. See, however, Veen, "Transformatie," 567–568 discussing the conclusions drawn from this passage by K. de Vries.

104 Huber, *Heedensdaegse Rechtsgeleertheyt*, 1.2.26.

105 Ibid., 27–28.

106 Ibid., 29.

Indeed Huber's civil law includes both written and unwritten law. The "written laws in Friesland are first the Roman … and secondly the Resolutions of the States [of Friesland]."[107] Huber sets out the formalities required for a Frisian law to take effect and notes also that "resolutions for the benefit of individuals or particular towns or localities … have not the force of law in respect of others" and are "indeed … altogether without force insofar as they may conduce to the injury of another person's vested right," unless publicity and consent requirements are met.[108] But Huber also describes a process for the cognizance of customary law:

> Unwritten law is the same as custom (*gewoonte*) which gradually obtained binding force through popular usage. It is called unwritten because it is never put into writing in its beginning, since its beginning is obscure. But when once adopted and settled it is put into writing. For instance, Costumen, that is, customs, are ocommonly put into writing in our ordinances.[109]

For customs to "have the same force as laws," they must be "righteous, general and certain":[110]

> Righteous, that is, not clashing with virtue, sound reason or the common law of nations. General, that is, adopted by the whole people or by the greater part of it. Certain, that is, of such long and frequent usage that there can be no doubt of them.[111]

Huber obviously draws on the Digest for his definition, but his requirement that a custom be righteous (*Rechtsvererdig*) goes beyond Roman law and essentially subjects customary law to the law of nations (*gemein recht der volkeren*) as well as to rationality and morality.[112] Huber seems intent on subordinating custom to learned law and the law of nations. He would not even regard long usage as going above them:

> We must not then regard as customs those usages which rather arise from ignorance of law then rest on sound foundations.[113]

[107] Ibid., 32–33.
[108] Ibid., 34–35.
[109] Ibid., 48–50.
[110] Ibid., 52.
[111] Ibid., 53–55.
[112] Ibid., 53 citing D.1.3.39: "A proposition does not hold good in analogical cases if it was not originally brought in on a rational ground but adhered to in the first place in error and thereafter by custom."
[113] Ibid., 56.

Huber presents two examples (regarding the valuation of trees planted by tenants and of household goods for usufruct): in the former, the Court of Friesland decided against what "long been the custom of the landlords," the latter what is "now everywhere usual . . . is in truth contrary to the principles of the law."[114]

What is more interesting is Huber's reference to *de stijl van de Cancellerie*, which "has as much force as lawful custom and should be upheld as such provided that it does not clash with clear laws (*wetten*) and ordinances."[115] This has been translated by Gane as "legal practice," while Huber seemingly cites Andreas von Gail's reference to *stylus iudicii*.[116] Judicial practice appears to be a more accurate translation, in the light of the – subsequent – equivalent passage in *Praelectiones*.[117] Gail himself, the "German Papinian," is an interesting authority, in the sense that in his *Observations* on the practice of the Reichskammergericht any sense of that Court's case law is lost under the weight of learned-law sources.[118] In any case, according to Huber such practice may be treated as custom but must not conflict with Frisian legislation or the other laws, i.e. Roman law or even the law of nations.[119]

This reference to *stijl* is distinguished from numerous references to practice (*practijke*) throughout the work, of which the most interesting for our purposes comes in Huber's chapter on notaries. In Friesland, "the original signed documents would have to be delivered to the parties, and the registration thereof, signed in the protocol by the notary, would have the force of proof, so that he could always have recourse to them."[120] This practice was in contrast to other territories, notably Holland, where "parties and witnesses are accustomed to sign the protocol, from which

[114] Ibid., 56–57.

[115] Ibid., 58 with reference to Andreas Gail.

[116] von Gail, *Practicarum Observationum*, 1.1.1. See also ibid., 1.1.14 and 1.65.8. But in the same edition, von Gail, *De Arrestis Imperii*, 7.13 actually uses the term *stylus Cancellariae* to refer to the chancery practice (*licet ista differentia in Grammatophylaciis, sive Cancellariis Principum*).

[117] Huber, *Praelectiones ad Pandectas*, 1.3.15 (*in foro vim Consuetudinum habere stylum Curiae, sive judicii, qui dicitur et praxis*).

[118] Dawson, *Oracles of the Law*, 221–222: "The principal purpose was to flesh out around the skeleton provided by Reichskammergericht decisiones the great body of opinion found in the learned others. But with Gail the skeleton was barely visible. References to the decisions or the practice of the Reichskammergericht were buried beneath copious citations to jurists' writings and ponderous structures of argumentation."

[119] See in more detail Huber, *Praelectiones ad Pandectas*, 1.3.15.

[120] Huber, *Heedensdaegse Rechtsgeleertheyt*, 5.25.9.

the notary takes copies signed by him, which then have the force of proof."[121] Apparently, however, this led to a practice of notaries neglecting their protocols and practice "barely discriminating whether an instrument was written by a notary, or by an attorney, village justice or school-master, so that equal justice is pronounced upon them, even without any witnesses and often almost on bare handwriting signed by a person." Huber acknowledges that "just as in other matters, practice becomes the mistress (*meestersse*) of Laws and Ordinances, so it has happened with the notaries." He calls this practice an "abuse" (*misbruik*) "the more surprising" because it flies in the face both of legislative reform ("as though the whole injunction on the subject had been left out of the new ordinance") and Roman law itself:

> This abuse is the most surprising since in the old ordinance a certain old note of a custom which must have existed in Friesland, as to proof by handwritings signed and sealed by a person, was expressly censured, disapproved and annulled and the new ordinance passed, to the effect that from thenceforth, in matters touching the credence to be given to documents or instruments the written law should be followed.
>
> We might reasonably wonder that in a country where the Roman law is so strictly observed, a custom could have been adopted, in spite of Ordinances and in spite of everything, so highly in conflict with those laws and with the customs of all nations and no less with the common weal (*gemeene nut*).[122]

Huber's immediate next step is to address himself to the notaries' self-interest and common sense and proceed with detailed practical guidance to notaries. The whole discussion can help us better appreciate the background of Huber's *actus* territorialism. What is of immediate interest, however, is what it tells us about Huber's legal hierarchies: Roman law constitutes the residual law of Friesland, except so far as abrogated by an express provision in provincial legislation.[123] Frisian law is also subject to natural law (defined more strictly) and the law of nations, which is defined more broadly to include doctrines common in the laws of all nations. In areas not covered by Roman law, Huber would allow

[121] Ibid.

[122] Huber, *Heedensdaegse Rechtsgeleertheyt*, 5.26.11–12.

[123] Ibid., 42 has an example relating to our treatment's marriage cases: "The law demands that marriages should be made known throughout the community, and ratified before the community; but because a money fine has been appointed in the case of transgressors, it is understood that the marriage, if proved in some other way, is not null and void but is left to the dispensation of the Imperial law as will appear later on."

gaps to be filled by drawing on the example of the "laws and customs of our neighbors" – Huber means primarily Holland in matters of commercial law.[124] Any practices or customs that were or are developed must operate within these confines.[125] Huber is a legal positivist but his positivism includes – indeed is powered by – learned law.

12.3.3 *Judicial Power and Discretion*

These attitudes are apparent in the guidance and advice to judges Huber provides across his work. His Judge must be "a man of honor, skilled in the laws and of good judgment," whose "duty is in general to lay down the law as dictated by the laws and ordinances."[126] Huber insists that a judge must be "skilled in the knowledge of the laws, which is also necessary in the highest degree, especially as the science of law is of very wide circumference and the most difficult of all branches of learning."[127] Requisite learning must be "in the common law, and in the particular law in use where he exercises his office."[128] In contrast, Huber plays down the importance of "practice": "a Judge, who has experience in the knowledge of the laws can soon acquire the practice, but a person who knows nothing but practice can never be fit for the office of a Judge":[129]

> Practice is treated by many as though it was something different from the science of Roman law and of the Ordinances of Friesland; but in truth practice is nothing else than the employing and applying of laws and ordinances, all doubts arising in practice having assuredly to be resolved out of the laws and ordinances; except that sometimes things prescribed in the ordinances may fall into long-continued disuse which is the sole point in which practice may differ from the knowledge of the laws; apart from that, it is nothing but a competence, obtained from experience to put into operation the contents of the laws.[130]

124 Ibid., 62.

125 Huber does not see much ground for local legislation ("local laws of individual towns"), which must in any case conform to the common law of Friesland. See ibid., 1.2.59–60. Such local laws were more prevalent in other Provinces, as will be seen in cases discussed in this Part. For an example of Frisian local divergence see Section 12.4.1.1.

126 Ibid., 4.15.6 and 24.

127 Ibid., 9.

128 Ibid., 13.

129 Ibid., 17.

130 Ibid., 16.

Huber on the contrary emphasizes the need of the judge possessing a "sound and accute judgment":

> The judgment of the judge must be both natural and civil – natural, that is, in agreement with innate sound reason; and civil, that is, justified by an observation of the circumstances in the light of human intercourse, so that the judgment is not in conflict with the received opinion of the rest of mankind; for private whims leading to a conception of things different to people's common comprehension are not suitable to the office of Judge.[131]
>
> It is true that the laws are founded on natural equity and that all legal judgments must agree with sound reason and be tested by it. It is also true that if a Judge should have to lack one of the two things, great learning in law or a sound and acute judgment to lack the latter would be much the more serious.[132]

The judge's "good judgment" will be guided by – and measured against – "sound reason" and the "received opinion of mankind," presumably as elaborated by jurists. "Natural equity" is here invoked as a foundation for the law, which the judge must apply. Indeed, the same applies to civil equity, as we have seen.[133] Civil equity must be considered "universally and not in respect of particular cases; for it often happens that a good and equitable law seems very unjust in reference to this or that particular case":[134]

> Some think that the Supreme Courts (*Souveraine Hoven*) may base their judgment on this particular [i.e. civil] equity, while the lower Judges (*Neder-rechters*) ought to adhere closely to the words of the law; but the truth is that neither superior nor inferior Judges may depart from the general law for reasons of equity peculiar to this or that case; for all Judges, even those from whose decision there is no appeal, have no higher honor than to be servants of laws. The laws will be entirely loose and uncertain if Judges were allowed to decide in each particular case whether they should be followed or not.[135]

We will search in vain for a statement in support of "judge-made law" or "the discretionary power of the judge." In fact, Huber provides two telling illustrations of how he perceives both equity and the role of the judge: the judge must enforce the law, even if in the particular case such

131 Ibid., 20.
132 Ibid., 11.
133 Ibid., 1.1.16 discussed at Section 12.3.
134 Ibid., 17.
135 Ibid., 1.1.18.

enforcement seems inequitable.[136] But, the judge should follow the spirit of the law rather than the letter, if the latter is "hard and inequitable."[137]

12.4 Sovereignty and Jurisdiction in Huber

The influence of Huber's thought on political and legal order on his conflicts doctrine will be a theme underlying the next two chapters. Given that our emphasis therein will be on the choice of law, the last part of this chapter appears the most appropriate venue for examining his doctrine on civil jurisdiction, which appears as a sidenote in Huber's conflicts treatment but was of immediate concern to him and has indeed colored how he is perceived by modern doctrine.

In "De Conflictu Legum," Huber defends his second axiom against those who "seem to be of a different opinion and deny that foreigners are subject to the laws of the place in which they act" (*in quibus agunt*). This is a notion as old as the gloss *si Bononienis*, but of course, Huber lives in a world with different legal hierarchies than Accursius. On the other hand, Huber himself has raised the stakes by stating that his second axiom covers those found either "permanently or temporarily" in the territory. But what does he mean by "temporarily" or "for a time" (*ad tempus*)? Let us consider his response:

> I admit this to be true in certain cases, as we shall see later. But the proposition that *all persons who act within the limits of a state are to be*

[136] Ibid., 19–20. The first one concerns a 1680 decision where the Court of Friesland applied the *Senatus consultum velleianum* in a case where "enforcing [the law] against [the creditors] seemed very inequitable, and for that reasons many members of the Court felt difficulty in giving absolution" (ibid., 19). The second case (ibid., 20) concerns judicial power to allow the alienation of minor's property when such a sale would "very advantageous" for the minor but not "absolutely necessary," as the law requires: "This seems inequitable but universal justice turns the scale since if the decision of what is profitable or not in these cases were once left to the Judge, the sale of such properties will be without check or restraint."

[137] Ibid., 21: "It is then not in the power of the judge to decide in any other way than the law lays down, although the reason which underlies the law may not apply in this or that particular case; however it is the duty and privilege of the Judge, in case the words of the law are hard and inequitable, and it nevertheless appears obvious that the intention of the legislator was not such, to follow the spirit of the law rather than the letter. For example the law says, *Whoso sheddeth man's blood, by blood shall his blood be shed.* If a man has shed blood in protecting his own person, according to the letter he would have to be punished; but the Judge will not punish him, because the intention of the law is beyond doubt. To such verbal cavillings the proverb "The highest law is the greatest injustice" refers.

> *deemed subject thereto* is absolutely certain, for it is in accordance both with the nature of the state and the practice of subjecting all persons found therein to its authority, and with that which is accepted by all nations in regard to personal arrest. Grotius maintains that he who contracts in any particular place is subjected as a temporary subject to the laws of that place. Nor is there any other basis (*ratio*) for the rule that foreigners are compelled to submit to mesne arrest for no other reason than that they are found in a place, except that the sovereign authority is deemed to extend to all persons who are found within its boundaries.[138]

Huber is here not concerned with defending territorial sovereignty: we shall in fact see below how his *actus* territorialism is encroaching upon the harder, *situs*-centered territorialism.[139] He is concerned with establishing a foundation for the idea that legal acts will be, in principle, valid everywhere as long as they are valid under the law of the place where they were made. And the first step to achieve this is to establish that a polity has jurisdiction over such activity "within its boundaries." Once this is established, the next step is to establish mutual recognition of the effects of such jurisdiction – his third axiom, about which he tells us that "none hitherto seems to have entertained any doubt."[140] Even though the verb "act" (*agere*) does not appear in the second axiom itself, Huber's preoccupation shows in its supporting passage, where he uses the verb twice, the second time in restating his proposition (*positio*), which is italicized in the original text. Even the reference to Grotius concerns acting. In fact, the reference is used to support the idea that contracting constitutes a voluntary subjection to the place of contracting and its laws.[141] Again, this idea is not new, but earlier jurists may have limited themselves to the idea of tacit agreement that the laws of the place of contracting be implied into the contract. Huber, like indeed Grotius, suggests that contracting in a place makes one a "temporary subject" (*subditus temporaribus*) as far as the reach of that place's laws is concerned. We may better appreciate how important this idea is for Huber's scheme once we realize that this is the only specific reference to another work in Huber's conflicts treatment – probably the only conflicts treatment, at least since

[138] Ibid., 2 in fine.

[139] See Section 14.2.3.

[140] See Section 14.4.1.

[141] Grotius, *De Jure Belli ac Pacis*, 2.11.5. See Section 11.3.2.3.

the fourteenth century, with no references to other works in concrete points.[142]

Having determined what Huber wants to establish, let us see how he supports it. The first line of argument regards the "nature of the State (*natura Reipublicae*)" and the "practice" or "custom" (*mos*) of "subjecting to its authority" all persons "found" in the polity (*subigendi imperio cunctos in civitate repertos*). The very definition of State and Sovereignty, as elaborated by Huber, necessitates the exercise of such jurisdiction over "those found within its boundaries" (*intra terminos ejusdem reperiuntur*). Huber presents this also as established in law. It is difficult to translate exactly the word Huber actually uses, *mos*. It is certainly more binding than "practice," but it is also more than an individual "custom" (*consuetudo*), which Huber has discussed in the immediately preceding chapter of his *Praelectiones*.

The second line of argument concerns "that which is accepted by almost all nations in regard to personal arrest." Being a practice accepted by all or almost all nations, it forms part of the law of nations according to Huber's own definition. If the first line of argument operates deductively, the second one operates inductively. But what precisely is Huber alluding to here?

12.4.1 Civil Jurisdiction over Foreigners in Huber

Huber's doctrine on civil jurisdiction has not been a matter of concern in conflicts historiography but it came to the fore with regard to the historical pedigree of process-based jurisdiction in US law.[143] Whereas inevitably our examination relates to that discussion, our own purpose must be to understand the thinking underlying Huber's doctrine.

Huber devotes the fifth book of *Contemporary Jurisprudence* to "the Judicial proceeding (*Regt geding*) itself, commonly called the Process (*Proces*)," beginning with a chapter on summons or "citation" (*citatie*)."[144] The choice of subject has to do less with the chronological or logical order of the stages of the process, and more with the inherent link, in the scholarship of this period, of citation/summons with establishing jurisdiction – a subject to which Huber has devoted much attention also

[142] See Section 13.2.3. The earlier Huber, *Heedensdaegse Rechtsgeleertheyt*, 1.3.8 cites Gail and Sandius when presenting his primary rule.

[143] See Section 2.6.2.2.

[144] Huber, *Heedensdaegse Rechtsgeleertheyt*, 5.1.1.

in his fourth book.[145] Citation is "the first and most necessary part," according to both civil law and the law of nature, "which do not allow a person to be condemned without first calling and hearing him."[146] It is defined as "a calling of one's opponent before the Judge under whose jurisdiction he is, in order to have a dispute ended by that Judge's judgment."[147] Huber distinguishes *ordinary* from *extraordinary*, or *edictal, citation*.[148] Domicilaries are summoned to court by ordinary citation, whereas non-domiciliaries by extraordinary citation.

Citation – and hence jurisdiction – is linked to the power of the judge over the defendant. This holds true not just with regard to jurisdiction over "foreigners," but also as the assertion and allocation of venue jurisdiction within the Province. Huber begins with the latter:

> In our definition it was said that the citation must be made upon one who is subject to the Judge's jurisdiction, on the ground that is, of domicile; for no Judge can have a summons served outside his area. When we have to cite a person not domiciled under the Judge, but subject for another reason to the tribunal, as on the ground of contract, transaction or otherwise, a petition to his magistracy is then necessary in order that he may be cited by it. This is called requisitorial citation and it is in the power of the judge to grant it or not. In case of refusal, no further proceedings may be taken against that person but if the defendant's Judge allows it, then a person who has submitted to another jurisdiction or who contracted at the specified place, may not legally except to it.[149]

So, in cases involving defendants with a domicile elsewhere in the Province, consent of their local judge is required so that they be cited in the first court and Huber encourages lower judges to not simply grant such consent without considering the actual case.[150] But when it comes

[145] Ibid., 4.22–33. This has inevitably led to some basic ideas recurring in two or even three different chapters of the work. In contast, Voet, *Commentarius ad Pandectas*, 2, treats of these matters, beginning with jurisdiction, in his commentary on the second book of the Digest, following the Digest's structure. As a result, his chapter on summons is separated by the one on jurisdiction by two chapters on the right of retorsion and on disobedience to a judicial order.

[146] Huber, *Heedensdaegse Rechtsgeleertheyt*, 5.1.2, with reference to Inst. 4.16.3 ("The beginning of every action is controlled by the part of the praetor's edict providing for summons to court. That is of course always the first step, getting the defendant before the person who will decide the case") and C.7.45.4.

[147] Ibid., 5.1.1.

[148] Ibid., 7.

[149] Ibid., 6.

[150] Ibid. See also Section 13.6.

to persons not found in the Province, citation may require an edict or more extraordinary measures:

> Extraordinary or edictal citation applies when the jurisdiction of the court has been founded over a foreigner who is not found in the province whether he is resident at a certain place or it is unknown where he may reside.[151]

An extraordinary citation is only possible in the specific instances set out by Huber. The only other way for the Frisian court to obtain jurisdiction would be to make a requisitorial citation and rely on the "Judge, in whose jurisdiction the party is domiciled ... to be good enough to have him cited."[152] That judge has the power, when faced with a requisitorial citation, to decide whether to adjudicate the case himself or to effect the citation of the party (to be tried by the requesting judge).[153] Huber notes that, for practical reasons ("the edictal [form] demands much formality and expense"), it is common to opt for the "requisitorial form," i.e. to still go through the Judge of the party's domicile, even in cases where a ground for extraordinary citation exists.[154] In such a case, however, there is "no reason" for the receiving Judge to refuse the service and if he does refuse, "edictal citation can still take place."[155]

So let us examine these instances:

> The principal cases in which jurisdiction can be founded over a foreigner are these. Firstly, when the legal proceeding has already lawfully (*wettelijk*) begun before the Court, and citation is necessary in regard to proofs or incidentals, and the party has not chosen a *domicilium citandi* here, that is, a place at which to receive it.
>
> Secondly, when a person is sued in an action relating to fixed property situated in the Province.

151 Ibid., 8.

152 Ibid., 5.1.15.

153 Ibid., 16 and 6.

154 Ibid., 17.

155 Ibid., 18. "The content of this is notified to the person cited by a letter of notice from the Sheriff who makes the service on the borders, and the case is then proceeded with here, no return being demanded as necessary other than that of the same Sheriff [citing a 1681 decision]." Regarding conflicts of venue jurisdiction within Friesland, Huber notes at this point that edictal citation "has no place" within the Province but (having previously listed the special circumstances that may necessitate such extraordinary citation within Friesland) he states that in those cases "the one Judge must request the other to have the defendant cited." Huber repeats that receiving judges "are neither obliged nor ought to allow this" in cases where jurisdiction of the requesting judge is based "on the ground of mere submission or place of transaction." Ibid., 18 and 7.

> Thirdly, when a person contracted in this Province, and has fixed property situated here.
>
> Fourthly, when a person has a part interest in a case brought and heard here, and which cannot be divided.
>
> Fifthly, when a foreigner is arrested in the Province personally or in his property, provided that in his own [province] such arrests are employed against Frisians.
>
> Apart from these cases, neither place of transaction nor submission can give course for edictal citation since they can only found jurisdiction when a party walks on to the summons (*met citatie beloopen is*).[156]

The first and fourth instances regard existing processes and correspond to procedural principles and the need for legal certainty without causing any prejudice to the foreign defendant. The second instance is a classic case of *forum rei sitae*, presumably extending to any litigation – including that is, marital-property or succession – involving immovable property situated in the forum. We would today speak of jurisdiction *in rem*, even though Huber phrases the entire subject as regarding whether jurisdiction can be over a person. Likewise, the third instance is a case of so-called *quasi in rem* jurisdiction: land in Friesland is used to anchor there a nonresident defendant in a contractual dispute. This is still substantially more limited than the subsequent iteration of the so-called *forum patrimonii*, which extended the anchor to movables and especially money assets, even unrelated to the case.

What is more remarkable is that neither the place of transaction nor even the party's consent to be sued in the forum, called "submission" (*submissie*) may by themselves constitute grounds for jurisdiction. Submission or voluntary subjection (*vrywillige overwerpinge*) was a common practice ("annexed to almost all contracts and instruments").[157] Huber views submission to another forum with suspicion, because "it will disturb the order of country and government and create disorder if the officers of the one place should exercise jurisdiction in the territory of another."[158] He is especially adamant that mere submission cannot establish jurisdiction over a resident of another Province: "no private person may extend the jurisdiction of a Judge from one country into another":[159]

[156] Huber, *Heedensdaegse Rechtsgeleertheyt*, 5.1.9–14. Gane translates *met citatie beloopen is* as "is caught with the summons."

[157] Ibid., 4.27.3.

[158] Ibid., 4.14.21

[159] Ibid., 31

> [I]f a resident of Holland or another Province happens to submit to the court of Friesland, then nevertheless that person may not be summoned before the court unless he is found and summoned within this Province; it being certain that the Frisian judges cannot have him cited in Holland because citation is an act of jurisdiction which no Frisian can have in Holland according to the clear law and to the advice of Sande.[160]

Huber outlines the consequences of this rule. First, he makes it clear that edictal citation may not be used:

> Citation for the purpose of such a case may not be effected by public announcement and posting at the frontiers of the Province, as we are accustomed to do in the case of foreigners, for that can only be done when the jurisdiction of the judge over the parties has already been founded and is in full force, which cannot be brought about by consent of parties; for they may only renounce their rights, while the establishing of jurisdiction is the work of the sovereign and not of private persons.[161]

Second, he cautions against judges accepting requisitorial citations too indiscriminately:

> It is necessary that inferior judges should take a little more care in regard to requisitorial citations, and not just let them take their course, as they do, allowing them to be served indiscriminately by their messengers. They ought first to hear the defendant upon them, and investigate the case; for they ought not to allow them in case of submission upon a made contact; but they may offer themselves to adjudicate.[162]

12.4.1.1 Arrest-Based Jurisdiction

This brings back us the fifth ground, arrest of a person or of the person's goods, whose availability Huber would condition on whether such arrests are employed against Frisians in the foreigner's own place.[163]

Huber defines arrest as "an attachment of the person or property of a debtor made with accompanying citation by his creditor with the

[160] Ibid., 28, citing Sandius, *Decisiones frisicae*, 1.1.3.

[161] Ibid., 29.

[162] Ibid., 5.1.6.

[163] Ibid., 5.1.13. Huber is more categorical in discussing submission, ibid., 4.14.31: "You will say that we may bring it about by means of arrest that a party found in our territory, but who has not submitted himself, may nevertheless be bound to appear before a Judge. My answer is that, just as those methods of arrest are unknown in the Imperial law so we in Friesland do not employ them; and even where they are employed it can make no difference, since there as elsewhere it is certain that no private person may extend the jurisdiction of a judge from one country into another."

authority of the magistracy."[164] In Roman law, such attachment was only permitted "when a debtor is absconding, or is with good reason suspected of an intention to run away" and again only until security was provided:[165]

> But practice in the present-day goes a deal further among most nations (*volkeren*) both in respect of persons and of property for everyone may have his opponent who lives abroad or in another jurisdiction and is found by chance at his creditor's place of residence, arrested and cited, with the result that he is thereby rendered court-bound (*bankvast*) and obliged to appear before his creditor's forum, though he is not confined, but merely ordered not to depart; and this merely for the convenience and advantage of the creditor, to the end that he should not be obliged to pursue the debtor to a distance.[166]

Huber speaks of practice (*practijke*), which he acknowledges to be widespread and to go a deal further than Roman law. But this practice does not constitute Frisian law:

> [J]ust as this is unknown in the Imperial law so also in Friesland we do not employ such a right of arrest, either between Frisians or against foreigners. I cannot have my debtor, being a Frisian, but living in another town or bailiwick, arrested and cited when he comes into the town or jurisdiction in which I live, in order to render him bound to my forum, but I must none the less seek him out before his own Judge.[167]

Having stated the law, Huber can now address actual contrary practice. It appears that arrest was employed as a means of obtaining jurisdiction both by Friesland's neighboring provinces and even by a major town within the province. Huber first addresses the latter case, which poses a problem of legal order as well as of major practicalities:

> Those only of the town of Leeuwarden claim to have such a right that they may cause other Frisians or foreigners found in their town to be arrested and cited, and so rendered court-bound. But possibly there is no more in this than that they introduced it after the example of other nations and for their own accommodation, which however cannot constitute a full right; for a single town or bailiwick may not introduce a special custom (*gewoonte*) against the law of the whole Province, and to the detriment and encumbrance or other inhabitants or persons. Meanwhile, since the

[164] Huber, *Heedensdaegse Rechtsgeleertheyt*, 4.31.1.
[165] Ibid., 2.
[166] Ibid., 3.
[167] Ibid., 4.

> people of Leeuwarden do cleave to the custom, and have judicial decisions given accordingly, it follows that the citizens and residents of that town may also be arrested and made court-bound in other towns and bailiwicks, in virtue of the right of retorsion (*recht van retorsie*), that is, that every person must submit to the steps which he takes against others.[168]

Huber now turns his attention to sister provinces, foreign territories, and persons not residing in Friesland:

> Against foreigners also there is no such law in Friesland, as that, being found here, we may without further reason attach them and compel them to appear before our judge without their being amenable to the Frisian tribunals in virtue of contract, crime, situation of property, submission made or otherwise. If however they are people from countries (*landen*) where the said usage obtains in arrests, then they must in turn be made subject to it here, for the reason applied just now to those of Leeuwarden; in such a case the arrest is simply a citation effected in word and act. But since all peoples lying round Friesland employ this method of personal arrest, a creditor in Friesland cannot easily go wrong in arresting foreign debtors; and practice is everywhere in favor of it, provided that a summons is asked for at the same time.[169]

In this passage, Huber provides a legal justification for the establishment of jurisdiction over transient foreigners. It is also given the legal form of citation ("a citation effected in word and act"). The passage concludes with a practical rule: this jurisdictional ground would be available in most cases ("one cannot easily go wrong").[170] But we need to look closer into the meaning of Huber's words.

Huber may have found a legal form for arrest, but he is very mindful that citation means jurisdiction and he does not see how such a jurisdictional ground is per se lawful. Whether he is concerned with the administration of justice within Friesland or with interprovincial cases, Huber does not hide behind existing Frisian practice or case law: absent legislative derogation, Frisian law follows the Roman law, which did not employ arrest as simply a means for obtaining jurisdiction over foreigners. Judged against Huber's definition of the law of nations, the practice does not seem to have acquired the status of law "through being observed by the whole human race or the greater part of it." If Huber had wanted to claim otherwise, he would have presented existing – apparently

[168] Huber, *Heedensdaegse Rechtsgeleertheyt*, 4.31.5, with reference to D.2.2.

[169] Ibid., 6–7.

[170] See, in more detail, ibid. 7–8.

established – practice in terms of a more abstract rule or deduce it from an axiom or a principle.

Huber nonetheless provides a legal foundation for arrest-based jurisdiction, conditional on the same practice being exercised by the foreigner's own territory. It does not seem to matter whether the latter is another Dutch province or perhaps a territory of the Holy Roman Empire (such as East Frisia), what matters is that they do employ this practice. It is easy to see the political rationale behind the reciprocal treatment proposed by Huber. But this condition also allows Huber to continue regarding arrest-based jurisdiction as not allowed in principle while providing a legal foundation for it in these cases. This legal foundation is found in both Roman (civil) law and the law of nations: the right of retortion or retaliation (*lex talionis*).[171] Huber cites the Digest and its title "The same rule which anyone maintains against another will be applied against him."[172]

12.4.2 *Res Judicata, Jurisdiction, and Huber on the Conflict of Laws*

Reciprocity brings us to the other matter touched by Huber's treatment regarding jurisdiction: the effects of judgments abroad.

Huber treats judicial decisions in the same way as private legal acts or legal instruments. A civil judgment, criminal sentence, even the pardon of a crime "will have effect everywhere" as long as they derive from someone having jurisdiction. Huber is not even concerned with the adequacy of the reasons that led to the decision as he asserts both the res judicata of foreign decisions and a double jeopardy rule.[173] Yet he also

[171] As to the law of nations see Grotius, *De jure belli ac pacis*, 3.4.13 and 2.18.7. As to Roman law, see Huber, *Praelectiones ad Pandectas*, 2.2; Voet, *Commentarius ad Pandectas*, 2.2.

[172] See esp. the beginning of D.2.2.1 (Ulpian): "This edict has the greatest equity without arousing the just indignation of anyone for who will reject the application to himself of the same law which he has applied or caused to be applied to others? 1. 'If one who holds a magistracy or authority establishes a new law against anyone, he himself ought to employ the same law whenever his adversary demands it. If anyone should obtain a new law from a person holding a magistracy or authority, whenever his adversary subsequently demands it, let judgment be given against him in accordance with the same law.' The reason of course is that what anyone believed to be fair when applied to another he should suffer to prevail in his own case."

[173] Huber, *Praelectiones ad Pandectas*, 1.3.App.6 ("[N]or is it proper for the magistrates of another state to prosecute or to permit to be charged again a party who has been acquitted or pardoned in another place, even without adequate reason"). Huber, *Heedensdaegse Rechtsgeleertheyt*, 1.3.24 adds "everywhere recognized and enforced without inquiry into the reason for it"). He claims this is so "in virtue of rule 3."

notes two exceptions, deriving from actual Frisian cases, where to acknowledge such an effect would constitute "danger or prejudice" to the legal order of the forum.

Huber discusses second a classic case of enforcement sought in a third country, raising questions as to jurisdiction of the judgment court. The case he mentions involves a contract, in which a citizen of Haarlem, in Holland, agreed to submit to the courts of Groningen.[174] When he was sued, however, he did not appear, resulting in a default judgment. Enforcement of the judgment was sought – and apparently granted – in Friesland. The case would not raise issues today, but Huber did not regard submission as by itself establishing jurisdiction over a nonresident, as we have seen above, and in his conflicts treatment he is very critical of the decision of the Court of Friesland to grant enforcement. What is more remarkable is that members of the Court had advanced arguments that could have just as well be drawn from Huber's own doctrine. Some judges had argued that, as long as the judgment was validly rendered according to the law of the place of the judgment court, the Frisian court should grant enforcement ("it was not open to the Frisians to inquire into the grounds on which the judgment was given"). But to accept this would defeat the very idea that "if a defendant cannot be found to the territory of the judge to whom he had submitted, he cannot by reason of the submission be proceeded against by contumacy," which Huber has staunchly defended above.[175] It is telling, in this regard, that Huber is critical of the decision of the court of the defendant's domicile (Haarlem) to allow the process to carry on in Groningen.[176] In contrast, he approves a decision by the court in Amsterdam not to allow enforcement of a Frisian judgment against an absent defendant.

The first case Huber brings up involves a case of forum shopping: the offender flees the territory and escapes the jurisdiction of the forum in order to be able to obtain an acquittal in a neighboring province and subsequently invoke this res judicata in Friesland, avoiding punishment. To allow this would "open the way too much for the evasion of the Frisian jurisdiction."[177] We will return to this notion – and especially this

[174] Huber, *Praelectiones ad Pandectas*, 1.3.App.6. Huber, *Heedensdaegse Rechtsgeleertheyt*, 1.3.26 discusses a generic case.

[175] Huber, *Praelectiones ad Pandectas*, 1.3.App.6.

[176] Ibid.: "Other adopted the view that the magistrate at Haarlem on being requested in his own city had allowed the process, which he ought rather not to have done."

[177] Huber, *Praelectiones ad Pandectas*, 1.3.App.6.

case – when discussing Huber's comity doctrine and his prejudice exception.[178]

Both cases illustrate Huber's emphasis on the territorial allocation of jurisdiction to adjudicate. Huber comes up with a strong rule in favor of the recognition and enforcement of judgments. He does not even declare exceptions properly speaking, but merely excludes those judgments whose recognition would cause "detriment to our own jurisdiction and prejudice to our own citizens."[179] The main such instance would be a judgment rendered in default against a foreign defendant: even permission of the court of the defendant's domicile may not suffice to alter such a violation of the jurisdiction of the natural forum of the case. In the second instance, the foreign court has legitimately obtained jurisdiction, at least *prima facie*, since the defendant has appeared and voluntarily submitted himself to that court. Such "submission" however aimed at evading Frisian jurisdiction: it is treated as if the defendant never crossed the border.

12.4.3 Jurisdiction Theories and Huber

In his typology of general theories of adjudicatory jurisdiction, Arthur von Mehren distinguished between theories based on power, fairness, or allegiance.[180] Power theories "justif[y] jurisdiction if power can be asserted either directly or indirectly over particular defendants," tend to regard as natural the distinction between jurisdiction over "persons" (*in personam*) and jurisdiction over "things" (*in rem*) and to establish general jurisdiction, in the sense that "adjudicatory authority extends, in principle, to any claim against the defendant."[181] Fairness theories reject the "central importance of power in jurisdictional thinking" the clear distinction between *in personam* and *in rem* jurisdiction and the idea of general jurisdiction, in favor of an analytical framework constituted by considerations such as "the parties' relation to the forum community independent of the underlying controversy, the underlying controversy's litigational relation to the forum community, and the controversy's substantive relation to the forum" and resulting in a system of specific

[178] See Section 14.4.4.
[179] Huber, *Praelectiones ad Pandectas*, 1.3.App.6.
[180] Von Mehren, "Adjudicatory Jurisdiction," 282ff.
[181] Ibid., 286.

jurisdiction.[182] Von Mehren implies a narrative of conceptual progress, from allegiance to power to fairness theories, that has global resonance but fits especially the US experience.[183]

Fitting Huber into this picture is more challenging than one might have imagined. Summoning the defendant constitutes the cornerstone of the jurisdictional system of Friesland; there is jurisdiction *in rem*; there are instances in which citation may be effected by a legal fiction; and it has become apparent that arrest-based jurisdiction was widely practiced in the area. Huber himself invokes sovereignty as a foundation of this system, including when he questions the power of the individual to bind himself into litigating a future dispute in a territory other than his own domicile. But it would appear that fairness considerations are at least as much at the roots of Huber's concern with default judgments and his advocacy of both formal (requisitorial citation) and substantive (control by the judge of the domicile) requirements for the exercise of jurisdiction over a nonresident signatory to a submission agreement.

With respect to arrest-based jurisdiction, Huber is mobilizing both Roman law and the law of nations in opposition against such practices. This is the only instance in which we shall see Huber invoking a reciprocity mechanism and the *lex talionis*, and this is remarkable compared with Johannes Voet's writings. Given how widespread the practice was so the fifth ground, even thus conditioned, would effectively cover almost every visitor to the Province. Therefore, by imposing a reciprocity condition Huber is engaged in a reconstructive effort: existing practice is only legitimated within a tightened legal framework. At the very least, the Frisians will not be disadvantaged and at best foreign states will be forced to reconsider.

12.5 Conclusion

The purpose of this chapter has been to provide the necessary context to understand Huber on the conflict of laws. Our examination has indeed illustrated that Huber is a child of his time: his doctrine is best understood in the context of his contemporaneous political and even theological struggles, as well as of seventeenth-century legal theory. In its turn, Huber's approach to the conflict of laws, including both the applicable law and civil jurisdiction, is an illustration of his political and

182 Ibid.

183 Ibid., esp. 283–284, 300–307.

jurisprudential ideas. This is a point which will be elaborated further in the remaining chapters of this book.

Huber was a republican, with a firm conviction in the rule of law. Sovereignty – more specifically, territorial sovereignty – appears as the fundamental idea of his political system. In fact, sovereignty constitutes a foundation for the legal edifice Huber constructs. On the one hand, it provides philosophical legitimation, to the highest echelons of power in a polity, as well as for the idea of an international states system. On the other hand, it legitimates the exercise of power by the remaining echelons and even justifies the notion of a customary "law of nations," which we see being invoked by Huber, on several occasions, as a body of law that sets limits on the exercise of a polity's power – a role played by the *ius commune* or even natural law in earlier authors. Huber's republicanism and the theoretical foundation provided by territorial sovereignty fuel the clear allocation of jurisdiction, both vertically and horizontally, an example of which we have seen in Huber's doctrine on civil jurisdiction and his restrictive approach to arrest-based jurisdiction. This explains moreover Huber's restrictive approach to jurisdictional agreements ("submission"), which he does not regard as conferring jurisdiction over a nonresident defendant – certainly not in themselves and, remarkably, even in some cases where this has been allowed by the courts of the defendant's own domicile.

Religion also plays a role in Huber's doctrine: it interconnects with state law and policy and influences the elaboration and ascertainment of superior norms. We saw that Huber opposes "natural" or "intuitive" law to "derivative" law, which includes not only the Civil law but also the divine law and the law of nations: in short, Reason is contrasted to "positive" law in a broad sense. It would be wrong to assume that Huber is so much motivated by anti-Catholicism as to impact his conflicts doctrine or as to reject Roman law or Medieval scholasticism any more than other seventeenth-century jurists, Catholic as well as Protestant. Huber's approach to Roman law is markedly different from the one of Medieval jurists: in his world, there is no fiction of a continuing Roman Empire whose law is directly binding upon all its peoples. Yet Roman law is omnipresent: the foundation of its relevance is the sovereign's decision to allow its application but in reality it surrounds and transforms the *ius proprium civitatis*. Huber obviously did not believe in the inherent power of legislation to bind the court of another country, but then neither did the Medieval jurists. Rather than rejecting "statutism," Huber examines theories of statutes in terms of Roman law and modern political constructs (such as sovereignty/territorium, law of nations), which again related to Roman law. In this environment, we can also understand better Huber's insistence on making the judge think about his decision but not to allow discretion or even to grant lawmaking primacy to the judges over legislators. For Huber, state sovereignty, via Roman law, leads to learned law. Legal doctrine holds the key – and to this aspect we must now turn.

13

Doctrinal Aspects of Huber's Conflict of Laws

13.1 Introduction

Huber's treatment of conflict issues forms, in both its versions, part of comprehensive – and systematic – doctrinal works. It must therefore be placed in that context. Section 13.2 of this chapter examines the legal style of Huber's conflicts treatment: the choices he made as to structure and the organization of his argument, on the one hand, and as to the use of authorities, on the other. Section 13.3 addresses the organization of the legal subject matter within our text. Section 13.4 examines the use of the form/substance distinction, and their corollaries. Sections 13.5, 13.6, and 13.7 address respectively the role of jurisdiction, party autonomy, and decisional harmony in Huber's choice-of-law system.

13.2 Legal Style

Huber was a prime example of the Dutch Elegant School, the seventeenth-century stream of moderate humanism that centered in the universities of the Low Countries. He had himself taught history and oratory at Franeker prior to his appointment to a law professorship. Besides his legal writings, which themselves demonstrate the breadth of his thought, Huber left behind him numerous works on history, education, philosophy, and religion. Even the style of his conflicts treatment is in marked contrast to that of Medieval texts such as the influential *repetitio* of Bartolus. Huber's language is markedly closer to classical Latin than that of Medieval jurists and there is a clear structure that follows a rational organization of the subject matter. Our examination should allow us to address two common misreadings of Huber's conflicts doctrine: that the three axioms are all are there is to it, and that Huber's orientation is purely practical.

13.2.1 Structure

The first observation that must be made about Huber's conflicts treatment – indeed, both its Latin and vernacular versions – concerns the very existence of a formal structure of the chapter itself. The chapter itself has a formally distinct – and prominent – place within the overall work.

Huber, in the spirit of his times – and in contrast to the manuscripts of Medieval scholars such as Bartolus – endowed his treatment in *Praelectiones* with an overall title, a title for each section, and even an outline of contents. The earlier versions, notably the vernacular ones, may contain titles per section but are divided even more diligently into paragraphs easy to reference. As to its substance, Huber's conflicts treatment is clearly divided between an introductory part that lays out its theoretical foundations and a second/main part that elaborates his doctrine. This doctrinal part itself is organized on the basis of general rules or principles, on the basis of which the subject matter of what we would today call "private law" is organized and examined.[1]

Both "De Conflictu Legum" and "Observance" constitute a separate chapter, given a prominent place at the beginning of the respective work. This is more obviously so in "Observance," but it is at least equally true of the *Praelectiones*, which are organized in the form of distinct commentaries for each Title in each Book of either Institutes or Digest. Unlike "Observance," this actually makes impossible a proper enumeration of "De Conflictu Legum" – the only standalone chapter of Huber's *Praelectiones*. We are clearly still quite far from the proper, standalone works of private international law: each of Huber's conflicts discourses is but one chapter in an extensive legal work – within which, moreover, neither was found to have merited comments or annotations in the several posthumous editions of either work in the eighteenth century. No matter how modern his doctrinal outlook may appear to our eyes, for Huber conflict of laws is a cog in his doctrinal machinery.

A vital cog nonetheless. In both cases, Huber's conflicts treatment is one of the very first chapters. In *Praelectiones*, "De Conflictu Legum" follows the discussion of the first three titles of the Digest: "Justice and Law," "The Origin of the Law and All the Magistracies and the Succession of the Jurists," and "Statutes, Senatus Consulta, and

[1] This structure – as well as the order of dealing with subjects – has indeed remained the same since Huber's first treatment in *De jure civitatis*.

Long-Established Custom" (to which it is attached).[2] In its turn, *Contemporary Jurisprudence*, which follows the structure of the Institutes as reworked in elegant jurisprudence, has the chapter on "The Observance of Frisian Laws in other Countries; and of those of other Countries in Friesland" coming third after the chapters on "Justice" and "Law."[3]

13.2.2 Rational Ordering

In much of the literature, discussions about or quotations from Huber tend to concern his three axioms, disregarding the rest of the text.[4] This obscures, however, the fact that Huber also creates three choice-of-law rules – one general and two more limited in their scope – which, he claims, emanate from his axioms, demonstrating how his rules resolve problems in all areas of legal subject matter. Even Lorenzen, who saw beyond the axioms and gave us the most accessible, and very learned, presentation of Huber's conflicts doctrine, entitled that section of his article "Application of Huber's Maxims" and structured it in accordance with Lorenzen's own hierarchy of topics and not in a way which could immediately give the reader a sense of Huber's structure, let along his priorities.[5]

[2] Voet, *Commentarius ad Pandectas*, 1.4.App. has his own treatment follow the fourth title ("Enactments by Emperors"). In the original edition, his treatment is entitled Part B to Title 4, whereas the editors of the 1829 edition have re-titled it as an Appendix to both Titles 3 and 4 together. See Gane, *Selective Voet*, 97.

[3] The importance of Huber's choice is made clearer once we consider Huber's literature output in its evolving entirety. The earliest version of the conflicts treatment is the first chapter of the second section in the third book of *De jure civitatis* (1672). A chapter identical to "Observance" is the titular "Last Chapter" of the sixth book of Huber, *Beginselen*. Allowing for the different purpose of *De jure civitatis* from both the Dutch treatises and *Praelectiones* – without exaggerating however – this evidences a growing realization of the importance of the subject. The idea of a chapter in the end of *Beginselen*, not following the numbering of the rest of the book indicates an awareness of the importance and the unique nature of the subject. Two years later, in the refined version of that treatise, the chapter has moved to the very front.

[4] See e.g. Kegel and Schurig, *Internationales Privatrecht*, 158; Symeonides et al., *Conflict of Laws*, 11 and 13 ("Unlike Huber, Story took the next step of erecting around these general parameters a comprehensive system of bilateral choice-of-law rules").

[5] See Lorenzen, "Huber's De Conflictu Legum," 139–154. Lorenzen examines, in comparison with the other preclassical writers, Huber on "Status and Capacity in General," "Capacity to Dispose of Immovable Property," "Capacity to Make a Will Disposing of Movable Property," "Form," "Movable Property," "Contracts," "Marriage," "Effect of Marriage Upon Property," "Marriage Settlements," "Intestate Succession," "Testaments,"

My thesis is that what the axioms do is to provide the *foundation* for Huber's three doctrinal rules. The axioms are of course important. Huber uses them so that, on the one hand, he can better justify the rules themselves and – more importantly – the solutions he gives on concrete problems or borderline cases. On the other hand, even though his doctrinal edifice is not radically different from the statutist theory of his time, the axioms do allow him to present a different conceptual scheme – a difference that would over time grow in importance and allow his legacy to outlive the demise of both Latin and the *usus modernus Pandectarum*.

Let us examine more closely the conclusion of § 1:

> In order to reveal the subtlety of this very intricate question [i.e. how transactions entered into in one place have force and effect in a different country or are judicially decided upon in another place], we shall employ three axioms, which, having been accepted, as their acceptance seems always necessary, seem able to grant us a clear way as to the remaining [questions].[6]

Huber's choice of the term "axiom" to describe the fundamental principles of his system is paired with the use of the term *Positio* to define his principal rule that flows from them.[7] In mathematics, axioms are fundamental principles impossible to demonstrate that ought to be accepted, by convention, in order to build a theory: demonstrable propositions (*theorems*) derive from the axioms.[8] Huber in fact begins his systematic work on the Corpus Iuris by this very distinction, drawn from mathematics, between *axiomata* and *positiones*.[9] Axioms "are nothing else

"Procedure," "International Jurisdiction in Civil Matters," "Foreign Judgments," and "Criminal Law."

[6] Huber, *Praelectiones ad Pandectas*, 1.3.App.1 in fine ("*Nos ad detegendam hujus intricatissimae quaestionis subtilitatem, tria collocabimus axiomata, quae concessa, sicut omnino concedenda videntur, viam nobis ad reliqua planam redditura videntur*"). Lorenzen, "Huber's De Conflictu Legum," 376, 402 translates axiomata as maxims.

[7] Huber, *Praelectiones ad Pandectas*, 1.3.App.3 princ. ("*Inde fluit haec Positio*"); likewise Huber, *Heedensdaegse Rechtsgeleertheyt*, 1.3.8 (*stellinge*). The – older and less systematic – vernacular text actually refers to "fundamental rules (*grondt-regels*), known to the Roman law" rather than to axioms. Ibid., 4. See also ibid., 36, 53. Reference to the axioms as "rules" is also found in Huber, *Praelectiones ad Pandectas*, 1.3.App.12.

[8] On the influence of Euclidian geometry on seventeenth-century philosophers such as Spinoza, Hobbes, and Descartes, dealing with demonstrative metaphysics see N. Jolley, "Metaphysics" in D. Rutherford (ed.), *Cambridge Companion to Early Modern Philosophy* (Cambridge: Cambridge University Press, 2006), 95–135, 96–101.

[9] Urlic Huber, *Praelectiones ad Institutes*, bk. 1, Proemium, § 2.

than statements needing no demonstration."[10] It is *positiones*, described as "fundamental rules of the Art, certified and valid, but with high inspection and explanation, where definitions, partitions, categorizations and conclusions are collected" that form the backbone of his system.[11]

Huber employs the term axiom for two reasons. First, the actual observance of these three fundamental propositions cannot be effectively demonstrated – but once they are accepted, the path to resolving conflicts issues is cleared. Second, his actual rules are derived from these axioms.[12]

Our thesis is further supported by considering also the conflicts treatment of Johannes Voet, written a few years later, and falling within the same tradition of *mos hollandicus*. Voet himself sets the essence of his approach in three questions on "statutes": first, what is the strict law applied on the subject by a jealous people; second, whether statutes may be extended "by comity;" third, whether they may be departed from by express or tacit agreement.[13] Voet's actual treatment is structured in terms of answering these three questions.[14] It is logically coherent – in fact, it attracted more scholarly admiration than Huber's – but also requires its reader to return to the same subject two or three times and often to also look elsewhere in the book in the hope for more. On the contrary, in Huber there is a marked divide between the discussions of the axioms (§§ 1–2) and the doctrinal discussion (§§ 3–15), which is organized on the basis of three rules and the legal subject matter:

10 Ibid. (*axiomata, nihil sunt aliud quam enuntiationes nullius indigae demonstrationis*). Watson, *Comity of Errors*, 4 (and 103 n. 15), aptly summarizes § 2: "Budaeus, [Huber] declared, had not absurdly said that rules of law were handed down by axiomata or by positiones, terms that he said were taken by the usage of mathematicians. 'For axioms are nothing other than statements that require no proof.'"

11 Huber, *Praelectiones ad Institutes*, Proemium, § 3 ("*Positiones videntur esse, regulae fundamentals Artis, certae quidem et validae, sed altioris indaginis et explicationis, veluti definitiones, partitiones et conclusiones inde collectae. In eo sensu, positionis vocabulo utitur Iustinianus* ... *Quando iuris aiunt duas esse positiones, publicum et privatum, nemque species quae collocantur, ut fundamenta detegendi et evolvendi materiam disciplinae, eleganter positiones appelantur*").

12 Huber, *Praelectiones ad Pandectas*, 1.3.App.3, 12, and 15. When it comes to the rule on personal status, Huber seemingly reverses his terminology: "From the Rules initially laid out this axiom may also be inferred" (*Ex Regulis initio collocatis etiam hoc axioma colligitur*: ibid., 12). *Regula* here may be seen as having a broader meaning than a legal norm. As to the axiom, this may be explained by the fact that this rule is essentially a balancing act proposed by Huber.

13 Voet, *Commentarius ad Pandectas*, 1.4.App.1. See Section 14.4.2 for the first and second and Section 13.6 for the third question and Voet's elaboration.

14 Voet, *Commentarius ad Pandectas*, 1.4.App. 2–11, 12–17, and 18–21 respectively.

invocations of the axioms – essentially the third axiom – are scattered in the text, as a justification of special rules or exceptions.[15]

13.2.2.1 A Novel Method

The comparison of the structure of the conflicts treatments of Huber and Johannes Voet illustrates further the effectiveness – and novelty – of Huber's scheme. Whereas Huber begins with his axioms (or fundamental rules), from which he derives rules which he applies to concrete situations, Voet, who is younger than Huber but follows the classic division of statutes and expressly honors the legacy of his own father in this regard, begins his discussion by presenting the three types of statutes: personal, real and mixed.[16] He then sets his rule that "strictly all statutes have territorial force only."[17] This evidently applies to real statutes.[18] As to personal statutes, Voet goes at length to refute the position of "many" that they must have "extraterritorial force."[19] Even "mixed statutes have in strict law no extraterritorial effect."[20] Having established his strict rule across the board, Voet then notes that "comity demands some relaxation of strict law." He then devotes the second half of his treatment to elaborating the impact of comity with regard primarily to mixed statutes and in certain cases, personal statutes as well.

Huber on the contrary makes no typology of personal, real, and mixed statutes. We will find these terms nowhere in his text, where the very expression "extraterritorial" is only used sparingly. Even "comity," which has been presented in the opening part, is seldom mentioned expressly in the doctrinal discussion that follows. The most important change that Huber brings is that, by dispensing with the traditional terminology of the theory of statutes, he is able to reverse the order of his material. A classic "theory of statutes" tends to begin with the discussion of real statutes and then personal statutes; "mixed statutes" can only be discussed subsequently and in relation to the other two categories, whether the notion is actually embraced, as by the Voets, or dismissed, as by Rodenburgh and the eighteenth-century French authors.[21] Moreover,

[15] See Sections 14.4.3 and 14.4.4.
[16] See Voet, *Commentarius ad Pandectas*, 1.4.App.2–4.
[17] Ibid., 5.
[18] Ibid., 6.
[19] Ibid., 7–9.
[20] Ibid., 10.
[21] See e.g. Rodenburgh, *De jure quod oritur*, 1.2 in fine; Boullenois, *Traité*, 1.25–28 (Obs. III); Dumouchet du Bac, *Traité*, 17.

Paul and Johannes Voet defined as "mixed" those statutes pertaining to the validity of an act.[22] Admittedly, while Huber's own three rules may look to us like bilateral conflicts rules (*règles de conflit*), functionally they correspond to the tripartite division of statutes. But Huber's equivalent of "mixed statutes" is granted very broad scope: legal acts, and most of their conditions of validity and effects. It is also placed first, and as the primary category.

For a seasoned scholar, the – longer – text of Johannes Voet has its rewards. He makes extensive use of authorities and combines an antiquarian style (in his allusions to phrases, sources, and his rhetorical tools) with a pragmatic directness and arguments that could find resonance with international-relations realists and particularist legal positivists from later days.[23] But Huber is arguably more effective and certainly more efficient. Voet did not break with the classic theory of statutes, but that scheme already made less sense for him than it did for past authors – resulting in a serpentine structure. Huber is eminently more readable than Voet and his doctrinal system appears less tendentious.

13.2.3 Practice and Pragmatism

It is common to point to the "essentially practical" character of Huber's treatment.[24] Contrasting him to the Voets, father and son, Lainé remarks that Huber:

> With the same elements [used by the Voets] he composed another system, made of short and striking (*frappantes*) formulas, not of eloquent dissertations. In him, no or few discussions, but principles, declared incontestable or quickly justified, applied to the diverse parts of law.[25]

Lainé is correct that Huber used the same building blocks as Voet. It is also true that Huber's work – both *Praelectiones* and *Contemporary Jurisprudence* – could certainly appeal to a broader audience of lawyers. But Huber's plain language and spare use of authorities should not obscure the deep thinking and results-oriented pragmatism underlying his attempt to "explain this subtle and confused subject simply and thoroughly."[26]

22 See P. Voet, *De Statutis*, 4.2.4; and Voet, *Commentarius ad Pandectas*, 1.4.App.4.
23 See e.g. Voet, *Commentarius ad Pandectas*, 1.4.App.2–4 and 5ff.
24 Lainé, *Introduction*, 2:107.
25 Ibid., 97.
26 Huber, *Heedensdaegse Rechtsgeleertheyt*, 1.3.55.

This pragmatism reflects on the use of illustrations and authorities. Both versions of Huber's conflicts treatment abound in practical examples drawn from the author's environment. Many of these examples come from actual cases to which Huber gives references; he even tries to gauge any consensus around the adopted position.[27] Huber certainly has his own opinions, for which he canvasses the readers, but for his work to have practical value he had to note where the opposite position holds or could come to hold.[28] Moreover, unlike the examples of redundant types of conflicts, often included in doctrinal works, even the "hypothetical" examples of Huber come from cases where conflicts are waiting to happen.[29]

Huber is more sparing with authorities. Decisions are used as illustrations, or at best as an indication of prevailing opinion.[30] References to Roman-law sources (the Digest) are only made in "De Conflictu Legum" in support of the axioms. Conclusion aside, the only other doctrinal works he cites in either chapter are: the *Practicarum Observationum* of Andreas von Gail (1526–1587), in "Observance of Frisian Laws," and *De Jure Belli ac Pacis* of Grotius in "De Conflictu Legum" – both in support of the second axiom.[31]

Huber does not present himself – at least not ostensibly – as engaged in a dialogue with other writers of his time or before. It is indicative that, when he expresses his disagreement with the idea that laws of capacity have extraterritorial effect, he names no supporter of that view, which had been supported by everyone until Paul Voet.[32] Huber does acknowledge in his conclusion to "De Conflictu Legum" that "[t]hese principles are such as would be capable of a fuller explanation, since there are writers on the Statutes who think differently on several matters," but he

[27] Huber, *Praelectiones ad Pandectas*, 1.3.App.6, 7, and 13 in fine; Huber *Heedensdaegse Rechtsgeleertheyt*, 1.3.15.

[28] See Huber, *Praelectiones ad Pandectas*, 1.3.App.6 and 13 in fine. Cf. ibid., 4, where no mention is made of a recent (1683) Frisian decision reported nonetheless in the earlier Huber, *Heedensdaegse Rechtsgeleertheyt*, 1.3.15.

[29] For a relative exception see Huber, *Praelectiones ad Pandectas*, 1.3.App.8: the occurrence of the Brabantine uncle-niece marriage such as the one discussed iappears highly improbable, but it seems likely that Huber mistakenly thought such an instance possible under Catholic practice.

[30] Huber, *Heedensdaegse Rechtsgeleertheyt*, 1.5.51.

[31] See Huber, *Heedensdaegse Rechtsgeleertheyt*, 1.3.8; Huber, *Praelectiones ad Pandectas*, 1.3. App.2. Sandius is cited alongside Gail in Huber, *Heedensdaegse Rechtsgeleertheyt*, 1.3.8 and on his own in Huber, *Praelectiones ad Pandectas*, 1.3.App.9.

[32] See the comprehensive presentation of Lainé, *Introduction*, 2:114ff.

still makes do with the minimal citations.[33] Readers who want more are referred to a collection of reported Frisian cases (where a lot of sixteenth-century authorities are cited in a report of a 1611 succession case).[34] The "recent work" of Rodenburgh "may be added" to them.[35] But in "Observance of Frisian Laws," where Huber claims to have explained the subject "according to the treatment of great jurists," reference is made to Rodenburgh's *Treatise concerning the law which arises from different statutes* as following Argentraeus and Burgundus.[36] Sande's work had been published more than forty years prior to the publication of either of Huber's works – in fact, the first edition dates from before Huber's birth, although there appear to have been successive reprints.[37] Rodenburgh's "recent" work also dates from 1643, although editions appeared in 1653 and 1676.[38]

We will on contrary find no references to the work of either Voet. Johannes Voet wrote his *Commentary on the Pandects* just after Huber's death, but the work of Paul Voet, available since the 1660s, is never mentioned by Huber anywhere in his text, including other chapters where Huber makes references to other works.[39] Johannes Voet in his turn reciprocated through no mention of Huber's work.[40]

[33] Huber, *Praelectiones ad Pandectas*, 1.3.App.15.
[34] Sande, *Decisiones frisicae* 4.8.7.
[35] Huber, *Praelectiones ad Pandectas*, 1.3.App.15.
[36] Huber, *Heedensdaegse Rechtsgeleertheyt*, 1.3.55.
[37] See Section 3.3.3.
[38] C. Rodenburgius, *Tractatus de jure conjugum . . . cum tractatione praeliminari de jure, quod oritur ex statutorum, vel consuetudinum discripantium conflictu.* Lainé, *Introduction,* 1:404 mentions as "second" edition the 1676 Brussels edition. The Harvard Law Library possesses a 1653 copy (*trajecti ad Rhenum*) – as well as 1699 copy (*Coloniae Agrippinae*) which I used. Huber gives no reference to the edition he is using, but I would regard the 1653 edition as more likely to have reached him than an edition from Brussels.
[39] See also Section 14.4.2, discussing "De Conflictu Legum" in comparison to both the treatment's earlier versions) and Paul Voet, who first used the word *comiter* in 1661: we find the word in *Praelectiones* (1689) but not the earlier versions.
[40] Yntema, "Comity," 29 points to Huber's "sparing of unnecessary citiations" and suggests that the "more generous in this respect" Jan Voet "with filial reciprocity fails to mention Huber." Of Frisian origin himself, Yntema then makes a distinction between the *doctrine hollandaise* of comity and Huber's *doctrine frisonne* (29). This lack of citations presents us with evidence of these jurists perceiving the subject as a peripheral – if necessary – one within their doctrinal systems, rather than suggesting feelings of personal slight. See e.g. a letter of 6 December 1684 by Johannes Voet to his "most esteemed friend" Huber, thanking and praising him upon receiving a copy of his *De Ratione Iuris*. See Hewett, *Ulric Huber*, 141–142 (translation in English) and 334 (reproduction of the Latin original).

This need not be taken to mean anything more than the orientation of Huber toward practical concerns, perhaps a certain traditionalism in his non-Frisian bibliography, a feeling he has a satisfactory grasp of the topic. But it also suggests that no "invisible college" of people writing on conflict of laws issues existed at the very time when, with hindsight, we could that the "Dutch school" was at its peak.

13.3 The Organization of the Legal Subject Matter

We now come to the organization of the legal subject matter itself. It has become evident that Huber's treatment follows a logical order – but to what extent do the choice-of-law rules adopted by Huber relate to his approach of substantive law matters?

Huber's structure is in marked contrast with the tripartite organization of legal matters into personal, real, and mixed statutes in works following the classic theory. For example, Johannes Voet structures his own treatment in abstract terms but, in his definitions of each category of statutes, provides a substantial number of examples for both personal and real statutes:

> [Personal] statutes are those which decide whether one is to be held citizen or foreigner; noble or ignoble; infamous or of sound repute or restored to good fame; of such an age or condition as to be able or not to leave his goods by last will; and whether a woman or minor is or is not to be allowed to make a contract without the consent of husband or guardian. You could equally well bring into this class the declaration of a prodigal; the grant of *venia aetatis*; the introduction from the practice of advocacy, from a forum, business or art; or contrariwise the admission to the practice of such things, when special admission is necessary, as it is for practicing the art of scrivener or notary or the like; and generally any case where the condition of a person is added to or taken from, so as to make him appear capable or incapable of performing various actions.[41]
>
> [To real statutes] belong rights of succession *ab intestato*; the order in which any persons are to be admitted in intestacy to any goods, whether by heads, stocks, lines or right of primogeniture; in what manner legitimates or illegitimates, blood-relations on a father's side or on either side are called to succeed; and many other like matters. Nor would you be wrong in referring to this class of statutes the prohibition of allowance of donations between spouses; the limits of the community of goods to be brought in between them by marriage; and dispositions by last will,

[41] Voet, *Commentarius ad Pandectas*, 1.4.App.2.

> forbidden in some places where only succession of *ab intestato* is in force, but allowed in others.[42]

For someone, like Voet, working with the classic distinction, there are three steps to be made: identify legal issues, classify them into the three categories of statutes, and work out the actual rules (doctrinal solutions) for each category of issues. Huber has spared himself the intermediate level of complexity of having to classify legal issues into real, personal, and mixed statutes. His conflicts rules are thus directly shaped by – and in turn reshape – substantive-law categories.

The protagonist in Huber's scheme is the *legal act*: the conditions for its validity, its content, and its effects. This is immediately evident with regard to Huber's primary rule: most of the subject matter – including marriage and even procedural acts – is presented in terms of legal acts and "transactions," and fitted under the *lex loci actus*. But even Huber's "personal" and "real" rule address legal issues that may often arise in relation to conditions for the validity of a legal act (civil status) and effects (over the transfer of real property).

13.3.1 Huber as an Institutist

This scheme certainly corresponds to the commercial and social realities and the political and economic thinking that constitute Huber's context.[43] But it also corresponds to the reconceptualization of law by Huber's time. Following the humanists, jurists adopted the organizational scheme of law propounded in Justinian's Institutes, namely the tripartite division of law into the law of persons, the law of things, and the law of actions. The Institutes' division into four books was technical: the law of things occupied Books II and III, as well as part of Book IV, where "tacked on, though awkwardly" is a last section on crime.[44] Following Hugues Doneau (Donellus), the tripartite distinction became one between persons, things, and obligations. Substantive law was thus

42 Ibid., 3.

43 See e.g. J. Whitman, "The Moral Menace of Roman Law and the Making of Commerce: Some Dutch Evidence," *Yale Law Journal*, 105 (1996), 1841–1889. Whitman studies Dutch authors – other than Huber – as an example of how "Roman law offered justifications for varieties of market behavior that Christian Europeans had long viewed as sinister and wrong" (ibid., 1854).

44 P. Birks and G. McLeod, "Introduction" in *Justinian's Institutes* (Ithaca, NY: Cornell University Press, 1987), 13.

distinguished from procedural law, as well as criminal law. Huber, and more generally the Dutch Elegant School and contemporaneous legal scholarship, adopted the Institutional scheme thus revised. This is apparent in *Contemporary Jurisprudence*, which is divided into six "books." Huber did not initially give titles to these books but, from the outset, he sets out his intention to devote the first book to the law of persons, as he did, the next three to the law of things (*saken*) and the last two to the law of actions ("*aktien*, dat is *rechts-vordering*").[45] The first volume's three books deal respectively with the law of persons, the law of things (property and succession), and the law of obligations, essentially contracts. In his second volume, however, Huber decided to treat "misdeeds" (*misdaden*) last; the fourth and fifth book deal therefore, respectively, with the state and the offices of justice and judicial proceedings properly speaking.[46]

The structure of Huber's conflicts treatment fundamentally serves the basic idea of his system, which is announced in the very first sentence, addressed by the axioms, and then finally elaborated in his primary rule. Huber tends to follow the Institutionalist division, and order, of topics as long as it fits his structure. As a result, he grants primacy to legal acts – which should have come third under the Institutionalist classification as indeed they are in most other schemes of the period – but he does place second his auxiliary rule corresponding to the law of persons and third his rule corresponding to the law of (immovable) things.[47] In discussing the application of his primary rule concerning legal acts, Huber begins with testaments, then contracts, and then actions and their effect. "Marriage" however – which falls under the law of persons and is discussed early in Book I of both the Institutes and his own systematic work – is discussed here last among the legal acts. This can be explained in two ways: on the one hand, conflicts of marriage laws has been a relatively recent addition to scholarly writings; on the other hand, it is a topic where political and moral sensitivities raise issues that necessitate a more complex analysis from Huber, and the acknowledgment of

[45] Huber, *Heedensdaegse Rechtsgeleertheyt*, 1.2.67.

[46] See ibid., 4.1.1, explaining the change in order compared to Huber, *Beginselen*, where crimes are treated in the fourth book ("since crimes and the prosecution of them differs entirely from civil actions, it will not be foreign to our purpose to keep crimes to the last, and now to pass to actions touching the law of persons and property").

[47] The order could also be explained by suggesting that the discussion about personal capacity is corollary to the discussion about legal acts, whereas the third rule constitutes an exception properly speaking to the primary rule.

exceptions to his primary rule. Testamentary and intestate succession are treated separately. The latter appears connected to the elaboration of the *lex rei sitae* rule and discussion of the law of property.

13.3.2 Contracts and Obligations

Cases involving contracts are as prevalent in Huber's conflicts treatment as testaments and related acts are in Bartolus.[48] Just like Huber's treatment of contracts is focused on the contract of sale and purchase, Huber's main examples involve the sale of goods, and he subsequently discusses actions on debt arising from the sale of goods and the effects of real remedies over goods. There are also marriage contracts as well as matters pertaining to the capacity to contract. What is not however immediately visible in the text is a scheme with the doctrinal distinctions elaborated by Bartolus: Huber's contractual conflicts appear instead permeated by the *lex loci contractus*.

We should not however assume that all matters are simply governed by the law of the place where the contract was made, without further ado. Having stated that the *lex loci contractus* will apply "not only with respect to the form of the contract but also as regards its substance," Huber goes directly to the most problematic case: performance in a place different from the *locus contractus*. Huber examines the sale of goods or "merchandise" (*merces*), when such sale is prohibited in one of these places:[49] the example used in "Observance" involves sale of "brandy or certain other commodities," which used to be forbidden in Friesland.[50] Such a sale is void if forbidden in both the place of contracting and place of performance.[51] As to the other cases, Huber distinguishes depending on where delivery has taken or is to take place. If the agreement was made and the goods were delivered in a place where no prohibition exists, the seller may bring action against the buyer even in a place where such a sale is prohibited. If, however, the goods are to be delivered in a place where such sale is prohibited, the contract is void and, even if the goods were delivered in secret, the seller may not recover the price in court. Likewise,

[48] Huber, *Praelectiones ad Pandectas*, 1.3.App.3 (sale), 7 (prescription of debt), 8–10 (marriage contracts), 11 (hypothecation of movable property), and 12 (capacity to contract).

[49] Ibid., 5.

[50] Huber, *Heedensdaegse Rechtsgeleertheyt*, 1.3.19–23. See in addition ibid., 6.19.17–20 on excises – and the inevitable smuggling – imposed by Friesland on wine and beer.

[51] Ibid., 1.3.20.

if such a contract was concluded in a place where such sale is prohibited, it is void *ab initio* and neither party may bring action on debt or to compel the delivery. In that case, however, if delivery did take place, Huber would allow the seller to recover on another legal basis, namely unjustified enrichment.[52] The same solution is given with regard to residents of a town where "it has been forbidden . . . to drink brandy," who "go just outside the jurisdiction of the town, and drink it there."[53] In such a case, "the traffic is legitimate" in that place and will give rise to claims anywhere but not in the town where such consumption is prohibited itself.[54]

Contractual analogies and emphasis on remedies under the law of the forum are also on display when Huber considers sales contracts again, in his discussion of procedural acts and judgments: prescription of a claim for the price of goods sold elsewhere is regarded as a matter that does not pertain to the substance of the contract but to the time and mode of instituting the action, "which are by themselves like a contract and a separate transaction."[55]

Huber's other examples of commercial transactions concern the effects of suretyship agreements. The principal case, discussed in both "De Conflictu Legum" and "Observance" concerned real sureties (*hypoteeken* or *pand-recht*), specifically claims to movable property used as security for a debt.[56] Hypothecation is defined as "the right which the creditor has on the property of his debtor, by way of security for his debt."[57] Such property included movables and even acknowledgments of debt. There

[52] Huber, *Praelectiones ad Pandectas*, 1.3.App.5 in fine ("if the purchaser should refuse to pay the price after delivery he would be bound not so much by virtue of the agreement asked why he delivered everything insofar as he would enrich himself at the expense of another"). Cf. Huber, *Heedensdaegse Rechtsgeleertheyt*, 1.3.21 ("unless equity on account of special circumstances might provide some extraordinary remedy against the avaricious purchaser").

[53] Ibid., 22.

[54] Ibid. An analogous solution applies to the criminalization of such behavior: see ibid., 23 and Section 14.4.4.2.

[55] Huber, *Praelectiones ad Pandectas*, 1.3.App.7 (*per se quasi contractum separatumque negotium constituit*). Lorenzen, "Huber's De Conflictu Legum" translates "quasi contract."

[56] Huber, *Praelectiones ad Pandectas*, 1.3.App.11; Huber, *Heedensdaegse Rechtsgeleertheyt*, 13.54: "In Friesland a prior hypothec gives a preference also removable property and acknowledgments of debt, even, according to Imperial law, against third parties in possession of them; but "if you lay a claim in Holland on such a bond you will fail, because you cannot deprive people of their property lawfully obtained there."

[57] Huber, *Heedensdaegse Rechtsgeleertheyt*, 2.46.1.

were various instances of legal hypothec and, pertinently to our text, hypothecation by agreement often referred to as "bond" (*verbandt*).[58] The law of Friesland, following Roman law, allowed the creditor who had obtained such security to oppose his right, in principle, even against a third party in actual possession of the property in question: this position was not shared by other provinces and indeed many Frisian authors, who thought that the rule might be adversely impacting commerce.[59] Accordingly, Friesland – but not Holland – allowed an older hypothecary creditor to take the movable from the hands of a subsequent creditor holding it as a pledge: even though Huber himself insists that this is the law in Friesland, he acknowledges the contrary "present-day practice of most nations" and observes that the practice in Friesland is rare "more because it is unfamiliar, than because persons have no such right."[60] This brings Huber to his conclusion that "if you lay a claim in Holland on

[58] Huber, *Heedensdaegse Rechtsgeleertheyt*, 2.47.

[59] Ibid., 1.3.54 and 2.49. See notably ibid., 2.49.12, where Huber argues that this Roman-law rule still holds in Friesland and cites case law to that effect, while noting its limited use in practice: "As to hypothecary action over movable property, it is said by the majority of writers that at the present day it has no application against a third party in possession, who has become owner or pledgee thereof, even though there was a special pledge, since commerce would otherwise be too much restricted. This is so firmly maintained among all nations, that among us too we do not see recourse had in insolvent estates against movables previously sold; and he who holds a pledge is not accustomed to hand it over to old creditors without compensation, as pawnbrokers and others would be obliged to do, if the hypothecary action applied to movable property. But, however, the rule that among us the Imperial law applies in everything, in which it has not been abrogated, is so strong that it would also have to hold good here whenever anyone wished to pursue it at law."

[60] Ibid., 2.50.40: "In the present-day practice of most nations this rule has also no application in respect of movable property delivered in pledge, which remains in the hands of second parties in possession, and cannot be taken from them by any older hypothecary creditors for the reason already mentioned, namely, that the right of pledge over movable property is not available beyond the time that it is found in the estate of the debtor; but since this rule is strange to the Imperial law, which has not been altered among us in this respect, we must also say, that creditors who have movable property under pledge in their possession, if the other creditors get to know of it, are bound to bring it into the common stock and allowed to be adjudged according to the order of preference. However, this seldom happens, more because it is unfamiliar, than because persons have no such right. Pawnbrokers, however, never return their pledges except upon satisfaction of their advances, in virtue of the concessions granted them by the authorities; although, according to strict law, such concessions would not hold good unless confirmed by the States, since judges and magistrates are not permitted to vary the common rights introduced by law."

such a bond you will fail, because you cannot deprive people of their property lawfully obtained there."[61]

Huber comes again to contracts – sandwiched between testaments and intestate succession – in his final section, in discussing those instances where *lex rei sitae* must apply in spite of the legal act made abroad. All instances concern acquisition of ownership over immovable property.

The first case concerned the sale of land in Friesland by a contract made elsewhere: the "notices" and "consents" provided in Frisian law must be observed.[62] Notices (*booden*) were "public announcements which the purchaser must cause to be given on three several occasions within the year at the church and before the tribunal of the place where the property is situated."[63] By consents (*consenten*) was meant "the confirmation of the sale by the authorities of the place where the property is situated . . . followed by an investing, conducted by the Judge in favor of him who has finally remained buyer."[64] Huber explains the policies – essentially publicity – underlying the requirement.[65] An additional public policy was apparently the "consent-fees" that had to be paid.[66]

The second example – found in both treatments – concerns the sale in Holland of corn (*frumentum*) still growing in Friesland "by the lasts" (*secundum lastas*).[67] The last was a substantial measurement unit based on vehicle capacity.[68] Frisian law prohibited "to sell or deal in any kind of grain for delivery by the last before it has been sown, or while it is still growing" and not ripe to be cut, with a view to protecting agriculture from "all too hazardous dealings" and husbandmen from being "too

61 Ibid., 1.3.54.

62 Ibid., 1.3.48.

63 Ibid., 3.5.2.

64 Ibid., 3.5.3.

65 Ibid., 3.5.10 ("It touches the public good that it should be known who are the owners of immovable property, and that nothing should be done to the prejudice of the law of the land. To that end it is also forbidden to bring any property by sale under the jurisdiction of another town or bailiwick without the consent of the States, no officials having the power to do such a thing").

66 It seems that these notices and consents would cost the buyer 1/56th of the land's value, to the benefit of the locality or – if below a certain value – the local officials: ibid., 4.

67 Huber, *Praelectiones ad Pandectas*, 1.3.App.15; Huber, *Heedensdaegse Rechtsgeleertheyt*, 1.3.49.

68 The *last* is defined by the *Oxford English Dictionary*, 8:671, as "a commercial denomination of weight, capacity or quantity, varying for different kinds of goods and in different localities." Originally the last must have corresponded to the quantity carried by the vehicle ordinarily used to transport the particular kind of merchandise (boat, wagon, etc.).

grossly cheated."[69] Such prohibition did not extend to "butter, cheese and other products of husbandry," deliveries of smaller quantities or agreements to deliver grain "when the persons have not in mind grain, which is expected to come from a definite piece of land."[70] Huber is evidently concerned with "avoid[ing] making the prohibition a nullity."[71] This is in effect a sale of specific future goods but by insisting on the characterization of a crop of growing corn as "attached to the soil and . . . part thereof," Huber makes the contract invalid and ineffective abroad, thus ensuring that Frisian farmers are protected from contracting away their future crops.[72]

13.3.3 Law of Persons

The first book of *Contemporary Jurisprudence*, on the law of persons, deals primarily with questions of marriage (including property), personal status and capacity, and curatorship. The role of family as a social and legal unit is apparent in Huber's work, even though there is no clear legal concept or category of "family relations" and family law itself does not appear as a grand doctrinal category until the early nineteenth century. In his conflicts treatment, however, which immediately precedes in the same book, we see that Huber deals not just with marriage but also with issues such as guardianship or parental power in terms of the validity of legal acts, rather than legal relations.

Huber lives in a world that has inherited from the Late Roman Antiquity the texts and many of the distinctions as to the status of persons, discarded some, and added some others.[73] Status and capacity mattered regarding the ability of certain classes of persons to make a will, enter into marriage without paternal consent, or alienate property.[74] In "De Conflictu Legum," Huber mentions "adolescents, unemancipated

[69] Huber, *Heedensdaegse Rechtsgeleertheyt*, 3.3.4 and 8–9.

[70] Ibid., 5–7.

[71] Ibid., 8. A few years later Voet, *Commentarius ad Pandectas*, 18.1.13, cites Sandius, *Decisiones frisicae*, 3.4.7 to the effect that "the sale of corn standing in the green has been forbidden in Friesland" and Groenewegen and Paul Voet to the effect that the "various prohibitory decrees on that matter . . . promulgated of old by the Counts of Holland . . . were abolished later by usage, and that thus the Roman law is followed in this subject both in Holland and at Utrecht."

[72] Huber, *Praelectiones ad Pandectas*, 1.3.App.15.

[73] Huber, *Heedensdaegse Rechtsgeleertheyt*, 1.4.

[74] Ibid., 3.54.

son, prodigals, married women" as persons under tutorship or curatorship.[75] The age of majority was set at twenty-five but there were frequently other distinctions according to age that allowed certain rights to persons above a certain age. For example, Holland granted the right to testation to both males and females "right from the very start of puberty," i.e. seven years of age, and Utrecht for men over eighteen and women over sixteen, whether they were under paternal power or not, whereas Friesland did not allow unemancipated sons to make a will.[76] At the same time, reaching majority did not automatically terminate paternal power. Roman law provided that *patria potestas* was terminated in the cases of death of the *paterfamilias*, emancipation, or appointment to certain "offices."[77] Voet suggests that such office has been widened by custom to include "any magisterial office or of the priesthood," including all civil magistrates of cities or free towns."[78] Yet in Huber's Friesland such "office" does not include these lower magistrates, "captains of horse … nor other captains, much less lieutenants or ensigns; not yet doctors, professors, ministers and such like."[79] By that time, marriage was also regarded as terminating parental power, provided – at least in Friesland – that it was consented to by the father: this further explains the stakes underlying Frisians' marriages without paternal consent.[80]

In his conflicts treatment, Huber himself draws a novel distinction between the status itself and actual capacity to enter into a certain legal act.[81] Status is conferred to a person by the law of his or her domicile: the person then carries his or her status everywhere. But it is up to the *lex loci actus* to determine whether that status grants capacity to enter into the legal act. A seventeen-year-old young male from Utrecht or Friesland who moved to Holland would be allowed to make his will there, whereas

[75] Huber, *Praelectiones ad Pandectas*, 1.3.App.12.

[76] Voet, *Commentarius ad Pandectas*, 28.1.44.

[77] Inst. 1.12, esp. 1.12.4 ("attainment of the patriciate, the highest of honours, releases a son from family authority as soon as he is given the imperial patent"): that was a rule promulgated by Justinian, whereas in republican Rome senators or even consuls would remain under *patria potestas*.

[78] Voet, *Commentarius ad Pandectas*, 1.7.10.

[79] Huber, *Heedensdaegse Rechtsgeleertheyt*, 1.12.44–47 citing a 1648 case involving a lieutant.

[80] Ibid., 49–50 (marriage "throughout Europe and particularly in Friesland, terminates the paternal power" provided that it "takes place with the express consent of the father, wherever that is required by law, for otherwise his power and his rights remain just as they were before").

[81] Huber, *Praelectiones ad Pandectas*, 1.3.App.12. See Section 14.2.2.

an unemancipated nineteen-year-old man from either Utrecht or Holland who moved to Friesland would still require paternal consent, but for cause to remove paternal power.[82] A Frisian priest still under paternal power in his homeland will have the same capacity as an unemancipated son in Holland, even though in Holland priests may not fall under paternal power. A priest of Holland would conversely enjoy the status of an emancipated son in Friesland. A person regarded as of age upon completion of his twenty-first year in his place of domicile has acquired the status of a major and is thus able to alienate his immovable property even in a territory where the age of majority remains at 25.[83]

13.3.3.1 Marriage

In *Contemporary Jurisprudence*, Huber states that "marriage, being the beginning of the human race and of all civic relations, should be treated first by us."[84] He sets out the doctrine on "marriages" by fitting the practice of his day – and the dictates of religion – into the skin of his Roman sources, beginning with the definition of marriage in contractual terms.[85] The two elements of marriage are "promise" (i.e. what constitutes such an express declaration) and "consummation" which involves the "benediction of the Church" and "cohabitation."[86] The three "further requirements" consist of capacity to procreate (essentially, a minimum age of fourteen and twelve years for male and female), "consent, not merely of the contracting parties but also of those under whose power the young people stand," and "regard for Blood-relationship."[87] Most of the actual discussion involves what constitutes such an express declaration, what constitutes valid consent, and marriage impediments due to kinship.[88]

[82] Huber, *Praelectiones ad Pandectas*, 1.3.App.13.
[83] Ibid.
[84] Huber, *Heedensdaegse Rechtsgeleertheyt*, 1.5.1.
[85] Ibid., 1.5.2–5: "Marriage is a union of man and woman, consisting in a very close and lifelong community of body and mind. By the term "union" we understand particularly the agreement by which man and wife accept and promise such community with each other. For it is from the mutual declaration of such an intention that marriage derives its existence and power. But the declaration must be an express declaration that they contract marriage or that they take each other for man and wife."
[86] Ibid., 21.
[87] Ibid., 33.
[88] Ibid., 5–20, 37–66, and 67–96.

These are precisely the problematic cases dealt with in Huber's conflicts treatment. Incidentally, they address the three main categories of issues regarding the validity of a marriage: issues regarding celebration, temporal impediments, and permanent impediments.

We have already discussed a case regarding a foreign marriage within the prohibited degrees of kinship. This would be regarded as a matter of substantive validity even today. Even though Huber does not employ such terms or distinctions, the solution he gives would respect the validity of such a marriage between Brabanters but not between Frisians, who would have thus circumvented the prohibition against such marriages in their own law. However, this solution is given in a case that Huber strongly disapproves of but can envisage a dispensation being validly granted in Catholic territories. He would on the contrary not tolerate a "scarcely supposable" marriage between second-degree relatives as too abominable and incestuous under the law of nations.[89]

The other two cases involve issues whose classification as matters of formal or substantive validity has varied across time. The first one – only treated in Huber's Latin text – concerns the effects, in Holland, of the marriage between a Frisian couple who were not wedded in Church but "agree to marry and recognize each other as husband and wife."[90] Even though this would not constitute a marriage in Holland, the Frisians will enjoy "without doubt" there the rights of spouses regarding marital property and succession rights under Huber's primary rule.[91] Contrary to what may appear, this case does not involve the requirement of a religious ceremony by itself – a matter that would eventually create a lot of conflicts and problems involving its characterization – but the requirement of publicity ("banns") that must precede such ceremony. Huber regarded the ceremony itself ("announcement and giving away in Church") an ecclesiastical matter, but the observance of the banns was "a consequence of political or juridical authority, and . . . subject to the jurisdiction of that authority to which ministers and elders could, in case of necessity, be compelled to bow."[92] We learn from Huber that in Frisia a marriage had "to be announced and made known on three different Sundays in Church, or if the parties are of some other persuasion, on three different court days in Court;" even a judicial dispensation

[89] Huber, *Praelectiones ad Pandectas*, 1.3.App.8.
[90] Ibid.
[91] Ibid.
[92] Huber, *Heedensdaegse Rechtsgeleertheyt*, 1.5.23.

"according to circumstances" to shorten the terms for the calling of the banns had to allow "at least six full days" between first and third publication and demand "a heavier penalty (*straffe*) for the third time."[93] An attempt to marry without the certificate of banns would incur penalties for the responsible ministers and magistrates and especially for those attempting to be thus married.[94] But Frisian law would nonetheless acknowledge the validity of such a marriage lacking "announcement in Church or Court," as long as "proof of betrothal is forthcoming from other sources."[95] In contrast, Holland and Utrecht – where the same rule as to three callings of the banns was in force – regarded such marriages *ipso iure* void, unless the parties had availed themselves of a lawful dispensation.[96] Johannes Voet would – controversially – not even allow a Hollander to marry in Flanders or Brabant a local girl without first calling the banns in Holland.[97]

Huber himself is most preoccupied with another case of a forum resident going abroad to marry in violation of forum requirements: unemancipated Frisians getting married in East Frisia without paternal consent. Friesland had taken seriously the idea that "the consent of the father is necessary to the marriage of his children, so long as they are still in his power."[98] Such a marriage would therefore be invalid and the same rule apparently held in all Provinces, as well in the Generality lands by decision of the States-General.[99]

The East Frisian cases appear to have touched upon a stong nerve of Frisian magistrates, as demonstrated by a comparison between the original text of *Contemporary Jurisprudence* and that of the posthumous editions that followed the new Provincial Ordinance of 1723, where the following passage has been added by Huber's son:

93 Ibid., 1.5.22.
94 Ibid., 22 and 23.
95 Ibid., 24: "The marriage holds good all the same, and the children born of it are legitimate and succeed to their parents; as has been frequently ruled by the Court, and as has been held even to the prejudice of another marriage and to the detriment of the children of the latter [citing a 1671 case]."
96 Voet, *Commentarius ad Pandectas*, 23.2.3.
97 Ibid., 4.
98 Huber, *Heedensdaegse Rechtsgeleertheyt*, 1.5.41. Consent of the mother was required for fatherless girls under twenty-five years of age: ibid., 44. Parental consent was still required for widows under the age of twenty-five: ibid., 45 and 59.
99 Voet, *Commentarius ad Pandectas*, 23.2.11.

> No ministers or magistrates may marry or give in marriage persons whose banns have been called elsewhere, unless it appears that they have had the banns called three times without objection at their place of domicile, that is at the place where they have had a fixed dwelling-place for at least half a year.[100]

The 1725 Ordinance strengthened the legal consequences of a marriage without paternal consent (or even maternal consent, where applicable). Originally, Frisian legislation forbade men under twenty-five years of age and daughters under twenty years of age who married without their father's consent from deriving any benefit from their spouses by last will, by gifts, by assignment, or in any other way.[101] This was the rule of the Perpetual Edict laid out by Emperor Charles V in 1540.[102] The new Ordinance not only expanded the scope of the prohibition even to older children "under the power of the father or the guardianship of the mother" – including widows under twenty-five years of age – and to benefits derived by the death of children born of such marriage but most importantly it declared such marriages invalid.[103] These developments were in line with the law in other Dutch provinces, where it was even held that such marriages were *ipso iure* invalid.[104] Huber himself had argued against the notion that such marriages were invalid but it would appear that Frisian authors had argued, and courts had held, otherwise.[105]

100 Huber, *Heedensdaegse Rechtsgeleertheyt* (1742), 1.5.23 in fine, prescribing a monetary penalty for officials and arbitral penalty (*arbitrale straffe*) for those who present themselves without the certificate of banns.

101 Ibid., 46 (1686 edition).

102 Art. 17, Edict of 4 October 1540.

103 Ibid., 46: "[F]or, over and above declaring the marriage null and void, it forbids a young man or woman under the power of the father of the guardianship of the mother, as well as a widow not yet twenty-five years old, who has contracted such a marriage, to reap any benefit from his or her spouse by last will, by donation, by assignment, by death of children born from such marriage, or in any other way."

104 Voet, *Commentarius ad Pandectas*, 23.2.11, with references to the 1580 Political Edict of Holland, as well as legislation and doctrine in Utrecht, Gelderland, lands administered directly by the States-General and even to Sande so as to show that Friesland followed the same rule.

105 Huber, *Heedensdaegse Rechtsgeleertheyt*, 1.5.58: "What reason is there then for our presuming nullity in addition to that penalty, when the Ordinance is silent on the question of nullity? In other places, where the Ordinance intends it, nullity is expressly enacted, but here neither the Ordinance nor the Imperial law provides it. But as has been said practice rules otherwise." In the posthumous editions, the following sentence has been added in fine: "And that is why in the new ordinance there is an addition to the effect that such marriages shall also be null and void."

13.3.3.2 Marital Property

In his discussion of marriage, Huber contrasts the "community of minds and habitation," with "community of goods" which "does not belong to the essence of marriage."[106] The patrimony of spouses has been a constant source of problems – since the Medieval beginnings of conflicts doctrine, as we have already observed in examining Bartolus – arising not only in the case of living spouses dissolving their marriage but also in the context of succession pitting the surviving spouse against the deceased one's heirs, or even the heirs of each spouse against the heirs of the other. Huber himself is faced with fewer polities – and obviously more divorces – than Bartolus was, but this was more than compensated by an even wider disparity between marital property regimes: whereas under Roman law spouses maintained their properties separate, many territories in Northwestern Europe followed the Germanic system of community property. These included Holland, where, unless the spouses had stipulated otherwise in an antenuptial agreement, all present and future property fell into community.[107] Friesland itself followed a variation of the separate-property regime: there was no community of property but there was a community of profit and loss, which of course created its own legal problems.[108]

Huber discusses in his treatments all three major conflicts problems regarding marital property that we find in preclassical doctrine. The first concerned the change of domicile. It was accepted that, upon marriage, the wife obtained the husband's domicile.[109] But what about the case where the couple moved to another province during their marriage? Huber answers that property acquired before the change of domicile would retain its status under the law of that first place, whereas new property would be subject to the law of their new domicile:

> If spouses who lived in places where marriage produces full community of property afterwards come to live in Friesland then from that time forth

[106] Huber, *Heedensdaegse Rechtsgeleertheyt*, 1.11.31. Likewise, Grotius, *Inleiding*, 2.11 treating "commixtion of property by marriage" (as well as "antenuptial contracts," immediately below) within the law of things as opposed to marriage which he treats within the law of persons. On the contrary Voet, *Commentarius ad Pandectas*, 23.2.68 discusses community propery in his chapter on Marriage.

[107] Voet, *Commentarius ad Pandectas*, 23.2.68.

[108] Huber, *Heedensdaegse Rechtsgeleertheyt*, 1.11.2 ("[B]ut others, and among them our countrymen, chose the mean, namely that, the property remaining in each one of the spouses, the fruits and revenues should be common between them").

[109] Voet, *Commentarius ad Pandectas*, 23.2.40

> Frisian law begins to apply, but the property which has previously become common remains common, even after the change of residence, without distinction between movable and immovable property.[110]

The second question involved immovable property acquired in another province that followed a different marital-property regime: should rights over such property be determined by the *lex rei sitae* or the law of the spousal domicile? Huber answers unequivocally in the affirmative, after taking note of the "controversy among the Doctors." To support his view he draws on the axioms he laid out in the beginning but also on the contractual nature of the relationship.

This view – which easily contrasts to the *situs* territorialism of d'Argentré and others – is common among Dutch authors. It follows as a consequence of the characterization of marriage as a contract or covenant and the incorporation of patrimonial relations between spouses into the doctrinal discussion of marriage: marriage is an *actus*; its effects to the spouses' property, the benefits and losses accruing from it are also treated in contractual terms, as the effects of the actus.

The third problem involved actual contracts.[111] The problem of a wife's property providing security for her husband's debts has been a recurring one, from ancient to modern times: we saw that Huber used it as his example in distinguishing civil from natural equity.[112] The Roman-law prohibition encapsulated in the *Senatus-consultum Velleianum* found appeal even in territories following customary law and community-property arrangements, as well as in Huber's Friesland, which had maintained a separate-property regime with community of profit and loss but gave the husband guardianship of his wife's property.[113] The matter is considered by Huber in the final chapter of his discussion of contracts, bearing the apt title "Who cannot be sureties, and women in this regard."[114] The woman could renounce her claim to remedy under the *Senatus-consultum Velleianum*, provided she had been "duly instructed" and certain procedural and transactional formalities were followed, which effectively made any such surety conditional on the

110 Huber, *Heedensdaegse Rechtsgeleertheyt*, 1.11.52. See also ibid., 1.3.App.34–35; Huber, *Praelectiones ad Pandectas*, 1.3.App.9.

111 The case is only discussed in Huber, *Praelectiones ad Pandectas*, 1.3.App.11, where Huber mentions that he was recently consulted in a similar case.

112 Huber, *Heedensdaegse Rechtsgeleertheyt*, 1.1.16–19. See Section 12.3.

113 Huber, *Heedensdaegse Rechtsgeleertheyt*, 1.10.4. See Section 9.3.6.

114 Ibid., 3.21.4–28.

observance of these formalities.[115] In Holland, on the contrary, the wife, in her share, was liable by her husband's surety, but she could opt out of community in the antenuptial contract.[116] Voet notes that such agreements were common, as indeed were also agreements reserving the woman the right to elect between reclaiming her dowry or participating in the profit and loss.[117] In Friesland, however, such agreements had to be "openly announced . . . for the purpose of giving such a condition binding force against strangers" and could only be antenuptial.[118] Otherwise, the wive could still have recourse against her husband or – perhaps more frequently – his heirs.[119] In the case brought up by Huber, the wife, upon being sued for one half of her husband's debt contracted in Friesland, pleads the stipulations of her antenuptial contract (*pactum dotale*) but stumbles upon the Frisian requirement of publication and the good faith of the creditors.[120]

13.3.4 *Testaments and Property*

Whereas Bartolus focused much of his attention on succession but begun with contracts, the reverse holds true of Huber, who begins with our familiar case. Friesland required seven witnesses – including the testator – and a notary would simply substitute the seventh witness.[121] Holland maintained the Roman law doctrines but also provided additional

115 Ibid., 18–24.

116 Voet, *Commentarius ad Pandectas*, 23.2.53 and 23.4.52 respectively.

117 Ibid., 23.4.52 and 53. These wives could still elect to provide surety and indeed Voet suggests that tax farmers' wives were compelled to do so: ibid., 56.

118 Huber, *Heedensdaegse Rechtsgeleertheyt*, 1.11.29

119 Ibid., 29 ("for between spouses themselves it is sufficient, to give rise to such an arrangement between them, that there has been a mutual agreement to that effect"). Voet, *Commentarius ad Pandectas*, 23.4.52 is more descriptive: "For among the people of Utrecht and the Frisians such antenuptial covenants do not prevent a wife being sued in whole on dissolution of marriage by creditors for debt which was contracted during marriage, though she will afterward have recourse for indemnity against her husband or his heirs; and would also correctly claim that her defense should be taken up by them when she had started to be sued by the creditors of her husband; such agreements therefore do not in terms of [C.2.3.25] stand in the way of creditors. They only exert their strength between husband and wife and the heirs of both of them, and the loss would be that of the wife if perhaps the estate of her husband has been unequal to paying off such debts."

120 Huber, *Praelectiones ad Pandectas*, 1.3.App.11.

121 Huber, *Heedensdaegse Rechtsgeleertheyt*, 2.12.21–37. An eighth witness would be required if the testator could not write his own name: ibid., 32.

options to the testator, including the "privileged" testaments before a notary and two witnesses, to which Huber makes reference.[122] A testament validly made in Friesland would not raise concerns in Holland and the reverse would certainly hold in accordance with Huber's primary rule. The actual problematic case mentioned – only in *Contemporary Jurisprudence* – concerned a testament made in the neighboring province of Overijssel by a Frisian, witnessed by seven witnesses, in conformity with the requirements of the law of Friesland (and Roman law). But "[this] form of will was in conflict with the local law of that Province." Huber would regard this testament null and void, but the Court of Friesland had recently held otherwise (1683).[123] There is also the example of the seventeen-year-old Frisian who made a testament in Groningen immediately upon arriving there as a student: that would not be a problem in his native Friesland, but Groningen did not allow minors under the age of twenty to make a testament "not even at the time of fatal illness nor as to more than moiety of their inherited property."[124] In that earlier case, the Court of Friesland held against the testament, "consistently with what we have said," but that decision was not unanimous.[125]

This is not simply a conceptual matter and not necessarily a matter of formalities. Testamentary succession was traditionally viewed with suspicion in the western, agrarian provinces of the Dutch confederation, especially with regard to hereditary land, up to Huber's time. Johannes Voet, who himself shares the Roman preference for last wills, notes the deep-rooted aversion of certain peoples to testamentary succession, generally or with regard to specific kinds of property.[126] As examples of "nations which were of old dissatisfied with the last directions of dying persons as to their goods and which were minded to reform the ancient

[122] Voet, *Commentarius ad Pandectas*, 28.1.20.

[123] Huber, *Heedensdaegse Rechtsgeleertheyt*, 1.3.15.

[124] Huber, *Praelectiones ad Pandectas*, 1.3.App.14.

[125] Ibid.

[126] Voet, *Commentarius ad Pandectas*, 28.1.2: "Not to mention that the ancient Germans were not satisfied by anything but legal succession according to Tacitus, there are peoples by whose laws all making of a last will is disapproved both in the case of movables and in the case of immovables, whether acquired or hereditary. There are those who have allowed it with movables, but not with immovables. Others have thought fit to allow such provisions as to acquired, but not as to hereditary immovables. Nor are there lacking those who have thought it just for a free disposition to be made by last will of all acquired, and of a certain part of heriditary immovables. Finally certain peoples have granted the right for dying declarations to be framed as to a definite share of immovables, whether acquired or hereditary."

laws for the better," Voet gives two examples from the province of Gelderland whose "old law" did not allow testaments. Zutphen first allowed a testamentary disposition for half of the testator's goods in 1604. Nijmegen initially "made it possible for dispositions to be made by last wish about immovables before seven *schepenen* and about movables before two of them," until in 1686 "a fuller and more complete form of testation" was fixed for all property.[127] Huber himself mentions the province of Groningen as not allowing testamentary disposition of immovables and alludes to the controversy involving the use of "deeds executed between living persons or in contemplation of death."[128]

This is actually what Huber is concerned with in his discussion of the effects of legal acts on immovables, in the final section of his treatment. We tend to approach that section as affirming – and setting the limits – of the *lex rei sitae* rule and indeed this is the spirit of Huber's explanation in both Latin and vernacular text. But the example he gives concerns a testament made, presumably at home, by a Frisian who has "fields and houses" in the Groningen Ommelands, where it is not allowed to dispose of such property by a testament. This also illuminates the distinction Huber draws, in *Praelectiones*, between what pertains to free disposition by each household (*ut dependentes a libera dispositione cuiusque patrisfamilias*) and incidents (*notae*) by law, which must remain unchangeable lest "general confusion and prejudice" results in the place where the land is situated.[129]

Respect for the local rules regulating the acquisition of property rights over land carries over into Huber's treatment of intestate succession, which comes at the very end. Huber's solution bears contractual analogies. Succession as to immovables will be determined by the place where they are situated. Succession as to movables will be determined by the law of the place where the defunct was domiciled.

13.4 Form and Substance in Huber

In our study of Bartolus, we observed that his eclectic system of rules and interpretative methods made frequent use of the distinction between solemnity requirements and the "substantive" *dispositio* of issues. The

[127] Ibid.

[128] Huber, *Praelectiones ad Pandectas*, 1.3.App.15; Huber, *Heedensdaegse Rechtsgeleertheyt*, 46–47.

[129] Huber, *Praelectiones ad Pandectas*, 1.3.App.15.

Voets have followed a similar approach, in carving a distinct category of mixed statutes that "prescribe the shape, manner, order and formalities of acts."[130] Moreover, such acts "have to be done by persons in and about things" but "do not deal principally either with persons or with things."[131]

Huber himself does not announce such a distinction: his *locus regit actum* rule appears to apply across the board, without differentiating *ab initio* between formal validity and substantive requirements. In explaining his *positio* or primary rule, Huber speaks of acts "properly executed" according to the law of a particular place (*secundum ius certi loci rite celebrata valent*).[132] The illustrations of the rule that Huber provides us with would be characterized today as pertaining to substance as well as form. This calls for a more careful examination of the cases Huber brings up and how he deals with them.

13.4.1 From Testaments to Contracts

Huber's first illustration of the *locus regit actum* rule involves the classic example as to the observance of formalities in acts *mortis causa*: namely the number of witnesses to a testament and the divergence between provinces following the original Roman rule as to seven witnesses and those derogating from it, usually by providing a more liberal regime of formalities.[133] More interesting is his treatment, in "Observance," of the testament made in Overijssel by a Frisian in form conforming to Frisian and Roman law but in conflict with the law of Overijssel.[134] The Court of Friesland held that "there was no reason to nullify and reject in Frisian land a testament made elsewhere by a Frisian," a ruling with echoes of modern *favor validitatis*.[135] On the contrary, Huber argues that "the deed was from the beginning null and void, and therefore can acquire no force among us without being made anew."[136] As mentioned above, Huber is addressing not just a diversity in formalities, but also a – longstanding if waning – hostility of neighboring provinces toward testamentary

130 Voet, *Commentarius ad Pandectas*, 1.4.App.4.

131 Ibid.

132 Huber, *Praelectiones ad Pandectas*, 1.3.App.3.

133 Ibid., 4. See also Huber, *Heedensdaegse Rechtsgeleertheyt*, 1.3.12–17. See also Section 13.3.4 (as to the substantive aspects of testamentary formalities).

134 Huber, *Heedensdaegse Rechtsgeleertheyt*, 1.3.15.

135 Ibid., with reference to a 1683 case.

136 Ibid., 14.

succession. While Huber's insistence on the absolute effect of his *lex loci celebrationis* rule led to a more severe result in this case, it would also allow testaments – and even deeds *inter vivos* – made in Holland, Utrecht, or Friesland, by citizens of the Eastern Provinces, to produce their effects. This is shown near the end of the treatment, where Huber, dealing with the case of the Frisian testator leaving behind land in Groningen, argues that Groningen law should only invalidate the acquisition of land and not the act itself (or acquisition of movables).[137]

When it comes to contracts, Huber declares on the outset that the validity of a contract made validly in the place of contracting extends over both its form and its substance.[138] The examples given in elaboration of the rule concern substance and third-party rights. Huber goes directly to hard cases, exploring the limits of the *locus actus*. The only case that actually concerns what we should regard as transactional formalities comes as Huber elaborates his *lex rei situs* rule: a contract made abroad for the sale of land in Friesland will require, apart from the formalities needed under the *lex loci conclusionis*, the fulfillment of the "notices and consents" required under Frisian law.

13.4.2 Formal and Substantive Validity of Marriages

The distinction of formal and substantive requirements as to the validity of a marriage is a staple of comparative conflict of laws. The only national conflicts tradition that eschewed this distinction has been US conflict of laws and this is not unrelated to the influence of the Dutch school upon the founding fathers of Anglo-American conflict of laws.[139] Huber indeed neither makes nor alludes to a distinction between form and substance, even though the three cases he uses – involving celebration,

[137] Huber, *Heedensdaegse Rechtsgeleertheyt*, 1.3.47: "I spoke of 'the law touching such property,' for if there is a diversity of laws in regard to the *form* of deeds executed between living persons or in contemplation of death in that case we merely follow the law of the place where the deed is executed, without distinguishing between movable and immovable property; just as has already been remarked, that a will legally executed in Holland is also good here with respect to immovable property, although, had it been made here in that form, it would have been null and void."

[138] Huber, *Praelectiones ad Pandectas*, 1.3.App.5.

[139] English law begun adopting the distinction between formal and substantive validity in earnest in the mid-nineteenth century with *Brook* v. *Brook* (1858) 3 Sm & G 481, (1861) 9 HLC 193. See Westlake, *Private International Law* (1890), 55ff.

temporal and permanent impediments – have raised centuries-long debates about their characterization in this regard.

The first one, marriage within the prohibited degrees, is to this day the classic issue of substantive validity.[140] This includes dispensations. Huber would apply the *lex loci celebrationis* with a vigilant eye toward evasive abuse by Frisians.

The second case involves what appears to be an unsolemnized marriage without Church benediction. In classical conflict of laws, religious – or in some countries, secular – requirements imposed by some states were regarded as a matter of substantive validity that was governed by personal law and modified the *locus regit actum* principle.[141] This takes us to the creeping formalization of marriage law in the Early Modern period – a process in which Huber's Dutch Republic represents a moment of transition, where past doctrines about present consent (and binding promises to marry) coexisted with administrative formalism by Church and State. The matter became one of form – observance of the banns – rather than of essence or substance. Hence the *lex loci actus* rather than any personal law would apply – unless perhaps evasion is involved.[142]

Administrative formalism also plays its part in Huber's third and most pressing case: marriage without paternal consent. The legal treatment of parental or guardian consent to a marriage is by definition linked to the age requirements set for marriage and majority. It has been traditionally regarded in most countries as a matter of substantive validity.[143] The notable exception has been English law, which was originally shaped by the reality of such conflicts occurring within a recently United Kingdom.[144] A recent tendency has been to subject the application of foreign law in such cases to a reasonableness test so that it should not apply if it fixes the age too low or too high by the standards of the forum.[145] As ought to be expected, Huber does not use such concepts. He endorses a sweeping application of *the lex loci celebrationis*, with the critical exception of the young Frisians who crossed Friesland's border to evade its law. As discussed above, this case can only be fully understood in the context of the

[140] Indeed, both *Brook* v. *Brook* and *Sottomayor* v. *De Barros* involved such cases.

[141] See Section 5.4.1.2.

[142] See Section 13.3.3.1 and also Voet, *Commentarius ad Pandectas*, 23.2.4 in fine.

[143] Rabel, *Conflict of Laws*, 1:209 ("The requirement of parental consent to the marriage of a minor is universally characterized as closely connected with the intrinsic requirement of consent of the party") and 266–269.

[144] Collins, *Dicey, Morris & Collins on the Conflict of Laws*, 923–925.

[145] See e.g. Audit, *Droit international privé*, 519–520.

banns requirements and sanctions imposed in Friesland but it nonetheless gave rise to an *actus* territorialist doctrine that would allow the marriage to be held valid anywhere but in Friesland.[146]

We will return to the question of evasion and prejudice in Huber's doctrine in the subsequent chapter. But it would appear that the more "substantive" a requirement is for Huber and his forum (for example, paternal consent), the more it has the potential to be allowed to interfere with the validity or effects of the marriage. Among issues of "substantive" validity, the less they have to do with administrative formalities the stronger the intra- and extraterritorial effect of their prohibition (for example, incest as compared to guardian's consent).

Carving up a distinct category of formal-validity requirements would help put a limit to the public-policy concerns of the forum: for example, Hollanders could become married in Friesland without ever setting foot in a church. On the other hand, the creation of a separate category of substantive-validity requirements, we allow more scope, and space, to the public policy of forum: for example, if we conceptualize kinship impediments to marriage as a matter of substantive validity, subjected to a more vigilant law than with regard to form, the uncle will remain unmarried to his niece as far as Friesland is concerned, even if they were married in Brabant and then remained there for some time (without changing their domicile). Friesland might even wish to claim that in its eyes this union could have no validity elsewhere, and convert other states to its cause. Huber himself makes no distinction between formal and substantive validity: his solution provides a liberal principle (in the spirit of *locus regit actum*) which is supported, or moderated by a strong intervention mechanism at the local level.

13.4.3 Procedure: or, Control by the Forum through Carving an Area of Form

At the beginning of *Contemporary Jurisprudence*, Huber notes that "all law has a threefold object: the person of every human being, the causes of

[146] The doctrine is stated by Rabel, *Conflict of Laws*, 1:269 (discussing US law with reference to *Sturgis* v. *Sturgis* (1908) 51 Ore 10, 93 Pac 696): "Although form and substance need not be distinguished in the United States since the law of the place of celebration governs both, on grounds of public policy the domiciliary law is occasionally taken into consideration with respect to parental consent no such attention would be given to a mere formality."

actions and the actions themselves, that is to say, the claims of law by which we maintain the right in relation to the person and the cause of action."[147] This may sound like our own distinction between substance and procedure. In his conflicts treatment, however, procedural matters are approached as a series of "transactions." It is even remarked that the "legal process is of itself like a contract, and therefore also involves its own observances."[148] Huber uses this contractual analogy not only in order to strengthen the argument for recognizing the effects of foreign judgments but also as a way of raising judicial process, from being the handmaid of the contract, to equal status.

This understanding corresponds to the extended ("remedial") scope of the procedural category in Huber. The prescription of claims is deemed a procedural matter, on the ground that the statute of limitations does not pertain to the substance of the contract but to the time and mode of bringing suit.[149] The same holds as to judicial remedies, such as immediate execution.[150] In fact, Huber invokes again a contractual analogy in order to resolve a conflict of procedures: a reason why "the mode and the law" of the place of execution "is always followed, even though the tribunal before which judgment was pronounced may have other laws and customs" is that "execution is of itself a separate transaction and ought to be governed by the law of its own place."[151]

13.5 Huber and the Conflict of Jurisdictions

Huber grounds his doctrines of both adjudicative jurisdiction and choice-of-law on similar ideas. He espouses an *enlightened* conception of *territorial sovereignty*, that emphasizes the mutual recognition of each other state's acts and judgments. Whereas Johannes Voet plays down the aggressive assertion of legislative and adjudicative jurisdiction by some states, Huber's forum respects the territorial sovereignty of other states and shows good faith toward its effects, as long as it is exercised duly and

[147] Huber, *Heedensdaegse Rechtsgeleertheyt*, 1.2.66.
[148] Ibid., 1.3.28.
[149] Huber, *Praelectiones ad Pandectas*, 1.3.App.7; id., *Heedensdaegse Rechtsgeleertheyt*, 1.3.29. See also ibid., 5.14 ("Duration of Actions," where prescription issues are discussed).
[150] Huber, *Praelectiones ad Pandectas*, 1.3.App.7; Huber, *Heedensdaegse Rechtsgeleertheyt*, 1.3.30.
[151] Ibid., 27.

in good faith. But his system has its safety valves, which may allow judicial and legislative jurisdiction to be extended, upon occasion.

However, the two sub-systems are not fully aligned. The choice-of-law sub-system revolves around the idea of recognizing legal transactions made abroad: its specific rules – as opposed to the axioms – are not about allocating legislative jurisdiction *a priori*, but rather about determining whether legislative jurisdiction has been properly exercised and whether prejudicial effects would arise by recognizing it.

In its turn, the adjudicative jurisdiction sub-system is more old-fashioned than the choice-of-law one. While the *lex actus* appears as something different from both "personal" and "real" statutes, no independent *forum actus* or *forum obligationis* appears to accompany it.[152] The lack of such a *forum*, in its turn, has to do both with the pragmatism and notions of justice that emphasize the defendant's domicile as a proper venue, and with the fact that here the *lex actus* is the law of the place where the contract was made, whereas in Savigny's *forum obligationis – lex obligationis* system it is the law of the place of performance, whose stronger "territorial" element may make a more pragmatic judicial venue as well. Generally speaking, Huber's jurisdiction system is more unilateral than the choice-of-law one.

13.6 Individual Autonomy in Huber's Conflict of Laws

In Huber's conflicts doctrine, it is the legal acts that constitute the basic material and principal subject. We will search in vain the text for references to individual freedom: the two types of subjects are the legal acts and the sovereigns who issue the laws and enforce the laws and acts. On the other hand, statutes are made by sovereigns and acts are performed by individuals. In this regard, it is significant that Huber states his fundamental question – and structures his treatment – not in terms of classifying and defining the reach of statutes but rather in terms of achieving a priori the universal validity of legal acts.

It has been suggested that "the doctrine of party autonomy is adumbrated" in "De Conflictu Legum."[153] There are admittedly more traces of party autonomy in Huber than in Bartolus. Huber does at some point state that "if the parties in contracting had another place in mind," the

[152] See Huber, *Heedensdaegse Rechtsgeleertheyt*, 4.22–33, 5.1.9–14 and Section 12.4.1.
[153] Yntema, "Comity," 27.

locus conclusionis "should not prevail."[154] But this remark must be seen in context, beginning with his citation of the *contraxisse* passage from the Digest: "Every person is considered to have concluded a contract (*contraxisse*) in the place where he had bound himself to pay (*ut solveret se obligavit*)."[155] The passage suggests that for certain obligations, the place in which performance is stipulated should be looked to as if the contract had been concluded there. In the case at hand, Huber is concerned with the case of Frisian men who got married in Holland and subsequently return to Friesland. We have seen that there was a veritable conflict of laws between Holland and Friesland regarding the patrimonial relations of spouses – the former opting for community property (managed or nuanced by a prolific practice of antenuptial contracts), whereas the latter largely maintained a separate-property regime following Roman law, with added complications involving husbands' guardianship of their wives' property, as well as community of profit and loss, that were also managed via private instruments. Such conflicts were a constant issue in preclassical conflict of laws (as indeed they have remained to this day). We have seen that, from Bartolus to Dumoulin, jurists had held that the law of matrimonial domicile – Friesland – and not the law of the place of marriage (and presumably place of conclusion of the dowry contract) should be looked to in order to determine the proprietary interests of each spouse, with Dumoulin invoking the parties' will as presumed under the circumstances.[156] But under the territorialist approach followed by d'Argentré and others in the intervening century and a half, the law of Holland being a real statute should apply over immovable property in Holland, and the law of Friesland over immovables in Friesland.[157] Ownership of movables will be determined under the law of the matrimonial domicile. As a result, if our couple lived in Friesland but maintained a furnished house in the province of Holland, they – and their heirs – will share ownership of the house, but Frisian law will determine ownership over the house's furnishings.

It is thus no accident that Huber alludes to the intention of the parties when it comes to the effects of marriage over property and not in his discussion of contracts. There is, to begin with, a factual difference: most

[154] Huber, *Praelectiones ad Pandectas*, 1.3.App.10.

[155] D.44.7.21. Llewellyn Davies, "Influence," 73 translates "contracted … bound to perform."

[156] See Section 9.6.

[157] See Section 14.2.2.

contracts have a clear *locus conclusionis*, which often may also be the place of performance between the parties. Moreover, at least one of the parties has an ongoing connection with that place, but even the other party may either have travelled there or be contracting via an agent or factor who is based in the *locus conclusionis*. Moreover, any transaction shall involve specific property and usually short-term consequences. On the contrary, a marriage tends to be celebrated – and the antenuptial contract concluded – at the original domicile of the bride, yet the couple tends to move to the groom's domicile soon thereafter and that becomes the domicile of the bride as well. As a result, the relationship between the *locus celebrationis* and the spouses begins weakening almost immediately. To subject, by default, land in Friesland to the community property rules of Holland just because the marriage was celebrated there would create problems which Huber wants to avoid without however abandoning his primary rule of *actus* territoriality. Such a solution should also achieve a secondary purpose: to maintain the unity of a person's property.

Huber's solution is better laid out in "Observance," where he explicitly defines the issue as one of determining the marital-property regime:

> If there is full community of goods at the place where the marriage was contracted and the spouses are resident, as there is in Holland where not otherwise stipulated, then the property situated in Friesland, both movable and immovable, and belonging to either of the spouses, is common to both, just as though it had been alienated or made common by a legal contract in Holland. This is founded on the tacit wish (*stilswijgende wille*) of the contracting parties, which, however, ceases to exist if the marriage has been contracted and celebrated in Holland, but the spouses intend to reside in Friesland where no community supervenes except that of profit and loss. In that case they cannot be presumed to desire to be governed by the law of Holland, but rather by that of Friesland, which they have in contemplation, and where they intend to live.[158]

Huber proposes that a single law should determine the rights over all marital property, movables as well as immovables, regardless of the place or situation.[159] His solution is grounded on the contractual nature of marital property, which allows him to invoke the "tacit wish" of the parties. In this regard, Huber is joining the long list of jurists, from the

[158] Huber, *Heedensdaegse Rechtsgeleertheyt*, 1.3.33–34.

[159] Regarding immovables, the rule obviously applies only to the determination of ownership claims and shares. The *lex rei sitae* will apply as to additional formality requirements and matters pertaining to the exercise of property rights over the immovables in question.

High Middle Ages to the twentieth century, who used the "intention of the parties" to justify *a posteriori* what they regarded as the best applicable-law solution.[160] In this regard, Huber could hardly be considered as a father of what we today think of as party autonomy. But we must also consider another passage from his vernacular text. Toward the end of "Observance," Huber notes, with regard to succession to movables, that "we are accustomed, both in affairs of death and in transactions between living persons, to follow the custom of the place where we are at the time."[161] And he continues:

> It is otherwise when a dying man or two contracting parties have said expressly (*uitdruckelijk*) what law they wish to be followed, for that law must then be followed everywhere; just as also, if persons, who engage in a transaction at a certain place, declare that they have in contemplation another place, where they intend to complete the transaction, the law of the latter place must be observed as regards that transaction.[162]

The passage (sandwiched between the rule *mobilia sequuntur personam* and the observation that the *lex loci actus* cannot prejudice the "vested rights" of the forum's government and subjects) is a rare reference in scholarly texts to actual stipulations by parties regarding applicable law to their legal acts. It must be viewed in the context of its time and other texts, which repeatedly invoke the presumed intention of the testator.[163] But, in the very least, it should invite more research into primary sources. The passage constitutes evidence that conflict of laws questions were considered in transactional and testamentary practice, which should come as no surprise given the role of notaries and notarial practice in the Netherlands of the Golden Age, especially considering the default norms concerning succession and marital-property claims and the diversity between the Provinces. But this does not necessarily imply anything more than the incorporation of the default norms of the chosen law into the transaction: there is a function of "objective localization" but we

160 See Hatzimihail, "Foundations," esp. 34–36.

161 Huber, *Heedensdaegse Rechtsgeleertheyt*, 1.3.51 in fine.

162 Ibid., 52.

163 See e.g. Grotius, *De Jure Belli ac Pacis*, 2.7.11: "Nevertheless this principle should be kept in mind that whenever there are no quite definite indications of intent it is to be believed that each person in regard to his accession had in mind that which the law or custom of his people approved such belief is based not only on the power of government but also on presumption regarding the voices of the deceased which has weight even with those who possess sovereign power."

should stop short of projecting modern ideas into a very different society with a different state of mind.

This is best illustrated by two relevant cases. The first one concerns Huber's legal treatment of agreements of submission or voluntary subjection to the jurisdiction of a court. We are told that such agreements were "very common" and indeed "annexed to almost all contracts and instruments."[164] Most of these agreements concerned choice of venue or even subject matter jurisdiction within Friesland, but Huber bears witness to an unmistakeable practice in contract and testamentary drafting. What is of interest to us here is that Huber appears much more circumspect about such agreements than a modern lawyer: Huber is clearly opposed to the idea that jurisdiction can be simply be unilaterally established (i.e. by means of an extraordinary citation) over a nonresident defendant who had made such an agreement; the only way would be for the Frisian court to request from the court of his domicile to compel the defendant to appear by effecting citation, but even in that case Huber cautions the judge of domicile to first examine the facts of the case before accepting such a request. Huber does not even accept in principle the idea that, if such a defendant is found in Friesland, jurisdiction could be grounded on his arrest; the only way for the Frisian court to obtain jurisdiction over the foreigner would be if he voluntarily appeared before the court – or if he were regarded as residing in Friesland.

The second one comes from the conflicts treatment of Johannes Voet, who has likewise also been called an early proponent of the "principle of private autonomy."[165] Indeed, Voet organizes his treatment as a response to three questions. The first two, to which we shall return in the next chapter, concern the position at strict law and the impact of comity.[166] The third one is the following:

> How far can anybody, whether citizen or alien, depart by express agreements from the provisions of municipal or provincial laws or be deemed to have departed from them by tacit covenants to be inferred from presumptions?[167]

Voet distinguishes between statutes that "concern primarily the right, convenience and favor of private persons" and statutes that "look to the

[164] Huber, *Heedensdaegse Rechtsgeleertheyt*, 4.27.3.
[165] Yntema, "Comity," 24.
[166] Voet, *Commentarius ad Pandectas*, 1.4.App.1. See Section 14.4.2.
[167] Ibid.

public advantage."[168] There can be no derogation from statutes belonging to the latter category, in which he includes not just laws that "touch upon public honor" but also "those which touch the public establishment of formality and shape for acts."[169] As to the former category, Voet draws another distinction, between prohibitive and dispositive statutes.

Prohibitive statutes are those "in which the doing of something is expressly forbidden." Voet's examples of *statuta prohibitiva* include the prohibition of donations or legacies between spouses, prohibition of testamentary disposition of immovable property, and restrictions to disposition of property following remarriage. Voet notes that "whatever has been made subject of agreement or of disposition by last will in reference to property situate in the territory of the prohibiting authority ought to be deemed of no weight."[170]

Statuta dispositiva contain "no prohibition, but simply dispositions of what appears to be in the interest of private persons" – for example, laws on intestate succession or laws establishing community property or another marital property regime. Such *statuta dispositiva* "may be departed from either by renunciations or by pacts and arrangements."[171] Voet notes that renunciation may even be by "tacit or presumed intention" – a rule that must been seen in the light of a presumption that "everyone is deemed in case of doubt to have intended in contracting to pattern and fit himself to the statutes of his domicile."[172] But the expression of such tacit intention requires an actual contract or testament: "where there is no act there is no tacit agreement, and by similarity of reasoning no testament."[173]

Voet has addressed in several pages of text what Huber said in several lines. Granted that to read modern or even classical ideas into Huber or the Voets would be historically doubtful but also unjust to their ability to address the problems of their time in a manner fitting to their own legal environment, we are observing in these texts an awareness of the power of the individuals to alter the equation as the law applicable to

[168] Ibid., 18.

[169] Ibid.

[170] Ibid.: "It would be in vain for a Hollander to bequeath to his wife immovables situated at Utrecht; in vain also for him to arrange a last will as to his immovables situated in a place where the making of the last will is totally forbidden."

[171] Ibid.

[172] Ibid., 19.

[173] Ibid., 21.

their act – both by their physical movement and by their words in contracts and acts *mortis causa*. This should be expected from a legal doctrine that places emphasis on legal acts and relies on a vibrant documentary practice. But we are far from a notion of party autonomy. Parties may depart from dispositive rules of the law otherwise applicable – essentially, what we mean by implication of terms. On the contrary, there is a marked awareness of the tendency of individuals to evade the system: if conflict of laws is perceived as a game between individuals and state laws, the Dutch jurists come on the side of the latter.

13.7 Harmony of Solutions

Systems espousing *actus* territorialism usually place strong emphasis on achieving decisional harmony. This emphasis shows in a relatively simple system of jurisdiction-allocating rules and in the rhetoric about safeguarding rights or transactions. This is certainly true of Huber, beginning with his theoretical foundations and the very first sentence of his treatment.[174] The circulation and extraterritorial effects of *negotia* is for him a *fact*, but even the Voets, though less concerned with decisional harmony, speak of *bene gesta* that should not be disturbed. Huber moreover proposes a system of very limited rules, with the *lex loci actus* as the primary rule. In its application, Huber tries to reconcile the forum's interests with the need for "international" harmony.

Where Huber is shown to be more concerned with decisional harmony than most others is in cases such as the testament made by a forum domiciliary abroad in conformity with the formalities prescribed by the *lex fori* but not the *lex loci celebrationis*. There may well be pragmatic reasons for Huber's solution, but it is contrasted both with modern and even classical doctrines ("false conflict," *favor validitatis*, nationality principle) and with the stance of Johannes Voet, who sees no reason for the forum to display comity to the *locus celebrationis* in such a case.

At the same time, the price for the simplicity of Huber's system is the discordance in the cases of prejudice. We shall consider at length these exceptions below, where they are broken down into cases of actual evasion, where something like an *ordre public* mechanism is triggered; cases where an auxiliary choice-of-law norm is carved out of the *lex loci actus*; and cases opposing to the foreign contract existing forum-born

[174] Huber, *Praelectiones ad Pandectas*, 1.3.App.1. See Section 14.4.3.

rights of good-faith third parties.[175] What is remarkable is that, even in such cases, Huber tries to minimize the impact of such exceptions.

13.8 Conclusion

In his presentation of Bartolus's conflicts treatments, J. A. Clarence Smith contrasts the great Italian with Huber's "methodless iconoclasm."[176] It must be obvious that I do not share this view, which however evidences a widely held misconception about Huber's doctrine, partly attributable to the emphasis placed on the three axioms by themselves, to the detriment of his three actual choice-of-law rules and the environment in which they are called to operate. Yet it the rules that constitute the essence of Huber's conflicts doctrine. The axioms provide the foundation for the rules. And it is the contemporaneous legal institutions and problems that give impetus to these rules.

From a jurisprudential point of view, Huber clearly works with rules, rather than standards. He advocates a system of one primary rule and two secondary rules. Apart from cases of evasion, even those instances where he claims an exception to comity on account of prejudice are morphed into rules. The theoretical discussion – in and around the axioms – and the discussion of the legal subject matter serve as interpretative material for the rules.

In a way, Huber plays the hedgehog to the Bartolan fox. Going back to Niboyet's scheme of contrasting characters, whereas Bartolus is analytical and eclectic, Huber is *synthetic* – in the sense that he is imbued by a spirit of synthesis and systematization and he is wary of too much detail interfering with the sense of direction he is trying to convey – and *dogmatic*, in the sense that his conflicts treatment is imbued by one fundamental theme, which he affirms and around which everything revolves. The fundamental idea however is not territorial sovereignty, but the universal validity of rights and legal acts (*negotia*, or the Voets' *bona gesta*) validly made in the place of their creation – and universal invalidity in the contrary case. Huber is certainly not methodless: his system moves from *axiomata* to *positiones*, from theoretical foundations to legal norms. He is also not that much of an iconoclast: his treatment may be one of the most clearly written, and concise, texts of preclassical scholarship but it was written for the Dutch jurists and an international

[175] See Section 14.4.4.

[176] Clarence Smith, "Bartolo," 160.

academic community working on learned law, in his time and soon thereafter. Huber appears to have eschewed the traditional concepts of the theory of statutes in favor of logical tools, but neither his solutions nor the legal thought that underlies his doctrine are very different from those of his contemporaries.

Huber cannot be studied without understanding the context, the jurisprudence, and the issues that fostered his work. But the last key to understanding Huber lies in the present. In the next chapter, we will consider how Huber has been approached in the historical consciousness of private international law and examine his theoretical foundations, and doctrine, in the light of present-day conceptions.

14

Huber's Conflict of Laws in the Conceptual Battlefield

14.1 Introduction

In the preceding chapters, we had the opportunity to examine in detail Huber's conflicts treatment and to draw connections to Huber's overall doctrinal outlook. In the process, we have come across common perceptions, or rather misperceptions, of Huber in conflicts literature. Having established the context, we have been gradually moving toward issues more specific to a doctrinal work in the conflict of laws. Our exercise is completed in this chapter, where Huber's doctrine is examined in the light of the basic conceptual oppositions of the conflicts discourse. Huber has been often described as a territorialist and as a unilateralist. He has also been perceived as thinking of the conflict of laws in terms of addressing or seeking to avoid a conflict between the "sovereignties" of different states. His famous three axioms are a recurring invocation in all these perceptions, as indeed is the concept of comity, with the origins of which Huber has become associated as none in classical and modern consciousness.

Addressing these perceptions requires us to, first, distinguish between the different ideas captured in a single word and, second, to look carefully into Huber's words and consider the solutions given on a subject-by-subject basis: it is the rules system that Huber constructs, rather than the axioms by themselves, that shall provide our answers. Section 14.2 examines Huber in relation to territorialist and personalist approaches. Section 14.3 addresses the subject of Huber and unilateralism. Inevitably, this leads us to a close examination of comity doctrine in Huber, including comparisons with the other leading jurists of the Dutch school: Section 14.4 is by far the largest in the chapter. Section 14.5, by means of an interim conclusion, asks whether Huber did approach conflict of laws as a conflict of sovereignties.

14.2 Huber and Territorialism

It is becoming apparent that the classic theory of statutes can only partly account for Huber's doctrine. In marked contrast to the Voets and other Early Modern jurists, Huber does not use the terms personal, real, or mixed statute – in fact, he does not even use the term statute itself. It must be noted that Huber deals with the same problems as the Voets and the doctrinal solutions he provides are fully compatible with their own conceptual framework – differences in terminology, policy preferences, and foundations asserted notwithstanding – and often similar. All of them are somewhat reluctant to allow the personal law of a party to follow him or her everywhere but they are also mindful of the need for transactional certainty. The three rules that Huber elaborates essentially correspond to the three categories of the classic theory of statutes, with the fundamental difference that in Huber, *statuta mixta* have given their place to an extended category of legal acts.

Huber is generally regarded as a territorialist, but a more nuanced picture is emerging as we examine the concrete aspects – and subjects – that constitute his conflicts doctrine. It is true that Huber's axioms are informed by a conception of territorial sovereignty. He espouses a states system built on the mutual respect of territorial sovereignty, as well as on the intercourse between nations, yet relying on a system of commonly accepted legal principles. But Huber's interest in both territoriality and sovereignty has more to do with his interest in describing a functioning system that produces satisfactory private-law results, and less with defending territorialism. His axioms do not constitute rules but rather operate as a theoretical foundation for a comprehensive doctrinal system dealing with conflict-of-laws matters, from jurisdiction to applicable law to foreign judgments. This doctrinal system is characterized by a territorialist conception of sorts – which we have defined as *actus* territorialism.

14.2.1 Huber and Actus Territorialism

The principal *rule* that Huber enunciated – though by no means invented – is indeed the *lex loci actus*. His conflicts treatment is permeated by the question of ensuring that legal acts will produce effects everywhere, provided they were made validly in accordance with the law of the place where they were made.

Such *actus* territorialism – as contrasted to a simple substantive policy in favor of validity – is at display in cases such as the Frisian's testament in Overijssel: that testament would be valid under the stricter formality requirements of Friesland, as well as in most other Provinces, but Huber regards it as invalid because it did not comply with the – excessive – additional formalities required in Overijssel.[1] Any number of modern approaches – application of personal law, *favor validitatis*, even a better-law approach – would have led to a different result, as indeed was held by the Court of Friesland, and even Johannes Voet would have sided with them.[2] While certainly influenced by policy considerations, Huber thus elevates the moment – and place – of creation of the act.

This emphasis on the act and the *locus actus* underlies Huber's doctrine even in less apparent aspects. For example, Huber invokes the intention of the parties to remove entire groups of cases from the reach of the *locus conclusionis* or *celebrationis*. But whereas modern doctrines of party autonomy eschew territorialist foundations, Huber, who evidently adheres to the notion of a "place" (*locus*) for the act, presents the intention of the parties as a means helping to ascertain the true *locus actus*.

Huber's actus territorialism is most prevalent in the fact that he makes no general distinction between the formal and substantive validity of acts: both are subjected, in principle, to the law of the place where the act was made. A close examination has revealed a more nuanced approach, and as a general manner Huber is much more cautious in that regard than Story and much of US classical conflict of laws. We shall accordingly explore the possible elements of other approaches in Huber's doctrine and their interaction with actus territorialism.

14.2.2 Actus Territorialism and Personalism

Taken by themselves, Huber's general axioms could appear like an explicit and absolute denial of personalism. Laws cannot have force outside the sovereign's territory: therefore, they cannot follow the sovereign's citizens abroad. Laws bind even temporary residents: therefore, nor do the laws of foreign sovereigns follow their citizens abroad.

The denial is not so absolute once we start examining the legal doctrine itself. The second rule that Huber comes up with is a "personal"

[1] Huber, *Heedensdaegse Rechtsgeleertheyt*, 1.3.15–16.

[2] Voet, *Commentarius ad Pandectas*, 1.4.App.9.

one: the characterization of a certain person as being under tutelage or guardianship, or as being an adult, is to follow that person – and thus produce legal effects – everywhere. This is not absolute territorialism, but it is not hard personalism either. In a personalist approach, a person is followed abroad by the rules of the place of origin as to that person's capacity and acquisition of rights: it therefore these rules themselves which determine that person's actual rights and disabilities. But in Huber's scheme it is simply the rule about the age in which majority is acquired that follows the person, i.e. only the characterization of that person as a major or minor: this is a second-order norm, selecting the "first order" rule of the place of the transaction to determine the actual result.

Huber's solution did not find much subsequent resonance and requires some effort to understand.[3] It can be best appreciated in the context of his contemporaneous doctrine, which had moved in more territorial directions than Medieval Italian jurists.[4] D'Argentré had distinguished between statutes affecting a person's general capacity (*de universali personae statu*) and those only limiting that person's capacity to make a certain act: only the former should be regarded as personal and then again as long as they did not touch upon real property.[5] By Huber's time, we see Johannes Voet, for example, devoting a considerable part of his treatment to explain why personal statutes do not have extra-territorial force.[6]

Things were more complicated in actual practice. Consider, for example, a case mentioned by d'Argentré himself near the end of his treatment: majority was achieved at 20 years of age under the custom of Bretagne, and at 25 years of age under the custom of neighboring Maine.[7] So, could a resident of Maine who was over 20 but less than 25 years old, with property (*magnas possessiones*) located in Bretagne, sell his holdings there? Citing especially Bartolus, d'Argentré answered in the negative: the

[3] Lorenzen, "Huber's De Conflictu Legum," 379 aptly remarks: "Huber is generally very lucid in his statements but in the matter of status and capacity it is difficult to get his exact meaning."

[4] In addition of the primary sources discussed here, see Lorenzen, "Huber's De Conflictu Legum," 378–381 and especially Lainé, *Introduction*, 2:114–217 (a comprehensive presentation of the evolution of preclassical doctrine on personal status and capacity over six centuries).

[5] Argentraeus, *Commentarii*, 218.6.14.

[6] Voet, *Commentarius ad Pandectas*, 1.4.App.7–9.

[7] Argentraeus, *Commentarii*, 218.6.46. Paris also set the age at 25. Ibid., nu. 49.

law of the young man's domicile should be followed. This is in apparent contradiction to what d'Argentré himself declared early in his treatment.[8] It was also the position adopted by French courts in the seventeenth and eighteenth century.[9] In the Spanish Netherlands, Burgundus defended the idea that incapacity in the place of domicile could not impact the conveyancing of land in another place: our minor could dispose of property in a territory that gave him this power.[10] He was criticized by Rodenburgh, who regarded such prohibitive rules as having a universal effect.[11]

We thus come to Johannes Voet, who also characterized the statute as personal but refused to acknowledge to such statutes an automatic extraterritorial effect.[12] Voet does take note of the arguments in favor of such extraterritoriality, including the absurdity of subjecting matters of capacity to the law of the place where the party has just found itself.[13] His solution is comity, which has led to "a relaxation of the rigor of the law as though by the common consent of all nations" with regard to movables but not immovables.[14] Huber himself mentions a case that led to a

[8] Lainé, *Introduction*, 1:331.

[9] See Lainé, *Introduction*, 2:122–123.

[10] N. Burgundus, *Ad consuetudines Flandriae aliarumque gentium tractatus controversiarum* (Antwerp, 1666), 1.8. See also the extensive discussion of Burgundus (and evidence of judicial adoption of his position in the Spanish Netherlands) by Boullenois, *Traité*, 1:127ff, who is critical and presents, in the same spirit, Dutch doctrine as a reaction against Burgundus.

[11] Rodenburgius, *De jure quod oritur*, 1.3.4–10, esp. 8.

[12] Voet, *Commentarius ad Pandectas*, 1.4.App.2, 8–9.

[13] Ibid., 8: "I do not deny that often the magistrates of the domicile are able best of all to judge of the condition, capacity and ripeness of a man's intellect and judgment for directing, alienating and so forth what is his. And yet we should just remember that it can also happen that the person born and brought up in a place where, by reason of the slow appearance of traces of strength of mind and capacity, anybody is held to be of age only on the completion of his twenty-fifth year, may move after barely attaining a span of twenty years to some other place where on account of a quicker maturing of intellects the twentieth year puts an end to minority, and the other way around. Yet I find that supporters of the opposite view lay it down that in such cases the new arrival becomes capable or incapable according to the law of his fresh domicile. I would like them to be advised by what right the magistrate of the new domicile converts more happily of his capacity or incapacity than the magistrate of the old. Why, he is welcoming as quite capable or incapable in virtue of his own law a new citizen who was unknown to him at the first moment of his arrival and whom the magistrates of the original domicile had appraised under another law on account of the slowness of intellect from which they believed persons born on their own soil to suffer. Everyone knows however that a change of climate does not mean an instant change of mind."

[14] Ibid., 12.

decision "by no means unanimous" as to the validity of the testament that a 17-year-old Frisian, Rudolph Monsema, made in Groningen: such a testament would be valid if made in Friesland but not in Groningen, where it was made. Huber takes pains to note first that Monsema made the testament "within fourteen days after he had gone there to learn pharmacy" and subsequently that "there was no intention to evade the law of the home country" which means that Friesland should be regarded as the testator's domicile.[15]

Viewed in this context, Huber's two-track approach constituted a valuable effort to overcome these tensions and reconcile the role acknowledged to the party's domicile in Early Modern doctrine with the needs of transactional certainty in the place of the transaction. In contrast to many others, Huber avoids drawing a distinction at that stage between the effects of capacity over movables and immovables. He acknowledges a role for the law of both the *locus domicilii* and the *locus actus*.

It is clear that the effect of Huber's doctrine is to let as many acts as possible stand, without violating the *lex loci actus* principle. If the adolescent comes from a province where the law allows for majority earlier than the *lex loci actus*, he will be treated as an adult.[16] If it is the *locus actus* which is more liberal, he will also be treated as a major.[17] The "confusion of laws," the burden placed "upon neighboring states . . . from the laws of other states," seems to arise only when the incapacity of the foreigner could invalidate a contract or testament.[18]

Huber's *lex domicilii* essentially serves transactional objectives and indeed is presented in *actus* terms. Huber does not speak of "place of origin" or something like that: his rule actually speaks of "personal qualities impressed upon a person by the law in any place."[19] The party's personal qualities are "impressed upon" at a certain moment and are often triggered by administrative formalities. In the case of prodigals or married men it is easy to determine which law impresses the personal quality: the law of the place where the declaration has occurred, in the

[15] Huber, *Praelectiones ad Pandectas*, 1.3.App.14.

[16] Ibid., 12.

[17] Ibid., 13.

[18] Ibid. Huber, *Heedensdaegse Rechtsgeleertheyt*, 1.3.44 is more straightforward: "Some would have it that whatever a person cannot on account of personal incapacity do in his native country, he can do nowhere, not even in places where such persons are allowed to do it; but it would cause too great inconvenience if in respect of persons who do business among us we had to be guided to such an extent by the law of another country."

[19] Huber, *Praelectiones ad Pandectas*, 1.3.App.12.

former case, the *lex matrimonii* in the latter case, and so forth. But one may well be married or be declared a prodigal in a place different from that where one has spent most of one's past life.

Minors raise a more interesting case. In *Contemporary Jurisprudence*, Huber notes that "he who is reckoned of full age in his own Province is of age in all Provinces."[20] This young man is very likely to have lived in one province prior to migrating – in the controversial period after he has reached the age in which majority is attained according to the first province but not according to the second – to another to continue his studies. But, what of a young man who had lived in Utrecht (where majority is attained at either 20 or 21 years of age) for his first nineteen years of life and then moved to Holland? Are we to give more credence to the possessive antonym "his own" (*sijnent*) in the Dutch text or to Axiom Two? If we are to rely on the Latin text, we could argue that, not having attained majority under the more liberal law of Utrecht while in Utrecht, the young man has not had the "personal quality" of majority impressed upon him by Utrecht law. Considering the relative ease of – and criteria to determine – a change of domicile, the critical issue would whether the young man would be regarded as having maintained his Utrecht domicile or as having changed it to Holland domicile upon moving.[21]

14.2.3 Actus and Situs Territorialism

It is clear that in Huber's work the *lex rei sitae* is taking a back seat to the *lex loci actus*. Conceptually, this is evident in the organization of the material and the relegation of the *lex rei sitae* rule to the end of Huber's conflicts treatment. This is almost the inverse of d'Argentré, who begins his conflicts treatment with things of the ground (*de rebus soli*), announcing that as to them all provisions of the *lex rei sitae* must be looked to, and only grudgingly acknowledges, at the very end of his treatment, a role for the *lex domilii* as imposing additional constraints as to capacity in contracts.[22] D'Argentré follows a bipartite scheme – the basic theory of dividing statutes into real or personal. He uses the idea of "mixed" as a tool, in order to characterize as real anything that even incidentally touched upon real property.[23] On the contrary, Huber not only elevates

[20] Huber, *Heedensdaegse Rechtsgeleertheyt*, 1.3.37.
[21] See Section 12.2.2.1 and Voet, *Commentarius ad Pandectas*, 5.1.92.
[22] Argentraeus, *Commentarii*, 218.6.2.
[23] Ibid., 6.

his equivalent of mixed statutes to primacy but also structures his entire treatment in a manner chipping away from the *lex rei sitae* and especially from what amounts to a discussion of "real" statutes.

The primary instance concerns questions of the validity of legal acts touching upon land. The subject features twice in Huber's text, if one also considers his discussion of the effects of legal acts. Even though there is no express mention of land in those sections, Huber's solutions are meant to apply to legal relations and acts *inter vivos* and *mortis causa* that affect immovable as well as movable property; this holds equally true of the debates to which Huber is taking part, as illustrated by our closer reading of the examples he is using. When he finally comes to immovable property, Huber affirms this: such law "regulates the act of making a testament and the testament having been properly made, the law of the country does not prohibit that act from being valid in respect of immovable property" and likewise "Frisian immovable property sold to persons in Holland in a manner prohibited in Friesland but valid where the sale takes place is deemed to be duly sold."[24] But Huber draws a line: this only holds true insofar as matters "depending upon the free disposition of [the immovables'] owners" are involved, such as the form of a contract or testament or the ability, in principle, to dispose of one's property. The *lex actus* will only apply "so far as no quality impressed upon it by the law of the place (*a Lege loci*) is injured or diminished."

Huber gives us three examples of such a "quality" (*character*) or "incidents" (*notae*), each of which presents its own interest as to how the *lex rei sitae* is approached. The first one concerns the administrative formalities that must be fulfilled for the sale of land in Friesland. Another one is interesting for different reasons: Huber is using the private-law rule about things like crops being regarded as immovable property as long as they remain attached to land in order to serve the Frisian policy of prohibiting contracts on future crops and exploitation of smaller landholders.

The third example presents substantive policy implications: recognizing that Frisian law cannot be used to undermine the prohibition, in Groningen, of testamentary succession into immovables ensures preservation of the intestate rights of blood-relatives and thus of a certain social order or structure in the neighboring province. It could be contrasted with the other testamentary case involving the two provinces, the one of

[24] Huber, *Praelectiones ad Pandectas*, 1.3.App.15.

the Frisian minor making a testament in Groningen, involving presumably property in Friesland: Groningen law applies in this case as well, leading again to the invalidity of the testament, but here the connecting factors are reversed: the act was made in Groningen and property is situated in Friesland, but the legal norm in question concerns capacity to make a testament and not directly the acquisition of immovables. It obviously doesn't hurt that, once the testament is invalid, Frisian law of intestate succession would apply to both movable and immovable property. But taken together, these two cases exemplify Huber's distinction between "free disposition" and "incidents."

Huber's *lex rei sitae* defends its particular content against legal acts, whether *inter vivos* or *mortis causa*. It can even prohibit a certain type of act, such as testaments, from having any effect on *res*. What it cannot do is to kill the act on its own: only *lex loci actus* could do that. It could even be suggested that the *lex rei sitae* operates in subsidiary fashion to the *lex loci actus*, and that Huber's *lex rei sitae* is not the same as the classic real statutes. It has a more limited task, which it does perform. What Huber's *lex rei sitae* does "kill" is any idea of subjecting intestate succession as a whole to one single law, irrespective of where the property included in the estate is located.

The fate of movables requires some special attention. The idea that they are governed by the law of their owner's domicile (*mobilia sequuntur personam*) was never questioned in preclassical doctrine, but it required explanation, especially in Early Modern territorialist systems. D'Argentré had dealt with the issue summarily, in the beginning of his treatment.[25] In contrast, Huber comes this matter last, as indeed does Johannes Voet, who considers movables after he has dealt with mixed statutes as well.[26] Application of place of domicile causes a stronger predicament for Voet, who has previously argued that, in strict law, neither personal nor mixed statutes have extraterritorial effect but has to acknowledge the *lex domicilii* for movable property. Indeed, whereas in "De Conflictu Legum" Huber treats of movables almost incidentally and in a single sentence, in his discussion of the law applicable to

[25] Argentraeus, *Commentarii*, 218.6.3 (*alia ratio est de personarum iure, in quo et mobilia continentur*). The medulla of § 3 bears the title *in mobilibus spectandus locus domicilii*).

[26] Voet, *Commentarius ad Pandectas*, 1.4.App.11.

intestate succession, Voet comes to movables as this special case, which he must fit into his system.[27]

Huber is less laconic in "Observance," which is more practically minded. In arguing for the "place where the deceased resided," he notes that "[*movables*] *form no portion of the country where they happen to be*, but are carried from place to place and *depend only on the good pleasure of the owner*."[28] Arguing in favor of the place of last residence, Huber draws an *actus* analogy: "just as we are accustomed, both in affairs of death and in transactions between living persons, to follow the custom of the place where we are at the time."[29]

We are left wondering whether this is supposed to be a personal or territorial rule: are movables conceptualized as *following the person*, or does the owner's domicile represent a situs, a means of localization to a territory? Most Early Modern jurists embraced the latter idea (movables "conceived as being in the very place of domicile"), including Voet himself, who acknowledges that it relies upon a fiction or presumption of law (*fictione seu malis praesumptione*) and in the end suggests that comity constitutes a better explanation.[30] Huber probably assumes such a fiction, but his approach and comparative emphasis on *actus* allows him to avoid entering into such discussions.

14.2.4 Huber and Public Policy Territorialism

In Chapter 4, we suggested that a third type of territorialism must be considered, in order to best account for doctrines aimed at fighting off the evasion of local laws as well as at safeguarding rights arisen under the local law from foreign acts. Such public policy territorialism indeed cuts through Huber's *actus* territorialism, but we will consider this matter in our discussion of comity and the exceptions Huber acknowledges to it.[31]

27 Ibid.: (the medulla of § 11 is: *Docetur, affectionem de statutis territorium non egredientibus non subverti ex eo, quod mobilia ubicumque sita devolvuntur ab intestate secundum leges domicilii defuncti*). This is indeed the first instance in his treatment where Voet makes actual use of comity.

28 Huber, *Heedensdaegse Rechtsgeleertheyt*, 1.3.51. This argument was taken further by Story, *Commentaries*, 311–312.

29 Ibid.

30 Voet, *Commentarius ad Pandectas*, 1.4.App.11 with reference to the authorities mentioned by P. Voet, *De statutis*, 4.2.8.

31 See Section 14.4.4.

14.3 Huber as Unilateralist

In order to answer the question of whether Huber can be considered a unilateralist, we must first ask ourselves what is meant by that term.

It would be conceivable, but wrong, to consider Huber as a late-stage *absolute unilateralist*. One may argue that Huber's doctrine is phrased in terms of the forum acknowledging effects to foreign acts, not applying foreign laws. Such an argument could rely upon the translation of *iura . . . exercita* in Huber's third axiom, as "rights" acquired, rather than "laws" applied.[32] This would be wrong, however, translation notwithstanding. Huber is using examples of legal acts and undoubtedly preoccupied with ensuring, at least in principle, the effects of legal acts validly made. But he is also using the *actus* paradigm as a tool in dealing with non-transactional regimes and situations. Translation notwithstanding, we could say that Huber is using the concept of a foreign act so broadly as to amount to what others would consider as foreign laws. The title of his Dutch-language conflicts treatment is, after all, about "the observance of Frisian laws in other countries and of other countries in Friesland."

"Absolute unilateralists" who allow foreign acts to produce effects try to reconcile the two sensibilities by reifying the legal act: the foreign legal act thus becomes a *fact*, a part of the real world that surrounds us. On the contrary, Huber not only links foreign acts with the foreign law, having founded his doctrine on a "world system" of sovereign entities, but also argues for the "free movement" of legal acts on grounds of policy (convenience of individuals, magistrates and states) rather than on reification theories such as "vested rights" already created.

It is even easier to conclude that Huber is not a *doctrinal unilateralist*, in any sense of that term. From a technical point of view, both axioms and the rules in Huber's treatment are addressed to each state individually, but they are effectively addressing all states and seeking a multilateral arrangement. Huber makes it clear that it is not the foreign State that determines unilaterally the scope of its own law. Everything – axioms, allusions to the law of nations, but also to the practice of nations and to comity – serves in buttressing Huber's rules against an aggressive forum. Here again, Huber is reminiscent of modern, "multilateral" – albeit imperfect – systems.

[32] Lorenzen, "Huber's De Conflictu Legum," 403 has opted for the former translation; Llewellyn Davies, "Influence," 65 for the latter.

On the other hand, we have already seen that Huber has registered in modern historical consciousness as a unilateralist. In some cases, this has been the result of superficially reading Huber's axioms as his conflicts rules. But for many others, such an understanding of Huber has to do with how we approach the content of the axioms and especially his reference to *comity*. Inevitably, this relates to the subsequent invocations of Huber and, more generally, to the uses of the concept of comity itself, especially in Anglo-American conflict of laws. The history of the concept of comity merits yet another study but it suffices to say that early Anglo-American conflicts lawyers such as Mansfield and Story attributed to Huber's comity doctrine a "discretionary" element, which was then blown out of proportions by their detractors, especially on the Continent, such as François Laurent. Even today the historical consciousness is shaped by suggestions such as that Huber "attempts to explain *why* the forum state will apply the law of another sovereign but not *when*" and his doctrine provides no "concrete guidance as to the circumstances in which the forum will or will not apply the law of another state."[33]

Such an understanding, if correct, would make it easier to call Huber a *political unilateralist*. On the other hand, our study has shown that Huber primarily espouses a doctrine of *actus territorialism*, which – although not absolute – does not support the idea that Huber would seek to extend Frisian law whenever to do so would "advance" the "policies underlying the law." This is obviously not to say that Huber is not mindful of the policies, and politics, of the forum: we have just seen how he uses personal law and *lex rei situs* in this regard and we have also been discussing several cases of exception to the general norms. But Huber makes a conscious effort to fit these exceptions, and objectives, into a multilateral system. From the perspective of modern conflict of laws, we may discuss the legal form of Huber's solutions. For example, in the case of sale of prohibited goods, Huber's solution functions not unlike a *loi de police*; but it could also be regarded as a secondary conflicts norm dealing with aspects of the performance of an obligation; or even an ad hoc exception similar to *ordre public*.

On the other hand, Huber's doctrine contains elements of a limited unilateralism. Some traces appear in the way in which the second and especially the third rules of his system are stated and justified. But we will

[33] Symeonides et al., *Conflict of Laws*, 10.

find even more fruitful examples in the exceptions to the comity doctrine and the third axiom. It is therefore to comity that we shall turn.

14.4 Comity in Huber's Doctrine

Comity is a word with different connotations.[34] In the common law tradition, it provided a foundation for early Anglo-American conflict of laws, most notably in the work of Joseph Story.[35] In the classical period, "comity of nations" acquired a new legacy thanks to the US Supreme Court, which famously defined it as "neither a matter of absolute obligation ... nor of mere courtesy and goodwill" and derived from it a reciprocity requirement for the enforcement of foreign judgments.[36] In the modern English doctrine of international commercial litigation, there is a new life for "international comity" as a standard against which the discretionary assertion of English jurisdiction, for example regarding injunctive relief such as anti-suit injunctions must be considered.[37] But in the Continental legal tradition, comity has been traditionally viewed with suspicion or hostility: for the school of international law, comity's association with territorialism was a reason to regard it as dangerous or redundant. It was also perceived as legitimating unilateral action by countries and their courts, to the detriment of learned concord that was supposed to lead to an international codification of private

[34] See J. Paul, "The Transformation of International Comity," *Law and Contemporary Probems*, 71 (2008), 19–38.

[35] Story, *Commentaries*, 2ff.

[36] *Hilton* v. *Guyot*, 159 US 113, 149 (1895) (Gray, J.): "No law has any effect, of its own force, beyond the limits of the sovereignty from which its authority is derived. The extent to which the law of one nation, as put in force within its territory, whether by executive order, by legislative act, or by judicial decree, shall be allowed to operate within the dominion of another nation, depends upon what our greatest jurists have been content to call 'the comity of nations.' Although the phrase has been often criticised, no satisfactory substitute has been suggested. 'Comity,' in the legal sense, is neither a matter of absolute obligation, on the one hand, nor of mere courtesy and good will, upon the other. But it is the recognition which one nation allows within its territory to the legislative, executive or judicial acts of another nation, having due regard both to international duty and convenience, and to the rights of its own citizens, or of other persons who are under the protection of its laws."

[37] See e.g. *Airbus Industrie GIE* v. *Patel* [1999] 1 AC 119, 136 ("comity requires that the English forum should have a sufficient interest in, or connection with, the matter in question": per Lord Goff) and *Star Reefers Pool Inc.* v. *JFC Group Co. Ltd.* [2012] EWCA Civ 14 at [21]. See for more Fentiman, *International Commercial Litigation*, 526–531.

international law. Finally, it suggests an element of discretion that goes against Continental ideas of legal certainty, and legal formalism.[38]

Given that the notion or at least the word *comity* was introduced by the jurists of the Dutch school, it should come as no surprise that classical and modern authors have tended to credit – or fault – the Duch jurists with whatever notion of comity they were using themselves in their own time and environment. For example, among modern scholars, Joel Paul, himself a policy-conscious progressive internationalist, associates Huber's comity with "sound judicial policy and reciprocity."[39] Among classical scholars, Meili, who called comity a "juridical bind alley," accused the Dutch school with placing the whole subject on a basis where it nearly perished."[40] Armand Lainé, so attentive to the nuances of Medieval Italian and Early Modern French doctrine, associates the Dutch school with the Anglo-American doctrine of his days. His criticism is simple: d'Argentré succumbed to the logical inconsistency of asserting, on the one hand, in the name of the law, the principle of absolute and strict territoriality, and admitting, on the other hand, that certain provisions are neither territorial nor absolute in their application; Johannes Voet and the others avoid this logical fallacy by asserting that law is territorial while accepting that this strict law can be tempered by purely gratuitous concessions (*concessions purement gracieuses*), but the

[38] See e.g. the passage from A. S. de Bustamante, *Tratado de derecho Internacional Privado*, vol. I (Havana, 1896), 456 as quoted and translated by Lorenzen, "Huber's De Conflictu Legum," 397: "Comity is a pretext for the evasion of the consequences of a strict territorial law. After the notion of such law is denied, it would be idle to combat it, for it becomes unnecessary. But it may not be amiss to observe that in its obscure and little defined concept, interest, courtesy, and reciprocity, ideas so important for the history of law, play a part ... The name of science cannot be given to them, nor can a practical and useful system be based upon them. They authorize simply concessions ungoverned by rule, the supposed independence of a State consisting in an adjustment of its conduct to that followed by other states, resulting ultimately in a real isolation between the people of different countries, and in making of courtesy and reciprocity a system of reprisal, instead of a furtherance of juridical relations."

[39] Paul, "Comity," 17: "For Huber, the idea of comity derived from the tacit understanding of sovereigns. It was custom, but not necessarily customary law. Comity was sound judicial policy and invited reciprocity. But it was not obligatory, and it was explicitly subject to the limitation by the application of foreign law not interfere with the rights of the sovereign or its subjects."

[40] Meili, "Specimen," 190 as quoted by Lorenzen, "Huber's De Conflictu Legum," 397, who also quotes Rolin, *Principes*, 1:79. Cf. Catellani, *Diritto internazionale privato*, 1:52–54.

result is worse: "for a theory, a defect even worse than assaulting logic, is to end up in nothingness."[41]

Over the past century, there have been several efforts at rehabilitation, or at least better understanding, of the Dutch school and especially Huber, whose doctrine on closer inspection appears less discretionary than Johannes Voet.[42] Any of these texts should have impacted the historical consciousness much more than it actually has. This section will attempt a more comprehensive examination of Huber's comity doctrine, in comparison with Paul and especially Johannes Voet. Our examination takes place at three levels. We shall first consider Huber's third axiom in itself, then consider how comity doctrine is being used as a foundation for the author's doctrinal system, and finally consider the exceptions allowed by the author to the application of his comity doctrine.

14.4.1 Huber's Third Axiom

The first step is to examine the axiom itself. Our subject of examination (to which we will be referring simply as "the axiom" below) is the version that appeared in *Praelectiones,* in 1689:

> Those who exercise sovereign authority so act from comity (*id comiter agitur*) that the laws (*iura*) of each nation having been applied within its own boundaries should retain their effect everywhere so far as they do not prejudice the power or law of the other government and its citizens.[43]

[41] Lainé, *Introduction,* 2:111 ("il est pour une théorie un défaut pire que celui d'offenser la logique, c'est celui d'aboutir au néant").

[42] The work of Kollewijn, *Geschiedenis,* is the most comprehensive examination of primary material. It inspired the concise presentation and rehabilitation of Huber by Yntema, "Comity," to which we shall return in this section. More recently, Watson, *Comity,* devotes a small book to "rehabilitating" Huber and blaming Story and others for misunderstanding him. The South African tradition of Roman-Dutch law, which has given us reliable translations into English of the basic texts, is aptly represented by Kahn, "Territorial School," and Forsyth, "Comparative Ethos."

[43] Huber, *Praelectiones ad Pandectas,* 1.3.App.2: "*III. Rectores imperiorum id comiter agunt, ut jura cujusque populi intra terminos ejus exercita, teneant ubique suam vim, quatenus nihil potestati aut juri alterius imperantis ejusque civium praejudicetur.*" Lorenzen, "Huber's De Conflictu Legum," 403 translates as "Sovereigns will so act by way of comity that rights acquired within the limits of a government retain their force everywhere so far as they do not cause prejudice to the power or rights of such government or of its subjects." My translation largely follows Llewyellyn Davies, "Influence," 65 (apart from the last phrase, where he follows Lorenzen).

Discussion of the axiom usually revolves around the concepts of "comity" and "prejudice," but before we get to these concepts we should examine the text more closely and in context.

The axiom contains a general proposition ("laws retain their force everywhere") and an exception, in cases the power or laws of another state or its citizens are prejudiced (to which the case of a "most revolting" transaction is subsequently added). The general proposition suggests a common practice among nations (acting *comiter* to apply foreign laws or, according to Lorenzen's translation to give effect to foreign rights) and an objective to be achieved (that the foreign *iura* "retain their effect everywhere"). As to the exception, it could either serve as an "escape clause," in a manner similar to moderate internationalist contemporary systems which allow an ordre public exception, or as a unilateralist defense of domestic policy. The choice would depend on the interpreter and the societal context.

The same structure is found in the axiom's earlier versions. In *De Jure Civitatis*, his first attempt (1672), Huber stated his third axiom as following:

> Third, the sovereigns (*summae potestates*) of every country mutually concede to each other, so that one's laws and legislation, have effect in another's territory, as long as this can be without prejudice to those conceding.[44]

This is more or less the phrasing used a decade later (1684–1686), when Huber stated the axiom in Dutch:

> Thirdly, the sovereign powers of every country assist each other with the object that the laws of each may be binding on its own subjects, although being elsewhere, so far as they do not conflict with the operation of the authority of the law of the other power.[45]

The differences in the wording between the axiom in *Praelectiones* and its earlier versions are as evident as their fundamental similarity in structure and central idea. It has been noted that "comity" is not mentioned prior

[44] Huber, *De jure civitatis*, 3.4.1.14: "Tertia, Summae Potestates cujusque Reipublicae indulgent sibi mutuo, ut jura legesque aliarum, in aliarum territoriis effectum habeant, quatenus sine praejudicio indulgentium fieri potest."

[45] Huber, *Heedensdaegse Rechtsgeleertheyt*, 1.3.6: "Ten 3. de Hooge machten van yder Landt bieden elkander de handt, ten einde, de Rechten van yder, op elk sijn onderdanen, schoon elders zijnde, soo verre gelden, als het niet is strijdig met de Macht of het Recht des anderen in sijn bedrijf." This is identical to Huber, *Beginselen*, 6.40.7. Paul, "Comity," 17 notes the first phrase (translated literally as "the high authorities of each country offer each other a hand") as supporting his reading.

to *Praelectiones*.[46] This is true but does not necessarily indicate a conceptual change for Huber. On the other hand, the later *Praelectiones* version is more precise and written in more elegant Latin with classical allusions.[47] Even the word *comitas* and its derivative, *comiter*, which is used here, have similar provenance.

The reference to *iura* ... *exercita* in the axiom has been translated as "laws ... applied." Lorenzen has instead read into the text "rights ... exercised." This may allude to the vested rights theories of classical Anglo-American conflict of laws of his time, but it is consonant neither with the argument of "De Conflictu Legum" – let alone the earlier versions who clearly refer to "laws" in an identical context – nor with Huber's conceptual context.[48] The verb *exercere* also has a positive connotation of coverage and *exercitur* here is best translated as applied. This is actually a key word to understand Huber's thought: in order for the law of a polity/*populus* to retain its effects everywhere, it must have first been *applied* within its own territory. We do witness here the development of Huber's thought: Huber's constant preoccupation is with the idea of country A's laws having effect in the territory of country B, but in his final version he refines his idea: such laws produce effect abroad because they have already been applied in their own territory.[49]

[46] Yntema, "Comity," 25 citing Kollewijn, *Geschiedenis*, 142.

[47] Some examples. First, *summa potestas* means "sovereignty" or "sovereign power." Huber, as we have seen, has in mind the highest authority of a State and hence his reference in plural (*summae potestates cujusque Reipublicae*) is replaced by the more precise *rectores imperiorum*. Second, in the phrase *iura legesque aliarum in aliarum territoriis*, the same word (*alius*) is used to indicate two different – in a sense, opposing even if *indulgentes* – polities. If indeed *iura legesque* is meant to correspond to Huber's vernacular phrase "laws and Ordinances" we have the opposite problem: the simple reference to *iura* in *Praelectiones* serves the same purpose. Third, words and phrases such as *rectores*, *exercita*, *teneant vim*, and even *civium* have Ciceronian (republican) roots. See e.g. S. Tzounakas, "Cato's laudatio Pompei in Lucan's De Bello Civili" in S. Tzounakas (ed.), *Praises of Roman Leaders in Latin Literature* (Nicosia: Stamoulis, 2014), 205–221, 207–210.

[48] See in this regard Voet, *Commentarius ad Pandectas*, 1.4.App.1 in fine (the term *statutum* includes "laws not only by lower magistrates but also by supreme emperors or peoples endowed with sovereignty (*non inferiorum tantum magistratuum sed et supremorum principum ac populorum majestate praeditorum jura*), whether enacted by express desire or brought in by the usage and customs or those who adopt them ... in fact, all laws of all nations (*leges omnes omnium gentium*) ... even the judgments and decrees of judges and magistrates in regard to individual persons, as when they are declared prodigals, infamous, granted *venia aetatis*, etc.").

[49] Even if we were to follow Lorenzen and translate *iura* here as "rights," it should be noted that the rights are exercised, not acquired or born, abroad; this allows for a more expansive definition of enforceable rights.

One might even suggest that, as phrased in *Praelectiones*, the third axiom follows logically from the first two axioms, rather than constituting an exception to them.

Our observation moreover explains the addition of the word "everywhere" (*ubique*) – another critical word often neglected in discussions of Huber. The word is not found in the earlier versions, where the situation is bilateral (with unilateral undertones). But in the polished version, the whole story is, at least in the abstract, about more than just the two countries whose laws are "in conflict." It is about their laws, whose effect is to be retained *everywhere*. I would argue this is about refinement and clarity rather than about a change in doctrine.[50] The early versions may not refer to effects *ubique* but their wording – *indulgent sibi mutuo*, *bieden elkanten* – paints an image of an active, collaborative effort to enable country A's laws to have effect in country B's territory. The Dutch version even suggests that this mutual assistance has the purpose of ensuring that Country A's laws continue to bind its subjects even when "elsewhere."[51] The use of that word (rather than, for example, "in the other") already indicates a more multilateral – as well as more abstract – wording.

Further evidence is provided in this regard by the discussion immediately following as well as preceding the axioms in "De Conflictu Legum."[52] We have seen above that Huber quickly states that "none hitherto seems to have entertained any doubt" regarding his third axiom and then passes to the justification of the second one, where he elaborated his own doctrine of strict territoriality.[53] From our discussion it must have been clear that Huber's territoriality is not so strict when applied to his actual doctrine; indeed, even his § 2 references in support of the second axiom, once put in context, indicate so.[54] Huber has used Roman-law authorities from the Digest in support of axioms one and two. But when it comes to his third axiom, he relies on the law of nations.

This brings him full circle from his opening remarks, immediately prior to stating the axioms. We have seen that Huber begins his treatment with an observation: "It often happens that transactions entered

[50] There is indeed no change in Huber's doctrinal solutions, from *De jure civitatis* to *Pralectiones ad Pandectas*.

[51] Huber, *Heedensdaegse Rechtsgeleertheyt*, 1.3.6.

[52] Huber, *Praelectiones ad Pandectas*, 1.3.App.2. This discussion reprises that in Huber, *De jure civitatis*, 3.4.1.11–13.

[53] See Section 11.3.2.3.

[54] See Section 12.4.

into one place have force and effect in the territories of a different state, or have to be adjudicated upon in another place."[55] In this sentence, he identifies the real problem in pragmatic, private-law terms (the legal effect – and effectiveness – abroad of transactions, and legal acts in general) and also lays the ground for his normative pragmatism, which has to account for the common fact ("often happens") that such foreign acts "have force and effect" and "have to be adjudicated."

In his second sentence, Huber refers to the political environment of his time ("the laws of every nation differ in many respects"). This is traced back to the "breaking up of the provinces of the Roman Empire." Since then, "Christendom has been divided into almost innumerable nations, not subject to one another and not sharing the same system of government." Huber thus identifies the problem as both a legal and a political one.

There is again a purpose in this observation of something which is evidently "well known." On the one hand, Huber must address his subject (and his audience) using the legal – and often, the political – language of Roman law: just like his peers, he relies on the doctrines and conceptual skeleton of Roman law and has to draw on Roman authorities. On the other hand, he is mindul that Roman law cannot provide a full solution to this problem.

This informs Huber's position. To begin with, "since the sovereignty of Rome extended to all parts of the world and was regulated by a uniform law it could hardly give rise to a conflict of different laws," we cannot look for answers in Roman law ("it is no surprise that there is nothing on the subject." Huber in this way justifies the lack of any reference to a Roman law authority (or even a classical reference) in the main body of his treatment. In the immediately subsequent sentence, he states that the "fundamental rules" (*regulae fundamentales*) should apparently be sought (*videntur esse petendae*) in Roman law. A third sentence cautions us ("although") that the question pertains more to the law of nations (*ius gentium*) than to the civil law (*ius civile*), "since that which different *populi* should observe among themselves clearly pertains to the law of nations."

It is against this background that Huber lays down his axioms. The first two axioms, which lay down an approach founded on territorial sovereignty, are supported by Roman-law authorities, as we have seen.

[55] Huber, *Praelectiones ad Pandectas*, 1.3.App.1.

No authority is cited in the third axiom itself, but we must look to the opening of § 2 that immediately follows the axiom. That passage contains a statement – that the fundamental rule will be found in the law of nations – and argumentation in support of the statement. Let us consider first the statement:

> From this we conclude (*ex quo liquet*) that this matter should be pursued according not to a single civil law (*ex simplici jure Civili*), but the common weal and the tacit consent of the nations (*ex commodis et tacito populorum consensu*).[56]

Huber begins the sentence emphatically: the verb *liquere* is used to indicate a clear judicial verdict and not a suggestion ("it appears") as often translated. The verb *petere* suggests a – juridical or forensic – pursuit. The word *simplici* is not a short form of the adverb *simpliciter* but the ablative case of the adjective *simplex*, which should be interpreted as unique. The word *commodum* is translated as "convenience" but is often used to convey an element of mutual or common benefit. We are using the words *gentes* and *populi* as interchangeable and translate both as "nations," but the latter word has stronger connotations of organized *polities*. This is not the Roman or even the Medieval *ius gentium*: it derives from the tacit consent of the States, as well as on their enlightened self-interest.

This interpretation is corroborated by Huber's statement in "Observance":

> From this it is clear that the decision of such cases is a part of the law of nations and not properly speaking of civic law in as much as it does not depend on the individual pleasure of the higher power of each country but on the mutual convenience of the sovereign powers and their tacit agreement with each other.[57]

Let us now return to *Praelectiones* and Huber's argumentation:

> [F]or although the laws of one nation cannot apply directly (*directe valere*) to another, yet nothing could be more inconvenient to the intercourse and various practices of nations (*commerciis et usu gentium*

[56] Ibid., 2: "*Ex quo liquet, hanc rem non ex simplici jure Civili, sed ex commodis et tacito populorum consensu esse petendam: quia sicut leges alterius populi apud alium directe valere non possunt, ita commerciis et usu gentium promiscuo nihil foret magis incommodum, quam si res jure certi loci validae, mox alibi diversitate Juris infirmarentur, quae est ratio tertii axiomatis: quod, uti nec prius, nullum videtur habere dubium.*" See Section 14.4.3. Llewyllyn Davies, "Influence," 65–66 translates "this subject is to be derived not simply from the civil law but from the convenience and tacit consent of nations."

[57] Huber, *Heedensdaegse Rechtsgeleertheyt*, 1.3.7.

> *promiscuo*) than that which is valid by the law of one place should be rendered invalid elsewhere owing to a difference in the law.[58]

Huber starts with an acknowledgment, which is the logical consequence of his first two axioms. He then asks us to acknowledge, in our turn, the problems that would be created if we were to follow a strict territorial approach to its limit: to allow "difference in the law" would cause something to be valid under the law of one place but not another. Under Huber's system, this should only be justified in the special circumstances defined in his exception.

14.4.2 Comity from Paul to Johannes Voet

Scholars who have examined Huber's comity doctrine have tended to distinguish between Huber's doctrine and the doctrine developed by the rest of the Dutch school, namely Paul and Johannes Voet.[59] A concise examination of these authors is necessary in order to better understand Huber and the discourse in which he is taking part.

The notion of comity is indeed first found in the conflicts treatment of Paul Voet. Voet draws on Roman-law authorities in order to conclude that, in principle, no statute extends beyond the territory of its legislator. He then lists several exceptions, of which the last of which is as follows:

> Finally, sometimes, whenever a neighbouring nation wishes to observe a neighbour's customs (*mores*) in comity and in order that many things well done (*bene gesta*) may not be disturbed, as accustomed (*de moribus*), statutes, their effect having been considered, tend to go beyond in the territory of their maker.[60]

Paul Voet supports his rule by alluding three times to common practice ("sometimes," "accustomed," "tend to"), adding then a pragmatic argument (not disturbing existing *bene gesta*), and finally concluding with a

[58] Huber, *Praelectiones ad Pandectas*, 1.3.App.2.

[59] Yntema, "Comity," 29 distinguishes between "the *doctrine hollandaise* of comity and the *doctrine frisonne* that in this field '*goet recht ende Justitie*' should prevail." See also ibid., 28 citing Kollewjihn, *Geschiedenis*, 132 about Huber appearing as "an isolated, paradoxical figure, whose works, highly regard in other countries, have had negligible influence in his own."

[60] Voet, *De statutis*, 4.2.17: "Denique *nonnunquam*, dum populus vicinus vicini mores comiter vult observare, et ne multa bene gesta turbarentur, de moribus, statuta territorium statuentis, inspecto effectu, solent egredi" (reference to D.49.15.7).

citation of a Digest passage, where the adverb *comiter* is used.[61] Both the adverb *comiter*, used by Paul Voet and Huber, and the noun *comitas*, which is subsequently used by Johannes Voet derive from the adjective *comis* – translated as courteous, affable, kind, obliging, friendly, loving.[62] Whereas *comitas* was used more to describe an attitude in social relations, *comiter* had more of a legal connotation, specifically with regard to the interstate relations of Ancient Rome, and may have been used as a formula in treaties: the emphasis, however, was on the willingness of commitment rather than discretion.[63] Indeed, the title of the Digest on "Prisoners of war, postliminium and persons ransomed from the Enemy," from which comes the passage cited by Paul Voet, was often associated with the law of nations.[64]

Whether Huber was inspired by the elder Voet's work or by his own reading of the Digest, he finally made use of the term *comiter* in *Praelectiones*, some time after Voet (of which there is no citation). The word is the same for Voet and Huber, but the use is different. To begin with, the notion of comity has made no difference to the substance of Huber's axiom, compared with its earlier versions, and only appears once more in the treatment, although Huber had several opportunities to use

[61] D.49.15.7 (Proculus). "I have no doubt that although free peoples and those bound to us by treaty are foreigners to us, there is no *postliminium* between us and them; for what need is there of *postliminium* between us and them, since they retain their freedom and rights over their own property in our own country just as in their own, and the same applies to us in their country? 1. A free people is one which is not subject to the control of any other people, a *civitas foederata*, one which has either entered into friendship under an equal treaty or under a treaty [which] includes the provision that these people should with good will preserve the *maiestas* of another people (*alterius populi maiestatem comiter conservaret*). it has to be added that the other people is to be understood to be superior, not that the [federated] people is not free; and insofar as we understand our client [states] to be free, even if they're not our equals in authority, dignity or power, so also those who are bound to preserve our *maiestas* with good will (*comiter conservare debent*) are understood to be free. 2. But persons from *civitates foederatae* may be charged in our courts, and we inflict punishments on them [if] condemned." See also Yntema, "Comity," 23: "Thus the authority of Justinian was adduced . . . to support the absolute conception of territorial sovereignty and to exemplify the principle of comity in his new doctrine."

[62] Lewis & Short, *Elementary Latin Dictionary*, s.v. comis. The word *comiter* itself is translated as "courteously, affably, kindly." *Comitas* is translated as "courteousness, kindness, obligingless, friendliness, affability, gentleness" but there are also incidents of it being used to indicate "too great liberality, prodigality."

[63] See ibid., with references to respective texts. Cicero, *Pro Balbo*, 16.36 stands out as to *comiter*.

[64] See e.g. Huber, *De jure civitatis*, 3.4.1.9.

it. Paul Voet's ninth exception to strict territoriality has become Huber's third axiom: the escape clause has become the foundation of an entire system. In contrast with Paul Voet, who simply acknowledges some degree of existing practice, Huber grounds, expressly, the comity doctrine to the law of nations and rejects the idea that Roman law could provide any authority.

Johannes Voet takes the next step. To begin with, he speaks of *comitas* – for example, *ex comitate* ("out of comity") – rather than the more formulaic or legalist *comiter*. Like Huber, Johannes Voet uses the notion of comity as a foundation of his doctrinal system. But he also keeps the basic idea of his father, namely that, in principle, all statutes – personal, mixed or real – fall under strict territoriality but exceptions are necessary, to a different degree for each category. Accordingly, Johannes Voet uses comity as a general doctrine addressing such cases:

> I shall first deal with the question, What should be the position in the strict law (*quid ex summo jure obtinere debeat*) when every people sets his teeth and strives to extend and protect its own laws so far as it can, meantime barring the laws of others out of its territory? The next question will be what general and polite concessions, licenses or endurances (*indulgeat, permittat, patiatur, ultro citroque*) does nation in comity allow reciprocally to nation in regard to the extension of statutes and decrees beyond the territory of the maker when otherwise bound by no law to allow them; and how far has this matter been fixed and settled in certain cases by various public agreements between related and neighbouring nations, so as to keep the limits of comity equal on both sides?[65]

Voet is certainly more eloquent than his father. But already his first question and his emphatically affirmative response to it, suggest that he does not regard the nations (*gentes*) bound by any superior law to exercise such comity toward each other. Of the several words he uses to describe the operation of comity, none conveys not just any suggestion that acting in comity is grounded in the law of nations, natural law, or Roman law, but not even a vague sense of moral commitment, or even a reference to existing practice like Paul Voet. In contrast, there are suggestions of reciprocity, and even any practice of agreements between polities is attributed to the pursuit of "equal" limits of comity. This attitude is demonstrated when Johannes Voet finally arrives to comity, having defended at length strict territoriality:

[65] Voet, *Commentarius ad Pandectas*, 1.4.App.1.

> But any private person will pass his life in the society of his fellow citizens with little happiness if he disdains to render mutual services to others and in turn to receive them from others to his own advantage. It may be that he could be said to inflict no wrong on anyone if, self-satisfied with a rigorous mode of life in spurning the delights of other men he leaves to others what is theirs and keeps what is his for himself, discarding all enjoyment of generous intercourse and service. Just in the same way the magistrates of different countries, showing no mutual obedience each to the other nor all to some third superior party, may never at any time remit anything of the rigour of their own law as explained above, nor by mutual comity generously approve, uphold and forward each the commands of the other. Then each will make the state of his subjects harder and involve it in many a trouble and difficulty. On the one hand each will confound, upset and annul the good acts, decrees and enactments of the others; and in turn on the other hand suffer his own to be confounded, infringed and set aside by the others on lines of retaliation and strict law.[66]

Rather than treating it as a matter of fact, Voet deploys here very strong arguments in favor of comity but all of them are pragmatic. In fact, Voet appeals to the self-interest of each State. States may very well embrace an absolute territoriality or indeed what we have been calling absolute unilateralism. But they – and their subjects – will inevitably suffer the consequences. The analogy with the *privatus* who can go through life without rendering – and receiving – mutual services to others, but probably with little happiness is indicative.

But contrary to Huber, Voet does hint at a legal ground in Roman law, to which he returns a few dozen pages later in his work, as he discusses the so-called *lex talionis* (right of retorsion or retaliation). We have seen Huber invoke *lex talionis* to explain why, even though he regarded arrest-based jurisdiction as contrary to the law of Friesland, he did accept the use of such practices against residents of those – essentially all neighboring territories – that used the practice.[67] Voet himself is more aggressive, even going as far as to suggest that, in the case of a prohibitive statute that applies across the board, preempting the effects of another territory's statute in all such cases, the magistrate of the latter territory "who sees his own laws shut out and barred elsewhere, may also in turn by right of retorsion deny the benefit of the provisions of his own statute to foreigners of yon place where the prohibitory statute is enforced, if, were that right of retorsion not employed a definite inequality will remain and

[66] Ibid., 12.

[67] Huber, *Heedensdaegse Rechtsgeleertheyt*, 4.31.55. See Section 12.4.1.1.

citizens would always have a worse standing than foreigners."[68] The example Voet has in mind is our familiar prohibition of testamentary succession in Gelderland, and apparently – and perhaps equally disconcertingly – in Flanders as well. Yet Voet warns against the dangers of such an approach.[69] This brings us back to the solution he proposed in the opening section of his conflicts treatment:

> But to prevent the rendering of service and comity between neighbor nations being vague, uncertain and often not reciprocal, and to prevent one denying to another what he has himself already won by comity, it has not seldom been settled, by special agreements or by long-standing customs worthy of observance like agreements, what service is to be rendered on either side. Thus many nations have agreed, and in many places it has prevailed by usage that judgments given elsewhere should on request be put into execution by the judge of another territory against property situate in his jurisdiction.[70]

This is as close as Voet's conflict of laws gets to the law of nations. Voet mentions customary practices. He also mentions several examples of agreements, notably concerning what we would be tempted to call judicial cooperation: enforcement of each other's judgments or even an agreement between Holland and Utrecht that their judges will not accept to judge a case involving two subjects of the other province.[71] It should come as no surprise that most examples concern Utrecht and Holland, Voet's native and adopted provinces, given the density of their relations and the volume of their economies. But this observation sheds further light on Voet's mentality: he is at the center of a small but vibrant, and legally diverse, world.

[68] Voet, *Commentarius ad Pandectas*, 2.2.5.

[69] Ibid.: "We must avoid being tide up in baffling wars and difficulties, such as we should avoid with all our powers, especially as between neighboring nations . . . [I]t will be far better than the uncertainties of gain or loss in succession should be mutually balanced in the uniform rule of succession laid down and kept both for foreigners and natives. Let our decision be the same in as many other matters as possible."

[70] Ibid., 1.4.App.17.

[71] Ibid.: "Besoldus tells us that by mutual consent and general custom judges in Germany can extend their sentences of banishment beyond the limits of their territory. We know that by a like consent Hollanders may extend such a sentence to the territory of Utrecht also, and the people of Utrecht in turn may extend theirs to the dominion of Holland. By special compact between the states of both provinces it was established that two Hollanders should not mutually sue one another at Utrecht, nor two men of Utrecht one another in Holland, and that the disobedient should be debarred from entry to the court by the judges who ordinarily possess in their own right the power to admit litigants of that class."

14.4.3 *Comity as Foundation*

Having established that comity is used as a doctrinal foundation for both Huber and Johannes Voet, we must consider whether there is a difference as to their doctrinal solutions. In the following section, we shall examine the exceptions each acknowledges to the application of comity. But what about the scope granted to its application in the first place?

For both Huber and Johannes Voet, comity is the essence that allows them to construct their doctrinal systems on the foundation of territorial sovereignty. Each of them chooses a different method of demonstration.

Voet provides the most vivid demonstration, by presenting two contrasting images: in the first, the conflict of laws is between polities jealously – and zealously – asserting the application of their law in all instances their own territory, whereas in the second, these polities have better considered their own – and their citizens' interest. In the same section where he presents the doctrine of comity, Voet brings up the different treatment of movable and immovable property as an example of how he perceives the operation of the doctrine: when it comes to immovables, magistrates would not "shift by comity even the breadth of a finger-nail from their real statutes, but set their teeth and cling to their own law."[72] But as to movables, "there has been a relaxation of the rigour of law as though by the common consent of all nations," and as a result "a rule based on comity has by universal practice prevailed that movables wherever actually found are governed in case of doubt by the law of the place in which their owner cherishes their domicile."[73]

When it comes to "mixed statutes dealing with the formalities of various acts," comity leads Voet, in principle, to the same solution as Huber's *actus territorialism*, declaring that it "has become just as common to disregard the reasoning based on strict law and power in its case and to regard the employment of these formalities . . . as sufficient for the validity of any act." Whereas Huber simply deduces his primary rule from his axioms and alludes to strong practice, Voet provides a policy rationale ("this rule appears to have been adopted for three reasons") and provides references to a score of jurists as well as to a case where he suggests that the Court of Friesland was "moved by the equity

[72] Ibid., 12.

[73] Ibid.

of the matter" to this effect.[74] This is no vacuus wording: when Voet returns to the subject, he takes the position that legal acts made abroad by a forum domiciliary, in accordance with the formalities required by the forum even though not conforming to the formalities of *lex loci actus* should be accepted as valid: strict law and justice must guide the forum judge and no serious consideration of comity counters this.[75]

When it comes to personal statutes, Voet refuses to draw a general rule as to "how far they operate in virtue of some comity (*ex quadam operantur comitate*) outside the territory of their legislator on property situated in foreign territory." The matter "cannot be settled by any fixed rules, nor be inferred from any universal principles commonly approved and accepted by the mutual tacit consent of nations," and Voet proposes to examine "each question in the proper setting of each subject-matter." His answer in those settings, notably regarding "the right of testation" can be summarized in simple terms: *lex domicilii* applies as to movables; *lex situs* as to immovables.[76]

Huber provides us with a single system, where his rules emanate from all axioms operating together: territorial sovereignty may constitute the basic foundation for the original valid creation of legal acts, determination of property rights over both immovable and immovable property, the conferral of personal status on subjects and the determination of capacity in accordance with the *lex loci actus*. But it is comity that allows these acts to produce effects everywhere and this gives meaning to the original exercise of territorial sovereignty. It is also comity that enables the forum to refuse such effect in its territory, in the case of prejudice. This reading of Huber is supported by considering instances in which he invokes or alludes to the comity doctrine as the foundation.

There is no express mention of comity in the first instance: Huber brings up the case of the Frisian who makes a testament in Holland in

[74] Ibid., citing 11 Dutch authors (but not Huber), 4 Germans, 2 Spanish and 4 French and the 1599 case presented in Sandius, *Decisiones frisicae*, 4.1.14.

[75] Ibid., 15: "And every magistrate by strict law (as discussed above and as found in use here) does rightly in protecting the force of his statute to the limit of his power. Surely he would be unjust to the person subject to him in respect of domicile or of property if he did not in regard to property lying in his own territory uphold the last will or contract of the man by whom he sees his own statutes in reference to formalities observed. Especially this is so when by safeguarding in this way the power of his statute he does not confound or upset things well done elsewhere and thus can nohow appeared to do any wrong to the magistrates of the other territory."

[76] Ibid., 28.1.44.

accordance with the more liberal formalities provided for in that province: the testament is valid in Holland, in accordance with the second axiom ("because while he was in Holland, although only temporarily, he was bound by the law of that place") and in Friesland, in accordance with the third axiom ("an act valid from the beginning, should be valid everywhere . . . and this applies without any distinction between movable and immovable property, as the law is and is observed").[77] It is interesting that, in the same passage in "Observance," Huber refers to the law of nations.[78] In the same text, Huber refers again to the third axiom as the basis for his pronouncement about the effects of judicial decisions.[79] There is also, in "De Conflictu Legum," an additional reference to the law of nations as a standard against which both the original application of East Frisian law and the refusal of authorities in Friesland to recognize it are judged, which we will consider below.

The one instance where Huber expressly mentions comity comes in the discussion of his second rule, according to which a person's personal status or capacity is determined in accordance with the law of the place of his or her origin (*lex domicilii*) but the capacity itself to do a certain act will be determined by the *lex loci actus*. We have seen that Huber's doctrine steers between a territorialist Scylla and a personalist Harrybdis. In "Observance," Huber simply states his rule: "everyone is recognized everywhere to have the capacity which he has in his native country, and he enjoys everywhere the rights which persons of that capacity there enjoy or are subject to."[80] He takes note that "[s]ome would have it that whatever a person cannot on account of personal incapacity do in his native country, he can do nowhere, not even in places

[77] Huber, *Praelectiones ad Pandectas*, 1.3.App.4.

[78] Huber, *Heedensdaegse Rechtsgeleertheyt,* 1.3.13: "I would say that if it was made in Holand or in some other Province according to the manner customary there, but by persons who usually reside in Friesland, then it holds good here also (in accordance with 2nd rule, sec. 5) both in respect of immovable and of movable property. This is stated as a consequence of 3rd rule, sec. 6); and also because the will of an owner of property as to such property executed in accordance with the law of the place where it is executed, must, according to the law of nations be recognized and enforced everywhere."

[79] Ibid., 24. If we examine precisely how Huber phrases his text as he moves in his treatment from contracts to judicial decisions (or, as he puts it, res judicata, *gewijde dingen*) we will find traces of him suggesting that his primary rule constitutes established practice or "usage." Gane translates *Diergelijk gebruik is 'er ten aenzien van gewijde dingen* (ibid., 24 princ.) as: "The usage is the same with respect to judicial decisions." The phrase must be seen in conjunction with Huber, *Praelectiones ad Pandectas*, 1.3.App.5 princ. (*Similem usum habet haec observatio in rebus iudicatis*).

[80] Huber, *Heedensdaegse Rechtsgeleertheyt,* 1.3.41.

where such persons are allowed to do it" but counters that "it would cause too great inconvenience if in respect of persons who do business among us we had to be guided to such an extent by the law of another country."[81] In "De Conflictu Legum," written for a more learned – and international – audience, he has better elaborated his justification. Persons who have obtained their majority at a younger age in a province have the rights associated with majority even in places where majority is obtained at a more advanced age, "because the other governments grant effect, in comity, to the laws and judgments of the other States over their subjects."[82] There is a condition: "so far as there is no prejudice to the law of [the forum State] itself and its own [subjects]."[83] The association of the law not just with the state but also its citizens (*suo suorumque iuri*) serves here as a counterweight to the other state's claim over its own citizens.

This is a subject discussed at some length by Huber, in "De Conflictu Legum" even more than in "Observance." Having invoked comity in support of the first (*lex domicilii*) leg of his rule, he turns to pragmatic or rather rationalist considerations to explain the second (*lex loci actus*) one. Huber reasons that it does not appear to him within reason (*non videtur habere rationem*) to hold that "whatever [a person] can do, or cannot do in his own country, he is "allowed to do, or prohibited from doing, everywhere." Such a solution "would produce too great a confusion of laws, and too great a burden upon neighbouring states from the laws of other states."[84] This is not simply a pragmatic argument. Huber uses the Greek word for confusion (σύγχυσις): even though this has been consistently translated as "confusion," Huber is probably aware of the ancient meaning of the word, which was indeed closer to mixture, not necessarily in a positive sense (hence the meaning of "confusion" eventually prevailed).[85] The notion of prejudice is used, together with comity, as the foundation of Huber's second rule. This contrasts with the

[81] Ibid., 44.

[82] Huber, *Praelectiones ad Pandectas*, 1.3.App.12 (*Quia Legibus rebusque judicatis aliarum Civitatum in suos subjectos quaelibet aliae potestates comiter effectum tribuunt; quatenus suo suorumque iuri quaesito non praejudicatur*).

[83] Ibid. The verbal similarities to the third axiom are evident, but there is no basis to follow Davies, "Influence," 75 who translates "to such state or to the rights of its citizens." The phrase *suo suorumque* is a standard one.

[84] Ibid., 13 (*Quae res mihi non videtur habere rationem, quia nimia inde σύγχυσις iurium et onus pro vicinis ex aliorus legibus oriretur*).

[85] See *Liddell-Scott-Jones Greek-English Dictionary*, s.v. σύγχυσις.

invocation of prejudice as the criterion underlying the exceptions to the application of the primary rule, to which we shall now turn.

14.4.4 *Comity and Exceptions*

The second leg of Huber's axiom concerns the exceptions to the application of comity. Huber argues that States "act in comity so far as this does not prejudice the power or law of the other government or its citizens." In all versions of the axiom, the temporal conjunction is maintained. The actual phrasing was refined – evolved from prejudice to "those conceding" (i.e. forum) in *De jure civitatis* to a reference to the power and rights of both government and citizens. But what does "prejudice" mean?

We will not find the notion in Johannes Voet, at least not as an abstract, general exception to comity. Voet does, however, after having considered all types of statutes via the prism of comity, list three exceptions to the application of his comity doctrine.

The first one concerns those instances where a person "in order to avoid the more troublesome and perhaps more expensive formalities of his domicile, a person has needlessly and in fraud of statute gone elsewhere for the purpose of completing the act, and then shortly returned."[86] This would make invalid the marriage of unemancipated Frisians in East Frisia and disallow the effects over property located in Friesland of a testament made by an unemancipated Frisian in a quick visit to a notary in Holland.

The second one concerns those who go to another place to make an act in order to avoid payment of dues to the fiscus.[87]

The third one concerns cases of an express legislative prohibition ("statute expressly forbids that an act shall be done outside the territory in any other way or with other formalities").[88]

86 Voet, *Commentarius ad Pandectas*, 1.4.App.14: "These things hold good as stated unless it should appear that in order to avoid the more troublesome and perhaps more expensive formalities of his domicile a person has needlessly and in fraud of statute gone elsewhere for the purpose of completing the act and then shortly returned. It would hardly be that in that case the validity of the act or testament should extend to property situated at the place of domicile. One who has deliberately and fraudulently spurned, evaded and cheated the laws of his domicile appears unworthy of any generosity or comity."

87 Ibid.: "And I should think that those are to be included in this class who, when heavier dues for sealed paper prevail at the place of domicile in the shape of payments to be made to the treasury, proceed in order to defraud the rights of the seal to some other place where such form of impost is unknown and return to the place of domicile after the act is finished."

88 Ibid.

Huber himself does not offer such a list. References to the third axiom or to prejudice are to be found in various cases throughout the treatment. Huber would share Voet's three exceptions. The fact that the scope of his own exception to the operation of comity is broader than Voet's is a result of Huber allowing a broader scope for the application of the foreign law as well.

There are two ways to examine Huber's exceptions. One is to go through the text and consider them case by case. The other one, which is followed in this section, is to group them into three categories, depending on the intended scope of the exception.

14.4.4.1 Fighting against Evasion

The first group involves those cases which, under normal circumstances, should be simply governed by the foreign law under the *lex loci actus rule* but in the specific circumstances discussed constitute an evasion of forum law. In a total of eighteen cases discussed by Huber, three involve such instances: the marriage of an uncle with his niece in Brabant; the marriage of underage persons in East Frisia; the testament of an unemancipated son in Holland.[89] All of them involve Frisians crossing the border to make a legal act they would not be allowed in their place of domicile: Huber's system triggers a mechanism to prevent evasion.

All these cases fall under what is called in modern French doctrine the *statut personnel*: capacity to make a testament, capacity to marry, incest prohibition. In late classical and modern doctrine, the possibility of a state's citizens avoiding that state's prohibitions or formalities by crossing over the border and engaging there in the prohibited or unfavorably regulated contact has been, has served as the "last line of defense" for arguing for a personalist approach in matters of capacity and status.[90] The problem of evasion (*fraus legis*) arises the moment a territorialist system is adopted – including the case when *another* state adopts a territorialist system and disregards the concerns of the state whose citizens are bent on evasion. Some writers have insisted on their *actus* territorialism, even in the face of evasion. For example, Joseph Story was reluctant to allow exceptions to the *lex loci celebrationis* with regard to

[89] Huber, *Praelectiones ad Pandectas*, 1.3.App.8 and 13; Huber, *Heedensdaegse Rechtsgeleertheyt*, 1.3.31–32 and 44.

[90] See e.g. Batiffol, *Traité élémentaire*, 296–297.

marriages.[91] Story's approach was influential in classical Anglo-American conflict of laws. On the contrary, Huber is keen not to allow the evasion of Frisian laws, and we have seen that this reflects a common attitude in Friesland and the Netherlands of his time. But he is equally intent on achieving this public policy objective while minimizing the disruption to his actus territorialist system.

The clearest example is the case of the unemancipated son making a testament: not accidentally, this is the least repugnant of the three cases. It is also a case where Huber must defend the application, essentially, of *lex loci celebrationis* against supporters of the *lex domicilii*. The son's testament is valid in Holland. It will also be valid in third states – remarkably, including those states whose law is even stricter or identical to Friesland's, in which he could therefore not have made a valid testament in the first place. It is only in Friesland where the testament will not stand, "because in that way nothing would be easier than for our citizens to evade our laws, as they could be evaded every day."[92] In discussing this case, Huber sounds almost apologetic.[93]

He is less reserved in the marriage cases. The case of the Brabant marriage is dispensed with quickly: in contrast to inhabitants of Brabant who "may not be troubled here on that account," "Frisians who have gone for that purpose to Brabant, and have there entered into forbidden wedlock after that fashion, would, if they returned after a short while be scarcely tolerated here, by virtue of the limitation to rule 3."[94] Recognition in this case would mean that Frisian law could be "evaded by the worst precedents."[95]

[91] Story, *Commentaries*, 103ff. Story makes allowance only for the case of an explicit prohibition in the law of a country to prevent its subjects only from marrying abroad contrary to its law (107–108). With regard to such rules, as for example Art. 174 of the French Civil Code, he notes: "The wisdom of such a course remains to be established; and it will be no matter of surprise, if hereafter we shall find a Frenchman, with two lawful wives, one according to the law of the place of the marriage, and the other according to that of his domicil of origin" (117).

[92] Huber, *Praelectiones ad Pandectas*, 1.3.App.13. See also Huber, *Heedensdaegse Rechtsgeleertheyt*, 1.3.42 ("They may, but it will not, however, hold good in Friesland, because it tends to supplant the Frisian law; elsewhere it can and will hold good").

[93] See Huber, *Praelectiones ad Pandectas*, 1.3.App.13: "On the other hand, it is true that . . . But elsewhere. . ." Of course the apologetic tone has to do with the fact that Huber is here fighting off the advocates of a personal law.

[94] Huber, *Heedensdaegse Rechtsgeleertheyt*, 1.3.31, with reference to the *res judicata* case discussed ibid., 25–26 (on which see immediately below in this section).

[95] Huber, *Praelectiones ad Pandectas*, 1.3.App.8.

The Brabant case acts as laying the ground for the East Frisia cases, which presented stronger practical interest.[96] In fact, Huber addresses himself to the East Frisian officials. In the Dutch text, it is remarked that "the Church and the administration of those countries ought not to have received such young persons to their undoing in this manner."[97] The Latin text includes a more abstract – but equally firm – statement:

> I consider that this obviously involves the subversion of our own law, and that, therefore, our magistrates are not bound by the law of the nations to recognize and give effect to such marriages here. And still more it should be held that those persons appear to act contrary to the law of nations who, by reason of their light-heartedness (*sua facilitate*), share with the citizens of another state, knowingly and intentionally, a law contrary to their paternal laws.[98]

It is interesting that Huber here accepts the law of nations as an objective point of reference: Frisian magistrates will not violate the law of nations by refusing to recognize these marriages, because they constitute an obvious subversion of Frisian law. It is on the contrary the East Frisian magistrates, whose light-heartedness (*facilitas*) leads them to "knowingly and intentionally" encroach upon the paternal laws of their (Western) Frisian cousins in a manner not looked favorably by the law of nations.[99]

But does this run-in of East Frisian magistrates with the law of nations affect the validity of these marriages? The normative prescription of Huber as far as the *effect* of the marriages *themselves* is concerned, is that *Frisian* magistrates "are not bound by the law of nations to recognize and give effect to such marriages here." Not bound. Here. Because "this obviously involves the subversion of our own law." But what about third states? Are they bound, under Huber's third axiom, to recognize these marriages, or does the term "another state" in the "prejudice clause" of the third axiom, mean instead that any state could take Friesland's

[96] Ibid., 8 ("The following observation also bears on this matter"). See Section 13.3.3.1.

[97] Huber, *Heedensdaegse Rechtsgeleertheyt*, 1.3.32 in fine.

[98] Huber, *Praelectiones ad Pandectas*, 1.3.App.8 in fine: "*Ego ita existimo, hanc rem manifesto pertinere ad eversionem iuris nostri; ne ideo non esse Magistratus heic obligatos, e iure Gentium, eiusmodi nuptias agnoscere et ratas habere: Multoque magis statuendum est, eos contra Jus Gentium facere videri, qui civibus alieni imperii sua facilitate, ius Patriis Legibus contrarium, scientes volentes, impertiuntur.*"

[99] The word *facilitas* can convey a variety of meanings, from easiness to levity and heedlessness. This ambiguity was probably intended by Huber: East Frisian magistrates may simply be too easy-going, or they may by neglect or even for gain facilitate this evasion of Frisian laws. Lorenzen translates as "slipperiness" and Davies, "Influence," 65 as "facility."

position with regard to the East Frisian marriage? The decision should be for the third state to make: if the marriage constitutes for some reason prejudice to its own power and laws, things would be simpler. Otherwise, *locus regit actum* may prevail.

The fourth case involves an exception to the recognition of the foreign *res judicata*:

> Titius struck a man on the head in Frisian territory. This man having lost much blood through the nose, and having drunk and eaten well, died the following night. Titius escaped into Overijssel. Having been apprehended there, voluntarily, as it seems, he is immediately tried and acquitted on the ground that the man had not died from the wound. This judgment is sent to Friesland and freedom from punishment is claimed for the acquitted.[100]

Huber notes that "the ground of acquittal was not inconsistent with the truth." In fact, even though in *Praelectiones* Huber recalls the case "from memory," in *Contemporary Jurisprudence* he describes it in detail, in the course of his discussion of homicide: it appears that it was originally thought that the man died – within an hour and a half – from Titius's blows but following a postmortem the doctors were nearly unanimous that the man had self-suffocated in his sleep.[101] What Huber and the Court of Friesland were concerned with was not that a guilty person got away, but that the said person – a notary, by the way – "had not the courage properly to face the law, but fled to Overijssel, and was there acquitted by the bailiff of Haeksbergen":[102]

> This decision the Court of Friesland refused to recognize as having been too much sought for, and apparently obtained by contrivance; and refused to grant the acquitted man his freedom here in this Province, unless he first again faced the law.[103]

[100] Huber, *Praelectiones ad Pandectas*, 1.3.App.6. The case is discussed by Watson, *Comity of Errors*, 10–11, who suggests the case also involved a conflict between the laws of Friesland and Overijsel, as to the definition of necessary causation. After reading the vernacular both on conflicts and on causation, one may be more reserved.

[101] Huber, *Heedensdaegse Rechtsgeleertheyt*, 5.13.12.

[102] Huber, *Praelectiones ad Pandectas*, 1.3.App.6 notes that "the ground for the acquittal was not inconsistent with the truth." Watson takes this to imply agreement with a laxer degree of necessary causation. In his discussion of homicide, Huber devotes much attention to the matter but essentially remarks that it is difficult to ascertain what is necessary and what is not, that "medicine is an art full of conjecture" and that the Judge should generally accept the doctors' opinion but first use his own judgment. See Huber, *Heedensdaegse Rechtsgeleertheyt*, 5.13.3–13.

[103] Huber, *Heedensdaegse Rechtsgeleertheyt*, 5.13.12.

In "De Conflictu Legum," Huber himself acknowledges that recognition of the judgment "was demanded by the people of Overijssel" but opines "that such an escape into a neighboring country and feigned proceedings appeared to open the way too much for the evasion of the Frisian jurisdiction, which is the basis of the exception to the third axiom."[104] The vernacular treatment, in fact, omits the interesting details of the case and only keeps the example of "a homicide flee[ing] from Friesland and go[ing] just outside the jurisdiction into another Province, where he gives himself up and is acquitted."[105] But it is equally forceful in its conclusion:

> It will not be unreasonable for the judges of the place where the crime was committed to demur to recognizing such a judgment and to giving effect to it within their own sphere, in as much as it appeared to tend to supplant their law and justice.[106]

Again, most modern conflicts lawyers would have sided with Huber on the substantive outcome. But what seems to indicate a weaker assertiveness than he is commonly associated with, is the way in which he defines the issue – i.e. as one of *fraus legis*, and not as a matter of Frisian sovereignty extending over Titius, or as an issue to be determined by the *lex loci delicti*. Moreover, we see the forum mobilized in the minimalist quest of not allowing the evasion of its own laws to walk on its *own* grounds. Huber's forum is not trying too hard to prevent the evasion from being perpetrated, and continuing to produce its effects, abroad: even in the case of the Frisian uncle and niece, the problem arises because they return to Friesland "after a while," i.e. not having abandoned their Frisian domicile. On the other hand, in the cases discussed the parties involved have a very strong connection with Friesland so if their marriage, testament, or acquittal is not valid there, it makes little difference if it would be valid in another place. Unless of course they earnestly leave Friesland, moving into a different domicile, in which case there would be no evasion.

14.4.4.2 Defending Local Laws

The second group involves cases where a legal act made validly abroad may not produce all its effects in all cases involving the forum. The cases involved are mostly contracts for the sale of prohibited goods, contracts

104 Huber, *Praelectiones ad Pandectas*, 1.3.App.6.
105 Huber, *Heedensdaegse Rechtsgeleertheyt*, 1.3.25.
106 Ibid.

for the sale of land while avoiding costly administrative formalities of the place of situation, and testaments disposing of land contrary to the *lex rei sitae*. In all these cases, evasion may well be involved but the intentions of the parties make no legal difference – and Huber makes no mention of or even hint at evasion. In technical terms, whereas the first group of cases is treated in a manner like the *ordre public* exception, this second group of cases is dealt with by a special choice-of-law norm.

Most of these cases indeed concern the acquisition of property rights over land and are discussed in the final section of Huber's treatment as examples of application of the *lex rei sitae* rule.[107] Having noted, in defense of his limited *lex domicilii* rule, the "great inconvenience if in respect of persons who do business among us we had to be guided to such an extent by the law of another country," Huber states:

> The same reasoning shows that in relation to immovable property, when the law touching such property varies locally, regard must always be had to the law of the place where the property is situated, because immovable property forms a physical part of a country or town, and the law of another country or town cannot attach or be applied to it without confusion and prejudice to the government of the country where the property is situated.[108]

Voet simply dealt with such matters as real statutes, for which there could be no question of comity.[109] Moreover, all three examples brought up by Huber would be characterized as prohibitive statutes, from which there could be no derogation by means of a legal act.[110]

Huber's lead case involves the lack of effects, over immovables in Groningen, of a testament made validly by a Frisian in Friesland. Huber notes that "the laws enacted relating to such property could not be varied by such dispositions without general confusion and prejudice to the state where the immovable is situated," before distinguishing between the norm that "regulates the act" and those pertaining to the qualities of immovable property: forum law (*lex rei sitae*) "does not prohibit that act from being valid in respect of immovable property so far as no quality impressed upon it by the law of the place is injured or diminished."[111] Huber is in this sense using the notion of "prejudice" in order to account

[107] Huber, *Praelectiones ad Pandectas*, 1.3.App.15.
[108] Huber, *Heedensdaegse Rechtsgeleertheyt*, 1.3.45. See Section 14.2.2 regarding ibid., 44.
[109] Voet, *Commentarius ad Pandectas*, 1.4.App.3, 5, 12.
[110] Ibid., 18.
[111] Huber, *Praelectiones ad Pandectas*, 1.3.App.15.

for the need to conform to the *lex rei sitae* with regard to the manner of acquisition of immovable property. In the case at hand, Groningen law of intestate succession is made mandatory when it comes to immovables, but testamentary succession continues to hold with respect to movables in Groningen and immovables elsewhere. In this sense, by characterizing the application of *lex rei sitae* in terms of a needed exception to comity on the ground of prejudice, Huber minimizes the – inevitable – disruption to his *lex loci actus* primary rule.

This also holds true with respect to the observance of the "notices and consent" requirements of Friesland for the sale of land located there.[112] These administrative formalities of the *lex rei sitae* are superimposed to the *lex loci actus*: the latter still determines the foreign contract's validity but the *lex rei sitae* must be complied with for the contract to produce its effects as to the acquisition of the immovable property in question.

The sale "by the lasts" of corn still growing in Friesland presents a different problem. This is about contracts for the bulk sale of growing crops, which was prohibited in Friesland (but no longer in other provinces such as Holland).[113] From a technical point of view, Huber is characterizing such a contract as involving the sale of immovable property, in order to subject it to the *lex rei sitae*, which "applies to things, which although not immovable, are attached to land."[114] From a doctrinal point of view, this may be a stretch given that this concerns a sale of specific future goods that must be detached from the soil to be sold but given that the prohibition intended to protect Frisian farmers and possibly to prevent alienation of their land, we can better understand the underlying policy. In Voet's doctrine, even if this prohibition is not characterized as a real statute, it would still be a prohibitive one from which there could be no contractual derogation; this would definitely settle the matter in Friesland but we can only assume that Holland would be motivated by comity in holding such a contract invalid.

By making *lex rei sitae* an exception to comity, Huber is limiting its potential scope without breaking with established practice. This holds at least as regards the first two cases, which would be generally accepted as falling within the *lex rei sitae*. The third case is different, but it is also not

112 Huber, *Heedensdaegse Rechtsgeleertheyt*, 1.3.48. See Section 13.3.2.

113 See Section 13.3.2.

114 Huber, *Praelectiones ad Pandectas*, 1.3.App.15.

an example of *situs* territorialism: Huber makes the choice of subjecting these contracts to *lex rei sitae* in order to ensure their invalidity everywhere.

This sweeping approach is contrasted with the cases involving the sale of prohibited goods (such as brandy), where Huber allows legal claims arising out of the contract – provided it was valid in the place of contracting – anywhere except for the place of the prohibition.[115] Even the criminal prohibition, in a town prohibiting consumption of brandy by its citizens just outside its territory, may take place in that town but may not interfere with claims pursued outside the town's territory.[116] For each of the two examples in which he holds that such transactions are not actionable in the place of prohibition, Huber invokes the prejudice exception. First, in stating that an agreement to deliver the goods in the place of prohibition would not be actionable "because it would conflict with the law and authority of that very territory."[117] Second, when consumption is prohibited and citizens simply "go just outside the jurisdiction of the town and drink [the brandy] there," there can be "no ground of claim in that town, because it tends to its signal inconvenience and disorder."[118]

The final case in this group involves conflicts of jurisdiction and Huber's position that submission in an agreement does not confer jurisdiction by itself over a nonresident defendant.[119] Huber argues that a judgment by contumacy in such a case should not be enforced in Friesland: "It would . . . be right to refuse to put such a judgment into execution as being prejudicial in general to our jurisdiction here and in particular to the inhabitants of this Province."[120]

115 Huber, *Praelectiones ad Pandectas*, 1.3.App.5 and especially Huber, *Heedensdaegse Rechtsgeleertheyt*, 1.3.19–23. See Section 13.3.2.

116 Ibid., 23.

117 Huber, *Heedensdaegse Rechtsgeleertheyt*, 1.3.20 (*om dat het soude strijden met het recht ende macht van de selve Landtschap*).

118 Ibid., 22 (*om dat het is tot merkelijk ongerijf ende vanordere desselfs*).

119 Huber, *Heedensdaegse Rechtsgeleertheyt*, 1.3.26 ("This they had no power to do unless they had reached him with his summons in their own jurisdiction or had caused him to be lawfully someone by his own magistrate who however need not have allowed that to be done"). See discussion at Section 12.4.1.

120 Ibid. See also Huber, *Praelectiones ad Pandectas*, 1.3.App.6: "*nor can effect be given to such judgments without detriment to our own jurisdiction and prejudice to our citizens*" (emphasis in the original).

14.4.4.3 Defending Local Rights: Third-Party Rights and Conflicts of Obligations

The third group of cases concerns instances where rights created abroad conflict with rights created in the forum's territory. There are two such cases discussed by Huber, both concerning the effects of security provided for a debt vis-à-vis third-party rights: real surety in one case, personal surety in the other. In both cases, the law of the place of contracting – under which the suretyship has been validly created – comes into conflict with a rule at another place: presumably the place of the third party's domicile, where the surety must be pursued.

The first case, discussed both in "De Conflictu Legum" and "Observance," involves the question of whether a creditor's right of priority, under a hypothecation by agreement, may be exercised over property – movables or acknowledgment of debt – in possession of a third party, presumably another creditor, whose claim may be inferior under Frisian – and Roman – law but not in Holland. Friesland is assumed to be the place of contracting as far as the hypothecation agreement between creditor and debtor is concerned. But when it comes to property, Huber makes no allusion to the rule *mobilia sequitur personam* or to the *lex domicilii:* we cannot know if the movable's owner is found in Friesland, Holland, or elsewhere. What matters is that the third-party possessor is in Holland and has rights to the personal property under the law of that province. Huber is categorical: "the rights of a third party to the movable cannot be taken away by the law of another territory."[121]

The second case brings us to the longstanding problem of married women providing security for their husbands and an interesting conflict of marital property laws: Holland, where the default regime is community property, which entails wives being automatically bound by the debts of their husbands, allows its women to opt out of community in their antenuptial contract. Friesland, where there is only community of profit and loss, allows its women to opt *into* undertaking sureties. The offside is that Friesland also subjects such opt-out conditions of marriage contracts to rigorous publicity requirements. As a result, these conditions are

[121] Huber, *Praelectiones ad Pandectas*, 1.3.App.11 (*quia ius illi tertio in ista re mobile quaesitum per ius alieni territorii non potest auferri*). See also Huber, *Heedensdaegse Rechtsgeleertheyt*, 1.3.54 ("if you lay a claim in Holland on such a bond against a third person in possession of an acknowledgement of debt, you will fail, because you cannot deprive people of their property lawfully obtained there").

therefore "not valid [in Friesland] unless [the marriage contract is] published, nor do they affect those who have reasonable grounds for being ignorant of them." Huber is mindful of the different policy choice that Holland has made: "Although a private contract, it is said to be valid in Holland to the prejudice of creditors to whom the husband is subsequently indebted."[122] Indeed, the contract will produce its effects against "those who have contracted" in Holland. But when it comes to creditors in Friesland, Huber is clear:

> If the law of the place [of contracting] in another state should conflict with the law of our state, where a contract was also entered into, which is inconsistent with the contract which was concluded elsewhere, it is more reasonable that we should follow our own law rather than the foreign law.[123]

It is interesting how the issue moves away from sovereignty and toward fairness to third parties and publicity. In both cases, Huber argues for the *lex fori* exception on "territorial" grounds, but the same result could have been made on the basis of publicity requirements and the need to protect good-faith parties.

14.5 Huber and the Conflict of Sovereignties Discourse

The Dutch school has often been regarded as epitomizing the idea of conflict of laws as grounded on state sovereignty. Discussions of comity and territoriality have added credence to this idea. Huber's very axioms are presented as the logical elaboration of the concept of sovereignty. Sovereignty is even invoked as the foundation of his system. Should we then classify Huber, and the Dutch school, among those who think of the conflict of laws as being a conflict between sovereignties?

Having reached the end of this study on Huber, we can say that the answer is, at the very least, more complicated. The Dutch school used sovereignty – to be more precise, its equivalent words in Latin or Dutch – as the foundation for their doctrinal systems and indeed the notion of sovereignty permeates Huber's treatment. But we must remember that doctrinal foundations are often employed *ex post* to justify solutions already accepted. As has been justly remarked, the potential of the seventeenth-century teachings invoking sovereignty was only used by

[122] Huber, *Praelectiones ad Pandectas*, 1.3.App.11.
[123] Ibid.

subsequent doctrine.[124] We have seen that even in his definition of sovereignty, Huber places a different emphasis than what we might have expected, but one that suits his objective – defending the Frisian commonwealth, and its governance system. When it comes to the conflict of jurisdictions, we saw him referring to territorial sovereignty in order to curtail the assertion of adjudicating jurisdiction by both Friesland and neighboring territories and the same applies even more with regard to the conflict of laws. Even though Huber uses the term "conflict of laws" and Voet does not, Voet may perceive such a conflict as potentially arising, whereas Huber approaches the whole matter in terms of allocating jurisdiction. "Sovereignty" is the foundation for the rules of such a jurisdiction-allocating system, but not its essence. To go back to his own distinction, "sovereignty" has to do with the axioms, not the *positiones*.

This is corroborated by the cases in which Huber, rather than draw on sovereignty-based arguments, considers individual interests, in order to come to conclusions that could have been equally reached on account of sovereignty. For example, in arguing against the extraterritorial effect of laws on personal capacity (i.e. a position supported by the doctrinal mainstream, from the Medieval Italians to the territorialists like d'Argentré and his Belgian/Dutch followers), Huber emphasizes transactional expediency, not the sovereignty of the forum or his own axioms – even though the notion of territorial exercise of sovereignty could have provided a very strong argument and indeed was the Achilles heel of d'Argentré's personal-law exception. Likewise, in characterizing matters such as prescription as procedural, Huber relies not on territorial sovereignty or on the political nature of jurisdiction, but on the judicial process being "of itself like a contract, and therefore also involving its own observances."[125]

We cannot tell why Huber made this choice of argument (indeed, why he decided to omit the sovereignty-based argument). Perhaps he thought that it is was superfluous, that his expressed position embodied sovereignty, but it is also likely that he thought he could not win the argument on the basis of political-theory arguments alone. It is at least equally likely, however, that Huber genuinely made up his mind on the basis of "substantive" considerations. In either case, it shows the limited utility of

[124] Kollewijn, *Geschiedenis*, 195–197.
[125] Ibid., 28.

the concept of a "conflict of sovereignties" in the exploration of preclassical conflicts law.

14.6 Conclusion

Huber has indeed had little influence on the subsequent evolution of Dutch and Continental conflict of laws, but significant influence in the development of Anglo-American conflict of laws.[126] This much is commonly accepted, although a more interesting question would be to consider the reasons for this divergent legacy: Is this a story of books circulating and jurists studying abroad, of chance encounters with texts? Was Huber's analysis considered as too simplistic by some and succinct enough by others? This is not the place to provide a definite answer, but what is certain after our lengthy analysis is that Huber has been misjudged by much of subsequent conflicts literature: his doctrine has been distorted and its sophistication underestimated.

Huber has thus been presented as a "territorialist." He has also been presented as a doctrinal unilateralist, but on closer inspection, he appears quite the opposite. His use of the concept of comity has been misinterpreted so much that has prompted entire books.[127] Yet it persists. In fact, Huber has been so persistently misread that people who have subsequently held opinions very similar to Huber's, notably *actus* territorialism, failed to mention him, or even attacked him in strong words.[128]

[126] See Yntema, "Comity," 28ff noting that Huber's iconoclasm led to him being ignored in his own country, while his "solution . . . clear, concise, practical, and modern, could not but appeal" to countries "where the problem of conflicts of laws awaited serious attention" (28), and furthermore: "[I]t is noteworthy that since 1700 the works concerned with private international law whose influence has been the most durable and extensive, those of Story, Savigny, Dicey and Niboyet for example, directly or mediately, have followed the main lines that Huber marked out – the sovereign authority of the national legislator, recognition of transactions as declared by the proper law, except when unduly prejudicial to the interests of the State or its citizens, and the effort by construction of a common law, whether derived from judicial decisions or from doctrine, to provide principles enabling the questions arising from the diversity of laws and commerce with other countries to be decided on a rational basis (31)."

[127] See esp. Watson, *Comity of Errors*.

[128] See de Vareilles-Sommières, *Synthèse*, 1:8. Livermore, *Dissertations*, 12ff, 26ff, as noted (and quoted) by Watson, *Comity of Errors*, 31–32. Livermore harbored more personalist views than Huber, but Watson may be partly right: while I do not believe that the proper reading of Huber would have lead to different doctrines taking hold in the US, in attacking Huber as the proponent of the "discretionary" doctrine of comity, Livermore yielded strong ground to his opponents.

A key reason for these misreadings has been the emphasis placed on Huber's three axioms by themselves, to the detriment of his three actual choice-of-law rules. However, it is the rules that constitute Huber's conflicts doctrine: the axioms provide the foundation of the rules. Once Huber's conflicts tract is studied in its entirety, as a doctrinal system, modern conflicts lawyers may feel that they share with Huber much of their sensibilities, vocabulary, and even methodological tools.

Let us take first comity. Huber certainly did not live in the thirteenth-century world in which the glossators thought themselves to be living. He presents his environment as a world of sovereign states, with formal equality and their own private-law regimes. Upon closer inspection, we shall observe that Huber's polities had their own complex internal structures, leading to internal as well as external conflicts of jurisdiction. Moreover, "Roman law" binds together these polities, even if it owes its legal existence to the sovereign state rather than a higher authority. Roman law is thus both part of domestic ("municipal" or "civil") law as well as the supranational body that, together with the emerging law of nations, ensures the ongoing "intercourse" (*commercium*) between them. This is where, and how, comity comes into play: a *foundation* for a system of rules allocating jurisdiction between the various polities, primarily those of the Dutch confederacy but potentially across the world. Like the Grotian law of nations, Huber's comity encapsulates law and history, pragmatism and morality, strict and soft power.

Once closely examined, Huber's conflicts system combines very active "international" and "private-law" dimensions. As to the former, Huber sought to structure the world-system in a way that reduced frictions and ensured positive, mutual respect among states. His depiction of how the world-system works certainly has idealist elements, but Huber also plays a pragmatic card. All his arguments about universal law or practice are intended to convince the foreign Leviathans, as well as the local ones, that they are bound. Furthermore, in his conflicts treatment, he pleads with the magistrates of East Friesland and other territories who would allow Frisian adolescents to marry without their guardians' permission.[129] In terms of modern international-relations theory, he is neither a utopian nor a realist.

[129] See especially Huber, *Heedensdaegse Rechtsgeleertheyd*, 1.3.32 in fine ("Rather one might remark that the Church and the administration of these countries ought not to have received such young persons to their undoing in this manner").

As to the latter, Huber tried to ensure the orderly making and universal effectiveness of legal acts, while drawing a line to ensure respect of fundamental forum policies. His *lex loci actus* is more considerate of substantive state policies, than, for example, Story's version: marriage prohibitions stand out in this regard. In modern, anachronistic, terms, Huber expresses a moderate liberal internationalist sensibility.

Modern internationalists tend to confuse two distinct "universalist" visions: on the one hand, the perennial urge of jurists and moralists to establish or defend a universal rule of their liking, and, on the other, the effort to achieve the mutual recognition of local solutions by those conscious of sovereignty or of losing the substantive-law argument. Huber clearly subscribes to the latter idea. Let us consider, for example, his position on marriages within the prohibited degrees. Huber regards as "too revolting" the idea of recognizing extraterritorial effects to a marriage in the second degree, which is "incestuous according to the law of nations" – and of course the Christian religion – to the point that it is highly unlikely to be permitted anywhere.[130] But he is far more tolerant regarding a hypothetical marriage of non-Frisian Catholics in the third degree, whether out of pragmatic considerations (he could not possibly change things), the desire to maintain decisional harmony, or the calculation that any moral damage from letting the "papist" dispensation have effect in Friesland could not outweigh the dangers from cracking holes to the general principle about the validity of acts.

Once Huber's conflicts tract is studied in its entirety, as a doctrinal system, modern conflicts lawyers may feel that they share with Huber much of their sensibilities, vocabulary, and even methodological tools. Huber's organization of the legal subject matter is not unfamiliar to us – certainly not as unfamiliar as Medieval doctrine. We discover clear, general choice-of-law rules that look very much like the multilateral, *a priori* norms of the present. But we also observe the employment of other subsequent techniques, including escape devices and incidental questions. Even his preoccupation with providing a foundation for his conflicts system, including a justification for both the dominant role of the

[130] On the contrary, marriage to one's brother's daughter (but not his sister's daughter, nor a marriage between aunt and nephew) was permitted in Roman law for three centuries, following a self-serving *senatusconsultum* of Claudius in 49 CE, which was narrowly interpreted until its repeal in 342 CE (see Inst.1.10.3; for the repealing constitution see *Codex Theodosianus*, 3.12.1). The pre-342 CE situation was known in Huber's time, through the *Regulae Ulpiani*, 5.6 and the narrations of Tacitus (*Annales*, 12.6) and Suetonius (*Claudius*, 26.3).

law of the forum at the beginning of the process and the application of foreign law, resonates with classical and modern scholarship. Medieval and other Early Modern writers might have engaged in similar exercises, but Huber is explicit about this and makes clear statements in a concise and readable manner – a factor that certainly contributed to his success in the Anglo-American world.

Yet Huber is still a long way from private international law as we know it. We find only traces of a – baroque – private-law taxonomy in his conflicts treatment. His thinking is familiar to a present-day private lawyer, but still different. His argumentation seems grounded on the concept of sovereignty, which modern conflicts lawyers have learned to distrust or at least play down. Upon closer inspection, we will see that he defines – and uses – differently these notions. The fault lines between private/public and domestic/international do not mean as much to Huber. We have seen him demonstrate, at times, a subtlety and sophistication not associated with conflicts doctrine in his era, yet modern conflicts lawyers are nonetheless likely to regard as naïve or "primitive" Huber's conflicts system of one general rule (*lex loci actus*) flanked by two exceptions (a very limited *lex domicilii* and *lex rei sitae*); likewise for its territorialist foundation and Huber's overreliance in the construct of *actus*. Even in his own time, Huber's rational simplicity confronted the prejudices and nuances of Frisian practice.[131]

Huber is different even when compared to modern advocates of a *lex actus* paradigm. Where Huber is simply speaking of the substantive law of the place where the act has been concluded, modern advocates speak of the "substantive law designed by the private international law rules" of the "place where [the act's] authors are found."[132] The modern *lex actus* rule has had conditions expressly attached to it: notably rules on legal evasion, the *ordre public* exception, and the party autonomy principle. Huber might not have disagreed with the effects of such conditions, but he certainly did not mention them in his rule. In short, he demonstrates a

131 See Section 12.4.

132 See Barnich, *Actes juridiques*, 141: "Tout acte juridique est soumis à la loi matérielle désignée par les règles de droit international privé de l'Etat où se trouvent ses auteurs, à la triple condition: 1o qu'il ne soit pas accompli frauduleuseument dans un Etat détérminé; 2o que la reconnaissance de l'acte ne soit pas contraire à l'ordre public du for et 3o que les parties à l'acte n'aient pas exercé la faculté qui leur était offerte de désigner un tribunal exclusivement compétent pour juger de l'acte, auquel cas il faudrait préferer les règles de conflit de ce tribunal."

far lower degree of awareness of the methodological and doctrinal distinctiveness of the conflict of laws.

In Huber's time, conflict of laws already existed as a distinct topic. But "conflicts lawyers" – and a distinct conflicts epistemology – are yet to be created.

PART V

Epilogue

15

Preclassical Conflict of Laws Configured

15.1 Introduction

After all this discussion, what is preclassical conflict of laws? Are we even right to use such a notion? What are its defining characteristics? What is its significance for us?

To write the intellectual history of a doctrinal field in a given period is to address a double-edged question. A period is defined by a minimum of internal coherence, as well as by its "external" differentiation from the adjacent periods. At the same time, these unifying characteristics coexist with internal divergences. The paradigm of an epoch is shaped by these defining ideas and the tensions generated, which over time give rise to a different environment and inspire new paradigms. Such a history is therefore a balancing exercise between concord and dissonance, our historical understanding inevitably coloured by the aspirations, sensibilities and tensions of subequent epochs.

This has certainly been the case with Medieval and Early Modern scholarship on the conflict of laws. We think of these works as consecutive reiterations of a "theory of statutes," in the sense that we believe that their principal occupation was to determine the spatial reach of *statuta* – legislative or customary norms. In order to perform this mission, "statutists" at first devised interpretative criteria to be applied to individual statutes and, over time, started grouping statutes together. The result was the classification of statutes into *personal* or *real.* Eventually, an intermediate category of *mixed* statutes was added – seen as a relic of doctrinal ingenuity as well as a testament to the inherent inadequacy of the statutist method. None seriously questions but few have actually considered to what extent statutists did come to organize their conflicts doctrine in terms of substantive legal categories: we assume that such categories were subordinated to the binary or tripartite distinction of statutes, which in this book are being called respectively the basic and the classic theory of statutes.

The result of these perceptions has been that we have often failed to understand the essence in the thought of these "primitive" forefathers, who are often associated in our historical consciousness with contemporary quarrels such as between "personalist" and "territorialist" approaches to the conflict of laws, multilateral and unilateral choice-of-law methods or the contest between private-law and public-law sensibilities. All too often, we have approached preclassical scholarship through the eyes of the classical jurists who replaced it. Yet these great jurists, the true founders of our discipline, were also human, children of their own age, with doctrinal aspirations and epistemological biases of their own. It is up to us, in the present, to decide if we would rather approach early conflicts scholarship via intermediaries, adding their biases to our own, or if we shall instead use the natural advantage of a more elevated vantage point, which we possess over our forefathers.

In this sense, writing *a* modern history *of* private international law requires as a first step, to reflect *on* the writing of history *for* private international law. Throughout this book, it has been advocated – and illustrated – that the real challenge is not the irrelevance of history to present-day concerns, but rather that we have failed to appreciate the true impact, and the richness, of both history and historiography. Only once some degree of such understanding has been achieved, can we proceed with the writing of history. A new history of private international law would have to grasp its internal dynamics. It must take account of its evolving relationship(s) to both domestic-law and international-law doctrine, but also understand the autonomous function of private international law, with its unique policies and methods. It must strike the appropriate balances in researching and writing history: balancing between adopting too intrinsic or too extrinsic a perspective in writing; between not taking context seriously enough or obsessing over it; between focusing on scholarly texts and keeping an eye for the practical side of things; between primary research and textual analysis. Such new history may find useful concepts in the social sciences and the humanities, notably with regard to the production of knowledge, the theoretical tools for approaching texts, and the operation of professional groups. It must also be mindful of historical methodology: respect its rigor and embrace the plurality in historical approaches. We should not be concerned about making history relevant for private international law; instead, we should be ambitious about making private international law relevant for history.

Having achieved a certain degree of elementary understanding in this regard, we proceeded with a close examination of two influential contributions of Medieval and Early Modern scholarship, which was guided by the conviction that preclassical conflicts doctrine can only be understood by first studying its context: its political and legal environment, the problems that preoccupied these jurists. The next step is to consider doctrinal solutions – including tools and concepts peculiar to the conflict of laws – as well as the structure of the works and the legal reasoning employed. The ambition of this book is to showcase such a different approach to preclassical scholarship and to contribute to a conceptual framework that invites discussion and closer examination of preclassical but also classical and modern texts, mindful of context, connections, and autonomy.

This concluding chapter consists of six sections. The first four seek to (re)define preclassical conflict of laws: after first asking if there is something in the typologies of statutes (Section 15.2), we shall consider the private-law impact of preclassical doctrine (Section 15.3), its political context and foundations (Section 15.4), and the construction of a preclassical conflicts discourse (Section 15.5). Section 15.6 addresses the move from preclassical to classical doctrine. Section 15.7 offers a general conclusion illuminating the persistent antinomies that defines private international law to this day.

15.2 *De Statutis*

Each of our two case studies revolved around a canonical text of the Medieval and Early Modern scholarship respectively. Whereas comparisons were drawn between these two texts and most of the principal texts of preclassical doctrine, this book does not purport to provide a complete history of Medieval and Early Modern conflict of laws. Our exploration has nonetheless shown that other preclassical works, some of which probably had more direct influence in their own time, appear closer to either the basic or the classic theory of statutes. It is nonetheless remarkable that such a theory does not feature prominently in either Bartolus or Huber. One could be of course tempted to argue otherwise: should we not perceive the binary distinction that Bartolus makes in the beginning of his commentary as an early example of a basic theory of statutes? What about the distinction between *statuta in rem* and *in personam*, famously made in the English case, and passed down through the centuries? Someone more daring might even suggest that Bartolus's treatment of contract choice of law is an early indication of conflicts doctrine chaffing under the binary discussion and gradually inserting an intermediate category. As to Huber, one would be even more tempted to see in his tripartite division an exact correspondence with the three categories of statutes in the classic theory.

Such temptation should come to no avail, however. There can be no question that both Bartolus and Huber do acknowledge that, of the norms (*statuta*) in force in a certain polity, some may only produce effect within the polity's jurisdiction, whereas others can produce their effect everywhere.[1] Conversely, the same polity will recognize the effects, within its jurisdiction, of some of the respective norms of a foreign polity but not necessarily all its norms. But this acknowledgment is only the starting point, not the theory, for either jurist. What is more interesting is that, for a variety of reasons, both these jurists attempted to treat the question of which norms should have what effect, likewise for both (for *all*) these polities – or at least in abstract terms. There can be no single answer as to why they embraced this abstraction: there were jurisprudential premises, political environment, practical considerations, and the influence of the "international" environment and audience to which they were addressed. But attempting to answer the question provides valuable insights, both as to preclassical scholarship itself and as to subsequent doctrine.

All this holds generally true for all preclassical jurists: if anything, the major dividing line that cuts across Medieval and Early Modern conflicts doctrine is not between the various statutist schools, but between scholarship – attempting to think in abstract terms and provide arguments that could decide multiple cases with several variables – and judicial practice – attempting to deal with the case at hand and often concerned with expanding the jurisdictional reach of the forum. The most important duality in preclassical doctrine may have been the need to provide compelling arguments to scholarly jurists as well as easy-to-use formulas to legal practitioners. The misreadings of both Bartolus and Huber show how difficult either task – let alone their coexistence – was.

Our own task must be to approach preclassical doctrine on its own terms, mindful of the limitations inherent in superimposing our own schemes, as well as those of our immediate forefathers. Let us consider Bartolus as an example of the Italian school. Although we do find sporadic references to a statute providing with respect (*circa*) either to things or to persons – a distinction going back to the Roman law on

[1] Jurisdiction is inherently linked – conceptually and practically – to *territorium*, especially in Medieval and Early Modern doctrine, but the former term conveys a broader meaning.

actions – we will find no mention – let alone a definition – of *statuta realia* or *personalia*.[2] What we will find, however, especially if we look at the context surrounding the text, is a treasure trove of concepts, problems, and rules, including choice-of-law norms still in force today, as well as legal constructs that were already becoming obsolete by his time: the text can even be used as discussion material for an advanced introduction to Medieval law and society. The distinctions drawn between prohibitive, permissive, and punitive statutes, or between *odiosa* and *favorabilia* are telling in both respects. What Bartolus has to offer us is a fascinating and multilayered treatment of conflicts questions. The same holds true as regards the explorations of other Medieval scholars into conflicts.

Over the next few centuries, the subject began to be defined in terms of a theory of statutes; from d'Argentré in the sixteenth century to the Voets in the seventeenth and Boullenois in the eighteenth, the primacy of the division between personal and real statutes was asserted and the subject matter was organized within these categories. The intermediate category of mixed statutes never seems to have acquired a life of its own, but it became very useful for the management of each author's system. The notion of mixed statutes allowed d'Argentré to expand the primacy of real over personal statutes: mixed statutes were treated as real and only statutes "purely" personal, as to both object and effects, had extraterritorial effect.[3] The same notion, however – now defined as pertaining to formalities of legal acts – enabled the Voets to acknowledge the universal effect of acts made under "mixed" statutes, in contrast to, certainly, real statutes but also, effectively, many personal ones.[4] *Statuta mixta* were therefore important to the evolution of the conflict of laws, but not as a legal doctrine per se, but rather for the two things that the *notion* signifies. First, an awareness that conflicts can best be solved if perceived in tridimensional and not bidimensional schemes. Second, an evolving sophistication in the argument of preclassical conflicts: whereas the concepts of personal and real statutes derive from general legal concepts of *in rem* and *in personam*, "mixed" is a new thing. Bertrand d'Argentré's mixed statutes are essentially a presumption in favor of real statutes. By the time of Johannes Voet, mixed statutes were a distinct legal category with its own legal rules.

[2] See Section 10.2.

[3] Argentraeus, *Commentarii*, 218.6.6. See also Section 14.2.3.

[4] Voet, *Commentarius ad Pandectas*, 1.4.App.4, 10 and 12.

This conclusion is bolstered by the relative skepticism toward the notion of mixed statutes of the eighteenth-century French jurists who nonetheless continue its use.[5] But it is especially illuminating when we consider our second author. Huber never mentions even the term *statutum*, let alone *personalia*, *realia* or *mixta*. His three rules do correspond to the three categories as developed by Johannes Voet: *lex rei sitae* for *statuta realia*, *lex domicilii* for *statuta personalia*, *lex loci actus* for *statuta mixta*. But the order is reversed: the counterpart to *statuta mixta* is Huber's primary rule, whereas the counterparts to both *statuta personalia* and *realia* have reduced scope. Where Voet would determine the extraterritorial effect of a *statutum personalium* by reference to the things it would impact, reaching results similar to d'Argentré, Huber splits would-be *statuta personalia* into those granting a status and those regulating actual capacity, in a manner not unlike modern techniques such as the incidental question. Where Voet asserts – or acknowledges – considerable power to the forum (both legislator and judge) to apply its law, Huber again employs another modern technique – employing auxiliary choice-of-law norms and even escape devices in order to manage the problematic cases that could be generated by his doctrinal system. Yet what is most remarkable is that, for all these apparently major philosophical and argumentative differences, Huber and Voet reach similar solutions in most cases.

Statuta personalia, *realia* or *mixta*, *prohibitiva*, *permissiva* or *punitoria*, *odiosa* or *favorabilia*, *circa rem* or *circa personam* constitute the language in which preclassical jurists sought to address an ongoing problem. Medieval jurists dealt with the problem by phrasing the question in terms of when local law may derogate from the *ius commune*. They employed a series of interpretative tools to that effect, as exemplified by Bartolus, who showcases a veritable toolbox of constructs, none of which is unique to the conflict of laws but all of which, taken together, constituted a doctrinal system. By the time of the Dutch school, the perspective seems reversed: Voet, especially, phrases the question in terms of when local law should give way to the effects of a foreign rule. But the problem continued to be the same: the allocation of political power was not that fundamentally different; and the answers given to these different questions were compatible.

[5] See e.g. Boullenois, *Traité*, 1:25–28.

Such concepts hold the key to understanding these jurists, but we must first identify the problem and then examine how it was conceptualized, what methods were used to address it and why they were eventually replaced.

15.3 Addressing Private Law Problems

Our examination of how Bartolus and Huber organized the legal subject matter had the twin objectives of gaining a better understanding of their environment and the problems that preoccupied them and considering the impact of these parameters on their conflicts system and its concrete rules. We have found evidently little of the grand categories of classical and modern doctrine: this is easily understandable in some matters that were only conceptualized as we know them in the Pandectist paradigm (such as family relations), but some attention should be paid to the lack of prominence of certain concepts – such as succession or even obligations – which were invented by the Romans and were important in Medieval and Early Modern law. We thus observed that even though succession-related issues take up most of Bartolus's conflicts treatment, their discussion is spread out: the making of testaments is treated in the third section, but then matters of capacity to make a testament, or capacity to inherit appear only, if persistently, as examples across the discussions about permissive and prohibitive statutes. Intestacy is not even expressly addressed in an example, except for the – imported – English case. This is in marked contrast to contracts, the second-most important topic in the text, which is treated first and in unitary fashion. Huber, who shares Bartolus's emphasis on these two subjects, treats both contracts and testaments as *species* of the same *genus* (legal acts); intestate succession is summarily dealt with together with property rights over immovables. In both cases, as well as in other conflicts treatments, the organization of the legal subject matter follows the author's argument, and especially the author's emphasis on specific problems.

The best way to understand how preclassical conflict of laws approached the legal subject matter is to think of it as organized along three axes, each centered on a major type of private-law institution.

The first axis concerns *legal acts*, especially contracts and testaments (acts *inter vivos* and *mortis causa*). In Early Modern doctrine, marriage is also included, whereas dowry contracts are an important staple of both Medieval and Early Modern doctrine. The principal conflicts norm for matters falling into this category was the *lex loci actus*, but that was never absolute: some matters – certainly prescription – were often subjected to another law, such as the law of the place of performance or the law of the place of the trial. We have seen this more vividly in Bartolus, but even Huber's strong embrace of the *lex loci actus* was not absolute.[6] Moreover, when it came to contracts pertaining to marital property, it was often successfully argued that the law of the marital domicile would apply in determining rather than the place where the contract was made.

The second axis concerns legal norms regulating the *acquisition of property rights.* Any discussions in this regard have concerned immovable (real) property, since it was generally accepted that acquisition of property rights over movables was determined by the law of their owner (*mobilia sequuntur personam*). Movables were moreover of lesser value and there were fewer legislative – or customary – attempts to control their transfer: we have seen examples of testamentary succession allowed with regard to movables but not with regard to immovables. As to immovable property, it was clear that the law of the place where it was situated (*lex rei situs*) should apply, but this did not settle the question of the scope of the rule. Clearly *lex rei sitae* would apply over the exercise of such property rights – for example, servitudes – but should a rule prohibiting testamentary succession over local land prevail over a foreign testament? What if the rule merely imposed additional formalities? Or prohibited certain persons from making such a testament? What about the effects of a marital contract made in a community-property territory over land in a territory that followed the Roman-law separate property regime?

The third axis concerns legal norms regulating the *status and capacity* of a person: for example, emancipation, legitimation, the capacity of a married woman to enter into contracts, the capacity to inherit. Such questions have been linked to so-called personal statutes and were subjected to the personal law of the person in question. That personal law was domicile: even though we have seen in the literature references to the place of origin or possessive antonyms to define the relationship between a party and his or her law, domicile was defined in more or less pragmatic terms and could be changed if someone really moved to another territory.[7] In the examples we have seen, tensions between this third axis and one of the other two usually arise in cases of a temporary move (or even without a move), where the party entered into a legal act

[6] See Section 14.2.
[7] See Section 12.2.2.1.

treated differently in the place of origin/domicile and the place of the act: for example, a testament by an adolescent student, a married woman's capacity to undertake debt obligations toward her husband's creditors. A different set of cases involves a person who should come to certain rights in more than one territories, but problems arise because he or she is denied the capacity to enter into these rights in one of these territories: for example, a Medieval Italian city statute prohibiting a wife from being named as her husband's heir in his will, or the succession rights of a person legitimated in accordance with a foreign city's law but not the *ius commune*.

It could be suggested that these three categories tend to correspond to the classification of statutes into mixed, real, and personal respectively.[8] This is not a literal correspondence: as we have seen, not all authors use the bipartite or tripartite division of statutes; among those who do, there is a diversity in the classification and organization of the legal subject matter; moreover, each of our three substantive categories may comprise more than one conflicts norm. But it is a functional correspondence, in the sense that the tripartite division of statutes tends to address the questions raised by the existence of – indeed, the coexistence and tension between – the three axes. Preclassical conflicts discourse is constructed in the successive attempts to resolve this tension.

The relative importance of these three categories was obviously different depending on time and place. For example, Ulric Huber's system corresponds more clearly with this typology: his system is moreover expressly oriented toward the legal act. We have seen that his equivalent to "personal statutes" revolves around legal acts and even his discussion of immovable property – with the exception of a remarkably brief discussion of intestate succession – also concerns the area that must be carved out of the *lex loci actus* in favor of the *lex rei sitae*.

But the same could also be told regarding Johannes Voet, even though the correspondence may be less apparent due to the serpentine structure of his treatment: Voet may not state a general *lex loci actus* rule, but in effect, the *statuta* of his time pertaining to legal acts and raising conflicts will regard either to formalities, or to capacity, or to the acquisition of property: as to matters of interpretation or implication of terms into a contract, these would be dealt with under the *usus modernus Pandectarum* or by a presumption of an agreement between the parties.

[8] See e.g the definition of personal, real and mixed statutes in Voet, *Commentarius ad Pandectas*, 1.4.App.2–4 as discussed at Sections 13.3 and 13.2.2.1.

In his turn, Bartolus has to devote substantial attention to institutions, such as emancipation and legitimation, which in Early Modern times, even though they continued to exist, raised considerably fewer practical and barely any political problems.[9] Legislative attempts to curtail testamentary freedom are definitely more widespread – and more diverse in their content – in Medieval Italy than in the Golden-Age Netherlands, where longheld testamentary restrictions mostly concern immovables and are seen as waning over time.[10] As a result, whereas the two Dutchmen subordinate the third category to the first (especially Huber) and the second (especially Voet, but also Huber), Bartolus discusses matters of status and capacity to a considerable degree in various parts of his *repetitio*, to the detriment of a unitary treatment of succession-related matters.

The panel is completed with the French authors, for whom personal statutes are as much as about civil and social status, and their legal consequences, as about the capacity to enter into legal acts.[11] It is interesting that d'Argentré, a *situs* territorialist, draws a very exhaustive typology of statutes touching upon the third category. He thus mentions – and characterizes as mixed, therefore real – statutes addressed to a person by reason of their immovable property (e.g. taxation); statutes regulating a person's capacity to dispose of immovable property (e.g. donations between spouses, minors disposing of land) as well as those determining the status of a person (e.g. legitimation) if they affect the acquisition of immovable property, and likewise as to statutes altering the capacity of persons regarding a specific legal act, if it involves disposition of immovable property.[12] But the most interesting case is the other category of mixed statutes he mentions: statutes that deal with the disposition of immovable property but have to consider the status of persons, namely

[9] Even as late as 1806, see van der Linden, *Institutes*, 1.4.2(2) on legitimation and 1.4.3(4) on emancipation. Kuehn, *Emancipation*, 1–2 cites Manlio Bellomo who traces the first criticisms of the legal concept of paternal power to the seventeenth century and notes that its disappearance coincides "with the structural transformation from the medieval to the modern family."

[10] See Section 13.3.4.

[11] Boulllenois, *Traité*, 1:51–74, adding to the usual examples commonly brought by "our Authors" (age of majority, emancipation or interdiction, power of husband over wife), laws on the birth status of children, legitimation, paternal power, but also excommunication, civil death or infamy, status of nobility, naturalization and declaration of alien status, as well as royal letters reestablishing the good status (*Lettres du Prince qui rétablissent dans la bonne fame et renommée*).

[12] Argentraeus, *Commentarii*, 218.6.8. See also Lainé, *Introduction*, 1:32–334.

whether they are nobles or commoners, as the primogeniture rule applies when nobles succeed and equal distribution when commoners are called as heirs.[13] Evidently, not only was land ownership materially very important for d'Argentré and sixteenth-century Brittany, but it was also strongly connected to personal identity and to the notion of family as a social unit. It is conceptualization and emphasis, more than the actual solutions given, that differentiates d'Argentré from Voet and Huber.

Legal acts have emerged from this elementary survey as the principal legal institution in preclassical conflict of laws. This is most evident in systems like Huber's, which were clearly conceptualized in such terms. But legal acts – contracts, testaments, but also unilateral acts of legitimation and emancipation – are also everywhere in Bartolus, upon closer inspection. Even d'Argentré, who places more emphasis on the consequences of immovable property and considers more strongly intestate succession is preoccupied with managing legal acts and subjecting them to the *lex rei sitae* when touching upon land.

The importance of legal acts explains the distinction between procedural and substantive matters. It has been suggested that the invention of this distinction was a foundational moment for conflicts doctrine, in the sense that it enables to at least contemplate the possibility that substantive matters may be governed by a law different than *lex fori*. This may well be so, although we should not exclude the reverse possibility of the distinction having been created in order to exclude procedural matters from the choice-of-law process. In any case, there is little significance in that question. What is more interesting is how the distinction is employed in Medieval and Early Modern texts. The distinction is certainly there and there is no question that as to procedural matters we should follow the law of the place of the trial (*locus iudicii*), to use the words of Bartolus, who indeed makes use of every opportunity to distinguish between "matters connecting the manner of conducting the case" and "matters concerning the decision itself." Bartolus himself seems to be using the distinction as a way of removing additional matters from the *lex fori*, including prescription.[14] Huber also employs the substance/procedure distinction but he is closer to the remedial approach of classical common law, which leads him to subject prescription to the

[13] Argentraeus, *Commentarii*, 218.6.8.

[14] Bartolus also refused to deal with questions of delict – indeed, of criminal wrong – simply in terms of applying forum law.

lex fori. It is nonetheless interesting that he assimilates (effectively subordinates conceptually) judicial process to contracts.

There is more to be said regarding the distinction between formalities and substantive validity of legal acts. This distinction has played an equally important if more variable role in the history of conflicts doctrine. This distinction has played an equally important, if more variable, role in the history of conflicts doctrine, but it can only be partly explained contextually, i.e. as the product of the "private law" jurisprudence at the time. It is generally accepted in preclassical doctrine that if the conflict concerns the formality requirements for a legal act, the law of the place of its making will be looked to (inspicitur locus contractus). We will on the contrary find little evidence – and this only as we near the dusk of our period – for an approach in favor of validity, as in the case where someone has made a testament abroad in conformity to his own personal law, but not to the *lex loci conclusionis.*[15] On the whole, the distinction between form and substance becomes more important in systems reluctant to acknowledge the extraterritorial effects of a legal norm making substantive dispositions: this explains why *solemnitas* becomes so important in Medieval conflict of laws, where the power of city law to make a substantive disposition regarding foreigners in its territory, let alone citizens abroad, contrary to the *ius commune* is strongly contested.[16] On the contrary, in actus territorialist systems, such as Huber's, formality is most important in constructing the language of *bene gesta* or *negotia* made in one place.

All things considered, the form/substance distinction seems to have been used by conflicts lawyers across time to distinguish between, and treat differently, "dissimilar" cases. In many instances, this technique has allowed them to facilitate the "circulation" of legal acts (from another perspective: the application of foreign law) while keeping certain cases under the control of the forum law – whether because they really think so or as the necessary tradeoff for the said facilitation. In some other cases, the distinction has been used conversely, in helping the *residual law* (forum law; *ius commune*, being forum law) control a case.[17]

The story of conflict of laws could in fact be told in terms of increased liberalization of the choice-of-law through the use of the form/substance

[15] See Sections 13.3.4 and 14.2.1.

[16] See Section 9.4.2.

[17] See e.g. the distinction between emancipation and legitimation of spurious children in Bartolus ad C.1.1.1, nu. 38, discussed at Section 9.3.6.

distinction. We saw Bartolus differentiating between "formalities" and substantive regulation in a manner allowing local formalities to produce acts with effects everywhere. We then observed *actus* territorialists, such as Huber – and the Anglo-American courts and authors who followed him – liberalize substantive requirements by subjecting them as well to the *lex loci actus*. Classical and modern doctrine further liberalized choice-of-law as to form, while regulating substance, eventually allowing most legal acts made validly in accordance with certain other laws other than the *lex loci celebrationis* to stand. This (*favor validitatis*) has remained the basic paradigm. Today, the reinvigoration of social, economic, and political liberalism and the concept of party autonomy have led to increased calls for an undifferentiating, liberal treatment of form and substance.

This brings us to the intention of the parties. Apologists of party autonomy have long claimed to have discovered solid foundations for the doctrine in preclassical scholarship, including Bartolus, Voet, and Huber. The historical accuracy of this claim has long been a matter of contention: the concept of party autonomy is grounded on the will theory of contracts, which only appears in the nineteenth century, but also in the idea of legal systems among which the parties may select. Such notions do not seem to exist in preclassical doctrine. The earlier references to the intention of the parties – certainly in Medieval texts, including Dumoulin – refer to the presumed intention of the parties, notably as a way of arguing in marital property cases that the intention of the spouses was that their marital arrangements be governed by the law of their matrimonial domicile (the husband's domicile) rather than the place where the marriage contract was made and presumably the marriage celebrated (the wife's original domicile prior to the marriage). This was a reasonable argument but it does not constitute evidence of party autonomy.

The same is true as to Huber's reference to the intention of the parties in "De Conflictu Legum." But we have found other references indicating express agreements or stipulations, about the law to apply to a testament or contract, or about submission to jurisdiction, notably in Huber's vernacular work and in Voet, in whose treatment the intention of the parties is one of his three questions, following the statement of strict law and the effects of the application of comity.[18] There is an evident

[18] Voet, *Commentarius ad Pandectas*, 1.4.App.1 and 18–21 (speaking in terms of individuals). See Section 13.6.

awareness of the power of the individuals to alter the equation as the law applicable to their transactions, both by their physical movement and by their words in contracts and acts *mortis causa* (Voet speaks of them "renouncing" statutes) but a careful reading would suggest that what is allowed is for parties to derogate from dispositive rules of the law otherwise applicable in favor of the rules of another polity. This observation is supported by the apparent wariness of the tendency of individuals to evade the system. I would suggest that we need a more serious study of scholarly works and research into the practices of individuals (testators, parties to marital and commercial contracts) before we conclude that no hybrid notion or practice of "party autonomy" existed in preclassical conflict of laws. But we are far from a concept of party autonomy.

Classical and modern conflict of laws has viewed *the individual* as the *subject* of a conflicts proposition. It has accordingly emphasized the image of the individual traveling away from local restrictions on the formal/substantive validity of an act or its content. Preclassical doctrine held, on the contrary, the individual rule (statute) or *actus* as its subject. There are moments, especially in the later jurists, such as the Dutch, reminiscent of the modern preoccupation with individuals evading the rule, but on the whole, the principal preclassical question was whether the statute (via the legal act) or the legal act (through the statute) may produce extraterritorial results. The different way in which the question was posed – and the answer was phrased – does not mean that the essential problem is different. But it has to do with the different premises – and different levels of consciousness – of preclassical doctrine compared to classical and modern. To these, we shall now turn.

15.4 Political Foundations and Legal Hierarchies

Preclassical conflicts doctrine developed in parallel with the elaboration of a concept of sovereignty – broadly defined to encompass Medieval notions of *iurisidictio* and *territorium*. Working out the implications of such evolving concepts was an ongoing project for Medieval and Early Modern jurists, including those who wrote on conflicts issues. Solutions given to conflicts issues impacted the political and social struggle of their time: this holds as true of the more "political" cases we have examined (such as the application of Medieval Italian cities' legislation over clerics in ecclesiastical courts or their jurisdiction over foreign mercenaries occupying territory abroad), as of cases with definable political stakes (such as the danger that evasion posed to Frisian ideas about the organization of the family) or even of seemingly technical questions (such as formalities of legal acts) that could nonetheless impact everyday life and the relative power of a polity and its institutions. But to recognize the normative implications of conflicts doctrine is not to say that it was either subordinate to the political dimension or simply an instrument of public or "interpolity" governance. All too often, an existing or imaginary political structure was invoked in order to support concrete "private-law" doctrinal solutions. Our story took us from a hierarchical world of institutional pluralism and jurisdictional privileges to a horizontal world of independent polities with clearly defined reach over territory and persons, but in both cases, the triangular relation between conflicts doctrine, governance objectives, and theoretical foundations appears to have persisted.

In the thirteenth century, we saw Accursius attempting to downplay the exercise of autonomous jurisdiction by local entities – but also other voices, more tolerant of the reach of local rules. Any success Accursius had was temporary: the *ultramontani* and especially the commentators had to redraw their scheme and accommodate the emerging political and intellectual reality surrounding them. In the process, this made them more tolerant of legal diversity, even of what we could call decisional dissonance: Jacobus de Ravanis would thus accept that a single person might die testate in some territory and intestate in another, because his testament was valid under the more permissive local law derogating from the *ius commune* but not abroad, until the next step was made by jurists arguing in favor of extending the effects of the testament – and thus indirectly of the statute – everywhere.[19] In any case, the political thought of Medieval jurists was still permeated by the notion of an imperial superstructure (or royal, in the case of French jurists). Local jurisdiction might be autonomous *jure* and especially *facto*; the jurists may have explained this state of affairs by evoking the delegation of imperial power or by reasoning by analogy; but the political super-structure provided the indispensable point of reference.

The text of Bartolus is emblematic of this move away from the glossators' maxim that "the statute does not bind the non-subjects." In the cases of conflicts between *ius commune* and city law, we witness city law gently being extended, in some cases, over foreigners and clerics; city law could even produce effects abroad. In the cases of conflicts between

[19] See Section 8.3.3.5.

city laws, the law of the "foreign" city obtains a – small – window for producing its effects. In the system of Bartolus, the *ius commune* serves a role similar to our international law, or federal law in federal countries. There are of course differences with these modern parallels: in law, all subordinate law, such as city law, existed by virtue of imperial authority i.e. of the *ius commune*; in reality, *ius commune* exists to the extent that the local authority has wanted it to. The *ius commune* also served as a common legal language, the interface connecting the localities: to make a modern analogy, it played the role of both *Rechtswissenschaft* and international law. Accordingly, in the hands of Bartolus it serves as an effective tool and a foundation for his conflicts treatment.

The case of Early Modern French lawyers is unique among preclassical jurists, in that they dealt with legal diversity under a single political authority – indeed, a single polity encompassing multiple jurisdictions. The French Kingdom had long seen itself as being independent from the revived Roman Empire while, at the same time, in possession of the imperial Roman political (and legal) armory. In private-law matters, part of the country followed Roman law, but most of it did not. Local customs had "sovereign" status but were also codified by royal decree. Whether in Paris or in the provinces, French jurists who wrote on conflicts came from judicial or government careers, or from legal practice. To understand the influence of political and professional context on French doctrine, it should be enough to consider two rough contemporaries: Dumoulin, moving between the French capital and universities in the adjacent territories of the Holy Roman Empire, involved in national politics as an effective advocate of central power (and author of an authoritative commentary of the Parisian custom) and d'Argentré, firmly anchored in his own province and defending the sovereignty of its Court (and custom) vis-à-vis the other provinces.

In contrast to the French, jurists from the Low Countries, mostly university professors, lived in a world where political authority was horizontally divided: Golden-Age Netherlands consisted of sovereign polities, acting in concert as a federation grounded on a careful, and delicate, institutional balance. Territorial sovereignty acquired additional political, as well as legal, importance: there could – and should – be executive cooperation and understanding, but no unifying legislative force. Political context, academic sensibilities, and jurisprudence explain the Dutch jurists' increased emphasis on providing foundations for their conflicts doctrines. Classical and modern scholarship has mistaken these foundations for the actual doctrine, and many have misread the foundations themselves for something more akin to political unilateralism, but a careful examination shows a different picture. Despite the differences both as to language and as to results in certain cases, both Huber and the Voets use sovereignty in tandem with comity in order to explain why and how legal acts should produce their effects everywhere and when exceptions must be made. But we can only understand the meaning of territorial sovereignty and the comity doctrine by looking at the actual problems dealt with, and the solutions given.

Territorial sovereignty thus provides a foundation for the valid creation of legal acts, as well as for the exercise of adjudicative jurisdiction by a State. Together with comity, it also acts as a limit to a more aggressive, or "unilateral" exercise of jurisdiction by a State. *Bene gesta* should produce universal effects, while the safeguards (Huber's "prejudice" exception) prevent evasion of the State's law or unsatisfactory results. Huber uses territorial sovereignty, and comity, in a way that allows him to minimize instances of decisional dissonance.[20]

There are differences in language – even literally, as the contrast between *comiter* and *ex comitate* has shown. Voet uses the concept of "comity" as an appeal to pragmatism and the sovereigns' self-interest; there is little hint of legal character, but the inherent rationality of acting *ex comitate* in most cases, also demonstrated by long-established practice should settle the issue. The image of "jealous" sovereigns aggressively defending their law is used both as a statement of "strict law" (*summum ius*) and as an argument that illustrates the benefits of acting *ex comitate.* In contrast, Huber strongly suggests a legal character for comity. Even his use of the adverb *comiter* refers to more legal precedents from Roman law and history. Huber clearly seeks to ground his conflicts doctrine on a juristic foundation, which he supports by both Roman law and the practice of nations. One gets the feeling that Huber's doctrinal system derives its content from the one and its legitimacy from the other (it is however unclear which is which). Huber plays natural law down in favor of a law of nations, which is no longer the Roman or even Medieval *ius gentium* but neither is it the *droit des gens* of a century later. As foundations go, this is a moment of transition as to the political foundation, having moved away from the High Medieval *ius commune,* but not yet near the law of nations of the late eighteenth or the international law of

[20] See Section 14.4.

the mid-nineteenth century. In that sense, if Huber sounds more like a classical jurist in his preoccupation with broad legal principles, a theoretical legal foundation, and working the exceptions into the system, both classical and modern doctrine may find resonance with the positivist Voet: concerned with the reason why, and the extent to which, States are truly bound and advocating agreements between states to take care of such matters.

For an additional example of the role of political foundations and the development of conflicts doctrine in the Medieval and Early Modern periods, we may consider conflicts of jurisdiction (i.e. adjudicative jurisdiction and enforcement of judgments). What we would think of as civil jurisdiction is treated seriously in other places in preclassical jurists' comprehensive doctrinal works, but there is, admittedly, scarcely any direct, and only some incidental, discussion of matters of adjudicative jurisdiction in preclassical conflicts treatments. This may be attributed in part to the learned-law environment of such texts, but a more important reason should be the limited awareness as to the special nature of the conflict of laws as a subject. To draw conclusions, we must consider broadly the works within which the conflicts texts are included.

From Bartolus we see that the adjudicative jurisdiction of the Medieval Italian city-states was grounded on the Roman-law bases of *iurisdictio* (and, so far as possible, their own long arm). In theory, the *ius commune* should make adjudicative jurisdiction more like venue jurisdiction but political aspirations and legal diversity (even within kingdoms recognizing no superior) had made this impossible. Bartolus's discussion of punitive judgments is in this regard fascinating, especially the forfeiture case where he starts from a very restrictive interpretation of a territory's *iurisdictio* under Roman law and then gradually empowers the territory by legal constructs allowing it to perform functions allowed to its fictionally superior authority. Roman law had a new life in the Early Modern Dutch Provinces, but the fiction of a hierarchy of *iurisdictiones* had been replaced by simpler political foundations, long-standing practice, and learned-law elaboration. We thus see in Huber a system of adjudicative jurisdiction, whose bases are not unfamiliar to modern doctrine, grounded on a rigorous territorial sovereignty and power theories of jurisdiction, mitigated by an equitable predisposition and considerations of mutual convenience. The fact that Titius could reasonably expect that an acquittal in Overijssel, over a case with which it had apparently little connection, could produce *res judicata* in Friesland is as telling as

Huber's account of why he failed.[21] There were even judicial cooperation agreements, as evidenced in J. Voet.[22]

There is no question that jurisdiction systems were more unilateral than the respective systems of applicable law.[23] This is understandable: jurisdictional issues were under the control of courts and practitioners, whereas questions of applicable law, rarer before courts, were more susceptible to learned doctrinal discussion. It would be difficult to speak of coordination between these two sub-systems (jurisdiction and applicable law), but the expansive assertion of adjudicative jurisdiction led to an increasing number of conflicts cases and thus further fueled the further development of conflicts doctrine.

15.5 A Conflicts Literature (and Discourse)

The idea of development characterizes the period between the High Middle Ages and the Age of Revolution. We began our journey with a cryptic one-sentence "rule" in the *Glossa Ordinaria.* Less than a century later, however, we witness Bartolus drawing on the work of his peers to provide a comprehensive treatment of the subject, which can still find much resonance seven centuries later. The Bartolan tract is certainly not exhaustive of the subject matter and could not be understood as a standalone work. It is not even a fully autonomous text. What is today called "Bartolus on the conflict of laws" is but a part – admittedly the principal part – of a *repetitio.* It is essentially nine questions with their answers, with no overall titles. Even the division in small sections we have been citing was made by subsequent editors of his works. But at least it represents an effort to approach the subject systematically, in one place – one would have to look through the entire work and put together several glosses in order to get an understanding or rather to recreate Accursian "doctrine." Even the changes in structure and additions in the content, between Bartolus's earlier *repetitio* on *de quibus* to his more mature and better-known *repetitio* on *cunctos populos* are indicative of a growing awareness of, and interest in, the subject.

[21] See Section 14.4.4.1.

[22] See Section 14.4.2.

[23] It is no coincidence that the only instance of political unilateralism in Huber, despite his attempts to contain Frisian jurisdictional assertions, concerns arrest-based jurisdiction of foreigners. See Section 12.4.1.1.

Bartolus is not unique: virtually all Medieval and Early Modern analyses of the conflict of laws form part of broad expositions of the civil law. Their place within such expositions gradually improves, during the Early Modern Era. Conflicts treatments appeared as part of separate books of jurisprudence, or in various places in commentaries on customary law or the Pandects, or even collection of cases. To such treatments one may also add numerous *consilia*, which however did not constitute systematic expositions of the subject and of which only a small number was really influential in the long run. In any case, by the seventeenth century, conflicts treatments appeared as independent chapters in large-scale doctrinal works. Again, it is interesting to note the evolution of Huber's conflicts treatment: from somewhere in the middle of an earlier treatise in Latin, to the last place of his Dutch-language treatise, to a prominent place in that treatise's reissue and then to an equally prominent place in his *magnum opus* on the Pandects – a privileged position also adopted by Johannes Voet – written in exemplary Latin.[24] In the mid-eighteenth century, we even have the first conflicts books – by practitioners who expected recognition and probably monetary recompense but had no ambition, or competence, to produce a comprehensive treatment of law. This appears however to have been a local phenomenon: it will take more than a half-century, after Boullenois, before the next influential book on the conflict of laws is published in the 1830s. Production of conflicts literature will only start in earnest late in the second third of the nineteenth century.

The mode of legal reasoning also evolved over this time. The original conflicts texts – such as the gloss on *cunctos populos* – cannot be understood outside of their context, but a standalone reading of Bartolus may be possible, even if it is considerably more rewarding to approach the text having in mind the political and jurisprudential foundations on which his doctrinal system is grounded, and for which we must look elsewhere in his work. The situation only partly improves by the sixteenth century. By the late seventeenth century, however, we witness structures more to the liking of classical and modern writers, which may moreover be read on their own. Huber's conflicts work begins with the statement of a geopolitical foundation, from which emanate his general guiding principles (from outside the conflicts field). We are then presented with general conflicts rules and immediately afterward we

[24] See Section 13.2.1.

witness their specification as to concrete categories of the legal subject matter.[25]

Savigny presents us with an emblematic moment in the story of the creation of a conflicts literature. His conflicts treatment is the bulk of a book – the last volume in an eight-volume treatise on the general part of private (civil) law, a monument of legal system-building. Compared to Story, Foelix, Schäffner, and several other authors of standalone conflicts treatises, this may appear as a slight regression – and is certainly proof that the move to a self-conscious field, let alone discipline, of private international law is not yet complete. But Savigny manages to underline the importance and doctrinal prerequisites of conflicts treatments. Bertrand d'Argentré or James Kent had placed their treatment somewhere in the middle, as a digression in the course of delving deeper in a substantive doctrinal question. The mature Huber and Johannes Voet treated conflicts issues at the beginning of their doctrinal work, where they discussed their jurisprudence and theory of sources. Huber had previously placed his conflicts treatment at the end of his treatise, but it was because it did not systematically fit anywhere – hence it was moved from last to third with no real changes in the text itself. So when Savigny placed the conflicts treatment at the end of his systematic work, it seemed as an acknowledgment of how vital and complicated the subject was. Instead of the conflicts treatment informing the substantive-law discussion or forming part of it, it is now the broad doctrinal discussion that is supposed to inform the conflict of laws. We could see this as the *true* recognition of the complexity of the field (after eons of *obiter* remarks to that effect). Actually, we could see this as the true recognition of the existence of the *field*.

Conflict of laws in the Middle Ages and the Early Modern Era did not even constitute a legal field and certainly not a legal discipline. We have seen little evidence of communication in real time even between people located in close proximity. And almost no consciousness that the conflict or collision of statutes and laws was a distinct department of the legal edifice. We could however speak of a preclassical conflicts discourse. We saw successive generations building on their predecessors, whether they cited approvingly, disparaged savagely, or simply ignored them. We also noticed that no historical consciousness separated the contemporaneous

[25] We could also look to Johannes Voet's apparent division of the law into the three parts of "hard" state law, equitable state practice and the role of individuals as a different kind of "modern" structure.

discussion on the conflict of laws from a "past" discussion. Late eighteenth-century scholars professing serious interest in the subject may have seriously misread Bartolus and other Medieval jurists – following their own sixteenth-century sources through which they were acquainted with early statutist thought – but they nonetheless feel compelled to discuss them. Even Story, who was acquainted with Bartolus through second- or third- hand references, still regarded him as a participant in the same discussion. Hence the idea that there is a continuous discourse that unites Medieval and Early Modern scholarship on this subject.

Preclassical conflicts discourse was nonetheless a very fragmented one. In marked contrast moreover to the classical period and the formation of a discipline, where communication between jurists and their works was immediate, in Medieval and Early Modern doctrine such communication has a generational lag: we have to come to mid-eighteenth-century Paris to find evidence of near-synchronous communication between jurists and even in that case we must take into account the disregard of these relatively recent doctrinal contributions in the Napoleonic Code, almost half a century later. The only truly alive "horizontal" conflicts discourse (i.e. where contemporaries were apprised of each other's work and interacted with each other, whether in concert or in opposition) was the Italian school – but of course, the conflict of laws was a marginal topic for the glossators and the commentators. As to the eighteenth-century Conference of Advocates, it might have had little impact on the broader fact, but the incitement to Boullenois, especially, by his peers or the market was a foreboding of things to come: Lainé might be excused his – rare – lapse into romanticism.

15.6 From Preclassical Conflict of Laws to Private International Law

In the Introduction of his influential *Digest on the Conflict of Laws*, Oxford Professor A. V. Dicey distinguished between a *theoretical* and a *positive* "method" of treating the "subject of the conflict of laws."[26] The theoretical method "has been adopted by a body of Continental writers, among whom by far the most distinguished is still Savigny."[27] These writers, "starting from the facts that the rules of private international law

[26] See Dicey, *Digest*, 15ff ("method of treatment").

[27] Ibid., 15.

which prevail in one country . . . are to a great extent the same as to the rules maintained in other countries . . . and that, under the influence of modern civilization, this similarity tends to increase," "consider private international law as constituting in some sense a 'common law,' tacitly adopted by all civilized nations":[28]

> They of course do not deny that whatever force this common law possesses within England, or any other country, is derived from the authority of the sovereign thereof. Nor do they overlook the fact that the legislation or judicial decisions of different states deviate more or less from the principles of the supposed common law. Their doctrine is, that such deviations ought to be avoided, that the fundamental principles of private international law can be ascertained by study and reflection, and that the soundness of the rules maintained, say in England, as to the extra-territorial recognition of rights, can be tested by their conformity to, or deviation from, such general principles.[29]

If belief in this "common law" is the first characteristic shared by the adherents to the theoretical method, the second one is "agreement in the view":

> [T]hat the object of a writer on the conflict of laws is to discover the principles of this common law of Europe, and starting from one principle, as, for example, that we must "discover for every legal relation (case) that legal territory to which in its proper nature, it belongs or is subject (in which it has its seat);" or that "the local law should be always applied by which vested rights are kept intact;" or that "every legal relation must be judged according to the local law of that territory within which it has come into existence," to show how in accordance with the fundamental principle assumed by the writer as the basis of his system, a consistent body of rules is, or might be, adopted by all nations for the determination of the questions proper to private international law. What may be the merit or demerit of the fundamental principles laid down by Savigny and others is, be it noted, not at present in question. What requires our attention is the aim proposed to themselves by the class of authors at whose head stands Savigny. Their object is to construct a logically consistent series of rules, which either actually do agree with the rules as to the choice of law upheld in different states, or ought, consistently with sound theory, to prevail in every state.[30]

[28] Ibid.
[29] Ibid., 15–16.
[30] Ibid., 16.

To this theoretical method Dicey contrasted the "positive" one, dominant in England, of "treating the rules of private international law in the main as part of the municipal law of any given country ... where they are enforced":

> This school starts from the fact that the rules for determining the conflict of laws are themselves "laws" in the strict sense of that term, and that they derive their authority from the support of the sovereign in whose territory they are enforced. ... [W]hatever the limits imposed on the scope of their inquiries by writers who follow the positive method [i.e. whether to examine the law of one country or more], the object of their labours is always in character the same. Their aim is to ascertain what are the rules contained in the law of a given country with regard to a special topic, namely extraterritorial recognition of rights.[31]

Dicey's description is perhaps the most illuminating picture of nineteenth-century conflict of laws, and probably finds some resonance to this day.[32] Dicey has conceptualized in an excellent manner the governance project of Continental private international lawyers, to which he opposed the "positivist" response – as well as his own more nuanced method.

Dicey's image can also illuminate the preclassical period – mainly by contrast to the classical one. The whole discussion Dicey describes would sound odd to preclassical ears. Preclassical writers tended not to make an explicit distinction between what the law *is* and what the law ought to be, at least with regard to the conflict of laws. They viewed their role in terms of the "positive" method, but the law they interpreted was often a law common among states, rather than the creature of a sovereign. Their work often entailed a "theoretical" element, in envisaging a "common law" as connecting tissue between states, but there is little evidence that they conceptualized "conflict of laws" *by itself* as this connecting tissue. The system of Bartolus goes beyond statutory interpretation into an actual allocation of legislative, and adjudicative, jurisdiction between polities; there may be an awareness of the importance and difficulty of the topic but there is no awareness of its unique character, nor distinct methodology, even as the interpretative methods and standards Bartolus is using turn into rules. An example is the so-called English case: from a modern perspective, his objective and the substantive results he would achieve are perfectly understandable or even compatible with our own

[31] Ibid., 18.
[32] Hatzimihail, "Conceptual Battlefield," 59ff.

doctrines and may not simply be explained in terms of statutory interpretation. With hindsight, Bartolus could even be seen as adopting a "unilateralist" approach relying on legislative positivism, but there is no consciousness in Bartolus of such ideas – which explains his subsequent misreading – and to read them into his doctrine defeats its context and our own objective of understanding his thought. The same could be argued of Huber, who presents us with a set of what appears more like proper "choice-of-law" rules and is nearer to the classical paradigm, or Voet, who in his own theoretical elaboration touches upon modern sensibilities. In that sense, Dicey's imagery is suggestive of the *limited consciousness* of preclassical conflicts lawyers. Their writings do indicate a certain degree of legal consciousness about the complexity of these issues and the need to treat them together, whether in order to provide a common doctrine or draw distinctions. But when it comes to *self-consciousness* of the matter forming part of a distinct subject that requires its own epistemology, methodology, and legal rules, we see only the first traces as the preclassical period draws to a close.

This was to change in the nineteenth century. When Dicey, referring to the "positive method" says that "the rules for determining the conflict of laws are themselves 'laws' in the strict sense of that term," he means laws requiring the sovereign's sanction. For the early nineteenth century "positive" writers, conflicts norms were "laws," i.e. legal rules on their own right. This is what preclassical conflicts writers lack, and this is probably what would have made the theoretical/positive distinction foreign to them. In this sense, preclassical conflict of laws appears as a genre or discourse pertaining to interpretation and jurisprudence, rather than as a legal field dealing with its own rules "in the strict sense of the term."

What changed? It has been common to associate the demise of statutist doctrine with the advent of the "national" codifications at the turn of the eighteenth and especially the early nineteenth century. Such explanations do not take adequate account either of the relative diversity of ideas within the preclassical paradigm, or of the continuing doctrinal development and the continuity between the late eighteenth and early nineteenth centuries. But this should not suffice: statutist doctrine was embodied in the new Codes – a legislative vindication of sorts? – and it certainly took some time until a new paradigm emerged. Neither does the surge in legal nationalism and the shattering of the common legal tradition, both commonly associated with the new codifications suffice. Statutist doctrines continued to persist, especially among conservative nationalists, as late as the end of the nineteenth century and if the emergence of unilateralist theories is linked to jurisprudence, the revival of some statutist ideas has been associated with some forms of legal positivism. Moreover, the common legal tradition was not shattered but rather its core was reconfigured once more: just as the Medieval *ius commune* gave its place to Early Modern traditions of natural law and the law of nations, these were succeeded by international law and positivist jurisprudence.

The Codes should be taken instead as epitomizing a broader development, which by the early to mid-nineteenth century had taken the concept of sovereignty to its intellectual completion, exemplified by Austinian positivism. Bartolus and Baldus may have toyed with the concept of *dominus mundi* and accepted cities with no superior power (*principes*) but it was inconceivable to the Medieval mind that even the Emperor could abrogate the *ius commune* as a whole. Huber and Voet, who constructed their systems on the basis of territorial sovereignty and considered Roman law as applicable as part of domestic law, because of its Reception and only so far as allowed by the local sovereignty, could never have imagined the possibility of the provincial assembly (the "States") abrogating Roman law as a whole. Huber is in fact using Roman law to supplant ancient Frisian customary law and reinterprets even the limited Frisian legislation in conformity with the *usus modernus Pandectarum*.[33] Even the royalist Early Modern French jurists could not have envisaged the sweeping replacement of provincial customs and jurisdictions by a national legislation and jurisdiction. By the early to mid-nineteenth century, however, this extravagant assertion of sovereignty was a historical fact: it is no accident that Carl-Georg von Wächter, the legal positivist associated in our historical consciousness with a version of absolute unilateralism and with "demolishing" the theory of statutes, was a senior official in the new German kingdoms. The world of conflicts law could no longer be the same.

The paradigm shift in the concept of law was paralleled by doctrinal and conceptual developments in the legal treatment of rights and private relations. The demise of the *actus* paradigm in favor of the concept of legal relation in an apt example. In Medieval and Early Modern times, it was possible to easily "localize" legal acts: most transactions had short duration in any case; long-distance commercial relations were often

[33] See Section 12.3.2.

"localized," as far as enforcement was concerned, via networks of commercial papers, partners and factors; even most conflicts of law that did occur involved small distance. It is no accident that the most challenging case to localize, in the preclassical era, concerned marital contracts – long-term relations where the place of contracting was supposed to lose connection to both parties soon thereafter. As the distances grew and new means of communication developed. It became more difficult to point to the *locus contractus* – or to acknowledge that it provided an appropriate anchor. Many legal acts became less easy to pin down to a certain locality.[34]

Changes in the political and social environment were even more important. Political and economic liberalism fostered legal individualism. On the other hand, the new states flexed their legislative muscles and sought to better regulate all aspects of life. Law was thus restructured into spheres of private autonomy and spheres of strong public interest. In both spheres, the focus was now less on acts and more on their makers – and their relations. The intellectual environment, and expanding societal needs, fostered doctrinal sophistication and the construction of private-law systems.

This brings us back to Savigny's so-called Copernican revolution, which we tend to view in terms of legal philosophy: Savigny created *secondary* (second-order) rules whose aim was to regulate not the factual cases themselves, but instead the statutes doing so. This would constitute a significant step toward the conceptual autonomy of our field, and the affirmation of its scholarly character: even though traces of aprioristic bilateral rules, or even second-order norms, may be found in certain preclassical writers, there is no indication that they conceptualized what they were doing in such terms. Savigny, on the contrary, elaborated a theory of second-order rules that laid the doctrinal foundations for an autonomous conflict of laws. He also brought to the spotlight the concept of legal relation (*Rechtsverhältnis*), which facilitated a move away from the narrowest versions of legislative positivism; it provided an alternative to an excessive rights discourse; finally, it helped the organization and reconceptualization of private law into grand categories. Contracts, along with civil wrongs, were conceptualized into the law of obligations. Marriage, and marital property, including marriage contracts, were grouped together into family law, along with relations between family

[34] Lando, "Conflict of Laws of Contracts," 244 talks of losing "the unity of place and time in the making and performance of contracts."

members. Testaments, along with intestacy, into succession law. Chattels, along with land, into property law. The concept of legal relationship pushed legal acts away from the foreground. Moreover, in seeking to locate these "legal relations" within a territorial legal system, Savigny seems to premise the existence of a coherent *legal system* for each state. This was probably the most important development.

From a technical point of view, what the preclassical jurists did was to examine the scope of statutes – first their personal, territorial, sometimes temporal scope, and eventually their scope in terms of subject matter. In this respect, their task *was* the interpretation of statutes and customs. They are thus different from the subsequent scholarship that will eventually try to move between *legal systems*, whereas its ancestors moved between legal rules. It is not the shift in method *per se* that is so important, as much as the fact that it represents major, as well as gradual, changes both in the *Weltanschauung* of conflicts writers and the structure of their legal thinking.

The change is *major* given the discursive power of concepts like *legal system* and the ethical premises involved in the classical choice-of-law paradigm. The change is also *gradual*, classical doctrine being the culmination of an effort started long before, in preclassical attempts to make abstract, general, even "value-neutral" categories out of "statutes" – in a way not encountered in what we have come to call "statutory interpretation" today. In comparing, with hindsight, Bartolus with Huber (who is less concerned about substantive results, and much more about evasion), we may discern the early steps of the long march to a classical paradigm which looks away from the policy of the statutes by fostering a category of (conflicts) norms clearly distinguishable from substantive law.

Preclassical conflicts doctrine, just like conflicts doctrine in general, but even more so, is steeped into the jurisprudential premises and argumentative techniques of its time. But there also seems to be some awareness of the distinct nature of the subject matter – in a hybrid manner, if compared with classical doctrine (hence the terms preclassical and classical). Furthermore, the "statutists" show awareness of – and identification with – a greater context. In a sense, they identify, although they are not explicit about it, as participants in "international" ("interlocal," "interstate") governance. This is another step toward the nineteenth century and legal classicism.

Preclassical writers did indeed enquire about the "legitimate spacious reach of statutes." But who was to determine this legitimacy? At the time of Bartolus, there was still the *ius commune* as a supposedly positive law from which the power of these statutes emanated. With the French jurists, there was royal power over and above the *coutumes*. With the Dutch, enlightened self-interest, and a republican power balance. In all cases, there was also a common law that bound together the laws of these polities. In short, local ("domestic") legislation tended to operate within certain jurisprudential bounds. Voet did note, at least as a rhetoric point, how defenseless preclassical conflict of laws would be against a "jealous" legislator or judge (*mordicus*), but only when the lawmaking power was unbound, was the rationality of the system truly put into question. In a world of legal positivism, jurists would have to salvage what they could. The early nineteenth-century jurists whom Dicey held out as adherents to the "positive method," such as Story, Foelix, and Wächter, opted for realism and forum positivism. The "theoretical" writers of the second half of the century embraced the utopia of a new paradigm and the construction of an international positivism.

Seen in this light, the declarations of François Laurent, in the spirit of Savigny and others in between, about bringing together Theory and Practice in the new science of private international law, gain new importance. Faced with the Leviathan, classical conflicts doctrine elaborated an autonomous jurisprudential milieu for the conflict of laws. Nineteenth-century jurists did solicit the aid of international law, but, imbued by their own positivist ideology, they sought to construct a truly common "private international law."

15.7 The Hedgehog and the Fox

In his essay on Tolstoy's historical skepticism, Isaiah Berlin draws on an epigram by the ancient Greek lyric poet Archilochus ("The fox knows many things, but the hedgehog knows one big thing") to draw a distinction between "hedgehogs" and "foxes":[35]

> For there exists a great chasm between those, on one side, who relate everything to a single central vision, one system, less or more coherent or articulate, in terms of which they understand, think and feel – a single, universal, organizing principle in terms of which alone all that they are and say has significance – and, on the other side, those who pursue many ends, often unrelated and even contradictory, connected, if at all, only in

[35] I. Berlin, "The Hedgehog and the Fox: An Essay on Tolstoy's View of History" in *The Proper Study of Mankind* (New York: Farrar, Straus and Giroux, 1997), 436–498.

> some *de facto* way, for some psychological or physiological cause, related to no moral or aesthetic principle. These last lead lives, perform acts and entertain ideas that are centrifugal rather centripetal; their thought is scattered or diffused, moving on many levels, seizing upon the essence of a vast variety of experiences and objects for what they are in themselves, without, consciously or unconsciously, seeking to fit them into, or exclude them from, any one unchanging, all-embracing, sometimes self-contradictory and incomplete, at times fanatical, unitary inner vision.[36]

Berlin warns that this dichotomy "like all over-simplifications of this type . . . becomes, if pressed, artificial, scholastic and ultimately absurd" but argues that like "all distinctions which embody any degree of truth, it offers a point of view from which to look and compare, a starting point for genuine investigation."[37] Berlin was concerned with the history of ideas, with literature as his main playground, but both his statements ring even more true for the study of doctrinal system-building in legal literature: Bartolus on the conflict of laws may look more like a fox, and Huber like a hedgehog, but any doctrinal system destined to survive the length of time requires both the attention to details, nuances, and contingencies and the exploration associated with the fox and the unifying vision associated with the hedgehog. The history of conflicts doctrine, with intellectual achievement meeting its match in the individual case or a reticent judge, may in fact be closer to what Archilochus himself probably meant: "the fox, for all its cunning, is defeated by the hedgehog's only defence."[38] But I would argue that there is a value in appropriating Berlin's distinction, as long as we understand it as embodying an *antinomy*, rather than an *antithesis* persisting in conflicts discourse.

Berlin's twin statement also rings true for the many attempts to conceive conflict of laws in terms of a binary opposition – between territorialists and personalists, universalists and particularists, conflictualists and internationalists, nationalists and internationalists. Each of these terms means different things to different authors – and readers – but there is "some truth" in them as long as we are aware of their limits. The conceptual maps they create might tell us a lot about both the history and the present sensibilities of conflicts doctrine. They can also have significant educative value. But, if taken too seriously, we may be unable to appreciate the many dimensions – and nuances – of the conflicts

[36] Ibid., 436–437.
[37] Ibid., 437.
[38] Ibid., 436.

discourse, as must have been demonstrated in this book. This is especially the case when it comes to early writings on conflicts issues: clearcut, "manichean" dichotomies may provide us with a starting point, but not with a reliable looking glass. Where their principal usefulness lies is in helping us understand the *tensions* through which the field is constituted.

This brings us to the other set of –isms, the ones about methodology. Conceptualism, eclecticism, empiricism, historicism. Understanding private international law requires evaluating both the reality on the ground and the theoretical aspirations of succeeding generations; an appreciation of the doctrinal sophistication of the conflicts discourse without succumbing to self-absorbed intellectualism (or elitism); an awareness of the close relationship with other legal subjects (especially those of private law and public international law), of the continuous need of our subject to be renovated by ideas, concepts, values developed elsewhere, while maintaining a certain intellectual (and value) autonomy.

To account for the dynamics of the field, we explored the idea of a triple "governance" function, unique to private international law.[39] We contrasted governance projects to doctrinal foundations, where grand theoretical ideas are incubated in order to support doctrinal solutions, rather than the opposite. We also considered the dialectic relationship between the global aspirations of doctrine and the local focus of practice. All these play out in the persistent, antinomic opposition between an external and an internal perspective.

Private international law discourse has indeed emerged through the tension generated by the *coexistence* of the two perspectives, and the different image and weight accorded to each by different theories. The evolution of the discourse could be, not without trepidation, compared with the balancing act involved in riding a mule. The mule-rider bends left, then right, and so on; he maintains his balance by bending a little bit,

[39] Having started with Savigny, the reader might excuse this final reference to his near-contemporary, Carl von Clausewitz: "War is more than a true chameleon that slightly adapts its characteristics to the given case. As a total phenomenon its dominant tendencies always make war a paradoxical trinity (*wunderliche Dreifaltigkeit*) ... These three tendencies are like three different codes of law, deep-rooted in their subject and yet variable in their relationship to one another. A theory that ignores any one of them or seeks to fix an arbitrary relationship between them would conflict with reality to such an extent that for this reason alone it would be totally useless. Our task therefore is to develop a theory that maintains a balance between these three tendencies.": C. von Clausewitz, *On War*, M. Howard and P. Paret (eds. and tr.) (Princeton: Princeton University Press, 1984), 89.

and not by standing straight, but should he bend too much in either direction he will fall. Private international law has accordingly struggled to maintain its balance by leaning toward either, or rather both, directions: the history of the conflict of laws shows the alternation of ideologies and emphases. Like the mule's walk, the process has been often slow, and sometimes painful. But what remains, what seems to have always been there, is the quest to achieve harmony through legal diversity and justice through formality, the use of the "external" level to bring peace to the "internal" – and a dialectics that stubbornly evolves.

BIBLIOGRAPHY

Primary Sources

Manuscripts

Bartolus da Sassoferrato. *Repetitio supra lege cunctos populos* [D.1.1.1]. Vatican City, Bibliotheca Apostolica Vaticana, MS Vat. Lat. 2589 fol. 68v–76v.

Original and Early Modern Printed Editions

Accursius. *[Corpus iuris civilis] commentariis Accursii, scholiis Contii, paratitlis Cuiacii. novae accesserunt ad ipsum Accursium Dionysii Gothofredi*. 1–6, Lyon: Horatius Cardon, 1604.

Corpus Iuris Civilis Iustinanianei cum Commentariis Accursii, Scholiis Conti, D. Gothofredi Lucubrationibus ad Accursium. 1–5, Lyon: 1627.

Alexander Tartagnus (Imolensis). *Consiliorum seu responsorum Libri VII*. Venice: 1610

d'Argentré, Bertrand. *Commentarii in patrias Britonum leges, seu Consuetudines generales antiquiss. Ducatus Britanniae*. 8th ed. Antwerp: 1664.

Azo. *Summa Azonis*. Venice: 1581.

Baldus. *Repertorium Lect. Baldi super Codice*. Lyon: 1539.

Commentaria in primum, secundum & tertium Codicis lib. Turin: 1576.

Commentaria in primam Digesti veteris partem. Venice: 1616.

Bartholomaeus a Saliceto, B. *Commentarii ad I, II, III, et IV Lib. Codicis*. Lyon: 1560.

Bartolus da Sassoferrato. *Commentarius super prima parte Codicis*. Lyon: 1533.

In Ius Universum Civile Commentaria. 1–6, 1562.

Omnia, quae extant, opera. 1–11, Venice: 1602.

Bouhier, J. *Histoire des commentateurs de la Coutume du Duché de Bourgogne*. Dijon: 1742.

Les coutumes du Duché de Bourgogne. 2 vols. Dijon: 1742–1746

Boullenois, L. *Questions sur les demissions de biens*. Paris: 1727.

Dissertations sur des Questions qui naissent de la contrarieté des loix et des coutumes. Paris: 1732.

Traité de la personnalité, et de la realité des loix, coutumes ou statuts. 2 vols. Paris: Guillaume Desprez, 1766.

Burgundus, N. *Ad consuetudines Flandriae aliarumque gentium tractatus controversiarum.* Antwerp: 1666.

Challine, P. *Méthode génerale pour l'intelligence des coustumes de France.* Paris: 1666.

Coquille, G. *Questions et responses sur les Articles des Coustumes de France.* Paris: 1644.

Dumouchet du Bac, P. *Traité sur les Questions Mixtes, ou Examen des Loix et Jurisdictions qu'on doit suivre pour décider les contestations entre les hommes de différentes Nations, de différentes Provinces, de différens Districts, &c.* Paris: 1787.

Froland, L. *Mémoires concernant l'observation du Senatusconsulte velléien dans le Duché de Normandie et diverses questions mixtes qui en dependent avec les arrests qui les ont decidées.* Paris: 1722.

Mémoires concernans la nature et la qualité des statuts; diverses questions mixtes de droit et de coutume, et la plupart des arrests qui les ont décidées. Paris: 1729.

Grotius (de Groot), H. *De Iure Belli ac Pacis.* Paris: Apud Nicolaum Buon, 1625.

Inleiding tot de Hollandsche Rechtsgeleerdheid. Middelburg: Pieter Gillissen, 1767.

Huber, U. *Heedensdaegse Rechtsgeleertheyt, Soo elders, als in Frieslandt gebruikelyt.* Leuwarden: 2 vols. 1686.

Praelectionum Juris Civilis Pars Prior, Quae est secondum Institutiones, Justinianaeas. vol. 1. Franeker: 1687.

Praelectiones Juris Civilis. vol. 1. Franeker: 1690.

Beginselen der Hedendaegse Rechtskunde, so eelders als in Frieslandt gebruik. 2nd ed. Leeuwarden: Nauta, 1696.

Beginselen der Rechtskunde gebruikelijk in Friesland, 2nd ed. Leeuwarden: 1696.

Digressiones Justinianeae. 3rd ed. Franeker: 1696.

De Jure Civitatis, Libri Tres. 4th ed. Franeker: 1698.

Praelectionum Juris Romani et Hodierni pars II Que ad Libros 21 priores Pandectarum. 2nd ed. vol. 2. Franeker: 1700.

Praelectionum Juris Civilis Tomi III. Leipzig: 1735.

Heedensdaegse Rechtsgeleertheyt, Soo elders, als in Frieslandt gebruikelyt. 4th ed. Amsterdam: Johannes Rotterdam, 1742.

Heedensdaegse Rechtsgeleertheyt, Soo elders, als in Frieslandt gebruikelyt. 5th ed. Amsterdam: 1768.

Jacobus (de Arena). *Commentarii in universum Ius Civile.* 1541.

Molineaus (Dumoulin), C. *Omnia quae extant opera.* vols. 1–4. Paris: Apud viduam Gervasii Alliot & Antonium Clement, 1558.

Omnia quae extant opera. vols. 1–5. Paris: Ioannes Guignard, 1581.

Odofredus. *Lectura super Codice.* Lyon: 1602.

Rodenburgius, C. *Tractatus de jure conjugum ... cum tractatione praeliminari de jure, quod oritur ex statutorum, vel consuetudinum discripantium conflictu,* Köln: 1699.

Sande, I. *Decisiones Frisicae, sive Rerum in Suprema Frisiorum Curia Iudicatarum, Libri V.* Leeuwarden: 1638.

Van der Linden, J. *Regtsgeleerd, practicaal en koopmans handbook.* Amsterdam: Johannes Allart, 1806.

Vattel, E. *Le droit des gens, ou des principes de la loi naturelle, appliquées à la conduite et aux affaires des Nations et des Souverains.* vol. 1. London: 1758.

Voet, J. *Commentarius ad Pandectas. In quo praeter Romani juris principia ac controversias illustriores, jus etiam hodiernum, & praecipuae fori quaestiones excutiuntur.* vol. 1. The Hague: 1698–1704.

Voet, P. *De statutis, eorumque concursu, liber singularis.* Amsterdam: 1661.

De statutis, eorumque concursu, liber singularis (Nova Editio Auctior & Correctior). Brussels: 1715.

Modern Era Editions

Barry, Andrew. *Bartolus, ad C.1.1.1* Available online at www.law.harvard.edu/faculty/cdonahue/courses/lhsemclh/RdgsDownloads/BartolConflFormatted.pdf

Bonolis, G. *Questioni di diritto internazionale in alcuni consigli inediti di Baldo degli Ubaldi: Testo e commento.* Pisa: E. Spoerri, 1908.

Guthrie, W. *Friedrich Carl von Savigny: A Treatise on the Conflict of Laws.* 2nd ed. Edinburgh: T. & T. Clark, 1880, 433–452 (Bartolus), 452–461 (Molinaeus), 462–508 (P. Voet), 508–516 (Huber).

Hänel, M. (ed.). *Dissensiones dominorum sive controversiae veterum iuris Romani interpretum qui glossatores vocantur.* Leipzig: 1843.

Meijers, E. M. *Tractatus duo de vi et potestate statutorum.* Haarlem: H. D. Tjeenk Willink & zoon, 1939.

Translations

Ancel, B. "Le commentaire de Bartole ad legem cunctos populos sure la glosse quod si bononiensis" in B. Ancel (ed.), *Élements d'histoire du droit international privé.* Paris: Panthéon Assas, 2017, 165–187.

"La Lectura de Balde sur Cunctos Populos" in B. Ancel (ed.), *Élements d'histoire du droit international privé.* Paris: Panthéon Assas, 2017, 188–204.

"Charles Dumoulin, Conclusions sur les Statuts et coutumes locaux" in B. Ancel (ed.), *Élements d'histoire du droit international privé.* Paris: Panthéon Assas, 2017, 241–251.

"Bertrand d'Argentré, Commentaire de la Coutume de Bretagne" in B. Ancel (ed.), *Élements d'histoire du droit international privé.* Paris: Panthéon Assas, 2017, 254–281.

"Ulrich Huber, Du conflits des lois différentes dans des États différents" in B. Ancel (ed.), *Élements d'histoire du droit international privé.* Paris: Panthéon Assas, 2017, 341–351.

"Jean Voet, De Statutis" in B. Ancel (ed.), *Élements d'histoire du droit international privé.* Paris: Panthéon Assas, 2017, 354–385.

"Johann Nikolaus Hert, De Collisione Legum" in B. Ancel (ed.), *Élements d'histoire du droit international privé.* Paris: Panthéon Assas, 2017, 387–406.

Beale, J. H. *Bartolus on the Conflict of Laws.* Cambridge, MA: Harvard University Press, 1914.

P. Birks and G. McLeod. *Justinian's Institutes.* Ithaca, NY: Cornell University Press, 1987.

Clarence Smith, J. A. "Bartolo on the Conflict of Laws." *American Journal of Legal History* 14 (1970), 157–183, 247–275.

Frier, B. W. (ed.). *The Codex of Justinian.* 3 vols. Cambridge: Cambridge University Press, 2016.

Gane, P. *Huber's The Jurisprudence of My Time (Heedensdaegse Rechtsgeleertheyt).* Trans. P. Gane. 2 vols. Durban: Butterworth & Co. (Africa) Ltd., 1939.

The Selective Voet; being the Commentary on the Pandects, Paris edition of 1829, and the Supplement to that work by Johannes van der Linden. 8 vols. Durban: Butterworth, 1955.

Llewellyn Davies, D. J. "The Influence of Huber's De Conflictu Legum on English Private International Law." *British Yearbook of International Law* 18 (1937), 49–63.

Lorenzen, E. G. "Huber's De Conflictu Legum." *Illinois Law Review* 13 (1919), 401–418.

Neff, S. *Hugo Grotius On the Law of War and Peace (Student Edition).* Cambridge: Cambridge University Press, 2012.

Tuck R. (ed.). *Hugo Grotius: The Rights of War and Peace.* 3 vols. Indianapolis: Liberty Fund, 2005.

Valladão, H. *Beale, Bartolo: Conflito de leis.* Rio de Janeiro: Estabel. Graph. Canton & Reile, 1938.

Ulrik Huber, Conflito de leis. Rio de Janeiro: 1951.

Watson, A. *The Digest of Justinian*, rev. ed. 4 vols. Philadelphia: University of Pennsylvania Press, 1998.

Secondary Sources

Ailes, E. H. "Substance and Procedure in the Conflict of Laws." *Michigan Law Review* 39 (1941), 392–418.

Ancel, B. *Les conflits de qualifications à l'épreuve de la donation entre époux.* Paris: Dalloz, 1977.

"Review of P. Dominguez Lozano, Las circunstancias personales determinantes de la vinculación con el derecho local. Estudio sobre el derecho local altomedieval y el derecho local de Aragón, Navarra y Cataluña (Madrid, 1988)." *Revue critique de droit international privé* 79 (1990), 238–241.

Histoire du droit international privé. Paris: Panthéon Assas Paris II, 2008.

"Le commentaire de Bartole ad legem Cunctos populos sur la glosse Quod si Bononiensis mis en français" in B. d'Alteroche (ed.), *Mélanges en l'honneur d'Anne Lefebvre-Teillard*. Paris: Editions Panthéon-Assas, 2009.

Éléments d'histoire du droit international privé. Paris: Panthéon Assas Paris II, 2017.

Anton, A. *Private International Law*. Edinburgh: W. Green & Son, 1967.

Armstrong, L. and Kirshner, J. (eds.). *The Politics of Law in Late Medieval and Renaissance Italy*. Toronto: Toronto University Press, 2011.

Asser, T. M. C. "Droit international privé et droit uniforme." *Revue de droit international et de législation comparée* 12 (1880), 5–22.

Eléments de droit international privé ou du conflit de lois. Trans. A. Rivier. Paris: 1884.

Audit, B. *La fraude à la loi*. Paris: Dalloz, 1974.

"A Continental Lawyer Looks at American Choice-of-law Principles." *American Journal of Comparative Law* 27 (1979), 589–603.

"Le caractère fonctionnel de la règle de conflit." *Recueil des cours* 186 (1984), 220–397.

"Le droit international privé en quête d'universalité (cours général)." *Recueil des cours* 305 (2001), 9–487.

Droit international privé. 4th ed. Paris: Economica, 2006.

Audit, M. "L'intérpretation autonome du droit international privé Communautaire." *Clunet* 130 (2004), 789–816.

Aynès, L., Gautier, P. Y., and Terré, F. "Antithèse de 'l'entité' (à propos d'une opinion sur la doctrine)." *Dalloz* (1997), 229–230.

Baker, J. H. *An Introduction to English Legal History*. 5th ed. Oxford: Oxford University Press, 2019.

Ballarino, T. *Diritto Intenazionale Privato*. 3rd ed. Padova: CEDAM, 1999.

Banu, R. *Nineteenth-Century Perspectives on Private International Law*. Oxford: Oxford University Press, 2018.

Bar, L. V. *Internationales Privat- und Strafrecht*. Hannover: Hahn'sche Hofbuchhandlung, 1862.

Theorie und Praxis des Internationalen Privatrechts. vol. 1. Hannover: Hahn'sche Hofbuchhandlung, 1889.

Barde, L. *Théorie traditionnelle des Statuts – ou Principes du droit réel et du statut personnel d'après le droit civil français*. Bordeaux: J. Pechade, 1880.

Barile, G. "La fonction historique du droit international privé." *Recueil des cours* 116 (1965), 305–376.

Barnich, L. "Le lieu des actes juridiques: paradigme perdu de droit international privé." Unpublished dissertation, Free University of Brussels, 2000.

Les actes juridiques en droit international privé. Brussels: Bruylant, 2001.

Barry, A. "Bartolus on the Conflict of Laws." Unpublished third-year (J.D.) paper, Harvard Law School, 1998.

Barry, H. "Comity." *Virginia Law Review* 12 (1926), 353–375.

Bartin, É. "De l'impossibilité d'arriver à la suppression définitive des conflits de lois." *Clunet* 25 (1897), 225–255, 466–495, 720–738.

"Les dispositions d'ordre public. La théorie de la fraude à la loi, et l'idée de la communauté internationale." *Revue de droit international et de législation comparée* 29 (1897), 385–427, 613–658.

"Les conflits entre dispositions législatives de droit international privé: Théorie du renvoi." *Revue de droit international et de législation comparée* 30 (1898), 129–187, 272–320.

Bartin, E. A. *Principes de droit international privé selon la loi et la jurisrpudence françaises*. vol. 1. Paris: Domat-Montchrestien 1930.

Basile, M. et al. *Lex Mercatoria and Legal Pluralism: A Late Thirteenth-Century Treatise and Its Aftermath*. Cambridge, MA: The Ames Foundation, 1998.

Baszkiewicz, J. "Quelques remarques sur la conception de dominium mundi dans l'oeuvre de Bartolus" in U. D. Perugia (ed.), *Bartolo Da Sassoferrato: Studi E Documenti Per Il VI Centenario*. Milan: Giuffrè, 1962.

Batiffol, H. *Les conflits de lois en matière de contrats: Etude de droit international privé comparé*. Paris: Recueil Sirey, 1938.

Traité élémentaire de droit international privé. Paris: LGDJ, 1949.

Aspects philosophiques du droit international privé. Paris: Dalloz, 1956.

"Observations sur les liens de la compétence judiciaire et de la compétence legislative" in H. Batiffol (ed.), *De Conflictu Legum: Essays Presented to Roeland Duco Kollewijn & Johannes Offerhaus at Their Seventieth Birthday*. Leiden: A. W. Sijthoff, 1962, 55–66.

"Le pluralisme des méthodes en droit international privé." *Recueil des cours* 139 (1973), 75–148.

Batiffol, H. and Lagarde, P. *Droit international privé*. 8th ed. vol. 1. Paris: LGDJ, 1993.

Baty, T. *Polarized Law*. London: Stevens and Haynes, 1914.

Bayly, C. A. *The Birth of the Modern World, 1780–1914: Global Connections and Comparisons*. Oxford: Blackwell, 2004.

Beale, J. H. *A Treatise on the Conflict of Laws*. 3 vols. New York: Baker, Voorhis & Co., 1935.

Bederman, D. *International Law in Antiquity*. Cambridge: Cambridge University Press, 2001.

Behn, M. *Die Entstehungsgeschichte der einseitigen Kollisionsnormen des EGBGB*. Frankfurt: Haag & Herchen, 1980.

Bellomo, M. *Ricerche sui rapporti patrimoniali tra coniugi: contributo alla storia della famiglia medievale*. Milan: Giuffré, 1961.

Bentham, J. *An Introduction to the Principles of Morals and Legislation*. reprint of 1823 ed. Oxford: Clarendon Press, 1879.

Bentwich, N. "Le développement récent du principe du domicile en droit anglais." *Recueil des cours* 49 (1934), 377–465.

Berlin, I. (ed.). "The Hedgehog and the Fox: An Essay on Tolstoy's View of History" in *The Proper Study of Mankind*. New York: Farrar, Straus & Giroux, 1997, 436–498.

Bezemer, C. H. *Les répétitions de Jacques de Révigny: recherches sur la répétition comme forme d'enseignement juridique et comme genre littéraire, suivies d'un inventaire des textes*. Leiden: E. J. Brill/Leiden University Press, 1987.

Birks, P. and McLeod, G. "Introduction" in P. Birks and G. McLeod (eds.), *Justinian's Institutes*. Ithaca, NY: Cornell University Press, 1987, 7–28.

Bisping, C. "Avoid the Statutist Trap: The International Scope of the Consumer Credit Act 1974." *Journal of Private International Law* 8 (2012), 35–62.

Blagojević, B. "Théories des statuts à la lumière de l'histoire générale de l'évolution de la société" in *De Conflictu Legum: Essays Presented to Roeland Duco Kollewijn & Johannes Offerhaus At Their Seventieth Birthday*. Leiden: A. W. Sijthoff, 1962, 67–81.

Boden, D. "L'ordre public: limite et condition de la tolérance: Recherches sur le pluralisme juridique." Unpublished dissertation, University of Paris I, 2002.

Bogdan, M. "Private International Law as Component of the Law of the Forum : General Course on Private International Law." *Recueil des cours* 348 (2011), 9–252.

Boggiano, A. *Derecho Internacional Privado*. vol. 1. Buenos Aires: LexisNexis, 2006.

Bonnichon, A. "La notion de conflit des souverainetés dans la science des conflits des lois." *Revue critique de droit international privé* 38 (1949), 615–635, 39 (1950), 11–32

Boosfeld, K. "Die beiden Statutenlehren: Geschichte eines rechthistorischen Missverständnisses." *Zeitschrift der Savigny-Stiftung für Rechtsgeschichte (Germanistische Abteilung)* 136 (2019), 76–93.

Borchers, P. "The Internationalization of Contractual Conflicts Law." *Vanderbilt Journal of Transnational Law* 28 (1995), 421–486.

Boüard, A. D. *Manuel de diplomatie française et pontificale, vol. II: Actes privés*. Paris: Picard, 1948.

Boucher, C. "La conférence des avocats et le droit international privé au XVIIIe siècle." *Clunet* 63 (1935), 45–58.

Breschi, B. "Alcune osservationi sul contributo recato da Bartolo alla teoria degli statute" in U. D. Perugia (ed.), *Bartolo Da Sassoferrato: Studi E Documenti Per Il VI Centenario*. Milan: Giuffrè, 1962, 49–59.

Brilmayer, L. "Post-modernism in American Choice of Law" in J. Erauw (ed.), *Liber Memorialis François Laurent*. Brussels: E. Story-Scientia, 1989, 695–705.

Conflict of Laws. 2nd ed. Boston: Little Brown, 1995.

"The Role of Substantive and Choice of Law Policies in the Formation and Application of Choice of Law Rules." *Recueil des cours* (1995), 9–111.

Brundage, J. *Law, Sex and Christian Society in Medieval Europe*. Chicago/London: University of Chicago Press, 1987.

Bucher, A. "Vers l'adoption de la méthode des intérêts ? Réflexions à la lumière des codifications récentes." *Travaux du Comité français de droit international privé* 12 (1993), 209–237.

Bucher, A. and Bonomi, A. *Droit International Privé*. Basel: Helbing Lichtenhahn, 2001.

Buckland, W. W. *A Text-Book of Roman Law*. 3rd ed. Cambridge: Cambridge University Press, 1963.

Buzan, B. and Little, R. *International Systems in World History*. Oxford: Oxford University Press, 2000.

Caglioni, D. "'Regnativa prudentia.' Diritto e teologia nel 'Tractatus testimoniorum' bartoliano" in D. Caglioni (ed.), *Théologie Et Droit Dans La Science Politique De L'état Modern*. Rome: École française de Rome, 1991, 155–170.

Calasso, F. *Medio Evo del diritto*. Milan: Giuffré, 1954.

"Bartolo da Sassoferrato." *Annali di storia del diritto* 9 (1965), 472–520.

Callé, P. *L'acte public en droit international privé*. Paris: Economica, 2004.

Calvo Caravaca, A.-L. and Carrascosa González, J. *Derecho Internacional Privado*. 6th ed. Granada: Comares, 2005.

Canning, J. *The Political Thought of Baldus de Ubaldis*. Cambridge: Cambridge University Press, 1987.

"Introduction: politics, institutions and ideas" in J. H. Burns (ed.), *The Cambridge History of Medieval Political Thought*. Cambridge: Cambridge University Press, 1988.

Ideas of Power in the Late Middle Ages 1296–1417. Cambridge: Cambridge University Press, 2011.

Cassesse, A. "Remarks on Scelle's Theory of "Role Splitting" (dédoublement fonctionnel) in International Law." *European Journal of International Law* 1 (1990), 210–231.

Castel, J.-G. *Droit international privé québécois*. Toronto: Butterworths, 1988.

Catellani, E. L. *Il diritto internazionale privato e il suoi recenti progressi*. vol. I, 2nd ed. Turin: Stamperia dell'Unione Tipografico-Editrice, 1895.

Cavers, D. "A Critique of the Choice-of-Law Problem." *Harvard Law Review* 47 (1933), 173–208.

Cesar, F. J. "Popular Autonomy and Imperial Power in Bartolus of Saxoferrato: An Intrinsic Connection." *Journal of the History of Ideas* 65 (2004), 369–381.

Chavannes, R. D. "E. M. Meijers and the Recodification of the Dutch Civil Code after World War II." Unpublished paper, University of Oxford, 1997.

Checchini, A. "Presupposti giuridici dell'evoluzione storica dalla 'Bartoliana' teoria degli statuti al moderno diritto internazionale private" in U. D. Perugia (ed.), *Bartolo Da Sassoferrato: Studi E Documenti Per Il VI Centenario*. Milan: Giuffrè, 1962, 61–105.

Clarence Smith, J. A. "Bartolo on the Conflict of Laws." *American Journal of Legal History* 14 (1970), 157–183, 247–275.

Medieval Law Teachers and Writers, Civilians and Canonists. Ottawa: University of Ottawa Press, 1975.

Clermont, K. and Palmer, J. "French Article 14 Jurisdiction, Viewed from the United States." *Cornell Law Faculty Publications* 13 (2004).

Collier, J. *Conflict of Laws.* Cambridge: Cambridge University Press, 2001.

Collins, H. *The Law of Contract.* 4th ed. London: Butterworths, 2003.

Collins, L. (ed.). *Dicey, Morris and Collins on the Conflict of Laws.* London: Sweet & Maxwell, 2012.

Collins, R. *The Sociology of Philosophies: A Global Theory of Intellectual Change.* Cambridge, MA: Harvard University Press, 1998.

Condorelli, O. "Bartolo e il diritto canonico" in C. Tudertina (ed.), *Bartolo Da Sassoferrato Nel Vii Centenario Della Nascita: Diritto, Politica, Società (Atti Del L Convegno Storico Internazionale, Todi–Perugia, 13–16 Ottobre 2013).* Spoleto: Fondazione Centro Italiano di Studi sul Basso Medioevo, 2014, 463–557.

Copolla, G. "Nascita e declino dell'adagio 'nemo pro parte testatus pro parte intestatus decedere potest'." *Teoría e Storia del Diritto Privato* 5 (2012), 1–172.

Cornu, G. *Droit civil: Introduction au droit.* 12th ed. Paris: LGDJ, 2005.

Courbe, P. *Droit international privé.* Paris: Armand Colin, 2000.

Currie, B. "Married Women's Contracts: A Study In Conflict-of-Laws Method." *University of Chicago Law Review* 25 (1958), 227–268.

Dawson, J. *The Oracles of the Law.* Ann Arbor: University of Michigan Law School, 1968.

de Nova, R. "A Historical and Comparative Introduction to the Conflict of Laws (General Course." *Recueil des cours* 118 (1966), 443–622.

de Vries, J. and van der Woude, A. *The First Modern Economy: Success, Failure, and Perseverance of the Dutch Economy, 1500–1815.* Cambridge: Cambridge University Press, 1997.

Delaume, G.-R. *Les conflits de lois à la veille du Code civil: Contribution à l'histoire du droit international privé français.* Paris: Sirey, 1947.

Les conflits de lois à la veille du Code civil dans les traités diplomatiques. Paris: Sirey, 1948.

Demangeat, C. *Histoire de la condition civile des étrangers en France dans l'ancien et dans le nouveau droit.* Paris: 1844.

Despagnet, F. *Précis de droit international privé.* 5th ed. Paris: Sirey, 1909.

Dhont, F. "'L'histoire, Parole Vivante Du Droit?' François Laurent En Ernest Nys Als Historiografen Van Het Volkenrecht" in B. Debaenst (ed.), *De Belle Époque Van Het Belgisch Recht.* Brugge: die Keure, 2016, 91–115.

Diago Diago, M. del P. *Pactos o Capitulaciones Matrimoniales en Derecho Internacional Privado.* Zaragoza: El Justicia de Aragón, 1999.

Dicey, A. V. *The Law of Domicil as a Branch of the Law of England Stated in the Form of Rules*. London: Stevens & Sons, 1879.

A Digest of the Law of England with Reference to the Conflict of Laws. London: Stevens & Sons, 1896.

Dniestranski, S. *Zur Geschichte und Theorie des internationalen Privatrechts*. Vienna: M. Perles, 1929.

Dodge, W. S. "Extraterritoriality and Conflict-of-Laws Theory: An Argument for Judicial Unilateralism." *Harvard International Law Journal* 39 (1988), 101–169.

Domingo, R. *The New Global Law*. Cambridge: Cambridge University Press, 2010.

Dominguez Lozano, P. *Las circunstancias personales determinantes de la vinculación con el derecho local. Estudio sobre el derecho local altomedieval y el derecho local de Aragón, Navarra y Cataluña*. Madrid: Ediciones de la Universidad Autónoma de Madrid, 1988.

Donahue, C. "Medieval and Early Modern Lex mercatoria: An Attempt at the probatio diabolica." *Chicago Journal of International Law* (2004), 21–37.

Donahue, C., Jr. "What Causes Fundamental Legal Ideas? Marital Property in England and France in the Thirteenth Century." *Michigan Law Review* 78 (1979), 59–88.

Why the History of Canon Law Is Not Written. London: Selden Society, 1986.

"Ius Commune, Canon Law and Common Law in England." *Tulane Law Review* 66 (1992), 1745–1780.

"Jus in the Subjective Sense in Roman Law: Reflections on Villey and Tierney" in C. Donahue Jr. (ed.), *A Ennio Cortese*. Rome: Il Cigno Edizioni, 2001, 506–535.

"Private Law without the State and during Its Formation." *American Journal of Comparative Law* 56 (2008), 541–566.

Law, Marriage, and Society in the Later Middle Ages. Cambridge: Cambridge University Press, 2009.

Drucker, A. "Soviet Views on Private International Law." *International and Comparative Law Quarterly* 4 (1955), 384–389.

du Plessis, P. and Cairns, J. (eds.). *Reassessing Legal Humanism and Its Claims: Petere Fontes?* Edinburgh: Edinburgh University Press, 2015.

Edwards, A. B. "The Appeal to Ex Aequo et Bono in the Seventeenth to Eighteenth Century Conflict of Laws." *Fundamina* 2 (1996), 261–284.

Ehlrich, E. "Internationales Privatrecht." *Deutsche Rundschau* 126 (1906), 419–433.

"Les tendances actuelles du droit international privé." *Revue de droit international privé* 4 (1908), 902–924.

Ehrenzweig, A. A. "The Transient Rule of Personal Jurisdiction: The "Power" Myth and Forum Conveniens." *Yale Law Journal* 65 (1956), 289–314.

"Beale's Translation of Bartolus." *American Journal of Comparative Law* 12 (1963), 384–385.

Elden, S. *The Birth of Territory*. Chicago: University of Chicago Press, 2013.

Elhoueiss, J.-L. "Personnalité et territorialité en droit international privé." Unpublished dissertation, Paris II Panthéon-Assas University, 2000.

Engdahl, D. E. "English Marriage Conflicts Law before the Time of Bracton." *American Journal of Comparative Law* 15 (1966), 109–135.

"The Canonical and Metaphysical Background of the Classic Dutch Marriage Conflicts Rule." *Nederlands Tijdschrift voor International Recht* 15 (1968), 42–67.

"'Full Faith and Credit' in Merrie Olde England: New Insight for Marriage Conflicts Law from the Thirteenth Century." *Valparaiso University Law Review* 5 (1970), 1–25.

Epstein, S. *Wills and Wealth in Medieval Genoa, 1150–1250*. Cambridge, MA: Harvard University Press, 1984.

Erasmus, H. J. "Natural Law: Voet's Criticism of De Groot." *Fundamina* 22 (2016), 40–52.

Ercole, F. "L'istituto dotale nella pratica e nella legislazione statutaria dell'Italia superiore." *Rivista italiana per le scienze giuridiche* 45–46 (1908), 191–302.

"Impero universale e Stati particolari: la 'civitas sibi princeps' e lo Stato modern" in F. Ercole (ed.), *Da Bartolo All'Althusio: Saggi Sulla Storia Del Pensiero Pubblicistico Del Rinascimento Italiano*. Florence: Vallechi, 1932, 49–156.

"L'origine francese della formola Bartoliana 'civitas superiore, non recognoscens est sibi princeps" in F. Ercole (ed.), *Da Bartolo All'Althusio: Saggi Sulla Storia Del Pensiero Pubblicistico Del Rinascimento Italiano*. Florence: Vallechi, 1932, 157–217.

Farrely, M. "The New Italian School of International Law." *Juridical Review* 5 (1893), 105–124, 197.

Fassbender, B. and Peters, A. (eds.). *Oxford Handbook of the History of International Law*. Oxford: Oxford University Press, 2012.

Fassberg, C. W. "The Choice-of-Law Problem: Continuity and Change." Unpublished S.J.D. dissertation, Harvard University, 1982.

Fawcett, J. and Carruthers, J. M. *Cheshire, North & Fawcett: Private International Law*. 14th ed. Oxford: Oxford University Press, 2008.

Feenstra, R. *Bibliografie van hoogleraren in de rechten aan de Franeker Universiteit tot 1811*. Amsterdam: Royal Netherlands Academy of Arts and Sciences, 2003.

Fentiman, R. "Domicile Revisited." *Cambridge Law Journal* 50 (1991), 445–463.

"Choice of Law in Europe: Uniformity and Integration." *Tulane Law Review* 82 (2008), 2022–2051.

International Commercial Litigation. 2nd ed. Oxford: Oxford University Press, 2015.

Figgis, J. N. "Bartolus and the Development of European Political Ideas." *Transactions of the Royal Historical Society (n.s.)* 19 (1905), 147–168.

Figueira, R. "Glossa Ordinaria: Roman Law" in C. Kleinherz (ed.), *Medieval Italy: An Encyclopedia*. New York: Routledge, 2004, 437–439.

Fliniaux, A. "Le manuscrit 141 de la Bibliothèque municipale d'Avranches et le problème de l'introduction en France au Moyen-âge de texte des compilations du justinien" in A. Fliniaux (ed.), *Atti De Congresso Internazionale Di Diritto Romano (Bologna Et Roma, 17–28 Aprile 1934*. Pavia: Tip. successori F.lli Fusi, 1934, 313–327.

Foignet, R. *Manuel élémentaire de droit international privé à l'usage des étudiants en droit et des candidats aux carrières diplomatique et consulaire*. 2nd ed. Paris: Arthur Rousseau, 1909.

Forsyth, C. "The Value of the Comparative Ethos to the Judicial Process in the Conflict of Laws" in C. Visser (ed.), *Essays in Honour of Ellison Kahn*. Cape Town: Juta, 1989, 151–172.

Private International Law. 5th ed. Cape Town: Juta, 2012.

Foster, J. "La théorie anglaise du droit international privé." *Recueil des cours* 65 (1938), 399–557.

Francescakis, P. *La théorie du renvoi et les conflits de systèmes en droit international privé*. Paris: Sirey, 1958.

"Quelques précisions sur les 'lois d'application immédiate' et leurs rapports avec les règles de conflits de lois." *Revue critique de droit international privé* 55 (1966), 1–18.

Frankenstein, E. *Internationales Privatrecht (Grenzrecht)*. vol. 1. Berlin: Rothschild, 1926.

Franzina, P. "Bartolus" in J. Basedow, G. Rühl, and F. Ferrari (eds.), *Encyclopedia of Private International Law*. Cheltenham: Edward Elgar, 2017, 158–163.

Gamillscheg, F. *Der Einfluss Dumoulins auf die Entwicklung des Kollisionsrechts*. Berlin–Tübingen: Walter de Gruyter–J. C. B. Mohr, 1955.

"Überlegungen zum Text und zur kollisionsrechtslichen Methode bei Bartolus" in O. Behrends et al. (eds.), *Festschrift Für Franz Wieacker Zum 70*. Göttingen: Geburtstag, Vandenhoeck und Ruprecht, 1978, 235–235.

Garcimartín Alvarez, F. J. "Regulatory Competition: A Private International Law Approach." *European Journal of Law and Economics* 8 (1999), 251–270.

Garlati, L. "Women's Succession from the Middle Ages to the Modern Era" in M. G. di Renzo Villata (ed.), *Succession Law, Practice and Society in Europe Across the Centuries*. Cham: Springer, 2018, 207–230.

Garnett, R. *Substance and Procedure in Private International Law*. Oxford: Oxford University Press, 2012.

Gaudemet-Tallon, H. *Récherches sur les origines de l'article 14 du Code Civil*. Paris: PUF, 1964.

"Le pluralisme en droit international privé: richesses et faiblesses." *Recueil des cours* 312 (2005), 9–488.

Getman-Pavlova, I. "The History of Private International Law: The Theory of Belgian Realism in the 16th Century." *Sociology International Journal* 2 (2018), 431–437.

Geuss, R. *Morality, Culture and History*. Cambridge: Cambridge University Press, 1999.

Giddens, A. *The Consequences of Modernity*. Stanford: Stanford University Press, 1991.

Runaway World: How Globalization Is Reshaping Our Lives. London: Routledge, 2002.

Gillis, J. R. *For Better, For Worse: British Marriages, 1600 to Present*. Oxford: Oxford University Press, 1985.

Gilmore, M. P. *Argument from Roman Law in Political Thought*. Cambridge, MA: Harvard University Press, 1941.

Giuliani, A. "Una nota sul bartolismo" in C. Tudertina (ed.), *Bartolo Da Sassoferrato Nel VII Centenario Della Nascita: Diritto, Politica, Società (Atti del L Convegno Storico Internazionale, Todi–Perugia, 13–16 Ottobre 2013)*. Spoleto: Fondazione Centro Italiano di Studi sul Basso Medioevo, 2014, 585–600.

Glenn, H. P. "The Nationalist Heritage" in P. Legrand and R. Munday (eds.), *Comparative Legal Studies: Traditions and Transitions*. Cambridge: Cambridge University Press, 2003, 76–127.

Goldschmidt, W. *Sistema y Filosofia del Derecho Internacional Privado*. 2nd ed. vol. 1. Buenos Aires: Ediciones Jurídicas Europa-América, 1951.

Gordley, J. *The Philosophical Origins of Modern Contract Doctrine*. Oxford: Oxford University Press, 1991.

Gothot, P. "Le renouveau de la tendance unilatéraliste en droit international privé." *Revue critique de droit international privé* 60 (1971), 1–36, 209–243, 415.

"La méthode unilatéraliste face au droit international privé des contrats." *Travaux du Comité français de droit international privé* (1979), 201–232.

"La place d'Henri Batiffol dans la doctrine." *Travaux du Comité français de droit international privé* 11 (1994), 21–31.

Grewe, W. G. *The Epochs of International Law*. Trans. M. Byers. Berlin: De Gruyter, 2000.

Gruber-Magitot, S. *Les conflits de coutumes en matière de contrats dans la jurisprudence des Parlements: de Dumoulin au Code Civil*. Paris: PUF, 1980.

Guterman, S. L. "The Principle of the Personality of Law in the Early Middle Ages: A Chapter in the Evolution of Western Legal Institutions and Ideas." *University of Miami Law Review* 21 (1966), 259–348.

Gutzwiller, M. "Le développement historique du droit international privé." *Recueil des cours* 29 (1929), 287–400.

"Internationales Privatrecht" in R. Stammler (ed.), *Das Gesamte Deutsche Recht in Systematischer Darstellung*. Berlin: 1931, 1511–1661.

"Das Internationalprivatrecht der Haager Konferenzen: Vergangenheit und Zukunft." *Annuaire suisse de droit international* 2 (1945), 48–68.

"Aus den Anfängen des zwischenstaatlichen Erbrechts: ein Gutachten des Petrus Baldus de Ubaldis um 1375" in M. Gutzwiller (ed.), *Zum Schweizerischen Erbrecht: Festschrift Zum 70.* Zurich: Geburtstag Von Peter Tuor, Polygraphischer Verlag, 1946, 145–178.

70 Jahre Jurisprudenz: Erinnerungen eines Neunzigjährigen. Neuauflage anlässlich des 100. Geburtstags von Max Gutzwiller. Basel: Helbing & Lichtenhahn, 1989.

Halpérin, J.-L. *Histoire du droit privé français depuis 1804.* Paris: PUF, 1996.

Entre Nationalisme Juridique et Communauté du Droit. Paris: PUF, 1999.

Harding, M. *Conflict of Laws.* 4th ed. Abingdon: Routledge, 2014.

Harrison, F. "Le droit international privé ou le conflit des lois au point de vue analytique, particulièrement en Angleterre." *Clunet* 7 (1880), 533–551.

On Jurisprudence and the Conflict of Laws. Oxford: Clarendon Press, 1919.

Hartwieg, O. and Korkisch, F. *Die geheimen Materialen zur Kodifikation des deutschen Internationalen Privatrechts 1881–1896.* Tübingen: Mohr Siebeck, 1973.

Hatzimihail, N. E. "Prehistorical Private International Law."

"On Mapping the Conceptual Battlefield of Private International Law." *Hague Yearbook of Private International Law* 13 (2000), 57–64.

"Pages of History: Friedrich Juenger and the Historical Consciousness of Modern Private International Law" in L. Pereznieto Castro, T. Treves, and F. Seatzu (eds.), *Tradition and Innovation of Private International Law At the Beginning of the Third Millennium: Liber in Memoriam of Professor Friedrich K. Juenger.* Hunington, NY: Juris Publishing, 2006, 81–123.

"Bartolus on the Conflict of Laws." *Revue hellénique de droit international* 60 (2007), 11–79.

"The Many Lives – and Faces – of Lex Mercatoria: History as Genealogy in International Business Law." *Law & Contemporary Problems* 71 (2008), 169–190.

"Genealogies of lex mercatoria" in N. E. Hatzimihail (ed.), *In Studies in Memoriam of Professor Anthony M. Antapassis.* Athens: Ant.N.Sakkoulas, 2013, 311–351.

"Reflections on the International Dimension of Private International Law" in R. Jafferali, V. Marquette, and A. Nuyts (eds.), *Liber Amicorum Nadine Watté.* Brussels: Larcier, 2017, 287–302.

"On the Doctrinal Beginnings of Private International Law." *Yearbook of Private International Law* 21 (2019), 101–133.

Hazard, G. C. "A General Theory of State Court Jurisdiction." *Supreme Court Review* 6 (1965), 241–288.

Helmholz, R. H. *The Ius Commune in England: Four Studies.* Oxford: Oxford University Press, 2001.

Herlihy, D. *Pisa in the Early Renaisance: A Study of Urban Growth*. New Haven, CT: Yale University Press, 1958.

Hermans, M. M. "Wat lazen Friezen aan het einde van de Middeleeuwen." *De Vrije Fries* 70 (1970), 7–38.

Herrmann, G. *Johann Nikolaus Hert und die deutsche Statutenlehre*. Berlin: De Gruyter, 1963.

Hertogh, M. (ed.). *Living Law: Reconsidering Eugen Ehrlich*. Oxford: Hart, 2008.

Hewett, M. "Quae Legentem Fefellissent, Transferentem Fugere non Possunt" in R. van den Bergh et al. (eds.), *Ex Justa Causa Traditum: Essays in Honour of Eric H. Pool*. Pretoria: UNISA, 2006, 163–171.

Ulric Huber (1636–1694), "De ratione juris docendi & discendi diatribe per modum dialogi : nonnullis aucta paralipomenois": with a translation and commentary. Nijmegen: Gerard Noodt Instituut, 2010.

Holland, T. E. *Elements of Jurisprudence*. 7th ed. Oxford: Clarendon Press, 1895.

Holleaux, D. *Compétence du juge étranger et reconnaissance des jugement*. Paris: Dalloz, 1970.

Horwitz, M. *The Transformation of American Law, 1780–1850*. Cambridge, MA: Harvard University Press, 1977.

Hudault, J. "Statut personnel et droit naturel dans l'oeuvre judiciaire de G. J.-B. Target." *Revue critique de droit international privé* 87 (1998), 1–25.

Ibbetson, D. *A Historical Introduction to the Law of Obligations*. Oxford: Oxford University Press, 1999.

Institut für Ausländisches und Internationales Privat-und Wirtschaftsrecht. *In memoriam Max Gutzwiller: Gedächtnisfeier der Juristischen Fakultät Heidelberg am 3. November 1989 im "Gutzwiller-Saal" des Instituts für Ausländisches und Internationales Privat-und Wirtschaftsrecht*. Heidelberg: Winter, 1990.

Irmer, H. B. G. *"Comity": Een studie van het Internationaal Privaatrecht van de Verenigde Staten*. Nijmegen: Berkhout, 1948.

Israel, J. I. *The Dutch Republic: Its Rise, Greatness and Fall*. Oxford: Oxford University Press, 1998.

James, H. *The Creation and Destruction of Value: The Globalization Cycle*. Cambridge, MA: Harvard University Press, 2009.

Janis, M. W. "Jeremy Bentham and the Fashioning of 'International Law'." *American Journal of International Law* 74 (1984), 405–418.

Jayme, E. *Pasquale Stanislao Mancini: Internationales Privatrecht zwischen Risorgimento und Praktischer Jurisprudenz*. Ebelsbach: Verlag Rolf Gremer, 1980.

"Considérations historiques et actuelles sur la codification du droit international privé." *Recueil des cours* 177 (1982).

"Identité culturelle et intégration: le droit international privé postmoderne." *Recueil des cours* 251 (1995), 9–268.

"Le droit international privé du nouveau millénaire: la protection de la personne humaine face à la globalisation [conférence]." *Recueil des cours* 282 (2000), 9–40.

Internationales Privatrecht: Ideengeschichte von Mancini und Ehrenzweig zum Europäischen Kollisionsrecht. Heidelberg: C. F. Müller, 2009.

Jessurun d'Oliveira, H. U. "The Artifact of 'Sham Marriages'." *Yearbook of Private International Law* 1 (1999), 49–83.

Jestaz, P. and Jamin, C. "The Entity of French Doctrine: Some Thoughts on the Community of French Legal Writers." *Legal Studies* 18 (1998), 414–435.

La doctrine. Paris: Dalloz, 2004.

Jitta, D. J. *La méthode du droit international privé.* The Hague: Belinfante Frères, 1890.

Johnson, W. S. "Exctinctive Prescription—Conflict of Laws—Sources of Quebec Rules." *University of Toronto Law Journal* 4 (1941), 109–130.

Jolley, N. "Metaphysics" in D. Rutherford (ed.), *Cambridge Companion to Early Modern Philosophy.* Cambridge: Cambridge University Press, 2006, 95–135.

Jones, P. *The Italian City-State: From Commune to Signoria.* Oxford: Oxford University Press, 1997.

Juenger, F. K. "A Page of History." *Mercer Law Review* 35 (1984), 419–460.

Choice of Law and Multistate Justice. The Hague: Martinus Nijhoff, 1993.

"A Third Conflicts Restatement?" *Indiana Law Journal* 75 (2000), 403–416.

"The Lex Mercatoria and Private International Law." *Louisiana Law Review* 60 (2000), 1133–1150.

"Some Random Remarks from Overseas" in K.-P. Berger (ed.), *The Practice of Transnational Law.* The Hague: Kluwer, 2001, 81–89.

Kadens, E. "The Myth of the Customary Law Merchant." *Texas Law Review* 90 (2012), 1153–1206.

"The Medieval Law Merchant: The Tyranny of a Construct." *Journal of Legal Analysis* 7 (2015), 251–289.

Kahn-Freund, O. "General Problems of Private International Law." *Recueil des cours* 143 (1974), 139–474.

Kahn, E. "The 'Territorial School and Comity School' of the Conflict of Laws in the Roman-Dutch Era" in *Huldigingsbundel Aangebied Aan Professor Daniel Pont.* Cape Town: A. A. Balkema, 1970, 219–239.

Kahn, F. "Gesetzeskollisionen: Ein Beitrag zur Lehre des internationalen Privatrecht." *Jahrbücher für die Dogmatik des heutigen römischen und deutschen Privatrechts (Jherings Jahrbücher)* 30 (1891), 1–143.

Kalma, J. J. and de Vries, K. (eds.). *Friesland in het rampjaar 1672.* Leeuwarden: Fryske Akademy, 1972.

Kegel, G. and Schurig, K. *Internationales Privatrecht.* 8th ed. Munich: C. H. Beck, 2000.

Internationales Privatrecht. Munich: C. H. Beck, 2000.

Kennedy, Da. "Primitive Legal Scholarship." *Harvard International Law Journal* 27 (1986), 1–98.

"Receiving the International." *Connecticut Journal of International Law* 10 (1990), 1–26.

"The International Style in Postwar Law and Policy." *Utah Law Review* (1994), 7–104.

"International Law and the Nineteenth Century: History of an Illusion." *Quinnipiac Law Review* 17 (1997), 99–138.

"New Approaches to Comparative Law: Comparativism and International Governance." *Utah Law Review* (1997), 545–593.

"The Disciplines of International Law and Policy." *Leiden Journal of International Law* 12 (1999), 9–135.

Kennedy, Du. "Form and Substance in Private Law Adjudication." *Harvard Law Review* 89 (1976), 1685–1778.

"From the Will Theory to the Principle of Private Autonomy: Lon Fuller's 'Consideration and Form'." *Columbia Law Review* 100 (2000), 94–175.

"Legal Formalism" in N. J. Smelser and P. B. Baltes (eds.), *International Encyclopedia of the Social & Behavioral Sciences*. Elsevier, 2001, 8634–8638.

The Rise and Fall of Classical Legal Thought. Washington, DC: Beard Books, 2006.

Kim, K. *Aliens in Medieval Law*. Cambridge: Cambridge University Press, 2000.

Kirshner, J. "Civitas Sibi Faciat Civem: Bartolus of Sassoferrato's Doctrine on the Making of a Citizen." *Speculum* 48 (1973), 694–713.

"'Made Exiles for the Love of Knowledge': Students in Late Medieval Italy." *Medieval Studies* 70 (2008), 163–202.

Marriage, Dowry, and Citizenship in Late Medieval and Renaissance Italy. Toronto: University of Toronto Press, 2015.

"Materials for a Gilded Cage: Nondotal Assets in Florence, 1300–1500" in J. Kirshner (ed.), *Marriage, Dowry, and Citizenship in Late Medieval and Renaissance Italy*. Toronto: University of Toronto Press, 2015, 74–93.

"'Pisa's Long-Arm" Gabella Dotis (1420–1525), Issues, Cases, Legal Opinions" in J. Kirshner (ed.), *Marriage, Dowry, and Citizenship in Late Medieval and Renaissance Italy*. Toronto: University of Toronto Press, 2015, 197–214.

Kirshner, J. and Pluss, J. "Two Fourteenth-Century Opinions on Dowries, Paraphernalia and Non-Dotal Goods." *Bulletin of Medieval Canon Law* 9 (1979), 65–65.

Koessler, M. "'Subject,' 'Citizen,' 'National,' and 'Permanent Allegiance'." *Yale Law Journal* 56 (1946), 58–76.

Kogan, T. "A Neo-Federalist Tale of Personal Jurisdiction." *Southern California Law Review* 63 (1990), 257–372.

Köhler, H. *Internationales Privatrecht*. Vienna: Springer, 1966.

Kollewijn, R. D. *Geschiedenis van de Nederlandse Wetenschap van het Internationaal Privatrecht tot 1880.* Amsterdam: Noord-Hollandsche Uitgeversmij, 1937.

Köpcke, M. *A Short History of Legal Validity and Invalidity.* Cambridge: Intersentia, 2019.

Koschaker, P. *Europa und das römisches Recht.* Munich: Biederstein, 1947.

Koskenniemi, M. *The Gentle Civilizer of Nations: The Rise and Fall of International Law 1870–1960.* Cambridge: Cambridge University Press, 2002.

From Apology to Utopia: The Structure of International Legal Argument. Cambridge: Cambridge University Press, 2006.

Kossmann, E. H. *The Low Countries: 1780–1940.* Oxford: Clarendon Press, 1978.

Krčmář, J. "Beiträge zur Geschichte des internationalen Privatrecht" in J. Krčmář (ed.), *Festschrift Zur Jahrhundertfeier Des Allgemeinen Bürgerlichen Gesetzbuches.* Vienna: Juristische Gesellschaft, 1911, 133–161.

Kretzmann, N. et al. (eds.). *The Cambridge History of Later Medieval Philosophy.* Cambridge: Cambridge University Press, 1982.

Kropholler, J. *Internationales Privatrecht.* 6th ed. Tübingen: Mohr Siebeck, 2006.

Kruger, T. "Habitual Residence: The Factors that Courts Consider" in P. Beaumont et al. (eds.), *Cross-Border Litigation in Europe.* Oxford: Hart, 2017, 741–754.

Kuehn, T. *Emancipation in Late Medieval Florence.* Rutgers: Rutgers University Press, 1982.

Law, Family and Women: Toward a Legal Anthropology of Renaissance Italy. Chicago, IL: University of Chicago Press, 1991.

"Law, Death and Heirs in the Renaissance: Repudiation of Inheritance in Florence." *Renaissance Quarterly* 45 (1992), 484–516.

Heirs, Kin, and Creditors in Renaissance Florence. Cambridge: Cambridge University Press, 2008.

"Property of Spouses in Law in Renaissance Florence" in M. G. di Renzo Villata (ed.), *Family Law and Society in Europe From the Middle Ages to the Contemporary Era.* Cham: Springer, 2016, 109–134.

"Materia Est Valde Periculosa: Interpreting Testaments in Quattrocento Florence" in M. G. di Renzo Villata (ed.), *Succession Law, Practice and Society in Europe Across the Centuries.* Cham: Springer, 2018, 249–270.

Laboulaye, E. *Histoire du droit de propriété foncière en Occident.* Paris, 1839.

Lainé, A. *Introduction au droit international privé.* 2 vols. Paris: Librairie Cotillon, 1888–1892.

"Etude sur le titre préliminaire du project de révision du Code Civil Belge." *Bulletin de la Société de législation comparée* 19 (1890), 315–341, 383–413, 449–470, 525–567.

"La rédaction du Code civil et le sens de ses dispositions en matière de droit international privé." *Revue de droit international privé* 1 (1905), 21–60, 443–479.

Lalive, P. "Tendances et méthodes en droit international privé (Cours général)." *Recueil des cours* 155 (1977), 1–424.

Lando, O. "The Conflict of Laws of Contracts - General Principles." *Recueil des cours* 189 (1984), 225–446.

"Some Features of the Law of Contract in the Third Millenium." *Scandinavian Studies in Law* 40 (2000), 345–501.

Lange, H. *Römisches Recht im Mittelalter*. Munich: C. H. Beck, 1997.

Laurent, F. *Droit civil international*. 8 vols. Brussels: Bruylant-Christophe, 1880–1881.

Avant-projet de révision du code civil. 6 vols. Brussels: Bruylant-Christophe, 1882–1885.

Principes de droit civil français. 33 vols. Brussels: Bruylant-Christophe, 1887.

Laurent-Bonne, N. "Droits savants et coutumes dans la France médiévale et moderne: l'exemple du don mutuel entre époux." *Revue historique de droit français et étranger* 92 (2014), 335–356.

Le Bras, G. "Bartole et le droit canon" in U. D. Perugia (ed.), *Bartolo Da Sassoferrato: Studi E Documenti Per Il Vi Centenario*. Milan: Giuffrè, 1962, 297–308.

Leflar, R. *American Conflicts Law*. Indianapolis, IN: Bobbs-Merril, 1967.

Lehmann, M. "Regulation, Global Governance and Private International Law: Squaring the Triangle." *Journal of Private International Law* 16, 2020, 16–30.

Lemarignier, B. *La conférence des avocats et les conflits des statuts concernant les effets du mariage au début du XVIIIe siècle*. Faculté de Droit et Sciences Économiques de Paris, 1961.

Lequette, Y. "L'influence de l'œuvre d'Henri Batiffol sur la jurisprudence française." *Travaux du Comité français de droit international privé* 11 (1991), 32–54.

Lesaffer, R. "International Law and Its History" in M. Craven, M. Fitzmaurice, and M. Vogiatzi (eds.), *Time, History and International Law*. Leiden: Brill, 2007.

European Legal History: A Cultural and Political Perspective. Trans. J. Arriens. Cambridge: Cambridge University Press, 2009.

Lewald, H. "Conflits de lois dans le monde grec et romain." *Revue critique de droit international privé* 57 (1968), 419–440, 615.

Link, C. *Herrschaftsordnung und bürgerliche Freiheit: Grenzen der Staatsgewalt in der älteren deutschen Staatslehre*. Vienna: Böhlau, 1979.

Lipert, K., ed. *Historischer Statutismus und Neo-Statutismus der USA*. Zurich: Juris-Verlag, 1979.

Lipstein, K. "Conflict of Laws 1921–1971: The Way Ahead." *Cambridge Law Journal* 31 (1972), 67–120.

"The General Principles of Private International Law." *Recueil des cours* 135 (1972), 97–230.

"One Hundred Years of Hague Conferences on Private International Law." *International & Comparative Law Quarterly* 42 (1993), 553–653.

Livermore, S. *Dissertations on the Questions which arise from the Contrariety of the Positive Laws of Different States and Nations* (New Orleans, 1828)

Llewellyn Davies, D. J. "The Influence of Huber's De Conflictu Legum on English Private International Law." *British Yearbook of International Law* 18 (1937), 49–63.

Lobban, M. "The Development of Tort Law" in W. Cornish et al. (eds.), *Oxford History of the Laws of England XII: 1820–1914 Private Law*. Oxford: Oxford University Press, 2010, 877–902.

Lokin, J. H. A., Brandsma, F., and Jansen, C. *Roman-Frisian Law of the 17th and 18th Century*. Berlin: Duncker & Humblot, 2003.

Lorenzen, E. G. "Huber's De Conflictu Legum." *Illinois Law Review* 13 (1919), 375–418.

"The Qualification, Classification or Characterization Problem in the Conflict of Laws." *Yale Law Journal* 50 (1941), 743–761.

Louis-Lucas, P. "Conflits de méthodes en matière de conflits de lois = Conflicts of methods as regards conflicts of laws." *Clunet* 83 (1956), 774–823.

Loussouarn, Y. "The French Draft on Private International Law and the French Conference on Codification of Private International Law." *International & Comparative Law Quarterly* 5 (1956), 378–394.

"Cours général de droit international privé." *Recueil des cours* 139 (1973), 269–386.

Loussouarn, Y., Bourel, P., and Vareilles-Sommières, P. D. *Droit international privé*. Paris: Dalloz, 2004.

Lunz, L. A. *Internationales Privatrecht: Allgemeiner Teil*. Berlin: Deutscher Zentralverlag, 1961.

Luther, G. "Der Einfluss von Bartolus auf das deutsche internationale privat- und Strafrecht" in U. D. Perugia (ed.), *Bartolo Da Sassoferrato: Studi E Documenti Per Il Vi Centenario*. Milan: Giuffrè, 1962, 309–331.

Magnus, U. "Introduction" in U. Magnus and P. Mankowski (eds.), *Brussels I Regulation*. 2nd ed. Munich: Sellier, 2012, 1–46.

Maiolo, F. *Medieval Sovereignty: Marsilius of Padua and Bartolus of Saxoferrato*. Delft: Eburon, 2007.

Makarov, A. N. *Précis de droit international privé d'après la législation et la doctrine russes*. Trans. E. N. P. Pereverweff. Paris: Marcel Giard, 1932.

Mancini, P.-S. "De l'utilité de rendre obligatoires pour tous les Etats, sous la forme d'un ou de plusieurs traités internationaux, un certain nombre des règles générales du Droit international privé pour assurer la décision uniforme des conflits entre les différentes législations civiles et criminelles." *Clunet* 1 (1874), 221–239, 285.

Mansel, H.-P. "L'adoption du principe de la nationalité par le EGBGB du 18 août 1896" in J. Erauw (ed.), *Liber Memorialis François Laurent*. Brussels: E. Story-Scientia, 1989, 869–779.

Maridakis, G. "Le marriage des Grecs orthodoxes hors de Grèce." *Revue critique de droit international privé* 41 (1952), 661-671.

"Introduction au droit international privé." *Recueil des cours* 105 (1962), 375–515.

"L'inapplicabilité du droit étranger à Byzance" in J. Limpens (ed.), *Liber Amicorum Baron Louis Frédéricq*. Ghent: Faculteit der Rechtsgeleerldheid te Gent, 1965.

Idiōtikon Diethnes Dikaion. 2nd ed. Athens: Ant.N.Sakkoulas, 1967.

Martin, J. A. *Conflict of Laws*. Boston: Little, Brown, 1978.

Martines, L. *Lawyers and Statecraft in Renaissuance Florence*. Princeton: Princeton University Press, 1968.

Mayer, P. "Les lois de police étrangères." *Clunet* 108 (1981), 277–345.

"Le mouvement des idées dans le droit des conflits de lois." *Droits: Revue française de théorie juridique* 2 (1985), 129–143.

Droit international privé. 6th ed. Paris: Montchretien, 1998.

McClean, D. "A Common Inheritance? An Examination of the Private International Law Tradition of the Commonwealth." *Recueil des cours* 260 (1997), 13–98.

"De Conflictu Legum: Perspectives on Private International Law at the Turn of the Century." *Recueil des cours* 184 (2000), 41-228.

McClean, D. and Beevers, K. *Morris The Conflict of Laws*. 7th ed. London: Sweet & Maxwell, 2009.

McDougal, L. "'Private' International Law: Ius Gentium versus Choice of Law Rules or Approaches." *American Journal of Comparative Law* 38 (1990), 521–537.

McEleavy, P. "Regression and Reform in the Law of Domicile." *International & Comparative Law Quarterly* 56 (2007), 453–462.

Meeusen, J. *Nationalisme en Internationalisme in het Internationaal Privaatrecht: Analyse van het Belgische Conflictenrecht*. Antwerp/Groningen: Intersentia, 1997.

Meijers, E. M. "Nieuwe Bijdrage tot het onstaan van het beginsel der realiteit." *Tijdschrift voor Rechtsgeschiedenis* 3 (1922), 61–93.

"L'histoire des principes fondamentaux du droit international privé à partir du Moyen Age, spécialement dans l'Europe occidentale." *Recueil des cours* 49 (1934), 543–682.

"Introduction à la publication d'oeuvres inédites de Balde et de Van der Keesel." *Revue critique de droit international privé* 35 (1946), 203–219.

"Contribution à l'histoire du droit international privé et pénal en France et dans les Pays-Bas aux XIIIe et XIVe siècles" in P.-C. Timbal and J. Metman (eds.).

Études d'histoire du droit international privé. Paris: Éditions du Centre National de la Recherche Scientifique, 1967.

Meili, F. "Die theoretischen Abhandlungen von Bartolus und Baldus über das internationale Privaat- und Strafrecht." *Niemeyers Zeitschrift für internationales Recht* 4 (1894), 269–269, 340–346, 446–465.

"Argentraeus und Molinaeus und ihre Bedeutung im internationalen Privat- und Strafrecht." *Niemeyers Zeitschrift* 5 (1895), 363–380, 452–472, 554–566.

"Ein Specimen aus der holländischen Schule des IPR (Ulricus Huber 1636–1694)." *Niemeyers Zeitschrift* 8 (1898), 189–200.

Mendels, D. "The Five Empires: A Note on a Propagandistic Topos." *American Journal of Philology* 102 (1981), 330–337.

Meredith, P. "Jeremy Bentham and the Fashioning of 'International Law'." *American Journal of International Law* 78 (1984), 405–423.

Merzyn, G. *Der Beitrag Benedikt Carpzovs zur Entwicklung des Kollisionsrechts*. Göttingen: O. Schwartz, 1963.

Meylan, P. "Les statuts réels et personnels dans la doctrine de Du Moulin" in P. Meylan (ed.), *Mélanges Paul Fournier*. Paris: Recueil Sirey, 1929, 511–526.

"Nemo pro parte testatus pro parte intestatus decedere potest" in P. Meylan (ed.), *Zum Schweizerischen Erbrecht: Festschrift Zum 70*. Zurich: Geburtstag Von Peter Tuor, Polygraphischer Verlag, 1946, 179–200.

Miaja de la Muela, A. *Derecho internacional privado*. 8th ed. Madrid: Atlas, 1979.

Michaels, R. "Two Paradigms of Jurisdiction." *Michigan Journal of International Law* 27 (2006), 1003–1069.

"Globalizing Savigny? The State in Savigny's Conflict of Laws Theory, and the Challenge of Europeanization and Globalization" in M. Stolleis and W. Streeck (eds.), *Aktuelle Fragen Politischer Und Rechtlicher Steuerung Im Kontext Der Globalisierung*. Baden-Baden: Nomos, 2007, 119–144.

"The New European Choice-of-Law Revolution." *Tulane Law Review* 82 (2008), 1607–1644.

"After the Revolution: Decline and Return of U.S. Conflict of Laws." *Yearbook of Private International Law* 11 (2009), 11–30.

"Legal Medievalism in Lex Mercatoria Scholarship." *Texas Law Review* 90 (2012), 259–268.

"Wächter, Carl Georg von" in J. Basedow, G. Rühl, and F. Ferrari (eds.), *Encyclopedia of Private International Law*. Cheltenham: Edward Elgar, 2017, 1825–1832.

Mills, A. *The Confluence of Public and Private International Law: Justice, Pluralism and Subsidiarity in the International Constitutional Ordering of Private Law*. Cambridge: Cambridge University Press, 2009.

"Rethinking Jurisdiction in International Law." *British Yearbook of International Law* 84 (2014), 187–239.

Party Autonomy in Private International Law. Cambridge: Cambridge University Press, 2018.

Mistelis, L. A. *Charakterisierungen und Qualifikation im internationalen Privatrecht : zur Lehre einer parteispezifischen Qualifikation im Kollisionsrecht der privaten Wirtschaft*. Tübingen: Mohr Siebeck, 1999.

Mohnhaupt, H. "Von den 'leges fundamentales' zur modernen Verfassung in Europa. Zum begriffs- und dogmengeschichtlichen Befund (16–18 Jahrhundert)" in H. Mohnhaupt (ed.), *Historische Vergleichung Im Bereich Vom Staat Und Recht: Gesammelte Aufsätze*. Frankfurt: Vittorio Klostermann, 2000, 35–72.

Mortensen, R., Garnett, R., and Keyes, M. *Private International Law in Australia*. Melbourne: LexisNexis Australia, 2006.

Motulsky-Falardeau, A. "Les aspects historiques de la qualification de la prescription en droit international privé." *Cahiers du droit* 55 (2014), 829–876.

Muir Watt, H. "Aspects économiques du droit international privé (réflexions sur l'impact de la globalisation économique sur les fondements des conflits de lois et de juridictions)." *Recueil des cours* 307 (2004), 25–383.

"European Federalism and the 'New Unilateralism'." *Tulane Law Review* 82 (2008), 1983–1998.

Muir Watt, H. and Fernandez Arroyo, D. (eds.). *Private International Law and Global Governance*. Oxford: Oxford University Press, 2015.

Nadelman, K. "Book review of Héléne Gaudemet-Tallon, Récherches sur les origines de l'article 14 du Code Civil." *American Journal of Comparative Law* 14 (1965), 348–350. .

Nadelmann, K. H. "Marginal Remarks on the New Trends in American Conflicts Law." *Law & Contemporary Problems* 28 (1963), 860–869.

"Wächter's Essay on the Collision of Private Laws of Different States." *American Journal of Comparative Law* 13 (1964), 414–428.

"Mancini's Nationality Rule and Non-Unified Legal Systems: Nationality and Domicile." *American Journal of Comparative Law* 17 (1969), 418–451.

"Internationales Privatrecht: A Source Book on Conflicts Theory Analyzed and Reviewed." *Harvard International Law Journal* 17 (1976), 657–677.

Neidhardt, A. H. "The Transformation of Private International Law: A Genealogy of the Family Antinomy." Unpublished Doctoral dissertation, European University Institute, 2018.

Neuhaus, P. H. "Die Krise im internationalen Privatrecht." *Deutsche Rechts-Zeitschrift* 3 (1948), 86–87.

"Savigny und die Rechtsfindung aus der Natur der Sache." *Rabels Zeitschrift* 15 (1949), 364–381.

Neumeyer, K. *Die gemeinrechtliche Entwickelung des internationalen Privat- und Strafrechts bis Bartolus*. 2 vols. Munich: J. Schweitzer, 1901–1916.

"Zur Geschichte des internationalen Privatrechts in Frankreich und den Niederlanden." *Zeitschrift für Völkerrecht* 11 (1920), 190–204.

"Das Kanonische Recht und Die Lehren Der Kanonisten in Ihrem Einfluss Auf Die Entwicklung Des Internationalen Privatrechts (1250–1357)." *Tijdschrift voor Rechtsgeschiedenis* 33 (1965), 177–197.

Ní Shúilleabháin, M. *Cross-Border Divorce Law*. Oxford: Oxford University Press, 2010.

Niboyet, J.-P. "Froland, les conflicts de qualification et la question du renvoi." *Revue de droit international privé* 21 (1926), 1–25.

"La théorie de l'autonomie de la volonté." *Recueil des cours* 16 (1927), 1–114.

Traité de droit international privé français. Paris: Sirey, 1944.

Traité de droit international privé français. 2nd ed. Paris: Sirey, 1947.

"Territoriality and Universal Recognition of Rules of Conflict of Laws." *Harvard Law Review* 65 (1952), 582–596.

Niboyet, M.-L. and La Pradelle, G. D. G. *Droit international privé*. Paris: LGDJ, 2007.

Niederer, W. "Ceterum quaero de legum imperii romani conflictu." *Revue critique de droit international privé* 49 (1960), 137–150.

Niedner, A. *Das Einführungsgesetz vom 18 August 1896*. 2nd ed. Berlin: Heymann, 1913.

Nishitani, Y. *Mancini und die Parteiautonomie im internationalen Privatrecht*. Heidelberg: Winter Verlag, 2000.

"Mancini e l'autonomia della volontà nel diritto internazionale privato." *Rivista di diritto internazionale privato e processuale* 37 (2001), 23–44.

Nuyts, A. *L'exception de forum non conveniens*. Brussels: Bruylant, 2003.

Nygh, P. E. "The Reasonable Expectations of the Parties as a Guide to the Choice of Law in Contract and Tort." *Recueil des cours* 251 (1995), 271–400.

Autonomy in International Contracts. Oxford: Oxford University Press, 1999.

O'Rource, K. and Williamson, J. "When Did Globalization Begin?" *European Review of Economic History* 6 (2002), 23–50.

Onclin, W. "La doctrine de Bartole sur les conflits de lois et son influence en Belgique" in U. D. Perugia (ed.), *Bartolo Da Sassoferrato: Studi E Documenti Per Il VI Centenario*. Milan: Giuffrè, 1962, 373–392.

Oppetit, B. "Le droit international privé, droit savant." *Recueil des cours* 234 (1992), 331–434.

Ormrod, D. *The Rise of Commercial Empires: England and the Netherlands in the Age of Mercantilism, 1650–1770*. Cambridge: Cambridge University Press, 2003.

Ourliac, P. and Gazzaniga, J.-L. *Histoire du droit privé français de l'an mil au Code civil*. Paris: A. Michel, 1985.

Pakter, W. "Les origines canoniques de la règle forum regit actum dans le droit international privé." *Recueil des mémoires et travaux publié par la Société d'histoire et des institutions des anciens pays de droit écrit* 11 (1980), 1–22.

Pamboukis, C. *L'acte public étranger en droit international privé*. Paris: LGDJ, 1993.

"Droit international privé holistique: droit uniforme et droit international privé." *Recueil des cours* 330 (2007), 9–474.

Idiōtiko Diethnes Dikaio. Athens: Nomiki Bibliothiki, 2020.

Paras, E. L. *Philippine Conflict of Laws*. 7th ed. Manila: Rex Book Store, 1990.

Paul, J. R. "The Isolation of Private International Law." *Wisconsin International Law Journal* 7 (1988), 149–178.

"Comity in International Law." *Harvard International Law Journal* 32 (1991), 1–79.

"The Transformation of International Comity." *Law & Contemporary Problems* 71 (2008), 19–38.

Pennington, K. *The Prince and the Law, 1200–1600*. University of California Press, 1993.

Philimore, R. *Commentaries upon International Law*. Berkeley: William Benning & Son, 1861.

Piccone, P. "Les méthodes de coordination entre ordres juridiques en droit international privé: cours général de droit international privé." *Recueil des cours* 276 (1999), 9–296.

Pillet, A. *Principes de droit international privé*. Paris, 1903.

Droit international privé: Résumé du cours, 1904–1905. Paris: Pedone, 1905.

"L'oeuvre de M. Lainé." *Revue de droit international privé* 5 (1909), 1–11.

Pollock, F. and Maitland, F. W. *The History of English Law before the Time of Edward I*. 2nd ed Reissue. Cambridge: Cambridge University Press, 1968.

Pontier, J. A. *Conflictenrecht: grondslagen, methoden, beginselen en belangen*. Nijmegen: Ars Aequi Libri, 1997.

Popkin, R. H. (ed.). *The Columbia History of Western Philosophy* New York: Columbia University Press, 1999.

Popper, K. *The Poverty of Historicism*. New York: Basic Books, 1957.

Posch, W. *Bürgerliches Recht VII: Internationales Privatrecht*. 3rd ed. Vienna: Springer, 2002.

Prak, M. *The Dutch Republic in the Seventeenth Century*. Cambridge: Cambridge University Press, 2005.

Prosser, W. "Interstate Publication." *Michigan Law Review* 51 (1953), 959–1000.

Putnam, T. *Courts without Borders: Law, Politics and US Extraterritoriality*. Cambridge: Cambridge University Press, 2016.

Quadri, R. *Lezioni di Diritto internazionale privato*. 5th ed. Naples: Liguori, 1961.

"Quelques considérations sur la contribution du Professeur Wengler au progrès du droit international privé" in R. Quadri (ed.), *Multitudo Legum Ius Unum: Festschrift Für Wilhelm Wengler*. Berlin: Inter Recht, 1973.

Quaglioni, D. "'Regnativa prudentia'. Diritto e teologia nel 'Tractatus testimoniorum' bartoliano" in D. Quaglioni (ed.), *Théologie Et Droit Dans La*

Science Politique De L'État Moderne. Actes De La Table Ronde De Rome (12–14 Novembre 1987), 1991, 155–170.

Raape, L. *Internationales Privatrecht*. 5th ed. Berlin: Valen, 1961.

Raape, L. and Sturm, F. *Internationales Privatrecht*. Munich: Valen, 1977.

Raath, A. W. G. "Aspects of Ulrich Huber's Theory of Universal Public Law and Post-Constitutional Contracting." *Tydskrif vir Hedendaagse Romeins-Hollandse Reg* 75 (2012), 206–222.

Rabel, E. *The Conflict of Laws: A Comparative Study*. 4 vols. Ann Arbor/Chicago: University of Michigan Press/Callaghan & Co., 1945.

Raeburn, W. "Dispensing with the Personal Law." *International & Comparative Law Quarterly* 12 (1963), 125–125.

Ranouil, V. *L'autonomie de la volonté: naissance et évolution d'un concept*. Paris: PUF, 1980.

Reese, W. M. "Choice of Law: Rules or Approach." *Cornell Law Review* 57 (1972), 315–334.

Reese, W. M., Rosenberg, M., and Hay, P. *Cases and Materials on the Conflict of Laws*. 9th ed. Westbury, NY: Foundation Press, 1990.

Rehbinder, M. *Die Begründung der Rechtssoziologie durch Eugen Ehrlich*. 2nd ed. Berlin: Duncker & Humblot, 1986.

Reimann, M. *Conflict of Laws in Western Europe: A Guide through the Jungle*. Irvington, NY: Transnational Publishers, 1995.

Renault, L. *Introduction au droit international*. Paris: Larose, 1879.

Richard, H. "La place du président Bouhier dans l'histoire du droit international privé." *Mémoires de la Société pour l'histoire du droit et des institutions des anciens pays bourguignons, comtois et romands* 32 (1973), 87–172.

Rigaud, L. "Contribution des canonistes aux plus anciens doctrines du droit international privé et influence de celui-ci sur le 'Codex juris canonici'" in L. Rigaud (ed.), *Actes du Congrès de Droit Canonique: Livre du Cinquantainnaire de la Faculté de Droit Canonique (Paris, 22–26 Avril 1947)*. Paris: Letouzey & Ané, 1950, 376–386.

Rigaux, F. "Rapport de synthèse: Pour une relecture de François Laurent en 1987" in J. Erauw (ed.), *Liber Memorialis François Laurent*. Brussels: E. Story-Scientia, 1989, 663–668.

Robertson, A. H. *Characterization in the Conflict of Laws*. Cambridge, MA: Harvard University Press, 1940.

Robinson, O. F. *Ancient Rome: City Planning and Administration*. London: Routledge, 1992.

Robinson, O. F., Fergus, T. D., and Gordon, W. M. *European Legal History*. 3rd ed. Oxford: Oxford University Press, 2000.

Rolin-Jaequemyns, G. "De la nécessité d'organiser une institution scientifique permanente pour favoriser l'étude et les progress du droit international." *Revue de droit international et de législation comparée* 5 (1873), 463–491.

Romano, G. P. "La bilatéralité éclipsée par l'autorité : développements récents en matière d'état des personnes." *Revue critique de droit international privé* (2006), 457–519.

"Le droit international privé à l'épreuve de la théorie kantienne de la justice." *Clunet* 139 (2012), 61–94.

L'unilateralismo nel diritto internazionale privato moderno. Geneva: Schulthess, 2014.

Le dilemme du renvoi en droit international privé : la thèse, l'antithèse et la recherche d'une synthèse. Geneva: Schulthess, 2014.

Rosenberg, J. *The Follies of Globalization Theory*. London: Verso, 2000.

Roumy, F. "L'ignorance du droit dans la doctrine civiliste des XIIe-XIIIe siècles." *Cahiers de recherches médiévales et humanistes* 7 (2007), 1–20.

Rühl, G. "Party Autonomy in the Private International Law of Contracts" in E. Gottschalk et al. (eds.), *Conflict of Laws in a Globalized World*. Cambridge: Cambridge University Press, 2007, 153–183.

Ryan, M. "Territory in the Political Thought of the Medieval Lawyers."

"Bartolus of Sassoferrato and Free Cities (the Alexander Prize Lecture, read 23 April 1999)." *Transactions of the Royal Historical Society (6th series)* 10 (2000), 65–89.

"Political Thought" in D. Johnston (ed.), *Cambridge Companion to Roman Law*. Cambridge: Cambridge University Press, 2015, 423–451.

Sack, A. "Conflicts of Laws in the History of the English Law" in A. Reppy (ed.), *Law: A Century of Progress, 1835–1935 (Contributions in Celebration of the Founding of the School of Law of New York University)*. New York: New York University Press, 1937, 342–454.

Salvi, S. T. "A Difficult Legacy. Initial Comments on the Inheritance Rights of Filii Clericorum in the Middle Ages and Early Modern Period" in M. G. di Renzo Villata (ed.), *Succession Law, Practice and Society in Europe across the Centuries*. Cham: Springer, 2018, 381–419.

Sánchez-Moreno Ellart, C. "The Late Roman Law of Inheritance: The Testament of Five or Seven Witnesses" in B. Caseau and S. Huebner (eds.), *Inheritance, Law and Religions in the Ancient and Mediaeval Worlds*. Paris: ACHCByz, 2014.

Savigny, F. C. V. "Über den Zweck dieser Zeitschrift." *Zeitschrift für geschichtliche Rechtswissenschaft* 1 (1815), 1–17.

System des heutigen römisches Rechts. 8 vols. Berlin: Veit, 1840.

Geschichte des Römischen Rechts im Mittelalter. 2nd ed. Heidelberg: J. C. B. Mohr, 1850.

System of the Modern Roman Law. Trans. W. Holloway. Madras: J. Higginbontham, 1867.

Private International Law and the Retrospective Operation of Statutes: A Treatise on the Conflict of Laws, and the Limits of Their Operation in

Respect of Time and Place. 2nd ed. Trans. W. Guthrie. Edinburgh: T. & T. Clark, 1880.

Sbriccoli, M. *L' interpretazione dello statuto: Contributo allo studio della funzione dei giuristi nell'età comunale*. Milan: Giuffrè, 1969.

Scelle, G. *Manuel de droit international public*. Paris: Domat-Monchretien, 1948.

Schiller, R. *Narrative Economics: How Stories Go Viral and Drive Major Economic Events*. Princeton: Princeton University Press, 2019.

Schlag, P. "Rules and Standards." *UCLA Law Review* 33 (1985), 379–430.

Schnell, J. "Über die Zuständingkeit zum Erlass von gesetzlichen Vorschriften über die räumliche Herrschaft der Rechtnormen." *Niemeyers Zeitschrift* 5 (1895), 337–343.

Schöffer, I. "The Batavian Myth during the Sixteenth and Seventeeth Century" in J. S. Bromley and E. H. Kossmann (eds.), *Britain and the Netherlands V: Some Political Mythologies*. The Hague: Springer, 1975, 78–101.

Schwander, I. *Einführung in das international Privatrecht*. 3rd ed. St. Gallen/Lachen: Dike, 2000.

Schwind, F. "L'influsso di Bartolo sulla evoluzione del diritto internationale privatto" in U. D. Perugia (ed.), *Bartolo Da Sassoferrato: Studi E Documenti Per Il VI Centenario*. Milan: Giuffrè, 1962, 503–512.

Scoles, E. et al. *Conflict of Laws*. 3rd ed. St. Paul, MN: West, 2000.

Sheedy, A. T. *Bartolus on Social Conditions in the Fourteenth Century*. New York: Columbia University Press, 1942.

Shreve, G. *A Conflict of Laws Anthology*. Cincinnati, OH: Anderson, 1997.

Siehr, K. "The Hague Conference on Private International Law and Germany." *Netherlands International Law Review* 40 (1993), 129–142.

"Revolution and Evolution in Conflicts Law." *Louisiana Law Review* 60 (2000), 1353–1360.

Das Internationale Privatrecht der Schweiz. Zurich: Schulthess, 2002.

Simó Santonja, V.-L. *Aportación al estudio de los estatutarios españoles*. Valencia: Diputación Provincial de Valencia, 1959.

Simon-Depitre, M. *Droit international privé*. Paris: Librairie Armand Colin, 1964.

Singer, J. W. "Real Conflicts." *Boston University Law Review* 69 (1989), 1–129.

"A Pragmatic Guide to Conflicts." *Boston University Law Review* 70 (1990), 731–819.

Sperdutti, G. "Théorie du droit international privé." *Recueil des cours* 122 (1967), 173–336.

Spiro, E. *The General Principles of the Conflict of Laws*. Cape Town: Juta, 1982.

Stein, P. "Bartolus, the Conflict of Laws and the Roman Law" in P. Stein (ed.), *Multum Non Multa : Festschrift Für Kurt Lipstein Aus Anlass Seines 70.* Geburtstages. Heidelberg: C. F. Müller, 1980, 251–258.

Legal Evolution: The Story of an Idea. Cambridge: Cambridge University Press, 1980.

Stille, A. L. G. A. "Asser et Rolin-Jaequemyns. Compte-rendu de quelques contacts personnels entre deux contemporains de Laurent" in J. Erauw (ed.), *Liber Memorialis François Laurent*. Brussels: E. Story–Scientia, 1989, 1089–1097.

Stone, P. "The Concept of Habitual Residence in Private International Law." *Anglo-American Law Review* 29 (2000), 342–367.

Storti, C. "Early 'Italian' Scholars of Ius Gentium" in G. Bartolini (ed.), *A History of International Law in Italy*. Oxford: Oxford University Press, 2020, 19–47.

Story, J. *Commentaries on the Conflict of Laws, Foreign and Domestic, in regard to Contracts, Rights, and Remedies, and especially in regard to Marriages, DIvorces, Wills, Successionsm and Judgments*. Boston: Hillard, Gray & Co., 1834.

Strikwerda, L. "Fries Recht in America. Over Ulrik Huber, Joseph Story en internationale contracten." *Groningen opmerkingen en mededelingen* 4 (1987), 55–78.

Sturm, F. "Comment l'Antiquité réglait-elle ses conflits de lois?" *Clunet* 106 (1979), 259–273.

Surville, F. "La théorie des statuts d'après Bartole et Dumoulin." *Clunet* 48 (1921), 1–15.

Surville, F. and Arthuys, F. *Cours élémentaire de droit international privé conforme au programme des facultés de droit*. Paris: Arthur Rousseau, 1895.

Swain, W. *The Law of Contract 1670–1870*. Cambridge: Cambridge University Press, 2015.

Symeonides, S. C. "Territoriality and Personality in Tort Conflicts" in T. Einhorn and K. Siehr (eds.), *Intercontinental Cooperation through Private International Law: Essays in Memory of Peter E. Nygh*. The Hague: TMC Asser, 2004, 401–433.

The American Choice-of-Law Revolution: Past, Present and Future. Leiden: Brill, 2006.

American Private International Law. Netherlands: Kluwer Law International, 2008.

"The American Revolution and the European Evolution in Choice of Law: Reciprocal Lessons." *Tulane Law Review* 82 (2008), 1741–1799.

"The First Conflicts Restatement through the Eyes of Old: As Bad as Its Reputation?" *Southern Illinois University Law Journal* 32 (2008), 39–82.

"Private International Law: Idealism, Pragmatism, Eclecticism." *Recueil des cours* 384 (2017), 9–385.

Symeonides, S. C., Perdue, W., and von Mehren, A. T. *Conflict of Laws: American, Comparative, International*. St Paul, MN: West, 1998.

Szászy, I. *Private International Law in the European People's Democracies*. Budapest: Akadémiai Kiadó, 1964.

ten Wolde, M. "Huber, Ulrik" in J. Basedow, G. Rühl, and F. Ferrari (eds.), *Encyclopedia of Private International Law*. Cheltenham: Edward Elgar, 2017, 876–880.

Teubner, G. "De Collisione Discursuum: Communicative Rationalities in Law, Morality and Politics." *Cardozo Law Review* 17 (1996), 901–916.

"Altera Pars Audiatur: Law in the Collision of Discourses" in R. Rawlins (ed.), *Law, Society and Economy*. Oxford: Oxford University Press, 1997, 149–176.

Thorne, S. E. "Sovereignty and the Conflict of Laws" in U. D. Perugia (ed.), *Bartolo Da Sassoferrato: Studi E Documenti Per Il VI Centenario*. Milan: Giuffrè, 1962, 673–689.

Timbal, P.-C. "La contribution des auteurs et de la pratique coutumière au droit international privé du moyen âge." *Revue critique de droit international privé* 44 (1955), 17–32.

Trias y Giro, J. D. D. and Trias de Bes, J. M. *Estudios de derecho internacional privado*. Barcelona: Sociedad General de Publicationes, 1921.

Trigger, B. *A History of Archaeological Thought*. Cambridge: Cambridge University Press, 2006.

Tsouca, C. "Les règles étrangères d'application immédiate et leur impact sur la nature méthodologique du droit international privé." *Koinodikaion* 3 (1997), 227–269.

Tudertina, C. (ed.). *Bartolo da Sassoferrato nel VII Centenario della Nascita: Diritto, Politica, Società*. Spoleto: Fondazione Centro Italiano di Studi sull'Alto Medioevo, 2014.

Tzounakas, S. "Cato's laudatio Pompei in Lucan's De Bello Civili" in S. Tzounakas (ed.), *Praises of Roman Leaders in Latin Literature*. Nicosia: Stamoulis, 2014, 205–221.

Vacari, P. "Utrum jurisdictio cohaereat territorio" in U. D. Perugia (ed.), *Bartolo Da Sassoferrato: Studi E Documenti Per Il VI Centenario*. Milan: Giuffrè, 1962, 735–753.

Valéry, J. *Manuel de droit international privé*. Paris: Fontemoing, 1914.

van Hecke, G. "The Catholic Origins and Calvinist Orientation of Dutch Reformed Church Law" in G. van Hecke (ed.), *Mélanges En L'Honneur De Jean Dabin*. Brussels: Bruylant-Sirey, 1963, 939–954.

van Hove, A. "La territorialité et la personnalité des lois en droit canonique depuis Gratien (vers 1140) jusqu'à Jean Andre (1348)." *Tijdschrift voor Rechtsgeschiedenis* 3 (1922), 277–322.

van Loon, J. H. A. "Quelques réflexions sur l'unification progressive du droit international privé dans le cadre de la Conférence de la Haye" in J. Erauw (ed.), *Liber Memorialis François Laurent*. Brussels: E. Story-Scientia, 1989.

Vaquette, T. *Cours résumé du droit international privé*. 1884.

Vareilles-Sommières, G. D. *La synthèse du droit international privé*. Paris: F. Pichon, 1897.

"Un Sedan juridique: Etude sur le droit des conflits successorales." *Revue de Lille* 13 (1902), 832–852.

Veen, T. J. *Recht en nut: studiën over en naar aanleiding van Ulrik Huber (1636–1694).* Zwolle: Tjeenk Willink, 1976.

Volken, P. "How Common Are the General Principles of Private International Law? America and Europe Compared." *Yearbook of Private International Law* 1 (1999), 85–102.

von Mehren, A. T. "Une esquisse de l'évolution du droit international privé aux Etats-Unis." *Clunet* 100 (1973), 116–157.

"Adjudicatory Jurisdiction: General Theories Compared and Evaluated." *Boston University Law Review* 63 (1983), 279–340.

Vrellis, S. *Idiōtiko Diethnes Dikaio.* 3rd ed. Athens: Nomiki Bibliothiki, 2001.

Wächter, C. G. V. "Über die Collision der Privatrechtsgesetze verschiedener Staaten." *Archiv für die Civilistiche Praxis* 24 (1841), 230–311, 25 (1842), 1–60, 161–200, 361–419.

Waelkens, L. *La théorie de la coutume chez Jacques de Révigny: Edition et analyse de sa répétition sur la loi De quibus (D. 1,3,32).* Leiden: E. J. Brill/Leiden University Press, 1984.

Wallerstein, I. *The Modern World System I: Capitalist Agriculture and the Origins of the European World-Economy in the Sixteenth Century.* Berkeley: University of California Press, 2011.

Wardle, L. D., Rogers, W. S., and Hogue, L. L. *Interstate and International Conflict of Laws: Cases and Materials.* Provo, UT: 1999.

Warlomont, R. *François Laurent, juriste, homme d'action et publiciste.* Brussels, 1948.

Watson, A. *Joseph Story and the Comity of Errors.* Athens, GA: University of Georgia Press, 2002.

Watts, J. C. *The Making of Polities: Europe 1300–1500.* Cambridge: Cambridge University Press, 2009.

Weber, H. *Die Theorie der Qualifikation: Franz Kahn, Etienne Bartin und Entwicklung ihrer Lehre bis zur universalen Annerkerung der Qualifikation als allgemeines Problem des Internationales Privatrechts (1890–1945).* Tübingen: Mohr Siebeck, 1986.

Wegner, A. *Geschichte des Völkerrechts.* Stuttgart: W. Kohlhammer, 1936.

Weinstein, J. "The Dutch Influence on the Conception of Judicial Jurisdiction in 19th Century America." *American Journal of Comparative Law* 38 (1990), 73–101.

"The Early American Origins of Territoriality in Judicial Jurisdiction." *St Louis University Law Journal* 37 (1992), 1–61.

Weintraub, R. *International Litigation and Arbitration.* Durham, NC: Carolina Academic Press, 2001.

Wessels, J. W. *History of the Roman-Dutch Law.* Grahamstown: African Book Co., 1908.

Westlake, J. *A Treatise on Private International Law, on the Conflict of Laws, with Principal Reference to Its Practice in the English and Cognate Systems of Jurisprudence.* London, 1858.

A Treatise on Private International Law with Principal Reference to Its Practice in England. London: Sweet & Maxwell, 1890.

Whincop, M. J. and Keyes, M. *Policy and Pragmatism in the Conflict of Laws*. London: Routledge, 2001.

White, G. E. *Tort Law in America: An Intellectual History*. Oxford: Oxford University Press, 2003.

Whitman, J. "Commercial Law and the American Volk: A Note on Llewellyn's German Sources for the Uniform Commercial Code." *Yale Law Journal* 97 (1987), 156–175.

The Legacy of Roman Law in the German Romantic Era: Historical Vision and Legal Change. Princeton: Princeton University Press, 1990.

"A Note on the Medieval Division of the Digest." *Tijdschrift voor Rechtsgeschiedenis* 59 (1991), 269–284.

Whitman, J. Q. "The Moral Menace of Roman Law and the Making of Commerce: Some Dutch Evidence." *Yale Law Journal* 105 (1996), 1841–1889.

Wieacker, F. *A History of Private Law in Europe with Particular Reference to Germany*. Trans. W. Tony. Oxford: Oxford University Press, 1995.

Wiecek, W. M. *The Lost World of Classical Legal Thought: Law and Ideology in America, 1886–1937*. Oxford: Oxford University Press, 1998.

Wickham, C. *Medieval Europe*. New Haven CT: Yale University Press, 2016.

Witte, E. "The Battle for Monasteries, Cemeteries and Schools: Belgium" in C. Clark and W. Kaiser (eds.), *Culture Wars: Secular-Catholic Conflict in Nineteenth-Century Europe*. Cambridge: Cambridge University Press, 2003, 102–128.

Witte, J. "The Catholic Origins and Calvinist Orientation of Dutch Reformed Church Law." *Calvin Theological Journal* 28 (1993), 328–351.

From Sacrament to Contract: Marriage, Religion and Law in the Western Tradition. Lousville, KY: Westminister John Knox, 1999.

Law and Protestantism: The Legal Teachings of the Lutheran Reformation. Cambridge: Cambridge University Press, 2002.

Wittman, T. *Das Goldene Zeitalter der Niederlande*. Leipzig: Koehler & Amelang, 1975.

Wolff, M. *Private International Law*. 2nd ed. Oxford: Clarendon Press, 1950.

Wood, D. P. "Extraterritorial Enforcement of Regulatory Laws." *Recueil des cours* 401 (2019), 9–126.

Woolf, C. N. S. *Bartolus of Sassoferrato: His Position in the History of Medieval Political Thought*. Cambridge: Cambridge University Press, 1913.

Yntema, H. "'Autonomy' in Choice of Law." *American Journal of Comparative Law* 1 (1952), 341–358.

"The Historic Bases of Private International Law." *American Journal of Comparative Law* 2 (1953), 297–317.

"Basic Issues in Conflicts Law." *American Journal of Comparative Law* 12 (1963), 474–482.

"The Comity Doctrine." *Michigan Law Review* 65 (1966), 9–32.

Ziegler, K.-H. *Völkerrechtsgeschichte*. 2nd ed. Munich: C. H. Beck, 2007.

Zimmermann, R. "Savigny's Legacy: Legal History, Comparative Law, and the Emergence of a European Legal Science." *Law Quarterly Review* 112 (1996), 576–605.

The Law of Obligations: Roman Foundations of the Civilian Tradition. Oxford: Oxford University Press, 1996.

"'In der Schule von Ludwig Mitteis': Ernst Rabels rechtshistorische Ursprünge'." *Rabels Zeitschrift* 65 (2001), 1–38.

"Was Heimat hieß, nun heißt es Hölle': The emigration of lawyers from Hitler's Germany: political background, legal framework , and cultural context," in J. Beatson and R. Zimmermann (eds.), *Jurists Uprooted: German-speaking Émigré Lawyers in Twentieth-century Britain*. Oxford: Oxford University Press, 2003, 1–71.

Zitelmann, E. "Der Name 'internationales Privatrecht'." *Niemeyers Zeitschrift* 27 (1918), 177–196.

Zuber, C. K. "Plague and Family Life" in M. Jones (ed.), *New Cambridge Medieval History*. Cambridge: Cambridge University Press, 2008, 124–154.

Zweigert, K. "Die Dritte Schule Im Internationalen Privatrecht: Zur Neuren Wissenschaftsgeschichte Des Kollisionsrechts" in H.-P. Ipsen (ed.), *Festschrift Für Leo Raape Zu Seinem Siebzigsten Geburtstag*. Hamburg: 1948, 35–52.

"Some Reflections on the Sociological Dimensions of Private International Law or What Is Justice in Conflict of Laws?" *University of Colorado Law Review* 44 (1973), 283–300.

Zweigert, K. and Kötz, H. *An Introduction to Comparative Law*. Trans. T. Weir. Oxford: Clarendon Press, 1998.

Zwierlein, C. "Resisting the Thomist Temptation: A Good Political Order According to Calvin" in K. Maag and A. Hujgen (eds.), *Calvinus Frater in Domino: Papers of the Twelfth International Congress on Calvin Research*. Göttingen: Vandenhoeck & Ruprecht, 2020, 125–148.

INDEX

CAMBRIDGE STUDIES IN INTERNATIONAL AND COMPARATIVE LAW

Books in the Series

158 *International Investment Law and Legal Theory: Expropriation and the Fragmentation of Sources*
Jörg Kammerhofer

157 *Legal Barbarians: Identity, Modern Comparative Law and the Global South*
Daniel Bonilla Maldonado

156 *International Human Rights Law Beyond State Territorial Control*
Antal Berkes

155 *The Crime of Aggression under the Rome Statute of the International Criminal Court*
Carrie McDougall

154 *Minorities and the Making of Postcolonial States in International Law*
Mohammad Shahabuddin

153 *Preclassical Conflict of Laws*
Nikitas E. Hatzimihail

152 *International Law and History: Modern Interfaces* Ignacio de la Rasilla del Moral

151 *Marketing Global Justice: The Political Economy of International Criminal Law*
Christine Schwöbel-Patel

150 *International Status in the Shadow of Empire*
Cait Storr

149 *Treaties in Motion: The Evolution of Treaties from Formation to Termination*
Edited by Malgosia Fitzmaurice and Panos Merkouris

148 *Humanitarian Disarmament: An Historical Enquiry*
Treasa Dunworth

147 *Complementarity, Catalysts, Compliance: The International Criminal Court in Uganda, Kenya, and the Democratic Republic of Congo*
Christian M. De Vos

146 *Cyber Operations and International Law*
François Delerue

145 *Comparative Reasoning in International Courts and Tribunals*
Daniel Peat

144 *Maritime Delimitation as a Judicial Process*
Massimo Lando

143 *Prosecuting Sexual and Gender-Based Crimes at the International Criminal Court: Practice, Progress and Potential*
Rosemary Grey

142 *Capitalism As Civilisation: A History of International Law*
Ntina Tzouvala

141 *Sovereignty in China: A Genealogy of a Concept Since 1840*
Adele Carrai

140 *Narratives of Hunger in International Law: Feeding the World in Times of Climate Change*
Anne Saab

139 *Victim Reparation under the Ius Post Bellum: An Historical and Normative Perspective*
Shavana Musa

138 *The Analogy between States and International Organizations*
Fernando Lusa Bordin

137 *The Process of International Legal Reproduction: Inequality, Historiography, Resistance*
Rose Parfitt

136 *State Responsibility for Breaches of Investment Contracts*
Jean Ho

135 *Coalitions of the Willing and International Law: The Interplay between Formality and Informality*
Alejandro Rodiles

134 *Self-Determination in Disputed Colonial Territories*
Jamie Trinidad

133 *International Law as a Belief System* Jean d'Aspremont

132 *Legal Consequences of Peremptory Norms in International Law*
Daniel Costelloe

131 *Third-Party Countermeasures in International Law*
Martin Dawidowicz

130 *Justification and Excuse in International Law: Concept and Theory of General Defences*
Federica Paddeu

129 *Exclusion from Public Space: A Comparative Constitutional Analysis*
Daniel Moeckli

128 *Provisional Measures before International Courts and Tribunals*
Cameron A. Miles

127 *Humanity at Sea: Maritime Migration and the Foundations of International Law*
Itamar Mann

126 *Beyond Human Rights: The Legal Status of the Individual in International Law*
Anne Peters

125 *The Doctrine of Odious Debt in International Law: A Restatement*
Jeff King

124 *Static and Evolutive Treaty Interpretation: A Functional Reconstruction*
Christian Djeffal

123 *Civil Liability in Europe for Terrorism-Related Risk*
Lucas Bergkamp, Michael Faure, Monika Hinteregger and Niels Philipsen

122 *Proportionality and Deference in Investor-State Arbitration: Balancing Investment Protection and Regulatory Autonomy*
Caroline Henckels

121 *International Law and Governance of Natural Resources in Conflict and Post-Conflict Situations*
Daniëlla Dam-de Jong

120 *Proof of Causation in Tort Law*
Sandy Steel

119 *The Formation and Identification of Rules of Customary International Law in International Investment Law*
Patrick Dumberry

118 *Religious Hatred and International Law: The Prohibition of Incitement to Violence or Discrimination*
Jeroen Temperman

117 *Taking Economic, Social and Cultural Rights Seriously in International Criminal Law*
Evelyne Schmid

116 *Climate Change Litigation: Regulatory Pathways to Cleaner Energy*
Jacqueline Peel and Hari M. Osofsky

115 *Mestizo International Law: A Global Intellectual History 1842–1933*
Arnulf Becker Lorca

114 *Sugar and the Making of International Trade Law*
Michael Fakhri

113 *Strategically Created Treaty Conflicts and the Politics of International Law*
Surabhi Ranganathan

112 *Investment Treaty Arbitration As Public International Law: Procedural Aspects and Implications*
Eric De Brabandere

111 *The New Entrants Problem in International Fisheries Law*
Andrew Serdy

110 *Substantive Protection under Investment Treaties: A Legal and Economic Analysis*
Jonathan Bonnitcha

109 *Popular Governance of Post-Conflict Reconstruction: The Role of International Law*
Matthew Saul

108 *Evolution of International Environmental Regimes: The Case of Climate Change*
Simone Schiele

107 *Judges, Law and War: The Judicial Development of International Humanitarian Law*
Shane Darcy

106 *Religious Offence and Human Rights: The Implications of Defamation of Religions*
Lorenz Langer

105 *Forum Shopping in International Adjudication: The Role of Preliminary Objections*
Luiz Eduardo Salles

104 *Domestic Politics and International Human Rights Tribunals: The Problem of Compliance*
Courtney Hillebrecht

103 *International Law and the Arctic*
Michael Byers

102 *Cooperation in the Law of Transboundary Water Resources*
Christina Leb

101 *Underwater Cultural Heritage and International Law*
Sarah Dromgoole

100 *State Responsibility: The General Part*
James Crawford

99 *The Origins of International Investment Law: Empire, Environment and the Safeguarding of Capital*
Kate Miles

98 *The Crime of Aggression under the Rome Statute of the International Criminal Court*
Carrie McDougall

97 *'Crimes against Peace' and International Law*
Kirsten Sellars

96 *Non-Legality in International Law: Unruly Law*
Fleur Johns

95 *Armed Conflict and Displacement: The Protection of Refugees and Displaced Persons under International Humanitarian Law*
Mélanie Jacques

94 *Foreign Investment and the Environment in International Law*
Jorge E. Viñuales

93 *The Human Rights Treaty Obligations of Peacekeepers*
Kjetil Mujezinović Larsen

92 *Cyber Warfare and the Laws of War*
Heather Harrison Dinniss

91 *The Right to Reparation in International Law for Victims of Armed Conflict*
Christine Evans

90 *Global Public Interest in International Investment Law*
Andreas Kulick

89 *State Immunity in International Law*
Xiaodong Yang

88 *Reparations and Victim Support in the International Criminal Court*
Conor McCarthy

87 *Reducing Genocide to Law: Definition, Meaning, and the Ultimate Crime*
Payam Akhavan

86 *Decolonising International Law: Development, Economic Growth and the Politics of Universality*
Sundhya Pahuja

85 *Complicity and the Law of State Responsibility*
Helmut Philipp Aust

84 *State Control over Private Military and Security Companies in Armed Conflict*
Hannah Tonkin

83 *'Fair and Equitable Treatment' in International Investment Law*
Roland Kläger

82 *The UN and Human Rights: Who Guards the Guardians?*
Guglielmo Verdirame

81 *Sovereign Defaults before International Courts and Tribunals*
Michael Waibel

80 *Making the Law of the Sea: A Study in the Development of International Law*
James Harrison

79 *Science and the Precautionary Principle in International Courts and Tribunals: Expert Evidence, Burden of Proof and Finality*
Caroline E. Foster

78 *Transition from Illegal Regimes under International Law*
Yaël Ronen

77 *Access to Asylum: International Refugee Law and the Globalisation of Migration Control*
Thomas Gammeltoft-Hansen

76 *Trading Fish, Saving Fish: The Interaction between Regimes in International Law*
Margaret A. Young

75 *The Individual in the International Legal System: Continuity and Change in International Law*
Kate Parlett

74 *'Armed Attack' and Article 51 of the UN Charter: Evolutions in Customary Law and Practice*
Tom Ruys

73 *Theatre of the Rule of Law: Transnational Legal Intervention in Theory and Practice*
Stephen Humphreys

72 *Science and Risk Regulation in International Law*
Jacqueline Peel

71 *The Participation of States in International Organisations: The Role of Human Rights and Democracy*
Alison Duxbury

70 *Legal Personality in International Law*
Roland Portmann

69 *Vicarious Liability in Tort: A Comparative Perspective*
Paula Giliker

68 *The Public International Law Theory of Hans Kelsen: Believing in Universal Law*
Jochen von Bernstorff

67 *Legitimacy and Legality in International Law: An Interactional Account*
Jutta Brunnée and Stephen J. Toope

66 *The Concept of Non-International Armed Conflict in International Humanitarian Law*
Anthony Cullen

65 *The Principle of Legality in International and Comparative Criminal Law*
Kenneth S. Gallant

64 *The Challenge of Child Labour in International Law*
Franziska Humbert

63 *Shipping Interdiction and the Law of the Sea*
Douglas Guilfoyle

62 *International Courts and Environmental Protection*
Tim Stephens

61 *Legal Principles in WTO Disputes*
Andrew D. Mitchell

60 *War Crimes in Internal Armed Conflicts*
Eve La Haye

59 *Humanitarian Occupation*
Gregory H. Fox

58 *The International Law of Environmental Impact Assessment: Process, Substance and Integration*
Neil Craik

57 *The Law and Practice of International Territorial Administration: Versailles to Iraq and Beyond*
Carsten Stahn

56 *United Nations Sanctions and the Rule of Law*
Jeremy Matam Farrall

55 *National Law in WTO Law: Effectiveness and Good Governance in the World Trading System*
Sharif Bhuiyan

54 *Cultural Products and the World Trade Organization*
Tania Voon

53 *The Threat of Force in International Law*
Nikolas Stürchler

52 *Indigenous Rights and United Nations Standards: Self-Determination, Culture and Land*
Alexandra Xanthaki

51 *International Refugee Law and Socio-Economic Rights: Refuge from Deprivation*
Michelle Foster

50 *The Protection of Cultural Property in Armed Conflict*
Roger O'Keefe

49 *Interpretation and Revision of International Boundary Decisions*
Kaiyan Homi Kaikobad

48 *Multinationals and Corporate Social Responsibility: Limitations and Opportunities in International Law*
Jennifer A. Zerk

47 *Judiciaries within Europe: A Comparative Review*
John Bell

46 *Law in Times of Crisis: Emergency Powers in Theory and Practice*
Oren Gross and Fionnuala Ní Aoláin

45 *Vessel-Source Marine Pollution: The Law and Politics of International Regulation*
Alan Khee-Jin Tan

44 *Enforcing Obligations Erga Omnes in International Law*
Christian J. Tams

43 *Non-Governmental Organisations in International Law*
Anna-Karin Lindblom

42 *Democracy, Minorities and International Law*
Steven Wheatley

41 *Prosecuting International Crimes: Selectivity and the International Criminal Law Regime*
Robert Cryer

40 *Compensation for Personal Injury in English, German and Italian Law: A Comparative Outline*
Basil Markesinis, Michael Coester, Guido Alpa and Augustus Ullstein

39 *Dispute Settlement in the UN Convention on the Law of the Sea*
Natalie Klein

38 *The International Protection of Internally Displaced Persons*
Catherine Phuong

37 *Imperialism, Sovereignty and the Making of International Law*
Antony Anghie

36 *Principles of the Institutional Law of International Organizations*
C. F. Amerasinghe

35 *Necessity, Proportionality and the Use of Force by States*
Judith Gardam

34 *International Legal Argument in the Permanent Court of International Justice: The Rise of the International Judiciary*
Ole Spiermann

33 –

32 *Great Powers and Outlaw States: Unequal Sovereigns in the International Legal Order*
Gerry Simpson

31 *Local Remedies in International Law (second edition)*
Chittharanjan Felix Amerasinghe

30 *Reading Humanitarian Intervention: Human Rights and the Use of Force in International Law*
Anne Orford

29 *Conflict of Norms in Public International Law: How WTO Law Relates to Other Rules of International Law*
Joost Pauwelyn

27 *Transboundary Damage in International Law*
Hanqin Xue

25 *European Criminal Procedures*
Edited by Mireille Delmas-Marty and J. R. Spencer

24 *Accountability of Armed Opposition Groups in International Law*
Liesbeth Zegveld

23 *Sharing Transboundary Resources: International Law and Optimal Resource Use*
Eyal Benvenisti

22 *International Human Rights and Humanitarian Law*
René Provost

21 *Remedies against International Organisations*
Karel Wellens

20 *Diversity and Self-Determination in International Law*
Karen Knop

19 *The Law of Internal Armed Conflict*
Lindsay Moir

18 *International Commercial Arbitration and African States: Practice, Participation and Institutional Development*
Amazu A. Asouzu

17 *The Enforceability of Promises in European Contract Law*
James Gordley

16 *International Law in Antiquity*
David J. Bederman

15 *Money Laundering: A New International Law Enforcement Model*
Guy Stessens

14 *Good Faith in European Contract Law*
Reinhard Zimmermann and Simon Whittaker

13 *On Civil Procedure*
J. A. Jolowicz

12 *Trusts: A Comparative Study*
Maurizio Lupoi and Simon Dix

11 *The Right to Property in Commonwealth Constitutions*
Tom Allen

10 *International Organizations before National Courts*
August Reinisch

9 *The Changing International Law of High Seas Fisheries*
Francisco Orrego Vicuña

8 *Trade and the Environment: A Comparative Study of EC and US Law*
Damien Geradin

7 *Unjust Enrichment: A Study of Private Law and Public Values*
Hanoch Dagan

6 *Religious Liberty and International Law in Europe*
Malcolm D. Evans

5 *Ethics and Authority in International Law*
Alfred P. Rubin

4 *Sovereignty over Natural Resources: Balancing Rights and Duties*
Nico Schrijver

3 *The Polar Regions and the Development of International Law*
Donald R. Rothwell

2 *Fragmentation and the International Relations of Micro-States: Self- Determination and Statehood*
Jorri C. Duursma

1 *Principles of the Institutional Law of International Organizations*
C. F. Amerasinghe

For EU product safety concerns, contact us at Calle de José Abascal, 56–1°, 28003 Madrid, Spain or eugpsr@cambridge.org.

www.ingramcontent.com/pod-product-compliance
Lightning Source LLC
LaVergne TN
LVHW010338220926
848484LV00004BB/925